Praise for *The Love-charm of Bombs*:

'An original and ingenious recreation of the Second World War in London as experienced through the lives of writers who also fought fires, drove ambulances or worked in the Ministry of Information . . . This is a highly readable interweaving of their individual stories – shocking, enjoyable, full of surprises' Michael Holroyd

'A fascinating and brilliantly researched group biography . . . an extraordinary tapestry of life in wartime, from September 1940 in London to the ruins of postwar Europe . . . This is a glorious mixture of history, literature and riveting gossip about war as – yes – an aphrodisiac . . . what remains with you at the end of this engaging book is the sense that Larkin was right, and that after the bombs, after the grieving, "what will survive of us is love"' *Daily Mail*

'One pleasure of this brave and original book is seeing these lives overlap, mirror each other, and diverge . . . Feigel shows the English in a new light: not cold or repressed, but a sensuous people for whom love matters most of all. She also shows why the period from September 1940 to May 1941, when we stood alone against the powers of darkness, remains the defining moment in our recent history' Peter J. Conradi, *Independent*

'A fine account . . . An absorbing and well-researched group biography of five prominent writers' Robert McCrum, *Observer*

'Intelligently written, seamlessly presented, and with something of the quality of a tapestry' Nicholas Shakespeare, *Daily Telegraph*

'Reads like an apocalyptic thriller . . . A fine book that brings the writers of the Second World War into the spotlight . . . The breadth and depth of Feigel's research is admirable, but this is not a dry account of famous lives. Her love and curiosity about her subjects is palpable and her writing style is simple but affecting . . . A thrilling insight to each writer's response to war, both published and private' *Independent on Sunday*

'A skillfully composed group portrait . . . Feigel is a good storyteller and responsive to the nuances of expression in the period' Tessa Hadley, *Guardian*

'Feigel writes with modesty and grace, never patronises or sentimentalises her subjects, and makes the reader glad to be sharing her ideas. *The Love-Charm of Bombs* is a bounding success as an account of wartime London and as a study of highly strung but tough characters under stress . . . I haven't for many a year read a book of literary scholarship with such impatience to know what happens next' Richard Davenport-Hines, *Sunday Telegraph*

'A strikingly original book. It succeeds in its ambitious combination of group biography and literary criticism . . . *The Love-charm of Bombs* excels in demonstrating that these years of bleakness and loss were also, for a fortunate few, a time of extraordinary excitement and literary aspiration' *Economist*

'Scintillating account of the lives of London litterateurs during the Blitz' *Scotsman*

'From these various fragments she has created a meticulously researched and elegantly rendered whole' *Newsweek*

'Feigel's method of juxtaposing writers in London brings out the drama and accidents of wartime, while her well-documented historical research supports both a detailed account of the German air raids and a broader outline of progress of the war' *Times Literary Supplement*

'Inspired . . . Feigel had an immense task in shaping these extraordinary stories of love, war and creativity. The later sections of Feigel's elegantly written, multifocal biography have the charm of a maze' *Sydney Morning Herald*

'It reads like a novel because there's great intimacy in this fugue-like composition of writers and their books and world events. Feigel has an ear for her subjects' individual voices, an eye for detail, a feel for contiguities and for the city of London. After the frenzy and intoxication of war, the dénouement of Bowen and Macaulay and Spiel, Greene and Yorke and their entourage of family and lovers, all coming to terms with the end of an era, all spent and striving to renew: that is the most moving and revealing section of this extraordinary book' Evelyn Juers, *The Australian*

'As an account of life in London under bombardment and as an examination of how a handful of gifted writers responded to the stress and anxiety of war, Ms. Feigel's intelligent and lucidly written book is continuously interesting and illuminating' *Wall Street Journal*

'Lara Feigel's ambitious fusion of criticism and biography . . . *The Love-Charm of Bombs* is a richly layered work . . . Her writing radiates with poignance and insight' *Boston Globe*

'A lovingly researched book that focuses on the experiences of five writers living in London during those suspenseful months . . . This is an enterprising, lively and original work, full of striking cameos and fresh insights' Miranda Seymour, *New York Times*

THE LOVE-CHARM OF BOMBS

DR LARA FEIGEL is a lecturer in English and the Medical Humanities at King's College London, where her research is centred on the 1930s and the Second World War. She is the author of *Literature, Cinema and Politics, 1930–1945* and the editor (with Alexandra Harris) of *Modernism of Sea: Art and Culture at the British Seaside* and (with John Sutherland) of the *New Selected Journals of Stephen Spender*. She has also written pieces for various publications, including the *Guardian*, *Prospect* and *History Today*. Lara lives in West Hampstead, London.

A Nosegay: A Literary Journey from the Fragrant to the Fetid (ed.)

Modernism on Sea: Art and Culture at the British Seaside (ed. with Alexandra Harris)

Literature, Cinema and Politics, 1930–1945: Reading between the Frames

New Selected Journals of Stephen Spender (ed. with John Sutherland)

THE LOVE-CHARM
OF BOMBS

Restless Lives in the Second World War

Lara Feigel

BLOOMSBURY

LONDON • NEW DELHI • NEW YORK • SYDNEY

for Humphrey

First published in Great Britain 2013
This paperback edition published 2014

Copyright © 2013 by Lara Feigel

The moral right of the author has been asserted

Map by ML Design

Bloomsbury Publishing Plc
50 Bedford Square
London
WC1B 3DP

www.bloomsbury.com

Bloomsbury is a trade mark of Bloomsbury Publishing Plc

Bloomsbury Publishing, London, New Delhi, New York and Sydney

A CIP catalogue record for this book is available from the British Library

ISBN 978 1 4088 3090 1

10 9 8 7 6 5 4 3 2 1

Typeset by Hewer Text UK Ltd, Edinburgh
Printed in Great Britain by CPI Group (UK) Ltd, Croydon, CR0 4YY

Contents

PART IV: *Approaching Victory*
June 1944–August 1945

PART V: *Surveying the Ruins*

PART VI: *Mid-century: Middle Age*

Introduction

It is six o'clock on the evening of 26 September 1940, at the end of the first month of London air raids. This is the final hour of daylight on one of the last days of an Indian summer. Soon it will be time to black out windows and to retreat indoors. Any light will be eliminated, leaving people to stumble along gloomy streets. And then the sirens will start wailing, as they have wailed every evening for the last two and a half weeks, and another night of bombing will begin.

Across London, people are making the most of this final interlude of peace before the bombers arrive. 'War had made them idolise day and summer,' the narrator observes in Elizabeth Bowen's wartime novel *The Heat of the Day*; 'night and autumn were enemies.' Between the dark and fearful nights, the days offer a brief holiday from fear. 'Out of mists of morning charred by smoke from ruins each day rose to a height of unmisty glitter.' In Marylebone, Bowen herself must shortly go on duty as an ARP (Air Raid Protection) warden. From the balcony of her terraced Regency house at the edge of Regent's Park she can see the empty boating lake where trees have started to shed their first autumnal leaves. The park is shut because of an unexploded bomb and the white terraces bordering the park look to her like scenery in an empty theatre.

Standing on her balcony surveying the park, Elizabeth Bowen presents an imposing figure. She is strong-backed and long-necked;

her face with its high cheekbones and tall forehead seems to many of her friends to have become more beautiful now that she has entered her forties. The narrator of Bowen's first novel *The Hotel* observes that everyone has an age at which they are most themselves. The Second World War is Bowen's own. As an Anglo-Irishwoman she has always had torn loyalties; in her childhood she was half at home in the Cork countryside and half at home on the Kent coast. Now she has found a home in wartime London and she paces the blacked-out streets with a vigorous certainty. She is a successful and popular writer who has already published ten books and is confident of her own powers. And literary success has brought social and romantic success. Since her early twenties Bowen has been married to Alan Cameron, an English civil servant. The marriage is contented but celibate and for two years before the war Bowen was engaged in a passionate affair with the Irish writer and one-time IRA gunman Sean O'Faolain. In the summer of 1941 she will fall in love with the Canadian diplomat Charles Ritchie, the man who will centre her world for the next thirty years.

A few streets south in Marylebone, Bowen's friend Rose Macaulay is in her flat in Luxborough Street, completing the day's writing before fear and noise make it impossible to concentrate. She is exhausted by the weeks of bombing, and is unlikely to have much sleep tonight. Later, she will go on duty as an ambulance driver, rescuing people trapped by debris or scalded by fire. Unlike Bowen, Macaulay is finding the intensity of wartime London more sad than exhilarating. She is almost sixty and is a frail though wiry and redoubtable woman. The arduous physical labour of her work as an ambulance driver distracts her both from her dismay at the war going on around her and from personal sorrow. For the last twenty years she has been in a secret but idyllic love affair with the married Irish novelist and former priest, Gerald O'Donovan. Ten years older than Macaulay, he is now dying and Macaulay can confide in very few people about the loss that she is preparing herself to face.

Macaulay's ambulance may well cross paths with the fire engine of Henry Yorke (better known by his pseudonym Henry Green). He is working as an auxiliary fireman just around the corner from Macaulay in Davies Street and has been constantly fighting fires since the bombing began. The duality of Yorke's names reflects a division between two identities. Henry Yorke is an upper-class socialite who works in his father's business, Pontifex, and spends most of his evenings at extravagant parties. Henry Green is an experimental novelist who writes strange and lyrical tales of factory life and bright young things. Unlike Macaulay, Yorke is enjoying the Blitz, which has come as a relief after months of sterile waiting during the so-called 'phoney war'. He is pleased to be a hero at last and to see his heroism reflected back by girls who look him 'straight, long in the eye as never before, complicity in theirs, blue, and blue, and blue'. And between shifts at the fire station he can make the most of this adoration, enjoying the absence of his wife and son whom he has evacuated to the countryside.

But Yorke is frightened as well as excited by fire and he does not look forward to the raids as much as Graham Greene. For Greene the real action of the day begins when he can leave his desk at the Ministry of Information in Bloomsbury and start his night-time duties as an ARP warden, often accompanied by his lover Dorothy Glover. Greene's wife and children, like Yorke's, are out of London and he is enjoying his independence. Emerging unscathed from the bombs each morning, Greene has conquered his lifelong boredom and found a way to feel urgently alive. Meanwhile for the Austrian writer Hilde Spiel, serving supper to her husband, parents and child in Wimbledon, the fading light heralds the tedium and fear of another wakeful night at home. Once the raid begins the family will pile their mattresses against the windows and listen to music on the gramophone, trying to drown out the noise of the bombs which they hope will land elsewhere.

These writers, firefighting, ambulance-driving, patrolling the streets, were the successors of the soldier poets of the First World War, and their story remains to be told. Like the poets in the trenches, Bowen, Greene, Macaulay and Yorke were participants rather than witnesses, risking death, night after night, in defence of their city. The Second

War was a Total War. No one escaped the danger and every ~~~oner~~ was vulnerable. While the fighting in the First World War ~~ok~~ place far away, the bombing of the Second World War was super-imposed onto a relatively normal London life. Books were written, parties hosted, love affairs initiated and broken off. But the books, parties and love affairs were infused with the danger of death; every aspect of life was refracted through the lens of war.

Looking back on the Blitz, Elizabeth Bowen described this as a period of 'lucid abnormality'; a moment outside time when she and her friends were 'afloat on the tideless, hypnotic, futureless to-day'. When a bomb exploded, nearby clocks ceased to function, remaining stuck at the time of the detonation. London was a city of shock-stopped clocks and for its inhabitants, the suspended present created a climate where intense emotions could flourish. 'It came to be rumoured,' Bowen recalled, 'that everybody in London was in love.'

Bowen, Greene, Macaulay, Spiel and Yorke floated dangerously on that futureless present. All experienced the war as an abnormal pocket of time. As writers, they observed the strangeness of war imaginatively. London became a city of restless dreams and hallucinogenic madness; a place in which fear itself could transmute into addictive euphoria. To stay in London was to gamble nightly with death. And so each day was unexpected; each moment had the exhilarating but unreal intensity of the last moment on earth. Their public war work became the backdrop for volatile individual private lives. For Bowen, 'war time, with its makeshifts, shelvings, deferrings, could not have been kinder to roman-tic love'. Bowen, Greene and Yorke spent the war in the kind of love that blazed with the raging intensity of the fires igniting their city.

Often separated, necessarily or wilfully, from their spouses, they immersed themselves in a makeshift present in which pre-war morality seemed less relevant. As the bombs fell outside, lovers huddled together in basements and shelters, or defiantly outfaced the raids in blacked-out bedrooms or torch-lit streets. The passionate love affairs in Bowen's *The Heat of the Day* (1948), Greene's *The End of the Affair* (1951) and Yorke's *Caught* (1943) all had their basis in the wartime lives of their creators.

The stories told here do not always concur with the official propaganda, which portrayed the Blitz as a scene of cheerful togetherness and courage, making the most of the 'London can take it' spirit that developed among Londoners. Documentary films from the period show cheerful groups of civilians resiliently flouting danger with communal singing and cups of tea. For the writers in this book, the reality was less wholesome and more reckless. To defy the nightly threat of death took more than staunch morale and national pride. They were too selfish to 'take it' for the sake of their city and too snobbish to sing together; they were more likely to be found drinking cocktails than tea.

Bowen, Greene, Macaulay, Spiel and Yorke all had moments of enthusing about the 'People's War', especially during the first months of the Blitz. They all felt briefly united with their neighbours and their colleagues in the civil defence services, and would all look back on this as a time of unusual community spirit. In 1969 Bowen reviewed *The People's War* by the historian Angus Calder, a book which challenged the commonplace image of national unity against a common enemy. She insisted that in fact the 'exuberance, during the early London Blitzes, was not a fake'. For her the myth of collective harmony, 'though bedraggled', persisted throughout the war; 'How else should we have gone on?'

But the exuberance referred to by Bowen was not quite the community spirit encouraged by government propaganda. Greene or Yorke, enjoying the sexual freedom enabled by war, indulged in a licentiousness that would not be officially encouraged; Greene's exuberance during the raids was symptomatic of a rather frightening glory in destruction for its own sake. So, too, it was a luxury to find the war exciting; a luxury enabled by class privilege (Bowen and Yorke had access to private shelters and to far more enticing food than rationing alone allowed) and also by the imaginative possibilities open to writers. Bowen later described her wartime writing as a 'saving resort', suggesting that writing allowed her to experience actual events on two planes at once. Writers and artists tended to be peculiarly receptive to the temporal and erotic freedom offered by the war in part because they could switch off from the danger and enjoy the raids as aesthetic events.

According to the fireman and short story writer William Sansom, the city bereft of electric and neon light took on a new beauty: 'By moonlight the great buildings assumed a remote and classic magnificence, cold, ancient, lunar palaces carved in bone from the moon.' In September 1940 Rose Macaulay recounted her experience of watching an air battle over London which she found 'most beautiful': 'the searchlights, and parachute flares, the fiery balls . . . and the sky lit up into gun-flashes, like sheet-lightning, and a wonderful background of stars.' Painters such as John Piper and Graham Sutherland depicted the raids in London as scenes of incandescent splendour, making the most of the surreal juxtapositions and the pinks, reds and yellows of the fires, glowing against the darkness of the blacked-out city.

For Bowen, in her review of Calder's book, the historian is in danger of falling into the same tendency to over-generalise as the government propagandists fell into at the time. 'We at least,' she writes, 'knew that we only half knew what we were doing.' She suggests that a picture of the war should be presented not just in terms of the actualities, but in terms of the 'mood, temper and climate' of the time. This is a climate best accessed through individual stories and through the intense, often strange war-writing of individual writers. Describing her own wartime short stories, Bowen wrote that 'through the particular, in wartime, I felt the high-voltage current of the general pass'.

Taken together, Bowen's statements can be seen as the impetus behind this book, which focuses on the lucidly abnormal particular stories of five writers in wartime London and post-war London, Ireland, Vienna and Berlin. In the process it attempts to tap into the high-voltage current of war, illuminating a ten-year period through the lives of five extraordinary individuals. The five writers are chosen for their own experiences and for their confluence in London in the Blitz. They were of different ages and nationalities and did not form a clear coterie in the manner of the First World War poets or of 1920s Bloomsbury. In a 1958 letter to her friend William Plomer, Elizabeth Bowen looked back on her contemporaries in the 1930s and 1940s as 'the only non-groupy generation'. Nonetheless, she did acknowledge a shared social world. 'What an agreeable life we all had, seeing each other *without* being a group,' she wrote.

By seeing each other without being a group, Bowen, Greene, Macaulay and Yorke were often in the same place at the same time, and shared friends, experiences and, at one remove, lovers. Before the war, Bowen had been the theatre critic for *Night and Day*, the short-lived magazine edited by Graham Greene; in 1949 she would correspond publicly with Greene in a series of letters called 'Why do I Write?' Bowen and Macaulay were close friends and were linked by their mutual friendship with Virginia Woolf. Bowen always attributed her initial success as a writer to Macaulay's help in finding a publisher for her first stories. And Bowen and Yorke were linked by the incestuous love triangles which tessellated in literary London. After Bowen's lover Goronwy Rees jilted her for the beautiful novelist Rosamond Lehmann in 1936, Lehmann herself found solace from Rees's callous waywardness in Yorke's arms.

In his autobiography, Rosamond's brother, the publisher John Lehmann (who at this stage was working with Virginia and Leonard Woolf at the Hogarth Press), described an 'imaginary but nevertheless imaginable' party, drawing together some of the people who drank pre-dinner cocktails in his flat during the war. He hoped in the process to produce 'a composite picture that would illuminate the anatomy of our wartime society in the most truthful detail'. In this scene there are partygoers from the Ministry of Information, notably Graham Greene, 'full of sardonic stories about muddle and maze-like confusion of action'; there are guests from the fire service – Stephen Spender, William Sansom and Henry Yorke, who tells 'extraordinary stories of his fellow firemen'; at the other end of the room is Elizabeth Bowen, 'in high spirits, radiating charm and vitality'; and then there is Rose Macaulay, 'symbol of some dauntless, indomitable quality of moral and intellectual integrity in the pre-1914 generation'.

Hilde Spiel is notably absent from this party. She did encounter Macaulay during the war, but this tended to be at gatherings organised by the PEN club rather than at more decadent parties. She was an enthusiastic reader of Bowen and Greene and would later translate both novelists into German. However she herself remained unknown to both of them in the 1940s, although the three almost crossed paths in Vienna in 1948. Spiel's presence here acts as a counterpoint to the more exalted lives of the other four protagonists; a reminder of the gloomy and often horrific reality of the war years and of the fact that the main events of the war took place outside London. Exiled from her native Austria, Spiel was in the strange position of attempting to avoid bombs dropped by her former compatriots. Both she and her German husband Peter de Mendelssohn were attempting to resist their position as exiles, starting to publish fiction in English and insisting on their allegiance to Britain. But it was still hard to read about the gradual destruction of their homelands without ambivalence; and there were continual indications from the British that they did not quite belong. The sense of displacement was compounded by financial anxiety and by Spiel's resentment that she had left behind a successful literary career in Vienna to become a housewife in suburban Wimbledon.

It was only after the war that Spiel came into her own and that the roles of the five writers were reversed. Bowen, Greene and Yorke all had a good war but a bad peace. Spiel, on the other hand, had the most exciting time of her life in post-war Berlin and Vienna, where she was sent as an Allied press officer. The ruined European cities provided the setting for a new kind of ecstatic vitality. But, as she blacked out her windows on 26 September 1940, Spiel found it hard to be hopeful that life would ever dramatically improve or that she would feel fully at home anywhere again. For now it was Bowen, Greene, Macaulay and Yorke who could claim the territory of the blacked-out city as their own.

PART I

One Night in the Lives of Five Writers

26 September 1940

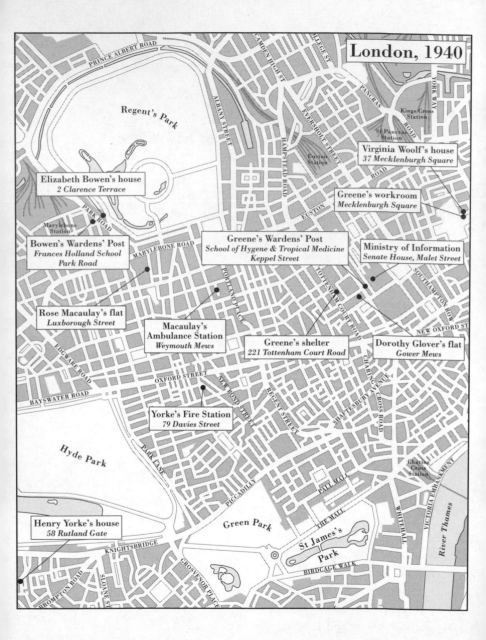

London, 1940

PRINCE ALBERT ROAD

Regent's Park

Elizabeth Bowen's house
2 Clarence Terrace

Virginia Woolf's house
37 Mecklenburgh Square

Greene's workroom
Mecklenburgh Square

Bowen's Wardens' Post
Frances Holland School
Park Road

Greene's Wardens' Post
School of Hygene & Tropical Medicine
Keppel Street

Ministry of Information
Senate House, Malet Street

Rose Macaulay's flat
Luxborough Street

Macaulay's
Ambulance Station
Weymouth Mews

Greene's shelter
221 Tottenham Court Road

Dorothy Glover's flat
Gower Mews

Yorke's Fire Station
79 Davies Street

Hyde Park

Henry Yorke's house
58 Rutland Gate

Green Park

St James's
Park

River Thames

Newsreel

By 26 September 1940 Londoners were gradually becoming accustomed to air raids. It was now clear that the war in Britain had finally begun after a year of false starts.

When war was declared the previous September, the government and public prepared for the immediate bombing of London. Graham Greene and Henry Yorke were not unusual in hastily evacuating their wives and children to the countryside. Both men readied themselves for the deaths they thought could not be long in coming, with Greene drafting his will and Yorke writing his autobiography. Greene prepared for the raids by finding a builder to put plywood under his skylight to prevent broken glass falling inside; throughout London people queued up to have gas masks fitted and attempted to build shelters in their gardens. But these precautions proved premature. The first year of war came to be known as the 'phoney war' because the expected invasion and aerial bombardment failed to materialise. Away from home, the Battle of the Atlantic was playing out at sea, but in London it was a period characterised by anticlimactic waiting. By the late autumn of 1939, people had stopped carrying gas masks and there was a ban on recruiting any more ARP wardens.

The war in Europe began in earnest in the spring of 1940. Germany invaded Norway and Denmark in April and the Low Countries and

France in May. Allied forces were quickly cut off in Belgium and then evacuated from Dunkirk. The Germans next pushed further into France, occupying Paris by 14 June. This was an unexpectedly dramatic victory which isolated Britain and gave the Germans and other Axis powers an immediate advantage in Europe. On 18 June Winston Churchill, who had now succeeded Neville Chamberlain as Prime Minister, predicted the beginning of the Battle of Britain. Two weeks earlier he had vowed never to surrender, fighting on the beaches, landing grounds, fields, streets and hills. Now he repeated that Britain would fight on, 'if necessary for years, if necessary alone', assuring the populace that they would look back on this as their finest hour. At this stage, people were expecting a full invasion. 'The prospect of invasion of England no longer absurd,' Hilde Spiel lamented in her diary after the Germans were victorious in Norway; 'This would mean death.' Official warnings blended with unofficial rumours suggesting that hundreds of German parachutists were about to land in Britain disguised as monks or nuns, with collapsible bicycles concealed beneath their habits.

The Battle of Britain did materialise that summer, but at first London remained unharmed. There were small daylight raids on coastal towns in the south and east in June and July and then, when the British Foreign Secretary rejected a final offer of peace from Germany on 22 July, the Germans embarked on an air battle, intending to wipe out Britain's air defences. Initially the Luftwaffe engaged RAF fighter planes in aerial combat. Then in August they attempted to destroy Britain's fighter defences, attacking airfields and radar stations. By the end of the month 1,333 people had been killed in raids. Nonetheless, these summer attacks were colloquially known as 'nuisance raids' and the British remained dismissive of their effects. 'There are two corrections I want to make to current Nazi propaganda,' the playwright J. B. Priestley informed the nation in a broadcast on 9 July:

> First air raids. There has been a great deal of German raiding lately, but
> the results, so far from being effective, either as regards military

objectives or civilian morale, have been so negligible that the general opinion here has been that these raids can only have been feelers, attempts to discover where the best defences are located.

The Nazis, he implied tauntingly, were not really trying.

However, during the second half of August the German bombers moved progressively inland and began to incorporate the suburbs of London in their attacks. On the night of 18 August bombs fell in Croydon and in Wimbledon, where Hilde Spiel was living. On 22 August the first bombs fell in central London, giving Churchill an excuse to order an air attack on Berlin, which materialised on 25 August. Hitler in his turn used the bombing of Berlin as a pretext to command a more sustained attack on London. On 4 September he announced to the citizens of Germany that in England they were asking scornfully, 'Why doesn't he come?' They would not have to wait much longer. 'He's coming! He's coming!' When the RAF dropped three or four thousand kilograms of bombs on Germany, Hitler boasted that the Luftwaffe would respond with several hundred thousand kilograms. 'When they declare that they will increase their attacks on our cities, then we will *raze* their cities to the ground!' Still defiant, Priestley boasted the next day that Londoners were going on as normal, despite the sirens. There were searchlights at night, making rapidly changing patterns in the sky, and 'many-coloured flares blazing like sudden comets'. But it was surprising, on the whole, what little difference it made.

He spoke too soon. On 7 September Göring declared that as a result of the provocative British attacks on Berlin 'the Führer has decided to order a mighty blow to be struck in revenge against the capital of the British Empire'. That night London suffered its first major attack. At five in the afternoon a swarm of planes flew in from Kent towards the London docks. By 6.30 much of the East End was on fire and the streets were strewn with fallen bricks and broken glass. Later on, heavy bombs landed in Chelsea and Victoria while others continued to destroy the East End. Looking back on that night, William Sansom recalled that:

when the western skies had grown already dark the fierce red glow in the East stuck harshly fast and there was seen for the first time that black London roofscape silhouetted against what was to become a monotonously copper-orange sky.

As a full-time auxiliary fireman, Henry Yorke was engaged in defending London from the start of the raids, risking his life night after night at the docks. 'I've fought fires every night since Saturday,' he wrote to Rosamond Lehmann on 11 September,

> have had three in one day and the two longest, Surrey Commercial Docks and St Paul's, lasted 12 hours without a relief. The Docks one was the worst, bombed continuously from 9pm to 3am in the middle of a timber yard alight and completely out of control. I was lucky to get out.

Elizabeth Bowen, Graham Greene and Rose Macaulay had longer to wait before they were directly involved, but by the third day of the Blitz the bombs were falling indiscriminately across London and no area seemed safe. 'I hear little by little of the various bomb-damages in London,' Macaulay told her sister on 8 September; 'Hoxton again was badly hit, even streets in Kensington and round Paddington.'

On 9 September, just around the corner from the area Greene was patrolling as an ARP warden, Virginia Woolf's Bloomsbury home in Mecklenburgh Square was hit by a high explosive (HE) and an unexploded bomb. Woolf went to London to survey the damage and found that the square was roped off to the public but she could peer in from behind. A house thirty yards away from theirs was completely ruined. 'Scraps of cloth hanging to the bare walls at the side still standing,' she reported; 'A looking glass I think swinging. Like a tooth knocked out – a clean cut.' The Woolfs started making urgent plans to move the Hogarth Press and all its equipment out of the house, but a week later the unexploded bomb exploded and the house and with it the Press was destroyed. ' "We have need of all our courage" are the words that come to the surface this morning; on hearing that all our windows are broken, ceilings down, and most of our china smashed,' Woolf observed in her diary. Bowen and Macaulay, both close friends of Woolf's, wrote to console her, terrified that their own homes would be next. 'When your flat went did that mean all the things in it too?' Bowen asked. 'All my life I have said, "Whatever happens there will always be tables and chairs" – and what a mistake.'

Churchill urged Londoners to remain resilient. 'Hitler expects to terrorise and cow the people of this mighty city,' he announced on the radio on 11 September. 'Little does he know the spirit of the British nation, or the tough fibre of the Londoners.' But the heavy raids continued throughout September. Several stations and major buildings in London were hit in the first week of attacks: Somerset House, White-hall, Westminster Abbey, the Houses of Parliament and Buckingham Palace had all been struck by 15 September, though none of these was seriously damaged. Meanwhile houses and flats throughout London were destroyed by explosion and fire. Gradually people learnt to tell the difference between the sounds of HEs, incendiary bombs, parachute mines (dropped from aeroplanes to detonate at roof level) and defensive guns. Initially, the anti-aircraft guns in London were non-existent but by 10 September guns had been brought in from throughout Britain. Only one shell in 2,000 reached its target but morale improved now that London was heard to defend itself so noisily. William Sansom described how on 11 September guns started up from every side as soon as the enemy bombers came droning down, creating a 'momentous sound that sent a chattering, smashing, blinding thrill through the London heart'. There had been gunfire before, but nothing like this. 'A violent medley of angry sounds, urgently accumulating like the barking of a pack of dogs, a rattling of pompoms and a booming of great naval guns.' At this stage there were raids by both day and night but on 15 September the Germans started concentrating their attacks on the night-time, deterred from daytime sorties by heavy Luftwaffe losses.

Politicians and journalists praised the resilience of Londoners engaged in defending their city. All the civil defence services were learning from experience and improving in efficiency and efficacy. Firemen now knew to keep the stirrup pump unlashed and to have water ready drawn. They had also become less fearful in dealing with fire. In a broadcast on

10 September, J. B. Priestley lauded the ARP services both for their organisation and for 'the quality of service given by the men and women acting as air wardens, fire fighters, and as members of emergency squads'; this service could not be bought with money and sprang instead 'out of a deep devotion to and love of this great city and its people'.

But despite a widespread determination to resist the Germans and keep going, Londoners were becoming cumulatively exhausted by the succession of all-night raids. 'To work or think was to ache,' Bowen wrote in *The Heat of the Day*. 'In offices, factories, ministries, shops, kitchens the hot yellow sands of each afternoon ran out slowly; fatigue was the one reality. You dared not envisage sleep.' Sleeplessness compounded anxiety. No one had any idea where the bombing would lead, or if London would end up flattened. 'How fantastic life has become,' Rose Macaulay wrote to her sister on 11 September. 'I wonder if London will soon lie in ruins, like Warsaw and Rotterdam.'

Increasingly involved in their local battle, Londoners became isolated from the war as it progressed in the outside world. William Sansom recalled how in this period 'out in the wide world of the war' Quisling had assumed power in Norway, Germany was extending its power in Romania, and ominously Hitler met Mussolini on the Brenner. Britain itself was involved in raids on western Germany and naval engagements in the Atlantic. 'But every night in the dark small world of London's intimate streets these matters receded, and under the urging drone of the bombers, the weaving searchlights, the thunder of bombs and the crack of guns the moments became vivid and active.' These were

> hot, cold, sharp, slow moments of intense being; moments that then extended themselves into hours, that brought with them the exhaustion of cold and sleeplessness, so that the total experience is most remembered as a curious double exposure of tensity and dullness.

Each night of the Blitz was a self-contained moment in itself. And as darkness fell on the evening of 26 September, Bowen, Greene, Macaulay, Spiel and Yorke waited anxiously to see what this particular moment would involve.

7 p.m.: Blackout

The blackout on 26 September began officially at 7.26 p.m. It had been a cloudy day after weeks of unreal autumnal sunshine. When the sun did break through in the middle of the afternoon, the trees and lawns in the London parks appeared to Elizabeth Bowen to freeze in the horizontal light. For Bowen, the scene below her white stucco house seemed especially still because Regent's Park itself was closed. She and her husband Alan Cameron were among only a few residents who had returned since the time bomb fell two weeks earlier. 'Through the railings I watch dahlias blaze out their colour,' she wrote in an article entitled 'London, 1940'. 'Leaves fill the empty deck-chairs; in the sunshine water-fowl, used to so much attention, mope round the unpeopled rim of the lake.'

Now the clouds had faded into darkness. Throughout London people pulled down black screens, tucking curtains into the corners of windows. The thick layers of cloth offered a sense of protection against the bombs, even if they would do nothing to impede the blast. Gradually, the streets began to empty and civilians waited uneasily inside their houses, prepared to make their way to the shelters if necessary. But for those in the Air Raid Protection services, the ghostly blacked-out streets were a terrain to be paced, surveyed and known. When darkness fell it was time for the ARP wardens to go on duty; for Elizabeth Bowen in Marylebone and Graham Greene in Bloomsbury to patrol their districts, making sure that there were no chinks in the blackout along the way. Both were rendered official by their attire. Greene had a Civil Defence armlet over his own clothes and Bowen was wearing a dark blue ARP uniform coat, although that July the local authorities had decided to save money by discontinuing these. Like all wardens, they were equipped with tin hats, whistles and respirators.

Bowen later described how in

> walking in the darkness of the nights for six years (darkness which transformed a capital city into a network of inscrutable canyons), one developed new bare alert senses, with their own savage warnings and notations.

The buses and cars in the street were almost invisible except for a tiny point of light at each side. Lenses on traffic lights were permanently covered by a black metal plate pierced by a single cross. Passing human figures had been reduced to shadows. It was hard not to trip over the kerb or the sandbags piled high on the pavements. Indeed, in the first month of the war casualties due to the blackout had exceeded British military casualties. But wardens were learning to feel their way around familiar pavements and to recognise each other's outlines as they passed, developing a new sense somewhere between the sense of touch and the sense of smell.

The districts were small enough for wardens to get to know a large proportion of the local residents, as well as learning the layout of the streets and the location of any potential hazards. Bowen was probably based at her nearest post, which was situated in the basement of Francis Holland School on Park Road, just behind her own street, Clarence Terrace. The wardens at this post patrolled a patch that went as far as Marylebone Station in the west, the Marylebone Road in the south and the Outer Circle of Regent's Park in the east. Greene was based at a post about a mile and a half south-east of the park, underneath the School of Hygiene & Tropical Medicine in Gower Street. He and his colleagues looked after an area bounded by New Oxford Street in the south, the Euston Road in the north, Gordon Square in the east and Gower Street in the west.

Tonight, Elizabeth Bowen was pleased to be back in London after two weeks away. She and Alan had been home since Monday. Clarence

Terrace, like all the streets off the park, was still officially 'closed'; there were barriers and bomb-notices at every entrance. Elizabeth reported to her cousin Noreen in neutral Ireland that it looked 'like a street in a city of the dead, with dead leaves and bits of paper blowing about'. Going to bed, she felt as if she was sleeping in the corner of a deserted palace. Each day, the postman took a flying run down the terrace, and Elizabeth left to buy loaves and bottles of milk, largely to feed Lawrence the cat. 'I had always placed this Park among the most civilised scenes on earth,' she wrote in 'London 1940';

> the Nash pillars look as brittle as sugar – actually, which is wonderful, they have not cracked; though several of the terraces are gutted – blown-in shutters swing loose, ceilings lie on floors and a premature decay-smell comes from the rooms. A pediment has fallen on a lawn.

On the night of the time bomb, Elizabeth had only had the chance to rush back into the house and pick up a box of 200 cigarettes, which seemed briefly more precious than anything else she could take with her. Away from home, she worried about her typewriter left uncovered as the dust blew through their suddenly emptied house. Elizabeth and Alan spent their first few days away from Clarence Terrace at the Mount Royal Hotel off Oxford Street, but after two days they were bombed out of Oxford Street as well. This raid, Elizabeth told Noreen, was 'as appalling a night as I ever wish to see', although as a member of the Home Guard Alan had relished being in charge, taking command of the hotel and issuing orders in a military voice as he directed the early morning traffic. Alan had enjoyed his adventure and now, returning after a week at the home of friends in the countryside, it was time for Elizabeth to enjoy hers.

Elizabeth Bowen described these September evenings as a time when 'after black-out we keep that date with fear. The howling ramping over the darkness, the lurch of the barrage opening, the obscure throb in the air.' In fact, though, she herself was more often exhilarated than afraid. On nights when Bowen was not on ARP duty, visitors to Clarence Terrace were expected to remain on the balcony to watch the display. 'I

Bond Street following the 17 September raid

do ap-p-pologise for the noise,' Stephen Spender recalled Bowen announcing dryly as she led her guests inside after a raid. 'The sound of the Boche bomber overhead is exactly like the enlarged sound of a wasp,' she informed Noreen dismissively; 'it makes the same priggish and consequential noise.'

In a section of her novel *The Heat of the Day* written during the war, Bowen pays testament to the strength of London itself in September 1940:

> The very soil of the city at this time seemed to generate more strength: in parks the outsize dahlias, velvet and wine, and the trees on which each vein in each yellow leaf stretched out perfect against the sun blazoned out the idea of the finest hour.

As an Anglo-Irishwoman, Bowen had always had an ambivalent identity, feeling neither fully British nor fully Irish. Now she was embarrassed

by Ireland's decision to remain neutral during the war and had identified completely as a Londoner, defiantly protecting her city. And if it
was London's finest hour, then it was also Bowen's own. She believed
herself to be invincible, partly because she prided herself on being the
same age as her century.

In her 1960 account of *A Time in Rome*, Bowen observed that
'twinship with one's century' brings 'the feeling of being hand-in-
glove with it, which may make for unavowed confidence'. She
attributed this feeling to Stella in *The Heat of the Day*, who finds that
'the fateful course of her fatalistic century' seems 'more and more her
own'. Both Stella and her creator had been too young to be actively
involved in the First World War, though Bowen had spent some time
as 'a pink, rattled, inexpert VAD' (Voluntary Aid Detachment) nurse
in an Irish hospital for shell-shocked soldiers after leaving school in
1918. Looking back, she saw herself at this age as resembling a rabbit
in the middle of the road. Now, as she and her century entered their
forties together, Bowen was determined to take responsibility for her
age. She, like Stella, would not die in the Blitz because the century
itself had more in store for her.

According to Rosamond Lehmann, Elizabeth Bowen gave in this
period 'an impression of abounding health and vitality'. The admiring
younger writer May Sarton recalled her friend as looking in this period
like a drawing by Holbein.

> Hers was a handsome face, handsome rather than beautiful, with its
> bold nose, high cheekbones, and tall forehead; but the colouring was as
> delicate as the structure was strong – fine red-gold hair pulled straight
> back into a loose knot at her neck, faint eyebrows over pale-blue eyes.

For May, Elizabeth was rendered human and approachable by her slight
stammer and her rippling laughter, which was rather like a purr.

Bowen was currently writing a family history in which she described
her grandmother, Elizabeth Clarke, in a passage that reads as an accurate self-portrait:

It is possible that Elizabeth's *manner* was part of her physical personality. As a girl in her early twenties she was (to judge by successive pictures) less nearly beautiful than in her later life. But her way of holding herself and her smiling candid calmness must always have been distinctive and beautiful. In girlhood, the fine open moulding of her face, her eyes set in like eyes in a Holbein portrait, her rather large mobile mouth must have been distinctive and strange. She always moved with deliberation; her voice was low-pitched; she must have been a mixture of aliveness and repose.

By 1940 Elizabeth Bowen herself was both distinctive and beautiful. She was alive and ready to pounce; to walk out fearlessly into the darkness of the blackout; to fall, as she would six months later, precipitously and consumingly in love.

Elizabeth Bowen, photographed by Howard Coster, 1942

Meanwhile Graham Greene was already in love. At thirty-six, he, like Bowen, was growing into himself. He was the author of ten novels

© National Portrait Gallery, London

Graham Greene, photographed by Bassano, 1939

– most recently *The Power and the Glory*, which had been published in March. Tall, with grey-blue eyes, he had always been austerely handsome, and now his youthful shyness had begun to dissipate as a result of literary success and sexual experience. He was often accompanied during the raids by his feisty and beguiling comrade-at-arms, Dorothy Glover. In general, Greene was more elated by the bombing than Bowen. Since childhood he had yearned, both romantically and depressively, for death. And, with Dorothy, the heady combination of danger and sex was especially alluring. Greene's friend the journalist Malcolm Muggeridge recollected the Blitz as

> a kind of protracted debauch, with the shape of orderly living shattered, all restraints removed, barriers non-existent. It gave one the same feeling a debauch did, of, as it were, floating loose; of having slipped one's moorings.

Greene himself looked back on this as a manic-depressive period: 'depressive when the bombs were at their worst and manic when one woke up in the morning to the sound of the glass being swept up and one was alive.'

When he had first joined the ARP training course, Greene was nervous that he would faint, as he had done as a young man hearing descriptions of accidents, or even once as an adult cutting his own finger. But like many other wardens he found that once he was equipped with a job to do he stopped being afraid of his emotions. John Strachey, another literary warden who wrote a war memoir which Greene admired, recalled his relief on beginning his duties that he was no longer at liberty to worry about his own safety. He observed that

> the instant that an individual is given even the simplest objective function, and becomes a member of an organised (and uniformed, this is notoriously important) group, the whole burden of deciding whether or not on any particular occasion to seek his or her safety is automatically removed.

A few years after the war, Bowen recollected that she had signed up as a warden because 'air raids were much less trying if one had something to do'. She described how a warden in an air raid stumped up and down the streets, 'making a clatter with the boots you are wearing, knowing you can't prevent a bomb falling, but thinking "At any rate I'm taking part in this, I may be doing some good."'

Where Bowen gained solace from a belief in her own invincibility, Greene was more bizarrely reassured by the certainty that he would not survive the Blitz at all. He later recalled that he was scared to begin with, but that soon he gave up the idea that he was going to survive and ceased to be frightened. As a warden, Greene could enjoy the cleansing moment of apocalypse that he had been longing for since his childhood. 'We were,' he wrote, 'a generation brought up on adventure stories who had missed the enormous disillusionment of the First World War, so we went looking for adventure.' Indeed, his sense of the First World War was so vivid that years later he dreamed that he was Wilfred Owen, waiting for battle in a dugout and writing Owen's own poems.

Greene was right in attributing this feeling to other members of his generation. In his 1938 autobiography, Christopher Isherwood described how 'we young writers of the middle twenties were all suffering, more or less subconsciously, from a feeling of shame that we hadn't been old enough to take part in the European War'. However, Greene was unusual among writers of his circle in enjoying the danger unequivocally. 'I can't help wishing sometimes,' he had written aged twenty-one to his future wife Vivien, 'that something would happen to solve all problems once and for all. Something like war with Turkey and Russia and Germany, which would destroy all thought of the future, and leave only a certain present.' As a teenager, he had staved off boredom and depression by playing Russian roulette with a loaded gun, enjoying the feeling that life contained an infinite number of possibilities until even playing with death became boring. In the 1930s, a restlessness set in, which he later interpreted as a desire to be a spectator of history. He looked forward to war as an entry into history and as a necessary awakening.

Once war was declared, Greene was initially disappointed by the lack of danger. During the summer of 1940, he often spent Saturday nights in Southend, which was an obvious entry point for German planes coming in from the sea. In an October 1940 article entitled 'At Home', Greene described the relief he had experienced once the Blitz started. The British, he wrote, had got used to violence so quickly because the violence itself had been expected for so long. Indeed, 'the world we lived in could not have ended any other way'. The squalor of England in the 1930s – 'the curious waste lands one sometimes saw from trains . . . the dingy fortune-teller's on the first-floor above the cheap permanent waves in a Brighton back street,' the landmarks, indeed, of the 'Greeneland' in which he set his own fiction – had called out for violence, like the rooms in a dream where you know that something is about to happen. In 1936, many writers had gone to meet the violence halfway in Spain; less ideological, perhaps less courageous writers such as Greene himself had chosen destinations like Africa where the violence was more moderate.

But, armed with a two-way ticket, these writers had an escape route;

according to Greene they were simply tickling their own moral sense. Those journeys were a mere 'useful rehearsal' which now helped them to adapt to a strange home, 'lying on one's stomach while a bomb whines across'. Now, it was easy to feel at home in London or the other bombed cities because life there was 'what it ought to be'. Like a cracked cup placed in boiling water, civilisation was breaking up at last.

> The nightly routine of sirens, barrage, the probing raider, the unmistakable engine ('Where are you? Where are you? Where are you?'), the bomb-bursts moving nearer and then moving away, hold one like a love-charm.

Greene was unhappy when he spent just a few days away from the city during the Blitz; he found safe areas 'unsavoury' in their evasion of the general condition of danger. Even the victims failed to evoke his sympathy. He too expected death in his turn and often envied the casualties of the bombing. As a Catholic, he believed that the dead were treated justly and that war could therefore bestow peace.

> The innocent will be given their peace, and the unhappy will know more happiness than they have ever dreamt about, and poor muddled people will be given an answer they have to accept.

Unlike many of the writers in his circle, Greene had never advocated pacifism. 'If war,' he wrote in the *Spectator* in December 1940, 'were only as pacifists describe it – violent, unjust, horrible, useless – it would have fallen out of favour long ago.' For him, the desire for war was a longing both for catharsis and for tribulation. By night, the Second World War provided both.

During the day, Greene was pen-pushing in the Ministry of Information. If it were not for his nights as an ARP warden, he would have been embarrassed to play so small a part in the violence that he saw as the real business of war. At the start of the conflict, Greene wrote to his wife describing the 'faint susurrus of the intellectuals dashing for ministry posts', dismissing Stephen Spender who had 'feathered his young nest in the Ministry of Information', though in fact Spender worked as a schoolteacher before he signed up as a fireman in 1941. Greene himself initially refrained from accepting a desk job. Called for his interview with the Emergency Reserve in the winter of 1939, he was asked what role he envisaged himself undertaking in wartime by officials who clearly expected to hear the word 'Intelligence'. As the interviewers leaned forward in their chairs, Greene had the impression that they were holding out to him, 'in the desperation of their boredom, a deck of cards with one card marked'. He helped them by taking the marked card and announcing 'the Infantry', asking only for six months to finish *The Power and the Glory,* which was actually already completed.

In fact in April 1940, two months before he was due to be called up into the army, Greene accepted a post at the Ministry of Information. He wanted to stay where he was, with time to write, even if working as a wartime civil servant would be boring. Greene was responsible for looking after the authors' section and had a tiny office carved out within one of the Ministry's rambling corridors, incongruously housed within the clean art deco lines of Senate House, normally the province of the University of London. According to Malcolm Muggeridge (now a colleague of Greene's), there were still intimations of the academic function of the building: 'scientific formulae scrawled on blackboards, the whiff of chemicals and dead dog-fish in one of the lavatories'. But now, like all Ministry buildings, this one teemed with people, moving about energetically. In a 1940 story called 'Men at Work', Greene described the 'high heartless building with complicated lifts and long passages like those of a liner and lavatories where the water never ran hot and the nail-brushes were chained like Bibles'. The building even had the stuffy smell of the mid-Atlantic, except in the corridors, where the windows were open for fear of blast and he expected to see people wrapped in rugs lying in deckchairs. Here, 'work was not done for its usefulness but for its own sake – simply as an occupation'. Propaganda, as far as Greene was concerned, was a mere means of passing the time.

Meanwhile, determined to get to the front one way or another, Greene was proposing a scheme for official writers to the Forces, equivalent to the war artists. When Evelyn Waugh visited him at the Ministry

of Information in May 1940, Greene tried to persuade Waugh to
support the idea, announcing that he himself wanted to become a
marine. While trapped in the soulless safety of Senate House, he and
Muggeridge entertained themselves by reading the file of letters from
writers offering their services to the Ministry and by dreaming up
imaginatively ludicrous schemes to throw the enemy off course.
Muggeridge later remembered Greene coolly exploring the possibility
of throwing stigmata and other miraculous occurrences into the battle
for the mind in Latin America.

The excitement and the danger of wartime came at night. When
Greene was not on duty as a warden, he would wander around anyway,
sometimes with Dorothy Glover and sometimes with Muggeridge,
who found that

> there was something rather wonderful about London in the Blitz, with
> no street lights, no traffic and no pedestrians to speak of; just an empty,
> dark city, torn with great explosions, racked with ack-ack fire, lit with
> lurid flames, acrid smoke, its air full of the dust of fallen buildings.

Muggeridge observed Greene's longing on these evenings for a bomb to
fall on him.

On nights like 26 September when he was on duty, Greene could
legitimately feel that he was actively involved in the war. The autumn
of 1940 was an especially satisfying moment for ARP wardens. From
the start of the war, official civil defence manuals had insisted on the
wardens' importance, stating that there would be a great need in air
raids for 'persons of courage and personality' with sound local knowledge to serve as a link between the public and the authorities. But
Violet Bonham Carter, President of the Women's Liberal Federation
and a close friend of Winston Churchill, reported in the *Spectator* in
November 1940 that during the phoney war wardens like herself had
been regarded as 'a quite unecesssary and rather expensive nuisance'.
They appeared to spend their days in basements, listening to gas lectures
in the intervals of playing darts, emerging at nightfall only to worry
innocent people about their lights or perform strange charades with the

traffic. Now that the raids had started, the wardens had their reward for months of training and waiting. 'We are conscious, as never before in our lives, of fulfilling a definite, direct and essential function.'

Bonham Carter was particularly proud that this new service was self-created and democratic; the wardens' posts were run by local authorities and staffed by volunteers. As civilians, the wardens were not subject to military discipline and were unfettered by red tape and rigid regulations; 'in an essentially human task we are allowed to behave like human beings.' Many of them did not even have uniforms; the only pre-requisite for the job was a tin hat. This kind of war work was especially satisfying for women like Bonham Carter who were determined to play an equivalent role in society to men. John Strachey considered that women who were sharing the danger of the war by engaging in civil defence work were undergoing some of the most satisfying and valuable experiences they had ever been offered. As far as he was concerned, a woman's life was no higher or more sacred than a man's, and it was 'mere cant' to pretend that it was.

Bowen, like Bonham Carter, was proud that she was risking her life alongside her male counterparts. In a longer draft of 'London, 1940' she outlined the liberating effects of war for women, who were no longer having to dress according to the expectations of male society.

> Those who don't like scratchy stockings go bare-legged. You see everywhere the trouser that comforts the ankle, the flat-heeled shoe for long pavement walks.

Both Bowen and Greene appreciated the opportunity the war gave them to become acquainted with their fellow wardens, with Bowen later describing the warden's post as a fascinating focus of life. 'We wardens,' she wrote, 'were of all types – so different that, but for the war, we would not have met at all. As it was, in spite of periodic rows or arguments on non-raid evenings, most of us became excellent friends.'

Bowen provided a tribute to these wartime friends through the character of Connie in *The Heat of the Day*. As tired as everyone else, Connie may occasionally slumber beside the telephone but she can, at any moment, 'instantly pop open both eyes and cope'. She also maintains standards, despite the privations of war, clipping on her earrings, even though they hurt, because 'going on night duty you had all the same to keep up a certain style'.

Working alongside women like Connie, Bowen was coming to believe in this as a democratic 'People's War'. In the earlier draft of the 'London, 1940' article, she stated that in the previous six months British class-consciousness had faced a severe challenge. The spell of the Old School Tie had lost its power; people walked the streets shabby, with grooming now limited to the effort to clean the brick dust from their faces and hair. Liberated from checking for signs of status, Londoners looked straight into each other's eyes. All over the place there was an 'exchange of searching, speechless, intimate looks between strangers'. Indeed, there were no strangers now; everyone was part of a collective community. 'We have almost stopped talking about Democracy,' Bowen went on, 'because, for the first time, we *are* a democracy. We are more, we are almost a commune.' Now that everyone faced the same risks as their neighbours, they were levelled by danger. 'All destructions make the same grey mess; rich homes, poor homes, the big store, the one-man shop make the same slipping rubble.' Identifying herself collectively with 'the people', she announced that this '*is* the people's war, for the people's land, and what we save we rule'.

Although Greene was dismissive of cantish propaganda, he, like Bowen, was sold on the idea of the democratic spirit of wartime London. 'This is a people's war,' he had declared in a review of British newsreels at the end of the first month of the war, suggesting that the American public should learn about the war in Britain through 'the rough unprepared words of a Mrs Jarvis, of Penge, faced with evacuation, black-outs, a broken home'. He was impressed by the courage of the civilians he saw every night, hurrying to the shelter, making do amid bombed buildings. Reviewing a theatrical revue-satire two months into the Blitz, he commended Edith Evans's portrait of a hop-picker returning to the fields from her bombed home. The 'unembittered humour', the 'Cockney repetitions that move one like the refrain of a

ballad' and the 'silly simple smile' came 'very close to the heroic truth
at which the world is beginning to wonder'.

For Greene, the camaraderie in the warden's post transposed wartime
London onto the comic world of his own stories. This was largely the
result of a colleague called Charlie Wix, the 'heroic raconteur' of the
post, whose chief occupation before the war had been giving evidence
in divorce cases. Anecdotes with punchlines like 'Mr Wix . . . what 'ave
you done with the bodies?' gave Greene entertaining material for his
war diary. Later, he realised that his most humorous stories all dated
from the Second World War, as though the proximity of death provoked
an irresistible urge to laugh. Together, the wardens united in the face of
the surprising nervousness of the police, who disappeared from the
streets during bad raids, with one mistaking a new heavy gun for a
landmine. And Greene found similar material for humour in the shelter at 221 Tottenham Court Road, which was on the edge of his patch
and was frequented chiefly by good-natured prostitutes from the bar

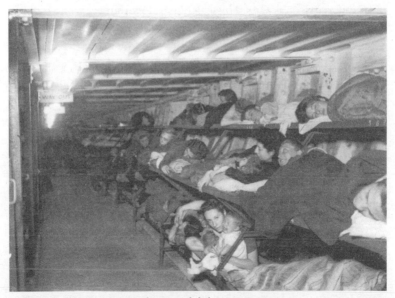

A London air-raid shelter, autumn 1940

opposite. 'Molly Hawthorn,' he reported in his diary, 'is a whore and likes it.' A former pillion girl, she became a prostitute when she discovered 'that people would actually pay her'. Before the war, she had married, but then her husband was called up and sent to Ireland 'and back she went to whoring'. Greene had wandered once again into Greeneland.

At 8.30 p.m. on 26 September the sirens in both Bloomsbury and Marylebone began to wail. The main sirens sounded for two minutes: a mournful and ominous howl, gliding slowly up and down between two notes. John Lehmann compared this to the noise of a dog in the extremities of agony. The warning was then taken up by the wardens, who sounded sharp blasts on their whistles, urging local residents to retreat into shelters. Once they had blown their whistles, Bowen and Greene had to visit the shelters in their district, making sure that people were settling for the night and that the paraffin lamps were still working. Now, with the sky lit up by searchlights, pedestrians watched as the battle played itself out high up in the sky, with the planes too far away to hear. The raiding bombers, arriving from the coast, were met by defending fighters, diving and curling, with both leaving white trails across the sky. Gradually the enemy aeroplanes approached the city, as they do in *The Heat of the Day*, 'dragging, drumming, slowly round in the pool of night, drawing up bursts of gunfire – nosing, pausing, turning'.

From now on the hum of aircraft overhead was punctuated by the noise of bombs dropping, mingled with the persistent sound of the pelting shells of the ack-ack guns, which were stationed near Bowen in Regent's Park. In his wartime diary Harold Nicolson, who was currently heading the Ministry of Information, tried to distinguish between the different layers of sound:

> There is the distant drumfire of the outer batteries. There is the nearer crum-crum of the Regent's Park guns. Then there is the drone of aeroplanes and the sharp impertinent notes of some nearer batteries.

FF-oopb! they shout. And then in the middle distance there is the rocket sound of the heavy guns in Hyde Park. One gets to love them, these angry London guns. And when they drop into silence, one hears above them, irritating and undeterred, the dentist's drill of the German aeroplanes, seeming always overhead, appearing always to circle round and round, ready always to drop three bombs, flaming, and then . . . Crump, crump, crump, somewhere.

The first bombs of the night were usually incendiaries: small cylindrical weapons about eighteen inches long with a magnesium alloy exterior and a core of thermite priming composition. These were dropped in clusters and were designed to start fires that would light the way for subsequent planes dropping more powerful high explosive bombs. The incendiaries sounded less threatening than the HEs, clattering down casually like trays of tin cans. But an official civil defence booklet warned the public that it was possible for one aeroplane to carry up to a thousand of these bombs, and that they were particularly potent because the whole of the device was combustible, with the exception of the striker mechanism and the sheet-iron tail fin. The Home Office had calculated that a single German bomber could start up to 150 fires spread over three miles. According to John Strachey incendiaries could be regarded either as harmless toys or as deadly menaces, depending on whether civilians were prepared to put them out with sand buckets and stirrup pumps. Three weeks into the Blitz, ARP wardens had become adept at using their tin hats to extinguish them as soon as they landed in the street and were becoming less dependent on the help of the fire brigade.

Now, the incendiaries punctured the darkness of the blackout, lighting up the ruins which already lined Marylebone and Bloomsbury. Both Bowen and Greene found the ruins eerily beautiful when illuminated at night. Greene frequently passed by the first bombed house he had seen, neatly sliced in half, in Woburn Square. Initially, exposed in cross-section, it had looked like a Swiss chalet: 'there were a pair of skiing sticks hanging in the attic, and in another room a grand piano cocked one leg over the abyss.' The kitchen seemed impossibly crowded with furniture until he realised that he had been given a kind of mouse-eye view from behind the stove and the dresser. These were the surreal scenes that would characterise much wartime visual art and that in turn would lead people to view pre-war surrealist art with new eyes. During this period the novelist Inez Holden surveyed Regent's Park with a surrealist painter friend. There were two or three odd stockings slung over the branches; purple damask draped on a tree; a brand new bowler hat balanced on a twig. Turning to Holden, the painter announced smugly: 'Of course we were painting this sort of thing years ago, but it has taken some time to get here.'

Since the night of the Woburn Square bombing, fresh gashes had been created in Greene's district every night. Two days earlier, the YMCA club on Great Russell Street was bombed, killing five people, including a member of the Home Guard. Tonight as the aeroplanes gathered overhead, Greene was waiting expectantly to see any new ruins the bombing might bring.

2

10 p.m.: Fire

At 9.30 p.m. Rose Macaulay set out for her 10 p.m. ambulance shift. By now the raid was fully underway. Incendiaries were falling throughout Marylebone and the blacked-out streets were lit up by fire and searchlights. Eighty German aircraft attacked London over the course of the night, flying in over Norfolk, Suffolk and the south coast. Despite the danger of the streets, Macaulay was relieved to leave her flat. During evenings at home, she spent the raids under the dubious protection of

Rose Macaulay in her flat in Hinde House in 1950

her kitchen table. 'Faith in tables is important,' she had informed her sister Jean in a letter earlier that week. But her faith was not strong enough to assuage her phobia of being buried under rubble: the result of seeing a succession of houses and blocks of flats reduced to piles of ruins from which the inhabitants could not be extracted in time to live. She would rather brave the explosions from the street, or from the relative safety of the ambulance station dugout.

The ambulance station was a half-hour walk from Macaulay's flat, through the side streets of Marylebone. Lurching along in the darkness, Macaulay presented a frail figure. Always tall, thin and angular, she had become bonier with age and was currently existing chiefly on a diet of tomato juice. But at fifty-nine, she was in fact still stronger than many of her younger colleagues at the ambulance station. As an undergraduate, she had spent her evenings scaling the university roofs, and was surprised when the other turn-of-the-century undergraduates at Somerville College did not wish to do the same. Now, she kept her climbing skills honed by clambering up and down the staff ladders in the stacks at the London Library. Volunteering to drive an ambulance in March 1939, she was unfazed by the regulations, which set the upper age limit at fifty, or by the application form, which asked volunteers to assess their ability to lift a person on a stretcher to the top bunk of an ambulance.

In the spring of 1940 official government decrees had stipulated that any female ambulance drivers over fifty should relinquish their duties, but Macaulay had managed to maintain her post. She had no inclination to rein in her physical courage or to surrender to the conventions of middle age. Nonetheless, close friends had been saddened to see her age visibly over the past year. They ascribed it to the war which, as a vocal pacifist, she had found hard to accept. 'My God, what a world,' she wrote to Rosamond Lehmann a week after the declaration of war; 'I feel still that it is a nightmare and that I will wake – but know it isn't.' A few friends, such as Lehmann herself, also attributed Macaulay's new frailty to the decline in health of Gerald O'Donovan, her secret lover and companion of the past twenty years. 'He is terribly weak,' Macaulay reported in the same letter to Lehmann; 'I don't think he'll get well ever.'

Arriving at the ambulance dugout, Macaulay tried out her new prize possession: a blow-up lilo that she had found in Selfridges earlier in the day. This, she told Jean subsequently, was 'a great stroke of luck': they had informed her previously that they would not have any more for weeks. She blew it up by mouth and put it ready for use on the floor, although she knew it was unlikely she would get much sleep that night. She then joined the other drivers, awaiting instructions as they listened to the bombs overhead. Earlier in the war, they had been given extra training during the periods of waiting, but on 21 September London County Council had announced that as long as the severe raiding continued it was desirable that 'any exercise or instruction which would deprive personnel of any opportunity there may be for sleep should be avoided'. Instead they could chat, play games and knit, and Macaulay was cheerful in the company of the other ambulance workers. Away from the ambulance station, she was a literary *grande dame*: the author of over twenty novels, many of them bestsellers, and a familiar, eccentric presence in literary London. Here she could discard that persona and take pleasure in the shared everyday preoccupations of wartime life. 'I like my ambulance colleagues, male and female,' she wrote to Virginia Woolf in October. 'You would too, I think. They teach me to knit, and are not unduly cast down by what they have to see and do.'

Not far from Macaulay, Henry Yorke was also waiting to be called out to a raid at his fire station, Sub-station 345V 'A' Division, at 79 Davies Street. Firefighters had the longest shifts of all defence workers; as a full-time auxiliary fireman, Yorke was on duty for forty-eight hours followed by a twenty-four-hour break. This suited him because the time off was long enough to make progress with his writing, which was more prolific than it had ever been despite the long hours of work. He could also go into the office of Pontifex, the family business he was helping his father to run, which specialised in making equipment for breweries and bathrooms. Charming, rich, funny and briefly single now that his wife Dig and six-year-old son Sebastian had been evacuated to the countryside, Yorke spent the evenings of his leave taking girls out to restaurants, bars and nightclubs, impressing them with tales of his heroic exploits. Rosamond Lehmann affectionately described Yorke in this period as

> an eccentric, fire-fighting, efficient, pub-and-night-club-haunting monk, voluble, frivolous, ironic, worldly, austerely vowed to the invisible cell which he inhabited and within which a series of intricately designed, elaborately executed, poetic yet realistic war novels were being evolved.

Henry Yorke, photographed by Cecil Beaton, 1949

On duty, both Macaulay and Yorke wore full official uniforms. She had been issued with a peaked cap and a dark blue drill coat, which some ambulance drivers complained was too insubstantial to survive many nights of bombing. Yorke was dressed in a dark blue uniform with silver buttons and red piping. He wore rubber boots and a tin hat and carried an axe and spanner in his blue belt. Auxiliary firemen were only issued with one uniform, and by the end of a shift both Yorke and his clothes were black with soot and soaked through from the water used to put out fires. Despite the excitement of his time off, Yorke found the long shifts draining. For the past two and a half weeks he had been continually busy fighting major fires. And conditions at the fire station itself were not helped by the fact that there had been no gas at the station for several days, which meant that there were no heaters to dry clothes and no hot food. He was also exhausted. 'Quite well but sleep the great difficulty,' he wrote to Rosamond Lehmann a week into the raids. Sleeping on duty was very difficult, and off duty Yorke was too busy writing and socialising to catch up on rest. In March 1939 he had told his friend Mary Strickland that his pre-war routine was 'to work myself silly and then go out . . . about once a week and get blind drunk and talk hard till 4am'. This had not changed, and his leave nights were often even later than his nights on duty.

Yorke had joined up with the Auxiliary Fire Service in October 1938, wanting to avoid being conscripted into the army so that he could continue his ordinary London life. In 1937 London County Council had established its own air-raid precautions committee, which in March 1938 approved proposals for the recruiting and training of 28,000 auxiliary firemen for the London Fire Brigade, preparing for a war which many already believed to be imminent. Yorke was about the seven-thousandth fireman to sign up and he was subsequently very proud of his low serial number. In order to join he needed a doctor's certificate confirming, as he put it, that he was 'not likely to fall down dead running upstairs' and references suggesting that he was a responsible person and was therefore unlikely to make the most of the looting opportunities provided by fire. Unlike even the police, firemen in uniform were allowed by law to enter any house, which some saw as an invitation to help themselves. Yorke spent the first eight weeks in his new profession being trained in the regular fire station. This was a course that no one failed, because the regular firemen were convinced they would be held responsible for any failures. This did not mean that they felt the need to make the course especially stringent. According to Yorke their teaching consisted chiefly of lectures in how much the regular London Fire Brigade hated the Auxiliary Fire Service. He was then deemed ready to fight fires.

At this stage Yorke was ambivalent about the war itself, although he could see no obvious alternative. In his 1940 memoir *Pack My Bag*, begun in July 1939, he described himself as unwilling to fight and yet 'likely enough to die by fighting for something which, as I am now, for

Firemen being trained before the war

the life of me I cannot understand'. But he wrote to Evelyn Waugh in October 1939 that the dangers of life as a fireman seemed preferable to 'what seems to be the alternative, domination by Hitler and the Mitfords on top'.

Initially, Yorke saw his decision to fight fires as a heroic one. Indeed, he later wrote that some of his fellow volunteers had joined up thinking that the AFS was a suicide squad, choosing the most dangerous job of all. As a result, he experienced the declaration of war as a personal death sentence. When he was mobilised on 1 September 1939, Yorke dressed himself in his prickly, still unfamiliar uniform, 'alone, frightened, sickened, sure of dying'. The autobiographically-inspired hero of Yorke's 1943 novel *Caught* is convinced as soon as war begins that death will follow. 'All that was real to him then was his death in a matter of days.' Yorke himself told Evelyn Waugh in his October 1939 letter that he could not believe he would survive, suggesting that Waugh should come to London and take a last look at the city itself as it would soon be in ruins. 'If you did come up then we could get together again for old times sake, just once more.'

Like Graham Greene, Yorke minded the fact that he had missed the chance to prove himself in the First World War, and, though he dreaded the prospect of imminent death, he now embraced the danger sentimentally. In *Pack My Bag* he describes his birth in 1905 as 'three years after one war and nine before another, too late for both' but not too late for the war which seemed to be coming upon him as he wrote. Hence 'the need to put down what comes to mind before one is killed', storing up memories as charms with which to die. 'We who must die soon, or so it seems to me, should chase our memories back standing, when they are found, enough apart not to be near what they once meant.'

This was a period when the public, too, saw firemen as heroes. In *Caught* Yorke writes that at the start of the war the Fire Service came second only to pilots in the eyes of the public. Old ladies gave auxiliary firemen money, aged gentlemen bought them drinks, street cleaners called them 'mate' and girls looked back yearningly as they passed by. But after pledging himself, gladiatorially, to an early and heroic death, Yorke was faced merely with the sustained inaction of the phoney war, which he found especially hard. 'His life in the Fire Brigade sounds undendurable,' Waugh observed in his diary after meeting Yorke for lunch in November 1939. 'Fire fighting is a waiting game,' Yorke wrote in a 1960 account of his time in the fire service. For forty-eight hours, he and the other firemen would wait through day and night, ready all the time to ride out with a pump to civilian fires in under sixty seconds. The focus, now, was on discipline in ordinary tasks, which the auxiliary firemen found unnecessary and demeaning. 'We come here ready for at least death, and then we get into trouble for not going under our beds,' Richard complains in *Caught*. Here Richard is distressed because the regular firemen hate him and because an old lady on a bus has announced that firemen are 'army dodgers'. In the original typescript of the novel the narrator explains that 'the Fire Service, now that there had been no raids, was as unpopular with the public as, in the first few days, it had been popular'.

The Blitz brought Yorke and other auxiliary firemen the chance they needed to prove that they were heroes after all. In his 1955 novel *Officers and Gentlemen* Evelyn Waugh was playfully dismissive of the activities of his auxiliary firemen friends in the Blitz. The book opens with a fire in a gentlemen's club in Piccadilly where, amid blazing flames, 'a group of progressive novelists in fireman's uniform' stand on the pavement opposite and squirt a little jet of water into the morning-room. The club's alcohol store room has been hit by the raid and the gutters outside are running with whisky and brandy, which the firemen apparently consume mid-raid. But in fact, the firemen did put themselves in more danger than Waugh, from his lofty position as a marine, suggests. Before 7 September, four-fifths of the London auxiliaries had not seen a real fire. They were now called upon to deal with conflagrations that in peacetime would have frightened regular firemen. And according to Yorke's friend William Sansom, who was also an auxiliary fireman in Westminster, it was a particular tradition of London firemen to begin their assault on the fire from within the building rather than from the safer ground outside. Years later Yorke recollected idealistically that the firemen were always brave when together with their crew.

> However frightened, they are hardly ever cowards. Behind them they have the crew, the other men on the appliance. They are like a small pack of hounds, cowards alone they may be but when together ready to take on lions.

Yorke himself often wanted to retreat into a shelter or lie down flat during raids, but when observed by his colleagues he waited to be hit instead. The danger and bravery were recognised by the public. 'We're absolute heroes now to everyone,' Richard boasts to his sister-in-law in *Caught*; 'Soldiers can't look us in the face, even.'

A hero at last, Henry Yorke was enjoying the Blitz. He liked learning to use the technical equipment of firefighting, becoming at home with

Firemen at work, autumn 1940

pumps, hoses, ropes, ladders and coupling pipes. His 1960 account of his time in the fire service goes into enthusiastic detail about the Dual Purpose (a wagon comprising a ladder on large wheels, a built-in tank of water with a pump, and a vacuum pump to raise water from a pond), the simple pump appliance and the special ladder, made in Germany, comprising a pump and three tubular ladders telescopically folded but joined together. Yorke's Blitz stories are filled with technical information. The fire in *Caught* is fought with pumps ineffectually supplied with water by remote pump operators and hoses which tear under pressure; the release in 'A Rescue' is achieved by means of complicated manoeuvring of firemen's ladders. For years afterwards, Yorke would be drawn to fires he could put out, proud to show off his technical prowess. Describing a 1951 fire in his local pub he informed his readers that they could:

judge of my delight to hear the old roar in the chimney, and to realise, as I entered the bar at midday, that I was to enjoy the most enviable moment of all to any ex-fireman, a nice little job in someone else's chimney.

Now that the firemen were lauded for their bravery one more, Yorke was in great demand. 'Who are you going out with tonight, darling?' girls asked each other as they prepared for nights out in the Blitz. 'Is it someone you'd like to die with?' In Yorke's case, it usually was. And he was happy to fall into the role of the endangered hero. Indeed, part of the attraction of the war was that, now it was no longer phoney, it gave him a series of roles to play.

Yorke seems always to have found an element of role play necessary in assuming a convincing public persona. Descriptions of him by others tend to characterise him as possessing an elusive emptiness. Acquaintances found him charming, lively and fun; as a result, he acquired new friends and mistresses with ease. But closer friends and lovers tended to experience him partly as a lack. Rosamond Lehmann's description of Yorke as inhabiting an 'invisible cell' accurately evoked his ability to keep his inner life private while in company, whether with fellow firemen or with lovers. Henry had told Rosamond at the start of the war that in times such as these 'the writer, our kind, must sink absolutely down to the bottom and remain anonymous'. In fact, this kind of behaviour was customary for him, so much so that friends and lovers tended in retrospect to wonder whether they actually knew him at all.

The architectural historian and London gossip James Lees-Milne, who was a friend of Yorke's in the 1930s, later described him as 'well read, articulate, but inscrutable. Inclined to be morose.' Although the two men saw each other frequently, Lees-Milne knew Yorke principally as an upper-class 'Bright Young Thing' who worked in the family business. Because Yorke had published his three novels under the pseudonym Henry Green, Lees-Milne did not at this stage even know that his friend was a writer. Indeed, the pseudonym itself was part of the role-playing. Henry Yorke did not want his social persona to be complicated by the novels, and at the same time the enigmatic writerly persona of

Henry Green was another role he could assume. For his part Lees-Milne observed in his memoirs that he had never been able to fathom

> what was going on in that dark head, beneath that sallow skin, under that sleek black hair, behind that straight, stern nose, those deep-set, wild bird eyes and that strange mobile mouth which changed shape and expression according to his thoughts even when he was not speaking.

Yorke appears to have been happiest and most alive when confident in assuming a role. In his twenties, he had enjoyed his time spent as a worker in the factory of his father's business near Birmingham. Here he could take on the role of the toff made good, discovering ordinary life as a worker among workers. 'The men, I loved them,' he stated in an interview which, much to the embarrassment of his parents, he gave to the *Star* in 1929. 'They are fine fellows, generous, open-hearted, and splendid pals . . . Of course, they knew who I was, but that made no difference.' In *Pack My Bag* he wrote that his experiences in his father's factory taught him how little money meant and literature counted, showing him the real satisfaction of making something with his hands. His schoolfriend the novelist Anthony Powell later recalled that Yorke was as happy during his time as a factory worker as he ever knew him to be.

The fire station was providing Yorke once again with the chance for camaraderie with the working classes. He was nicknamed 'the Honourable' by the other volunteers, whom he found tended to be domestic servants and hotel staff as well as burglars who had joined up hoping to loot the bombed houses they were saving. But, secure in his role, he at least liked to convince himself that he felt at home with them. And he enjoyed listening to the other firemen talking and gossiping, taking mental notes for the novel that would become *Caught*. 'The behaviour of my AFS unit gets more and more fascinating,' he had written to Mary Strickland in July. 'It will make a good book one day.' He was learning a new, communal language in which getting the flames down became 'putting the light out', the other firemen were known as 'cock' and children became 'nippers'.

In *Caught* Yorke satirises Richard Roe's sense that he can merge with the firemen around him. Richard is convinced that he has become indistinguishable from the other firemen, at least in appearance.

> In his dirt, his tiredness, the way the light hurt his eyes and he could not look, in all these he thought he recognised that he was now a labourer, he thought he had grasped the fact that, from now on, dressed like this, and that was why roadmen called him mate, he was one of the thousand million that toiled and spun.

He announces happily that 'It brings everyone together, there's that much to a war.' But in fact this kind of anonymity is never possible. The narrator makes it clear that Richard merely lets himself 'drop into what he imagined was their manner of talking'. He goes to great lengths to ingratiate himself with the regular firemen, buying them drinks in the bar, but is never in fact accepted as one of them. Nonetheless, Yorke does portray Richard as content to be caught up in this myth.

According to William Sansom, some integration did inevitably occur among firemen forced to spend such long periods in each other's company. For Sansom, the effect of the long shifts was to imbue the men with semi-military discipline and to concentrate life more at the station than at home. While waiting for fires the men at most sub-stations went into the local pub together to drink draught ale.

But the night of 26 September came at the end of a busy shift for Westminster firemen. The previous night an HE and an unexploded bomb had fallen at the junction of Denbigh Street and Belgrave Road, and firemen were called in to rescue people trapped in a vault shelter underneath the pavement, where water was dangerously pouring in from a broken mains. They were responsible for attempting to restrict the fire and for pumping water out of the flooded basements. At one stage the firefighters found dead bodies, killed by the bomb, floating in the water. That morning the officer in charge of Westminster stretcher parties had gone to inspect the unexploded bomb at just the moment that it exploded. His head was caught in the blast and he died later that day. Firefighting was turning out to be as dangerous an occupation as Yorke had feared it would be at the start of the war.

After a day of attempting to catch up on sleep at the fire station, Yorke and his crew were now ready for the next batch of incidents. Shortly after 11 p.m. there was a series of explosions between Oxford Street and Mayfair. At 11.21 p.m. the Curzon cinema was hit, with half the stage damaged by fire, heat, smoke and water. But the most notable incident in Westminster on the night of 26 September was the bombing of Old Palace Yard, close to the Houses of Parliament, by an HE at ten minutes after midnight. This was the first time the Parliament had been directly affected by the bombing. The western frontage of the buildings, including the main public entrance, was badly damaged and the tip of the sword on the bronze statue of Richard the Lionheart was bent forward by the blast. Inside the building, doors were broken and ceilings brought down. Some of the glass in Westminster Abbey was blown out by the

The Houses of Parliament following the 26 September raid

force of the explosion. Although no one was killed, eleven people sustained injuries from the splintered glass and the plaster falling from the ceiling. After the wardens on the scene had reported the incident, the injured people were treated by nurses from the British Red Cross who were stationed in the building. Firemen from across the borough, including from Yorke's sub-station, were immediately summoned to the scene.

By now, much of London was ablaze. In *Officers and Gentlemen* Evelyn Waugh recalled his visual memories of the Blitz at this time, describing the sky over London as turning a glorious ochre, as though a dozen tropical suns were simultaneously setting round the horizon.

> Everywhere the searchlights clustered and hovered, then swept apart; here and there pitchy clouds drifted and billowed; now and then a huge flash momentarily froze the serene fireside glow.

These lighting effects made it easier for the drivers of fire engines to navigate as they drove at full speed to an incident through the blackout, although the glare of the fire was also dangerous in attracting more bombers.

As an auxiliary fireman, Yorke travelled with a trailer pump rather than an ordinary fire engine. These had been produced in vast quantities in the lead-up to war and were light appliances, easily handled by two or three firemen, which could pump 350–500 gallons of water a minute, as opposed to the 900 gallons pumped by regular fire engines. They were towed into action by light vans which carried the hose and other equipment. On the way to the fire, Yorke sat forward on his seat, apprehensively looking out for a bomb, or a crater not marked out with lamps, or for glass that would cut the tyres. Tonight, as always, the AFS were first on the scene of the fire, supervised by the regular members of the Fire Brigade who were stationed at the auxiliary sub-stations. They only called on the regular fire brigade to come and extinguish fires if they were beyond the control of the trailer pumps.

As the firemen set to work to put out the fire at the Houses of Parliament, more bombs continued to fall. Three more HEs landed on the building before one in the morning, and a cluster of incendiaries was then dropped at 1.53 a.m., damaging the gas mains. The firemen did not leave the scene when the bombers reappeared and so they were in serious danger of being hit by the explosion. Once you were the direct target of a bomb you had time to duck but not to get out of the way altogether as it landed. According to the literary ARP warden Barbara Nixon, HE bombs did not so much fall as rush at enormous velocity to the ground, issuing a tearing sound and a whistle as they descended. These bombs consisted of a high explosive mixture contained in a steel case, fitted with a fuse and exploder. They varied from 100 to 2,000 pounds in weight, although most were under 500 pounds. A 1940 air-raid manual described their destructive effects as being twofold. There were the effects of the blast, which was the air pressure created by the explosion, and those of the fragmentation, which was the breaking up of the steel case of the bomb into jagged pieces or splinters. These splinters were about an inch wide and were projected in large numbers in every direction at twice the speed of a rifle bullet.

Yorke and his crew tackled fires by attaching the trailer pump to a street hydrant outside and hauling a rope up the stairs to connect the pump to the fire. If a strong jet of water could be concentrated on the seat of the fire, then the conflagration as a whole could be brought under control, but it was often hard to access the seat of the fire in time to stop it spreading. Yorke always had difficulty hearing over the noise created both by the fire itself and by the pumps, and also found it arduous to breathe. The smoke came in hot waves which made his eyes run and his throat tickle, bringing on a painful cough. He found that the thick, cold smoke of a continuing fire was worse than the hot smoke of a recent explosion:

This gripped by the throat. Until you could break a few windows you were throttled, but if you had a head cold it was miraculously cured. You lost so much mucus by the eyes and nose.

For Yorke, the fighting of fires was at once a practical, communal task and an intensely personal, dreamlike experience. In his short story 'Mr Jonas' he describes all his fellow firemen withdrawing into themselves when faced with a fire, as though each 'had come upon a place foreign to him but which he was aware he had to visit'. The fire became an imaginative landscape which Yorke inhabited as 'something between living and dying', caught between hope and fear, 'betwixt coma and the giving up of living'. In this state he could find the fire itself abstractly beautiful, retreating into a visual experience which seemed to have nothing to do with the actual immediate danger. When faced with a fire in *Caught*, Richard initially sits still before the immensity. The flame is 'a roaring red gold', pulsing rose-coloured at the outside edge; 'the perimeter round which the heavens, set with stars before fading into utter blackness' is 'for a space a trembling green'. The sheds burning at the docks become

> a broken, torn-up dark mosaic aglow with rose where square after square of timber had been burned down to embers, while beyond the distant yellow flames toyed joyfully with the next black stacks which softly merged into the pink of that night.

But caught up in the solitary, imaginative experience of fire, Yorke was then suddenly awakened into the actuality of danger. Yelling and receiving instructions, he experienced the scene once more as real.

3

1 a.m.: Rescue

As the fires across London were gradually brought under control, rescue workers and ambulance drivers could attend to the people trapped underneath the debris. Now that the spectacular lighting effects were starting to fade, the human costs of the bombing were becoming more apparent. At one in the morning, Rose Macaulay was dispatched to an incident in Camden Town, where the inhabitants of two fallen houses were buried under ruins. The night of 26 September 1940 was one of Macaulay's most active on duty as an ambulance driver, and she recounted it three times: immediately afterwards, in a letter to her sister Jean, and two weeks later in an article in *Time and Tide* and in a letter to Virginia Woolf.

The incident was not far from the ambulance station but it was still a hazardous drive. With her headlights dimmed, Macaulay found it difficult to avoid hitting patches of rubble in the street. Describing the Blitz in her 1942 *Life Among the English,* she recalled the darkness of these nights, when 'cars crashed all night into street refuges, pedestrians, and each other' and dust from pulverised buildings settled on the windscreens.

Macaulay had always been a reckless driver. Indeed, she signed up with the ambulance service in March 1939 partly to put her courageous motoring skills to good use. In a 1935 catalogue of *Personal Pleasures*, Macaulay included three separate entries on the joys of driving. The first, headed 'Driving a Car', opens by lyrically extolling speed and the open road:

> To propel a car through space, to devour the flying miles, to triumph over roads, flinging them behind us like discarded snakes . . . here is a joy that Phaethon, that bad driver, never knew.

Another entry, more ambitiously headed 'Fastest on Earth', records her joy on returning to her parked car to find a leaflet on the windscreen advertising 'Fastest on earth'. Seeing this as a personal accolade, she is tempted to keep it there as testimony to her car's prowess. As she rolls through the streets,

> the other cars, yes, and even omnibuses, may yield to me and my Morris pride of place in the Hyde Park Corner scuffle, at the Marble Arch roundabout, and dashing up Baker Street.

Driving an ambulance enabled Macaulay to fulfil her ambition to take pride of place on the road. It also gave her the chance to get her hands on the clanging bells that she admired in the fire engines that she also included in *Personal Pleasures*.

But since she first signed up to drive an ambulance, Rose Macaulay's enthusiasm for speeding had been chastened. The current ill-health of her lover, Gerald O'Donovan, began in June 1939, when Rose and Gerald had a car accident on a motoring holiday in Wales. Swerving to the wrong side of the road as she approached a corner, Rose ran into an oncoming car. Gerald suffered serious head injuries, which were followed by a stroke. For several weeks his chances of life were uncertain. Devastated, Rose informed Jean that 'if he dies, you won't be seeing me for some time'.

In fact, Gerald did not die until 1942, but Macaulay never overcame her guilt at hastening his demise. The climax of her final published novel *The Towers of Trebizond* (1956) is a reenactment of her own accident. The first-person heroine Laurie kills her lover Vere by driving recklessly. She rushes self-righteously through a green light, knowing that a bus is charging across its own red light. The accident is not completely her fault, but she apportions the blame unequivocally:

> I knew about the surge of rage that had sent me off, the second the lights were with me, to stop the path of that rushing monster . . . I had plenty of time to think about it; no doubt my whole life.

Unlike Gerald O'Donovan, Vere dies instantaneously after the crash. By fast-forwarding the years between crash and death, Macaulay made clear the pattern of cause and effect she perceived as operating between these two events.

The imagined guilt of *The Towers of Trebizond* did have its basis in an experienced reality. For the first few months after the accident, it seemed that the crash would hasten Gerald's death more immediately than it in fact did. Rose began to mourn with all the intensity of a grieving widow, and to blame herself, not just for the accident, but for the imperfections in his life. In *Trebizond* Laurie immediately condemns herself for coming between Vere and his wife for ten years, observing that 'he had given me his love, mental and physical, and I had taken it; to that extent, I was a thief'. Rose herself had taken Gerald's love, mental and physical, for twenty years. Her sense of his impending death, coinciding with the increasing certainty of war, left her desolate. Once war began, it was hard to regain immediate confidence behind the wheel. Driving through London in her ambulance, she relished the empty roads and the speed legitimised by her siren. But she could no longer see herself as invincible.

Arriving in Camden Town, Macaulay found the incident post which the warden had marked with the customary two blue lamps placed on top of each other. She was confronted by the remains of two houses, now reduced to an enormous pile of ruins. Immediately, she was struck by the odour of gas, seeping through the pits and craters in the rubble, and by the unmistakable smell of the explosion itself. According to John Strachey the raw, brutal stench of a bombing incident was not so much a smell as 'an acute irritation of the nasal passages from the powdered rubble of dissolved houses'. But on top of this there was the acrid overtone left by the HE bomb itself, as well as the 'mean little stink' of domestic gas. For Strachey, 'the whole of the smell was greater than the sum of its parts. It was the smell of violent death itself. It was as if death was a toad that had come and squatted down at the bottom of the bomb craters of London.'

When Macaulay joined the workers at this particular incident, a rescue party was hacking away, trying to free the people trapped inside.

Rescue party at work, autumn 1940

Everyone was coughing, and people cried out from under the ruins, calling for help. The street was flooded with water where a main had burst. 'Dust,' Macaulay wrote in the *Time and Tide* report, 'liquefies into slimy mud.' Meanwhile the bombing went on noisily around her.

> Jerry zooms and drones about the sky, still pitching them down with long whistling whooshs and thundering crashes, while the guns bark like great dogs at his heels. The moonless sky, lanced with long, sliding, crossing shafts, is a-flare with golden oranges that pitch and burst and are lost among the stars.

There was nothing Macaulay could do except to wait for the rescue workers to complete the excavation, hoping all the while that no new bomb would fall on the site. The men were busy sawing, hacking, drilling and heaving. She stood by, encouraging the people inside, assuring them that they would be out soon, although she had no idea if this was true or not. Here was her own burying phobia played out, and she was glad to be on her side of the rubble. The cry of 'My baby. Oh, my poor baby. Oh, my baby. Get us out!' was heard from underneath the ruins, and Macaulay passed milk to the baby and water to the mother. 'All right, my dear. We'll be with you in ten minutes now,' the rescue workers called out at regular intervals throughout the night as they worked on, carefully dislodging one bit of rubble from another. But it was clear to Macaulay how much they still had to shift before they would reach the baby, who might well not make it through the night. The atmosphere remained convivial, despite the danger. Macaulay was impressed by the rescue workers who were, she reported to her sister the next day, 'very nice and matey. I like their way of calling every one (including the ambulance women) "mate".'

The planes continued to drone over their heads. There was a crash as a bomb landed, a few streets away, which made Macaulay and the rescue workers duck their heads involuntarily. The air glowed with new flames. The next bomb could easily wipe them out. One of the workers swore up at the planes and then, alerted by his friend as to the presence of a lady, apologised to Macaulay. 'Sorry Miss, excuse my language.' She assured him that she felt the same way herself. Eventually, the first human form emerged from the ruins. It was a seventy-four-year-old woman, 'gay and loquacious'. She was followed, half an hour later, by her married daughter, who had a grey, smeared, bruised face and vomited into the surrounding dust. 'Oh my back, my legs, my head. Oh, dear God, my children.' The woman was reluctant to leave her children and drive away in Macaulay's ambulance. Macaulay promised her that they would be out soon as well. In fact, they turned out to be dead, their bodies crushed and maimed by the rubble. Two boys of eleven and twelve, two babies of three and one. 'If only,' the woman moaned, 'they didn't suffer much . . .'

London was free of enemy aircraft by 4 a.m. but fifteen bomber planes returned an hour later, flying in from Dungeness. Then as dawn approached, the final bombers departed. Now the rescue party left, to be replaced by the next crew. 'Only,' Macaulay observed, 'inside the ruins the personnel remains the same.' It would be ten the next morning before the mother and baby were at last freed from the debris, though thankfully the baby was still alive. Now Macaulay stood on the pavement with a rescue worker, who was drinking a cup of cocoa provided by the mobile canteen. 'It's like this every night now,' he observed. 'This and fires. How long will people stick it? Where'll it all end?'

Macaulay helped her patients onto stretchers. The official guidelines instructed ambulance workers to lie the patient on top of a blanket folded sideways to avoid direct contact with the canvas or metal bed portion. 'This adds to his comfort and keeps him warm, thus reducing shock.' She followed this advice and then joined her colleague in lifting the stretchers into the ambulance, relieved to have agency again. The hardest part of the night was always the passive waiting, when she was unable to help the rescue workers or to determine the outcome of their

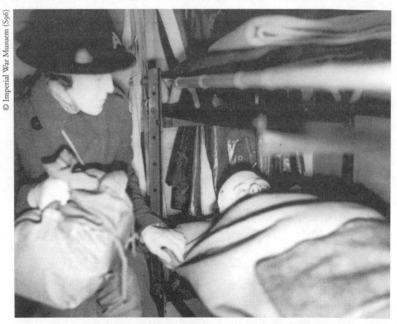

A London ambulance driver with patients, autumn 1940

efforts. She cleared the dust off the windscreen and drove off, while an ARP warden shone a torch on her wheels to make sure that she did not puncture them on the rubble. Ambulance drivers were supposed to keep to sixteen miles an hour, but most of them ignored the speed limit. Macaulay tended to become more tentative once she had patients in her charge. In *The Towers of Trebizond* she would have no qualms in labelling herself a murderer. She did not want other lives on her conscience as well as O'Donovan's.

She deposited her patients at the hospital, where ambulances pulled up at the stretcher entrance. Macaulay was never an enthusiastic hospital visitor. She had experienced her share of hospitals in the First World War, when she signed on as a VAD nurse, despite her extreme squeamishness. According to Jean, this was a foolish choice given that Rose 'tended to vomit or faint at the sight of blood or the mere mention of horrors'. Macaulay endowed Imogen, one of the heroines of her 1923 novel, *Told by an Idiot*, with her own nursing experience, describing her as 'an infinitely incapable V.A.D.' who 'did everything with remarkable incompetence, and fainted or was sick when her senses and nerves were more displeased than usual by what they encountered, which was often'. She recorded her own revulsion during the First World War through the character of Alix in her 1916 novel *Non-Combatants and Others*. Here Alix is suddenly and violently sick after she hears her shellshocked cousin describe the leg of a friend which he pulled out of the trench, 'thinking it led on to the entire friend, finding it didn't'. Her cousin Dorothy, like Jean an efficient and successful nurse, retorts impatiently: 'You'll never be any use if you don't forget *yourself*, Alix. You couldn't possibly nurse if you were always giving in to your own nerves.'

By the time of the Second World War, Macaulay had overcome her squeamishness enough to deal with her patients. Like nurses, ambulance drivers had to contend with nauseating gore. A Watford-based volunteer later recalled that the duties of an ambulance driver included tying together broken legs at the knees and ankles, and covering exposed intestines with her tin hat to keep infection out and the guts in. But Macaulay was still happier on this side of the entrance to the hospital; more at home in a van than a ward.

Now, having relinquished her patients, she returned to the ambulance station where, after raids, male and female drivers took their turns in their respective decontamination rooms, brushing off the dust that ended up coating their entire bodies, even getting under their tin hats and into their hair. She then went home to bed, relieved to find that her own flat remained intact. Macaulay knew that she was lucky to have survived the night. In the last three weeks of bombing, eight ambulance drivers had been killed and twenty-seven ambulances or adapted cars had been destroyed. And she was always less resilient than the rescue workers. 'It is all in the night's work to them,' she observed to Jean, and 'perhaps it will be to me sometime, but I am still an amateur at it and it rather gets one down. One wonders all the time how many people are at the moment alive under some ruin, and how much they are suffering in body and mind.'

———

Two weeks later, Macaulay published her account of her night in Camden Town in *Time and Tide*. Here, she did not minimise the misery she had witnessed. The government had instructed newspapers to maintain as optimistic as possible a stance towards the bombing, preventing them from including pictures of corpses or severely wounded bodies. But Macaulay refused to sanitise war. Her report contains moments of cheerfulness – she recounts the rescue worker's embarrassment that he has sworn at the Germans in front of a lady – but these serve to emphasise the bleakness of the overall situation. She ends the article by juxtaposing the rescue worker complaining that 'It's like this every night now' with the 'bland voice' on the radio the next day. 'There were a few casualties,' the radio states dismissively, 'but little material damage appears to have been done.'

This, Macaulay declares, is 'a sample corner of total war'. Here, there are civilian bodies entombed under dust and rubble; elsewhere, 'men are being burnt alive, blinded, shot, drowned, smashed to bits when their planes crash'. Having evoked the full horror of the dead children and their trapped, bruised mother, she insists that 'civilian war deaths are no worse than those of the young men in the fighting forces': 'it is

no worse that women should be killed than men'. Macaulay rejects the
apologetic cant of propagandists. She lauds the rescue workers for their
bravery, but does not allow this bravery to exonerate the brutality of
war. The dead pilots and the dead civilians are 'all part of the blind,
maniac, primitive, stupid bestiality of war, into which human beings
periodically leap, spitting in civilisation's face and putting her to
confused rout'.

Both Macaulay and *Time and Tide* risked government disapproval
by publishing this piece. Macaulay informed Virginia Woolf that *Time
and Tide* had doubts about whether they should print it at all, because
the censors had requested the press 'not to be too vivid about these
affairs'. They did in fact cut one sentence. Macaulay initially included
the rescue worker's despairing 'How long will people stick it?', but her
editors decided that the censor might 'boggle' at it. 'Accounts of raids,'
she told Woolf, 'have to be cheery – communal meals and singing, and
people shouting "We can take it".'

Macaulay's refusal to shout 'We can take it' herself perhaps belied the
fact that she was all the time taking an awful lot, and taking it with
remarkable courage. Aged fifty-nine, she was engaged in arduous
manual labour. While angry and sceptical about the war itself, Macaulay
always undertook her ambulance duties enthusiastically. Training in
August 1939, she wrote to thank her friend Daniel George for his
contribution of a 'mortified elephant' to a literary animal book they
were collaborating on, observing that 'he must have felt just as I did
this afternoon when I couldn't put a stretcher together after taking it
apart. Only I didn't cry and weep.' By June the following year she could
announce proudly to Jean: 'I am improving my bandaging to-day; also
stretcher bearing.' Now, driving a heavy van, lifting up wounded
patients and risking her own life, she resembled the ideal civilian
invoked by government propaganda.

By working as an ambulance driver, Macaulay had discovered a way
to be involved in the war effort, valiantly and stoically, while also rejecting war. She found refuge from sadness and pain in the camaraderie of
her fellow workers and in her own bravery, but this did not make her
shock at what was going on around her any less intense. Macaulay was

torn between involvement and detached disbelief, and this division was manifested by the split between her dual roles as ambulance driver and writer. By working in her ambulance and doing her best to mitigate the suffering caused by fighting, she was taking part in the war. By writing articles, she made it clear that she had not accepted the war itself, even if she accepted her role within it.

The chief appeal of ambulance driving was that it was a manual rather than a cerebral task, which enabled her to commit herself physically but not intellectually to the war effort. Shortly after the declaration of war she wrote to Rosamond Lehmann that she was dreading the onslaught of bombing – 'it will be hateful seeing people hurt and killed and terrified' – but that she would rather be in an ambulance than offer her services to the Ministry of Information, as writers were being asked to do.

> In my job, my mind is free in a sense, and all I have to think of is avoiding collisions and finding the cases and bringing them in; in a Ministry, one's mind would be sucked in too.

She had experience of working in a Ministry in the First World War, when her stints as a nurse and a landgirl were followed by a period working for the Department for Propaganda in Enemy Countries. It was in the Ministry, indeed, where she first met Gerald O'Donovan, who was then her boss. For Macaulay, to work for the Ministry of Information as Graham Greene was doing would be to condone implicitly not just the war effort but the war itself. And just because war seemed like the only option did not mean that war itself became acceptable.

Macaulay's divided attitude and role were partly the result of her experiences in the First World War. Then, young and idealistic, she accepted war's sacrifices. In a poem called 'The Garden', she insisted that the soldiers who 'fell dumb in the spring-time of age' had not 'lost all':

> Nay, see how they have won
> For their drifting dust a goodly heritage –
> A garden, full of flowers and the sun.

This was the dust that Macaulay's childhood friend Rupert Brooke had welcomed in 'The Soldier', anticipating that England's 'rich earth' would conceal the 'richer dust' of his own, ennobled corpse. In April 1915, Brooke was bitten on the lip by a mosquito while sailing on a Royal Navy ship to the Dardanelles. He died of blood poisoning a few hours later and was buried on the island of Skyros. In the end, his dust did not blend patriotically with the earth of his homeland; his death failed to ennoble.

Rupert had been a key figure in Rose's adolescence. The two had spent their early years a few doors away from each other in Rugby, before the Macaulays moved to Italy in 1887. After her return to England in 1894, Rose reconnected with Rupert, and they became neighbours again in Grantchester in their twenties. In a later memoir Rose looked back on idyllic days spent paddling together in the Grantchester meadows. By 1911, Rupert was living partly in London and Rose, now a published poet and novelist, was a frequent visitor. After the two young writers came joint first in a poetry competition, they took on literary London side by side. Rose later recollected her envy of Rupert, 'who walked about the streets without a map, often with a plaid rug over his shoulders'. She could not remember whether it was she or Rupert who first met Naomi Royde-Smith, a sophisticated literary hostess who would introduce her to people who seemed to her, 'an innocent from the Cam', to be more 'sparklingly alive' than any in her home world. War temporarily cut Rose off from the stimulating world of literary London she was just starting to enjoy, and severed her irretrievably from Rupert. Six months after his death, she recorded her unhappiness about 'the death at the war of several intimate friends of mine – Rupert Brooke was one – the sort of people who just can't be spared'.

For Macaulay, as for many of her generation, Rupert Brooke's death had revealed the futility of a conflict that quickly looked set to have no end. Her disillusionment, combined with her physical revulsion from the carnage she had witnessed as a nurse, was a driving force behind her commitment to the pacifist movement in the 1930s. In *Non-combatants and Others* Alix finds in pacifism an outlet for her own visceral pain at the indignities of war. 'As I can't be fighting in the war,' she announces,

'I've got to be fighting against it. Otherwise it's like a ghastly nightmare, swallowing one up.' Alix looks to pacifism as a source of personal strength, which will save her from her own weakness.

Like Alix's, Macaulay's politics were personal. The campaigning publisher Victor Gollancz described her politics as 'on the side of the angels (my angels) but hardly profound'. 'I hate party politics,' Macaulay announced in 1942, wondering whether to accept an invitation to join the Council of the Liberal Party. In Macaulay's 1921 novel *Dangerous Ages*, Nan, an unmarried writer who is the most autobiographical figure in the book, does not bother to use her vote because she finds all the parties and all the candidates equally absurd. She is unable to believe that there is a right and a wrong in politics, seeing only 'a lot of wrongs'.

Nonetheless, Macaulay herself did pledge support to pacifism; when it came to matters of war and peace, there was a wrong and a right worth campaigning for. She was an active supporter of the League of Nations in the 1920s and a sponsor for the Peace Pledge Union in the 1930s. Her arguments in favour of peace tended to be more passionate than practical. In 1937 she wrote a lengthy pamphlet, *Open Letter to a Non-pacifist*, which argues eloquently against war, but presents pacifism as at best a risky gamble, albeit one on the side of the gods (or angels). War itself is seen as a barbaric act that mocks so-called civilisation. Macaulay is virulently dismissive of arguments that savagery should be attacked with its own weapons.

> Our civilisation, our barbarism is built on that age-old, bloody, trampled ground; we have measured knives against knives, cannon against cannon, bombs against bombs, poison against poison, torture against torture.

The resulting world was a disordered mess. And if civilisation went under in hatred and lies, blown to bits by the bombers, it was going to be pretty difficult to put the pieces together again.

> All will be hate, fury, tyranny, dictatorship, brutality, fear – the bestial and stupid aftermath of war.

Macaulay advocates a brand of pacifism based on passive resistance to mass aggression. The individual, mugged in the street, can fight back; the country, attacked by barbarous forces, cannot. She admits that the gamble of pacifism may fail, owing 'to lack of courage and endurance on one side, or excess of barbarism or ingenuity on the other', but insists, idealistically, that even then, the experiment would have been worth trying. Optimistically, she suggests that even if the tyrants successfully invade and capture a country – even if the Nazis occupy Britain – it is possible that life might be made so uncomfortable and difficult that the tyrant will get 'pretty tired' of jailing and shooting the population and decide to give it up. 'Or, again,' she adds, more realistically, 'he might not.' But even then, the pacifist must not descend to the barbarian's level.

Macaulay's experiences in the First World War taught her that she must not fall into the trap of accepting propagandist rhetoric again. But at the same time, they taught her that if there was going to be a war, it was better to be involved than to look on from the outside. Then, she railed against her own helplessness before she joined up as a nurse. 'Oh it's you that have the luck,' she lamented in a poem addressed by 'Many Sisters to Many Brothers', 'out there in blood and muck'; 'In a trench you are sitting, while I am knitting.' Her work as a nurse and then a landgirl enabled her to play a direct part in working towards the outcome of the conflict. In *Non-Combatants and Others* Alix is appalled by the war, but finds that it is impossible to escape. Waking up in the night, her forehead hot and her feet cold, she stares into a darkness illuminated by a vision of the 'things happening across the seas: dreadful things, ugly, jarring, horrifying things'. War presses round her; 'Every one talked it, breathed it, lived in it.' 'I believe,' she says to her brother, 'it's jealousy that's demoralising me most. Jealousy of the people who can be in the beastly thing . . . Oh, I do so want to go and fight . . . I can't bear the sight of khaki; and I don't know whether it's most because the war's so beastly or because I want to be in it.'

Now, in the autumn of 1940, a tin hat on her head and dust caked on her hands, Macaulay was in the war. For as long as she was in charge of her ambulance, questions of war and peace were irrelevant. Instead she was assailed by more urgent questions of life and death; of trapped limbs, thirsty mothers and crying babies.

Despite being exposed to the butchery of war on a daily basis, Macaulay had abandoned her commitment to pacifism. In the early months of the war, Macaulay was finishing *And No Man's Wit*, a novel set in the aftermath of the Spanish Civil War, in a world increasingly gripped by fascism. The title of this novel comes from John Donne's 'An Anatomie of the World', which is quoted at greater length in the epigraph:

> The Sun is lost, and the earth, and no man's wit
> Can well direct him where to looke for it.
> And freely men confesse that this world's spent . . .
> 'Tis all in peeces, all cohærance gone;
> All just supply, and all Relation . . .

In her 1937 pamphlet, Macaulay still believed that wit might offer a means to redeem the sun and the earth. Two years later, she was less sure. At the end of the novel Kate Marlow, a feisty but exhausted English doctor, is asked by a Spanish fascist whether she is a pacifist. 'Oh, what does one mean by pacifist?' she asks, in return. 'I think war is horrible and cruel and grotesque, of course, and belongs to the dark age as much as the rack and the thumbscrew do.' She is not certain, though, that nothing is worse; indeed it is worse, she suggests, 'to let more and more people be tortured and enslaved without protest'. But '*is* war the only way to stop it, and have we tried all the others?' In the end, she admits despondently that she does not know what she thinks; 'one's altogether confused'.

Even after Macaulay signed up to drive an ambulance in March 1939, she still hoped that war could be avoided. At the start of the war, she was prepared to go to almost any lengths to avoid bloodshed. Two weeks after war was declared, she wrote that 'if Nazism *really* can't be defeated except by war, I say, let it win (for a time) in spite of all its horrors and cruelties. It is less irrevocable than war.' A month later, she informed her sister that she had been thinking the situation over, and it seemed 'an appalling indictment of our civilisation and intelligence that we can't remove from the scenes into a Home for the mentally

unsound a man obviously so mad as [Hitler] is getting'. Then, she
insisted, unrealistically, 'we could have peace at once'. If the 1937
pamphlet was the work of a naive idealist, then these 1939 musings were
the deliberations of a fantasist. Grieving for her dying lover, Macaulay
could not accept the mass death that would result from war, although
she could no longer propose a viable alternative.

Over the course of the first year of the war, Macaulay regained some
of her own strength. Gerald O'Donovan recovered from his stroke and,
although he was then diagnosed with cancer, his condition became
temporarily stable. When Macaulay was not busy ambulance-driving
or writing, she was happily and intrepidly cycling round London,
lunching with friends amid the ruins. Later, in October, she assured
Jean that she felt 'very well again now, and able to cope with life'. As a
result, she was able to escape from her sense of war as a personal nightmare and to assess it as a public event. And so, in the *Time and Tide*
article, while bemoaning the 'blind, maniac, primitive, stupid bestiality
of war', she admitted that there was no alternative. To accept the 'still
more blind, maniac, primitive, stupid bestiality of Nazi rule over
Europe' would be to spit at civilisation 'even more earnestly' – 'not even
the most pacific pacifist can see (so far as I can discover) any third way'.
Where once she advocated the passive acceptance of Nazism, she was
now strong enough to accept war as the price that must be paid in
fighting against it, condemning anyone who thought otherwise: 'pacifists should surely be the first to hate an order which is based on armed
terrorism, which glorifies war, whose leaders proclaim that prolonged
peace is ignoble and makes man decadent'. There was no longer the
suggestion that it might be enough merely to pronounce Hitler insane
or to attempt to bore the Germans into abandoning their wicked ways.

Macaulay's role as an ambulance driver contributed to her renewed
spirit. Cleaning her ambulance, bandaging her patients, she was glad to
have exacting tasks to distract her from sorrow. She was glad too that,
unlike in the First World War, she could engage in these tasks on equal
terms with men. This time she was spared the disjunction between
sitting in a trench and knitting at home. In an article written in autumn
1940 about the role of women in wartime, she observed that it was only

in the ambulance services that the sexes were on the same footing and doing exactly the same work. In the fire service, they were not allowed to go out to the fires with pumps; in the air service, they could not obtain jobs as pilots; and even on the omnibuses, they could be conductors but not drivers.

At the end of August 1939, anxiously waiting to hear whether war would be declared, Macaulay had reported her preparatory activities to her sister. She and her friends were busy buying blackout material, filling in cracks in their windows and stockpiling sand. 'I think,' she observed, 'this is a good thing, as it gives people something they feel useful to do, and may actually diminish effects of raids, and therefore lessen fear and prevent collapse of nerves in crowded districts, and prevent a bad raid being a knock-out blow.' It was even more useful to feel that she was helping others, and it was this that made the war bearable for her. Helping people, she was able to forget herself, as Dorothy instructed Alix to do in *Non-combatants and Others*. As a result, she found the nights when she was on duty much easier to bear than the nights when she was crouching under her table at home, experiencing each thud as a personal threat. 'I rather wish I was ambulancing tonight,' she wrote to Jean on 11 September, feeling her house rock, listening to the continuous pounding of the bombs dropping. 'I am expecting my ceiling to collapse and the furniture from the flat above to come through on to me.' Ambulancing would at least distract her from anxious expectation.

However, the anxiety itself remained intense. 'Where will it end?' the rescue worker asked Macaulay on 26 September, and it was her own question throughout the war. For Greene, the destruction would bring a necessary apocalypse which would cleanse both his own life and the world. The gamble with death might well pay off; he might emerge stronger than ever. For Elizabeth Bowen and Henry Yorke, wartime life was too exciting to succumb to despair. Ultimately, Macaulay could not enjoy the danger as they did because she could not believe that either she or the world would survive it. 'There is so little time,' she wrote to Virginia Woolf, 'and one feels (a) sleepy (b) disintegrated. I expect this war is thoroughly demoralising. We shall emerge (as far as we do emerge) scattered in wits, many of us troglodytes.'

4

6 a.m.: All Clear

Soon after Rose Macaulay arrived home for bed on the morning of 27 September, the all clear siren began to sound across London. This was a single note, sustained for two minutes. It was as haunting a wail as the danger signal, but Londoners had learnt to find it reassuring after three weeks of bombing. As yet no one had assessed the total damage of the night but in all there had been 481 fires reported. Of these, six were classified as serious, requiring up to thirty pumps; sixty-five were medium, including twenty in central London; and 409 were small. Each of the small fires could have caused the level of destruction that Macaulay found at her incident in Camden Town.

All over the city, people now began to emerge from the shelters and wander home. The previous day *The Times* had issued a report urging shelterers not to crowd immediately into the streets after the all clear sounded, but most people found it difficult to resist the urge to go outside into the dawn. The returning daylight brought the brief, ecstatic holiday from fear that Bowen described in *The Heat of the Day*. Seen through relieved, exhausted eyes, the ruins and barrage balloons became especially picturesque once they were tinged with pink from the sunrise.

In Wimbledon, Hilde Spiel now removed the mattresses from the windows and returned them to the beds, where the family had been trying to sleep on uncomfortable bare bed frames. She had slept very little that

Courtesy of Christine Shuttleworth

Hilde Spiel, *c.* 1939

night. There had been bombing planes above Wimbledon almost all the time, and one of the night's six serious fires was in Merton High Street, just a mile south-east of Spiel's flat. Spiel and her husband, daughter and parents remained inside their cramped flat during even the most severe raids. The three-storey concrete apartment house had no air-raid shelter or cellar and they were reluctant to go to the dark and uncomfortable public shelter. At the start of the war, the government had expected raids to be clear-cut events lasting up to an hour, and the shelters had not been built as all-night refuges. In November a Wimbledon doctor wrote angrily to Parliament complaining about the 'glaring deficiencies' in the borough's shelters.

There are no bunks, and the Shelterers sleep either on the wet floors or on the wet benches. The Sanitary accommodation is inadequate and in the Trench Shelters is indecent as the closets are covered by a sacking curtain which exposes to view the person sitting on the seat.

Spiel and her family would rather remain at home where between sirens and thuds they played Schubert records for consolation or listened to Beethoven symphonies on the radio. Spiel later wrote that 'since those days that heroic music has never again moved me so passionately'.

Hilde Spiel's husband, Peter de Mendelssohn, usually managed to ignore the raids, writing away at his desk as the bombs crashed around him. He worked at the Ministry of Information by day so the nights were the only time he had to write his own books. Too focused to be distracted by danger, he was determined to make his name as a novelist in England. Hilde found it harder to remain calm than her husband did and she resented his mental seclusion. Like him, she was buoyed up by the resilience of the English. She later wrote that enduring the bombing was easier in London than elsewhere 'because of the daily example of English stoicism, English equanimity, English humour, which lay before your eyes'. But she was worried about her eleven-month-old daughter, Christine, whom they periodically wondered about sending to wait out the war in America. The official ARP Guide assured Londoners sheltering in their homes that although any house hit by an HE bomb was 'almost sure to collapse', the danger of houses falling as a result of nearby explosions was very small. This did not provide much reassurance when there were bombers directly overhead, though, especially as the guide added that 'other dangers of a less spectacular kind' such as blasts and splinters could cause more casualties than direct hits. Hilde was also distracted by the anxious screams of her mother, Mimi, who was hysterically frightened by the raids and showed no inclination to mimic the calmness of the surrounding Londoners.

In the preface to her wartime stories, Elizabeth Bowen recalled her awareness throughout the war that compared with those on the continent the British could not be said to suffer. 'Foreign faces about the London streets had personal pain and impersonal history sealed up behind the eyes.' For Spiel the Blitz was more difficult than it was for Bowen because whereas Bowen was surrounded by friends and admirers, and was successfully pursuing a glamorous literary career, Spiel was abruptly cut off from friends and from a literary scene in which she had been just beginning to shine.

When Hilde Spiel left Vienna for London in 1936 she was the author of a prize-winning novel, *Kati on the Bridge*, and was feted and adored in Vienna's café society. She was a passionate young woman of twenty-five, sustained by illusions and by intense and impulsive love affairs with men who were about to change the world. Everything, including politics, was personal. In 1930 she had joined the socialist torchlit march around the Ringstrasse, pressurising her mother to join her in signing up to the Social Democratic Workers' Party. But her own party membership was largely the result of a love affair with a socialist newspaper editor and she was prepared to lay aside political commitments when they impinged on more pleasurable aspects of life. Devastated by the brutal defeat of the elected socialists in the Austrian Civil War in February 1934, she became determined to leave Austria. However, she was even more determined to complete her studies first. And in the meantime she enjoyed herself, winning second prize for the best suntan at the local swimming pool that summer.

In her early twenties Hilde took on one brilliant older man after another as her mentor – philosophers, writers, political thinkers – attending their lectures, sometimes accompanying them around Europe, adoring and adored in turn. Writing, loving, trying out herself and life for size, she was sustained by Vienna itself, which provided her with 'a climate of the most beautiful illusions'; this was a city in which the increasing menace of fascist brutality coincided with a longstanding tradition of courtly chivalry. Hilde's father Hugo had two deep scars to the left of his chin as a result of youthful duels. Before Hilde's mentor, the philosopher Moritz Schlick, was shot dead as a Jew in the summer of 1936 he rode a horse each day in Vienna's Prater. Sometimes the intensity of life in Vienna with its dramas and contradictions became unbearable. Periodically Hilde escaped alone with her skis to the Alps where she threw herself down mountains, forcing herself to achieve more and more exhausting physical feats.

Shortly before their move to London in 1936 Hilde had accepted Peter de Mendelssohn's insistent claim that she was destined to be his wife. Two years earlier Peter had arrived in Austria from exile in Paris with an unanswered fan letter from Hilde in his pocket, announcing to

Hilde Spiel (*left*) on the boat on her way to London, 1936; Peter de Mendelssohn, 1939

friends en route that he was on his way to Vienna where he was to marry a girl called Hilde Spiel. He had been recently liberated from his first marriage after his wife left him to return to her father's German estate, fed up with the privations of exile in Paris. Hilde was swayed by Peter's energy and determination; and she had, after all, written that fan letter professing herself to be 'enchanted' by his novel a year earlier. A month after Peter's arrival, she noted in her diary that he was 'definitely the man for me'. But she remained independent, falling in love in April 1935 with an Italian diplomat called Tino ('a man like a tree, handsome, tall, mustached, and a fascist by conviction') and then in 1936 with the gloomy Italian writer Alberto Moravia.

When she did finally marry Peter and move to London later that year, Hilde was expecting an adventure. The move was politically motivated. Hilde was racially Jewish and it was clear to them both that Hitler would soon encroach on Austria. But Hilde also considered herself an urbane Anglophile and she was excited by the prospect of a new life in England. However by September 1940 she had found herself, aged twenty-nine, a penny-pinching housewife who spent her days looking after her small daughter and parents in a suburban terraced house, queuing at the fishmonger's shop and meting out ration coupons while she waited for her husband to return from work. Gradually, fear and monotony were muting her emotions. She would look back on the whole war as a 'dreary and wretched' period offering merely 'varied but still monotonous danger'. She felt that she was gradually deterred from expressing violent emotions, both by the example of English stoicism and under the pressures of the otherwise unbearable war. The calmness with which she forced herself to confront the bombers circling Wimbledon came at the expense of strong feeling and, she later realised, of creative inspiration.

For both Hilde and Peter the Blitz was doubly difficult because they were aware that the aeroplanes were piloted by their compatriots. In a 1975 essay on 'The Psychology of Exile', Spiel described the 'split consciousness' or 'schizophrenic spiritual and mental attitude' of Austrians and Germans who, more than the British, had 'to welcome the horrible evil of war because otherwise a terror without end stood in view'. A pacifist by inclination, Spiel, even more than Macaulay, had to lay aside her horror of war and be grateful to Britain for fighting her homeland. At the same time, she could not forget that the bombs falling from the sky were potentially dropped by former friends. She and other exiles were longing for the defeat, 'even the annihilation . . . of those whose fibres were bound with theirs through origins, childhood experience, landscape, friendship and blood relationships'.

In September 1940, Hilde Spiel was also in a more difficult position than Bowen, Macaulay, Greene or Yorke because she had dependants in immediate danger from the bombs. A week later, Peter would evacuate both Hilde and Christine to Oxford, but for now Christine was at risk as much as her parents. Christine had been born in Cambridge on 31 October 1939, two months after Britain's declaration of war. With hindsight in her autobiography Hilde wondered what had induced them, in the brief breathing space between the Munich crisis and the outbreak of war, to think of bringing a child into the world. It was, she decided, 'Peter's zest for life, his most irresistible characteristic as a young man, which carried me along with him.'

Now, Christine inspired her mother with a helpful determination to survive but also with a more paralysing fear. Since the air attacks on Britain began in the summer, Hilde had been worrying about her daughter's safety. 'France conquered. We still live,' she noted on 25 June in the small appointment diary where each night she distilled the personal headlines of the day in cramped English handwriting. 'Yesterday the first air attack since last September. I would like to at least try to save Christine.' Wondering in August if they would ever love life again, Hilde wrote at the bottom of that week's page in her diary that she was 'never yet so despondent and without hope', seeing her daughter as the only reason to live. 'We are daily threatened by an invasion which signifies our certain death. Sometimes I would choose that of all other choices. But I have Christine and I love her so and want to see her growing up.'

Hilde's anxiety for her daughter was exacerbated by her mother's excessive fears. Since arriving in London in August 1938, Hilde's mother and father Mimi and Hugo Spiel had seemed more like children than parents and Hilde felt burdened by their sudden helplessness and by their continual presence in her already crowded home. She was aware, though, that Mimi was entitled to hysteria. In Vienna, Mimi had been as warm, charming and elegant as her daughter. She was temperamentally cheerful but easily broken, and in the past two years the Spiels had endured their share of the personal pain and impersonal history which Bowen saw as clouding the faces of exiles from the continent. In April 1938 they had watched in disbelief as thousands of Austrians apparently welcomed the Nazis into Vienna. They had then made a dangerous and circuitous journey to London, losing their livelihood and possessions in the process.

Hilde and Peter had been trying to persuade Mimi and Hugo to leave Austria since 1937. They themselves saw exile as the only possible course of action, even for non-Jews such as Peter. In a broadcast which Hilde described as encapsulating 'exactly how I felt at that time', Peter

Hugo (*left*) and Mimi Spiel in Austria before the war

later stated that emigration from a totalitarian country was necessary because it rendered impossible the retreat into a false compromise. If, he said, a person blocks a path for himself 'of which he knows that outwardly it is convenient, but inwardly will take him to hell, then this cannot be in vain'.

For Hilde's parents, exile was vital not just morally but practically. Although they had both converted to Catholicism, they were racially Jewish; it was evident to Hilde long before it became evident to her parents that they would be in danger in the event of a Nazi takeover. Spending Christmas with the Spiels in 1937, Peter begged them to leave the country, but Mimi protested that she could not bear to abandon her friends or her beloved suburb of Döbling. 'The SS will march through Döbling,' Peter insisted; 'your friends will betray you, or they will be in dreadful danger themselves.' By the time the Spiels had admitted the truth of Peter's claims, it had become much harder to leave. 'It is horrible and unbearable,' Hilde wrote in her diary as she learnt the news about the *Anschluss* in April. 'My parents are in the line of fire. The devil is in charge.' That June Ferdinand Kuhn, the American foreign correspondent in London, promised to help Hilde by granting her parents an American affidavit. But it was not clear that they would be able to get out. 'At night I dreamt that my father was brought to me half thrashed to death at the border,' she wrote. 'I saw all, his body full of wounds and blood.'

By September 1938, the Spiels had in fact managed to get out of Austria, and Hilde and Peter rushed to Bandol in France to meet them. But reaching Bandol on 10 September, Hilde learnt that her parents were stranded in Zurich with no money, having been refused entry to France. She sent the last of her own money and returned to London, where her parents finally arrived, exhausted, on 19 September 1938. Hilde led her fearful mother around the town, frightened by the news of Hitler's increasingly forceful encroaches on Czechoslovakia. They waited anxiously for the impending war, and then felt personally let down by the British when Chamberlain signed the Munich agreement on 29 September. 'The Czechs are betrayed,' Hilde wrote in her diary. 'There will be no war. Should one not leave Europe?' She later recalled that 'if we ever experienced England in a moment of shame, then it was on the day of Neville Chamberlain's return from his last meeting with Hitler . . . The jubilation in the land, the headlines about this illusory promise distressed us greatly.'

A year later the war which Hilde had desired and feared came at last, but the British betrayed the Spiels once again, this time more personally, by sending Hugo to an internment camp in the summer of 1940. Initially, German and Austrian refugees had been treated more liberally than in the First World War. Some were interned immediately after the outbreak of war, but the Home Secretary, John Anderson, urged Parliament to 'avoid treating as enemies those who are friendly to the country which has offered them asylum'. He was keen to differentiate Britain as a liberal democracy from Germany with its discrimination against 'aliens'. However, in the spring of 1940 when the invasion of Britain began to seem more probable, the popular press urged the government to round up refugees on the grounds that they could easily be enemy agents. 'In Britain you have to realise that every German is an agent,' the *Daily Mail* proclaimed in May 1940. At this point a third of the 'enemy alien' population was interned and no German or Austrian was free from suspicion. There was even a police swoop on Hampstead Public Library.

For Hugo Spiel, the internment came at a particularly bad time. In Vienna, he had invented a new mode of producing synthetic rubber. At the time of his move to London he was engaged in a patent dispute to gain recognition for his discovery. It became evident that he was unlikely to win the dispute, but he was nonetheless offered a post at DuPont in America in which he would use his skills. He was interned just at the moment when the immigration papers had finally been obtained, and Hugo and Mimi were unable to take up places which had already been booked for them on an ocean liner. By the time that Hugo came back from internment, all non-military shipping across the Atlantic had been suspended. The Spiels were forced to remain in London, dependent on the limited financial support of the Woburn House refugee aid organisation and on the help of Hilde and Peter, who themselves spent most of the war on the verge of bankruptcy.

Hilde and Peter were more secure in their British identity than Hilde's parents. On first arriving in Britain, Peter had found a job working as the second-string London correspondent for two Czech newspapers whose London headquarters were based in the offices of *The Times* and run by a former Viennese acquaintance of Hilde's, Peter Smolka. At the age of fourteen Smolka had stolen Hilde's seat at a foundation congress of the Paneuropa movement. Now he had become a colleague, as Hilde frequently ended up helping her husband with his work during political crises. She also took a job herself, working for the Austrian screenwriter Berthold Viertel, who had previously provided Christopher Isherwood with his first foray into filmmaking by employing him as his co-writer for *Little Friend* (1934). By March 1939 Czechoslovakia no longer existed as an independent state and Smolka's newspapers were shut down. Luckily, he immediately acquired and reactivated a news agency called Exchange Telegraph, and Peter de Mendelssohn could continue to assist him. Once war was declared, the agency was taken over by the British government and run by the Ministry of Information via neutral Portugal. Smolka was transferred to the Russian section of the Ministry and Peter de Mendelssohn became the director of the agency. He was an employee of the British government, which rendered Hilde and Peter safe from the threat of internment, and meant that Peter could use his influence in helping to free Hugo Spiel.

Both Hilde and Peter were determined to make the best of exile, embracing England and all things English, and attempting to integrate as much as possible. They even started to write their letters to each other in English. Although Hilde's first love was for France, she came to appreciate England very quickly, chiefly through reading the novels of Virginia Woolf and Elizabeth Bowen (whom she would later tell Christine was her favourite author). Evacuated to Cambridge while she waited to give birth in October 1939, Hilde wrote to Peter that she had got hold of Bowen's *The Death of the Heart*.

It's always a stroke of luck if one finds something decent, and this is extremely lovely and beautiful! It's something no man could ever write, and so very subtle and civilised that one cannot understand how people could live elsewhere than in a Regency house facing Regent's Park, full of grief and disparity and hushed up strange emotions, and it really makes you long for a life in which all that is important.

Reading Bowen's novel made Hilde yearn to become more English herself.

Let's live at Regent's Park one day, Pumpki, and have thick carpets and aquanine curtains and beautiful flower-vases and an old housekeeper creeping inaudibly up and down the stairs! But seriously the Bowen book is very very lovely and I wish you'd read it some day.

Meanwhile Peter was less beguiled by England, but in his own way was committing to an English literary and historical tradition. 'I have a fascinating idea for a book,' he wrote back to his wife, 'but of course one can't write it. Namely the history of England and the world during the past three years, starting from the assumption that Edward VIII had not abdicated but married Mrs Simpson and remained King.' He also wrote to tell her that he was making successful inroads into the London literary scene, enclosing a 'very charming little letter' from J. B. Priestley about his own forthcoming novel.

For both Hilde and Peter, entry to literary London was facilitated by the work of English PEN. Before the war started, PEN's president Margaret Storm Jameson (known to the public as Storm and to friends as Margaret) and secretary Hermon Ould were organising events to bring refugee writers into contact with established English authors in an attempt to make the visitors feel at home. Hilde Spiel later wrote that

> what the PEN club did for all of us cannot be sufficiently praised . . . the Germans, the Austrians, the Czechs, then the rest of the refugees from Hitler's Europe . . . were all taken to the hearts of a succession of motherly women and selfless men, made welcome, and from then on incorporated into the community until they were able to found their own centres for writers in exile . . . In no other country had I encountered such a group of true humanists and tolerant moralists.

She was particularly grateful to Storm Jameson who, at a dinner for Austrian and Czechoslovakian writers at Paganini's restaurant in February 1939, welcomed the gathered company to their new home:

> Some of you are exiles from your own country, but here you are not exiles. You are our friends, you are our brothers. Here, in this room, it is England, and it is also Europe . . . Please be at home here.

Both Hilde and Peter were able to remain members of English PEN, only nominally joining the Austrian and German centres in exile. Both published novels in English within their first couple of years in England, with Hutchinson publishing Spiel's *Flute and Drums* in 1939. Through PEN Hilde and Peter made a handful of good friends, but of course these were not quite friendships of equals and Hilde was painfully aware of the potential for misunderstandings. Invited to dinner with Peter's publisher Peter Wait and his wife Dodo, Hilde and Peter took 'next Saturday' to mean 'this Saturday' and arrived a week early. They were surprised by the lack of other guests, but reassured to be offered drinks. Then, half an hour later, they were told apologetically that they would have to excuse their hosts, who were expected in Kensington soon after eight. Hilde later expressed gratitude to Dodo for helping them over the social faux pas tactfully, rather than pointing it out. It was from Peter and Dodo that Hilde and Peter learnt the basic principles of English life, namely: 'don't fuss; don't ask personal questions; don't touch the teapot (this was reserved for the hostess); tea in first, milk after; understatement and stiff upper lip'. But there was also something unnatural in the resolutely unspoken nature of English communication, and a patronising element in the controlled superiority. In retrospect Hilde found that

> the consideration for foreigners that they showed on this occasion, as they did in all things, was undoubtedly bound up with a certainty, inborn in the British, that nothing else was to be expected from the non-British, with an unshakeable belief – unshaken to this day, even by the loss of an empire – in their self-evident superiority.

Hilde's sense of herself as an outsider was compounded by the fact that she felt sidelined in suburban Wimbledon, where they had moved from Notting Hill in November 1939, mistakenly thinking that they would be safer from air attack away from the centre. At first Hilde was beguiled by the green calmness of her new surroundings. 'I am so happy to be here in Wimbledon,' she wrote in her diary in April 1940. 'Beautiful trees, the garden charming.' But in her autobiography she complained that she had spent at least a third of her life in that 'beautiful, green utterly bourgeois district' and in all that time they were never invited into a single English household there or involved in the social structure. When they were especially lonely during the Blitz, Hilde and Peter braved the dangers of crossing London and went to visit English friends in Chelsea or Kensington or to see the exiled community of German-speaking émigrés in Hampstead.

Hilde and Peter had moved to Wimbledon partly at the suggestion of their friends the Austrian writer Hans Flesch-Brunningen and his wife Tetta. They had known Flesch since 1937 when he had approached them in the office of *The Times* one day when Hilde was at work with Peter, politely requesting practical advice. After he took his leave with hesitant courtesy, Hilde suggested that Peter should run after him and invite him to dinner. This was the beginning of a close friendship which Peter would later come to regret. Flesch was fifteen years older than them and he initially took the younger couple on as protégés. He dedicated his novel *The Blond Spider* 'to Hilde and Peter in friendship' in 1939 and gave the name Hilde to the beautiful and almost incestuously beloved sister of the hero of his 1940 novel *Untimely Ulysses*. Although he wrote these novels in English, he found it more difficult than Hilde and Peter did to adapt to his new surroundings and he was always impressed by the energy with which they entered into their new life. At the same time he impressed Hilde with his old-style Viennese dignity and quiet intelligence; when she allowed herself to be homesick it was often to Flesch that she turned.

Flesch was one of the few Austrians or Germans with whom Hilde and Peter were prepared to socialise frequently. Since moving to London they had both been determined to avoid becoming part of the community of exiles, however tempting it seemed. Occasionally they went to the Laterndl club nights on Hampstead's Finchley Road, where Austrian émigrés sang Viennese folk songs and performed their own poems. Hilde enjoyed the nostalgia but found it dangerous. In a later film script called *Anna and Anna*, where she juxtaposed her own story with that of an imaginary alter ego who had stayed in Vienna, Spiel made the Anna in London dismiss the exiles at the Laterndl, saying that she does not know 'whether it makes one happy or unhappy to cling so much to home', suggesting that it is like living in an evacuated room. 'We are in England,' she insists to her émigré friend.

In the 1975 essay about exile, Spiel complained that émigrés often suffered from a '*chez nous* syndrome', moaning continually that everything in London was worse than things were at home and deriding the cold-ness of the English people and their draughty houses. Her own mother was among these grumblers and Spiel was determined not to join their ranks herself. But she was often aware that she had more in common with the impetuous sensibility of her exiled friends than with the restraint of her English hosts, and she was frequently overcome by longing for home. She would later describe how, during the raids, whenever she listened to those records of Beethoven and Schubert, the Pfarrplatz in Vienna appeared before her eyes.

> A small village square: on the left a farmhouse, where the Eroica symphony was written; another on the right; and in the middle the little church of St. Jakob.

This homesickness was made harder by the fact that she had very little to remind her of her past. Almost all her parents' possessions had been confiscated in Hamburg during their escape. Among the items lost were most of Spiel's own library of books, her pictures and photograph albums, Alberto Moravia's letters and her long-treasured piano arrange-ments from *Tristan und Isolde*, which had a thumbmark on the top right corner of each sheet where the page was turned.

'Exile is an illness,' Spiel states in the exile essay. 'An illness of the mind, an illness of the spirit, and even sometimes a physical illness.' Here she sees the exile as unable to learn to be a good international European. 'We are rooted where we were born, grew up and learnt to live.' Most frighteningly, she views the exile as incapable of return, quoting Carl Zuckmayer's description of exile as the journey without homecoming. According to Zuckmayer, the exile may go back, but the place, when he finds it, is no longer the same one he left. This, for Hilde Spiel, constituted the recurring nightmare of the war. In 1946 she recounted how she had dreamt, again and again, that she was

> back in Vienna – an enemy presence in my native land, with English coins in my pocket, English words on my lips, while my mother tongue seemed frozen in my throat. The ghostly streets through which I

passed . . . the interiors – antiquated and intimidating with their huge cupboards and tables, whose carved eagles' heads and lions' paws frightened me, although they seemed to have come from the contents of my grandparents' house – they all threatened me with discovery, betrayal, court martial, death.

Nonetheless, when the all clear sounded on the morning of 27 September 1940, Hilde's relief at having survived another night was strong enough to suspend any wider anxiety about her life as an exile. For as long as daylight lasted, she could stop worrying about Christine and be pleased instead to have another day to live. Soon Hilde would escape the bombs by taking her daughter away to Oxford. Now it was almost time for Peter to leave for work but she herself could sink into a deeper sleep, grateful merely to have a mattress on the bed once more.

PART II

The Blitz

September 1940–May 1941

5

'War, she thought, was sex'

Graham Greene and Henry Yorke, autumn 1940

In Henry Yorke's *Caught*, Prudence, yearning for one lover while evad-ing the embraces of another, ponders the relation between love and death. 'War, she thought, was sex.' Prudence at once accepts and regrets the allure of the serviceman. 'This was a time,' the narrator muses, 'when girls, taken out to night clubs by men in uniform, if he was a pilot she died in his arms that would soon, so she thought, be dead.' Sex, already imbued with the language of surrender, seems to follow naturally from the imminence of death. Guaranteed neither world enough nor time, seduced by danger's erotic charge, girls abandon themselves in a daze of giving. In the darkness of the blackout, each clicking footfall was loaded with mystery. Elizabeth Bowen observed in *The Heat of the Day* that the wartime city night brought out something provocative in the step of even the most modest women. 'Nature tapped out with the heels on the pavement an illicit semaphore.'

Liberated by the atmosphere of unmarriedness, wartime Londoners fell in love quickly and passionately. For all five of the writers in this book, during the initial autumn of the Blitz death became a real and constant possibility for the first time. The proximity to death brought with it an intense consciousness of being alive that was conducive to sexual passion. This was particularly the case for Graham Greene, who was straightforwardly in love for the first time in his life.

Graham and Vivien Greene on their wedding day, 1927

In 1927, aged twenty-three, Graham Greene had married Vivien
Dayrell-Browning. Two years earlier, infatuated and unsure of himself,
he had promised her a 'monastic marriage'. 'You'd always keep your
ideal of celibacy, and you could help me to keep the same ideal . . . And
the whole thing would be an adventure finer than the ordinary
marriage.' Graham was lacking in self-knowledge and was too sexually
diffident to expect any lovable girl in her right mind to do more than
put up with his attentions anyway. Celibacy, in the service of a Catholic ideal (he converted to Catholicism in order to gain Vivien's hand),
seemed preferable and achievable. The ideal was short-lived. The
Greenes did have enough sex to produce two children, but not much
more than that, and Graham turned to prostitutes and occasional
mistresses when his commitment to monasticism faltered. Twelve
years later, on the day that the Second World War was declared,
Graham looked out of the window of his Bloomsbury workroom in
Mecklenburgh Square and caught the eye of his landlady's daughter,
looking out of the window opposite. Short, square and boisterous, this
was Dorothy Glover. By the time of the Blitz, the 'love-charm' of sirens

and bomb-bursts gained its appeal from the presence of Dorothy. As a shelter warden herself, she accompanied Graham on his nightly forays through the raids and shared his bed, defying death by making love as the bombs fell outside.

Just before war was declared, Graham had sent Vivien and the children to live with his parents in their cold, overcrowded house in Crowborough, Sussex, armed with only a few suitcases, a kitten and a canary. In common with many of his friends, Graham hoped eventually to evacuate his family to America or Canada in order to escape an invasion he believed to be imminent. His initial letters to his wife were tender and solicitous. 'I miss you so much,' he reported to her on 30 August 1939, 'particularly in the evening, which makes me rather moony and uncommunicative over my pint.' 'There's one thing you must never doubt at all,' he promised her on 4 September, 'that you are the only person I have or ever will love.'

By October it had become clear that, at least in the short term, Graham was having a better war than Vivien. 'Dear love,' he assured her, 'don't ever think I like this separation. It wouldn't have happened if we'd known how the war was going to turn out.' He promised that if Ribbentrop did not start dropping bombs soon they would revise their whole scheme. Gradually, Graham's letters to Vivien became less naturally loving and Vivien's letters to Graham became more anxiously demanding. In December 1939 Vivien pleaded with Graham to be well for his visit to her on Saturday: '(I mean, not pub crawl the night before so you have a tummy ache darling)'. During the early years of their relationship, Graham and Vivien had developed a shared language of love in which kisses were stars, meted out and dropped from a distinctly disembodied sky, and sexual embraces were the cosy nuzzlings of two furry cats. 'You are a kitten that will never grow up,' Graham had told Vivien in their courtship. Now that the couple were in their thirties, she had grown up but their relationship had not. The adolescent language had come to seem tired, but they had not been able to metamorphose into a new register. Graham continued to sign himself 'Tyg' and Vivien to wonder how his whiskers were withstanding the gale.

The only moment of sexual longing in Vivien's surviving wartime letters is expressed as a desire to put 'a lot of stars' on her husband's 'anxious muzzle'. Waking up in the night in December 1939, she had been brooding 'rather affectionately by degrees' on 'Wuff'. If only he had been there, 'what a responsive cosy cat you'd have had'. 'Perhaps you woke up feeling sleek and caressed,' she wondered, 'because I'd been thinking of you.' In fact Vivien later stated that 'in a physical sense the marriage ended just before war was declared', blaming this on Graham's reluctance to have children in wartime and suggesting that their marriage might have fared very differently if the pill had been in existence. Clearly, Graham did not have the same reticence with Dorothy, which suggests a more entrenched sexual reluctance on one or both sides of the marriage.

In Greene's 1948 novel *The Heart of the Matter*, Scobie has come to hate the pet name his wife has given him but he still continues to use it because 'it always worked'. 'Comfort, like the act of sex, developed a routine.' In January 1940 it was to the language of cats that Graham turned when Vivien complained that 'it is so awful being a schoolgirl after having been a proud housewife for 12 years', wondering if they would ever have their teas together again. 'Darling darling one, don't feel so sad,' he urged. 'It won't take any time to get back to normal, and our teas . . . cats can see in the dark, and we'll come creeping along to find each other.' Two weeks later, Vivien wrote to Graham begging to be allowed to come and look after him. 'You wouldn't see much of me,' she promised. 'I would banish you to work and only notice you really at tea time. You would have a meal on a tray in your study when you liked.'

But Graham was reluctant to have Vivien in London because she would intrude on his life with Dorothy. By the time that the Blitz started, he and Dorothy were spending every night together in her flat in Gower Mews. Graham pretended to Vivien that he was still living in Clapham, explaining when she failed to catch him on the telephone that in the morning he could not hear the phone when he was shaving, while at night there was always the chance that he was out, or in bed. The Blitz brought an end to the charade, as it was too dangerous to cross London and sleep in Clapham. He now claimed to be living in his workroom and simply popped to Clapham a couple of times a week to check that his marital home was still standing. Most weekends, he visited Vivien and the children, whom he had moved from Crowborough to Oxford in July, when the Battle of Britain made Sussex a target for Nazi aeroplanes. During the week he spent as much time as possible with Dorothy.

Unlike Vivien, who was a goddess to be adored ('my love, you are a saint' Graham had assured her in 1925), Dorothy was a fellow-adventurer and drinking companion. In later years, Vivien was dismissive of Dorothy, who was 'square and small' and was quite a lot older than Graham, 'and looked it'. Malcolm Muggeridge described Dorothy as 'a person who, on the grounds of attractiveness, was absolutely a non-starter'. But in *The Heart of the Matter* Scobie falls in love with his mistress, Helen, precisely because she is plain. He has no sense of responsibility towards the beautiful, the graceful and the intelligent, all of whom can 'find their own way'. Instead, it is 'the face that would never catch the covert look, the face that would soon be used to rebuffs and indifference' that demands his allegiance.

Dorothy's lack of physical vanity made her easy to spend time with. The cartoonist David Low recalled her as 'happy, small, rather stoutish, not smart but very friendly – she radiated friendliness. She gave you a sense of feeling at home in her company – she had a nice laugh.' Her good humour contrasted with Vivien's anxiety; her bravery contrasted with Vivien's cowardliness. 'From the first raid,' Greene said later, 'she was courageous, oh yes, and showed no fear of any kind.' David Low recollected meeting Graham and Dorothy after a raid, when papers from a bombed office were flying all over the street, and watching as the lovers picked up the fragments and read them to each other, roaring with laughter. He also remembered watching the chief warden taking a government official on a tour of the Bloomsbury shelters and coming across Graham and Dorothy entwined in the shadows. 'Just look at that pair,' said the official in disgust. 'But,' responded the chief warden, 'that is Mr Greene, one of our best wardens, and his nice wife.'

Dorothy was thirty-nine, a theatrical designer who in her youth had danced in the chorus of theatrical revues. According to Malcolm

Muggeridge, Graham was 'devoted' and 'extraordinarily good' to Dorothy. Certainly, he set about helping her with her career, sending a play she had written to his agent. He also authored a series of picture books with illustrations by Dorothy and even managed to get her employed as his secretary at the Ministry of Information. For the first time, Graham was in a relationship that combined physical acceptance with the collaborative partnership of a marriage. Unlike Vivien, Dorothy could accept the seedier side of Graham's sexuality. An enthusiast of cheap lodging houses, Graham took Dorothy to a lodging house in a road opposite Paddington Station on the first night of their affair. He could also take her to nude reviews, although Muggeridge recollected that Greene was careful during the Blitz to make 'a special act of penitence and other appropriate liturgical preparations in case death came upon him unawares'. On one occasion Muggeridge accompanied Greene to the Windmill Theatre to gaze 'balefully at the nudes; rather pinched and ravaged in the footlights' glare, yet still bound by law to keep absolutely still'. Muggeridge thought that the spectacle appealed to Greene 'for its tattiness and seediness' – the guise in which he most liked the Devil's offerings to be presented. Greene explained to his friend how the *cognoscenti* knew just where to sit to get the best view, and how, as the front rows cleared, spectators at the back pressed forward to take their places; 'wave upon wave, like an attacking army'.

On the night of 18 October, Graham and Vivien's Clapham house was bombed. It was not a heavy night of bombing, but south London was badly hit in the early morning. A pub was demolished near the Greenes' house, leaving forty people trapped. Arriving to check on the house the next morning, Graham was confronted by fire engines stationed outside it. Writing to his mother he reported that he had arrived to collect some belongings at 8.30 a.m. and found a scene of devastation. There had been no fire and no flood and the structure was still standing, but the workshop in the garden was destroyed and the back of the house had been struck by a blast. It was impossible to get beyond the front hall. He was still hoping to save some of his books and Vivien's ornaments but he told his mother that it was 'rather heartbreaking that so lovely a house that has survived so much should go like

that'. Vivien was devastated. Visiting the ruin to rescue some possessions, she walked 'in tears on the edge of the front room looking down
at the deep frightening cavity two floors below and all the rafters and
rubble and dirt'.

Graham was distressed to lose some of his books (he did manage to
rescue some by making a chute and pushing them down) but he soon
found that he was largely relieved by the loss of the house itself. 'It's sad
because it was a pretty house,' he reported to his agent in America, 'but
oddly enough it leaves one very carefree.'

There had been a large mortgage on the house so Graham was
rescued from a heavy financial burden. But it was evident to Vivien and
to Malcolm Muggeridge that Graham felt released by the loss chiefly
because it portended the destruction of his marriage, offering the
promise of release from moral responsibility. Looking back on the
bombing he wrote that he 'simply felt relieved that I didn't have to be
backwards and forwards, backwards and forwards all day, and lose my
lunch every day, whenever there had been a raid and there were raids
most days, to see that the thing was there'.

Henry Yorke, who was more cautious about material wealth than
Greene, would have been more distressed if the Yorkes' house in
Rutland Gate in Knightsbridge had been bombed. But he was content
only to be there one day in three and happy, too, that Dig and Sebastian
were safely absent in Herefordshire, where they were staying with Dig's
family. Henry had married Adelaide ('Dig') Biddulph, a distant cousin,
in 1929. Initially he had been courting her younger sister Mary (known
as 'Miss'), while his friend the novelist Anthony Powell was in love with
Dig (although Powell was aware that he had neither the money nor the
status to satisfy her titled parents). 'To the great scandal of the servants
Mary and I spent the night together at Forthampton,' Yorke boasted to
Powell in 1928; 'Her wisdom is terrific.' But he was also involved in
exchanging letters with Dig, falling in love by correspondence. In 1928,
'Miss', perhaps tired of waiting for Henry, became engaged to a guards
officer, Monty Lowry-Corry. Henry took Dig to Oxford to meet his

Henry and Dig Yorke on their wedding day, 1929

undergraduate friends, who were all agreed as to her beauty and general niceness. The following April, he wrote to tell Evelyn Waugh, who had not yet met Dig, that he was getting married. He informed his friend that his future wife hid 'a stupendous intellect behind an enormous capacity for idleness and an appearance of innocuousness'. Henry and Dig were married in July.

Dig herself, though always good-natured, cultured, sociable and polite, was almost as inscrutable as Henry. In a 1960 account of a holiday the couple spent in Ireland at the time of the Munich crisis in September 1938, Yorke gives a brief portrait of the marriage. Walking from one creamy Irish beach to another, the couple are companionable but restrained. 'We had been married for years, were fond, just did not say much to one another, so stayed comfortably quiet.' Settling on a beach, there is a brief moment of intimacy when they hold hands, but they are interrupted by an 'aged crone' who undresses and then wanders naked into the sea. Years later, Yorke could still recall enough of the scene to describe the well-preserved, unwrinkled belly of the woman, and the 'bush of hair black and enormous'. At the time, he reports, the Yorkes themselves 'did not say a word'. The woman leaves and Dig tells Henry that she would now like her tea. They wander inland, avoiding another naked couple they have seen on the neighbouring beach, and Dig announces to her husband that she is 'beginning to find Ireland creepy'.

What emerges in this account is a commitment both to the unsaid and to the status quo of the marriage. There is a sense that their companionable silence can continue in the face of any amount of embarrassment or emotional upheaval. In 1939 Yorke wrote in *Pack My Bag* that he saw mutual shyness as 'the saving grace' in all relationships: 'the not speaking out, not sharing confidences, the avoidance of intimacy in important things' made living, 'if you can find friends to play it that way, of so much greater interest even if it does involve a lot of lying'.

This seems to have been the day-to-day reality of the Yorkes' marriage. From the start, Henry had affairs, and even resumed the sexual relationship with Dig's sister. Dig was prepared to ignore these for the sake of propriety. She had been brought up as an upper-class hostess in a family where emotions were rarely discussed or prioritised and were secondary always to manners. 'It seems so *gauche*,' Dig announced in 1939 when told that anti-aircraft gunners seemed unable to hit their targets. As a result the Yorkes were better equipped to stay together in the long term than the Greenes. It was easier to have mental and physical privacy in a large house with servants than in a rural cottage, and Dig was well prepared for a marriage in which her position as a wife was more important than the continual and complete adoration of her husband.

According to the daughter of one of Henry's mistresses, Dig pretended that any unpleasant events were not actually occurring and concealed any negative emotion behind a manner of 'the most brilliant feyness'. For his part, Henry treated Dig with a respect that Graham Greene was increasingly failing to show to Vivien. It was clear to all but the most innocent of his mistresses that Henry had no intention of

leaving Dig, and when Dig was with Henry in London the Yorkes
entertained as a unit, inviting Henry's mistresses to the house as guests.
This did not, however, prevent Henry from falling in love, sensuously,
passionately and self-indulgently. And in wartime, there was no short-
age of girls ready to die, night after night, in those arms that would
soon perhaps be dead.

At the beginning of the Blitz, Henry Yorke was in the midst of an
intense and sexually charged friendship with Rosamond Lehmann.
Lehmann was a successful novelist herself and was a radiant presence
on the London literary scene. Stephen Spender later described her as
one of the most beautiful women of her generation: 'tall, and holding
herself with a sense of her presence, her warmth and vitality prevented
her from seeming coldly statuesque'. Rosamond had been married to
Wogan Philipps since 1928, and for the last four years had been involved
in a fervent and painful love affair with Yorke's friend, the caddish and

Rosamond Lehmann, c. 1943

charming writer and academic Goronwy Rees. The affair had begun during a weekend with Elizabeth Bowen at Bowen's Court in Ireland, when Goronwy was ostensibly in love with Elizabeth herself. Elizabeth was deeply hurt by the behaviour of both guests, complaining to her friend the philosopher Isaiah Berlin that Goronwy had visited Rosamond's bedroom in the night and upset Elizabeth's innocent niece, who was forced to listen through the thin partition wall.

Goronwy was generally believed to be fairly heartless. The poet Louis MacNeice once complained that Goronwy's famous charm 'takes an ell if you give it a millimetre', stating that he 'would have made a wonderful travelling salesman'. But, at least at the start, Goronwy seems to have been as infatuated with Rosamond as she was with him, and it was through Goronwy that Rosamond met Henry Yorke, whom Goronwy brought to stay with her in 1937. Now that her affair with Goronwy was losing momentum on his part if not on hers, Rosamond was finding consolation in this new friendship. She and Henry met frequently for evenings in London in 1939 and 1940, with Henry concealing the meetings from his wife. On 11 September 1940, a few days into the Blitz, Henry wrote to Rosamond that he looked on their two days spent together before the bombing began as 'a goal to get back to again if chance allows because it was the best of life'. 'Yes, it *was* the core of life,' Rosamond wrote in reply; 'I'm so glad we had it.'

It is unclear whether this was actually a sexual relationship. Rosamond later claimed that she had never gone to bed with Henry, though she had a tendency subsequently to deny sexual encounters, also claiming that nothing had happened with Goronwy Rees at Bowen's Court. Either way, she was ultimately preoccupied with Goronwy throughout this period, and neither she nor Henry seems to have had any intention of falling in love. Rosamond told Henry gratefully at this time that he was 'one of the few disinterested affection-givers (I don't know how to put it!) that I know'. For his part, Henry was more able to surrender himself in love affairs with younger women, perhaps because they were more easily impressed by the roles he assumed. He and Rosamond drifted apart in the autumn of 1940 and the following January he admitted to her that he had been avoiding her in the autumn because 'war is entirely unnatural and I can't see anything but pain in meeting people one cares for'. Instead he had been busy writing 'like a beaver' and seeing new friends, 'most of them very young'.

There were two very young women on the scene during the autumn of 1940: Ann Glass and Rosemary Clifford. Henry's affair with Rosemary Clifford began in the summer of 1940, when she seems to have been engaged in war work that brought her to the Davies Street fire station. That August she was working in Whitehall, missing their proximity – 'it's like swimming in a stagnant pond when you've been used to the sea' she wrote on 25 August – but dreaming happily about Henry in his absence. She had just tried to imagine him by climbing onto the roof in Park Street behind Park Lane, where she thought she could smell his hair on the wind. 'Have I told you I miss you?' she asked him, 'because I do – which is a nuisance. If we should meet again – I'm dark and rather grubby.'

Meanwhile Henry had begun his pursuit of Ann Glass, whom he had first come across at the beginning of the war as a teenage debutante and recently met again. 'You are now old enough for me to ask you out,' he informed her, and out they went, to one bar, restaurant and nightclub after another. A few months into the affair Ann looked back on a typical evening together, wishing they were 'back in the Lansdowne or the Conga or a sort of heavenly mixture of both, suspended above time in a golden dream of swing and brandy and enchanted conversation'. Ann was working for MI5 by day and that autumn her parents had taken a room for her at the Dorchester Hotel, where Henry visited her. Ann and Rosemary were probably not the only girls Henry was 'dying with' at this time. In *Pack My Bag* he characterised himself as someone who had always enjoyed first experiences too much, adding that this applied to people as well.

> How wonderful they seem the first few times, how clever, how beautiful, how right; how nice one seems to them because so interested, how well it all goes and then how dull it becomes and flat.

Having affairs with several girls at once was one way to assuage the flatness.

Ann and Rosemary themselves were both aware of each other's presence in Henry's affections and, too young and too impetuous to have mastered Dig's insouciance, they were periodically jealous. 'Darling, This is very tiresome having to write because I can't put it beautifully like Miss Glass,' Rosemary declared, thanking Henry for her copy of *Pack My Bag* in November; 'but you know if I tried to tell you I should have to put my head in a pillow and become embarrassed.' 'Would you like to know how you look when you're asleep?' she asked, by way of summoning him back to bed; 'your face loses all its creases and becomes very serene.'

The atmosphere of these affairs finds its way into Yorke's novel *Caught*, where the sheaved heads of pretty young girls collapse on the blue shoulders of pilots, drowsy with drink and sex, 'gorged with love, sleep lovewalking'. When the servicemen depart to fight overseas, the firemen inherit the girls they leave behind 'hunting for more farewells', seeking another man with whom they can spend their last hours, to whom they can murmur 'darling, darling, darling it will be you always', the 'I-have-given-all-before-we-die, their dying breath'.

Richard falls sensuously and easily for Hilly, a driver at his fire station, enticed by 'the bloom, as he said to himself, of a thousand moist evenings in August on her soft skin and, on the inner side of her lips, where the rouge had worn off, opened figs wet on a wall'. He takes her to a half-dark nightclub filled with the 'naked, fat round shoulders' of chalk-white girls, where jazz singers croon of the foreign land of the south which becomes 'everyone's longing in this soft evening aching room'. When the lights go out, 'to have what little he that minute had', he kisses her on the mouth and is answered by the feel of 'opened figs, wet at dead of night in a hothouse'. 'Oh darling,' he says, 'low and false', 'the months I've waited to do that.' He strokes the inside of her right arm, his lips still wet from hers, caught up in 'this forced communion, this hyacinthine, grape dark fellowship of longing'. Hilly herself opens up, enfolding his fingers in her hand, her eyes filling with tears as she settles down 'not, as she told herself, for long, to love Dickie'.

From this point, Richard and Hilly go to bed together on his days of leave. As their bodies meet, Richard experiences relief that is 'like the crack, on a snow silent day, of a branch that breaks to fall under a weight of snow' as his hands move 'like two owls in daylight over the hills, moors and wooded valleys, over the fat white winter of her body'. In bed, in love, he experiences what he has previously found only when drunk and comes to want nothing more.

> The small warm movements of her were promises she made, and which she was about to fulfil. He had no further questions. He had the certainty of her body in his arms. He grew hot.

Writing to his publisher John Lehmann, Henry Yorke referred dismissively to this as Richard's 'silly thing with Hilly'. But it is misleading to see this affair, any more than Henry's own, as merely a frivolous distraction from the real business of firefighting, parenting and writing. Some of the most evocative and beautiful descriptive language in *Caught* goes into these accounts of Richard and Hilly. Both Richard and Henry himself were self-indulgent and sentimental in their love affairs, and both were under no illusions about their own commitment to these women. However there is still a seriousness to the sensuality; a sense that it is at these moments, playing the role of the maudlin hero, that they are most vitally alive.

During this period Henry was seeing very little of his wife and son. In the phoney war he had been able sometimes to work four days and nights at a stretch and then to take forty-eight hours off, which gave him time to go back to the country to visit them. He was now too busy to be allowed to do this. Dig seems to have remained cheerful, or at least less needily lonely than Vivien Greene, in his absence. But Henry did not make the situation easier for her by sending her letters imploring 'DON'T COME UP TO LONDON' or playing a practical joke involving telephoning her to say that he was in a burning building and unlikely to emerge alive.

Yorke describes the predicament of wartime wives in *Caught*, where the men who take girls out to nightclubs have come back to London from the countryside earlier in the day, leaving their wives dragging along the station platform, 'hanging limp to door handles' from which they are snatched off by porters. In the published version of the novel, Richard's wife is dead, and his son Christopher is looked after by Richard's sister-in-law, Dy. However, this was a response to anxiety from the Hogarth Press, who thought that the censors would object to a fireman being portrayed as engaged in an adulterous affair. Initially Dy was the wife rather than the sister-in-law, and was evacuated rather than dead. This made the original version of the story in part a tribute to Dig, offering an assurance that Henry's love was unaltered, in spite of his adultery.

In the original typescript Richard, though still self-indulgently in love with Hilly, comes to miss his wife with equivalent sentimentality. Indeed, her absence leads to 'a new year's turn of love' on his part, as well as a first love for his son. On leave, visiting Dy in the countryside, Richard is overcome by sensuous longing. 'Now that he was back in this life only for a few days, he could not keep his hands off her'; the touch of her magnolia skin is a promise 'of the love they had one for the other, and of the love they would yet hold one another in'.

> He could not leave her alone, stroked her wrists, pinched, kissed her eyes, nibbled her lips while, as for her, she smiled, joked, and took him to bed at all hours of the day with her, and lay all night murmuring to him.

These passages are a testament to Richard's continued desire for his wife which Dig, reading it, could have taken as a sign of Henry's own feelings. But there is an unreal quality to the writing. We might expect Richard's feelings for Hilly to be falsely idealised, but there is an equivalent lack of everyday knowledge in his relationship with his wife that seems more odd. The kind of love that flowers between them seems to be the love of strangers; not merely rendered strange by war and absence, but strange to each other because fundamentally unknown. There are also uncomfortable revelations, such as when Dy takes off all her clothes to come naked into bed with Richard and he observes the unusualness of the act: 'as a rule he had to beg before she would take off her nightdress.' However this is nonetheless a scene where Yorke can

evince sympathy for his wife's predicament. Dy is visiting Richard in
London, and she sobs with longing for 'the darling flat and you'.
Although Richard is bemused by her tears, and has begun the scene by
wondering if his wife can smell Hilly on his skin, he does all he can to
comfort her. He assures her honestly that 'it's everything to have you
both again' and kisses her neck, so that she lies back 'slack', happy in
the arms of her husband.

6

'Ireland can be dementing'

Elizabeth Bowen, autumn 1940

In October 1940 Elizabeth Bowen abandoned Clarence Terrace to the nightly bombs and travelled by boat to neutral Ireland. The crossing, by train and boat, took a day, and it was then a long bus ride from Dublin to her ancestral home, Bowen's Court, in County Cork. For most of the journey the countryside undulated gently until suddenly, as the bus drew near Mitchelstown, the towering Galtees mountain range came into view in coloured peaks. Beyond Mitchelstown, Bowen entered the familiar lonely countryside surrounding Bowen's Court, which was squared in by mountains on three sides: the Ballyhouras in the north, the Kilworth Hills in the east and the Nagles mountains in the south. This was majestic, aloof scenery and Bowen's 'high bare Italianate house' always seemed both dreamier and more austere than usual on Bowen's wartime trips to Ireland. The journey west lengthened the days, as Stella finds in *The Heat of the Day*, arriving at just such a house in the war. As she stands looking down the length of a large room at a fire burning in a white marble fireplace, the hour seems outside time: 'an eternal luminousness of dusk in which nothing but the fire's flutter and the clock's ticking out there in the hall were to be heard'. In her fatigue, it feels as though it is another time, rather than another country that Stella has come to.

Bowen's business in Ireland was both personal and official. She was visiting Bowen's Court and catching up with old friends in Cork and

Dublin. She was also reporting on the situation in Ireland for the Ministry of Information, and was renting a flat overlooking the bustling park in Dublin's principal Georgian square, St Stephen's Green, from which to do this. Bowen's sense of her own Irish identity had lessened since September 1939. From the start of the war, it was clear that Ireland was going to remain neutral. The Irish Prime Minister, Éamon de Valera, leader of the nationalist Fianna Fáil party, was determined to keep Ireland out of the war for the sake of economic stability, safety (Ireland's army was small and ill-equipped) and the symbolic importance of Ireland's independence from Britain. It was evident that Ireland could not enter the war without reopening the civil war of 1921–2. Bowen respected the decision, but if she was pro-neutrality for Ireland then she was also pro-British. She could sympathise with the point of view of the British, who saw Ireland's opting out of the war as cowardly, irresponsible and dangerous, given the strategic importance of the Irish ports to the British war effort and self-defence. Once England was under threat Bowen had begun to identify, loyally and romantically, with her adopted homeland, and to feel impatient with the Irish intransigence.

In the spirit of reconciliation – hoping to be an ambassador who could explain the British and the Irish to each other – Bowen had written to the Ministry of Information in the spring of 1940 offering her services as a spy. She was sent to Ireland that July, soon after the fall of France. Writing to Virginia Woolf, Bowen reported that she felt it was important to go, hoping as she did to 'be some good', but that she felt low at going away.

> If there's to be an invasion of Ireland, I hope it may be while I'm there – which I don't mean frivolously – but if anything happens to England while I'm in Ireland I shall wish I'd never left, even for this short time.

In Ireland, where the war was referred to only as 'the Emergency', she would feel separated from the crisis.

In fact she was back in good time to witness the first bombs falling on London that September. Now, only two months into the bombing, it was sad to leave London again, but relations between Britain and Ireland were at their most volatile and Bowen hoped to ameliorate the situation. In 1938, Britain had handed over control of three Atlantic seaports at Cóbh, Berehaven and Lough Swilly to the 1922 Irish Free State, giving the Irish full control over their own defences and thus making Irish neutrality possible when the British were at war. Churchill, then an MP, was highly critical of this move and now, as Prime Minister, he was determined to use the Irish ports to defend Britain. Given that Ireland was arguably just as much at the mercy of German invasion as Britain (as demonstrated by the cases of other neutral nations such as Belgium and Holland), Churchill could not understand why de Valera refused to accept that this was in Ireland's interests as well. The tension was exacerbated by British losses in the Battle of the Atlantic, the focus of Britain's war efforts in the first year of the war. In the autumn of 1940, a succession of British ships were sunk by German submarines in the Irish Sea. As far as Churchill was concerned, the losses had only occurred because the British could not use the south and west coasts of Ireland to refuel their flotillas and aircraft. Determined to pressurise the Irish, he gave official credence to popular stories that the Irish were allowing German submarines to refuel on the western coasts.

As a passionate supporter of Churchill, Bowen was increasingly impatient with Irish politics. 'Ireland can be dementing, if one's Irish,' she had written to Virginia Woolf before her visit in the summer. It was all the more dementing if one had just experienced a frightening two months of bombing, and fully appreciated the strategic importance of the ports. But at the same time, Bowen could still understand the reasoning behind neutrality, and was loyally committed to explaining it to the equally intransigent English. Reporting back to London on 9 November, she described the unfavourable reaction of the Irish public to Churchill's remarks about the Irish ports, stating that even if de Valera wanted to be amenable, public opinion would now be defiantly against compromise. She was aware that the 'childishness and obtuseness' of Eire could not fail to be irritating to the English mind. But she reminded those in Britain that any suggestion of a violation of Eire could be used to implement enemy propaganda and weaken the British case. The British might feel that Eire was making a fetish of her neutrality, but this assertion of her neutrality was Eire's 'first *free* self-assertion' and she had invested her self-respect in it. In addition, 'it would be sheer disaster for this country, in its present growing stages, and with its uncertain morals, to be involved in war'.

As far as Bowen was concerned, it was possible for Eire to retain her neutrality and still lease her ports to the British. But this, she lamented, was a notion 'the popular mind here cannot grasp'. Any mention of involvement in the war and the public began to fear the immediate bombing of Ireland. And 'one air raid on an Irish city would produce a chaos with which, in the long run, England would have to cope'. For her part, Bowen was attempting to create consensus by assuring the Irish that England had no wish for Ireland to enter the war. She urged the War Office to arrange for 'a tactful broadcast, apparently *to* England, but *at* Eire', making this clear.

Bowen's own sympathies, as an Anglo-Irishwoman living in England, were complex. In a later interview she described the Anglo-Irish as 'a race inside a race' – 'a sort of race carved out of two races'. She was Irish enough to see that war would divide and destroy her native country, but English enough to see the need to do whatever it took to defeat Germany. More than anything else, she was enough of a native to see that the English were handling the Irish in the wrong way. And Bowen had always been able to sympathise with the Irish Republicans in their impatience with the British. Her 1929 novel *The Last September* depicted the Troubles which engulfed Ireland a decade earlier from the point of view of an Anglo-Irish family who have almost as much sympathy with the Republican rebels who are trying to burn the Big Houses down as with the British soldiers who are attempting to protect them.

The book is set in Danielstown, a Big House modelled on Bowen's Court. This house, loftily perched on high steps at the top of a lawn, is surrounded by a 'screen of trees', which press in 'from the open and empty country like an invasion'. It is the setting for the 'ambushes, arrests, captures and burnings, reprisals and counter-reprisals' that, as Bowen would later write in a preface to the novel, 'kept the country and country people distraught and tense'.

The British patrolled and hunted; the Irish planned, lay in wait, and struck.

Inside the house, the Naylors, an Anglo-Irish couple, preside over their wistful niece Lois and rebellious pro-IRA nephew Laurence, hosting tennis parties while they wait for their house to be burned down. 'One can only say,' Bowen goes on in the preface, 'it appeared the best thing to do.' But their position was not, she adds, only ambiguous; it was 'more nearly heart-breaking than they cared to show'. Inherited loyalty to Britain pulled them one way; their own temperamental Irishness the other.

The Naylors resent the interfering presence of the British almost as much as the Irish do themselves. 'This country,' Sir Richard complains, 'is altogether too full of soldiers, with nothing to do but dance and poke old women out of their beds to look for guns.' 'I'm not English,' says Laurence to Gerald, an English soldier who is courting Lois, when Gerald arrives at the house and proudly announces that he has captured a local Republican revolutionary called Peter Connor. Gerald is shocked when Sir Richard declares his intention to send Peter's mother some grapes. 'I had no idea,' he exclaims, perplexed, 'these people were friends of yours.' Meanwhile, only a few days earlier, Lois has had a secret encounter with Peter Connor, who appeared, garbed in a trench coat with 'a resolute profile, powerful as a thought', beside her on a dark shrubbery path in the grounds. Indeed, her unwitting meeting with Connor was charged with just the sexual possibility that is lacking from most of her assignations with Gerald. As a suitor Gerald is too careful, too prosaic – in the terms of the novel, too English – to be a satisfactory object for Lois's unfocused longing.

Since the publication of *The Last September*, Bowen's own inclination to sympathise with the Republicans had been strengthened by her two-year affair with a real-life Peter Connor figure, the Irish writer and one-time IRA gunman, Sean O'Faolain. The pair had met early in 1937, though both had already privately admired the other's work. Editing a collection of short stories in 1936, Bowen informed William Plomer that the only 'real pleasure' had been O'Faolain's *Midsummer Night's*

Madness collection, which she thought '*grand*'. 'Have you met him?' she asked Plomer, curiously; 'Is he nice? He might possibly be quite dim.' O'Faolain, meanwhile, had read Bowen's *Friends and Relations* and 'fallen utterly in love with this author who had Turgenev's triple trick of presenting reality to me as close-up as if it were a ball balanced on her five finger tips'. Just when he was despairing of the future of the Irish novel, hope had arrived. Accordingly, he arranged a meeting through their mutual friend, the literary editor of the *Spectator*, Derek Vershoyle. O'Faolain wrote to Bowen to announce his admiration in advance. 'I find so much trembling loveliness in your books that they have given me quite a bad time,' he announced; 'lonely folk shouldn't read lovely books.' He could only hope that she played fair and carried the aura of her imagination about her real self.

The meeting was a success; a month later O'Faolain was writing to Bowen mentioning how much he would 'love to run down there [to Kildorrey] and see your home', though his wife Eileen 'could hardly come at the moment'. Would 8 May be possible? By the summer of 1937, Bowen was reporting to another former lover, Humphry House, that 'I am, we are, someone and I are, very much in love'. 'It doesn't feel like a love affair,' she added; 'it feels like a marriage.' She described O'Faolain as 'the best (I think, without prejudice) of the younger Irish writers', adding proudly that he had fought with the Irish in the Anglo-Irish war, then the Republicans in the Civil War, though he was not at all like anybody's idea of an ex-gunman, being instead 'a very gentle person with fair hair – or hair, at least, about the colour of mine'. Sean, like Elizabeth, was the age of the century, though they were doing very different things in the same years of their lives. Both were married and anxious not to hurt their spouses, so they were trying to pay for their happiness by 'being very good'. All this had increased her allegiance to Ireland: 'I feel wedded to the country, and rooted there.'

Born only a few months and a few miles apart, Elizabeth and Sean were nonetheless enemies by birth. For centuries, his Catholic, Republican ancestors had hated the Protestant landed gentry who inhabited Bowen's Court. May Sarton later recalled how Elizabeth 'at one time suffered from the taunts of one man she loved who was Irish; there was never, there could not be, a perfect equilibrium after centuries of such hatred on one side and condescension on the other'. For Sean's daughter, the novelist Julia O'Faolain, who was a small child during the affair, this was sex 'as synecdoche': the coming together of two Irelands; the fiery liaison of the daughter of the Big House with the man who burned such houses down. Years later Elizabeth recollected Sean watching her as she locked up Bowen's Court for the night, heaving an iron bar into place and fastening the hall door with chains. '*Here*,' he told her, 'was a Big House ready for a siege!' Simultaneously, they were stirred by complex race memories; she was aware that her own first Irish ancestor had come from Wales, while Sean was descended from the ancient inhabitants of the land.

But Elizabeth discovered a new side of Ireland through Sean. As a child in Dublin, Elizabeth had been oblivious to the Irish revival that was going on around her. For her Irish contemporaries, this was the era

Elizabeth Bowen and Sean O'Faolain at Bowen's Court, *c.* 1938

when W. B. Yeats and Lady Gregory founded the Abbey Theatre, revived Celtic art and translated Celtic fairy stories. But Elizabeth Bowen recorded in *Bowen's Court* that 'so complete was my parents' immunity from the Irish Revival that *I* only heard of this for the first time when I was at school in England, about 1916'. Since then, she had read her way through the new Irish canon and met Yeats at a dinner given by her friend Maurice Bowra. But it was through Sean that she had direct access to the movement, and was introduced to Yeats in a domestic setting. 'I met some of the grand old boys,' Elizabeth reported to William Plomer in 1938; 'like Yeats, with whom I spent an evening, who was an angel, in his own house, less showy and more mellow: he has a superb white cat.' In his autobiography, Sean O'Faolain recalled that Elizabeth made such a hit with the ageing poet that Yeats's wife kept imploring Sean not to take her away: 'He likes her! He likes her!' Sean also introduced Elizabeth to his contemporaries. Frank O'Connor came to stay at Bowen's Court where she described him chanting in the library, 'dropping his head back as did Yeats', recalling 'the magnificence of the Midnight Court, poetry and bawdry of an Ireland before the potato had struck root'.

Sean increased Elizabeth's political range, enlisting her sympathy for the Republican rebels. As far as he was concerned, *The Last September* was extremely successful as a portrait of dreamy girlhood and countryside. He had no hesitation in judging it Elizabeth Bowen's 'loveliest novel', and later misremembered this as the novel that had caused him to fall in love in advance of meeting her. In fact, when he first courted her, he had no idea that she had written an Irish novel, and he read it in April 1937, just before going to stay with her at Bowen's Court. Finishing it at breakfast ('an unfair test'), he wrote her an ecstatic letter of congratulation, commending it as 'entirely Irish – if that matters a damn' (and for Sean O'Faolain, of course, it did). He could smell the hay; he adored the 'un-underlined atmosphere'; but he was longing for 'the "enemy" to come into the foreground a bit'. Sean, who was happy to identify with the romantic, dangerous figure in the trench coat, wanted Peter Connor to come upon Lois in the dark shrubbery. He later characterised Elizabeth Bowen's standard plot as the encounter between 'the kid and the cad'. Now, asking her if 'the wall between Danielstown and Peter Connor's farm' could be scaled, he was prepared to be the cad for the coltish girl he persistently regarded Elizabeth herself to be.

Sean swaggered into Elizabeth's life with all the charismatic eloquence of his hero, Daniel O'Connell, whose biography he was then writing, and insisted that she look the rebel straight in the eye. The encounter was exhilarating, painful and enlightening. Together, Sean and Elizabeth could chip away at the wall between the Big House and the Republican's farm, and Elizabeth could find a way to engage authentically with the other side of the struggle, interrogating the credentials of her Anglo-Irish ancestors. The result was *Bowen's Court*, a book that would be published in the middle of the war in 1942, but which she was already researching in 1938 and writing, in Sean's presence, in the summer of 1939. Sean himself is perhaps most romantically acknowledged here in her portrait of Daniel O'Connell, whose 'eloquence was to rush through remote and downtrodden Ireland like an incoming tide, filling dead reaches, lifting the people, carrying them'.

Bowen's Court is the history of Elizabeth Bowen's own house, set in the context of five hundred years of Irish history. It is both an attack on an imperialist power and a defence of a dying way of life. Bowen is clear in apportioning blame to the English for most of the bloodier aspects of Irish history. In the seventeenth century, 'the chivalric element disappeared from the struggle' between the English and the Irish. 'The complete subjugation and the exploitation of Ireland became the object of the English burgess class.' The Union of 1800 which brought together British and Irish church and state was, she states unequivocally, 'a bad deal'; 'a tragedy that puts uninformed comment quite out of countenance'.

But Bowen is equally clear in maintaining that the Anglo-Irish should not be taken for English and blamed accordingly. For the Union to take place, prominent Anglo-Irish 'were bought, to their lasting dishonour, by peerages, by advancements in the peerage, and by sums down'. They were attracted, masochistically, by the English, but Bowen insists that this attraction was 'too unwilling to be love'. And the

Bowens themselves, for all their faults, had an ethic of 'politeness to England, rather than loyalty'. They lived on good terms with their Irish neighbours and, although it would be presumptuous to say that they were popular, their hardnesses were pardoned and their vagaries suffered. She never heard ('why should I?') any remark about 'the Irish' prompted either by panic or by the wish to insult. The Anglo-Irish may not have done much but, for centuries, 'we did believe we did something: we lived well, we circulated our money, we, consciously or unconsciously, set out to give life an ideal mould'.

Elizabeth Bowen's affair with Sean O'Faolain was curtailed by war. From the start, it was evident to her that if and when war broke out between Britain and Germany, her place would be with her husband in London. During the Munich crisis in September 1938, Alan summoned Elizabeth to Clarence Terrace on what turned out to be a false alarm. On 30 September, she reported to Isaiah Berlin that Alan had telephoned her two days earlier, suggesting that she should cross that night to cope with aspects of the National Emergency in London. Crisis had been followed by anticlimax; she had done nothing but eat figs, read the ARP handbook and try on her gas mask. Feeling that more time in Ireland was owing, she arranged to return to collect some belongings and see friends in Dublin; she was not ready to leave Sean. Thankfully, the crisis was averted, and over the course of the next year Elizabeth spent much of her time in Ireland, meeting Sean fairly frequently in Cork and Dublin. He also visited her in London. In January 1939, Elizabeth wrote to ask Virginia Woolf if she had time to see a friend of hers from Ireland, who 'wants to meet you so very much'. Virginia wrote back offering tea to Elizabeth and 'the man with the Irish name' ('I've never read him, but am sure he's nice'). Later Sean recollected the sight of the profiles of the two women – 'Virginia's exquisitely, delicately beautiful, Elizabeth's not beautiful but handsome and stately' – bent over a ring-casket Virginia Woolf had inherited from Ottoline Morrell.

Sean's final visit to Elizabeth's house in Clarence Terrace took place on 31 August 1939, the day before Germany invaded Poland. In his autobiography, Sean O'Faolain recalled how, as they 'lay-abed, passionsated', Alan rang from the office to tell Elizabeth that the British fleet had been ordered to mobilise, 'which means war'. Elizabeth thanked her husband unemotionally; awkwardly, Sean made a joke; Elizabeth replied, dryly unforgiving, that this sort of tasteless humour '*is* the sort of thing that war "does to people", isn't it'. In a 1940 account of a journey around Ireland made during this period Sean O'Faolain rewrote the event altogether, claiming more heroically that he was in fact at the foot of Croagh Patrick mountain in Mayo, a traditional site of Irish pilgrimage, on the day that war was declared.

In October 1939, Sean made one final visit to Bowen's Court, where he found Elizabeth trying to haul the house into the twentieth century – getting a telephone put in, and having the house wired for electricity. It was clear that this was the end of the relationship; Elizabeth was about to decamp more permanently to London. After casting herself in the enjoyable role of the feisty *cailín* of a Republican gunman she was ready to identify herself as the loyal wife of an English civil servant. To an extent, Sean envied Elizabeth her role in the war. While staying at Bowen's Court, he wrote an article entitled 'Irish Blackout' for the *Manchester Guardian*, where he described the anxious atmosphere in the Irish countryside: 'Tradition has been broken. The heart is dishevelled. Continuity has been blotted out.' He was deafened by the 'silence from across Europe', blinded by the 'total darkness of the mind'. 'We sit wondering what it must be like in London, Berlin, Warsaw, conjuring furnace towns, flying men, and complaining beasts.' A year later, Elizabeth Bowen would write in her short story 'Summer Night' that 'in the heart of the neutral Irishman indirect suffering pulled like a crooked knife'.

The affair was officially over. However, Bowen listed O'Faolain among five other friends and relatives she had met in Dublin in her first report to the British government in July 1940. It is possible that it was more than a cursory meeting; that her letter to Woolf was disingenuous and her decision to visit wartime Ireland was the result of more than just a sense of political duty. Either way, she remained sufficiently in touch with O'Faolain for him to publish an article by her on 'The Big House' in the first issue of *The Bell*, Ireland's new literary magazine, which he edited throughout the war.

This article of October 1940 comes out of the writing of *Bowen's Court* and reveals Bowen thinking urgently about the role of the Big House in contemporary Ireland. In his letter about *The Last September* O'Faolain told Bowen that she should write about a Danielstown Big House 'that was at least aware of the Ireland outside'; 'that, perhaps, regretted the division enough to admit it was there'. Bowen's article is an attempt to explain the Big House to those on the outside of its walls; to protest that it is not as isolated as it seems ('one's own point of departure always seems to one normal') and to elucidate its appeal – the 'peculiar spell' cast by the dead who lived there and pursued the same routine within the house and now provide 'a sort of order, a reason for living, to every minute and every hour'.

Rather than defending the privilege of the inhabitants, Bowen assumes that everyone now knows 'that life is not all jam in the big house'. Expensive sacrifices must be made and 'new democratic Ireland no longer denounces the big house, but seems to marvel at it. Why fight to maintain life in a draughty barrack?' From amid the bombs in London, Bowen asks herself the same question. Can the Big House justify its existence and the sacrifices that must be made on its behalf in a time of war? The answer is that it can; that the social discipline – the subjugation of the personal to the impersonal – is now more relevant than ever. And, even with the bolts and chains that O'Faolain saw as preparing the way for a siege, the Big House is not designed to exclude but to bring together. The big rooms demand that we 'scrap the past, with its bitternesses and barriers, and all meet, throwing in what we have'; the doors, which stand open all day and are only regretfully barred up at night, welcome the stranger, just as much as the friend.

In Ireland in November 1940, a month after he had published her article, Sean took Elizabeth out for a final lunch. They went to Jammet's, Dublin's best restaurant. Before the war, Virginia Woolf had visited Dublin and despaired at the impossibility of cultural revolution 'when the best restaurant in the capital is Jammet's, when there's only boiled potatoes in the biggest hotel in Dublin'. Now, the food at Jammet's seemed positively opulent in contrast with the wartime rationing that had affected even London's grandest establishments. Elizabeth later recalled how during the war British journalists, happy to arrive in Dublin, headed on arrival straight to Ireland's finest restaurants, first to eat, then to type 'gargantuan stories of Irish eating' for the papers represented.

Yet this was not, according to Sean, 'a happy lunch':

> She did not say why she was revisiting our well-fed and neutral Dublin from her bombed and Spartan London, and I did not ask lest I should touch the nerve of some private crisis at Bowen's Court, and a lunch is a lunch even if between foiled lovers. As it was I blundered almost with my first words, saying with a gush of false gaiety as I shook out my table-napkin, 'Well, Elizabeth? So it is taking a world war to divorce us?'

Uttering these 'insensitive words', Sean remembered his blunder of the previous August; Elizabeth gave him the same reply – this was the sort of thing that war 'does to people'. 'Presently,' Sean O'Faolain later reflected, 'we outdid one another in fatuity.' He said floridly, 'I am afraid, Elizabeth, that I am content too often to let life ride me down. Whereas I always imagine you riding down life astride a powerful, prancing dappled horse.' 'I have never before felt so completely a leader!' she replied.

During lunch, Sean was oblivious of the fact that Elizabeth was using him once more as material for the Ministry of Information. 'I was able,' she wrote in her report, 'to see again, over tea or sherry, people whom I had met elsewhere, and to continue conversations that had promised to be interesting. Ostensibly I was in Dublin on holiday and "having a rest".' Again she listed O'Faolain among her contacts, and it was from his point of view that she described Dublin society as 'suffering from claustrophobia and restlessness'. The intelligentsia was minding the suspension of travel to and from Britain and was frightened of parochialism; the resulting deliberate escapism could be dreary, though she was struck by 'the intelligence (if not always the wisdom) and the animation of the talk'.

In his autobiography, O'Faolain claimed that a few weeks later he gathered that Dublin gossip was suggesting Bowen was there for the Ministry of Information. If this was true, then the gossip did not reach very far; James Dillon, the leader of the Opposition and the subject of several of Bowen's interviews, later expressed complete surprise when he found out about her reports. Whether he learnt the news then or later, O'Faolain found it distressing: here was another example of what war did to people. And Sean's Elizabeth, the romantic dreamer, may have thought that she wanted to help the war effort but would have been devastated if Ireland had abandoned her neutrality: 'the very thought of Ireland at war would have torn Elizabeth's heart apart'. He was right, of course: Bowen never questioned the judiciousness of neutrality as a policy. Her passionate love of Ireland, which had intensified during the relationship with O'Faolain, continued into the war and beyond. She had signed up as a spy partly to protect the interests and reputation of the country she loved. But O'Faolain underestimated the detached pragmatism with which she hoped, in her letter to Virginia Woolf, that she could 'be some good' in mitigating the tension between the two countries. O'Faolain would claim Bowen again and again as an Irish writer. 'She is an Irishwoman, at least one sea apart from English traditions,' he insisted in a 1956 account of her fiction; she knew English life only 'as an exile with an Irish home'. He could not accept the extent of her practical investment in Britain winning the war.

For her part, Bowen was still more loyal to O'Faolain than her Ministry of Information report might suggest. While she was in Ireland, he asked her to review his new novel, *Come Back to Erin*, for the December issue of *The Bell*. The resulting piece is a generous tribute to the man she had loved. Opening with the statement that '*Come Back to Erin* is the ironic title of Mr O'Faolain's latest, and greatest, novel', Bowen found that the book was too large to come inside the scope of a short review: 'To give the range of humanity, at its highest and lowest, is probably the first task of the novelist: Mr O'Faolain has done this.' He had regained the 'magnificent objectivity and the poetic fullness' of *A Nest of Simple Folk*, which he had posted to her before his first visit to *Bowen's Court*. And he had produced a tragedy devoid of cheap tricks, cynicism and sentiment. To read the book was to suffer, to an extent. But there was a tenderness, a 'love of man in the writing that leaves a sort of sweetness about the heart'.

Elizabeth Bowen remained in Ireland until the end of January 1941. Alan joined her for Christmas and then she was alone once again, in the severe seclusion of Bowen's Court. 'To be here is very nice,' she wrote to Virginia Woolf at the beginning of January,

> but I no longer like, as I used to, being here alone. I can't write letters, I can't make plans. The house now is very cold and empty, and very beautiful in a glassy sort of way. Every night it freezes. There are some very early lambs which at night get through the wires and cry on the lawn under my windows.

Boxed in by the barren mountains, she was feeling claustrophobic with no one to talk to. And, whatever British journalists might say about the luxurious conditions in Ireland, rationing made country life difficult. There was no petrol at all, so she was completely immobilised – 'at least immobilised until we get new ideas about time'. She had a bicycle but found it impossible to think while cycling; she would much rather have had a horse. Meanwhile, in another world and another time, the bombing in London continued, and it was almost time to return.

7

'How we shall survive this I don't know'

Hilde Spiel, Graham Greene and Henry Yorke, autumn 1940–spring 1941

Hilde Spiel also left London in October 1940, though she was less reluctant than Elizabeth Bowen to leave the bombs behind. She and her daughter were evacuated to Oxford where they stayed with their friend Teresa Carr-Saunders and her husband, who was the director of the London School of Economics, in an old English manor house on the Isis. Peter de Mendelssohn was less liberated by his family's departure than Greene or Yorke. He would not have been averse to a wartime affair, but he had a novel to write in the evenings, a severe lack of money, and was constrained by the continued presence of Hilde's parents. Hilde herself was pleased to escape both Wimbledon and the bombs. The countryside around the Isis was beautiful, and Oxford felt decidedly more cosmopolitan than the dreary London suburbs.

Away from London, though, Hilde grew more fearful. She no longer had to set an example of English stoicism for her hysterical mother and she became preoccupied with the more nightmarish aspects of the war. 'This morning at 8am I dreamed that you and I left a restaurant and in the vestibule were both shot dead,' she wrote to Peter. 'I still remember falling down on the floor next to you and saying quite calmly: just kiss me goodbye in case we should die. It wasn't really unpleasant and now I quite know what it feels like.' Meanwhile, reading about the bombing in London, she was anxious about Peter's safety. 'My darling, I am horrified at the thought of what you're going through in Wimbledon,' she complained a few days later. 'Sixty bombs in one night – it is incredible, dearest, will this wretched Ministry never evacuate London? . . . How we shall survive this I don't know . . . If the Americans don't save England it'll be hopeless.'

Hilde now had little faith in the British ability to win the war without America. As a result, she and Peter looked into the possibility of escaping as a family, first to America and then to the Azores. But the plans proved too complicated and Peter was indecisive. On 11 October 1940 he told Hilde that he was now convinced that it was too late, and that he was relieved by this outcome. 'The Azores would have been a perpetual nightmare to me.' He apologised to her for 'all the heart-searching confusion I caused you with my indecision and even damaging ideas' but he was praying that he had done the right thing. From the beginning of the war he had hated the idea of leaving Europe. 'If England fights, it fights not just for itself but also for us,' he had reminded Hilde in 1938; 'we are Europeans.'

Later, Hilde agreed with Peter. In her autobiography she wrote that 'it would have seemed like desertion . . . to leave the sinking ship while others, less directly concerned in the resistance to Hitler's tyranny, were risking their necks'. But at the time, she was less prepared to put her principles before her safety, and at first she was devastated that they had missed their chance to escape. 'I have not much faith in our "luck" left, in our personal luck, I mean, since we've missed the chance of going to America,' she told Peter.

> I really had a sort of mystical belief until then in our future and felt supported simply by the fact that we are such nice and talented people, and that it would be such a waste to let us go down. Well, I'm not so sure now. I don't believe England is going to win soon enough to let us escape, physically and psychologically.

Hilde was still wondering about sending Christine to safety alone, perhaps accompanied by Erika Mann, Thomas Mann's daughter, who was about to cross the sea in a military convoy protected by British destroyers. Peter, writing to Hilde to describe how this would work, announced that he was 65 per cent for and 35 per cent against the idea, though there was a danger that the ship would either be bombed or would get stuck in the Azores, where it was stopping en route. He wanted Christine to be safe and he wanted Hilde back with him in London, not least because he was finding it exhausting looking after her parents without her.

> We must . . . make a determined effort to get the Spiels a house and to organise our life. I can simply not do it alone. It would be very lovely if Mummi could come back.

But Hilde's lack of faith in their own luck made her doubt that God would have any mercy on the boat Christine was sailing on. At the same time, succumbing to a hysteria not dissimilar to her mother's, she announced that even if Christine was safer in Oxford than on a military convoy on the Atlantic, it would be a safety bought at the price of a lifetime of fascism.

> I know that England will be defeated and therefore I'd rather have my child drowned in the attempt to escape this than suddenly find herself in an England ruled by Mosley and Tyler Kent.

By the end of October, they had abandoned any thought of sending Christine across the sea alone, and Hilde settled into life in Oxford. Peter was relieved that his wife and daughter were safe. Coming back from a visit to Hilde in Oxford at the end of October he told her that his return to London had convinced him that

> wherever you are – provided it is warm – you will be better off than here. This is no longer a place for women and children. Not that things have become any worse. On the contrary last night was quite harmless, we all slept soundly through everything, but two days away from it make you forget the general picture, and that general picture is nerve-racking and ghastly.

Both Hilde and Peter were finding moments of escapism in visits to the cinema. In November Hilde saw *Waterloo Bridge* and sank happily into the world of Robert Taylor and Vivien Leigh ('the only person I know to look heavenly in an old beggar's hat'). Fed up with 'the Spiel faces' in Wimbledon, Peter went to see a new biopic of the actress Lilian Russell. 'It moved me to tears,' he told Hilde, 'although there isn't really very much to it.' What had moved him was

> the thing with which I had completely lost touch – you know: human voice, laughter, tears, a little music, someone talking of love – do you understand? In short, feeling, sentiment, human warmth. How one loses these things in this life of ours, in this daily bombing routine. Suddenly you come up against a note of music, a ripple of laughter, a beautiful face, a smile – and it just overwhelms you. How poor we have become through this war. The simplest, human things are suddenly a revelation, forcing tears into your eyes, for no reason at all. It is as if, after a long time, somebody says something nice and warm and personal to you – something you had completely forgotten existed.

Hilde wrote back, assuring her 'dearest Pumpi' that she could understand how he felt.

> It happened to me whenever we heard music or saw a film or read something beautiful, ever since this horror started. It is incredible how little of our life is left. Very often now, in the peaceful countryside, I remember the joys of earlier days, and it seems unbelievable that I should ever have been unhappy in the midst of these wonderful things and adventures.

Living amid the English restraint of the Carr-Saunders family, she was missing the intensity of life in Vienna. In a short story called 'Another Planet' written at this time she describes a true episode that occurred during her stay. Here, evacuated with her daughter to a house on the Thames a couple of miles from Oxford, the narrator is bemused by the formality of her host family. The four children, all younger than twelve, speak with the same decorous, joking expressions as the adults, with any regression into baby-speak frowned upon by their demanding parents. At first the narrator is impressed, if not enraptured, but then one Sunday lunchtime the family meal is interrupted by the arrival of a neighbour, who tells the twelve-year-old son Edmond that his dog, Benjamin, has been run over and gruesomely killed.

All eyes turn to look at Edmond. The dog has been an object of great tenderness for him; perhaps the sole tenderness he has experienced, brought up in a family that avoids kissing or touching. Edmond, unsurprisingly, starts to cry. But he is ignored by his family. His parents gaze at him sternly and his siblings survey him awkwardly, until his mother interrupts him with a 'Will you control yourself, Edmond', and he pulls himself together, continuing to eat his soup. Order has resumed for everyone except the narrator, who loses her self-control and breaks down in tears.

> I cried about Benjamin, about the suppressed feelings of a strange child, and out of homesickness for a country in which one could sob unrestrainedly when a sorrow befell one. I could not repress my tears. I stood up from the table, excused myself, and went up to my tower. No one looked at me, no one uttered a word.

In 'Another Planet' the narrator immediately packs her bags and leaves; her hosts expect no less. The reality was more compromising. Hilde Spiel remained with the Carr-Saunders family for a few more weeks but then at the start of December she and her daughter returned to London. She recorded on 3 December that the Blitz was now 'only once or twice a week, but then very bad'. There were no bombs over Christmas, and the war news was now focused on north-east Africa, where the British were fighting an offensive battle against the Italians on land. 'The Greeks are driving the Italians out of Albania,' Virginia Woolf had reported in her diary on 8 December.

> Perhaps this is the turning point in the war. But it dribbles out in such little drops. One can't always catch them. The war slowly enacts itself on a great scene: round our little scene.

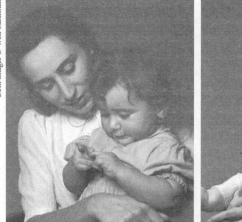
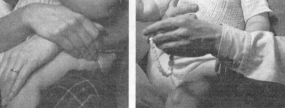

Both images © Wolf Suschitzky

Hilde Spiel and Peter de Mendelssohn with Christine, *c.* 1941

The respite in the bombing of London gave people a chance to survey the damage, and Harold Nicolson complained on Christmas Day that the city was beginning to look very drab. 'Paris is so young and gay that she could stand a little battering. But London is a charwoman among capitals, and when her teeth begin to fall out she looks ill indeed.' Areas like the City of London and the East End that had been badly bombed were now too much of a mess for maps to be of much use. It was no longer clear where the normal ground level was situated amid the cliffs and slopes of rubble. Throughout London, back gardens were deteriorating into wastelands of weeds and long grass and 'To Let' notices were proliferating now that so many former inhabitants had fled to the countryside.

By January 1941 the British could celebrate the growing success of their troops in Africa, but the bombing of London had begun again. There had been a series of particularly damaging raids between

Christmas and New Year (141 people were killed in London on the night of 27 December alone, including fifty in a public shelter in Southwark). On 30 December James Pope-Hennessy and the society photographer and aesthete Cecil Beaton visited the City of London, still in flames from the night before, researching a book called *History Under Fire*. Beaton recorded clambering among 'the still smouldering ashes of this frightful wasteland' as the icy winds beat around corners and they ran around the glowing mounds of rubble. 'We could not deny,' he admitted, 'a certain ghoulish excitement stimulated us, and our angers and sorrows were mixed with a strange thrill at seeing such a lively destruction – for this desolation is full of vitality. The heavy walls crumble and fall in the most romantic Piranesi forms.' For Beaton, the Blitz offered a ready-made aesthetic experience which could transcend the human suffering it caused. This was harder for Hilde Spiel, who could never forget the political reality of the war or the human costs of the dropping bombs. But Hilde and Peter too became more reckless. On the evening of 3 January they left Christine with Mimi and Hugo and went to the cinema to see Chaplin's *Great Dictator*, although the sirens were already wailing when they set out. Returning to Wimbledon, they had to run up the hill to their flat because there was an air battle playing out around them.

Still missing home, Spiel began to write a new novel called *The Fruits of Prosperity*, set in late-nineteenth-century Vienna. This opens with a panoramic sweep of Vienna in 1873, when the Kaiser is planning the future, confident that though the century is old, he himself is young. The focus then shifts to the novel's hero, Milan Todor, a young Croat who is journeying to Vienna to seek his fortune, leaving behind an idyllic countryside home. Observing Vienna through the eyes of a stranger, Spiel was able to indulge in a lyrical survey of her home town. Milan is at once overwhelmed and bewitched by the colours, smells and sounds of the city; it feels like drinking from a wonderful sea. Leaning against a wall, he briefly remembers home – the scent of early apples, wafted by the breeze to the floor, the husky laugh of the milkmaid in the dim barn – only to dive, overwhelmed, into the new jungle of the town, dazzled by the sunlit glass, sparkling metal and shining walls.

Like Bowen, writing about Bowen's Court while living in Regent's Park, Spiel found it reassuring to write about the lost age and world of her ancestors while the bombs fell around her in wartime Wimbledon. It was a strange book to write in English; Spiel herself felt it to be 'an impertinence'. In fact it did not find a publisher until she had translated it into German forty years later. But in the meantime it enabled her to bring together her new language with the culture in which she had grown up. And she unified the two worlds still more by including a section where Milan goes to London on a business trip. Expecting English colour and charm, he is hit by the smell of Virginia tobacco, coal and fumes, and is followed into the hall of his Russell Square hotel by a December fog. While in London he enters polite society and is bemused by the customs and titles, thinking that an acquaintance's first name is 'Mylord'.

For Hilde Spiel, despite the excitement of the new book, the year did not begin well. They were bankrupt and had to borrow money again. Hugo was searching desperately for work and he and Mimi were very depressed. Meanwhile the raids continued with increasing violence into January, and were rendered particularly unpleasant by a period of freezing weather. Visiting London from Sussex on 13 January, Virginia Woolf walked along the river, lamenting 'the desolate ruins of my old squares; gashed; dismantled; the old red bricks all white powder, like a builder's yard . . . all that completeness ravished and demolished'. The firemen in particular found the cold gruelling, struggling to unblock the turntables of their engines, which were immobilised by ice, and to climb up icy ladders wearing damp uniforms frozen stiff in the cold. On 24 January the 'air correspondent' of the *Spectator* announced that a new phase of the air war was about to begin, which would be completely different from what had gone before. For the past four months the German Air Force had been carefully husbanding its strength, which had been shattered in the autumn. Only two of the six Air Fleets of the Luftwaffe had been in constant action against Britain throughout the winter. The rest had been kept in the background.

Now with the approaching return of good weather we must expect more
intensive operations. We are better prepared to face them than we have
ever been, as well as to carry the war on into Germany. Air operations
are likely to overshadow all else this spring.

The correspondent's guesses about German policy were accurate. Hitler
issued a directive on 6 February stating that immediate efforts would be
made

to intensify the effect of air and sea war, not only to inflict the heaviest
possible losses on England, but also to give the impression that an invasion of Britain is planned this year.

In fact, though, there were fewer raids in February than in previous
months because the German bombers were deterred by the cloudy and
foggy weather. Just as the raids were easing off, British morale was
boosted by the news of continued successes against the Italians in North
Africa. By February Britain could free up troops from Africa and offer
them to help Greece resist the German-Italian assault on the Balkans,
hoping to persuade Yugoslavia and Turkey to join in opposing the Axis
powers. On 9 February Churchill triumphantly informed the nation
that British affairs had prospered 'far better than most of us would have ·
ventured to hope'. The success against Italy in the western desert was
cause for 'strong comfort and even rejoicing'. He was grateful to the
public in London and other big cities for standing firm in battle despite
their lack of military scarlet coats and assured them that 'in the end,
their victory will be greater than far-famed Waterloo', promising that
the attacks would shorten as the days lengthened. Two days later Harold
Nicolson announced in his diary that it was universally believed that
'unless Germany can knock us out within the next three months she
has lost the war'.

However, morale began to decline in March when the heavy raids on
Britain were resumed. London was once again a prime target. On 8 March
a major London raid resulted in damage to Buckingham Palace and the
demolition of the glamorous underground Café de Paris, previously

advertised as the safest restaurant in town, where thirty-four people were killed and eighty injured. The destruction was compounded by another major attack the following night, with bombing in twenty-two London boroughs. The situation was becoming increasingly bleak. On 20 March Spiel recorded in her diary that they had experienced 'the worst attack so far' the previous night. This had involved the largest number of incendiary bombs (122,292) to be used in any attack on Britain.

By the end of March, 33,118 civilians had been killed in air raids. However, between 20 March and the middle of April there was a brief lull in the London bombing as attacks became concentrated on the north of England, with major raids in Hull, Bristol, Coventry and Birmingham in particular. The London diarist Anthony Heap expressed wry gratitude to the Germans for spreading the Blitz 'fairly over the country' and giving the provinces their due share alongside London. 'The effect is that we now have time to digest our weekly dose before being served up for with another.'

Spiel made the most of the respite to enjoy some pleasant distractions from the war. She went to the theatre to see Joyce Grenfell and Peter Ustinov in comic mode on 5 April. Then on 16 April she had tea with her close friend Henrietta Leslie at Buszards tearoom on Oxford Street. This was a bastion of civilised English life. In the windows decorated cakes and buns were piled high; inside guests sat on cushioned chairs and ate sandwiches and scones off tiered cake stands. Twenty-five years earlier, Virginia Woolf had been taken to Buszards by Leonard as a birthday treat during the First World War; as early as the nineteenth century a guide to London had enthused about this 'emporium of cakes', describing Buszards as a favourite spot for ladies during the season. Henrietta Leslie herself, a middle-aged Englishwoman who combined feistiness and warmth, fitted in perfectly. Spiel had met Leslie through PEN, and found now that it was as if she was sitting with 'a piece of good old England, the pre-last war England with its Labour Movement, Fabians and suffragettes. She is a good and kind person and likes us nearly as much as we like her.'

But Spiel's peaceful tea preceded an especially unpalatable dose of bombing. Graham Greene would always look back on 16 April 1941 as

London during the 16 April raid

his most dramatic night as an ARP warden. The raid, which came simply to be known as 'the Wednesday', began at nine in the evening and lasted seven hours. Bloomsbury, Oxford Street, Chelsea and Lambeth were all badly hit, and in a single night there were 2,250 fires, 100,000 homes destroyed and 1,180 people killed. This was destruction on an unprecedented and shocking scale, though soon it would be overshadowed by the level of devastation the British inflicted on Germany. Greene wrote in his diary that it was the worst raid central London had ever experienced, though of course for him there was an anarchic exhilaration to be gained from the destruction which was not there for Spiel. When the sirens started at nine o'clock, Greene was drinking in the Horseshoe pub with Dorothy Glover. They left hurriedly, hoping to find a restaurant still open for dinner. But all the usual places were either full or closed. They finally managed to get served at Czardas in Dean Street, where they sat apprehensively in front of the plate-glass windows. By ten o'clock it was obvious that this was 'the real blitz'. The restaurant was shaken by bomb bursts. Walking back to Dorothy's flat in Gower Mews, Graham wished that he had his steel helmet. Dorothy was on duty first and Graham went with her to fire-watch on the roof of a garage, where they saw 'the flares come slowly floating down, dribbling their flames: they drift like great yellow peonies'.

Greene was on duty at midnight, but when he reported at his post he found that there had not yet been any incidents in his district. At a quarter to two, he had still not been called out to an incident, and he planned to sign off at two thirty. But then the flares came down right where he was standing with two other wardens at the corner of Alfred Place and Tottenham Court Road.

> White southern light: we cast long shadows and the flares came down from west to east across Charlotte Street. Then a few minutes later, without the warning of a whistle, there was a huge detonation. We only had time to get on our haunches and the shop window showered down on our helmets.

Greene ran down Alfred Place towards Gower Street, which was ravaged on both sides. There were women bleeding from cuts on the face standing in the street in dressing gowns, and Greene was told that there was someone hurt on the top floor above RADA, the Royal Academy of Dramatic Arts. He ran with two other wardens and a policeman up four littered flights of stairs to find a wounded girl lying on the floor. 'Bleeding. Stained pyjamas. Her hip hurt. Only room for one man to lift her at a time. Very heavy.' They took it in turns to carry her while the girl, though in pain, apologised to them for her weight. Once they got downstairs a stretcher party came and took her away. Walking along Gower Street, Greene passed one injured civilian after another standing bleeding in doorways, wearing pyjamas which were grey with debris and dust. 'These were the casualties of glass.'

Returning to the post, Greene discovered that the blackout boards had been blown out of the walls and that there was no one there to tell him what to do. He found the Incident Officer at the corner of Gower Street and Keppel Street and was ordered to the Victoria Club in Malet Street, where 350 sleeping Canadian soldiers had been hit by a parachute mine. 'What are a warden's duties?' Greene asked in his diary; 'the lectures no longer seemed clear. Soldiers still coming out in grey blood-smeared pyjamas: pavements littered by glass and some were barefooted.' A soldier appeared and told Greene that there was a man trapped on the stairs. He and the other wardens took a stretcher and went into the building, where they found a twenty-foot drop into what seemed the foundations of the building. It was difficult to think or act amid the confusion of darkness, fire and noise. 'One wished that things would stop: *this* was our incident, but the guns and bombs just went on.'

Eventually they found a body, although only the head and shoulders were visible. Quiet and slumped, this man had become merely a peaceful part of the rubble. ' "'s this him?" "No. He's a goner." ' But there was another stretcher party working on the stairs and they could not locate the body they were looking for, so they made their way down with the corpse. 'Perhaps it wasn't a corpse,' Greene wondered in retrospect.

As they carried the body downstairs, Greene found that time went very slowly. The clock-stopping effects of the bombs often permeated the whole night so that civil defence workers lost all sense of time. Now Greene wanted to get out and escape the claustrophobic suspended world. He shouted for stretcher bearers to take over and then helped to light their way out as they carried the body away. While the wardens were making their way outside, another stick of three bombs came whistling down and Greene lay on the pavement with a sailor on top of him. His hand was cut by broken glass so he hurried back to the post to have it dressed. He observed in his diary that a street accident was horrible and random, but the casualties of war were more disturbing because 'all this belonged to human nature'.

More bombs landed while Greene's hand was being dressed, and he found himself on the floor once again. The windows had blown in. 'One really thought that this was the end, but it wasn't exactly frightening – one had ceased to believe in the possibility of surviving the night.'

He began an Act of Contrition but in fact he was to be disappointed again; as always, he had survived. After attending to two more incidents, Greene called in at the shelter in Gower Mews where Dorothy was acting as shelter warden. He found that she was fairly cheerful but very relieved to see him. A warden had reported sighting Greene in the Victoria Club: 'I think he was all right. He was covered in blood, but I don't think it was his blood.'

'Looking back,' Greene wrote in his Blitz notebook, 'it was the squalor of the night, the purgatorial throng of men and women in dusty torn pyjamas with little blood splashes standing in doorways, which remained. These were disquieting because they supplied images for what one day would happen to oneself.' Two days after the raid, he wrote to his mother that the attack had been the worst yet, although 'one's first corpse in the Canadian place was not nearly as bad as one expected. It seemed just a bit of the rubble.' It had been disquieting but also exciting. Recreated in his diary, the purgatorial images of thronging crowds in bloody pyjamas seem to provide the material for a fantasy that may be nightmarish but is nonetheless appealing in its visionary intensity. And as always, when the glass was swept away the next morning and he and Dorothy awoke in her flat in Gower Mews, there was the vital sensation of being alive.

The spring of 1941 was the most optimistic point in the war for Greene. Since his house had been bombed in October, he had been consistently cheerful. 'I've been leading a chequered and rather disreputable life,' he had reported proudly to Anthony Powell in December, taking perverse delight in the ruins: 'London is extraordinarily pleasant these days with all the new spaces, and the rather Mexican effect of ruined churches.'

In September, he had left the Ministry of Information, when the Director General Frank Pick restructured the department and axed Greene's post. Since then he had been working in the more congenial surroundings of the *Spectator*, where he was the literary editor. Dorothy Glover had remained at the Ministry of Information, where she was responsible for commissioning caricatures and cartoons. The war, Greene told his American agent Mary Pritchett in March, was good 'for someone like me who has always suffered from an anxiety neurosis'. The only thing bothering him was the loneliness of Vivien in Oxford.

Graham was only visiting Vivien once a month now, and even then he had to stay in bachelor accommodation at the King's Arms pub as there was not enough space for him to share his wife's room at Trinity College, so his visits did little to assuage her need for comfort and normality. 'Do you ever *really* miss me or am I the termly tea out with relations?' she wrote to Graham at the beginning of April. She was wondering about leaving Trinity to keep house for her brother Pat, but would reconsider this if Graham gave 'a baffled woof' and came 'lolloping up bristling'. 'Make up that big brilliant mind of yours,' she urged him, 'because you'll turn round and see what you THOUGHT was Pussy purring on the mat was *really* just the white enamel refrigerator turning on and off.' It was hard for her to keep up the hostility for long, though. Soon she was writing again thanking Graham for his tenderness and feeling 'dreadfully bewildered by everything and very incompetent and unsuccessful'.

Perhaps because she was suspicious about Dorothy, Vivien was keen to join Graham in London, and went as far as offering him an ultimatum. Graham put her off stridently, and even managed to reprimand her for her selfishness. He insisted that it was highly likely that he was going to be killed, and if she were to be killed too it would leave the children to be 'bandied about among strangers for charity'. Self-indulgently morbid, he informed her that he would rather walk out into the street and be killed by himself than risk this: 'In the last war anyway people didn't have their wives following them into the trenches.'

Nonetheless, Graham felt guilty that he was enjoying the war so much more than his wife was. 'She has the thin end of things,' he told Mary Pritchett, asking her to drop Vivien a line if she had time. 'I have a most interesting and agreeable time in London. It all seems most right and proper.'

Henry Yorke, too, was on duty during the April raids, and he returned during his leave days to Rutland Gate where Rosamond Lehmann was currently staying with him. She had arrived in London in March, broken-hearted now that she was bereft of both husband and lover. The previous November Goronwy Rees had decided to marry a girl called Margie Morris. In a letter to Dig Yorke, he announced that his proposed bride was 'very young and not at all clever and rather tough and I adore her'. It was not, he said, possible to describe someone you were in love with, so he was not going to try, but he hoped that she and Henry would meet Margie soon and would approve of what they found. 'I only hope,' he added with apparent ingenuousness,

> I am as lucky as Henry has been, you and he are the only people I know who are an encouragement to get married. I'm rather alarmed at what I've done, so please write. Also it has caused terrible trouble with Rosamond, who tells me I'm behaving like a lunatic, but there isn't anything else I could or wanted to do. You see how really undependable I am, it rather alarms me but now I feel I shan't have any need to be undependable any more.

The example of Henry and Dig seems to have been one that Goronwy wished to follow literally. By February 1941, now married, he was writing to Rosamond suggesting they should resume their relationship and see something of the beauties of Cambridge together. For her part, she was furious, complaining to her friend Dadie Rylands that Goronwy could not 'suffer *one single pang*, not even uneasiness, over me'. Meanwhile, her children disapproved of her and her husband had finally left her for another woman. By the time she came to London she was inconsolably miserable, 'rejected and isolated and hoping I'd be killed by a bomb'. Henry invited her to stay and, in the spirit of friendship, attempted to help her pick up the pieces of her life.

Henry himself had also had a difficult few months. In February one of his closest friends, the travel writer Robert Byron, had died when his ship was torpedoed on the way to Persia, where Byron was to report on Russian activities. Henry was grateful for Rosamond's company when, every three days, he appeared from fire-service duty black with soot and joined her for breakfast before disappearing for his day of writing. In the evening he re-emerged and he and Rosamond went out for a drink before he departed to a nightclub with one of the women whom Rosamond later described as 'his rota of ridiculously young girls'.

Both Rosamond and Henry looked back on this as an important moment in the war. For both, the quiet pleasures of sympathetic friendship were more important and more fulfilling than the love affairs they were engaged in at the time; less self-indulgent, more grown-up and more honest. In June 1943 Rosamond wrote to congratulate Henry on *Caught* and to thank him for

> your perfect goodness to me at the time when sirens, chaos and death seemed my only companions, and every hour another proof of waste and exile. I thought I was done for. Your figure re-appearing at intervals, so remote yet so friendly, gave me a little focus of re-assurance and stopped the unending pinch under my ribs.

The next day Henry wrote to thank her, telling her how much her approval of his writing meant. 'One writes for about 6 people, of whom you are one, and when you approve one feels justified.' He too often thought back to 'those days when we sort of shared a life contentedly and with so little fuss' and assured her that if life ever hurt more than usual 'and begins to tear me in pieces I was only thinking on Thursday (it's true) that I should come straight to you'.

Rosamond paid more public tribute to Henry in the 1954 article in the *TLS* entitled 'An Absolute Gift', where she described his wartime persona as 'an eccentric, fire-fighting, efficient, pub-and-night-club haunting monk'. This was ostensibly an article about *Loving*, nine years after its publication, but was actually more of a personal offering of friendship to a man whom she thanked for the 'life-line flung to a fellow-writer during the years of war' and for providing 'an example, personally observed, deeply admired and never forgotten, however poorly followed'.

The example was of his own double life as a firefighter and a writer, living according to the self-imposed regime he had prescribed. She had found the example inspiring at a time when, though she does not state it here, she was too distraught to write, but she was most grateful for the lifeline, which 'had life itself involved in it, the survival of one's instinctive necessary faith in the individual constructive human spirit'. Here she quotes a statement made by Henry in a wartime letter where he told Rosamond that 'these times are an absolute gift to the writer. Everything is breaking up. A seed can lodge and sprout in any crack or fissure.' This image of regeneration germinating immediately and inevitably out of ruin is defiantly positive, suggesting not so much Graham Greene's delight in destruction as an acceptance of that same destruction as the necessary background to the more joyous and fertile aspects of the war. For Rosamond it showed that Henry himself was 'perfectly centred in the times, free to settle nowhere, everywhere, at home in ruins, on fruitful terms with rubble, explosions, flames and smokes'.

In this article Lehmann captures Yorke's elusiveness, while thanking him for being present and kind enough to help bind her once more to life. Unusually among his friends, she was allowed to get to know him well enough to see at once the enigmatic empty vessel and the more serious, passionate man exposed in the novels, and she was able to reconcile the two. Jeremy Treglown has suggested that Rosamond Lehmann paid insightful but less sympathetic tribute to Henry Yorke in the character of Rickie in her 1953 novel *The Echoing Grove*. There are external similarities. Married to Madeleine but also in love with her sister Dinah, Rickie wonders whether he has 'married the wrong sister'. There are also more fundamental parallels, in that Rickie is a character who fades out at will,

> slipping his identity; intently, idly playing with all possibilities, selecting one substitute-identity, then another, to fill out – or scale down – or put a frame round the amorphous semi-transparent mass of low-powered energy that seemed himself.

In this elusive, empty state, Rickie is liable, like Henry, to assume roles, and is also easily though transiently moved by others.

> Any piece of humanity could invade him like a cloud and like a cloud pass through and out of him. Any woman could move him. 'Anything in skirts.'

That spring in 1941 Rosamond could observe Henry being moved by his rota of skirted women but could also see beyond his semi-transparent exterior to a more hidden character that she admired.

The 16 April raid was the first in a series of bad nights. On 18 April Buszards tearoom was destroyed. Spiel could not believe that she had been there for such a peaceful tea only two days earlier. She felt as though it were her own childhood memories that had been dashed into fragments as that 'old, stuffy, solid place' was obliterated. Trudging around Wimbledon as she attempted to find enough food to feed her family, siphoning off the little energy and enthusiasm she did have to help her parents and daughter, Spiel was finding that it took very little to make her succumb to despair. The tearoom was a symbol at once of the world she had lost (the plush cafés of old Vienna) and of the world she had gained (the solid Edwardian backdrop of Woolf or Bowen's novels). A single bomb had casually destroyed both worlds at once; the flattened tearoom portended the ruins that she knew would greet her when she did finally return home to Austria.

In the meantime the war overseas continued to be depressing. Britain was doing extremely badly in the Battle of the Atlantic, with 412 British, Allied and neutral ships lost at sea between March and May 1941. In April Churchill ordered the British press to stop reporting shipping losses, believing that the news aided the Germans and lowered British morale. At the same time, the British were losing ground in the desert campaign in North Africa because Germany had now sent troops to join the battle. And attempts to thwart the German assault on the Balkans were failing as Turkey had refused to join Britain in defending the region and Hitler had focused his efforts on Yugoslavia. German forces destroyed Belgrade from the air at the start of April and Yugoslavia capitulated on 17 April. This enabled the Germans to surround the Greek army in Albania and Eastern Macedonia, leaving the British fighting a losing battle in Greece. On 21 April the British decided to admit defeat and evacuate Greece.

Harold Nicolson reported that there was 'a wave of defeatism sweeping the continent'. Among the defeatists was Hilde Spiel, who announced in her diary on 23 April that Greece was as good as conquered. 'This war is going to last five years, unless we are to lose it. Yes I cannot imagine how we'll ever win.' On 27 April she noted the 'very sad war news. Good old Winston spoke today on the radio, grim and determined, but somehow less cheering than before.' Certainly, Churchill as always made the best of the situation, insisting that he had returned from a recent tour of bombed cities 'not only reassured but refreshed' and that it was just where 'the savage enemy has done its worst' that morale was 'most high and splendid'. Indeed, he had been encompassed by an exaltation of spirit which lifted mankind into a heavenly realm. He excused the defeat in Greece on the grounds that Britain had never expected to succeed alone and that it was only as a result of the fall of Yugoslavia that the defence of Greece had failed. But it was all very well Churchill finding the bomb damage refreshing for the morale it inspired. As the raids continued, Spiel at least was losing resilience and was longing for the raids to stop, experiencing the nightly tests of endurance as more hellish than heavenly.

8

'So much else is on the way to be lost'

Rose Macaulay, May 1941

For Rose Macaulay, this period of the Blitz was even bleaker than it was for Hilde Spiel. During the spring of 1941, she was knocked back by one sorrow after another. In January, her sister Margaret underwent an unsuccessful operation for cancer and returned home in agonising pain from which the doctors refused to release her. When off duty at the ambulance station, Rose made exhausting journeys up and down to Margaret's home in Hampshire. Never comfortable with illness, she found her sister's pain difficult to bear, and was then grief-stricken by Margaret's death in March.

On 28 March Virginia Woolf disappeared, leaving a suicide note for her husband. She was suspected to have drowned herself in the river Ouse. Woolf had suffered from nervous breakdowns throughout her life; this time she believed that she would not recover. For a generation of writers, Woolf's suicide, coming as it did in the middle of the Blitz, brought home the relationship between the public atrocities of war and private suffering. Woolf's decision to drown herself was not in itself a response to war; but her illness was exacerbated by a war which she found overwhelming both in its destruction of her own home and in its more general savagery, brought oppressively into her sitting room on the radio each night. Elizabeth Bowen, who had stayed with the Woolfs in Sussex only a month earlier, wrote to Leonard that as far as she was concerned 'a great deal of

the meaning seems to have gone out of the world. She illuminated everything, and one referred the most trivial things to her in one's thoughts.'
This was not, like the First World War, a conflict in which everyone in
Britain knew someone who had been killed. But it was a war even more
barbaric in its methods, even more all-encompassing in its destruction.
And if, as seemed perfectly possible in 1941, Britain was to lose, the barbarism would continue seamlessly into post-war life.

In June 1940 Virginia Woolf had recorded debating suicide during
an air raid with Kingsley Martin and Rose Macaulay. Both Woolfs had
a suicide pact with Stephen Spender in the event of defeat and Macaulay,
like Woolf, was on the German black list in Britain. The actuality of
Woolf's suicide now took on an eerie inevitability for Macaulay, whose
obituary for her friend appeared in the *Spectator* on 11 April. Here she
described Woolf's pre-eminent 'personal charm' and the 'warm and
gleaming' quality of her talk. 'It amused her to embellish, fantasticate
and ironise her friends,' she added, aware that she had been the subject
of some scorn herself. In the early days of their acquaintance Woolf,
herself a participant in a celibate marriage, had dismissed Macaulay in
a letter as 'a spindle shanked withered virgin'; even once they had
become friends Woolf described Macaulay in her diary as 'a ravaged
sensitive old hack'. But Macaulay now forgave Woolf: 'nothing that she
touched stayed dull'. The article ends on a note of anguish: 'The gap
she leaves is unfillable, her loss (and now when so much else is on the
way to be lost) intolerable, like the extinguishing of a light.'

Rose Macaulay's sense that 'so much else is on the way to be lost'
betrays her anguish as a lover as well as a friend. Woolf's death, coming
so soon after Margaret's, had made her painfully aware of the fragility
of the people she loved and of Gerald O'Donovan in particular. He,
like Margaret, had been diagnosed with cancer; it was only a matter of
time before it took hold. Then on 18 April, the same day that Leonard
Woolf identified his wife's battered body, Mary O'Donovan, the youngest of Gerald's children, died of septicaemia at the age of twenty-three
after swallowing an open safety pin. This, Rose lamented, was 'a
wretched way to lose someone – much worse than enemy action, which
would seem normal'. Grieving with Gerald over his daughter's death,

she began to fear the impending death of her lover. The relationship with Gerald was the most important in Rose's life and she now became consumed by dreading the end she knew would come.

Rose Macaulay (*left*) and Gerald O'Donovan, *c.* 1920

Rose Macaulay and Gerald O'Donovan had fallen in love while working together at the Ministry of Information in 1918. He was her boss, heading the Italian section in the Department for Propaganda in Enemy Countries. She was thirty-six and resolutely single; he was forty-six and married. Love, when it came, was unexpected and overwhelming. In her 1918 novel *What Not*, written during the first months of love, Macaulay marvelled at the 'continual, disturbing, restless, aching want' caused by the proximity of the beloved. Her heroine, also in love with her boss, finds that there is now 'no peace of mind, none of the old careless light-hearted living and working':

> what was it, this extraordinary driving pressure of emotion, this quite disproportionate desire for companionship with, for contact with, one person out of all the world of people and things, which made, while it lasted, all other desires, all other emotions, pale and faint beside it.

A former Irish Catholic priest, Gerald O'Donovan had begun his career in 1897 as the second curate at Loughrea, a small town in County Galway, in the west of Ireland. For seven years, he ambitiously attempted to reform a troubled parish, fighting widespread drunkenness with temperance societies, and raising money to encourage the local Celtic revival in the arts. Here O'Donovan worked together with Irish revivalists including Lady Gregory and the painter Jack Yeats, the poet's brother, whom he commissioned to work on motifs for St Brendan's Cathedral at Loughrea. The art was a success but the town remained impoverished; in O'Donovan's 1913 novel *Father Ralph* the eponymous priest sees the 'muddy red of a stained glass window' as distilled from 'the blood of the poor'. O'Donovan reproached himself for deflecting the town's limited funds into art rather than into housing or education. The local inhabitants blamed him for enjoying fundraising trips to America and dinners with Lady Gregory too much to be committed to the needs of his parish.

In 1904 O'Donovan left Loughrea, cheered off by much of his parish, but believing himself to be a failure. He spent the next four years wandering between Ireland, America and England, eventually settling in London in 1908. Throughout this time, he was a priest without a parish, but in 1908 he left the priesthood. Two years later he married the twenty-four-year-old Beryl Vershoyle, whom he had met at a house party in County Donegal and proposed to after five days. Beryl described herself in her twenties as 'gay, young and enthusiastic'. Gerald, recently released from his vow of celibacy, fell for her easily. Beryl remembered Gerald at this time as 'considerably older, and exceedingly brilliant intellectually', adding that 'nobody thought me at all up to his standard, which was true, and I was humbly aware of it'.

By the time that Gerald met Rose, he was the progenitor of two children and two novels. At first, he was funded by Beryl's family money. Then, after short spells in the Service Corps and the Ministry of Munitions and a period in publishing, he was posted to the Ministry of Information in late 1917. Rose arrived at the Ministry a few months later and the two fell in love in the spring of 1918, when Beryl was pregnant with Gerald's third child. There is no directly autobiographical account of the start of their relationship, but Rose Macaulay reworked it compulsively in her novels, right up to her death in 1958.

Rose and Gerald first appeared as Kitty Grammont and Nicky Chester in *What Not*, Macaulay's prescient novel of post-war bureaucracy and eugenics, published during the First World War in 1918. Here, true to life, Chester heads a civil service department, though in the novel it is the satirically named Ministry of Brains, a department set up to encourage (and indeed enforce) superior intelligence throughout Britain. He is detached, fiery and impressive; 'his manners were bad' but 'he set other people on fire'. Kitty is his intelligent employee; 'something of the elegant rake, something of the gamin, something of the adventuress, something of the scholar'. She is impressed by Chester's 'interesting appearance', judging him to be, like Gerald, 'a brilliant failure' with 'a queer, violent strength'. And when he smiles, she feels as though 'someone had flashed a torch on lowering cliffs, and lit them into extraordinary and elf-like beauty'.

Gradually, the two spend time together socially as well as professionally, and Kitty observes that behind the work relationship, 'so departmental, so friendly, so emptied of sex', there is a 'relationship quite other and more personal and human' developing rapidly. Then, when Chester says goodnight to her at a house party and holds her hand 'but as long as all might or so very little longer', she is struck by a look in his eye which sends her up to bed 'with the staggering perception of the dawning of a new and third relationship . . . something still more simple and human'. 'One might surmise,' she observes, that 'he might fall very deeply in love before he knew anything much about it'. She, on the other hand, observes herself carefully, 'step by step, amused, interested, concerned'. This way, she asserts to herself confidently, 'is the best; not only do you get more out of the affair so, but you need not allow yourself, or the other party concerned, to be involved more deeply than you think advisable'.

Rose Macaulay mocks Kitty here, and by extension she mocks herself. Kitty, capable, detached, treating life as a 'decidedly entertaining' game, inherits Macaulay's own public persona. But all the time that she thinks she is in control of her own part in the flirtation, she is in fact plummeting into a passion that she is no better able to restrain than Chester. She begins sleeping badly, 'her thoughts turning and twisting in her brain'. Then the two of them are caught in a futuristic street aeroplane when something goes wrong with the machinery and they crash to the ground. Kitty bangs her head and faints; Chester believes her dead. Once she awakes he informs her, with ministerial restraint, 'I have bitten my tongue and fallen in love.' Kitty becomes giddy, finding that seas seem 'to rush past her ears'. Asked what she feels, she replies, 'cool and yet nervous, "I expect I feel pretty much the same as you do about it."'

Five years later, Macaulay reworked the scene in *Told by an Idiot*, a family saga that takes its central characters from the Victorian to the Georgian period. This is a detached novel, which does not dwell in the heads or hearts of any of its characters for long, but two women emerge as heroines, and both fall problematically in love. The first and most sustained heroine is Rome Garden, 'negligent, foppish and cool', an urbane thirty-one-year-old who likes 'to watch life at its games, be flicked by the edges of its flying skirts'. She falls in love, requitedly, with Mr Jayne, another brilliant, laconic and 'gracefully of the world worldly' man, whom Rome finds 'conceited, clever, entertaining, attractive and disarming, and the most companionable man of her wide acquaintance'. Both coolly English, they refrain from confessing their love until in a moment of unrestrained passion Mr Jayne insists that they should stop pretending: 'I love you more than any words I've got can say. You know it, you know it . . . dear heart . . .' He draws her up from her chair and looks into her face, 'and that was the defeat of their civilisation, for at their mutual touch it broke in disorder and fled. He kissed her mouth and face and hands, and passion rose about them like a sea in which they drowned.'

Macaulay repeatedly reimagined not only the initial meeting but the dilemma that keeps the lovers apart. In *What Not*, she shied away from adultery. Instead, Chester and Kitty are unable to be together because Chester has mental deficiency in his family and so, in the new order set up by the Ministry of Brains, is uncategorised, and forbidden to marry. Kitty, meanwhile, is class A, and must therefore marry and reproduce with someone of her own rank. Although this is intended to seem laughable to the reader, both of them take the Ministry seriously enough for it to keep them apart. Initially, they agree to mere friendship, but Chester finds the 'farce' of their 'beastly half-way house' intolerable, maintaining that they have to be 'more to each other – or less'. He urges Kitty to marry him secretly but she, high-minded, refuses. 'Let's be sporting,' he pleads; 'We're missing – we're missing the best thing in the world . . . I thought you never turned your back on life'; 'My dearest dear, I love you. Can't you . . . can't you? . . .' 'I love you,' she returns; 'I think I worship you.' But they agree to separate, and as they walk on together, the April afternoon itself cries out to them in its beauty, 'like a child whom they were betraying and forsaking'.

The separation does not last. 'The fact remained,' the narrator declares, with the wisdom of personal experience, that 'when two people who love each other work in the same building, however remote their spheres, they disturb each other, are conscious of each other's nearness.' Kitty is very far from being 'amused, interested, concerned' by her own feelings; she is struck by that 'continual, disturbing, restless, aching want'; 'no longer may life be greeted with a jest and death with a grin'. In the middle of the night, with aching, fevered head she writes Chester notes promising to marry him whenever he likes. But waking up, she is determined to give him his chance to stick by his principles. In the end, his presence overpowers her resolve. Seeing him again after several months, she admits that there is no good in living 'if you can't have what you want'. Chester announces that he has wanted her 'extremely badly these last three months. I have never wanted anything so much.' The two agree to get married.

In *Told by an Idiot* Macaulay made the obstacles separating the lovers more realistic, confronting the subject of adultery. Mr Jayne, like O'Donovan, is married. But Macaulay protected Rome from moral infamy by making Mr Jayne's wife less palpably present than Beryl O'Donovan. She is a mad Russian woman, safely hidden away in Russia, whom Mr Jayne can honestly claim never to have loved. Nonetheless, Rome is principled. 'I'm not,' she insists, 'going to take you away from your wife.' Mr Jayne avows that 'his love, his passion, his spirit, and his soul' are Rome's alone and encourages her to see civilisation as an arbitrary construct 'of society's making, that binds the spirit's freedom in chains'. The two endure a winter in which civilisation fights 'its losing battle with more primitive forces over the souls and bodies of Miss Garden and Mr Jayne'. Rome maintains that they can only be friends; Mr Jayne is unable to meet her with self-control; Rome retreats to 'the city of that name' with her father.

However, Mr Jayne follows his beloved to Italy and, spending time with the man she loves, walking in the warm sunlit air, Rome is 'caught into a deep and intoxicated joy':

> The bitter, restless struggling of the last months gave way to peace; the happy peace that looks not ahead, but rejoices in the moment. The tall and gay companion strolling at her side, so fluent in several languages, so apt to catch a half-worded meaning, to smile at an unuttered jest, so informed, so polished, so of the world worldly . . . take Mr Jayne as merely that, and she had her friend and companion back again, which was deeply restful and vastly stimulating. And beneath that was her lover, whom she loved; beneath his urbane exterior his passion throbbed and leaped, and his deep need of her cried, and in her the answering need cried back.

Ensconced in this moment of idyllic mutual need, Rome responds more favourably to Mr Jayne's sense that their fates are entwined. Although she still favours the claims of civilisation, and of his wife and children, she admits that neither of them can be 'happy, or fully ourselves, without being together'. She promises to take a week to decide, and he lifts his hands to her face. 'You are so beautiful,' he says, speaking, according to his self-deprecating narrator, 'inaccurately';

> There is no one like you . . . You hold my life in your two hands. Be kind to it, Rome. *I love you, I love you, I love you.* If we deny our love we shall be blaspheming. Love like ours transcends all barriers, and well you know it. Take your week, if you must, only decide rightly at the end of it, my heart's glory.

For an Oxford-educated, quintessential English gentleman, Mr Jayne sounds suspiciously Irish here. For an atheist who is irritated when Rome strays into religious arguments, he also sounds distinctly Christian. Mr Jayne is so closely associated with Gerald O'Donovan that he slips into his voice. His argument, that love transcends barriers, and that to deny the gift of love is to blaspheme, comes straight out of O'Donovan's own account of the relationship in his novel *The Holy Tree*, which had been published a year earlier. After Gerald's death, Rose Macaulay described this book to Rosamond Lehmann as 'his real work, the one I love'. 'In it,' she wrote, 'he put his whole philosophy of love, through the medium of Irish peasants – all the things he used to say to me about love and life, all he felt about me, all we both knew.'

The heroine of *The Holy Tree* is a passionate, uneducated Irish girl called Ann. Times are hard and Ann marries a decent but prosaic man called Joe without love, in order to save her family from bankruptcy. All the time she yearns for love, and is struck by it, innocently and delightedly, when Brian appears from afar, bringing with him dreams of founding a new and saintly community in the town. She becomes 'weak to think of him, or to talk of him'; he 'was always in her dreams. And, when she woke in the night, it was like as if he was in the room with her.' From the start, religious and human sensuality fuse in Ann and Brian's love. During their first kiss she has the sense of being 'in a holy place'; 'It wasn't on the earth at all they stood, but before the throne of God.' She walks in a new world, infused with the soul of her lover. Brian tells her that love is 'the wonder of God' ; not 'the flesh alone, or the spirit alone, but the perfect union of them both'.

When Ann is swayed by the disapproval of her family, and of her community, Brian quotes the Yeats poem from which the book takes its title:

> Beloved, gaze in thine own heart,
> The holy tree is growing there;
> From joy the holy branches start,
> And all the trembling flowers they bear.

Obediently, Ann looks into her heart and sees the holy tree, 'the like of which never grew and blossomed in the world before'. But she, like Kitty and Rome and like Macaulay herself, is swayed by convention. She realises that she cannot have both Brian and her child, Bessie, who is 'woven into the very woof of her heart'. She sees, like Kitty, that she must allow Brian to live according to his own principles so that he can fulfil his great plans. 'A sort of god he was among the people, the way he worked on them . . . Real love was to add to his power for the good of the world.' She will 'offer up her love to save him', sacrificing herself for the higher good.

Brian is distressed by her decision. He pleads with her to return to the holy tree, and not to look instead in the 'bitter glass'. He insists, like Mr Jayne, that they will be 'two stunted souls wandering about the world . . . unsatisfied desire searing our souls as well as our flesh'. 'It's life or death now,' he urges her; 'Life is the adventure of the soul . . . the only one.' But she remains firm, and it is only after he goes away to try to help rescue a boat that she realises she has made a mistake. Waiting for her lover to return, Ann resolves to deny him nothing: 'He was the light of the world and the light in her heart.' But Brian dies in the rescue attempt. Joe, returning safely, tells Ann that Brian was too reckless to survive. Ann realises that by rejecting Brian, 'she broke the dream in him'. And now, by dying, he has broken the dream in her.

The Holy Tree was a warning and a commendation to Rose Macaulay. In 1918, unwilling to embark on an affair with a married man, she came close to breaking Gerald's dream. By 1922, when the novel was published, they were lovers; she had found the holy tree in her heart. He celebrated that tree, but reminded her of the price they would both pay, were she to change her mind. In *Told by an Idiot* Rose accepted both the tribute and the lesson. Before Rome has a chance to make up her mind about her lover, Mr Jayne's Russian wife returns and has her husband abruptly murdered. Rome is bereft by Mr Jayne's untimely death. She is overcome by 'a faint weariness, as if nothing were very much worth while'. 'My dear,' she whispers, 'in tears, to the unanswering, endless night', 'Come back to me, and I will give you anything and everything . . . But you will never come back, and I can give you nothing any more.' Rose herself had been granted the chance to repair her mistake, and was keenly aware of what she might have lost.

Once Rose and Gerald committed to each other as lovers, they were able to find ways to see each other frequently. Both travelled extensively, and so it was easy to prolong their separate travels to spend time together. Between these trips, they met in London. At the beginning of their relationship they were seen together publicly, but then, fearing gossip, they became more secretive. Their love affair was known only to a handful of people, with Victor Gollancz later describing it as 'the best-kept secret in London'. Publicly, they retained the pretence of friendship. Rose was even invited regularly to Sunday lunch in the O'Donovans' home, accepted (with misgivings) by Beryl as a family friend. Indeed, she acted as godmother to the O'Donovans' granddaughter Mary Anne.

Rose and Gerald's relationship blended companionship, love and sexual passion. Friends and acquaintances tended to doubt Rose's sexual proclivities, perhaps because Rose Macaulay's public persona was both too briskly matter-of-fact and too quirkily eccentric to be immediately feminine or sensual. Several friends saw her as less an embodied woman than a disembodied voice booming down the telephone. Looking back on his first meeting with her in the 1920s, Anthony Powell recalled her as 'at immediate impact, prim, academic, rather alarming . . . It all seemed very chilly and Cambridge.' In fact nothing could, he said, have been further from a true assessment of her character. But not everyone made it through the chilly exterior. During an acrimonious exchange with the rivalrous popular novelist Ethel Mannin in 1931, Storm Jameson was outraged to be told that she was 'the clearest case of sexual frustration she knows of except Rose Macaulay'. Three years earlier, Woolf had made the dismissive reference to Macaulay as a withered virgin, announcing to her sister that she had never 'felt anyone so utterly devoid of the sexual parts'.

Certainly, there was an androgynous quality to Rose Macaulay, which was often noted by friends, and which finds its way into her girlish, neutrally named heroines. Several of her books feature coltish girls and young women, who shy away awkwardly from sexual contact. In *Keeping up Appearances*, the twelve-year-old Cary Folyot is so appalled by learning about sex from a secret reading of Freud's *The Interpretation of Dreams* that she resolves to become a nun to avoid the whole 'beastly' business. Macaulay was also frequently publicly dismissive of sex. She was impatient with the younger generation for placing too great an emphasis on it. In Macaulay's 1921 novel *Dangerous Ages*, Neville, a forty-three-year-old woman, mocks her daughter Gerda's continual emphasis on sex, suggesting that 'There *are* other things . . .' Gerda admits that there is also drawing and poetry, beauty, dancing and swimming; 'But the basis of life was the desire of the male for the female and of the female for the male.' At the same time Neville's mother, Mrs Hilary, is trying to allay the embitteredness of old age by embarking on a course of psychoanalysis. Both she and her analyst are lampooned by the narrator for their simplistic emphasis on sex. Mrs Hilary now misinterprets the behaviour of her daughters because she has learnt from her analyst 'the simple truth about life; that is that nearly every one is nearly always involved up to the eyes in the closest relationship with some one of another sex. It is nature's way with mankind.'

But Rose Macaulay always insisted nonetheless on the importance of sexual desire within love. In a 1927 letter to Jean she reminded her sister that though love between a man and a woman 'is the important part of their desire for each other', the originator of that love was 'mere animal desire'. The 'sexual parts' that Virginia Woolf found lacking in Macaulay's social persona are consistently evident in Macaulay's decidedly unvirginal novels. The post-war editor of the *TLS* Alan Pryce-Jones recalled Rose Macaulay flashing out a retort to the Woolfs and Mannins of the world, complaining that 'It is stupid to think that just because I never cared to marry I have no experience of life.' Life includes sex here. In even Macaulay's most ironically detached novels, there are moments when the author's pulse quickens, seriously and sensually, with the pulse of her characters, male and female. There is the aching want in *What Not* and the passion that rises about Rome and Mr Jayne in *Told by an Idiot* – that sea in which they drown when he kisses her mouth and face and hands. 'While you hold me I can't think,' Rome complains, just as O'Donovan's Ann finds that 'her limbs and every organ of her' quiver 'like fiddle strings under the bow of his love', blowing duty and God and religion out of sight. Even in *And No Man's Wit*, on the whole a detached comic novel, Macaulay takes Ramón's desire for the slippery, mermaid-like Ellen seriously. In answer to Guy's cynical profession that 'the longer I live the less it seems to matter particularly about sex', Ramón maintains that sex matters, 'to the imagination and to the body': 'Each such experience, when it is achieved, satisfies a dream that one had . . . if one didn't satisfy it, it would haunt the body and the mind.'

Rose Macaulay's own sensuality and embodiment are apparent in her frequent descriptions of the delights of swimming. Almost all of her heroines swim enthusiastically. In *What Not* Chester and Kitty pass 'amphibious days' on the Ligurian coast where Rose spent her childhood, swimming out for a mile, then lying on their backs and floating. In *And No Man's Wit* Ramón's beloved, Ellen, is so enthusiastic a swimmer that she turns out to be infused with mermaid blood, and is contented only when she can leave behind the constraints of dry land. 'Bathing' features prominently in *Personal Pleasures*, where Rose Macaulay muses lyrically on the joys of being 'lapped in the clear, thin stuff, so blue, so buoyant, so serene, you can conceive no reason for ever leaving it'. She is familiar with that 'reeling goddess', pleasure, but, bathing on an August afternoon off the Ligurian coast, 'we know you at your most reeling, your most zoneless. Such felicity seems to know no limit.'

Gerald O'Donovan was sensually drawn to Rose's maritime self. He repeatedly associated Ann with water in *The Holy Tree*. Although the sea is frightening, Ann cannot help loving it; 'To swim out agin the waves of a morning . . . was to feel alive.' It gives 'a delight to her heart that nothing else could give'; she can breast waves ten times higher than other bathers. Ann's body is beautiful and she enjoys her sense of her own embodiment, which she feels most strongly when in contact with the water. After bathing, she thinks that 'to run bare naked along the strand, and dry herself in the warm breeze, 'd be heaven itself'. Gerald may have been remembering times when he and Rose had swum naked together. In a 1936 radio broadcast on the pleasures of bathing, Rose suggested that swimming is best when undertaken naked:

> if one is so fortunate as to find a place and a time when one can bathe without a bathing suit, it enormously increases the pleasure of a bathe. The feeling of water, even river water, against one's bare skin is delightful.

Neville opens *Dangerous Ages* with a naked dip in the sea, finding that this is a moment when it is enough simply to be alive.

Neville may disapprove of her daughter's public analysis of sex as the basis of every emotion, but she enjoys her own sensuality and mourns the fading of her beauty in middle age. Macaulay mocks Neville's daughter Gerda, but she also mocks herself, through Neville, for disapproving. And within the novel Macaulay identifies simultaneously with Neville and with Gerda and Neville's sister Nan, two women who love. Few of Rose Macaulay's friends would have recognised her in Gerald O'Donovan's Ann, that naively ingenuous peasant girl who seems incapable of a satirical remark. Yet Rose was proud of her role in *The Holy Tree*; proud that Gerald inscribed Yeats's lines about the holy tree in her copy of the novel. She shared Ann's delight in the body; delight in swimming, running naked along the strand, and in kissing and touching her lover, glad of 'the feel of his arms, and of his lips'.

Now, in the summer of 1941, Rose was achingly aware that she would soon lose Gerald's touch for ever. She spent the beginning of May 1941 undertaking the difficult task of sorting through her sister's belongings. Then on 10 May, London was the target for one final, brutal bombing

London after the 10 May raid

attack. This was the last and perhaps the heaviest night of the London Blitz, with 507 aircraft bombing London in a single night, many of them returning for a second attack. There were over a thousand Londoners killed and similar numbers wounded; the British Museum and the Houses of Parliament were both damaged and 12,000 people were rendered homeless. On 11 May Rose came back from sorting through Margaret's belongings to find that her own flat had been destroyed. A bomb had landed on the building at 2 a.m. and at 4 a.m. the fire brigade had reported that the ensuing fire was out of control. Among other possessions that Rose lost in the flames were all her letters from Gerald and her inscribed copy of *The Holy Tree*, bidding her to find the strength of love in her own heart. That strength now failed. For the past eight months, she had distracted herself from personal sorrow by throwing herself into ambulance driving, socialising and writing. Once war had invaded her home, she could not help but feel its blows personally. It was as a preemptively bereft lover that she confronted the ashes of her accumulated fifty-nine years of possessions.

Rose wrote a series of disbelieving letters to her friends in the immediate aftermath of the bombing. In a letter to Storm Jameson, she explained the origins of the fire – 'it got first an HE, then fire started, and wasn't put out' – adding that 'everything was consumed'.

> I can't start again, I feel. I keep thinking of one thing I loved after another, with a fresh stab. I wish I could go abroad and stay there, then I shouldn't miss my things so much, but it can't be. I loved my books so much, and can never replace them. I feel I am finished, and would like to have been bombed too. Still, I suppose one gets over it in the end.

To Daniel George, with whom she was collaborating on the literary animal book that was one of the things keeping her going, she wrote on a scrap of paper:

> House no more – bombed and burned out of existence, and *nothing* saved. I am bookless, homeless, sans everything but my eyes to weep with. *All* my (and your) notes on animals gone – I shall never write that book now.

Ten days later she added that it would have been less trouble to have been killed by the bomb herself. Her sense that she should have been bombed too seems to come together with her background consciousness of Virginia Woolf's suicide in a letter to Victor Gollancz:

> Luxborough Towers have fallen down. Saturday night I returned there after the weekend to find it bombed and burnt to bits – *everything* – destroyed. I am desolated and desperate – I can't face life without my books . . . I have no clothes, no nothing. I feel like jumping into the river.

She attempts to manufacture some characteristic stoicism, but fails: 'soon hope to feel rather better (or doesn't one?)'.

In these letters, Rose's books become the focus of her sense of loss. Both in public and in private she poured all her sadness into grieving for these lost volumes. In another letter to Storm Jameson, two days later, she described the loss of her books as leaving a gaping wound in her heart and mind and listed the missing volumes:

> all my lovely seventeenth century books, my Aubrey, my Pliny, my Topsell, Sylvester, Drayton, all the poets – lots of lovely queer unknown writers, too – and Sir T Browne and my Oxford Dictionary.

There were four generations of books here. Macaulay was related on both sides to the historian Thomas Babington Macaulay and came from a family of Cambridge academics and clergymen. She had inherited a large collection of seventeenth-century volumes, which she had used to immerse herself in the relevant period when writing a biography of Milton and a historical novel, *They Were Defeated*, in the decade before the war. By reading and writing her way into the seventeenth century, Rose had found a way to gain access to the lost Cambridge world of her father and uncles, and to explore a period whose political turbulence and violence resembled and illuminated that of her own era. As a result, losing the seventeenth-century volumes she seemed to lose a decade of her own life.

Rose was more upset about the destruction of her Oxford Dictionary and her seventeenth-century collection than she was about the loss of her own work. She was distressed about the notes for the animal book, which she described to Jameson as her heart's blood, but relatively unbothered by the loss of her unfinished novel: 'I don't mind that so much, nearly.' Her grief for her books was in part a way of mourning publicly for her lost letters from Gerald and the death that she knew would soon come. Later, it would become clear that the loss of the letters was even more wrenching than the destruction of her precious volumes. But her grief for her dying lover was also entangled with her grief for her books, and with the seventeenth-century collection in particular.

The relationship with Gerald had all along been in part a literary collaboration. In the early days, he had helped her hone her own writing and develop her characteristic style. For the past twenty years, reading and writing had been mutual activities. Although they were often physically separated, they could always connect to each other through the books they loved and shared. This would have been one way in which she could have survived the permanent physical separation imposed by his death, and now she had lost it with the demolition of the volumes they had read together. And the vanished editions of Milton (inherited from her father) could have served as an especially poignant reminder of Gerald.

While writing about Milton, Rose had come to identify the seventeenth-century poet with her own lover. Milton too had been a failed revolutionary, not of his age; 'a superb and monstrous alien' in seventeenth-century England, exhorting vainly for liberty in all things before 'his cause and his world shattered in ruins about his ears'. Milton's marriage, too, had been unhappy; Milton's wife had been unworthy of him intellectually and disappointing sexually. In her Milton biography Rose Macaulay chastised Milton for failing in the 'important art of perceiving what a young woman is like behind her pretty face' and described how Milton had blamed his own sexual inexperience for the failures of his marriage. Gerald, too, had been sexually inexperienced when he chose the pretty young Beryl as his bride. And it is Gerald who seems to emerge, understood and accepted, in Rose's description of Milton's marriage in a letter to the medieval scholar Helen Waddell:

> I wish one of his wives had been of a mental stature he could have had to take into account – it would have been interesting and might have given a different list to Paradise Lost and Eve. I feel his capacities for love were so immense, and never fully (body and mind together) satisfied.

Now both Rose and Gerald had found a love that satisfied body and mind together and they were about to lose it. With the lost books she lost the echoes that could have reverberated down the years, keeping going the life they had shared.

Rose spent the first night after the bombing with her sister Jean in Romford, and then busied herself with finding a new place to live. She also had to spend considerable time at the Town Hall on the Marylebone Road, filling in forms to claim compensation for her lost possessions. Ordinary household insurance did not cover war damage, so compensation came from the War Damage Commission, and might take months or even years to arrive. In the meantime Rose's cousin Jean Smith lent her clothes and several of her friends offered her places to stay. However, she wanted to retain her independence, even now, so she took a bed-sittingroom in Manchester Street before moving around the corner to a flat in Hinde Street on 12 June. Just before she moved, Victor and Ruth Gollancz furnished her with a new Oxford Dictionary and Rose wrote effusively to thank them:

> my darling Dictionary again, in the same vestige and habit as I have always known it – and I was transported to Jerusalem the golden from the dreary limbo where I have been trudging lately . . . I begin to feel I can live again. The O.D. was my Bible, my staff, my entertainer, my help in work and my recreation in leisure – nothing else serves.

Her new flat was small; there was only a bedroom and a sitting room in addition to the kitchen and bathroom. But she only had the furniture that she had inherited from Margaret to fill it with, so she did not mind the lack of space. And her first act on moving in was to put her new Oxford Dictionary on its shelf; her one reminder of the life she had lost.

———

Rose Macaulay spent the summer of 1941 clambering around the ruins of her old flat, beginning the compulsive haunting of ruined buildings that would continue for the rest of her life. She was hoping to find books or letters surviving amid the debris, but in fact the only objects to survive were those contained in her old kitchen dresser, which had been sheltered by the roof of the building when it collapsed in the fire. Here she found some glasses and crockery, a jar of marmalade, some tea and an old silver mug.

In September Rose tore herself away from the rubble and attended the International PEN congress in London, which began with a lunch at the Savoy Hotel on Piccadilly and was conducted mainly in the French Institute in South Kensington. This meeting, which brought 470 delegates together to discuss 'Writers and Freedom', was a brave event to hold at this stage in the war, especially because it involved international speakers travelling from Europe and America. And for most of the audience it offered a moment of hope, showing that literary and political discussion was still possible despite the violence that was tearing their world apart. This was particularly the case for Hilde Spiel, who was pleased to be asked to help with the preparations and to have a chance to get to know Storm Jameson, whom she found 'very very charming'. Jameson herself began the Congress with a speech insisting that the war was or could be a social revolution and that afterwards the duty of the English writer would be to convince the English that they were responsible for Europe and could not evade this duty out of indifference or modesty. Here at least the fate of England was seen as bound up with the fate of Europe. And later that afternoon a 'Mr Smith' from Scotland Yard came to talk to Hilde and Peter about being naturalised as British citizens.

On the fourth day of the congress, Peter de Mendelssohn gave a speech on 'Writers without Language' where he compared two types of exiled writer, those for whom it was impossible to change languages because their identity was bound up with their mother tongue, and those who were able to start writing in the language of their host country. He gave J. B. Priestley as an example of the kind of writer who would be able to change linguistic currency. 'I am an Englishman', he imagined a hypothetical Priestley saying in Germany, 'true enough, but I am also a European. Where I am is Europe, and as I happen to be in Germany I declare Germany to be Europe, at least for the time being.' These were of course Peter de Mendelssohn's own sentiments, and both he and Hilde were starting to feel secure in their new British identity. In the world after the war, Peter stated, the émigrés who had changed language (as opposed to the refugees who had merely sought temporary refuge) would help build a great bridge which would span the waters and re-connect the continents and their peoples. He would help Storm Jameson in the task she had set the post-war writer. These were popular sentiments. Hilde reported in her diary that Peter's speech had been well received by the audience.

But Rose Macaulay remained unaffected by these notes of optimism ringing out around her. For her the rows of seated delegates remained less real than the charred ruins of her flat or the gradually atrophying body of the man she loved. Margaret Storm Jameson, meeting Rose on the way out at the end of the day, listened to her friend talking rapidly and watched as her smile flickered and her small head bobbed in a strange simulation of her usual animated state. She felt sad that old age could come upon someone so suddenly. But it was evident to Margaret that age alone could not account for the sad fatigue underlying Rose's show of liveliness. She wondered if Rose was still saddened by the bombing of her flat in May but guessed that her friend was weighed down by a more complex grief. 'You're very tired,' Margaret observed. Rose moved down a step, paused, and looked back at her friend. 'Margaret, you don't know what it's like to watch the person you love dying.' Margaret later wrote that she could feel the anguish pricking the ends of her fingers.

In November, Rose Macaulay wrote an article on 'Losing One's Books' for the *Spectator*. This opens with brisk, impersonal aloofness and with a characteristically whimsical linguistic aside:

> It happened to me last May to lose my home with all contents in a night of that phenomenon that we oddly called *Blitz*, though why we should use the German for lightning for attacks by bombs I do not know, unless to appease by euphemism, like calling the Furies Eumenides. Anyway, whatever the thing was called, it destroyed my flat, leaving not a wrack behind, or rather, nothing but wracks.

The tone then becomes more emotional, as she describes the charred remains of the wreckage, smelling of mortality, which troubled her with hints of what had been. A page of the Oxford Dictionary telling of hot-beds, hotch-pots, hot cockles, hotes and hotels; a page of Pepys.

'When the first stunned sickness begins to lift a little, one perceives,' she says, 'that something must be done about lost books.' When out, she climbed her ruins. When in, she made lists. A list of books she had owned ('that is the saddest list; perhaps one should not make it'), a list of books that could be replaced, another of books that could not be replaced, another of good riddances. She goes on to list books in each category. Among the irreplaceable books are her Baedekers, which are now hard to find; 'and anyhow,' she adds curtly, 'travel is over, like one's books and the rest of civilisation'. The article ends abruptly:

> One keeps on remembering some odd little book that one had; one can't list them all, and it is best to forget them now that they are ashes.

It is clear, though, that Rose Macaulay has not forgotten them. The description of list-making in this article reveals the continued obsessive nature of Rose's grief for her books. Although London was not seriously bombed again until 1944, the war continued horrifically elsewhere. Meanwhile Gerald was probably in the final months of his life. Yet Rose spent her time making lists of books, allowing the two sources of sadness to fuse in her own mind and finding in her lost volumes a way of giving public expression to private grief.

PART III

The Lull

June 1941–May 1944

9

'You are the ultimate of something'

Elizabeth Bowen, Graham Greene and Rose Macaulay, summer 1941–summer 1942

The raid of 10 May 1941 which flattened Rose Macaulay's flat was the last attack on so brutal a scale that London would suffer for three years. The summer following the Blitz came as an unreal period of calm after a gruelling nine months of bombing. At first, Londoners waited anxiously for another attack. 'We are puzzled why, in this lovely weather, the Germans have not seriously attacked us by air,' Harold Nicolson wrote in his diary in June, wondering if they were 'equipping their machines with some new device, like wirecutters'. Quickly, it became evident that the focus of the German war effort was now on Russia. On 22 June Hitler reneged on the non-aggression pact with Stalin and invaded the Soviet Union. Russia was unprepared for the attack and within three weeks of the invasion German forces had penetrated 450 miles into Russian territory. Churchill denounced Hitler on the radio as 'a monster of wickedness, insatiable in his lust for blood and plunder', who had terrorised Europe into submission and was now carrying on his butchery and desolation by victimising the multitudes of Russia and Asia. But in London the butchery was now experienced at a distance. 'War moved,' as Elizabeth Bowen observed in *The Heat of the Day*, 'from the horizon to the map'; daily life could resume again.

Graham Greene found the lull frustrating and longed to escape into a war zone. Even at the height of the Blitz in December 1940 he had told Anthony Powell that he was keen to do Free French propaganda in West Africa from a base in Liberia. His sister Elisabeth, as secretary to the regional head of the Secret Intelligence Service (SIS, popularly known as MI6) in the Middle East, was doing her best to pull strings to get both her brother and Malcolm Muggeridge accepted as overseas agents. Finally, a mysterious 'Mr Smith' invited Greene to a party that turned out to be part of the vetting process for spies. On 20 August he informed his mother that in two or three months he would be going out to West Africa, supposedly working for the Colonial Office. 'The pay is very good, and the job interesting,' he told her. Before he could start, the SIS decided Greene should be instilled with some military discipline, so that autumn he attended a four-week training course at Oriel College, Oxford. He reported to John Betjeman that he had been taught how to salute with a little stick under his arm while marching and, without success, to ride a motorcycle. He was also trained in the specific skills befitting an intelligence officer: to assume and inhabit another identity, use surveillance technology and choose and obtain information from local agents.

Most Londoners were more appreciative of the peace than Greene was. As in the phoney war, the calm was unreal. But after eight months of 'taking it' people felt entitled to a lull, and the impulsive spirit of the Blitz continued into the summer. Waking up from the long months of sleeplessness and fear, Londoners emerged grateful to be alive, and continued to float on the tideless present of war. 'Everyone has a sort of false armistice feeling,' Hilde Spiel observed in her diary; 'drinks, paints her finger-nails, makes love to young girls, and says: ce Noel à Paris!'

It was in the summer of 1941 that Elizabeth Bowen began the affair with Charles Ritchie that would heighten her experience of the next four years of war and dominate the rest of her life. 'Beloved, I can't believe any human being can ever have made another as purely wholly unchangeably and yet increasingly happy as you have made me,' she would write to him four years later, as the Red Army liberated Warsaw. She had been passionately in love before. But now, surrendering herself to the frightening exhilaration of complete vulnerability, she was reconfiguring her sense both of love itself and of herself as a woman who loved. 'For me, you are the ultimate of something. Till I met you, I did not imagine that such an ultimate could be reached. Now I rest in it, and cannot go beyond.'

Elizabeth and Charles had met at a christening during the brief lull in the London Blitz in February. 'She says it began when she saw me standing outside the church after the christening,' Charles recorded in his diary that September. He found this hard to believe. 'It smells to me of literary artifice,' he observed. He was less prepared for love than she was, and was particularly unprepared to fall in love with a woman whom he found on first impressions to be 'well-dressed middle-aged with the air of being the somewhat worldly wife of a don'. In his diary that evening he indifferently catalogued her 'narrow intelligent face, watching eyes' and 'cruel, witty mouth', not suspecting that four months later they would be lovers.

Charles Ritchie

Charles was six years younger than Elizabeth, and at once her junior in youthful irresponsibility and her senior in cynicism. A Canadian diplomat, he had been posted to London in January 1939 and was treating the commission as a holiday. A few months before war was declared he was yearning either for a new mistress or for the chance to risk his life in an aeroplane stunt. In fact his war would be pretty much risk-free, but it did bring a succession of mistresses. 'Wartime London was a forcing ground for love and friendship,' he wrote in a subsequent introduction to his diaries; 'for experiments and amusements snatched under pressure'. In January 1941, a month before he met Elizabeth at the christening, he listed his 'symptoms of sexual happiness' in his diary: 'I am temporarily cured of my mania for seeing things in a straight line'; 'Time no longer seems to be slipping away from me'. The ballerina who was the object of this happiness was about to depart on tour and he was already looking forward to 'early and varied infidelities' during her absence.

A month after meeting Elizabeth, Charles complained that he was sick of his 'present hectic life – the work, the miscellaneous love affairs and the mixed drinks', yearning only for Victorian evenings in the company of a wife and adoring daughters in a small provincial town. A bald patch was appearing on his head, marriage was hovering on the horizon as the only dignified course, but still he squeezed the last drops of pleasure out of his final months of youth. In May 1941, looking back on the extraordinary feeling of happiness and completeness he had experienced during the Blitz, he had a premonition that it must mean that he had gone as far as he could go and that retribution must follow. A week later, emerging once again from the bed of his ballerina, he observed that when he died they would find 'some woman's name written on my heart – I do not know myself whose it will be!' That summer, retribution came in the form of love; from now on, adolescent escapism would always be tinged with guilt. And it became increasingly clear that the name written on his heart would be that of Elizabeth Bowen.

For Elizabeth and Charles, the unreal climate of the summer of 1941 was the ideal climate for love. 'We go,' Charles wrote, 'from one cloudless, high-summer day to another in a kind of daze. The parks are full of soldiers and girls in summer dresses. It is difficult to get a table in a restaurant. My friends indulge their love affairs and their vendettas.' For Elizabeth at least, love was immediate and consuming. In a passage which she later excised from the first draft of *The Heat of the Day*, she described the dawning of love.

> It was not that she had been taken by surprise. To find oneself fallen into love is, however surprisingly, not surprising: in this state culminates, with a commanding calm, some suspended expectation of the whole being. It was, more, that it seemed inconceivable to be in love now.

Love, once acknowledged, brought the recognition that it had been developing for months. Elizabeth accepted love's vulnerability fearlessly; Charles allowed himself to be entranced by a woman he frequently characterised as a witch; together they drifted, dazed and absorbed, from day to day.

In early September, on one of the last, borrowed days of summer, they visited the rose garden in Regent's Park. They had been talking about going to see the roses for days, but Charles found it hard to escape the office before nightfall and it began to seem as if they would not see them together. Then, spontaneously, Elizabeth telephoned to say that if they did not go it would be too late, as the blooms were almost over. So he put away the Foreign Office boxes in the safe, locked up the files and took a taxi to Regent's Park. This was a perfect moment outside time that both would later see as marking the blooming of their happiness. The rose, flowering delicately and luxuriously in the midst of war, came to be a leitmotif of their love. So much so that Charles later added an extended account of the scene to his diary when he edited it for publication after Elizabeth's death:

> As we walked together I seemed to see the flowers through the lens of her sensibility. The whole scene, the misty river, the Regency villas with their walled gardens and damp lawns, and the late September afternoon weather blended into a dream – a dream in which these were all symbols

soaked with a mysterious associative power – Regent's Park – a landscape of love. A black swan floating downstream in the evening light
– the dark purplish-red roses whose petals already lay scattered – the
deserted Nash house with its flaking stucco colonnade and overgrown
gardens – all were symbols speaking a language which by some miracle
we could understand together.

Queen Mary's rose garden, Regent's Park, 1938, photographed by H. F. Davis

Both Elizabeth and Charles later memorialised this lull in the war in
London as an era of unbroken mutual love. The roses are recreated at
the opening of *The Heat of the Day* where, on just such a perfect
September evening, 'great globular roses, today at the height of their
second blooming, burned more as the sun descended, dazzling the
lake'. In 1950 Elizabeth wrote to Charles regretting that they had not
found the time to walk in the park together on his last visit to
London.

A particular gentle tract of our happiness belongs to it – walks after lunch, walks when we were coming back here to this house for tea. So much so that the park has become you for me.

In 1961, lunching with Elizabeth off whisky and sardine sandwiches at her hotel in New York, Charles recalled that twenty years ago they used to lunch off sardine sandwiches at Clarence Terrace in the early days when she lay stretched on the hard narrow Regency sofa in her little upstairs drawing room.

Looking back, Elizabeth and Charles yearned wistfully for the early, unconscious days of their love affair. Elizabeth Bowen pays tribute to this gentle entwinement in an early chapter of *The Heat of the Day*. Here she describes the genesis of love as more than a dream:

> More, it was a sort of growing, smiling regard, a happiness of which it seemed that the equilibrium became every day surer. The discovery together, for the first time, of life was serious, but very much more than serious, illuminating; there was an element of awe. Miraculously, unhindered, the plan of love had gone on unfolding itself.

Stella and Robert both start to feel that they are only fully alive in each other's presence. Though singly 'each of them might, must, exist, decide, act; all things done alone came to be no more than simulacra of behaviour: they waited to live again till they were together, then took living up from where they had left it off.' Together, they acquire a doubled awareness, an interlocking feeling, which intensifies everything around them so that all they see, know or tell one another is 'woven into the continuous narrative of love'. They do not tell one another everything, though: 'Every love has a poetic relevance of its own; each love brings to light only what is to it relevant. Outside lies the junk-yard of what does not matter.'

Among the irrelevancies which Elizabeth Bowen left out were the details of her day-to-day life with her husband, Alan Cameron. Charles and Alan were acquainted. They crossed paths at parties and, from time to time, in Elizabeth's own drawing room. Later in the war Charles came to stay with Elizabeth and Alan while he recovered from flu; one December the three of them ate their Christmas lunch together at Clarence Terrace. Nonetheless, the poetic relevance of both the marriage and the affair each excluded the other, and both men tolerated the situation. The Cameron marriage was based on companionship rather than sexual attraction, and for ten years Alan had accepted the existence of Elizabeth's lovers. For his part, Charles was intent on marriage to a younger and more pliable woman than Elizabeth. 'My fancy turns more and more to marrying and settling to a routine life of small pleasures,' he announced in May 1942, observing again the bald spot beginning on the back of his head.

Alan Cameron, c. 1940

Elizabeth had married Alan Cameron in 1923 after a brief courtship involving long country walks and literary discussions. She was twenty-four and eager to embark on adult life. 'I and my friends all intended to marry early,' she stated in a short autobiography she wrote in 1972, 'partly because this appeared an achievement or way of making one's mark, also from a feeling it would be difficult to settle to anything else until this was done. (Like passing School Certificate.)' Although Alan was only six years older than Elizabeth, he was a war veteran and a civil servant with a public role, and she looked up to him as a guiding adult. 'Do you real-ise how – in the worst sense – *young* I am?' she wrote to him five months before they married. 'You are a real person who has come in contact with real things, and I've lived altogether inside myself, all my experiences have been subjective.' She was aware of the part played by invention in her love of him. 'My love of you seems very childish – I mean sexless and imaginative'; 'I have only got to know you from a succession of glimpses, like a person walking parallel with one through a wood'.

Elizabeth's love for Alan remained sexless, though not childish. She was still a virgin when she began her affair with the literary critic Humphry House in 1933. 'Why, Elizabeth,' he asked her a year later,

> did you not tell me when we first slept together that you were a virgin? I thought you had some malformation: for you said only: 'I am as diffi-cult as a virgin.' I could not know you were one: and had I known, with what more tender slowness I would have come to you, and how much less gloom would have sat across that breakfast tray!

But although Alan did not enable Elizabeth to mature sexually, he did help her to grow up. Through him, she became an adult herself. He equipped her with new clothes and shoes, grooming her and endowing her with confidence. She remained dependent on him to sustain her as both a woman and a writer. To many of Elizabeth's literary friends, Alan seemed an odd choice of husband. Peter Quennell described him as striking an unwittingly discordant note; his 'temperament and tastes were those of a well-educated civil servant'. May Sarton initially found Alan not at all the man she might have imagined as Elizabeth's husband: 'He was quite stout, had a rather Blimpish look, a red face and walrus mustache, and spoke in a high voice, near falsetto.'

But Elizabeth's friends had no doubts about her loyalty to Alan. May saw at once that he was extremely kind and sensitive, and saw Eliza-beth's internal tensions as keeping 'her every relationship in suspense except perhaps that with her husband'. Each day, at 5.40 p.m., Alan came home to Elizabeth, asked her where the cat was, and enquired about her day. He complained about the practical matters she should have attended to; she looked flustered, laughed and pretended to be helpless. 'Alan's tenderness for her,' wrote May, 'took the form of teasing and she obviously enjoyed it. I never saw real strain or needling between them, never for a second. Love affairs were a counterpoint . . . But the marriage was truly "home".' May herself, though jealously possessive of Elizabeth, found visiting her a lonely experience without Alan present to spread his balm of kindness among guests when Elizabeth was too imaginatively preoccupied to do so. In *Bowen's Court* Bowen describes the marriage of her ancestor Henry III as offering a homecoming or return:

> I believe his love for his wife to have been from the first domestic rather than passionate. At the same time, that love was enduring, noble and happy: Margaret was his cousin, his mother, his only friend.

Elizabeth's own need for the stability provided by her marriage became particularly evident in wartime. 'War makes us more conscious, anxiously conscious, of the value of everything that is dear and old,' she wrote in a 1942 essay on the home, at the height of her affair with Charles. 'Above all, the home means people – their trust in each other, their happy habits of living, the calendar, year by year, of family life.'

The happy habits of the dear and old formed a secure base from which Elizabeth could explore the intoxication of the new. Since the 1930s, she had been involved with a succession of lovers. The passionate affair with Humphry House was succeeded by the abortive liaison with the caddish Goronwy Rees and then by the two-year affair with Sean O'Faolain. The role of these men was partly to compensate for the deficiencies in Elizabeth's marriage, which was limited conversationally as well as sexually. In 1942 in a rare moment of complaint to Charles, Elizabeth grumbled that Alan was like a character in a Chekhov play who always repeated the same lines at his entrances and exits. But arguably, Elizabeth loved multifariously not because of Alan's inadequacy as a husband but because of her own extreme capacity for love; for open-ing herself to other people. In 1937 May Sarton had spent a single night in bed with Elizabeth, which she saw as prompted by Elizabeth's sensi-tivity 'to atmosphere, to place, to the total content of a moment'. Elizabeth, May wrote, 'was willing to go deep into friendship in a few days or even hours if she felt an affinity'.

Elizabeth herself explicitly associated this quality with her gift as a writer. Writing to Humphry House, she worried that what he said about her 'overwhelming love' for him made her feel dishonest. She warned him against mistaking 'an artist's impulse and wish for every-one to live at full height for an ordinary or better woman's craving for love', insisting that she was a writer before she was a woman. She lived, from moment to moment, at full height. Alan, Humphry and subse-quent lovers each believed that they were the most important person in her world because, when she was with them, she believed it too.

For Elizabeth, this precluded remorse. In October 1941 Charles recorded that Elizabeth had informed him that a sense of guilt seemed to be specifically 'a middle-class complaint – not enough humility and sense of limitations'. She did not feel guilty because she lived according to her own, rigorous code of conduct. May Sarton wrote that Elizabeth made it clear by her own life that it is possible, with sufficient adven-turousness, discretion and discipline, to 'engage in extramarital affairs and keep one's dignity and one's personal truth intact, without hurting one's life partner'. Whether or not Alan was in fact hurt, Elizabeth, who was often judgemental about the conduct of her friends, condoned her own behaviour.

The tideless present of wartime London was the ideal habitat for a woman who was already able to exist intensely in the present moment. Elizabeth could tie herself powerfully to several people at once because she met each of them in a separate world; each encounter shut out past and future. 'Vacuum as to future,' she wrote in *The Heat of the Day*, 'was offset by vacuum as to past.' And of course in wartime, when any moment could be their last, many of the inhabitants of London were experiencing the world in similar terms. Henry Yorke's lovers who died each night in each other's arms were the 'campers in rooms of draughty dismantled houses' described by Elizabeth Bowen in *The Heat of the Day*. 'The extraordinary time,' Bowen observed in a passage that was cut from the final draft of the novel, 'exonerated, contented, transfixed' wartime lovers. They were exonerated from guilt, transfixed in the moment. A moment, she wrote in the publisher's blurb for the book, has the power 'to protract itself and contain the world'.

Charles Ritchie was less capable of surrendering to the protracted moment than Elizabeth Bowen. He was always aware of the future; of the woman he must eventually marry, the life he wanted to lead. In June 1941, shortly before he began his affair with Elizabeth, he observed in his diary that years of promiscuous love-making had, in the words of Robert Burns, hardened 'a' within' and petrified the feelings. Less accepting of vulnerability than Elizabeth, he distrusted his love for her and constantly compared his feelings for her with his feelings for other women. 'Would I ever have fallen for her if it hadn't been for her books?' he asked himself in September. 'I very much doubt it . . . It's as if the woman I "love" were always accompanied by a companion spirit infinitely more exciting and more poetic and more profound than E herself.' He resented their roles as older woman and younger man. 'She treats me as though I were a boy,' he complained; 'I am perpetually showing off to her, like a male coquette.' It was only in bed that their roles reversed. Here her face – 'powerful, mature, rather handsome' with a family resemblance to Virginia Woolf – was eclipsed by her body, 'that of a young woman. The most beautiful body I have seen. It is pure in line and contour, lovely long legs and arms and small almost immature firm breasts.' On her side, Elizabeth too was conscious of Charles's comparative youth. In *The Heat of the Day*, which is dedicated to Charles, she makes Robert 'five or six' years younger than Stella and describes 'his youthfulness – something moody, hardy, and lyrical which his being some way into his thirties had no more than brought to a finer point'.

By December 1941, the joys of the respite from bombing were starting to fade as winter set in. As a Canadian, Charles Ritchie was appreciative of the chance to survey the peculiar landscape of wartime London:

the tree-lined avenue in Hyde Park, echoing with the noise of soldiers' boots at dusk, alive with desire; the girls, watching the soldiers watching them, twisting and turning and giggling as they walked; the young men in guards uniforms drinking martinis in expensive restaurants; the aesthetes dancing in the Ritz bar after a day at the Ministry of Information; or the prostitutes lining Piccadilly while just behind them an old man made a bonfire of dead leaves in Berkeley Square. But he was depressed to observe a general deadening of feeling that winter.

> The capacity for sympathising with other people's troubles seems to have completely dried up. Do we ever think of the thousands of starving people in Europe? Do we sympathise with the sufferings of the Russians? I doubt it . . . It seems that now the response to suffering is dead . . . We have long ceased to find the war thrilling – any excitement in the movement of historic events is gone.

Londoners may have ceased to be thrilled, but the news from both North Africa and Russia was hopeful. In Africa the British had launched an attack on 18 November which resulted in the retreat of the German and Italian forces from the Libyan port of Tobruk. In Russia the Germans had been victorious in the Ukraine but were held up outside Moscow in November. 'Old men in clubs are puzzled by the Russians' successful resistance,' Charles Ritchie observed; people were surprised that so backward a country could manage the organisation of a modern war. On 6 December the Russians startled the Germans by counter-attacking with 100 fresh divisions.

The next day, the Japanese attack on the American fleet in Pearl Harbor brought the war in the Far East to centre stage. Churchill went to America to confer with Roosevelt, with whom he had signed a 'Joint Declaration of War Aims' in August, and Britain waited to see if the Americans would finally fully commit themselves to the war in Europe. Ritchie reported that Londoners were sardonically delighted by the Japanese invasion because it would bounce the Americans into battle.

The picture is that of an over-cautious boy balancing on the edge of a diving-board running forward two steps and back three and then a tough bully comes along and gives him a kick in the backside right into the water!

The final kick was provided by Hitler himself on 11 December, when Germany declared war on America. Meanwhile there was news of British losses in the Far East. Japan captured Hong Kong on Christmas Day and the Japanese advanced towards Singapore.

In London, the war was still experienced on the map. On leave from the marines, Evelyn Waugh described London itself as 'crowded and dead. Claridge's slowly decaying. Wine outrageous in price and quality, sent round daily from the Savoy. Newspapers always late and usually deficient.' Graham Greene, like Waugh, was pleased to return to the action, boarding a ship for West Africa in December. Once on board, he was told that two other ships had been torpedoed on the ship's previous convoy. He was getting closer to the danger once again. On 3 January 1942 Greene arrived in Freetown, Sierra Leone, a place he had fallen in love with on a visit seven years earlier. He recorded in his journal that 'it felt odd and poetic and encouraging coming back after so many years. Like seeing a place you've dreamed of. Even the sweet hot smell from the land . . . was oddly familiar.'

Sierra Leone was crucially positioned, at the border of French Guinea and close to Senegal, both of which were in the hands of Vichy France. Freetown itself was a necessary port of call for all shipping convoys from Egypt or North Africa. The broad aim of the British in West Africa was to gain ground for the Free French. In September 1940 Evelyn Waugh had been involved in Operation Menace, an unsuccessful mission to take the port of Dakar in Senegal and install General de Gaulle. This was Britain and the Free French's first offensive and they hoped that control of Dakar would be a preliminary to winning the whole of French West Africa for the Free French cause. However, the Vichy authorities surprised the attacking forces by refusing to transfer their loyalty to de Gaulle and instead opening fire on the British ships. Their primary weapon was the battleship *Richelieu*, which was equipped with formidable fifteen-inch guns. 'Dakar has set us back badly,' Rose Macaulay observed to her sister at the time; 'De Gaulle obviously misjudged.' This was Waugh's first overseas assignment in the marines and he found the defeat dispiriting. Reading letters from home about the raids in London while waiting for a ship back to Britain from Gibraltar in October, he felt less heroic than those who had stayed behind. 'Henry Yorke no doubt fighting fires day and night. The armed forces cut a small figure. We are like wives reading letters from the trenches.'

Now the *Richelieu*, which had been damaged in the battle, was being repaired in Dakar. If it was seaworthy, the ship would represent a considerable potential threat to British shipping, so Greene's chief task in West Africa was to obtain information about the state of the ship. Initially, he was flown to Lagos for three months' further training; while there he spent his time coding and decoding information, socialising with the colonials and turning cockroach-hunting into a sport. In March 1942 he was ready to start his posting in Freetown, which he found was unbearably hot and subject to severe water shortages. 'Nothing that I ever wrote about this place is really bad enough,' he told his sister. In Lagos, Greene had been officially working for the Department of Trade, but he was now instructed to assume the identity of an employee of CID Special Branch, despite the fact that he spent very little time in police headquarters. His job was bureaucratic, chiefly involving decoding and replying to telegrams, writing reports and processing the reports of his agents. Ambitiously, Greene wondered about opening a brothel in the Portuguese territory of Bissau, just down the coast from the *Richelieu*, in which the Madam could obtain information from the clients. However, his superiors in London discouraged the venture.

Spying appealed to both the romantic and the novelist in Greene. 'I suppose . . . that every novelist has something in common with a spy,' he wrote in his autobiography; 'he watches, he overhears, he seeks motives and analyses character, and in his attempt to serve literature he is unscrupulous.' He liked subterfuge and he liked storytelling, and at moments he could now believe that he was instrumental in the war effort. For years afterwards, he had self-aggrandising dreams about his own spying activities, imagining on one occasion that he and his brother Raymond were espionage agents in Hamburg. Cornered by the Nazis, they snatched their attackers' guns, clubbed them and shut their bodies in a cupboard before escaping in an aeroplane.

However, he did not quite leave wartime London behind. It was in Africa, missing the excitement of the Blitz, that Greene began work on the novel that would become *The Ministry of Fear*. On the journey there he had read a detective story by Michael Innes which inspired him to attempt his own detective fiction. Lying awake at night in the bunk in his ship, half hoping that a warning siren would herald a return to England, he decided to write a thriller, wanting it to be both fantastic and funny. The resulting novel is a faithful portrait of London in the Blitz. There are untidy gaps between the Bloomsbury houses, and fireplaces are left halfway up walls where the rest of the room has been blasted away. A summer fete on a Sunday afternoon is accompanied by the sound of broken glass being cleared as workers sweep up the debris from the previous night's bombing.

Wartime London was more enticing imagined in Africa than experienced in actuality. For Charles Ritchie, the winter of 1941 came as an anticlimax. 'After being the centre of the world's stage London has become unexciting,' he observed in his diary. 'We are not as heroic, desperate and gay as we were last winter. London seems drab. The tension is removed – the anxiety remains.' He was still in awe of Elizabeth. 'I should hate to lose her friendship,' he reflected on 21 December. 'It would be shattering to quarrel with her. I have so much more respect for her than I have for myself.' But it was becoming clear that her love went deeper than his, and neither of them was happy with this. On 11 January 1942, Japan declared war on Holland and Elizabeth brought Charles a cyclamen. 'E is sad,' he reported, 'because she loves me more than I love her. It is sad for me too in another way.' He was all the more troubled to recognise an unconditionality in her love. 'She sees through me more and more and still loves me, which is a most painful situation for me.' As Elizabeth's love deepened, Charles wished that she could make it less obvious. 'A little indifference goes such a long way with me

– indeed my system requires it, like the need for salt'; 'it is better for me to love more than I am loved.'

In her letters to her lover, Elizabeth always insisted that Charles was a better man than he himself was prepared to admit. But she was aware, too, that he was habitually unfaithful to her; aware that those years of promiscuous love-making had deadened his feelings. 'I told her the other evening that I was a crook,' he recorded in his diary in April 1942, 'which was a guarded way of saying that I had been and would continue to be unfaithful to her.' Two weeks later he described a 'desolating' evening with Elizabeth, where he attempted to convey that he did not love her, only to take her 'sadly to bed', which was a 'fiasco'.

For her part, Elizabeth retained her faith in the relationship. In 'Summer Night', the tale of disappointed love which Elizabeth had written before she met Charles, the heroine wonders if her lover has broken her heart and knows only that he has 'broken her fairytale'. Elizabeth kept her own fairy tale intact because she was unassailable in both loving and dreaming; confident in believing in the myth of their love. And it is fairy tales and dreams that Charles continually associated with Elizabeth. 'She holds me by the imagination,' he observed in September 1941. 'My daylight feelings, solid affections and passions are on another plane.' 'One of the luxuries of this love affair,' he wrote after a day trip to Kew in May 1942, 'is the giddy feeling of being carried along on the tide of her imagination.' 'I am in love with E imaginatively,' he wrote the next day, 'she even has a strange beauty like a woman in a tapestry.' 'Of what is her magic made?' he wondered the following week. 'What is the spell she has cast over me?' Walking, once again, in Regent's Park, sitting on the bank by the canal watching the swans pass by, he was both fascinated and disturbed by her flashes of insight, like summer lightning. Charles was discovering 'more and more of her generous nature, her wit and funniness, the stammering flow of her enthralling talk, the idiosyncrasies, vagaries of her temperament'. Bewitched, he observed with fateful prescience that 'this attachment is nothing transient but will bind me as long as I live'.

In the spring of 1942 Rose Macaulay was acutely aware of the binding strength of love as she waited for her lover to die. That February Gerald O'Donovan was admitted to King's College Hospital where he was informed that his colorectal cancer was an inoperable malignant growth. The doctors decided to operate as a palliative to prevent future pain and told Rose that he was unlikely to get through the operation. In fact he survived, but the growth turned out to be more widespread than they had expected. His life expectancy was shortened from eighteen months to considerably less. Gerald had known that he was unlikely to survive the operation, but did not know that it was not a cure. 'It's not too easy talking on that basis,' Rose told her cousin Jean on 25 February. She was finding it hard to concentrate on anything else.

> It gives one a queer dazed feeling – a sudden precipice yawning across a road that has run for nearly 25 years. First Margaret, then he. No doubt life must be thus, when one reaches my age. Perhaps, for him (as for her) it may be better to slip out before worse befall us all.

Here, for the first time, she acknowledged Gerald's letters as the source of much of her anguish at the bombing of her flat the previous May. 'I find it is minor things that stab deepest,' she wrote; 'the destruction of all his letters at Luxborough, for instance. Why didn't I move them in time?'

Over the next few months Rose Macaulay wrote a short story called 'Miss Anstruther's Letters' in which she made the role of the letters in her grief explicit. Commissioned by Storm Jameson, the story was published only in America, offering Macaulay the chance to publish with relative anonymity as she could assume that none of her London acquaintances would come across it. This is one of the most haunting and personal pieces that Macaulay ever wrote and is the only fiction that she published in the ten years between *And No Man's Wit* and *The World My Wilderness*.

'Miss Anstruther's Letters' is an elegy for Rose's burned possessions and an anticipatory elegy for Gerald. It is an account of a woman whose life is 'cut in two' when her flat is bombed, leaving her as 'a ghost, without attachments or habitation'. Unlike Rose herself, Miss Anstruther is present during the bombing, and has a chance to save some of her possessions. Confused and rushed, she rescues her type-writer and portable wireless. It is only after a gas main has burst, feeding the fire, that she remembers her lover's letters, and by now it is too late. With 'hell blazing and crashing all around her', she sits down helplessly in the road, 'sick and shaking, wholly bereft'. Her lover, unlike Gerald, died a year earlier; she has not yet had the courage to reread his letters. Only fragments of phrases remain in her memory: 'Light of my eyes'; 'the sun flickering through the beeches on your hair'.

Like Rose, Miss Anstruther spends the succeeding days combing her ruins for relics of her past. She finds only a fragment of a letter, written during a quarrel: 'leave it at that. I know now that you don't care twopence; if you did you would . . .' Twenty years ago, Miss Anstruther refused to commit to her lover; this was his remonstrance. 'She had failed in caring once, twenty years ago, and failed again now, and the twenty years between were a drift of grey ashes that once were fire, and she a drifting ghost too.'

Macaulay's story is painful in its candid portrayal of loss. Gerald had inscribed a new copy of *The Holy Tree* for her, but most of the memen-toes she had of the relationship had been destroyed in the bombing of her flat. It is only in 'Miss Anstruther's Letters' that the letters become central to her sorrow at the destruction of her possessions, and that the scale of this sorrow is explained. The public mourning for her books had enabled Rose to express her private grief at the death she now felt to be imminent. It was Gerald whom she could not face life without; Gerald whose impending death made Rose wish that she had been killed too. By writing 'Miss Anstruther's Letters', Rose Macaulay created one final relic of Gerald O'Donovan which, once published, could not be destroyed by bombs. At the same time, she assured Gerald that his death would not lessen her love. Like Miss Anstruther, she too would be left as a mere ghost of her former self.

In June Macaulay wrote an article about the war that blended anger with despair. Powerless in preventing Gerald's death or in preventing the bloodshed of war, she railed against the rhetoric of politicians. 'Is there anything to be said,' she asked, 'for the smug, pompous and tedious clichés which most of our public speakers drop about like worn coins whenever they speak? There are some phrases whose reiteration becomes nauseating: among them are "the freedom-loving nations", "the common peoples of Britain" . . . "retribution".' These phrases could not be uttered except in a smug voice and she wished that a concerted effort could be made to rid public speaking of platitude and sentimentality and allow it to resemble intelligent conversation. More angrily, Macaulay complained that they were being told again, as in the last war, that their enemies (and in particular the Italians) 'don't like cold steel'. 'Does any one,' she asked dismissively, 'like steel, either cold or hot, when it is plunged into them without (or even with) anaesthetics? This kind of exultant taunt seems to add an edge of barbarity to the accounts of the assaults of painful weapons of war on agonised human flesh and blood.'

On 26 July 1942 Gerald O'Donovan died. Rose had spent the previous day with him, managing to communicate with him although he was only semi-conscious. He became unconscious after she left and died the next morning. In a letter to Rosamond Lehmann, Rose tried, as always, to be buoyant, grateful that 'he didn't linger on in pain'. She was comparing him with her sister Margaret, whose final weeks of agony she had found hard to bear. 'Isn't it odd,' she asked Rosamond helplessly, 'with all this dying, so inevitable, we haven't yet learned to accept it. We are unadaptable about that. It still comes as a shock. It's all this loving we do. Worthwhile, but it doesn't fit us for losing each other.' She felt empty and dead and without purpose, and longed, as she had after her flat was bombed, to escape, perhaps to neutral Portugal, hoping that a change of scene would help her begin again. This is the new beginning Rose had found impossible to contemplate after the bombing of her flat. Once the death she had dreaded for so long had come at last, she began to see starting again as a possibility. 'He was the dearest companion, you know,' she added, looking back. 'And had such a fine, brilliant mind . . . Well, it's over if things are ever over.'

Rose was doubly bereft and exiled by Gerald's death. She was left without her partner and lover of twenty years, and she was denied the opportunity to grieve. Only a handful of close friends could know the scale of her loss, and very few of these had any intimate knowledge of Gerald himself. Two weeks later, Rose wrote an anonymous obituary for Gerald in *The Times*. Signed by 'a friend', it was painfully detached and impersonal. She described his 'in parts brilliant' novels and his 'wide and versatile interests', listing his successive careers as sub warden of Toynbee Hall, publisher, and head of the Italian section at the Ministry of Information. She let a note of affection intrude when she mentioned his recent work assisting Czech refugees, adding that 'his sympathetic understanding of their problems was a characteristic example of the generous help he always gave to those in need'. She ended with a restrained but personal tribute to the man she loved: 'As a friend he never failed; his wise judgment and unstinting interest were always on tap behind his reserve and behind the sometimes sardonic wit that was his Irish heritage. To know him was to love him.'

It is in her subsequent novels that Rose Macaulay's more effusive tributes are found. It is also in her fiction that she allowed the full force of her grief to surface. Rose did not write novels for some time after Gerald's death. Looking back on the period in a 1951 letter to her spiritual mentor and friend, a priest called Hamilton Johnson, she wrote that she was too unhappy to write fiction: 'I always talked over my novels with my companion, who stimulated my invention; when he died my mind seemed to go blank and dead.' When she did return to novel-writing, her grief for Gerald remained central to her work. In Macaulay's 1950 novel *The World My Wilderness*, Helen, a middle-aged English woman who lives in post-war France, mourns the death of her second husband, who was killed by the Resistance during the war: 'Her want of Maurice grew no less; it hungered in her night and day, engulfing her senses and her reason in an aching void.' Six years later in Macaulay's final novel, *The Towers of Trebizond*, Laurie is shattered by the death of her married lover Vere: 'And now the joy was killed, and there seemed no reason why my life too should not run down and stop now that its mainspring was broken.' For a companionship like theirs to end is 'to lose a limb, or the faculty of sight; one is, quite simply, cut off from life and scattered adrift, lacking the coherence and the integration of love'. Life will, she supposes, proceed, 'but the sentient, enjoying principle which had kept it all ticking, had been destroyed'.

Earlier in the novel, Laurie recalls an occasion when she and Vere fantasised about the life they might have shared. On holiday, wrapped in the bliss of togetherness, understanding each other, laughing at each other's jokes, allowing love to be their fortress and their peace, they wonder 'how long we should live in this doped oblivion if we had been married'. Laurie supposes, sensibly, that 'the every-day life which married people live together after a time blunts romance'. But neither she nor Vere thinks they should mind that, if they had all the other things to do together, and could plan their holidays and argue about the maps and the routes. She imagines that they would be very fair about equal turns of driving. They would like their children. And, crucially, 'marriage would still be our fortress and our peace, just as love was now when we could be together but could be a sadness and a torment when apart'.

In *The Towers of Trebizond* Macaulay allowed herself to depict a full adulterous affair that resembled her own. Here Laurie and Vere are placed in the same dilemma as Ann and Brian in *The Holy Tree* or Rome and Mr Jayne in *Told by an Idiot*. But Vere's wife, unlike Mr Jayne's lunatic Russian, is a reasonable woman who adores him. Vere convinces Laurie that he is fonder of his wife because of Laurie; 'men,' Laurie adds, 'are given to saying this'. But, justifying her own conduct, she states that

> really she bored him; if she had not bored him, he would not have fallen in love with me. If I had refused to be his lover he would no doubt, sooner or later, have found someone else. But I did not refuse, or only for a short time at the beginning, and so we had ten years of it, and each year was better than the one before, love and joy gradually drowning remorse, till in the end it struggled for life.

By 1955, Macaulay had come to regret the selfishness of adultery, but she could not regret a relationship that could have been so happy, had it been allowed to flourish normally. There does not seem to have been any question of allowing this to happen. Rose Macaulay is clear throughout her novels that she disapproves of divorce; Gerald might have come a long way since his days as a Catholic priest, but he does not seem to have inclined towards separation. Indeed, many of Rose's friends assumed that she would not have wanted to marry anyway; she was too independent and happily self reliant. Rose and Gerald's mutual friend the writer Marjorie Grant Cook later insisted that marriage to Gerald would have been a disastrous mistake on Rose's part, although Marjorie's own rather intense feelings towards Gerald may have influenced her opinion.

Certainly, Macaulay was scathing about marriage in several essays and novels. In a 1920s article entitled 'People who Should Not Marry' she maintained that

> some men and women might well prefer to live alone, meeting their beloved only when it suits them, thus retaining both that measure of freedom . . . enjoyed by the solitary, and the delicate bloom on the fruit of love which is said to be brushed off by continual contact.

She expressed this more strongly in an essay on the 'Problems of Married Life' in *A Casual Commentary*, where she states that 'to be with the beloved just enough – that is passionately moving and contenting', while 'to be with the beloved too much – that is surfeit and thraldom'. Later in this book, Macaulay inquires 'Into the Sanctity of the Home', challenging the assumption that people who have families are morally superior to those without. What is sanctity, she wonders, and how can one acquire it? 'How does one know whether sanctity adorns one's home or not?' Can the home of a bachelor or a spinster have sanctity? Can a flat have sanctity? Can a boarding-house? Presumably, they cannot. Gerda holds out against marrying the man she loves in *Dangerous Ages* on the grounds that marriage is 'a fetter on what shouldn't be fettered' and that it has the same Victorian fussiness as antimacassars. Macaulay was also often dismissive of child-bearing. In Macaulay's 1920 novel *Potterism*, Jane dismisses babies as 'a handicap, like your frock (however short it was) when you were climbing', complaining that babies make women ill before they arrive and need care and attention afterwards. Denham, the heroine of *Crewe Train* (1926) is so distressed to find herself pregnant that she goes out of her way to encourage a miscarriage.

But there is both a defensiveness and an ambivalence in many of these accounts. Macaulay adds in 'Problems of Married Life' that to be with the beloved insufficiently is 'annihilating anguish of the soul', with the sudden seriousness of this phrase jarring within this delicately comic essay. And she did not quite put the weight of her own conviction into 'People who Should Not Marry'; the carefully placed '*is said* to be brushed off' allows for the possibility that in fact the delicate bloom of love might remain. The light-hearted cheer with which she dismissed marriage is belied by the earnestness with which Laurie, in *The Towers of Trebizond*, imagines marriage as a fortress and a peace.

Writing to her friend Sylvia Lynd about Gerald's death, Rose celebrated the fact that the story of her love affair had been 'a good one', adding that 'it might have ended worse – perhaps in weariness, faithlessness, or nothingness, or a mere lessening of love'. She wondered if this constancy was 'the reward of sin'; had their love survived because it was spared the strain of years of constant household use? Gerda or Denham, even Kitty, might say that it had; Rose Macaulay, bereft and desolate, had more faith in her own constancy. 'Perhaps our love would have survived intact; it might, I think, because there was such a fundamental oneness – but who knows?' She would, she admitted, 'like to have a child or two of his', though it would have created complications. Later, writing to Hamilton Johnson, Rose admitted the sin in the relationship but insisted that, given the chance, it would have succeeded as a marriage:

> Oh why was there so much evil in what was in so many ways so good? Why did it have to be like that, all snarled up and tangled in wrong, when if we had been free it would have been the almost perfect thing.

10

'*Can* pain and danger exist?'

Elizabeth Bowen and Henry Yorke, July–December 1942

In July 1942, Charles Ritchie accompanied Elizabeth Bowen to Ireland. The war was going badly for the British and it was a relief to escape the atmosphere of helpless apprehension in London. Since January 1942, British forces had suffered setbacks on all fronts. The public learnt of defeats in Singapore and Hong Kong in the Far East and of a particularly humiliating reversal at Tobruk in North Africa. In a speech to the House of Commons in April, Churchill acknowledged that there had been 'a painful series of misfortunes in the Far East' but insisted that 'the violence, fury, skill and might of Japan' had exceeded anything they had been led to expect. As for the Middle East, 'by what narrow margins, chances and accidents was the balance tipped against us no one can compute'. 'Even Hitler makes mistakes,' he added rather plaintively in a broadcast to the world in May. Churchill's popularity fell to a wartime low of 78 per cent in June and he faced a vote of no confidence in the House of Commons at the start of July.

In Russia, Stalin's beleaguered forces fought on heroically against Hitler's, while Stalin pleaded with Britain and America to open a second front in western Europe to relieve the unrelenting attack on the eastern front. Meanwhile Hitler had responded to the bombing of the old German cities of Lübeck and Rostock by retaliating with the so-called 'Baedeker raids' on Britain. The Nazi Deputy Head of the German Information and Press Division coined the phrase 'Baedeker raids' as the targets all featured in Baedeker's *Great Britain: Handbook For Travellers*. 'We shall go out to bomb every building in Britain marked with three stars in the Guide.' Severe attacks on Bath, Norwich, Exeter, Canterbury and York were the result.

This visit to Bowen's Court in July 1942 was the first of many trips Charles would make to the house which Elizabeth soon came to think of as their home. Elizabeth stayed on after he had left. Bowen's Court was a dreamy house and from now on its dreaminess would be perennially associated with her longing for Charles. Alone, detached from reality and time, she could continue in a fantasy of togetherness, returning to their shared life by entering familiar rooms or gazing at familiar views. In *The Heat of the Day*, Stella visits Ireland in the autumn of 1942 and spends her days thinking about Robert. She wakes from a deep sleep to be confronted by Robert's face. She wanders through sunshafted beech trees, struck by 'a breathless glory' which travels through the layered foliage, mysteriously illuminated by the dappled light.

In the secluded Irish countryside, Elizabeth could assess her relationship with both Charles and the war from a distance. Charles's image remained vivid, while the war seemed at times to recede into unreality. Most people in England in this period who were not directly subject to bombing or fighting felt torn between the competing realities of their day-to-day personal life and the war going on elsewhere. In Ireland, where the war really could seem to disappear altogether, this duality was thrown into relief. The question implicit in all Bowen's wartime accounts of Ireland is whether it is possible or even desirable to escape the war; whether Irish neutrality made the country a peaceful haven or an irresponsible hiding place.

Bowen's Court, which had been published shortly before Bowen's arrival in Ireland, celebrates the enchanted quality of the house and its surroundings but is also dominated by the presence of death. The Ireland of Bowen's book is a mystical country in which 'the light, the light-consumed distances, that air of intense existence about the empty country . . . the great part played in society by the dead and by the idea of death' creates an 'unearthly disturbance' in the spirit. Her own house – for centuries the focus of generations of intense living on the part of her ancestors – is peopled by the ghosts of the dead.

Bowen's awareness of these ghosts had become even more powerful in wartime. She had come from a city that still shimmered with the blood of the recent dead, and the deathliness of Ireland reminded her of this. At the same time, the palpable sense of centuries of Irish dead buried around her had the effect of comfortingly opening up time, suggesting that this war, like others, would pass. Bowen had to decide whether the Irish dead would lull her into forgetfulness or stir her into remembering the war going on elsewhere.

In an afterword to *Bowen's Court* written in 1963, Bowen described how the house shielded its wartime inhabitants from the world outside:

> Only the wireless in the library conducted the world's urgency to the place. Wave after wave of war news broke upon the quiet air of the room, and in the daytime when the windows were open, passed out on to the sunny or overcast lawns.

Here was 'peace at its most ecstatic' – a sustaining illusion that conjured away the war. She supposed that 'everyone, fighting or just enduring, carried within him one private image, one peaceful scene. Mine was Bowen's Court. War made me that image out of a house built of anxious history.'

However, the history remained anxious. The ancestors whose presence pervaded the house had left an atmosphere of apprehension that could not quite be dispelled. '*Can* pain and danger exist?' Bowen asked herself, surveying the empty countryside from the steps of her peaceful house. The question itself contained the possibility that they could. 'The scene was a crystal in which, while one was looking, a shadow formed.' The Elizabeth Bowen who was the author of *Bowen's Court* may have been a romantic dreamer who had spent the war immersing herself in the history of her dead Anglo-Irish ancestors. But there was another Elizabeth Bowen who was in Ireland writing war reports for the Ministry of Information and for whom pain and danger could and did exist. She at least was unable to sustain the fantasy that the war stopped just because she herself was no longer attending to it. In the afterword to *Bowen's Court* she went on to state that the 'war-time urgency of the present, its relentless daily challenge' affected her view of the past. 'In the savage and austere light of a burning world, details leaped out with significance.' The waves of news breaking upon the quiet of the library inflected everything that she saw around her.

That news was dominated by the epic battle playing itself out in Russia. By 15 July the Germans were at the gates of Voronezh and Rostov, and the British government was debating whether or not to start a second front. It was a difficult decision to make. Harold Nicolson reflected in his diary that if Britain created a new front as a forlorn hope, just to show support, there would be a defeat as disastrous as Dunkirk. If they did not, they would be accused of letting down the Russians. The Germans then began to close round Rostov, leaving the Russians in danger of being cut off from their oil supplies. By August the Germans were pushing into Stalingrad. But in Ireland, the news took a long time to get through. Bowen reported to the Ministry of Information from Cork on 31 July that the country as a whole was experiencing a 'greater degree of cut-offness, since last year, with regard to up-to-date war news'. Papers were scarce and arrived late; there were few wireless sets. As a visitor from England, she was eagerly questioned about the war by people who she felt were using it as 'a form of escapism'. She herself may have been escaping the war by coming to Ireland, but the Irish were apparently escaping their own realities by attending to the war.

The news that did get through was heavily censored. Irish newspapers and radio stations were obliged to maintain a balance between the perspectives of the two sides in their war coverage. As a result, news of bombing in either Britain or Germany, and of the fighting in Russia, had to be brutally edited, because the facts alone were too distressing not to induce people to question the morality of Eire's neutral stance. When radio stations did decide to present an opinion, they balanced it with a view from the opposite side. Thus, the Irish heard regular broadcasts from the pro-Nazi writer Francis Stuart, a former IRA gunman once championed by Yeats (and married to his muse Maud Gonne's daughter), who was a direct contemporary of Elizabeth Bowen and Sean O'Faolain. Stuart, who had taken up a post at the University of Berlin in 1940, was now regaling the Irish public with tales of the amazing heroism of the German army in Russia.

As always, Bowen divided her time in Ireland between Bowen's Court and Dublin, and she found that the writers, journalists and politicians whom she met in Dublin now railed against both censorship and, to an extent, the whole policy of neutrality. 'Eire feels as strongly, one might say as religiously, about her neutrality as Britain feels about her part in the war,' Bowen had explained to English readers in an article in the *New Statesman and Nation* in April 1941. 'She has taken a stand – a stand, as she sees it, alone.' However, many former enthusiasts for the policy were now losing patience. Bowen's own cousin Hubert Butler had initially championed neutrality as an active anti-Nazi stance that would enable the Irish to combine pacifism with working, as Butler himself was doing, to save European refugees from Nazi persecution. In the autumn of 1940, when both the British and the Irish were expecting a joint attack from Germany, this sense of the Irish collaborating with Britain in defeating Hitler was still tenable. But by the summer of 1941, Butler was already starting to feel more disillusioned. He complained in *The Bell* that Ireland was surrounded by 'an ocean of indifference and xenophobia', fiercely guarding its own insularity.

Since the autumn of 1940, both de Valera and his policy of neutrality had confronted a passionate opponent in the figure of James Dillon, the deputy leader of Fine Gael, the main opposition to de Valera's Fianna Fáil party. From the start of the war, Dillon had suggested that there was a thin line between neutrality and indifference, protesting against the isolationist element of neutrality. In a debate in Ireland's parliament, the Dáil, on 17 July 1941, Dillon stated explicitly that neutrality was 'not in the true interests, moral or material, of the Irish people'. The Irish knew that the Allies were on the side of right, and it was mere fear of German bombing that deterred them. Dillon's views carried little weight. As far as de Valera was concerned, the Irish had 'no responsibility for the present war'. And public opinion remained against Dillon, especially after he gave a speech in February 1942 insisting that Ireland could not stand aloof from the world conflict and that duty and history forced Ireland to be on the side of the Allies. Dillon reminded the Irish of their friendship with America and warned them that

> if, in some awful hour, our people commit the supreme folly of accepting in exchange for the traditional Irish-American alliance any form of co-operation from the Nazi-Fascist Powers of Europe, it will be merely the introduction to a development which will end in this country being turned into a German Gibraltar of the Atlantic.

Bowen had met Dillon on each of her visits since November 1940. On first impressions, she liked him, though she could see why he was widely disliked. She reported that he held some views which 'even I distrust, and which are abhorrent to many Irish people whose integrity I respect . . . He is less parochial in outlook than most Irishmen: in fact, not parochial at all.' In her report of 9 February 1942 Bowen noted that 'Mr Dillon's uncompromising attitude is said to have lost him a good deal of support'. The country was frightened of him, believing that he would like to bring Ireland into the war. In fact, Bowen thought that Dillon merely wanted to open the pros and cons of Irish neutrality to the 'fair and reasonable debate' prevented by de Valera who, as far as Dillon was concerned, had broken the country's spirit with his exploitation of the widespread fear of German invasion or bombing.

By the time of Bowen's 20 February report, Dillon had resigned. She was not surprised. His speech had been too dramatic, stirring up 'an almost neurotic anger and fear' among people who had already 'lost face – with themselves, with each other'. In Dublin, he had lost the support even of those who thought Ireland should have entered the war in the first place. Bowen continued to meet Dillon after his resignation, and on 31 July she reported his belief that the general fervour on the subject of Eire's neutrality was beginning to lapse. For Dillon, this fervour was rooted first in national vanity and second in fear, both of which were on the decline. As far as he was concerned, the public was demoralised by the acknowledged timidity of Eire's attitude. Children and young people had less respect for their leaders and suspected the older generation of 'dishonesty, of turning the blind eye'.

Bowen was inclined to agree with Dillon. At the beginning of the war Eire, preparing to defend her neutrality, had 'claimed the right to regard herself as a land of heroes'. Now, most of that 'heroic illusion' had been stripped from neutrality. Instead she thought that it had come to be seen as 'a dreary and negative state – the sheer negative of "not being in the war"'. Having accepted the reality of the war, even within the seclusion of Bowen's Court, Bowen now demanded that the Irish accept it too. The glory of neutrality was fading and she applauded the fact that the Irish were candid enough to admit 'this drop in height', no longer regarding participation in the war with the same entrenched reluctance as they had two years earlier.

Perhaps most of all, the Irish resented the fact that they had all the deprivations of the war effort without the moral high ground of fighting a war. In his editorial for the January 1942 issue of *Horizon*, which was devoted to Ireland, Cyril Connolly declared that the predicament was serious, warning his English readers to 'stop thinking of Ireland as an uncharitable earthly paradise': 'The shops are full of good things to eat, the streets of people who cannot afford to buy them. Light and heat are desperately short, for there is very little coal, and turf is scarce through lack of transport.' For Stella, visiting Ireland in *The Heat of the Day*, the exciting sensation of being outside war concentrates itself in the 'fearless lights' possible in a country without a nightly blackout. As her ship draws into the Dublin harbour, the windows appear to blaze out. Dazzling reflections in damp streets make Dublin seem to be in the midst of a carnival. Yet Stella does not realise that in fact fuel and candles are rationed here as well; she alone is burning up the house's supplies for months ahead.

Meanwhile Sean O'Faolain and his circle were still committed to neutrality as a policy, but resented the anaesthetising effects of Irish isolationism. O'Faolain complained about the 'queer feeling of unrealism' resulting from the lack of clear war news, comparing the perpetual silence and guarded reticence to the atmosphere of a genteel tea party. On her February 1942 visit to Ireland, Bowen had reported that her 'general impression of Eire – or rather, Dublin – on this visit was that the country was morally and nervously in a state of deterioration'. She was left with the impression of isolation.

O'Faolain countered Ireland's remoteness by including frequent discussion of European, Ulster, British and Anglo-Irish culture in his monthly literary magazine *The Bell*. The July 1942 issue was devoted to Northern Ireland, which O'Faolain lauded for its capacity to 'live and act in the Now' ('Belfast has immediacy. Ulster has contemporaneity'). He also insistently retained an even-handed approach to British and to Anglo-Irish culture, emphasising its role within Ireland. In his November 1942 editorial, he dismissed the 'small but very vocal number of people' who called themselves Gaels and were determined to throw aside the Anglo-Irish strain in Irish life. These Irishmen with 'their backs to the wall' were acting and thinking, he complained, as if Landlordism still existed. They went on hating England as if it were still the nineteenth century. They were 'unable to begin to build a free Ireland because their minds stopped dead thirty years ago in an Ireland that was not free'.

In O'Faolain's new Ireland, there was plenty of room for the Anglo-Irish, and Bowen's frequent appearances in *The Bell* were evidence of this. Between August and November 1942 she featured in four successive issues. There was a review of *Bowen's Court* in August, an interview with her in September, a short story ('Sunday Afternoon') in October, and an extract from *Seven Winters*, Bowen's short autobiographical account of her Dublin childhood, in November. The division inherent in Bowen's position in Ireland was clear in these articles. She was represented in *The Bell* partly as a voice from England; a reminder of the wider life going on outside Ireland. But she was also there as an anachronistic vestige of the lost world of Big Houses and dreamy countryside that O'Faolain himself had enjoyed for the two years of their affair. If the Irish were aware that they were in an unreal position in relation to Britain and Europe, then they (or perhaps more specifically O'Faolain himself) could displace some of this unreality onto the Anglo-Irish now represented by Bowen.

This is evident in the August review of *Bowen's Court* by D. A. Binchy, who was generous but somewhat patronising both to Bowen herself and to the Anglo-Irish in general. As a scholar of linguistics, Binchy was well qualified to point out Bowen's 'minor errors' (she was mistaken, for example, in her explanation of her 'perfectly regular pronunciation of her straightforward Celtic surname'). But he was impressed by her frankness in condemning the abuses of power exercised by her ancestors, and he was prepared to admit that the Anglo-Irish had played a crucial and even a beneficial role in the cultural history of Ireland. For Binchy, it was a tragedy that the new Ireland, in whose construction the Anglo-Irish might have been involved, had been built without them, 'nay against them'; 'and that it is infinitely the poorer therefore no one, except the professional patriot and the synthetic Gael, is likely to deny'. He pronounced this overall 'a grand book', in which Bowen had been led by the spirit of her house through the corridors of its own past.

The October edition story, 'Sunday Afternoon', was effectively a description of Elizabeth Bowen's own wartime trips to Ireland which made explicit her role as a visitor from the battlefield to a scene of unreal peace. Henry Russel, an Anglo-Irishman living in London, returns to the Big House and the old friends 'in whose shadow he had grown up'. Arriving, he joins the group on a lawn unchanged for centuries and is asked 'What are your experiences? – Please tell us. But nothing dreadful: we are already feeling a little sad.' For Henry, arriving from a bombed city in which his own flat has been completely destroyed, the atmosphere is one of suspended charm. The 'sensations of wartime that locked his inside being' are gradually dispelled 'in the influence of this eternalised Sunday afternoon'.

However, Bowen complicates the divide between Britain and Ireland by suggesting that involvement in the war does not necessarily entail emotional engagement. It is not enough simply to be aware of the war, and reality may reside in the fields of Cork as much as in the bombed streets of London. Where initially it seems that the Anglo-Irish are living in an anaesthetised detachment while Henry is engaging with

destruction and pain, it becomes clear that he in fact is the anaesthetised one. Under the influence of the beauty of the setting and of his
hostess, an older woman he loved from a distance in his youth, Henry
comes to protest at returning to 'the zone of death'.

> The moment he had been dreading, returning desire, flooded him in
> this tunnel of avenue . . . He thought, with nothing left but our brute
> courage, we shall be nothing but brutes.

Politically, this is a complex story. If, as she had hoped in her letter to
Virginia Woolf, Bowen did do some good in Ireland, it was because she
insisted throughout the war on the intricacy of the Irish situation, and
of the relationship between the English and the Irish. O'Faolain saw
Bowen's Ministry of Information reports as a betrayal of herself and of
Ireland. In fact, from the start she saw this as something she was doing
as much for the sake of Ireland as for England. She hoped to explain
the nuances – the dementing intransigence – of each to the other, and
her appearances in *The Bell* provided her with a public voice in Ireland
with which to do this. She was convinced by her own, modest success.
In her 12 July report to the Ministry, Bowen urged the British government to grant more travel permits to responsible and intelligent Irish
people, in genuine sympathy with the Allied war effort, who 'could do
untold good over here'. 'I think I have stressed,' she added, 'in all my
Reports, the immense importance in this country, of personal impressions and personal talk.'

   An opportunity for talk was provided by her interview with the Irish
writer Larry Morrow, who was known in *The Bell* as the anonymous
'Bellman'. This took place during her summer visit and was printed in
the September issue of the magazine. They met at the Shelbourne Hotel
on St Stephen's Green, which was Elizabeth Bowen's favourite hotel in
Dublin (she would later write a book about it) and was just along the
Green from her Dublin flat. Although this was an interview of Bowen
by Morrow, the talk went in both directions. Morrow was struck by
what he saw as the 'aristocrat's capacity' for 'impressing one with sudden
and surprising degrees of solicitude for her listener's physical, spiritual

and intellectual welfare'. Bowen had questioned the questioner, presumably partly in the service of her Ministry of Information reports.

Bowen used the interview as a chance to prove her own Irish credentials. She enthused lyrically about Cork. 'If Elizabeth Bowen has any regrets in her life,' Morrow informed his readers, 'which one doubts – it is that, in all other respects a Corkwoman, she was born in the city of Dublin . . . "I'm *frightfully* proud of Cork", she will tell you, screwing up her eyes . . . "Ever since I saw Cork, as a small girl, I have regarded it as my capital city." ' And she presented herself matter-of-factly as an Irish novelist. 'As long as I can remember I've been extremely conscious of being Irish – even when I was writing about such very un-Irish things as suburban life in Paris or the English seaside.'

Larry Morrow, beguiled by Bowen's aristocratic charm, colluded in the exercise, even granting her a Celtic affinity with the Irish natural world. The colour of her eyes, he said, looked as if it had been scooped from the Irish Sea. In general, he seems to have been struck by just the enchanted timelessness that Bowen herself associated with Ireland. This was Bowen as an ethereal spirit from the Cork countryside, rather than as a professional writer visiting from a war zone. Morrow regretted that the meeting had not occurred two hundred years earlier in the Long Room at Bowen's Court instead of at the Shelbourne Hotel. But Miss Bowen was not long in dispelling his regrets: 'For she has surrounded herself with an atmosphere so intensely sixteenth- and seventeenth-century that with her one loses all sense of Time.' Quite apart from her immersion in her own family history, she possessed 'a curious timelessness, that is at once a contempt for Time and a cherished regard for it'. That timelessness was evident in her clothes ('the floppy hat of dark brown felt, the folds of the biscuit-coloured linen dress'), in her endless cigarette-smoking, and in her Holbein face. 'If you know your Holbein even tolerably well, you will have seen Elizabeth Bowen many times – in a dozen or so family portraits,' with their 'flat delicacy of tone' and lines 'that are not so much painted as etched on the canvas'.

By 15 August the German army was advancing into Stalingrad and Elizabeth Bowen was back in London, dining with Charles Ritchie once again. Here was reality, abruptly cutting into her Irish fairy tale;

reality that took the form of the blacked-out ruined streets and the beloved, balding figure of her lover. In *The Heat of the Day* Stella's journey home from Ireland is dominated by a sense of returning to Robert. The train creeps, with 'the timidity of an intruder', into a London whose built-up density is strongly felt. Her heart misses a beat; her being fills like an empty lock; with a 'shock of love' she sees Robert's tall turning head. Charles did not meet Elizabeth at the station, but she appeared at his flat, soon after her arrival, armed with flowers. For Charles, she seemed 'somehow less remarkable' than she had in Ireland – 'to have "lost height" '. 'I wonder if the spell is broken or if it just happened to be an off night,' he pondered. 'All the same my existence has come to life again since she came back.' The Irish had been more gallantly susceptible to Elizabeth's charms. 'Miss Bowen caught me in her sea-green eye and I sank full fathom five,' Morrow reported to his readers. But Charles, too, was bewitched. 'What is the spell she has cast over me,' he had asked in the spring. It was a spell that in his more courageous moments he could name as love; and, either way, he could rarely deny its power for long. 'Spent the day with dearest Elizabeth to whom I owe everything,' he wrote in his diary in September.

———

For Henry Yorke, who could escape neither the built-up density of London nor the war itself, this was a depressing period. His love affairs had been curbed by the return of Dig at the end of the Blitz in the summer of 1941. The time he spent in the fire service had once again taken on the tediously expectant quality of the phoney war. Stephen Spender, who joined the fire service in the autumn of 1942, found that in the absence of more serious concerns his superiors paid excessive attention to disciplinary matters such as the untidiness of his hair. 'It is like their deciding that, after all, Virginia Woolf is not quite suitable to be a washroom attendant,' he complained grandly to T. S. Eliot. Like Yorke, Spender appreciated the camaraderie. 'It would be true to say that we were like a family,' he observed in his journal that December. But he felt infantalised by his fireman's dungarees which he thought reduced the firemen to 'a childish-looking uniformity', turning middle-aged men into caricatured adolescents.

Given the lack of fires, Yorke had now been given leave to spend four weeks at a time working at Pontifex, which he found anticlimactic after the excitement of the Blitz. 'I sit in my swivel chair,' he wrote to Mary Strickland in July 1942, 'swivelling and biting my nails just as I used to do.' Time spent in the office was helped by the fact that the Yorkes' company was prospering for the first time in several years. They had now adapted their technology to make cordite, used in making shells, as well as machines that produced penicillin. Both were needed by Russia, and by the end of the year Yorke had processed orders that would bring in half a million pounds. But this did little to cheer him up personally and the desultory mood of the time goes into a story called 'The Lull' which he sent to John Lehmann in October.

This comprises a series of scenes showing firemen engaged in the depressing task of waiting for fires to fight. They sit around in a bar, telling tired and disconnected anecdotes and, whenever a stranger comes in, start reminiscing about their experiences in the 1940 Blitz. Recounting these stories is enough to make them feel that they are living again, 'if life in a fire station can be called living'. 'We want another blitz,' the barman remarks at one point. They are, the narrator states, 'seeking to justify the waiting life they [live] at present, without fires'. This waiting life is compared to the experience of changing fast trains where a traveller on a crowded platform 'cannot be said to command his destiny'. Even on a day's leave, a well-educated (and clearly autobiographically inspired) fireman called Henry listens helplessly to his female companion reciting Verlaine in the park, sleepy and unsure how to react. Yorke gave the manuscript of the story to Ann Glass and the girl seems to have been modelled on her. She is crisp and direct, informing Henry that he is 'the worst-read man I've ever met' when he fails to recognise Verlaine. Eventually Henry suggests that they should abandon the park and go to the cinema instead. The girl jumps at the suggestion and they hurry off, 'arm in arm, to the USA' for an afternoon of escapism. The story ends with a patrolman sitting on the roof convinced that he is in the middle of saving men from a fire.

Another fireman announces that if Hitler does not put another Blitz on soon 'we shall all be crackers'.

John Lehmann was happy with 'The Lull' and published it in *New Writing* after suggesting just a couple of small changes. But he was less happy with *Caught*, and was trying to persuade Yorke to cut the affair with Hilly from the book. This was when Yorke suggested making the change involving killing off Richard's wife and replacing her with her own sister. 'I have been thinking over *Caught*,' he wrote to Lehmann in November. 'Why should Richard Roe be married? Couldn't he be a widower? With a sister in law keeping house for him.' The Hogarth Press's lawyer was anxious about the adultery, but there would be no adultery if Richard was a widower. 'Tell me what you think. Because I'm afraid Richard's silly thing with Hilly is inevitable and essential to the make-up of the book.'

The compromise was accepted and Yorke spent the next couple of months rather callously killing off Richard's wife. This, on the whole, was simply a question of the occasional insertion or deletion. Part of the oddness of the final text is the bizarrely living quality of the dead woman who haunts Richard's imagination, and this is because in the original writing she was in fact alive. Thus 'he could not leave his wife alone' becomes 'he could not, this time, leave his wife's memory alone'. In the final version, as in the typescript, on the morning of Richard's return 'his wife went with him for a stroll before the car came to the door'; the arm he clutches at above the elbow in the typescript becomes simply 'the arm, which was not there' in the printed novel. Whole conversations with his wife become, verbatim, conversations with the sister-in-law, with the simple explanation that 'he had begun talking to her as though she was her dead sister'. This was a somewhat strange thing to be doing while living in the same house as Dig, not least because of the ambiguously incestuous relationship it ends up implying between Richard and his wife's sister, whom people at the fire station assume is actually his wife. The novel in its original form was largely flattering to Dig, but it surely became more problematic now that he had killed her off so easily. Perhaps it was easier to be unsentimental once he was again cohabiting with his wife.

The year ended well for Britain and badly for Henry Yorke. For Britain, the situation at sea was dire, but the war was going far better on land. November 1942 was the worst month of the Battle of the Atlantic, with 117 Merchant Navy vessels sunk in a single month. 'There is a great advantage, I think, in our not publishing the shipping losses,' Churchill announced to the House of Commons. Apart from the obvious loss of ships and lives, this created a crisis in food and supplies, preventing imports from America. Luckily, this news was overshadowed by the reports of the Allied victories in North Africa. On 4 November, General Bernard Montgomery, now Commander-in-Chief of the Eighth Army, won the twelve-day battle of El Alamein, recapturing all the major ports and towns the Allies had previously lost, and then on 13 December he crossed the border into Tripolitania. Churchill congratulated the 'noble Desert Army' for avenging the previous defeat at Tobruk: 'Taken by itself, the Battle of Egypt must be regarded as an historic British victory.' Meanwhile on 22 November the Russians had encircled the German army in Stalingrad.

El Alamein was the first British victory and was believed by many to be a turning point in the war. In *The Heat of the Day* it is celebrated even in Ireland, where Stella is told enthusiastically by the Irish servants that 'Montgomery's through' and that 'It's the war turning', with the war breaking in on and belying the unreal tranquillity of Stella's visit. But Henry Yorke was drinking too much and was fed up with his work at Pontifex and with editing *Caught*. For Yorke, the war news was now less real than his own daily life, and that daily life itself felt increasingly unreal as well. On Christmas Eve, writing to thank Evelyn Waugh for the launch party for Waugh's new novel *Put Out More Flags* he congratulated his friend on the book, which he saw as 'the best work you have done, or so it seems to me' and admitted that he had been too drunk to work out how they came to part or how he reached home. 'Am very depressed, lonely, and overworked,' he added, while thanking Waugh for his book which had cheered him up and made him think 'everything was real again'.

11

'Only at night I cry'

Hilde Spiel and Henry Yorke, spring 1943

In *The Heat of the Day* Bowen describes how '1942, still with no Second Front, ran out'. Stella and fellow Londoners experience 'nothing more than a sort of grinding change of gear for the up-grade' as they start their 1943 calendars. But in fact there was still news coming in from North Africa. The Eighth Army captured Tripoli on 23 January and continued their march towards Tunisia. And sporadic bombing began again in London. On 18 January Hilde Spiel reported the first raids for two years in her diary. 'First made me very nervous, mostly because of Christine. Second 5am excited me less!' Three days later she complained that the 'beastly Luftwaffe' had bombed a school in Catford, south London, and killed about forty small children. 'Heartrending.' Hilde was already feeling hysterical and on edge because she was in the final month of a difficult pregnancy. She had been operated on the previous March, and told to avoid becoming pregnant in the near future. It became clear that she should have heeded this advice when, four months pregnant in September, she suffered a small heart and breathing attack. Now she was waiting anxiously for the baby to come to term.

On 31 January the Germans finally capitulated at Stalingrad after a five-month battle in which 200,000 men were killed. For the Allies, the Russian victory came as a sign that the Third Reich could be defeated after all. Hilde Spiel spent the first few days of February in severe pain

Catford school on the night of the 20 January bombing

while builders crashed around upstairs creating a third bedroom and doctors tried to hurry the baby into the world by dosing her with castor oil. Her parents, who were now living in a small apartment in Notting Hill, hovered in the sitting room; Peter paced around nervously, making things worse. On 8 February Hilde was taken to the London clinic by ambulance, only to find that her labour pains mysteriously ceased. The next day she gave birth to a dead girl she had intended to call Brigid. There had been four hours of contractions, after which the baby came too quickly, swallowed water and could not be revived. Her doctor, a former leading light at the Berlin Charité hospital, was absent at the crucial moment. Distraught, Hilde described the 'tiny, perfect, absolutely waxen little baby girl . . . quite utterly dead' in her diary. She wondered if the baby had known that Hilde most wanted a boy and therefore 'did not dare to come into the world'. 'But I would have loved her,' she protested, 'after a short disappointment, I would never have made her feel she should have been a boy.'

The next day Hilde observed that she was 'breaking down only rarely'. However, she had to comfort Peter, who collapsed in her arms in the afternoon. She began to feel that she had failed him at the decisive moment. 'This, I suppose, is the most tragic thing that has happened to me,' she wrote. 'I'm surprised at my strength. Only at night I cry.' She was keeping going with the aid of mild drugs, injected with morphine each evening. But her breasts were now uncomfortably engorged with milk and she was still in pain. By the following week she was finding Peter a great help and she noted that 'in a way' he was the ideal husband for her. At the same time, she was developing a strange attachment to her doctor, Dr Löser, and was waiting expectantly for his visits. On 15 February she returned home, appreciating the blue sky and the breeze in the park, 'glad to be alive'. Dr Löser had promised to visit her on Sunday but now said he might not be able to stay for tea. 'Made me unhappy,' she wrote. 'Absurd, how fiction he cared helped me over these days. One more blow.' The next day she had what she described as a 'nervous break-down': 'terrific heartbeat and hot and cold sweat, thought I could die'. Her family rallied round and she focused on appreciating what she still had, noticing how clever and pretty Christine was becoming. Dr Löser cancelled his visit on Sunday but came the next day and had a 'tonic' effect: 'Very charming. Suggests rest until July in any case.'

As she recovered physically, Hilde found that she felt more depressed. She spent the rest of February and March writing her novel, which she often thought very bad, and putting away the baby things in mothballs. During this period the bombing continued intermittently, and people were sleeping in Wimbledon Station. Returning at night, Hilde and Peter climbed over outstretched legs, inadequately covered by rough blankets, crawling children who had escaped from their mothers, and snoring old men; 'scenes from Dante's Inferno'.

Hilde was lonely in Wimbledon, where they had very few friends, and she increasingly felt as if she had no real identity. She was grateful for the support of the community:

the goodwill, the consideration and helpfulness of all around us, from our neighbours in Wimbledon Close to the housewives with whom I stood in line for hours at the shops of the beefy butcher Higgins and the popeyed fishmonger Burgess.

But despite the solidarity between strangers in a time of emergency, there was always a distinction between the British and their foreign guests. 'As Great Britain had always described itself as "*of* Europe" but not "*in* Europe", so we were well aware that we were "*in* England" but not "*of* England".' Since October 1941 Hilde and Peter had been naturalised as British citizens, but there were still obstacles to full integration. When their home help Mrs Sims left in November 1941 she had told Hilde dismissively that sometimes in their house she felt she was not in England, but in a foreign country. In December 1942 Peter was informed that as a German he could not be elected to the managing committee of English PEN, despite the fact that everyone wanted him to be.

Now that the height of the Blitz and the euphoria of its aftermath was over, Hilde had more time to miss Vienna. In her 1975 exile essay she wrote that it was possible to avoid homesickness when they were enduring the misery of the bombing, but that as soon as the danger abated and the inhospitable circumstances became halfway tolerable, the gnawing pain returned.

> The vision of home broke over us in several simultaneous impressions, comparable to a collage: Viennese vistas, a curved shape, a faded shop sign which says 'Saint Florian's', a lush and green meadow in the Salzburg countryside covered in dandelions, a bright Sunday morning in the hall of the musical society. Or a single, overpowering moment, a piece of the past captured: summer heat in one of the gardens in Döbling, complete silence, the smell of food from the house, and a feeling of infinite comfort, being at one with one's existence in this world.

Hilde Spiel described in her autobiography how the memories of home, which she suppressed with difficulty, kept breaking out despite her efforts to embrace life in London. She dreamed of Heiligenstadt, of walks in the Prater with their dog Diemo, long dead, and of the contours of the Salesianerkirche on the Rennweg. Talking to her mother she reminisced happily about forgotten figures in their suburb of Döbling. Their laughter stopped abruptly when they wondered what fate had befallen these former acquaintances.

The homesickness was partly assuaged by contact with Austrian friends; notably with Hans Flesch-Brunningen, who was still a frequent visitor to Wimbledon, and sometimes took Hilde to the theatre in town. 'I was so pleased to see him,' she noted in her diary when he visited her in hospital after her operation. Writing *The Fruits of Prosperity* also enabled Hilde to take nostalgic forays into Vienna. It involved a lot of research, and she had some of her happiest London afternoons that spring in the domed reading room of the British Museum. Here she sat under a green reading lamp, suspended in space and time, with reference books heaped up on the desk. She appreciated the community of readers who surrounded her, some of whom were now her friends.

Courtesy of Christine Shuttleworth

Hilde Spiel, *c.* 1943

After the stillbirth of their baby, relations between Hilde and Peter had become strained and volatile. Perhaps as a result of this, *The Fruits of Prosperity* had become a book about a difficult marriage. Spiel's hero Milan, settled in Vienna, falls in love with Stephanie, the beautiful daughter of his mentor and patron Carl Benedict. Stephanie herself is in love with Andreas, a brilliant but feckless composer whom her father sensibly refuses to allow her to marry on the grounds that he is too self-obsessed to make her happy. Desperate with longing, Stephanie arrives one day at Andreas's studio where she finds him in the arms of a rival, who advises her cattily to go home and get married.

Returning home, swooning with distress, she is greeted by Milan, whom Herr Benedict has invited to move into the family home. After several months in which Milan climbs the ladder at Herr Benedict's firm and proves himself a worthy son-in-law, Stephanie succumbs to Milan's adoration and agrees to a loveless marriage. At first, even when Stephanie lies crying beside him on their wedding night, Milan is so delighted to have her in his bed that he does not mind her coldness, which he believes will pass. Gradually, however, he succumbs to the (reasonably chaste) embraces of loose girls in rowdy bars and then, on his visit to England, embarks on an ardent affair with a young English-woman called Queenie Lorrimer. Here at last is mutual passion; electricity and lightning spring between them when they touch; together they lose sight of past and future; 'so long as they remained entwined, joined by skin and hair, they were united by one flame'.

Meanwhile Stephanie, driven to desperation by loneliness, has visited Andreas, who is delighted to see her and takes her immediately to bed. The experience is perfunctory but salutary. She realises at last that she has been idealising him for all these years; he is no longer the man she once loved. Where her faith in Andreas ends, her trust in her husband begins. She writes an impassioned letter to Milan, begging him to forgive her and come home and promising a new life. Abandoning Queenie without even an explanation, Milan returns to his wife, who tells him about her unsatisfactory encounter with Andreas. Jealousy and possessiveness push Milan into outraged madness. Forgetting who she is, he hits her wildly, and then makes passionately violent love

to her. It does not surprise him that for the first time the moment of
lust is shared. Now calmer, Milan tells her that he has been unfaithful
as well. 'Then why did you hit me?' Stephanie asks. Milan laughs.
'Because I am a man, and you are a woman.' They are both satisfied
with the explanation. 'If they could only love each other always as they
had that night, they would need only this simple law and would spend
the rest of their days in satisfied happiness.'

When Hilde was first introduced to Peter's mother in Germany, she
was surprised when the older woman took it upon herself in a reserved
but not unfriendly manner to warn her future daughter-in-law against
Peter's violent fits of anger and changeable moods. This was, she
explained, the unaccountable temperament he had inherited from his
Baltic forebears. Peter himself saw his character in similar terms; it
could not be changed. At first, in the excitement of love and of their
new English life, imbued with confidence as a much-desired and
passionate woman, Hilde had found his fits of temper relatively easy to
deal with. Now, it was becoming harder; she had become vulnerable
and tearful and she wanted to be reassured, looked after and adored.

In *The Fruits of Prosperity* Hilde Spiel seems to be in part reassuring
herself that violent outbursts can be compatible with adoration; that,
indeed, such outbursts are necessary proofs of love. Stephanie and Milan's
marriage is weakest when it lacks passion; when she is too detached to be
tempestuous. Hilde suggests that passion can be restored through a crisis,
and that violence is preferable to emotional stultification. She was prepared
to put up with angry scenes for the sake of that emotional engagement
with life that the war was in danger of eliminating altogether.

In April 1943 Hilde and Christine were evacuated to Cambridge to
escape the renewed sporadic bombing attacks. While Hilde was away,
the Wimbledon flat was burgled, and all Hilde's jewellery was stolen.
This jewellery was all that she had left of her earlier, grander life in
Vienna, and she was devastated. 'I should have thought we'd had quite
enough bad luck already,' she wrote to Peter on 30 April. 'This burglary
is dreadful. I am quite desperate about it – all I ever had! I was so
unhappy last night I couldn't sleep at all.' Like Rose Macaulay, hopelessly listing the books she had lost, Hilde sent Peter a list of her lost

jewellery. There was his aunt Olga's sword-brooch, a Chinese silver ring, a golden necklace with a heartshaped medallion in which there had been a photograph of Christine, a pair of silver earrings, a silver chain with a coin, a small garnet pendant . . . Peter replied sympathetically, promising to replace what he could and sending her war news and literary essays cut from the newspaper. These included an essay by Arthur Koestler, another émigré writer who had entered literary London with rather more success than Hilde and Peter and whose novel Hilde had read earlier in the year. Hilde wrote back, grateful to Peter for his sympathy about her jewellery:

> The vision of my beloved golden brooch etc is still before me and makes me sad. It is sweet of you to want to replace what you can. If only jewellery weren't so damn expensive now. Anyhow, if I could have a little every few months, I should be so grateful. It is so dreadful to have to give up glamour.

She was also appreciative of the newspaper cuttings, and wished he was there to discuss them. But the literary news reminded her how cut off they were from present-day life, and she urged Peter to do what he could to change this. They could go to lectures together, and try to get the *Horizon* crowd or Koestler himself to meet in town for a meal. 'Now, for instance, one might write to him. If you did, you wouldn't get a rebuff, I'm sure.'

Throughout 1943 Peter de Mendelssohn was writing columns for the *New Statesman* about the political situation in the Far East; increasingly, he was becoming preoccupied with politics. In *The Heat of the Day* Bowen observes that at this stage of events 'war's being global meant it ran off the edges of maps'; what was happening in Japan 'was heard of but never grasped in London'. Peter was attempting to rectify this situation, but now his wife urged him to focus more of his attention on literature and on life itself.

> I have a feeling that politics play too great a part in your thoughts, held against the fact that you do not really believe in a cause, and are not

really vitally interested in the betterment of mankind. Why not recognise this and devote one's free thought to the things one believes in, like art, and literature, and the importance of emotions.

Aged thirty-one, Hilde Spiel was wondering how best to live. In the context of a demoralising war in which even her few glittery trinkets had been taken away, was it still possible to have an intense emotional life and to commit herself to literature and the life of the mind? Need looking after Christine preclude her from playing a part in the current of her time?

In *The Fruits of Prosperity* Milan, having fathered a second child with Stephanie, tries to persuade her to leave the lax morals and sullied air of the city and to move back with him to rural Croatia. Stephanie knows that it would be the right thing to do. Despite their new-found happiness, they are becoming corrupted by the city. At masked dances they flirt dangerously with other partners; after one such dance their sleep is filled with visions of enticing danger and iniquitous love. In the countryside, Milan would be happier, the children would be healthier, and even Stephanie's mother would be more contented. But what joy would there be? She likes going to balls, to opera houses, to dances where handsome men take her in their arms. She likes sitting in front of the mirror preparing for a glamorous evening, placing a flower in her hair. They decide to compromise, and live in a garden suburb of Vienna not unlike Wimbledon. Stephanie is happy but she wonders if she has betrayed something important to her, which had been the goal and true purpose of her life. Meanwhile Milan is fearful; he worries that his happiness rests on too fragile a basis. And their anxieties prove prescient. They go to a crowded concert where a fire breaks out. The smoke causes Stephanie to faint, but Milan manages to revive her by carrying her onto the balcony. He urges her to jump; she is too frightened; they make their way to the stairs, where they end up suffocating. As Milan dies he dreams of the clear streams and lakes of Croatia. The novel ends with a vision of Milan engulfed in his native river.

Stephanie has to decide between the health of her children and her own mental survival. In the end it is clear that she should have agreed to move to Croatia. The Manichean fire that ends their lives is symbolic of excess; of a city doomed to consume itself in fire. But Hilde Spiel, writing the novel from the fresh air and boredom of Wimbledon and Cambridge, was not wholly convinced. She, like Stephanie, longed to sit in front of a mirror and put a flower in her hair; she longed for attention, for glamour and for emotional intensity. Surely it was time to allow a little bit of the excitement they had lost to seep back into their new life in England.

In February 1943 Henry Yorke went with his new lover Mary Keene to stay with the painter Matthew Smith at Stratford St Mary in Suffolk, where Matthew had rented a house called Weavers. Writing to thank Matthew at the end of the month, Henry said that he had gone home 'refreshed (not quite as a lion, those halcyon days are past, or is it an eagle, but rather as a donkey that has been allowed to drop its burden) back home to the endless round of war, scrubbing floors one moment and directing the production of cordite plants the next'.

He was refreshed by the countryside, by the break from both office and fire station, by the escape from upper-class life into bohemia, by Matthew, whose work he would increasingly admire, and, most of all, by Mary. 'To Mary To Mary To Mary' Henry wrote in a copy of *Party Going* which he had inscribed to her at the end of January. Mary was twenty-one years old, at once impetuous, confident and vulnerable, with enormous grey eyes, creamy skin, long blonde hair and a metal lower leg. She was branded by the poet Ruthven Todd as 'the most beautiful English girl I ever saw' and later claimed to be commonly known as one of the two most beautiful women in London. In 1939, aged seventeen, she had embarked on an affair with Louis MacNeice, who a few years later described her in his poem 'The Kingdom':

> Too large in feature for a world of cuties,
> Too sculptured for a cocktail lounge flirtation,
> This girl is almost awkward, carrying off

The lintel of convention on her shoulders,
A Doric river-goddess with a pitcher
Of ice-cold wild emotions. Pour them where she will
The pitcher will not empty . . .
    . . . Vitality and fear
Are marbled in her eyes, from hour to hour
She changes like the sky – one moment is so gay
That all her words are laughter but the next
Moment she is puzzled, her own Sphinx,
Made granite by her destiny . . .

© Ralph Keene, courtesy of Alice Kadel

Mary Keene, *c.* 1943

Bewitched, MacNeice wrote to Mary during the affair that 'in the centre of the most haunting chaos . . . it is still possible to think of you, the star, in the heart of the whirling nebulae. I do.' Now, just when he had begun to be engulfed by the dreariness of the war, it was Henry

Yorke's turn to think of her, and he did too, as he began the novel that would be called *Loving*.

Set in an Anglo-Irish Big House in wartime neutral Ireland, *Loving* tells the story of the day-to-day life of a group of servants and their employers, working, dancing, stealing, worrying and, of course, loving. Although the war presses in on the house, with the servants wondering if they should go back to England and enlist, the Irish setting allowed Yorke and his characters to escape to the same heady fairy tale world that had greeted Bowen when she arrived in Ireland the previous summer. Yorke later said that he was given the idea for the book by a manservant in the fire service who told him that he had once asked an elderly butler what he liked most in the world. For Yorke the reply evoked a whole setting. 'Lying in bed on a summer morning, with the window open, listening to the church bells, eating buttered toast with cunty fingers.' The anecdote captures the tone of the novel, which is both carelessly sexual and extravagantly sensuous. Written in a spare prose style that can whirl lyrically into passages of thick, languorous beauty, it is certainly the most loving of Yorke's novels, and at the heart of it is Edith, a young English serving-girl with creamy skin and huge eyes. Edith is universally adored: by the butler, Charlie Raunce, whom she eventually marries; by his young assistant, Albert, who gazes at her from a love-struck distance; by the children of the house, who will do anything for her; by Kate, her friend and fellow-servant, who at one stage undresses her and massages her back; and most of all by the narrator himself, who follows her around with the same amazed infatuation as his characters.

At the opening of the book Edith sticks a peacock feather 'above her lovely head'; a few pages later Raunce appraises 'the dark eyes she sported which were warm and yet caught the light like plums dipped in cold water'. Naked to the waist in the bedroom she shares with Kate, Edith's skin shines 'like the flower of white lilac under leaves'. When she opens the window and gazes out into the morning, the soft bright light strikes her 'dazzled dazzling eyes'.

Watching Edith watching the fire, Raunce is mesmerised as 'her great eyes become invested with rose incandescence that was soft and soft and soft'. 'I never seen anything like your eyes they're so 'uge not in all my experience' he says later, falling for her, gradually and then more precipitously, as the novel progresses. Early on, Edith and Kate are cleaning the house's old ballroom when they decide to turn on the gramophone and dance, 'wheeling wheeling in each other's arms' around the mirrored room. Raunce comes in and sees 'two girls, minute in purple, dancing multiplied to eternity in these trembling pears of glass'. He tells them off but is unable to take his eyes off Edith; from this point he becomes more and more enraptured. 'I could fall for you in a big way,' he finally says, adding as he sees her back stiffen with attention, 'for the matter of that I have.' 'I didn't realise I could love anyone the way I love you,' he declares once they have begun to talk of marriage. 'I thought I'd lived too long.'

For her part Edith often thwarts easy adoration with her matter-of-factness. She is sometimes hard, and often surprisingly careless about ordinary morals. Her moment of triumph comes when she spots her mistress in bed with her lover and spreads the gossip, proprietorially and triumphantly. She plunders peahen eggs from her employers and then even briefly steals one of her mistress's rings, wondering about never returning it. 'I'd sell it an' save the money for a rainy day,' she claims. She often greets Raunce's devotion with impatient humour. 'You tell that to them all Charley' is all she says to his first declaration of love. But at this point her words are belied by 'the excitement and scorn which seemed to blaze from her'. And throughout she has moments of loving sensuality that shift the whole register of the novel into a passionate seriousness not often found in Yorke's work. 'I love Charley Raunce I love 'im I love 'im so there,' she tells Kate. 'I could open the veins of my right arm for that man.' Gradually she becomes more open with Raunce, looking 'full at him seriously with her raving beauty'. She assures him that the twenty-year age gap is unimportant. 'I like a man that's a man and not a lad.' And when he kisses her she kisses him back with such passion, 'all of her hard as a board', that he flops back flabbergasted, 'having caught a glimpse of what was in her waiting for him'.

By the time she met Henry Yorke, Mary Keene was not in fact a cockney like Edith, though she had been born in extreme poverty in east London and raised partly in an orphanage and partly by her violent mother. Aged eleven she was sent out to buy paraffin and was knocked down by a lorry, losing her right foot. She was given a metal lower leg and sent to a school for the disabled, where most of the other children were mentally handicapped and Mary was barely educated. As a teenager she ran away from home, working in sewing sweatshops and frequently going hungry. Then, aged sixteen, she began modelling for art students including Lucian Freud at Cedric Morris's art school in Dedham. From this point she moved into a bohemian world of artists and writers. She lost her East End accent when she decided it sounded ugly and searched for a grander and freer world. This seemed to be offered by Ralph ('Bunny') Keene, whom she met in a nightclub during a wartime police raid and married in January 1941. He had been an art dealer and had now started a film company. The marriage was initially passionate but both Mary and Bunny had other lovers from the start.

Through Bunny, Mary met Matthew Smith, who had been represented by the art gallery Bunny worked at in the 1930s. Matthew began a series of drawings and paintings of Mary that he would continue for the rest of his life. Matthew Smith was an instinctive and tactile painter and painting Mary was a sensual act. These paintings, in which he coated the body of the woman he desired in thick swathes of bright, unexpected colours, show Mary as angry and vulnerable, conscious of her own beauty but diffident in its display. The Mary of Matthew's pictures is the sphinx of MacNeice's poem, with vitality and fear marbled in her eyes, endowed with the huge glistening eyes of Henry Yorke's heroine. By this point Matthew was an extremely successful painter whose own marriage had been broken up by a series of affairs with young female muses. He was in his sixties and initially intended Mary for his son Dermot. But after he had taken Mary and Dermot out for an introductory tea he caught hold of Mary's hair as it blew out behind her and uttered a snarl of desire. In fact Mary was more interested in father than son; her proclivities, like Edith's, were for men and not lads. But her attention was distracted from Matthew when Augustus John's daughter introduced her to Dig Yorke, who then introduced Mary to her husband.

If Mary was not actually a cockney, she was certainly not from the Yorkes' own set, and she would have had no more qualms than Edith about stealing a ring. During the weekend with Henry and Matthew at Stratford St Mary, she stole nightdresses from Ida Hughes Stanton, the owner of the house Matthew was renting. Returning and finding them gone, Stanton summoned the police, who sent Mary for trial; she was put on probation. 'You know of course that I do not *approve* of what Mary did and I feel bruised in every direction,' Matthew assured his hostess, pleading with her to drop the charges. Meanwhile Henry sent Mary an amused telegram suggesting that she might like to read *Moll Flanders*, Daniel Defoe's tale of a loveable, thieving harlot. 'I have been guessing all this time especially since your telegram, how you have taken the latest news of me,' Mary replied. She had asked Matthew to tell her the story of *Moll Flanders* and the tale had made her blood boil. 'I can see no reason for reading it at the moment. It seems curious to me that you should have taken it in such a literary way. I am very upset, but not because I stole. Do come and see me as soon as you come back.'

The relationship between Henry and Mary was no less difficult than the relationship between Raunce and Edith, and was considerably more tempestuous. 'I have a great hangover, and a huge grazed bruise on my forehead and a little black eye all because of a great dramatic meeting with beloved Henry,' Mary wrote to Matthew at this time. 'It was so madly gay, and we talked a great deal about you.' But it was serious, on both sides. For his part Henry seems to have lost interest both in drink and in other women. He wrote to Rosamond Lehmann later that spring that he was busy working on producing the goods ordered by Russia – hard work which he found was slowly killing him. 'Believe it or not I don't drink at all now, practically. Though I still make a feeble pass at the youngest girls, like an old fool of 80.' This is of course typically disingenuous. For one girl at least, the passes were not feeble. 'Darling, darling, darling', Henry began his letters to that 'river-goddess with a pitcher / Of ice-cold wild emotions'. 'Pour them where she will', MacNeice had written, 'The pitcher will not empty'; Henry Yorke had begun to drink from the pitcher and he was finding it compulsive.

12

'Alas, what hate everywhere'

Graham Greene, Rose Macaulay, Henry Yorke and Hilde Spiel, March 1943–May 1944

On 1 March 1943 Graham Greene was pleased to arrive in London after over a year away. Africa had been an exciting experience, but he had quickly become infuriated with the English abroad. Two months earlier he had written to his brother Raymond suggesting that Churchill's reference to the 'majestic' services of West Africa in the war had been ironic.

> As far as I can see their contribution has been confined to cowardice, complacency, inefficiency, illiteracy and thirst . . . Of course one is referring only to the Europeans. The Africans at least contribute grace.

He was also still not sure that he was actively taking part in the war. The previous July he had admitted to envying Raymond's sense of doing a useful job. Graham himself was beginning to suspect that he would be more valuable in a munitions factory, and was sure he would prefer 'any factory town to this colonial slum'. In fact, Sierra Leone was crucially positioned, but Greene's doubts about his own strategic importance were realistic. Later Kim Philby, then Greene's boss and already (though not to Greene's knowledge) a Russian counterspy, recalled Greene's doubts about the relevance of his work in Freetown to the war against

Hitler and was inclined to agree. Certainly, Montgomery's success in North Africa had made West Africa less critical.

When his father died in November 1942, Greene felt guilty about being away from England at the time when his mother needed him most. 'I feel it was rather a selfish act taking on a job abroad at this time, and I ought to have been home,' he wrote to her. Later, he recalled how, learning about his father's death in two telegrams delivered in the wrong order (the first about his death, the second about his illness), he felt unexpected misery and remorse. He arranged for mass to be said for the dead man every day by an Irish priest in a West African church, although he thought that if his father knew he would regard the gesture with the same kindly amusement that he regarded the whole of Graham's Catholicism. Greene paid for the mass by giving the priest a sack of rice to distribute amongst his poorer parishioners.

In January 1943, hearing that London was being bombed again, Greene decided that it was time to come home. 'I felt sick in the stomach when I heard the Germans had started on London again,' he told his mother; 'I feel I'd be of much more use back wardening. One feels out of it in this colony of escapists with their huge drinking parties and their complete unconsciousness of what war is like.' He had been hoping that they might be bombed in Africa too, but the hope had faded. His desire to return was partly a wish to be of use, but it was primarily his usual longing to experience the war. Writing to Raymond after their father's death, Graham admitted that the prospect of immediate peace would fill him with gloom. War had 'not yet touched enough people of ours to alter the world'. Luckily, Kim Philby considered that Greene could be more usefully employed in London than in Freetown. He later recalled that 'after the North African landings, SIS interest in West Africa waned, and we left MI5 in possession of the field'.

Returning to London, Greene was delighted to be reunited with Dorothy Glover. He had missed her while in Africa, where he was uneasily jealous of his brother Hugh, who took Dorothy into his own bed in Graham's absence. In the summer of 1942 Hugh wrote to Graham about an illustrated guide to the sights of London he was planning to write with Dorothy. 'Doll wrote to me about the bawdy book she's planning with you,' Graham replied. Wistfully, he asked his brother for details about his lover – 'I wish you'd told me how she was looking, whether she seemed well, could down her pint of Irish as readily, etc' – and asked him to send her his love. Hugh tried to placate Graham by sending a girl of his own in his brother's direction. Graham promised to look out for her but said that he did not 'feel inclined really for a playmate', adding that 'life is quite complicated enough as it is, and I'm still in love!' Normally he would be grateful for his brother's 'tasteful and reliable pimping', but he had become terribly 'one-idea'd'. In fact, being 'one idea'd' did not preclude him asking colleagues for directions to the nearest brothel or for help in procuring 'French letters' (one intelligence officer collected eleven condoms for Graham from passengers on the boat to Freetown). But emotionally, two women were enough. That October, writing to console his sister Elisabeth about her own relationship difficulties, he told her that

> things can be hell, I know. The peculiar form it's taken with me the last
> four years has been in loving two people as equally as makes no differ-
> ence, the awful struggle to have your cake and eat it, the inability to
> throw over one for the sake of the other.

Vivien was now aware of the relationship with Dorothy but had hoped that the passion would have cooled during Graham's extended absence. In fact, the affair was now flourishing and it was the marriage that was cooling. While Graham was in Africa, Vivien wrote to him declaring and demanding love but trying not to overwhelm him. 'Won't it be nice when we don't have to look forward to weekends again but all live together,' she wrote in March 1942, wondering if after so much time alone 'family life is a bit claustrophobic' and urging him to 'think of the nice home made bread and the cubs thirsting for information'. That April she was disturbed by a letter from Graham in which he mentioned missing his wife's intelligence. 'I don't altogether fancy that,' she responded, informing him that she felt 'suspicious and prick eared', as she would rather be attractive than intelligent. A week later, she told him despondently that she was 'so VERY tired of being on my own and having no companion and being basketless', wondering if he missed his cat and thinking sadly that when he was in tropical latitudes a cat must sound rather hot and furry.

Graham meant it when he told Vivien that he respected her intellectually. He relied on her to make literary decisions for him in his absence, instructing his agent to run past Vivien the final draft of the script for a projected play of *Brighton Rock*. Earlier in the war, he had taken Vivien's advice in entitling his novel *The Power and the Glory*. But increasingly, Vivien was losing her hold over him, and his letters to his wife after his return were more apologetic than impassioned. In April 1943, arriving for the night at the King's Arms during a visit to Oxford, Graham wrote to Vivien assuring her that, contrary to appearances, he loved her and wanted to make her happy. 'You are the best, the most dear person I've ever known,' he wrote; 'Life is sometimes so beastly that one wishes one were dead, and I go to places like Mexico and Freetown in a half hope that everything will be finished,' but each time he came back and asked her 'to like me and go on liking me'. He had never wanted to be old, but with Vivien he could be old and happy. Indeed, sometimes he wished he could twist a ring and skip twenty years and be old with her, 'with all this ragged business over'.

The ragged business in question was sexual desire, and it was far from over. Throughout his life, Greene was pulled between the competing forces of pity and desire. He was unusually susceptible to pity. In *The Heart of the Matter* Scobie finds that it is when his wife is least attractive that he loves her most, and that at these times 'pity and responsibility reached the intensity of a passion'. For Greene himself, pity incited the kind of love that made him write letters like this one to his wife. He could declare love with a certainty that he did not habitually feel because, like Scobie, he believed that 'in human relations kindness and ties are worth a thousand truths', and because at that moment, touched by the passion of pity, he genuinely believed in the force of his own desire to make Vivien happy.

Ultimately, in *The Heart of the Matter*, pity is enough to motivate Scobie to kill himself in the hope that his death will leave his wife and mistress happier than he is able to make them by being alive. 'One forgets the dead quickly; one doesn't wonder about the dead – what is he doing now, who is he with?' Graham ended the letter written in the King's Arms by assuring Vivien that, although he had told a lot of lies in the last thirty-eight years, one thing was true: 'I hate life and I hate myself and I love you.' The self-hatred and the love were strong enough to make him declare the following month that life would have been better for Vivien if he had 'been torpedoed or plane crashed because a novel sort of vitality would have been handed over to you after the first shock'. But unlike Scobie, Graham was not about to commit suicide for the sake of his wife. There was still the thrill of being alive when the glass broke in the morning and as pity for Vivien gave way to desire for Dorothy.

Since his return to London, Greene had been working at the SIS headquarters in St Albans, where he was the second in command in the department responsible for overseeing the agents in neutral Portugal. After his boss Charles de Salis was moved to Lisbon in August, Greene took over as the head of the London desk. Here he was partially responsible for Malcolm Muggeridge, who was the SIS man in Mozambique and had been sent to Lisbon in 1942. Like Ireland, Portugal had been neutral since the start of the war. At this point it was a hub for both Allied and Axis intelligence. British and American agents used Lisbon as a departure point for Africa and the Germans went to Lisbon to collect information about Allied Atlantic convoys.

In the early years of the war, Portuguese officials had tended to collaborate with the Axis powers, turning a blind eye to the clandestine German radio stations operating out of Lisbon. But by the time that Greene began working in London the Portuguese government was starting to recognise the need to collaborate with the Allies, given that they were looking increasingly likely to win the war. Under Greene's leadership, SIS succeeded in convincing Portugal's leader, Antonio de Oliviera Salazar, of the extent of Portuguese collaboration and persuaded him to close down the German radio stations and informer networks. The chief tasks for Greene's staff were to gather enemy information and to disseminate false information back. Material came in from agents in Portugal and from the decodings of cryptographers. Since 1940 the British intelligence services had been breaking the codes produced by the German Enigma machine, one of their most secret systems of communications, gaining information which would prove extremely valuable in several areas of the war.

Greene did not visit Portugal during the war, but Malcolm Muggeridge had found on his 1942 visit that it seemed more like going to another world than simply going abroad: 'Lisbon, with all its lights, seemed after two years of blackout like a celestial vision when we landed there by night.' He wandered around the streets, marvelling at the shops and at the extensive menus in the restaurants, wondering if this was how the British would live again one day.

This was the sight that met Rose Macaulay's eyes in March 1943, when she embarked on the trip to Portugal that she had longed to make immediately after Gerald O'Donovan's death. She had endured a miserable winter. She was consumed by all the desperate 'aching want' of Gerald that she had attributed to Kitty in *What Not*, but this time without the knowledge that he still existed elsewhere. She had now given up ambulance driving and, like other Londoners during the lull, was demoralised by the disjunction between her own comparative safety and the savagery of the war news coming in from Europe, North Africa and the Far East. Hearing about the battles and bombing taking place offstage, Macaulay oscillated between incomprehending indifference and visceral horror. James Lees-Milne, meeting Macaulay for the first time in January, noted in his diary that his first impression was of 'a very thin, desiccated figure in a masculine tam-o-shanter, briskly entering the room'.

Now Macaulay spent two months in Lisbon, relishing the vibrant colours and smells after the mutedness of wartime London, appreciating the freedom from war, and distracting herself from sadness with work. The result was a compendious account of travellers who had visited Portugal throughout the ages. Like many of Rose Macaulay's non-fiction books, it was longer than anticipated – so much so that *They Went to Portugal* (1946) would eventually be followed, after her death, by the posthumously edited collection *They Went to Portugal Too*

(1990). Looking back on her Portuguese labours, Macaulay told Hamilton Johnson that the book 'entailed a good deal of hard work and research'; part of an attempt to 'deaden' her unhappiness.

But Lisbon was more than just an excuse for stultifying labours. For Macaulay, the city enabled a slow renewing of life. Unlike Greene in Africa, Macaulay had no compunction about exiting the war, and she was happy to immerse herself in the new culture. While in Lisbon, she wrote an article called 'Lisbon day: London day', comparing life in the two cities. Here she enthuses that you would know blindfolded at any hour of the day or night which of the two capitals you were in. The voices, the smell, the whole rhythm of the city is different. 'Open your eyes, and the cities might be two planets.' It is clear which planet she would rather be on. 'The one has light, colour, radiance, pale luminousness, a precipitous slant, a lilting jangle and blare of noise; the other darkly and impersonally hums, waves of sound well and die, as if winds beat on a forest.' She contrasts the wail of trams with the howl of sirens at home. And where the easiest way to get around wartime London is on a bicycle, in Lisbon it is pleasanter to walk, because the walker is 'confronted at each turn of the street by a merge of delicate colours, golden ochre, rose pink, terra cotta, the clear deep delphinium blue which is the blue of Lisbon'.

Macaulay was entranced by the beauty of Portugal. In an article on the political situation there called 'A Happy Neutral', Macaulay praised the Portuguese for their lack of war-consciousness, commending them for preserving their own neutrality and peace. 'Pleasure in this fact communicates itself through the clear and sunlit air of Lisbon, seeming to heighten the gay, pale colours of the city.' She ended by describing Portugal itself as gloriously neutral: 'that is its gift from the gods and to Europe; a gift never, one hopes, to be snatched away'. This was an optimistically rose-tinted view; Greene's agents had encountered a more corrupt version of neutrality. But certainly, neutrality was Portugal's gift to Macaulay herself. This 1943 trip began a gradual process of renewal that would continue in peacetime, as she clambered, methodically and urgently, around the ruins of the post-war world.

Away from neutral Portugal, the war was proceeding dramatically. As a result of the decrypting of the German naval Enigma codes, the Battle of the Atlantic had turned in favour of the Allies. They could now plot German U-boat courses and had increased the number of warships protecting shipping convoys. In the first half of May the British and Americans also achieved a conclusive victory in the Middle East. Tunis fell to the British and Bizerta to the Americans, and by 12 May the Germans and Italians had surrendered. The Allies took 250,000 prisoners, with only 650 men from the Axis armies escaping. 'We cannot doubt that Stalingrad and Tunisia are the greatest military disasters that have ever befallen Germany in all the wars she has made, and they are many,' Churchill informed the House of Commons in June. That summer saw the fall of Mussolini, who was voted out by the Fascist Grand Council on 24 July. The new Italian leader, Marshal Pietro Badoglio, began negotiations with the Allies for peace and then on 8 September Italy capitulated. Hilde Spiel reported that she was in 'best spirits' as a result; 'continent somehow comes nearer'. Meanwhile the Russians were gaining ground in the Soviet Union, recapturing Kharkov at the start of August.

At the same time, Britain was carrying out a series of brutal bombing attacks in Germany, which Spiel was finding difficult to take in. 'If they shorten the war, they're inevitable,' she wrote in her diary in May 1943, 'but one shudders at the amount of human suffering.' This major bombing offensive had been in preparation for two years. In a speech to the London County Council in July 1941 Churchill announced that it was time 'the Germans should be made to suffer in their own homeland and cities something of the torment they have twice in our lifetime let loose upon their neighbours and upon the world'. At the start of 1942 Arthur Harris, the newly appointed Commander-in-Chief of Bomber Command, was told to focus his operations on destroying the morale of the enemy civilian population. Prior to this, British bombers had approached the country singly and a large proportion of them had been successfully intercepted by German fighters, using the efficient German radar system. Now Harris decided to send in streams of several hundred bombers at once, swamping the German defences. The result was the bombing of Lübeck and Rostock in March and April and then the first '1000-bomber-raid' on Cologne in May, destroying almost 13,000 buildings. Heavy raids continued into 1943, and were now directed at Italy as well as Germany. A British night raid on Wuppertal on 29 May resulted in a firestorm which engulfed the entire city, killing 2,450 civilians. In June British bombers dropped fifteen thousand tons of bombs on Germany in twenty nights. The German defences were now severely depleted but Hitler refused to release extra aircraft to protect Germany, preferring to meet terror with terror and focus the Luftwaffe's efforts on attacking Britain. On 24 July, British bombers set out to raid Hamburg in the first night of a major mission brutally named Operation Gomorrah. They dropped 2,300 tons of high explosive and incendiary bombs in the first few hours, which was as much as the combined tonnage of the five heaviest German raids on London. And they continued to pound Hamburg for three more successive nights, culminating in a final savage attack during the night of 27 July when 2,326 tons of primarily incendiary bombs were dropped within an hour. This created a terrifying firestorm across the city, in the centre of which a hurricane-style wind uprooted trees and asphyxiated people. Eight square miles of Hamburg were burned out, leaving 37,000 German civilians dead; a figure almost equivalent to the total of British civilian deaths for the whole of the Blitz.

Amid the unreal green of springtime Wimbledon, Spiel tried to imagine the German rubble, aware that she had never seen anything like this scale of destruction. As always, she was in an ambivalent position. As someone who had given up everything for the sake of freedom, she had even less sympathy than her British contemporaries for the Germans who had stayed behind. But she was also more painfully aware than most Londoners of the physical reality of the cities that were being destroyed and aware, too, that she and her husband would now have no home to which to return.

Spiel was not alone in her ambivalence about the raids on Germany. In a survey at the start of 1944 only six out of ten Londoners gave 'unqualified approval' to the British bombing campaign of the previous year. There was also a pacifist campaign against the bombing policy, spearheaded by the Bishop of Chichester and the writer Vera Brittain among others. Rose Macaulay wrote to her cousin Jean in July 1943 complaining about 'this horrible smashing and bombing', glad to hear about the protests. 'What kind of a shambles will Europe be after this war?' she asked. 'And, alas, what hate everywhere.' Like Spiel, Macaulay was finding the news difficult to take in, and finding it hard to focus on ordinary life. She was keeping busy writing her book about Portugal but was feeling extremely weak. Meeting her at a lecture shortly after her return from Portugal, James Lees-Milne observed that 'she must be an unhappy woman', stating derisively that she had the 'dried-up look of the unenjoyed'. Certainly, she was grief-stricken and worn out, and continued to feel weak as the summer advanced. 'At present I feel indescribably exhausted,' she told Jean in August, 'as if at the bottom of a deep pit, and every movement like a climb up a steep bank. Tired heart, my doctor says . . . It is collapsing, and makes one very lethargic and inclined to despair.' Jean wrote back anxiously and Rose rallied, insisting that she had exaggerated. 'Heart not "collapsing" (which implies getting worse) but merely "slightly collapsed" – my doctor's expression, and only, I take it, means tired.' It would right itself in time, with rest and dietary improvement.

By September Macaulay was indeed starting to feel restored and on 16 September she had lunch with Graham Greene at Boulestin's in Covent Garden. This was a treat for both of them. Boulestin's was the most expensive as well as one of the most sumptuously decorated restaurants in London; the province of the writer, interior designer and chef Marcel Boulestin, who for the past twenty years had been writing bestselling French cookery books and even appearing on the television, attempting to convert the British to good food. Cecil Beaton once described the restaurant as the prettiest in London; the walls were painted with circus-themed murals, the windows were hung with patterned yellow brocade curtains, and the room was lit by hanging silk balloon lights. Entering the restaurant from the bomb-damaged London streets, Macaulay and Greene settled down amid the cushioning opulence to enjoy rather better food than wartime rationing usually allowed for. It was an appropriate setting in which to talk about

Portugal, and Macaulay was delighted to have a chance to discuss the country with an expert. She was also stimulated by Greene's energy; now that he was back in London, he was enjoying the war again, and his high spirits were invigorating.

Greene was now busy running the Portuguese desk at SIS and was also prospering as a writer. *The Ministry of Fear* had been published shortly before Henry Yorke's *Caught* in June. Both books received largely positive reviews and promising sales. *Caught* in particular was praised for its honesty. Stephen Spender, asked to comment on the book as a fellow fireman, found it was 'too sour and bitter and gossipy' but did think that it was genuine and that anyone who had experienced life in the fire service would agree. Looking back on it, John Lehmann thought that '*Caught* mirrored, with something like genius, the compound of tragedy and comedy that was the truth of the war, the heroism that showed itself in spite of an extreme distaste for and distrust of heroics.' Even for people who found the pettiness of the firemen problematic, Yorke was now firmly established as one of Britain's major war writers. Philip Toynbee, reviewing both *Caught* and *The Ministry of Fear* for the *New Statesman*, was relieved to encounter 'two proper novelists, bravely immune to the general decay' of the English novel. He admired both books for their 'honesty of purpose and their high measure of achievement' and praised Yorke for converting observed fact into imaginative truth.

One pleasant afternoon in Boulestin's was not enough to distract Rose Macaulay from her distress at the news of events outside Britain. As September advanced and the blackout began to steal more and more of the day, the war was starting to seem endless. This was the fifth autumn of a war which still did not seem likely to come to a decisive end in the near future.

The news was dominated by accounts of the battles in the Mediterranean. After Italy signed an Armistice with the Allies on 8 September, the Germans occupied the country by force. The Anglo-American army landing near Salerno hoped to encounter surrendering Italians but instead met ferocious German counter-attacks. At the same time, Montgomery's Eighth Army was landing further south in Taranto but was blocked by German demolitions and mines. The German forces nearly broke through to the coast on 14 September and although they then went onto the defensive it was evident that the conquest of Italy would be long drawn-out. 'Poor Rome, and poor Italy,' Rose Macaulay wrote to her cousin Jean in September, 'with all these tough-guys fighting to the death across her body, when she had hoped to be out of it all! They are fighting among such precious things – Pompeii and Paestum and everything – like bulls in china-shops – no use to hope they are being careful, I am sure they are not.' In fact there was not actually any fighting in Pompeii, but the battles continued all around it. Meanwhile the long-drawn-out battles in eastern Europe were still weighted in favour of the Allies. All this time Stalin was continuing to retain the upper hand against the Germans in Russia, recapturing key communication points in the Ukraine in September and pressing on towards Kiev. On 6 November Stalin entered the Crimea from the Caucasus, declaring that 'Germany is standing on the edge of a catastrophe!'

In October 1943 Mary Keene told Henry Yorke that she was two months pregnant and that the child was his. He initially responded with shocked confusion and then wrote her a loving but careful letter, in which he avoided any personal acknowledgement of paternity. 'Very confused at first then a tremendous illumination with a welter of feelings underlying it.' It would take her away, which was sad, but not, he hoped, for long. And he was sure that the mother-child bond would 'cement everything into a sort of keep', guarding her from unhappiness. She was too honest for this world, and was often hurt by the fact that other people were not as openly honest as she was. 'Children at any rate at first are so dead honest that one can trust oneself to them entirely.' They were sacred when they were small, because they were the perpetuation of life. Nothing, of course, made so much day-to-day difference as a child or, for a woman, took up so much time, but hopefully she would not regret it. 'Being yours I shall love it and I only hope it will not make any fundamental difference to you.'

It is clear in this letter that Henry's involvement with Mary's child was going to be limited. It would be 'yours' and not 'ours'; it would take up her time and not his. While hoping that she would not change and would not be taken away, he was already acknowledging that her priorities would alter and their relationship would wane. At this stage, Mary hoped that Henry might leave Dig and marry her. This was misguided, and if she had been more experienced with the upper classes she would probably have expected less. Henry thought it was great fun to be with a former cockney who stole nightdresses, but she was hardly the material for a Mrs Yorke. Anyway, he had no intention of leaving Dig. The child made no difference, if anything hastening the end of the affair.

At this point Dig herself was becoming proprietorially involved in the relationship with Mary. When they were all in London, the younger woman was invited to the family home. Dig and Mary even exchanged letters in which they addressed each other as 'darling'. Mary accepted the situation but resented the presence of Henry's wife in the affair. She told Matthew that she found Dig 'miserable', very cross and suspicious, and that he was wrong to think all was well between Dig and Henry. She showed Dig an expensive new dress, implying that Henry had bought it for her. Two years later Mary would write to Matthew that she had been 'quite dazzled' by meeting Dig, who was looking 'almost voluptuous' and very beautiful, adding acerbically that she herself 'should like to do as she does, sit back drinking noting watching and listening while Henry and his various friends play cat and mouse'.

In the 1950s Mary Keene wrote a novel called *Mrs Donald* in which she vented some of her own anger and confusion about her position in the Yorkes' marriage in this period. The central relationship in the novel is between Violet, a young woman of about Mary's age who has several siblings and an abusive mother, and Louis, a poet-painter who seems to be a composite of Louis MacNeice, Henry Yorke and Matthew Smith. Violet is overwhelmed by Louis: both by her love for him and by the force of his personality. Walking to meet him she feels herself entering 'his great world', becoming 'blindly caught up in it'. She imagines him, 'dark and magnetic', drawing her into a dangerous but enticing vortex as she struggles to save herself from drowning. Violet is as beautiful as

Mary. She receives, 'broadside on, the heady impact of admiration from strangers' who watch her openly. Their eyes become pivots as she moves before them in a circle of flame.

The affair by its nature can exist only in the present; 'they stood eternally in the burning glass of the present moment – no past, no future'. This is the same distortion of time, heightened by the effects of war, that Elizabeth Bowen and her circle found exhilarating. But for Mary or Violet it is disempowering, especially when they are liable to become pregnant and trapped. Violet's future is in the hands of the wife, a woman called Dinah, who is a caricatured version of Dig and is even more present in this affair than Dig was in Henry's. At one point Violet becomes angry with Dinah and asks her 'Why don't you work instead of talking and moaning?' She then shouts incoherently at Louis, who watches her dispassionately, 'enjoying her anger, not distressed for her sake', much as Henry, early on, enjoyed goading Mary about *Moll Flanders*.

Dinah is presented as constraining Louis, who is himself portrayed as selfish and weak. Louis wants merely 'to love what he could see – the perfect beauty of created things', which of course includes young women. He is oppressed by the thought of 'his family's inalienable right'; interrupted by Dinah he feels her presence like that of a steamroller. Briefly he contemplates leaving Dinah, but he does not have the strength. Instead, he merely sets off for an afternoon with Violet, 'innocent in a world of innocence'. Louis thinks of his wife 'left deliciously behind', but then takes Violet back to the house, where they are confronted with Dinah, whose mind they feel 'like walls which she circled'. Louis feels Violet flow over him like bright light, and flows back 'as if she was bringing him a wonderful new species of love'. But yet Violet knows that she is merely being flaunted to Dinah 'as a larger self'. She grabs the poker and stirs the fire, feeling like a ghost in a puppet world, 'chatting to them gaily while her real self lay struggling, limbs thrashing beneath her' and while Dinah, slow and deliberate, presides with the tea.

Then, with frightening complacency, Louis and Dinah reveal themselves as the unit they were all along. They show Violet photographs of themselves in their youth. 'Us at your age,' Louis says; 'our grand friends.' They sit back together, 'delighted with her, and intensely gay'; she realises that she is merely their creation, 'their new idea, their new dimension, the new real-life heroine of a romance they were beginning'. Dinah and Louis both gorge themselves on the luxury of Violet's beauty before Louis takes Violet to bed in the room next door. Violet, understandably, feels disengaged from the experience. She rolls to face the wall, feeling that the sex is 'something he wanted – not she', and that it hardly concerns her. At this point, in what seems to be wish-fulfilment on Mary Keene's part, Louis longs to start something inside Violet 'so that she could accept him as a man'. 'Through his child she would love him.' Violet uses this fantasy to imagine a shared future, feeling that she belongs to Louis; 'that the past was over and the future had come'. If she can live up to the idea he has formed of her then she will figure always in his dreams.

This scene is repeated, with Dinah becoming more closely and more voyeuristically involved in the affair. At one point Violet sits on Louis's lap in front of his wife, looking straight at Dinah and finding that the older woman's admiration gives her greater freedom. Later the lovers tumble onto the floor to have sex as Dinah rises to go to bed. Surrendering to his need, Violet gives herself up to Louis, 'turning from her own revulsion', concerned to be beautiful and relieved that 'she must be so in a splendour of extremity on the floor'. But, inevitably, she is discarded. Louis gives her a book of his poems inscribed simply 'from L to V' and the date, but no love. He then departs abroad with his wife, reminding himself that Violet has no claims and promising merely to send a postcard.

Mrs Donald is a bitter book, jagged in its anger at all three of the figures in its central love triangle. Mary Keene exonerates herself for her part in this warped *folie à trois* on the grounds that Violet is overpowered by the artistic older man and becomes a helpless automaton. To some extent she absolves Henry, suggesting that Louis is merely weakly drawn to the beautiful, though she also shows him as callous, manipulative and unfeeling. But she does not acquit Dig, whom she portrays as predatory and unnatural. Ill-equipped for simple, sensual pleasure herself, Dinah sits watching while her husband takes his mistress to bed, demonically controlling the lives of both her husband and his mistress.

Apart from the situation with Mary, Henry Yorke's life was complicated in the autumn of 1943 by the aftermath of the publication of *Caught*. Bizarrely, the novel had attracted the attention of the Germans, and a German publisher was proposing to translate and publish it. John Lehmann was keen to allow this but Yorke was unsure. 'I know there is nothing we can do to prevent the Germans pirating if they want to,' he wrote to Lehmann in December.

> The difficulty is whether our allowing a German translation is to invite Goebbels to make use of the book. I feel we should get leave from the MOI to send it out of the country. I can't think of anything worse than to have people saying that's the man whose books were used for German propaganda in the last war.

Yorke was right to be anxious. Although there are moments of heroism in *Caught*, it is one of the most ambivalent portraits of the civil defence services in the Blitz. The firemen in Yorke's novel make mistakes, stab each other in the back, fail to do their duty in order to avoid jeopardising their pension, and generally put the individual above the collective good. If published in Germany, it was unlikely to be used for anything other than negative propaganda.

While writing to Lehmann, Yorke expressed his distaste for a review of *Caught* by Jack Marlowe which Lehmann had recently published in *New Writing*. Here Marlowe focused on the ambivalence of *Caught* towards the firemen it portrayed, stating that it 'would not make anyone think the better of the British war-effort', but insisting that the novel did still provide propaganda 'for the vitality of imaginative literature in England under the most difficult conditions'. Reading the article hurriedly, Yorke complained to Lehmann that Marlowe had failed to engage with his book and was just 'turning the words out for money.' He ended his letter by wishing his friend a barbed 'all the best for 1944, though no doubt we should all be better dead'.

It is apparent that the various strains of wartime, work and impending illegitimate fatherhood were telling on Yorke, and ten days later he wrote to apologise to Lehmann.

My dear John, I'm sorry for my mad letter and Jack Marlowe, it was written in a moment of desperation in the bloody office when everything was going wrong and I was in a state of unnecessary savagery.

Rereading Marlowe's article he had decided that it was in fact complimentary and it was merely 'persecution mania' that had made him read it as he had. 'There are times I'm insane and that was one of them,' he admitted.

———

While Henry Yorke was suffering from persecution mania, Peter de Mendelssohn followed Rose Macaulay to Lisbon. For the last four years, his news agency, the Exchange Telegraph, had been run out of Portugal. Now, it had been rendered redundant by Reuters and it was his task to disband it. On 21 December he returned home in time for Christmas, happy and well fed, 'full of stories and presents, like Father Christmas'. Joyfully Hilde and Christine unpacked gifts of bananas, oranges, lemons and silk stockings. Once again, the bright colours of Lisbon could enliven the blacked-out world of wartime London, although Peter himself was pleased to be back in London, where his literary career was going well even if his job prospects were now uncertain. On 9 December he had finally joined the committee of PEN, which had adapted its criteria to incorporate nationalised Europeans.

Random bombing raids continued over Christmas and into January. Hilde Spiel distracted herself from fear by reading Alain-Fournier's escapist novel of idyllic childhood, *The Grand Meaulnes*, which she found 'one of the loveliest books that there is'. She was also playing Schubert quintets and the Mendelssohn violin concerto on the gramophone. But by 15 January she and Peter were quarrelling and she was exhausted by the bombs; 'I can't stand it any more,' she wrote in her diary.

On 20 January the RAF dropped over 2,300 tons of bombs over Berlin. The Luftwaffe retaliated the next day with an attack on London and south-east England, setting fire to Westminster Hall. This was nothing like the German raids of the Blitz; most of the remaining German bombers were now deployed in the Mediterranean and Russia. But there were heavy casualties in London for the first time since 1941, so it came as a shock. The following week Rose Macaulay reported to her cousin Jean that it had been a 'noisy night', suggesting that it might be 'a start of a noisy season – pre-invasion (our invasion, of course)'. She was waiting anxiously for the war news from the rest of Europe. On 22 January two Allied divisions had landed at Anzio, just south of Rome, and found themselves besieged by the Germans, which meant that the main Allied armies had to change course to relieve the Anzio forces. At the same time the main Allied forces were failing to get through the German Gustav Line on the Garigliano and Rapido rivers. 'All this Rome landing,' Macaulay complained.

> Surely there must soon be terrific resistance. It can't go on so smoothly as this. It is horrid to think of all that country being bashed to bits – shelling the Appian Way, the Germans in Frascati, soon the attack on Rome. I suppose we have a very bad few months ahead now.

The January bombing of London was the start of what became known as the 'Little Blitz'. This was indeed a noisy season, largely because of the new anti-aircraft barrages that had been spread throughout London. These contained a device which emitted several hundred rocket projectiles at a time in square formation, with the intention of enclosing the invading German aircraft. William Sansom described the 'Little Blitz' as the period when nerves in London were at their lowest ebb since the start of the war; a time of bombing when 'the perverse vivacities and the do-or-die ebullience of the old Blitz were not so evident'.

Wimbledon was bombed again severely on 4 February, but Hilde Spiel tried to ignore the raids and begin a new novel. Her writing was violently interrupted on 19 February when towards 1 a.m. a stick of bombs descended on the old people's home directly opposite, killing twenty-five people. In her autobiography Spiel wrote that she could 'still hear today the shrill, highpitched screams of the severely injured victims'. Their own small block of apartments withstood the full impact, but the air pressure crushed the inner walls, splintering the wood and shattering the glass. After the first bomb landed, Hilde ran into Christine's bedroom and bent over her daughter.

> Then came the earth-shaking explosion opposite. The wall at the side of the crib collapsed, falling, thank God, in the other direction. My leg was injured. Peter's upper lip was split; the blood pouring, he ran to the nearest doctor, who stitched the wound without anaesthetic. All the residents of our building sat around together in the entrance hall for a while, until the all clear sounded. Conscious of having escaped danger by a hair's breadth, we found relief in hectic gaiety.

During the raid, their cat Ha'penny disappeared. The next morning he returned, carefully picking his way through a sea of broken glass. Meanwhile the apartment had been transformed into a surreal scene. Hilde's new strawberry-red blouse was nailed to the wall by splinters, looking like a scarecrow. A huge reproduction of Van Gogh's nurse holding the ribbons of a baby's cradle was peppered with holes. All the rooms except one were uninhabitable. The bombing, as Graham Greene had noted in the first London Blitz, did not pause to enable people to recover from their private tragedies. Hilde spent the rest of February attempting to make the house inhabitable while they were still subjected to heavy nightly attacks. 'We had not expected more,' she complained in her diary on 26 February. 'These are among the most miserable weeks of my life.'

Returning to London at the end of February, Evelyn Waugh found everyone scared of air raids and, 'in contrast to my own health, very grey and old'. He reported to his wife that the damage to London was negligible but the inhabitants were very frightened. Wiltons restaurant had disappeared and the biographies in the London Library were buried in plaster. At the beginning of March Hilde and Peter decided to evacuate Christine to Cambridge. On 6 March Hilde accompanied her daughter to the house of a doctor and his wife, who were going to look after Christine alongside their own small children. 'It felt difficult for me to separate from her, but there is no other choice,' Hilde noted stoically. She herself remained in London, where the raids became sporadic after the middle of March.

In April Henry Yorke left London to spend some time in his parents' house, Forthampton Court, in Gloucestershire. This was a journey of escape. Yorke was less preoccupied by the war than many of his contemporaries, but for the past few months the mood of the war had been reflected in his personal life, which was greyer and less hopeful than it had been during the Blitz. In London, it was clear that with Mary the moment of exhilaration had passed, but in Forthampton Henry could rekindle his desire for Mary in the form of languorous longing.

In *Pack My Bag* Yorke describes his days spent fishing in Forthampton as amongst the happiest in his life; days that nothing could take away as, before he went to sleep at night, he returned to the river: 'under the blankets, one's thoughts like pigeons circling down out of the sky back to their dovecot set down where the river, sweeping to the sea, makes another turn like the last those birds make coming out of the evening'. It was these fishing trips that had sustained him at the start of the war, 'facing a slow death in the shelter they have made our basement into', taking with him these memories 'like a bar of gold' as the siren went and 'frightened we begin to forget'. Now he and his ten-year-old son Sebastian could share the experience and they fished every day, catching, as he told Mary, huge eels with heads like greyhounds. There was a great ham on the sideboard, the weather was good and he was sleeping in the bed Mary had been allocated when she visited Forthampton the previous year. But he was missing Mary and wished she was there. In her absence he had discussed her with Sebastian during one of their fishing trips. Sebastian announced that 'women had men beat' because they had only to threaten to go away and the 'wretched men were done for'. All women, father and son agreed, were excessively sly. But Mary, Henry suggested, was an exception. 'Oh Mary,' Sebastian answered. Henry asked if Sebastian thought she was beautiful and his son replied that her face was beautiful but her body was too thin. 'So now you know darling, now you know,' Henry informed his mistress.

On 14 May Mary Keene gave birth to a daughter she called Alice. Henry wrote to congratulate her. 'Darling. I'm so very very happy for you that you have got through with it and that it's a girl. I'm sure you'd rather have a girl to be nice to than a boy.' They had spoken on the telephone and he found it extraordinary to hear her voice so soon after she had given birth. The moment that she felt like having visitors he would come round. Alice was registered as the child of Bunny Keene, and Bunny believed himself to be the father. It later transpired in their divorce proceedings that 'sexual intercourse appears to have continued right up to the time they parted' in 1945 and that it was therefore possible for Bunny to have fathered the child. Mary, who had a more accurate idea of the dates, was always convinced that it was in fact Henry who was the father. For his part Henry accepted sufficient responsibility to agree to pay for the divorce proceedings that she was shortly to begin against Bunny.

Despite the pleasures of the father-son fishing trips, Henry Yorke does not generally seem to have been very moved by fatherhood. At a time when it was unusual for members of his class to have only one child, he never wanted to have more children with Dig, ostensibly because of the considerable extra expense children incurred. After Alice's birth, it became apparent that he had not loved Mary in a way that would make him want her child. The relationship had been passionate and serious, on his side as well as hers. He missed her and was finding life increasingly depressing in her absence, though he also missed the headier excitement of the Blitz. But if Rosamond Lehmann was right that Henry Yorke was at best a 'disinterested affection giver' then there was only so far that disinterested affection could go. In *Mrs Donald* Mary would berate Louis for failing to be distressed simply because Violet was upset. There is a point at which love requires sympathy to transmute into self-interested empathy, mutual vulnerability and need. These qualities are certainly present in Yorke's novel *Loving*, which Rosamond Lehmann saw as 'the most compassionate work of one never overtly compassionate', exhibiting 'a tenderness unusual in this tender and harsh writer'. But this tenderness was starting to evaporate. It turned out that Mary was not ultimately a part of Henry; as a result their child, if Henry did indeed believe Alice was his, could not be a part of him either.

PART IV

Approaching Victory

June 1944–August 1945

13

'Droning things, mindlessly making for you'

Hilde Spiel, Graham Greene and Elizabeth Bowen, June 1944–January 1945

On 4 June 1944 the Allies finally entered Rome. Two days later Londoners awakened to news of the D Day landings in Normandy. Five miles of sandy beaches were dotted with troops. 'D-Day has come,' Charles Ritchie wrote in his diary. 'It had become a hallucination – something like the Second Coming or the End of the World.' 'D-Day!' Hilde Spiel announced in disbelief. 'We start the attack of Europe. Frightfully exciting. The BBC bringing it all near.' The assault had been many months in preparation. That spring the Allies had attacked German bridges and communications in Occupied France from the air, as well as continuing to devastate German cities in an attempt to render the Germans incapable of producing war supplies. Now 132,000 troops landed on the beaches, arriving by air and sea.

There was widespread celebration. John Lehmann held a party at his flat in Shepherd Market. Henry Yorke, Rose Macaulay, Rosamond Lehmann, Louis MacNeice, Cecil Day-Lewis and Rex Warner were among his guests, suspending their separate anxieties to rejoice in a shared wartime moment as they had during the Blitz. Churchill congratulated the troops in Rome for 'a memorable and glorious event' which rewarded the intense fighting of the last months in Italy. He described the vast operation of the D-Day landings as 'undoubtedly the

most complicated and difficult that has ever taken place'. Determined
to get to France, Charles Ritchie persuaded his superiors that he should
deliver a message of good wishes to the Canadian troops on behalf of
the Prime Minister. He went by troopship, accompanying 460 infan-
trymen – 'stolid, cheerful English faces', who looked mostly like boys
in their teens.

Arriving at the beautiful French beach, which was now overrun with
troops, Ritchie became aware that the war was in fact far from won.
Although the German defences at the beachheads had been quickly
overwhelmed, the advance inland was slow. And in the middle of June
it became clear to Londoners that the Germans were going to continue
the fight as long as possible. On 14 June, Harold Nicolson announced
in his diary that there had been 'mysterious rocket-planes falling in
Kent'. It was all 'very hush at the moment', but on 16 June the Home
Secretary Herbert Morrison revealed that they were pilotless planes.

A V-1 flying over London, 1944

Now, Nicolson could see them clearly, since they were 'illuminated like little launches at a regatta': 'They fly slowly and low, and it is a mystery how any of them get through at all. They make a terrific noise like an express train with a curious hidden undertone.' The V-1s (*Vergeltung-swaffe Eins*), promised in Germany as 'Hitler's secret weapons', had arrived.

With the deployment of these new weapons, the landscape of London changed once more. Now that there were no pilots involved, bombs could drop at any time of the day or night. The blue skies that had once ushered in a brief holiday from fear now contained the possi-bility of danger. And the usual defensive measures were no longer possible. People received very little warning about the approach of these small planes with ominously burning tails and rarely had time to retreat into a shelter. In *The Heat of the Day* Elizabeth Bowen describes the V-1s as 'droning *things*, mindlessly making for you, thick and fast, day and night', which tear 'the calico of London, raising obscene dust out of the sullen bottom mind'. Sustained V-1 attacks on London began on the morning of 16 June. Within the first three days of the deploy-ment of V-1s, 499 people were killed. There was almost continual defensive gunfire until 18 June, when a bomb hit the Guard's Chapel attached to the Wellington Barracks and killed 119 members of the congregation. After that the attacks became more isolated and it became evident that this new phase of bombing was more a personal than a collective nightmare, as the destruction tended to affect individuals rather than whole communities.

On the evening of 17 June, Hilde Spiel and Peter de Mendelssohn dined at the Savoy with Hans Habe, Hilde's first love from her school-days in Vienna, who was now working as an Instructor in Psychological Warfare for the Americans. They stayed too long.

As we came out of Wimbledon station toward midnight, countless aircraft clacked over our heads, a sound like that of a hundred diabolical sewing machines. It was not the bombs, but the shower of metal that rained down from the defensive artillery that made us flee again and again into shop doorways; our journey punctuated by minute-long

pauses, we finally traversed the endless Wimbledon Hill Road and the
Ridgway as far as The Downs.

Hilde, pregnant again, decided it was time to join her daughter in
Cambridge. Christine remained with the doctor's family and Hilde
moved in nearby as the lodger of a female German scholar. 'A clever,
educated, grumbling old woman . . . I sleep, sleep, sleep.'

Hilde stayed in Cambridge until September, seeing Christine every
day and worrying about Peter's safety and fidelity. On 23 June he admitted that he had spent the night with his feisty and beautiful literary
agent Juliet O'Hea, who had dined at their house in Wimbledon in
February, advising Peter and Hilde on their manuscripts. At the time
O'Hea seemed to be one of the few people in London who admired *The
Fruits of Prosperity* and she had left Hilde feeling encouraged about the
novel's prospects of being published. 'Life is really absurd,' Hilde
observed now. 'Cried a lot. It's hard to sit here watching him start an
affair with her. I'd rather go back to the bombs.'

Pregnant, exiled and insecure about her own literary career, Hilde
was jealous of Juliet O'Hea, who had a more assured role in literary
London than she did. Juliet was single and childless, and so could be
less fearful among the bombs. The affair would flatter Peter by affirming his own sense of belonging in the literary scene and there was a
danger that it would also make him see Hilde as a dowdy outsider. But
the uncertainty about Peter intensified Hilde's own feelings for him
and they had an unusually joyful weekend together in Cambridge. 'I
was incredibly happy. I've hardly ever been so much in love with him,'
she wrote in her diary after he had gone. Over the next few weeks she
thought of him constantly, worrying about the bombs in London,
devastated at the end of each weekend when he left her alone once
more. 'Peter and I have never lived with each other more happily,' she
observed at the end of July, though the previous week he had confessed
to nearly going to bed with Juliet O'Hea again. 'If only he's spared!' she
begged, warding off both the V-1s and his seductress.

For Graham Greene, the V-1s were particularly disturbing because
he had dreamed them into existence. A few months earlier, he dreamt

that he woke up in bed and saw a small plane flying across the window with fire coming out of its tail. Although he was working for the government and had heard stories that a secret weapon was about to be unleashed by Hitler, he had no knowledge of the specifics and so was extremely surprised when the first V-1s appeared and he was confronted with exactly the same image he had seen in his dream. A week into the attacks, on 22 June, Greene wrote in his diary that 'one had thought of the Luftwaffe as defeated, unable to put on a show of this magnitude – there had been nothing like it since the spring of '41'. That Monday he had heard one explode, and from St James's off Piccadilly he had seen a pillar of black rising behind the Academy. 'I had to put on glasses, the air became so thick with brick dust.' Meanwhile, Dorothy Glover was in Tottenham Court Road during another explosion. Greene reported that the road was in an awful state: 'windows, doors and frames had been blasted from Torrington Place to Store Street'. The actual demolition was confined to a few slum houses which had been reduced to rubble, painting the buildings in Tottenham Court Road cream-coloured with clear fine dust.

The alarms had become so frequent that Londoners often forgot whether there was one on or not. In *The Heat of the Day* Louie is unable to tell the difference between the siren and the all clear. Graham Greene and Dorothy were now living in a top-floor flat in Gordon Square, which they had rented extremely cheaply because of its vulnerability to attack. During noisy raids, they sometimes hid in the cupboard under the stairs. From here, on 23 June, they could hear a bomb falling in Russell Square. The top floors of their own building sounded as though they were being crunched in a fist, although in fact the only glass to break was several doors away. Occasionally they took a mattress to the semi-basement at the bottom of the house. At other times, they just stayed in bed. Although *The End of the Affair* describes Greene's relationship with Catherine Walston, not Dorothy Glover, the accounts of reckless love-making amid the bombs recall his experiences with Dorothy during this period of the war, transposed from their Bloomsbury flat to Graham's marital home in Clapham Common:

We had only just lain down on the bed when the raid started. It made
no difference . . . the V1s didn't affect us until the act of love was over. I
had spent everything I had, and was lying back with my head on her
stomach and her taste – as thin and elusive as water – in my mouth,
when one of the robots crashed down on to the Common and we could
hear the glass breaking further down the south side.

In *The End of the Affair*, this moment of bombing becomes the occasion
for a tortured contract between Sarah and the God in whom the characters gradually come to believe. By the end of the book there is the
suggestion that God is directly involved in the outcome of the bombing. This is also implied in several entries in Greene's diary from the
summer of 1944. On 23 June he stated matter-of-factly that the Germans
'must surely have been having a national day of prayer' to be granted
such perfect bombing weather – 'cloudy and cold and windy'. 'Six
down during the night', he reported on 27 June; 'another rainy cloudy
day – we certainly seem meant to suffer'. 'An odd thing,' he observed
on 2 July, 'is the personal indignation one feels with God as the appalling weather continues: I lay in bed yesterday morning muttering angrily
to myself about it. One thinks of him as a person unjustly taking sides.'
The war was transmuting into an apocalyptic battle between right and
wrong, presided over by a contrary deity.

By the time of the V-1 attacks, Greene had resigned from the SIS and
was working for the Political Intelligence Department (PID) of the
Foreign Office, who had promised to send him to France in the event
of an invasion. This meant that he was now based in Grosvenor Street,
in London. On 30 June Greene heard a big explosion during lunch
and, getting back to the office, learnt that it was a bomb in the court-
yard of Bush House, the BBC overseas service headquarters where his
brother Hugh worked. He reported in his diary that the telephone was
off and he did not know when they would receive news of Hugh's
whereabouts. Later that afternoon he announced that Bush House had
suffered, but the telephone was now working. 'Hugh is all right, and
the bomb seems to have fallen by the Waldorf.' This was one of the
worst single attacks of the war. As the dust cleared after the explosion

onlookers saw corpses strewn across the pavements and a line of burned-out buses along the side of the road. Forty-eight people were killed.

For Greene, this had been a shattering day. During this period, he seems to have stopped revelling in the destruction for its own sake, instead starting to worry about the danger, perhaps because he was enjoying life too much to desire death. Insead, he kept up his spirits by reminding himself that 'the moment always exaggerates' – the damage was rarely as bad as it sounded – and observing the resilience of other Londoners. Once, an old woman yelped in terror in the queue at the local butcher and the butcher promptly leapt out from behind the counter and kissed the woman, providing a happy distraction for onlookers. But as the destruction escalated it was hard to forget about it. 'Had dinner at the Coquille to improve my morale – not very successfully,' Greene reported at the end of the day on 30 June. That night he was kept awake by 'an endless series of bombs coming over – I counted about 12 explosions: very little sleep'. By 10.20 the next morning the alert was still on. He and Dorothy escaped to the countryside for the day but the bad weather and the heavy raids continued. 'A bad night with over 40 explosions between 12.45 and 9,' he began his diary entry for 3 July. In the brief intervals of sleep between bombs, he had even dreamed that he was in a raid. Since then, it had poured all day and his secretary had asked if she could take a long lunch hour because her grandmother had suffered from bomb blast; later she heard that her other grandmother was trapped under the debris of her house.

The V-1 bombardment continued into July but by the end of the month only one 'doodle-bug' in seven penetrated the anti-aircraft and barrage-balloon screens. On 6 July Churchill told the Commons that it would be a mistake to underrate the serious character of this form of attack, but assured them that the Allies were doing their best to destroy the firing-points from which they were launched. He noted that on average the V-1s had killed one person per bomb, which was, he claimed, 'a wonderful figure'. On 13 July Charles Ritchie announced in his diary that morale had improved: 'we are getting used to the buzz-bombs and also fewer are coming over. People are beginning to come to life again – to ring up their friends and go to restaurants.' Greene, now released from government duties and working as publishing director at Eyre and Spottiswoode, was still on duty as a warden at night but was usually to be found taking authors for long and drunken lunches by day.

Resilient as always, many Londoners were patching up their homes. Among these was Elizabeth Bowen. Her house in Clarence Terrace had been scathed by two blasts and she and Alan cleared up the damage. In a subsequent account of her life during the war, she recalled that she wrote continuously throughout, interrupted only by the occasional necessity to clean up her house from time to time, when it had been blasted. 'Nobody', she added, 'who has not cleaned up a house in which every ceiling has come down and every window has been blown in knows what cleaning-up can be like: glass-dust and plaster from old ceilings are most pervasive.' In 1944 Bowen published an essay called 'Calico Windows', describing the experience of living in a patched-up house. Her windows filled with opaque creamy calico, she, like many other Londoners, was 'tied up, sealed up, inside a tense white parcel', embedded within a 'new, timeless era of calico' in which 'the old plan for living has been erased'. Going out into the world, she returned to the 'tense, mild, soporific indoor whiteness', dreamily cut off from the thunder of world events.

Bowen was dismissive of people who gave up too easily. Her story 'Oh, Madam', written during the 1940 Blitz, portrays the owner of a Regent's Park house as betraying both the house itself and the loyal servant who tries to keep it going when she announces her intention to pack up the house and depart for the countryside. The story is a monologue, addressed by the servant to her mistress. The servant has spent the days since the attack attempting to restore order, although it becomes clear that the house has barely survived. The windows are gone, the ceilings have fallen through, the stairs are covered in plaster. Even the inhabitants are ghosts. The servant is ashen with dust; the mistress goes white with shock. From the start, the servant assumes that her mistress has returned for good and that they will restore the house together. 'When we just get the windows back in again – why, madam, I'll have the drawing-room fit for you in no time!' She is counting on their shared loyalty to the house, which 'has been wonderful, madam, really – you really have cause to be proud of it'. 'Hitler can't beat you and me, madam, can he?' It then transpires that the mistress is intending to leave. The servant is shocked and disillusioned. *'But you couldn't ever, not this beautiful house!'* 'But, madam, this seemed so much your home.'

Bowen was more hardy than the mistress in the story. In *Bowen's Court* she attributed her own wartime courage to her anxiety twenty years earlier, during the Irish Troubles, when her father wrote to her and told her to prepare to see Bowen's Court burned down.

> I read his letter beside Lake Como, and, looking at the blue water, taught myself to imagine Bowen's Court in flames. Perhaps that moment disinfected the future: realities of war I have seen since have been frightful; none of them have taken me by surprise.

But on 20 July a V-1 landed across the road, blew the house hollow inside and wrecked every room. Charles Ritchie reported in his diary that Elizabeth and Alan had at last decided to move out now that the ceilings were down and the windows were broken and they were lucky to have escaped being killed. There came a point when, like the woman in 'Oh, Madam', she had to give up, though she, like the servant in the story, was proud of how sturdy her house had been so far. Charles hated the destruction of Clarence Terrace and felt that Elizabeth was without her background; a dignified retreat to Bowen's Court seemed called for.

> Her nerves have been under a terrible strain. But she is resilient, if she can get away and get some rest she will be all right. And in the midst of it all she is still trying frantically to write her novel.

The novel was *The Heat of the Day*, which Elizabeth Bowen had first started planning after her return from Ireland in August 1942. That September she told Charles that she was on the point of beginning 'a new novel of our Present Discontents'. By November she knew that it would open in Regent's Park. 'I like to think that the atmosphere of wartime London will be preserved in E's new novel,' Charles wrote in

February 1944, 'and that things we have seen and felt together will be preserved there. Of course what I would like best would be to find a romanticised portrait of myself but I shall be lucky, I daresay, not to be mentioned.'

These wishes were to be granted. Robert was indeed a romanticised portrait of Charles, down to his long, elegant hands, the 'fairness, not quite pallor' of his skin and the 'flame-thin blueness' of his eyes. 'How proud Charles must be,' Rosamond Lehmann wrote to Elizabeth after the book's publication, praising her friend for 'the unbearable re-creation of war and London and our private lives and loss'. 'You do, you really do, write about love.' Chapter five, which Bowen was writing as the bombs fell around her in 1944, situates Stella and Robert in the suspended present of wartime, exploring the aesthetics of wartime temporality. They meet (unlike Elizabeth and Charles) during a bomb-ing raid, and their first sighting of each other is interrupted by a detonation. Introduced to each other in a bar, they turn to look at each other and at first glance see in each other's faces 'a flash of promise'. Immediately, Stella finds herself not beginning to study but in the middle of studying Robert. Then she turns to wave goodbye to the friend who has brought her across the room before she and Robert fix their eyes expectantly on each other's lips. At this moment a bomb whistles and lands elsewhere, demolishing the moment.

Always afterwards, both lovers see Stella's gesture of goodbye and the expectant stare as frozen photographs. And the freezing of time seeps into their first months together so that, transfixed in the moment, they seem to stay 'for ever on the eve of being in love'. This changes one October morning when the stakes of the danger become apparent. For Stella, loving Robert is associated 'with the icelike tinkle of broken glass being swept among the crisping leaves and with the charred freshness of every morning'. At the start of the Blitz, she is buoyed up by the lightness of loving no particular person now left in London. During the September raids she is 'awed, exhilarated, cast at the very most into a sort of abstract of compassion'. Then, in October, she wakes to discover that lightness gone. 'That was the morning when, in the instant before opening her eyes, she saw Robert's face with a despairing hallucinatory clearness.'

As the V-1s fell around her in 1944, Bowen described the sensation of loving against a background of danger. She had never been without ties in London; Alan had been there with her throughout the war. But the specific sensation of waking up uncertain if her lover has survived the night is one she first experienced during the attacks by the V-1s, when the isolated nature of the attacks made it even harder to know if any particular house was safe.

Elizabeth did not retreat to Bowen's Court, and she and Charles continued to meet frequently after she and Alan left Clarence Terrace. On 12 August Charles reported that Elizabeth had moved to a flat belonging to Clarissa Churchill (niece of Winston), 'high up in a monstrous new block of flats overlooking Regent's Park'. There, gazing out towards the house she had recently evacuated, she was writing a short story called 'The Happy Autumn Fields'. She told Charles about it excitedly while he lay on the sofa looking out at the sky.

This is a story set in the confines of a bombed house. With calico 'stretched and tacked over the window', Mary sleeps amid ruins. She has spent the day sorting through her things and has come across photographs of her ancestors wandering through a cornfield in Ireland. The Ireland of the story is the Ireland of Bowen's Court. 'I was thinking about the fields round here,' Elizabeth would tell Charles, looking back on the story from Ireland in 1945, 'blonde and crisp with stubble, criss-crossed with belts of bronze-brown beeches.' As in Bowen's article, the calico induces dreams and she has wandered into the consciousness of Sarah, a girl in the photograph, talking to her suitor, Eugene, in the presence of her jealous sister Henrietta.

Mary's own lover Travis intrudes on her sleep, waking her up in order to try to persuade her to leave. 'In your normal senses you'd never attempt to stay here. There've been alerts, and more than alerts, all day; one more bang anywhere near, which may happen at any moment, could bring the rest of this down.' Mary stares sleepily over his shoulder at the calico window. Travis announces that he has taken a room for her in a hotel and is about to get her a taxi. 'I can't get into a taxi without waking,' she complains, unwilling to abandon her dream. She is frantic at being delayed in London, while the moment awaits her in the cornfield; it is grotesque to be saddled with Mary's body and lover. Mary persuades Travis to leave her in peace for two hours and returns to her dream, which darkens as the rupture between sisters is completed. 'It is *you* who are making something terrible happen,' Henrietta is lamenting to Eugene, just when in Mary's London the house rocks, the calico window splits and more ceiling plaster falls. There is the enormous dull sound of the explosion and Mary lies with lips pressed close, scarcely breathing, her eyes shut.

It is too late now to go back. Mary weeps on the bed, 'no longer reckoning who she was', waiting for Travis. 'How are we to live without natures?' she asks him, on his return. 'We only know inconvenience now, not sorrow.' The source, the sap dried up, or the pulse stopped, before either of them was conceived. She is 'drained by a dream': 'I cannot forget the climate of those hours. Or life at that pitch.' Mary's experience resembles Henry Russel's in Bowen's earlier story, 'Sunday Afternoon'. Once again, Bowen returns a character to Ireland, though this time only in a dream, in order to teach her to find the source, the sap and the pulse lost to her in the deadening air of bombed London. Bowen would always look on her experiences in London during the war as some of the most exciting in her life. But, from the confines of that new, monstrous block of flats, in the savage and austere light of wartime, she dreamed urgently of a world unchanged. In January 1941 Bowen had asked Virginia Woolf if, when her flat was bombed, all the things in it went too? 'All my life I have said, "Whatever happens there will always be tables and chairs" – and what a mistake.' Now her house was almost destroyed, and she clung desperately to an ideal of home which she located in the Irish countryside and in the heightened emotions that were the saving luxury of its more privileged inhabitants.

Despite dreaming of Ireland, Bowen was determined to stick out the remainder of the war close to home. Churchill himself insisted that there was no need for evacuation and that anyone who wanted to leave London must do so at their own expense. And Bowen and many of her acquaintances downplayed the danger of the 'doodle-bugs'. On 13 August Harold Nicolson reprimanded his sons for their apprehension about the V-1s, maintaining that it was a useless form of attack.

The anxiety it causes to individuals is limited in space and time. In space, because one gets to know the line it is taking and nine times out of ten it is not on one's own line. In time, because the actual moment of personal danger is only a few seconds.

Later that week Stephen Spender assured Christopher Isherwood in America that the V-1s were more of a nuisance than anything else. He was frustrated because the windows and ceilings of his top-floor flat had been blown in and he now had to go down to the shelter almost every night, but he was not especially frightened.

Nonetheless, during the summer and autumn of 1944, a large number of Londoners followed the example of the woman in Bowen's 'Oh, Madam' and retreated to the countryside. Hilde Spiel in Cambridge was receiving frequent reports from Peter about the bombing in Wimbledon. 'Tonight the doodlers are doing their worst,' he wrote in the middle of August.

> There is a warning literally every fifteen minutes, and each time, just one comes over. A little while ago one cut out just above the house, or so it seemed, and I heard it swish down. When it exploded I was sure all our windows would go again, but to my surprise found them all intact. There was a huge red glow on the horizon and a mushroom-shaped column of dark smoke rising into it. Quite fantastic, and I would have enjoyed it more if the whole performance hadn't given me a slightly odd sensation in the stomach.

Isolated in Cambridge, Hilde continued to worry about Peter's safety and to feel periodically jealous of the fun that he was having in London. On 22 August Peter was involved in another PEN congress, held at the French Institute in South Kensington. That morning a large V-1 had dropped in front of the Institute, destroying much of the neighbourhood, and there was a general feeling that the congress should be abandoned. Peter convinced the rest of the committee to go ahead on the grounds that the neighbourhood was no more dangerous than anywhere else in London and that the organisers were not responsible for the safety of the audience, who were all grown-ups with five years of Blitz experience. He boasted proudly to Hilde that he had rescued the congress, and that although the Institute was badly blitzed, the hall itself had been usable once they pulled down the black-out blinds to cover the broken windows. The speeches had been excellent. E. M. Forster was 'absolutely brilliant'; all in all it was 'first-class intellectual entertainment'. For her part Hilde was pleased that Peter had become so integral a member of the PEN committee but she wished that she could have been there too.

While the PEN congress was in session at the French embassy, one of the decisive battles of the Second World War was being fought in Paris. On 14 August the Allies had simultaneously launched Operation Tractable, which entailed a drive into Falaise and a westward thrust towards Paris, and Operation Dragoon, which involved landing 94,000 men on the French Mediterranean coast in a single day. The Falaise drive met with heavy resistance but the troops landing on the coast managed to push nearly twenty miles inland within four hours. In Paris, excited by the news of the landings, the police laid aside their uniforms and joined the Resistance on the streets. The next day, a general strike started, with thousands of employees of the Paris metro, police and postal service demonstrating against the Germans. By 19 August this escalated into full-scale war as the French fought the Germans in the streets, raising a tricolour flag, singing the Marseillaise and setting up barricades as they waited expectantly for the Allies to arrive. On 23 August Peter de Mendelssohn wrote to his wife that the news from Paris had really got him by the throat. He now realised how much he had been longing for this moment throughout the war. It was clear to him that it would only be a matter of weeks before the whole of France was liberated. On 24 August the Free French General Leclerc sent a vanguard of his Second Armoured Division to Paris, entering the city the following morning. At 2.30 p.m. on 25 August the German Commander of Paris surrendered and an hour and a half later General de Gaulle entered the city.

'Isn't the war going with a swing?' Peter asked Hilde on 24 August. But, as a German, he was starting to feel ambivalent about the news.

Tonight's headlines in the paper just take one's breath away. They make your eyes swim and your thoughts reel. I'm no longer able to contemplate the news calmly and objectively. By tonight I think the boys must be in Versailles or very near it. This is the one and only time I wish I could be a Frenchman, for one day – when Leclerc's men enter the capital. But I fear I would choke myself to death. I've been thinking about it all evening. It is an incredible time for all the allies, for all the suppressed and oppressed, for all the exiled and hunted – except, somehow for us. I know this is a bad and treacherous and ungrateful thing to say and even to think. But somehow I just cannot help it. What are we going to get out of it, you and I and the rest of us? Ours is the shabbiest lot of all. What do I inherit from this great moment of triumph and exuberance? The dreadful, grey, hopeless task of going to reform my former countrymen, this band of thieves and murderers and abject criminals.

Meanwhile the Russian army had entered Finland, Poland and the Balkans, and Peter had been reading the official Russian account of the discoveries of the concentration camp at Lublin, which the Russians had liberated in July. On 12 August *The Times* had summarised the report of the Russian writer Konstantin Simonov, who visited the camp and found permanent and mobile gas chambers and floors strewn with the passports and identity cards of victims. The article reported that the naked victims in this camp had been packed so tightly in their cells that they died on their feet as the poison gas was pumped in. Apparently the officials used to crack grisly jokes with their victims, a favourite remark being 'I'll see you in the stove soon.' There were reports, too, that SS men amused themselves by saying to victims coming to their senses after being clubbed, 'Well, you're in Heaven now. Did you guess there were SS men in Heaven?' Reading these accounts had made Peter de Mendelssohn wish never to see a German again.

What an execrable, damnable, accursed lot they are, all of them, the whole lot! Yet there I shall go, back to the old country, and no one to greet with a smile, an open word, no one to love, nothing – not even the

sight of their cities, of the playgrounds of my childhood and youth –
will make my heart beat faster. Oh, to be a Frenchman and to return
home on the high tide of hope and happiness.

The war continued to 'go with a swing'. At one o'clock on 4 September Harold Nicolson heard that the British Second Army had occupied
Brussels and that hostilities between Finland and Russia had ceased.
Then at 9.30 p.m. he turned on the French news and heard that the
British troops had crossed the Dutch border. Since D-Day they had
taken 300,000 German prisoners in France alone. The German Army
was in utter confusion.

On 10 September, Hilde Spiel returned to London, seven months
pregnant, undeterred by her husband's warnings that a new weapon
was about to be deployed against them. In the early morning hours
after her arrival, they were awakened by 'the ear-splitting sound of the
first rockets landing on London and the echo of their breaking
through the stratosphere that followed'. These were the first V-2s,
long-range missiles which travelled faster than the speed of sound.
They were forty-six feet long and five feet in diameter, and landed
with an extremely loud double bang that made people up to ten miles
away think they were about to be hit. Hilde and Peter's son Anthony
Felix, 'conceived among bombs, to be born among bombs', appeared
at ten in the evening on 14 November. There were two flying-bomb
attacks in the area of the London Clinic, where Hilde gave birth, and
a rocket landed near enough to shake the walls. 'Up in my room, in
my joy over my child, I took little notice of the V1s and V2s,' Hilde
Spiel recalled in her autobiography. 'As terrible as the rockets were
with their double thunder, we learned to adopt a stoic attitude
towards them. One could not predict when and where they would
land, and neither warning nor defence was possible, so we simply
paid no attention to them.'

The British government was determined not to boost German
morale by reporting the success of the rockets so they were kept out of
the news for almost a month, until details were revealed in the *New
York Times*. All this time, the battles in Europe dragged on. In France,

the Allies captured Boulogne and Brest in September and then breached the Siegfried Line into Germany on 15 September. On 21 October they took the garrison of Aachen, the first German city to be captured. Belgium was liberated at the start of November and the American army entered Strasbourg on 23 November. In the East, Soviet and Yugoslav forces took Belgrade and then entered East Prussia in late October. But the British were distressed to learn about the fall of Warsaw to the Germans in late September, after a Polish uprising was given insufficient support by Soviet troops. On 5 October Churchill paid tribute to 'the heroic stand' in Warsaw, lamenting that 'terrible damage has been inflicted upon this noble city' and promising that the epic of Warsaw would not be forgotten. All in all it was evident that the war would continue for some time, not least because of the resilience of the Japanese in the Far East, a battle front that still seemed remote to most Londoners.

Hilde Spiel spent the winter at home in Wimbledon where, on 1 December, she noted in her diary that she had now lived for five years. 'Boring and dangerous. Dear god, let me never again experience this.' Lying in bed, she felt angry but also very much in love with Peter, whom she resented for having more fun over the past two years than she had done. And now he was about to go away. Since he had disbanded the Exchange Telegraph a year earlier, Peter had been working for the Supreme Headquarters Allied Expeditionary Forces (SHAEF) as deputy director of the Allied News Pool. On 5 December he was sent to Paris, in British military uniform, leaving Hilde at home with their baby. 'You should comfort yourself with the knowledge that you have not missed much,' Peter wrote to Hilde, shocked by what he was seeing. 'Paris is outwardly the same – beautiful, clean, delightful – but inwardly it has changed terribly, not with advantage. Conditions are chaotic. (It is incredibly, bitterly, cold and raining all the time.)' They would have to get used to the fact that Europe was no longer the same as the world they had left behind before the war. Visiting Paris at the start of January, Charles Ritchie found that the heroic arches and spectacular perspectives had become ironic – 'the backdrop for their humiliation and their bitter unresigned endurance'. Although Peter de Mendelssohn was meant to come back on 18 December, he did not in fact arrive until the 23rd, full of tales of new Sartre plays and of the excitement of the continent. In the meantime there were more rockets, but on 15 December Christine was finally brought back from Cambridge. 'The baby doesn't interest her,' Hilde reported. She now did her best to ignore the V-2s, wrapping up her son in his pram, leaving him outside the house for fresh air, and taking her daughter shopping. 'We were all "in God's hands," whether we believed in him or not.'

During the V-2 attacks, Elizabeth Bowen had remained on the outskirts of Regent's Park and, as soon as she could, she returned home. By October, she and Alan were back in Clarence Terrace. She was, she told her friend Susan Tweedsmuir a few months later, 'so glad to be reinstated in what again seems a house, that we really have nothing to grumble about'. There may have been no cause for public complaint, but privately Elizabeth was preparing for one of the greatest personal sorrows of the war. Charles Ritchie had been posted back home to Canada. That December, during their final month of living in the same city, Charles bought Elizabeth a necklace for Christmas. It was made, he recorded in his diary, of large white amethysts flecked with mauve lights, alternating with small purple amethysts. He had been planning to buy topazes but fortunately had heard just in time that they were considered unlucky. 'I wouldn't want to give her an unlucky present – our future looks unlucky enough without that.'

In January 1945 Charles departed for Canada. 'I suppose I could have gone on year after year representing my country abroad without knowing much about what was going on at home.' But as it was, he was in for an intensive period of re-education and felt like a new boy at school. The letter Elizabeth wrote him on the eve of his departure was a manifesto of her faith in his love.

> We are so close to each other in understanding, closer than words could make us that I think you must know this . . . You know, too, don't you, that you take with you my real life, my only life, everything that is meant by my heart. I am in your keeping. And you are in mine.

She was aware that the last four years had seen him vacillating between love and detachment, and that he had not been faithful to her. She knew that he was seriously considering marriage to his cousin, Sylvia Smellie. 'E says she would not mind me marrying S so much, it would be like "marrying myself",' Charles had written in his diary in December. Yet Elizabeth kept her belief in the fairy tale alive because she was now unable to imagine happiness without him.

During the war Elizabeth Bowen wrote an essay called 'The Art of Reserve, or, The Art of Respecting Boundaries' warning her readers of the potential hazards of unrestrained love and friendship. 'We rush, we storm our approaches to other people,' she complains here, wondering 'what is at fault – the age we live in, fever and insecurity?' It is because people matter so much – 'perhaps they matter too much' – that 'we risk disillusionment, tragedy, when we pursue them wrongly'. She advocates quietness, which will allow the infinite possibilities within a single human relationship to unfold slowly and deliberately – 'magical silences, delicious chance meetings, the sweet-smelling hour in the garden after the rain, the evening by the fire, the sudden talk by the window looking out at the snow'. She urges her readers to learn how to pause and to respect boundaries.

There is a note of regret here; she chastises herself, together with her readers. Throughout her life, Elizabeth crashed noisily into friendships which she often had to extricate herself from heartlessly when they became too consuming. And she did not heed her own advice when it came to love. Here there was no pause and no restraint. 'She said she thought that if we had married we would have been perfectly happy together,' Charles had written just over a year into the relationship in November 1942. Her only chance of survival was to convince him that he felt it too. And there were moments when he did, though he found it hard to admit. 'E has become the centre of my life,' he observed in February 1943.

As usual I struggle with my love for her and with a lamentable but characteristic panic. I insist in my own mind that I do not love her, because I am not 'in love' with her; that however is true in a narrow sense in that I do not desire her. Yet what I feel for her is quite different from friendships . . . Of course with E I have found the perfect companion and intelligence and above all a power of expression superior to my own . . . insensibly she has put at a distance not only all rivals, but all rival memories . . . I am being absorbed by a love which wishes to penetrate and possess.

In February 1944 he observed less romantically that it was impossible for him to express adequately what she had been to him without sounding as though he were writing an obituary for *The Times*. Through her, he had grown up, and he wished for both their sakes that they could have met ten years earlier. It is unclear what might have been the result of this. Elizabeth would still have been married. Perhaps Charles thought that if Elizabeth could have wrought her consuming magic while he was still in his twenties he might have been saved from his own callousness; that without those extra ten years of transient love affairs he might have been able to live up to Elizabeth's own unwavering image of his steadfastness.

But for her part, Elizabeth exonerated herself for her lack of restraint and wove Charles into her own image of unchanging love. 'Outside us neither of us when we are together ever seems to look,' Stella claims to Robert in *The Heat of the Day*. 'How much of the "you" or the "me" *is*, even, outside of the "us"?' It is too late to ponder the merits of retaining or reinstating the boundaries between them when their consciousnesses have already merged. And that merging is itself inextricable from the war which forms the background of their love. They are 'the creatures of history, whose coming together was of a nature possible in no other day'. War itself effects 'a thinning of the membrane between the this and the that'; and 'what else', the narrator asks, 'is love?'

14

'A collective intoxication of happiness'

January–June 1945

By January 1945 the German army was largely confined within the boundaries of Germany itself, although there was still some fighting in Hungary, Poland, northern Holland, Scandinavia and northern Italy. It was clear that the war would be over within a few months. 'Let us be of good cheer,' Churchill told the Commons on 18 January; 'Military victory may be distant, it will certainly be costly, but it is no longer in doubt.' On 4 February, Churchill, Roosevelt and Stalin met at the Black Sea resort of Yalta in the Crimea to decide on the future of post-war Europe. Between them they divided Germany into four zones (France was to have one as well), decided on questions of German reparation and reconstruction, and agreed to cooperate in the planned United Nations organisation. Around them, the war continued, with the Allies doing everything in their power to force the unconditional surrender of Germany. On 13 February Britain and America began three nights of brutal bombing in the German city of Dresden; by 15 February, the resulting firestorm had destroyed fifteen square miles of the city centre. 'I feel the war may end any week, do you?' Rose Macaulay wrote to her friend David Ley on 14 February. 'I mean, the European part of it. There will be horrible celebrations and exultations, which I shan't like. But what a relief, all the same.'

However, the bombing of London continued into March, and according to William Sansom a new neurosis was developing. People were anxious about being killed by the last bullet. On Sunday 20 March London was hit by its last V-2, which landed just inside Hyde Park by Marble Arch. Lying in bed, late in the morning, Graham Greene heard 'a huge crash, followed by a terrific rumble and the sound of glass going', and went to Hyde Park to survey the damage. A week later, the V-2 attacks stopped altogether. The final rocket explosion was heard on 27 March and the last flying-bomb arrived the next morning. The Allies had overrun the launching sites in Holland. 'It really looks at last as though the war might be over soon,' Greene wrote to his mother. 'One feels one won't have much energy for peace.'

In Europe, the last stray territories were falling to the Allies. Warsaw was conquered by the Russians on 17 January and Budapest in March. On the western front, Britain and America cleared the west bank of the Rhine, capturing Cologne. The British and Americans began simultaneous offensives from the north and south of the Rhine, encircling the remaining 325,000 German troops defending the Ruhr at the start of April. Then amid the triumphant accounts of victories came news of a sadder kind. On 12 April Roosevelt died, aged 63. Churchill now reported that Roosevelt had already been visibly weakening at Yalta:

> His captivating smile, his gay and charming manner, had not deserted him, but his face had a transparency, an air of purification, and often there was a faraway look in his eyes.

However, the critical state of the President's health was not known to the general public and his death came as a shock. 'Early this morning Peter woke me to tell me that Roosevelt had died last night,' Hilde Spiel wrote in her diary. 'Dreadful shock.' She found that everything seemed suddenly overshadowed by Roosevelt's death.

> Vienna is freed, war closing to its end, everything looks well, Peter works a lot and earns a lot of money making a good career as well, and

there I sit quite disheartened and disconsolate over Roosevelt. He was the embodiment of integrity and human decency.

Henry Yorke spent the spring of 1945 worrying about the welfare of Mary Keene. He would never quite acknowledge responsibility for her daughter Alice, but he did now join Matthew Smith in trying to find somewhere for Mary to live. While they addressed this question, Mary took Alice to stay with Dylan Thomas and his wife Caitlin. She was pleased to escape both the bombs and Bunny Keene, whom she was now in the process of divorcing.

Henry missed Mary in her absence and was jealous of Dylan Thomas. 'Darling, darling, I'm so very glad the journey went off all right,' he wrote after her departure in February. 'Everything here is horrible. Fog today too.' The previous day a bomb had gone off above the Yorkes' house in Trevor Place. His letter ended plaintively:

I can't sleep.
My new book is no good.
So altogether I'd better stop.
I miss you terribly.
Love from Henry

Mary began by enjoying her stay in Wales. She was missing Henry and, perhaps most of all now, Matthew. 'I think about you always as I used to think about Henry,' she had written to Matthew the previous autumn. 'Oh I adore you my darling like no one else on earth.' But she liked being with Dylan Thomas. 'I don't take Dylan nearly so seriously as you do,' she told Henry, adding provocatively that the poet had taken her 'very much under his wing'. For his part Henry filled her in on gossip from the office, complained about the lack of pretty girls and teased her about life in Wales, asking if the innkeeper gave sufficient food to his dogs.

I fear they are ravening for poor little Alice, the little innocent can't know what a succulent feast she would make, particularly in these years of lean dog biscuits. I have your shriek in my ears as I write this and that must be my comfort for it is all I have.

At the beginning of March, Mary's peaceful life in Wales was shattered when a neighbour, jealous over reports of Thomas's flirtation with his wife, entered the cottage with a gun and began to shoot at random. 'Dearest dearest,' Mary wrote, reporting the incident to Henry, 'tears will be falling on this letter before I'm halfway through.' She described how the flimsy asbestos walls were flecked with machine-gun bullets, doors had been broken in and a madman with a gun in one hand and a hand grenade in the other had generally terrorised them. 'I feel as weak as a kitten.' She was overcome with a sense of her own 'alone-ness and innocence'. She wanted to come back to London but she did not want to be a burden for Henry and Matthew. 'When in trouble I have the feelings of an institution child, my anxiety is not that I have nowhere to live but that I am a responsibility to my friends.'

Both Henry and Dig wrote back immediately to comfort her. 'My dearest darling,' Dig's letter began, adding that she had missed Mary 'dreadfully' and hoped she would come back soon. 'What a terrible experience you had, I was horrified! You might have been shot. I know I should have dreamt about it every night if I'd been you.' She then recounted the gossip from London (chiefly that she had seen a lot of Matthew, who had been very nice and very amusing), before observing that Mary's time in Wales sounded extraordinary and asking provocatively 'would I have liked it, do you think?' Henry's letter was more consistently consoling. 'My darling darling darling, what a day and what an escape,' he began. 'You must have had the most terrible shock, and I only hope you are beginning to get over it now.' He assured her that he was doing all he could to find her somewhere to live. He and Matthew met almost daily and Henry did all the talking while Matthew sat there saying 'I know I know I know'. And he promised her that she would never be in real need so long as he and Matthew were alive, adding that 'little Alice must always be on a bed of roses'. A week later he told her rather heartlessly about a claim he was making with the insurance company for jewellery that had been stolen from Dig. The man at Cartier was going to 'prepare a "scheme" of a few "pieces" for her, which means I suppose that she will be literally brilliant with diamonds quite soon'.

Mary replied caustically that she was glad to hear about Dig's jewellery, wondering if he could 'slip in a bit for me'. She felt terribly separated from him. 'I don't dream or dare think of seeing you.' Her news was of police interrogations (she had informed the policeman that the shooting was worse than anything she had experienced in the Blitz) and of her impending appearance in court. She was losing patience with Dylan, who now seemed to be 'an extraordinarily abnormal person', and was spending her days waiting for the post and longing for the city. It is clear from her letters that her expectations of Henry were becoming lower and lower in his absence, and in this respect she was realistic. Henry missed her, but he had moved on and retreated into the safety of his day-to-day life with Dig. Mary later wrote to her daughter Alice: 'There was a hole there. He only really existed in other people. He was living off the fat of other people and once the fat had gone, he would go.' This was a statement written in bitterness but it is not dissimilar from opinions expressed by more friendly observers. Henry had been awakened by his wartime experiences into a form of passion he had rarely experienced before. Now it was over and he had indeed gone.

But that passion had been memorialised in *Loving*, which had come out in March. Near the end of the month Henry told Mary that all 5,000 copies of *Loving* had been sold five days before publication, and that, given the paper rationing, there was no more paper to print new copies. He was generally gratified by the ensuing reviews, and especially pleased with the praise of friends. 'Your letters about my books give me the most intense pleasure,' he wrote to Rosamond Lehmann, who had written admiringly after being sent an advance copy, adding that 'you are one of the very few, the two or three, I will take praise from'.

────────

The war in Europe was now almost over. 'Armies monotonously victorious,' Evelyn Waugh observed cynically on 13 April. The previous evening he had been at a party at Cyril Connolly's with Elizabeth

Bowen. 'Gloomy apprehensions of V Day. I hope to escape it.' After encircling the Germans in the Ruhr the American army continued eastwards, crossing the Czechoslovakian border on 19 April. Meanwhile the Russians had begun a final offensive on Berlin and by 22 April the city was held from both sides. Three days later the Americans met the Russians on the Elbe, cutting the German army in half. As well as defeating the Germans, the British and Americans were anxious to contain the Russians, who had already set up Communist governments in Poland and Austria. Hilde Spiel was worried about the situation in Vienna but cared most of all about the resumption of peace. 'The war hurries rapidly to an end,' she announced jubilantly on 28 April. The next day the German forces in Italy surrendered unconditionally and on 30 April Hitler committed suicide. 'Hitler reported dead!' Spiel wrote in disbelief on 1 May.

Elizabeth Bowen heard about Hitler's death in Hythe, where she had spent happy summers with her mother as a child. When she had arrived in Kent, the beach was covered in barbed wire and the cheerful seaside villas were deserted. Now she told Charles that the sea front was open again; miles of coils of rusty barbed wire had been snipped away and triumphantly flung back. On 2 May, the commander of German troops in Berlin surrendered to the Allies. Bowen celebrated the peace at the house of her friend Lord Berners in Faringdon in Oxfordshire, where the fountain was turned on for the first time since the war.

> There was a breathless pause, then a jet of water, at first a little rusty, hesitated up into the air, wobbled, then separated into four curved feathers of water. It was so beautiful and so sublimely symbolic – with the long view, the miles of England, stretching away behind it, that I found myself weeping.

She thought a fountain was a better way to celebrate peace than the bonfires that were taking place in villages throughout England, though admittedly it was less democratic. This fountain made her think of the spectacular fountains at Versailles and the Villa d'Este in Tivoli, which soon would no longer be sealed off by war. The world seemed to be opening up once more and Elizabeth hoped that one day soon she and Charles could look at a fountain together, expanding their shared world onto the Continent.

On 8 May Britain celebrated VE Day, rejoicing at the Victory in Europe. The public had been expecting the declaration since early the previous day, when the Germans were informed by their Foreign Minister that the war was over. People waited expectantly with flags, which could be purchased without the usual obligatory ration coupons. Finally, at 7.40 p.m., the BBC interrupted a piano recital with the announcement that the next day would 'be treated as victory in Europe Day, and will be regarded as a holiday'.

Initially, the news seemed anticlimactic. In the days leading up to the announcement, Elizabeth Bowen described to Charles Ritchie the general atmosphere of paralysis and apprehension in London, with 'everyone wondering what they ought to *do*'. The declaration on the radio did not actually seem to change anything.

> I switched off the wireless and said to Alan, 'Well, the war's over,' and he said, 'Yes, I know,' and we gave short gloomy satirical laughs, went into the dining-room and sat on the window sill for about an hour, quite unable to rally, he furious because he hadn't made any arrangements about his office, and I furious because I hadn't got any flags. The park looked as dark as a photograph and was quite empty; and I thought, well, I knew one would feel like this.

Later in the evening, the sky blazed white, and they laid aside their churlishness and walked out into the streets that Elizabeth had patrolled in total darkness for several long years of war. They found Marylebone Town Hall floodlit. To Elizabeth it looked so much like a building in heaven that she burst into tears.

Gradually, London filled with flags. By the following afternoon when Churchill and his ministers assembled on the balcony of the Ministry of Health in Whitehall to announce the end of the war, the city was ready to celebrate. A vast crowd of people gathered at the corner of Whitehall and Parliament Square. 'God bless you all,' Churchill told them. 'This is

Churchill addressing the VE-day crowds

your victory! . . . In all our long history we have never seen a greater day than this. Everyone, man or woman, has done their best. Everyone has tried . . . God bless you all.' Spontaneously, 'Land of Hope and Glory' swelled up from below. Churchill began to conduct the chorus and was rewarded with a rendition of 'For he's a jolly good fellow'. Elizabeth Bowen, always a loyal fan of Churchill, joined in the celebrations, which she found impressive and beautiful. 'On a monster scale,' she wrote to Charles, 'it was like an experience in love. Everything, physically – beginning and ending with the smell of sweat, so strong and so everywhere that it travelled all through this house by the open windows – was against exultation, and yet it happened.' Walking to Westminster Abbey she found that 'after a crise (which happened quite early on) of hysterical revulsion and tiredness, I passed beyond . . . and became entered by a rather sublime feeling'. But Elizabeth felt out of place on the streets. 'The intelligentsia', she reported, 'remained in bed, drank and thought.'

Graham Greene stayed in London to celebrate VE Day with Dorothy. 'Having watched the blitz through I thought I'd see the peace in London,' he explained to his mother. 'LOVE AND HAPPY PEACE TO YOU – GREEN' he wrote in a cable to his wife. 'Your wire *quite* admirable and pie-worthy,' she replied enigmatically. Vivien took their son Francis through Oxford to see the illuminations, gazing at the floodlights, rockets and bonfires – 'huge leaping pyres'. She had a small party, serving iced coffee and cake to friends. 'Drawing room looked lovely and I had one window quite up and cushions on the balcony window sill.' But she minded Graham's absence. 'I so missed you to go about with. Oxford is a good place for such things as the architecture looked so lovely: no street lights, just windows, and coloured lights and firelight.'

Graham and Dorothy went to St James's Park to watch the celebrations. 'There was precious little to see but some floodlighting,' he told his mother, 'and still less to eat or drink. Everything very much more decorous than the Jubilee or Berkhamsted in 1918.' In *The End of the Affair* Greene attributes his experiences to Sarah Miles and her husband Henry. 'It was very quiet beside the floodlit water between the Horse Guards and the palace,' Sarah records in her diary. 'Nobody shouted or sang or got drunk. People sat on the grass in twos, holding hands. I suppose they were happy because this was peace and there were no more bombs. I said to Henry, "I don't like the peace".'

Sarah, wanting her lover beside her instead of her husband, wishes that she could begin again but knows that she cannot. Greene himself was accompanied by his lover. However, the love affair with Dorothy had now started to take on the same claustrophobic quality as his marriage. Writing to Vivien in 1948, lamenting his failures as a husband, Graham told his wife that since 1944 he had failed with Dorothy 'just as completely as at Oxford'. 'Especially during the last four years, though the strain began much earlier, I have caused her a great deal of misery.' In *The Heart of the Matter* Scobie tells his mistress that it is a mistake to mix up happiness and love. Graham continued to love (and to pity) Dorothy, but she was no longer a straightforward source of happiness.

Returning to Oxford, Graham attempted to pacify Vivien by suggesting they should have a third child. Vivien had always wanted another
son, who was to be called Mark, but Graham had been reluctant to
have more children in wartime and was not particularly interested in
spending time with the children they already had. Vivien later recalled
the occasion at the end of the war when Graham suddenly turned to
her and said 'Have Mark'. 'I felt a sort of outrage,' she said.

When he suggested having Mark, I thought to myself, 'You've had all
these women and you live with them and you say you love them and
then come back after all these years to me, and expect to pick up everything just as it was,' and I said to him, 'no, no, nothing like that,' and he
said, 'oh, very well,' quite cheerfully.

Hilde Spiel and Peter de Mendelssohn found VE Day more of a satisfying climax to the war than Greene did. They celebrated the German
capitulation itself at the home of Kingsley Martin, the editor of the
New Statesman. Then on 7 May Peter called Hilde from the Ministry
and told her to come immediately into town. They walked down
Piccadilly looking at the endless crowds of excited people. The next day,
like Bowen and Greene, they joined the thousands of Londoners
wandering dizzily through a city whose lights were allowed to flare up
again after five and a half years. They were part of the crowd singing
'For he's a jolly good fellow' up to Churchill on his balcony. Near the
end of her life, Spiel looked back on this as the pinnacle of her happiness in London. 'Never before or after have I experienced such a
collective intoxication of happiness, never again such certainty of being
at home here and nowhere else.'

The next evening, the government put on a display of searchlights.
These were the same flares that had lit up the sky in wartime, but now
Londoners could enjoy the lighting effects without worrying about the
damage they portended. Walking home at midnight from a dinner
party, Elizabeth Bowen watched the searchlights from Grosvenor
Square: 'each one staggered and whirled around the sky, scribbled,
darted, and crashed into others'. The tips of the lights met, as though

pinpointing an enemy plane, but this evening they seemed to be drunk, collapsing against each other for support; 'they also managed to look extremely lewd'. Elizabeth walked towards the park and, once she was halfway down Baker Street, the searchlights began to send up vertical pillars of light, so that 'the whole of the darkness above London became a Gothic cathedral'. They then tipped over, dripping white rain towards the ground. 'I suppose', Elizabeth wrote to Charles, 'that everyone, in those two days, found one thing that was in *their* own language, and seemed to be speaking to them, specially. The searchlights were mine. For me they were the music of the occasion.'

In the aftermath of war, Elizabeth Bowen began to take stock. Quickly, she began to look back on the war as an exhilarating period and to find what followed anticlimactic. With the threat of death removed, everyday life became less precious. Without Charles, life had lost its sheen. 'I would not have missed being in London throughout the war for anything,' she would write in an autobiographical note in 1948; 'it was the most interesting period of my life. It was interesting to see the quiet old English capital converted into a high-pressure cosmo-politan city.' Now, Elizabeth wrote to thank those who had helped her to live at high pressure. There was Cyril Connolly, who had helped to make the war a positive experience instead of a 'deteriorating dead loss' by hosting parties with 'real spirit': 'I know that many of us owe you a lot, and I do personally.' There was William Plomer, who had been 'completely incarcerated' in naval intelligence but could not have made 'less fuss'. Writing to Plomer, she reflected that she was lucky to have had 'such a good war – if you know what I mean'.

15

'The days were listless and a flop'

Summer 1945

For most Londoners, the summer of 1945 was a muted period in which the bright lights of victory faded into a greyer peace. Elizabeth Bowen was pleased to retreat to Ireland at the beginning of June and to enter the languid world of Bowen's Court, with its tempo of 'slow motion, reflectiveness, ease'. Each time she arrived at the house, she had an uncanny sense of surveying a life that had continued in her absence. On this occasion, she reported to Charles that she would not be surprised when first entering the house if she found ferns growing on the staircase or a mythical animal crouching outside her bedroom door. She was missing Charles, and had embarked on the dual existence that would continue for the rest of her life. Part of her was engaged in the daily routine, entertaining, socialising, visiting the local church. But most of her was in the virtual realm of letters, ensconced in the secret psychic space she shared with Charles. 'You take with you my real life, my only life,' she had told him in the letter she sent him away with.

Now, Elizabeth was distressed because, owing to slow postal services and Irish censorship, she had not received a letter from him for a month. She had realised that her week 'really, focuses internally on what you say, how you are and what you tell me you're doing'. In the absence of a new letter she returned to old ones, reading and rereading them until she knew them by heart. Everything else that she read was

inflected through him. Enjoying *Antony and Cleopatra*, she demanded
that he should read it again, when he had time. It had become crucial
to know that her mental experiences were in some way shared. Fortunately Bowen's Court was receptive to the felt sense of absent presences.
It had always been a ghostly house, and it was easier to keep Charles's
ghost alive here than it was in London, where the flux of new visitors
erased the traces of those who had departed. 'I look round and see the
corduroy armchair, near the fire, that you sat in; and can almost see you
in it.' Ireland itself was 'conducive to dreams' and she was 'making
plans, seeing pictures, building castles in the air' around their future.
'There are such lovely places round here – river valleys, woods, sides of
mountains, that you and I never had time to see. I long to wander
about them.'

For Hilde Spiel, the euphoria ebbed as the anxieties of everyday life
returned. 'No more danger from the skies, but money problems, food
problems, worries about my parents, as before.' Since the beginning of
the year, Peter de Mendelssohn had repeatedly disappeared on visits to
France, sent by SHAEF. Now, in June, he was sent to Germany to set
up contacts with writers and journalists for SHAEF Information Services Control. His time for reforming that 'band of thieves and
murderers and abject criminals' in Germany had come. After Peter left
for Berlin, Hilde was alone in witnessing the gradual decline of her
father. Throughout the war Hugo Spiel had looked for work, with little
success. On 6 April 1941 Hilde noted in her diary that he had gone to a
factory in Enfield to find a job as an assembler, but that he did not pass
the physical assessment. Two weeks later she reported that he was working with the rubble clearers, which also involved joinery work and
repairing windows. 'He does it all happily.' He continued to clear
rubble periodically for the next few years.

At the end of the war Hugo Spiel was briefly given a job as a laboratory supervisor for the Ministry of Supply in Leeds, and then as a
director of research. His technique for producing synthetic rubber had
attracted attention at last; the renowned scientist J. D. Bernal had taken
an interest in him and suggested recommending him for membership
of the Royal Society. But then the rubber plantations in the Far East

were reclaimed and Hugo was dismissed, becoming unemployed once
more. In June 1945 he was clearing rubble again, a fact unsuspected by
Hilde, whom he tried to protect from his shabby desperation. When
she did find out, she put a stop to the job, but she herself, as always, was
short of funds. She was too busy translating Peter's wartime novel *The
Hours and the Centuries* for a Swiss publisher to earn any extra money.

Together Hilde and her father attempted to find a more dignified
alternative to rubble-clearing. However, Hilde had little patience with
Hugo's attempts to set himself up as a translator, and wrote a letter
explaining to him the harsh economic laws of the literary world. In her
autobiography she castigated herself for her heartlessness:

> I would have treated him more gently if I had understood then that his
> life was over, that exile was killing him as surely as a German concentra-
> tion camp would have done.

In July 1945 Hugo died. Returning exhausted from an abortive search for
work, reckless as ever, he ran himself a cold bath. His wife found him dead
in the chilly water. Hilde had to borrow money to pay for the cremation.
'Everything now is being lived already before one has a chance to do it
oneself,' she observed in her diary, 'and all emotions are second hand.'

Hilde's letters to Peter were delayed and it was weeks before he heard
about his father-in-law's death. In the meantime he wrote cheerful
letters about his escapades in Germany, where he was now temporarily
seconded to the Americans as the press officer for their zone. 'At odd
moments I wonder whether it was right for me to come out here and
leave you alone,' he wrote from Bad Homburg at the end of June; 'but
the more I think of it the more I feel it was right. These weeks are
among the most important in my life.' He felt lucky because he was the
right age to realise the full implications of the scenes he was witnessing.
'I am old enough to be about and really see it all with mine own living
eyes, and I'm young enough to understand what it means. Few people
do around here, I find.'

Peter became even more jubilant once he began work in Berlin,
where he arrived on 7 July. 'This', he announced to Hilde the day after

his arrival, 'is the crowning adventure of this whole fantastically adventurous business.' He had only been in the town for two days but had 'lived a life already, or rather relived it', visiting nightclubs, wandering through ruins, elated by the 'crazy town'. The nightclub he had been to the previous night – 'wild, noisy, cheap, vulgar' – reminded him of Berlin of the early 1920s.

Loud shrill music, megaphones, jazz, loud dresses, fiercely painted and powdered faces, young men who haven't eaten for days in smart suits which are smart only at a distance – all fiercely pretending they are still there, they are alive, trying to drown their despair and misery in this hectic outburst of amusement [amid] a colossal ruin, brown, grey, black ruins, street after street, block after block.

There had never been anything like it anywhere. 'What a story, what an unbelievable story.' It was the most exciting job he had ever had.

At the same time, he needed Hilde's help with the more mundane aspects of life. Could she send a large tin of Normacol (a laxative), toothpaste, a towel, pyjamas, shoes, handkerchiefs and cigarettes? Could she ring up Kingsley Martin and promise Peter's *New Statesman* report? Oh, and could she get on with translating Peter's novel; he wanted to send it off as soon as he returned. A week later he informed her dramatically that Berlin was 'boiling in sweltering summer heat, and the stench and odour that rises from the canals and river arms of the inner city, still packed with thousands of rotting human bodies, make one really sick'. But he was managing to feel at home in a country mansion in suburban Zehlendorf, where the Allies had set up their headquarters. The chairs and sofas were comfortable, there were large French windows opening out onto the terrace, and there were drinks and American cigarettes on the coffee table. It was a perfect lazy summer evening and the night before he had gone to a party hosted by a forty-year-old German woman wearing a transparent white silk dress with a bunch of roses in her hair. This was a gathering of musicians, singers, theatre and film people, decorated by 'girls big and small, pretty and very pretty'. Peter drank heavy, sweet red Caucasian wine and talked to old and new acquaintances on the terrace.

'My darling,' Hilde wrote to her husband,

> life is so queer, so unbearably ironical that I cannot know what to do,
> what to say. Today three letters came from Berlin and Hamburg, and it
> is clear that you had, or perhaps still have, no idea of what has happened.
> How ghastly it all is. While you went to the German singer's party I
> walked about here like a ghost, tearless, comforting my mother and
> aunt, crying noiselessly at night so as not to wake up my mother who
> slept in the same room.

She was perplexed by their disparity: 'This is clearly the moment in my life when I would have needed you most, when you, on the other hand, need me least. How is that possible?' She was also distressed by the ease with which he seemed to have settled into communicating with that band of murderers and traitors he had once so high-mindedly derided. 'Much of what you describe disgusts me,' she told him. 'You know how tolerant I am, how ready to compromise, how unwilling to hate.' But she found it intolerable that he could just forget 'so much suffering and torment, the dark years, all the martyrdom, hunger, annihilation'.

And the dark years were also their own. For years she had given Christine a goodnight kiss without knowing whether the next morning she would find her alive or torn in pieces. Now she looked at helpless émigrés of her parents' generation and the furrowed faces of ordinary people on the Underground and found, bitterly, that something in her resisted these fraternisations over Caucasian wine. Since the Allies had liberated the concentration camp at Belsen on 15 April it had become even harder for many people in Britain to tolerate the Germans. On 19 April Richard Dimbleby broadcast a report about his first impressions of the camp, describing the day he had visited it as the most horrible of his life.

> I picked my way over corpse after corpse in the gloom . . . Some of the
> poor starved creatures . . . looked so utterly unreal and inhuman that I
> could have imagined that they had never lived at all.

That summer the British public could see newsreels at the cinema showing film footage of the atrocities.

Peter did not receive Hilde's letter until later in the month, so he continued to write to her triumphantly about his exploits in Berlin. On 17 July he reported that he had been entrusted with the task of preparing the publication of the first and probably only American-licensed German newspaper in Berlin. He was extremely excited.

> This is the crowning event, and I'm immensely happy that the long and not always easy road has led me thus far. Beyond accomplishing this I have no ambition in this field, and after accomplishing it, I shall gladly return home and cultivate my literary garden.

He begged Hilde not to be angry with him for not coming home any earlier, adding:

> I don't want to write a lot of stuff about how much I long to be home and how I miss you all. That is so completely understood that I don't have to make a lot of words about it. I want to come home and stay at home, with you and the children . . . But I must first complete this job . . . Please Mummili, let me do it and don't feel angry and frustrated about it.

Meanwhile he was still waiting for the Normacol. Perhaps she had not yet received his letter?

On 21 July Peter finally did get a letter from Hilde, berating him for not writing, but he had still not received the critical letters about her father. He told her crossly that he had written conscientiously, from wherever he was, approximately three times a week. 'I'm quite innocent,' he added. Hilde had said that she would like to hear a little more about how much he was missing her, failing simply to take it as read, but Peter did not have much patience with her demands.

> To answer your letter quickly . . . I think we have evolved a very good system of letter writing, in that we limited the formalities (which are

understood, namely how are you, I'm well) to a minimum, and write
with extreme egocentrism (does that word exist? I wonder). You just
rattle off all the news and views you have, and I rattle off mine, and we
just assume that we love each other and all the rest. I think this is very
good.

He did at least thank her more fully for translating his novel, which she
had now finished.

You've done well, my Mummi, it was a big job, and doing it on the side
along with all your other chores can't have been easy. I'm very, very
grateful, and very happy that you also enjoyed it.

This rather patronising gratitude was not enough to console Hilde for
her serious money worries or her grief at her father's death. But there
was nothing that she could do except to wait for her earlier letters to
arrive.

All this time London was preparing for the election on 29 July, in which
Churchill's Conservative party was vying for power against the Labour
party, led by Clement Attlee. Labour was promising Britain the social
reforms that politicians on both sides had often claimed they were
fighting for during the war. In December 1942 the economist and civil
servant William Beveridge had published the popular Beveridge Report,
setting out proposals in health care that would form the basis of a
welfare state. Churchill responded cautiously at the time, reluctant to
make promises that he would not be able to fulfil. Since then some
progress had been made – notably R. A. Butler's August 1944 Education
Act, which created a tripartite system of education – but there was still
a long way to go and the Conservative government under Churchill
seemed unlikely to commit to a full course of social reform.

   In April 1945 the Labour party issued a manifesto called *Let Us Face
the Future*, demanding decisive post-war action to ensure full employ-
ment, the creation of a national health service and a housing programme.

They insisted that 'the problems and pressures of the post-war world threatened our security and progress as surely as – though less dramatically than – the Germans threatened them in 1940.' At this stage Labour seemed more likely than the Conservatives to provide the reform the public felt was owing to them, and this became clearer in the run-up to the election. The electorate was becoming gradually more disillusioned with Churchill. On 4 June Churchill made his first radio campaign speech, in which he assured the nation that a socialist government would be untenable in Britain because it would be unable to allow public expressions of discontent and 'would have to fall back on some form of Gestapo'. This did not go down well with people who had just been fighting the Germans and were inclined towards some form of socialism. His public appearances in London that summer were greeted with muted enthusiasm.

Returning from Ireland and finding London 'rude, lewd and untidy' after the decorum of Dublin, where she had stayed for a few days, Elizabeth Bowen spent the final week of June campaigning. The electioneering itself, she told Charles, was getting more and more idiotic on all sides; at intervals loudspeaker vans dashed around Regent's Park. She was supporting a Liberal candidate who had decided at the last moment to stand in South Marylebone, although she knew it was a 'lost cause'. The Liberal party, under the leadership of Archibald Sinclair, was never a serious contender. Alan was planning to vote Labour on the grounds that the Labour candidate was a woman. 'His 1912 feminism,' Elizabeth explained to Charles; 'I ask him whether he wants the country run by Jews and Welshmen?' Graham Greene approached the election with similar flippancy. 'Reluctantly I shall vote Conservative,' he informed his mother. 'The Socialists are such bores! But if there was a Liberal I'd vote for him.'

In the event, Labour won a resounding victory, gaining 393 seats, while the Conservatives were left with 197 and the Liberals with 12. Peter de Mendelssohn, learning of the results in Berlin, was delighted. 'For once it feels good again to be a Britisher,' he wrote to Hilde. 'We are, after all, awake and not merely a people of overaged, somnolent share-holders and dividend earners.' Social insurance, land reform, housing, schools; all the reforms for which the British had waited so patiently could now be pushed through.

Graham Greene remained flippant even after the results were declared. Lunching with the writer Walter Allen at Rules he saw the headline 'SOCIALISTS IN' plastered across the *Evening Standard*. 'Damn!' he exclaimed. 'Don't you approve, Graham?' Allen asked. Greene told him that he did not care one way or another and had not bothered to vote himself, but he had been planning to make a prank call at three o'clock, assuming that the Tories would win. 'There won't be any point in doing so now,' he complained. It turned out that he had been intending to ring the Reform Club where the editor of the *Spectator*, Wilson Harris, lunched every day. Harris was Greene's former boss and a long-term enemy, and was also a Churchill-supporting MP. Greene was going to pretend to be speaking from the Cabinet Office and tell Harris to call at 10 Downing Street at 3.30, making him think that he was about to be offered high office.

Elizabeth Bowen was more earnestly disappointed by the election and it became clear that her sympathies were with the defeated Conservatives. The results, she told Charles, were 'a terrific psychic shock to me'.

> I felt sick, and shortly afterwards was. I don't think I minded the Socialist walkover: it was the complete collapse and failure and ignominy of the people who represent the ideas I support that got me down. In a flash I saw so many things that I had been trying to hide from myself.

She was angry with the Conservatives for conducting their own campaign with 'a tactlessness, a sheer psychological ineptitude, that was shattering'. They had insisted to the public that Churchill had won the war on their behalf when in fact most people were convinced that they had won the war themselves: 'Ma by standing in the fish queues, little Herbert by helping with the fire-watching'. She felt that their voting was a reflex of indignation at being told anything to the contrary.

Although she was distressed by the Labour victory (and especially by its scale), Elizabeth was infuriated with the Conservative party. Indeed, she would not have wanted the Conservatives to win by an enormous majority either. 'Obviously, from the point of the good Conservative, the Party needs a good purge' she informed Charles. She was even in favour of Labour 'doing some heavy bulldozing work within the next two years or so' and, especially, of their breaking 'Big Business'. Her own Conservatism was driven more by a respect for tradition than by a commitment to Tory economic principles. She had always hoped that the aristocratic Tories would eventually repudiate 'Big Business', though she had now come to see this as hopelessly unrealistic.

Elizabeth's horror at the election results was more a response to the lamentable failure of the Conservatives and the Liberals (who had lost half their seats) than to the change of government. She empathised passionately with them for their defeat and was personally sad to lose Churchill, who had been a hero for her throughout the war. However she was prepared to accept the presence of Labour and of the welfare state they would create. What she could not tolerate was the levelling that was evidently about to ensue. She had lost the spirit of camaraderie that she had demonstrated in letters and essays written during the Blitz. In that first draft of the 'London, 1940' essay she expressed just the kind of belief in the war as a 'People's War' that she now repudiated in dismissing the popular conception of Ma in the fish queue and Herbert on the roof fire-watching. 'It is the people's war,' she had stated there, 'for the people's land, and what we save we rule. And we have it in us. It is this stir of big power in little people, the wide-awake look in the eyes, the nerve in the step, that makes this autumn in Britain a sort of spring.'

The problem was that this sense of camaraderie existed alongside a more elitist sense of entitlement. Charles noted in his diary in 1941 that Elizabeth always managed to get hold of large quantities of smoked salmon; even during the Blitz the rich home was quite different from the poor home. He expressed hopes that Elizabeth shared when in December 1941 he prayed in his diary that after the war God should leave them their luxuries, even if they had to do without necessities.

Let Cartiers and the Ritz be restored to their former glories. Let house-parties burgeon once more in the stately homes in England. Restore the vintage port to the clubs and the old brown sherry to the colleges. Let us have pomp and luxury, painted jezebels and scarlet guardsmen, – rags and riches rubbing shoulders. Give us back our bad, old world.

Elizabeth, like Charles, saw the rise of the working classes as heralding a failure in taste. While she could accept some sharing of wealth and welfare, she bristled at the thought of popular culture displacing the older modes of life that she loved.

And Elizabeth Bowen was not the only one to repudiate her wartime enthusiasm for democratic levelling in the immediate post-war period. Henry Yorke, who had gone further than Bowen in applauding the breakdown of class distinctions, at least within the fire service, was immediately fearful of the high levels of taxation that would be brought in by the Labour government. Taxes had already doubled between 1938 and 1945 and looked set to go up more, just at the point when Yorke's family business was successful for the first time in years. Ultimately, his loyalties were with the conservative upper classes. He may have feared the domination of the world by the Mosleys in 1939, but he and Dig were the first people to write to Diana Mosley when she was put in prison the following year. 'Another lot who are put out are those who for some years have been mildly pink,' Elizabeth Bowen wrote to Charles on the day of the election. 'They are now in a great (and I imagine for some time unnecessary) fuss about their investments. Also they are faced by the fact that their political ideas are no longer daring.' She wished that Proust were there to mock the hypocrisy of the aristocracy as they eagerly contradicted themselves.

At the beginning of August Yorke delivered his new novel, *Back*, to the Hogarth Press. An early mention of it occurs in a letter to Rosamond Lehmann in March, where he wrote that it was 'all about a man whose nerves are very bad: and as far as I can tell will be no better or no worse than anything else I have done.' Despite this relative optimism, it had been a hard book to write. 'I've been working like mad,' he told Mary Keene in June. 'The new book is being difficult.' And he was writing it at a time of general unhappiness. 'It's very sad. Nothing but work, work, work and not getting anywhere,' he complained.

Although *Back* is set in 1944, it is a novel that reflects Yorke's own sense of post-war deflation. Its central character, Charley Summers, experiences the end of the war as a period of anticlimax, having lost a leg fighting overseas and been sent home. He feels displaced by civilian society, primarily because Rose, a girl he was having an affair with before the war, has died. The plot of the novel hinges on a case of mistaken identity. Charley becomes convinced that Rose's illegitimate half-sister Nancy is Rose herself, who has only pretended to die. It takes him several months to forget Rose and fall in love with Nancy, having now been persuaded that she is a separate person. The mood and setting of the novel feels pallid after the impassioned lyricism of *Loving*. There is the occasional enthusiastic description of Rose: 'crying, dear Rose, laughing, mad Rose, holding her baby, or, oh Rose, best of all in bed, her glorious locks abounding.' But on the whole Charley finds her harder and harder to remember and his love for Nancy is more quietly admiring than ardent. Sex is presented as merely a brief respite from unhappiness rather than a source of joy. Contemplating an affair with his secretary, Charley muses that 'this was the sole promise there was in being alive'. It is the only aspect of life that is not unremittingly bleak.

Back is in part a novel about confused, illegitimate fatherhood. Rose's father, Mr Grant, has fathered Nancy during a brief affair, and although he acknowledges this second daughter he is never a committed father to her. Charley always suspects Rose's son Ridley of being his own child rather than Rose's husband's, but searches in vain for 'an echo of his own face in those cheekbones'. In fact the narrator tells us that 'unknown to him' the child has nothing to do with him at all, 'except in so far as he was a reminder of his Rose'.

Implicit here is a rejection of Alice that may have been partly behind Mary Keene's violent antagonism to the book. Her copy of the novel, which is not inscribed by Henry, contains an angry piece of personal literary criticism on the back page. Here Mary complains that 'Charley (he is called Charley as one calls a child) Summers can't react to anyone. He is them and not himself. So they have to be both themselves and him. He has no active love, but a sickness, which is mainly bewilderment.' She adds that the war is blamed for this state but that this is suspect and that if Charley Summers were a boy just reaching puberty all would be understandable. Rejected, Mary took refuge in a scathing dismissal of the man she had loved who, she suggests, was himself incapable of love in the first place. Certainly Henry Yorke presents Charley Summers as a man unable to access his emotions easily, though in fact he himself seems to be no more forgiving of his central character than Mary is. Unlike *Loving*, this is a book that does not encourage easy empathy between reader and characters, although Mary was right to see that the muted mood of the book was Henry's own.

During the summer of 1945, the war against Japan was finally drawing to a close. It had been a long-drawn-out and costly struggle. Even on VE Day newspapers had reported more British soldiers lost in the fighting in Burma; for people with relatives overseas and for anyone outside Europe the war was still going on. On 21 July America appealed to Japan's leaders to surrender, warning them that their opportunity was passing rapidly and that a refusal would result in the almost total destruction of the country. No surrender was forthcoming, and on 6 August America dropped the first atomic bomb on the Japanese city of Hiroshima. President Truman announced that this was 2,000 times more powerful than any bomb dropped before. Its impact was catastrophic; most of Hiroshima was destroyed within minutes. In Britain, people debated the ethics of the act. According to the *Manchester Guardian* the Allies had already dropped the equivalent of one and a half times the Hiroshima bomb on Cologne and its use was 'entirely legitimate'. On 7 August Evelyn Waugh noted that newspapers, 'as often miles wide of public conscience', were jubilant about the bomb, forecasting vast benefits to the world by its discovery. But Victor Gollancz was representative of many of his contemporaries when he complained that it was 'further debasement of the human currency'. On 9 August Evelyn Waugh reported that the newspapers had now started to express consternation about the new bomb, hurriedly catching up with public opinion. That day a second atomic bomb was dropped on Nagasaki. As the world looked on in horror at the extraordinary destructive power of the new weapon, the Emperor of Japan, Hirohito, began negotiations for a Japanese defeat. He capitulated in part because he was frightened by the Russian success in occupying Manchuria and he had decided that he would rather Japan was occupied by the Americans than the Rusisans. On 15 August he announced the unconditional surrender of his country. Because of the time difference, the British heard the news on 14 August, and 15 August became VJ Day, celebrating victory over Japan.

VJ Day itself was experienced fairly universally as an anticlimax. King George VI opened Parliament with a speech proclaiming the nationalisation of the coal mines and of the Bank of England; crowds lined Piccadilly Circus and Trafalgar Square. But it was hard to celebrate with the same enthusiasm as in May. In Wimbledon Hilde Spiel was looking after her children on her own once again. At the beginning of August Peter had briefly returned at last, but his visit had been too short for them to resume the usual rhythms of their lives. She was disappointed that he was too caught up in his own adventures and successes to empathise fully with the pain that she had experienced during his absence. And her distress was compounded when she was given a clear indication of their continuing status as exiles. When the atom bomb was dropped on Hiroshima, Hilde and Peter were at Kingsley Martin's cottage in Essex. The assembled guests were all deeply stirred by the news of the bomb. Hilde thought of her father, whom the news would have roused to enthusiasm as a scientist, but still horrified as a moral human being. Kingsley Martin announced: 'This means the end of the war.' Turning to Hilde and Peter, he observed, 'I expect you will go back to your own country now?' 'Then we knew,' Hilde later wrote, 'though we did not admit it to ourselves, that nine years of assimilation into the English world had been in vain.' They had spent much of the war in the company of Kingsley Martin, defying the German bombs together; they had celebrated the first signs of victory with him; and he, more than most British people, was anxious to remember the humanity lurking within every German. But it did not occur to him that nationality could ultimately be anything less than immutable.

By the time of VJ Day, Peter was back in Berlin and Hilde wrote to him describing the celebrations. For her the day began with a domestic crisis. Her domestic help, Mrs Stanhouse, rang at eight in the morning and announced that as it was VJ Day she would not come. 'I was genuinely angry,' Hilde told Peter, 'and cried: The Fools!' There was no bread, meat or vegetables in the house. But then Beate, the nanny, went out hunting for food and returned with some rolls, having stood in a bread queue of fifty people, and they all settled down to another great day. 'One will miss them in time, but at the moment they're just five for a penny.' As it was pouring with rain, she did not hang out the flags, in case they were soaked. Towards lunchtime, the sun came out, spirits rose and Hilde and the children roamed around the town.

> It was, well, very much like other V-days, but in some ways they hadn't timed it quite so badly after all, what with the Opening of Parliament and this, that and the other. In scorching heat we stood outside Buckingham Palace for an hour and a half, looking at the queer sights . . . soldiers stuck all over with flags leading a snake round and round the square, two nuns in a taxi, and crowds, crowds, crowds.

By chance, Hilde lined up exactly where the Cabinet and the House of Commons walked into St Margaret's church for the Thanksgiving service and so she had a clear view of Churchill, Morrison, Attlee and Eden, followed by the other MPs. 'Churchill wrung my heart,' Hilde wrote, 'walking with hands clasped at the back, gloomy and solemn like Beethoven, and not stirring to acknowledge the crowd who cheered him more than Attlee.' She found it a curious situation. As far as she was concerned, nobody would have wanted the Conservatives back and everybody liked Attlee, who seemed a modest and decent man. But there was 'something in Churchill that grips your heart, and you can't resist him personally'. Unlike Elizabeth Bowen, Hilde thought that it was admirable for the country to have voted Labour, 'against one's sentiment obviously'.

From Germany, Peter did his best to repair their marriage, wondering if he had shown enough sympathy during his visit. 'My sweet, I was glad and happy to be back home again,' he wrote to Hilde on 9 August.

It was good and restful to share your room with you, I loved and enjoyed every minute of it. Now that you've got over the worst of it – without my being able to help you at all – I must tell you how immensely I've admired the fortitude and bravery with which you have mastered this dreadful situation. It gives me the creeps, even now and in retrospect, to think that you were in this fearful mess at the time, all alone. How good you were, my mummili – it's been a packet, and you've carried it all the way. I did not want to speak about it all while I was home, because I wanted to do nothing that might weaken you or revive anything you had already overcome. That is why I was cool and, perhaps reserved even – but that was because I wanted to strengthen and reinforce your own coolness and steadiness so painfully acquired. I think you understand. I knew not how to deal with it all.

Just before VJ day, Hilde and Peter's son Anthony was christened. Hilde presided alone in Peter's absence and Hans Flesch-Brunningen was god-father. Remarkably, Juliet O'Hea was godmother, together with their friend Joyce Arrow. Juliet was still attempting to sell Hilde's novel and the two women had been 'most cordial and polite' with each other on the telephone that February. Hilde was still extremely jealous but had decided that Juliet represented less of a threat to her marriage when contained within the family structure. As godfather, Flesch helped Hilde to organise the event. Increasingly, he was taking on the role of *Hausfreund*, the gen-tleman friend who was a normal feature of the lives of most women in 1920s Vienna. In Austria at least, this could be compatible with marriage, and as things stood Peter seems to have accepted the other man's role in their lives. Certainly, he did not have much room to complain; he was leaving Hilde to do almost everything for the family alone. At the end of July he relinquished all responsibility for the christening to her.

About the christening – I really want to leave this to you. I should have liked, of course, to be present, but I can see that it gets postponed further and further, and after all, as you say, it isn't such a frightfully important occasion and you should perhaps really go ahead without me. I think I'm for it.

Hilde sent Peter a description of the event, and he wrote back worried that too much fuss was being made of Anthony and not enough of Christine, given that Hilde had described Christine as looking 'quite sweet' while Anthony was 'immensely admired'. 'Is it possible that my little muffin is being neglected in any way, Mummi?' Peter asked. He felt sorry and apprehensive and was tempted (though not enough to act on it) to rush home and take care of his daughter.

> She is our first child, and it was for her that we lived through these five terrible years – at least I did – and I will never allow her to suffer the slightest bit of unhappiness because now she is no longer the only one.

Anxious, sad and herself feeling neglected, Hilde cannot have seen this as a welcome piece of interference. It was lucky that there were friends like Flesch to make London a less lonely place to be.

For Elizabeth Bowen, VJ Day was merely depressing. 'You know how I felt about VE Day,' she wrote to Charles.

> But that sort of thing can't happen twice. The days were listless and a flop, the nights orgiastic and unpleasant. (Violent anti-Yank demonstrations in Piccadilly, etc: a lot of fights all over the West End and people beaten up.) The most enjoyable human touch was that the poor Queen's hat – powder-blue – fell to pieces on her during the return drive from the opening of Parliament, owing to being saturated with rain. The crowd would not permit her to put up an umbrella.

As far as Elizabeth was concerned, feeling was exhausted. And there was a pervasive sense of guilt ('wrong, I think') about the atomic bomb. Elizabeth was relieved to leave London and return once more to the unchanging world of Bowen's Court.

PART V

Surveying the Ruins

1945–9

Post-war Europe 1945–9

Once the half-hearted excitement of VJ Day had passed, a new era of post-war living began. In the immediate aftermath of the war, Bowen, Greene, Macaulay, Spiel and Yorke took stock and surveyed the world that remained. All five were disappointed by London in this period. Labour immediately started to put in place the reforms they had promised; the buildings damaged by war were gradually repaired. But after the intensity of wartime life, the post-war period seemed grey and slow. Moments out of time, suspended between past and future, gave way to a continuum in which life was measured once again in years and decades rather than in days and weeks.

Bowen, Greene and Yorke in particular had all had an exciting war, and looked set to have a less exhilarating peace. All three had found a kind of spiritual home in wartime London, seizing each unexpected day and each dangerous, blacked-out night. All three were unusually alive to the imaginative possibilities of the moment, and had appreciated the war's power to contract time and suspend the present, whether in the moment of bombing or in the wider temporal climate created by the uncertain tomorrow. They would never again be able to value the present moment so wholeheartedly.

Macaulay's war had been intense too, but tragic rather than ecstatic in its intensity; if she had dwelt in the present moment, then the moment itself had threatened to engulf her in sorrow and pain. She found the prospect of post-war London as dispiriting as Bowen, Greene and Yorke. However she experienced less of a disjunction between war and peace, embarking instead on a period of gradual recovery.

It was Spiel who learnt to inhabit the post-war present most successfully; Spiel, who had found the war itself miserable and unrelenting, who was able to have a better experience of peace than of war and who found in post-war Vienna the suspended present that the others had found in wartime London.

For all five writers, if intense experience was possible in the post-war world it was to be found outside England. Although for most people in Britain travel was severely restricted at this time, Bowen, Greene, Macaulay and Spiel all managed to journey to Europe. And if Europe was not always feasible, then Ireland was. Bowen, Greene, Macaulay and Yorke all made trips to Ireland in the years following the war, enjoying the relative plenty still possible in a country that had experienced the past six years as merely an 'Emergency'. This was a period of deciding how and where to live in the post-war world. Journeys outside Britain were voyages of exploration or return, which offered a chance to try out potential destinations and ways of life. They also presented the opportunity to inspect the landscapes left behind by war and to assess how the world had changed.

During the war, Londoners had become acclimatised to the black and white landscape of their city. In wartime at least, the monochrome streets were rendered briefly beautiful by strange lighting effects. Bomb sites glowed yellow, red and pink in the fire and under searchlights; ruins turned familiar landscapes into odd, other-worldly scenes. But now the greyscale city became more monotonous. The gashed holes and crumbling ruins were bleakly depressing rather than dramatically beautiful, except in areas such as the City of London, where plants had begun to sprout amid the still ghostly, empty streets. And the colourless feel was reinforced by the continued austerity. Rationing was tightened in February 1946 to release supplies for the British Zone in Germany; even bread was rationed in May. In the winter of 1946 Britain was hit by dangerously severe cold weather, widespread power cuts, labour strikes and a fuel crisis.

For these five writers, to leave Britain was to be jolted awake by ruins on a less human, more frightening scale in Germany or Austria, or to be rejuvenated by the colours of southern Europe, or soothed by the dreaminess of the Irish coast and countryside. For Bowen, the greyness of London could be forgotten amid the green of Ireland. Here the ruins were older and more romantic; the wistful landscape evoked the grandeur of a past that was being neglected in London, where a new world was insistently being forged. This was Ireland's appeal for the English as well; Greene, Macaulay and Yorke were all relieved to escape to a country where time seemed slower and nature more luxuriantly green. They all enjoyed the continued opulence of Dublin's Shelbourne Hotel and the relative ease and plenty of the Irish countryside. And Macaulay was also more energetically awakened by a trip to the coast of Spain and Portugal, where she swam in one glittering bay after another, rediscovering the sensual pleasures of water and sunlight.

Like Macaulay, Spiel was reawakened by travel, though for her it was the total destruction of Vienna and Berlin that enabled her mental renewal. The very horror of the ruined landscapes ended a period of anaesthetisation, convincing her that the most exhilarating experiences in the post-war world were to be found as a British subject occupying a defeated, desecrated European city. Greene and Bowen were less enamoured of post-war Vienna than Spiel was, but they too were excited by the chance to experience history in occupied Vienna, revolutionary Prague and humiliated Paris. In Europe and in Ireland the intense moment of the war in London that had ended in the spring of 1945 could be recaptured; pockets of time could be hollowed out of these new and strange landscapes.

16

'The magic Irish light and the soft air'

Elizabeth Bowen's return to Ireland, 1945

Shortly after VJ Day, Elizabeth Bowen returned home to Ireland. She and Alan arrived by boat in the south, steaming up the estuary of the river Suir and landing at Waterford, where they were greeted by rows of high decaying buildings along the quay and a smell of wood smoke in the damp morning air. Elizabeth was ready to leave behind the ruins in London and return to a country whose decay had begun centuries earlier and whose ruins blended unobtrusively and romantically into the landscape.

There was no doubt that this was a homecoming. 'It is impossible', Elizabeth Bowen wrote in a 1946 essay entitled 'Ireland makes Irish', 'to be *in* this small vivid country and not *of* her . . . What has proved so winning, so holding, is, I think, the manner of life here – life infused with a tempo and temperament bred of the magic Irish light and the soft air.'

Soon after her arrival in August, Elizabeth announced to Charles that Ireland, now that she had come back, seemed 'very amiable and good and sweet'. During the war, Elizabeth had been a Londoner who often identified with England. That had changed on the day of the 1945 election, when she decided that it was an advantage to be Anglo-Irish and to disassociate herself from the situation in England. She told Charles that she was happy to 'belong to a class, that potted at by the

Irish and sold out by the British, has made an art of maintaining its position in vacuo'. As a result, she felt entitled to escape again now. 'I stare at the outside of this house and think my ancestors didn't care a damn about English politics, and how right they were.'

Elizabeth appreciated the Irish because, unlike the English, they were responding to peace with straightforward enthusiasm.

> Quite illicitly – I mean, in view of their having been neutrals – everybody is enjoying peace madly; going about with shining and beaming faces. In fact the Irish are the only people I have met so far who are really just getting 100% kick out of world peace. They also remark with justifiable smugness that they always knew this war would end up in Bolshevism, and they are gladder than ever they kept out of it.

It took impressive insouciance on the part of the Irish to enjoy the peace unequivocally. After Hitler's death at the end of April, de Valera had somewhat ignominiously followed official protocol for neutral countries by formally offering his condolences to the German Minister in Dublin. As far as the British were concerned, Ireland now had no right to celebrate the peace. Churchill tempered the jubilatory note of his VE Day broadcast with a taunt at 'the action of Mr de Valera' who, 'so much at variance with the temper and instinct of thousands of Southern Irishmen who hastened to the battle-front to prove their ancient valour', had denied the Allies access to the ports. 'This was indeed a deadly moment in our life, and if it had not been for the loyalty and friendship of Northern Ireland we would have been forced to come to close quarters with Mr de Valera or perish forever from the earth.' De Valera retaliated, shocked by Churchill's suggestion that given sufficient necessity Britain might have been forced to violate Ireland's neutrality, by accusing Churchill of disregarding the autonomy of small nations in a manner comparable to Hitler. He nonetheless thanked Churchill for avoiding the temptation on this occasion. It was hard for the strong to be just to the weak 'but acting justly always has its rewards'.

Unlike Churchill, Elizabeth Bowen did not grudge her compatriots their moment of glory. Politically, she had now lost patience with

England as well as Ireland; personally, she was grateful that the Irish at least were entering the post-war era with style and gaiety. Elizabeth was also appreciative of the comparative luxury available in rural Cork. Here at least, Ireland did seem to be the land of plenty it was portrayed as during the war. Elizabeth informed Charles that although there was not much soap (a deficit remedied by the supplies he sent from Canada), there was, thanks to the kindness of friends, plenty of cream, peaches, eggs, meat, lobsters and butter. 'The sense of profusion, ease, courtesy, leisure, space drips like warm honey over one's nerves,' she added gratefully, though she was aware that elsewhere in the country things were still as bad as in England. 'The food in all Co Cork houses (other than mine where it is rather haphazard) is simply marvellous,' she boasted in September, 'swimming in cream and cakes and hot scones running with melted butter. I suppose, strictly, Irish country house life is the last form of comfortable, old-fashioned existence left anywhere in Europe. How absolutely furious it would make the British.' Most of all, Elizabeth appreciated the silence of Bowen's Court because it gave her the imaginative space she needed to write and the leisure to think, uninterrupted, about Charles. 'This house', she wrote to him shortly after her arrival, 'was built by that long-ago, unconscious Bowen for you and me to be happy in. That July when you and I were here it reached its height. It will again when you're back. I often wonder what time of year that will be.'

Elizabeth had arrived at the house with Alan and, practically, they were in the process of arranging their future there together. She told William Plomer that their plans were fluid. They still had Clarence Terrace but had sublet the top floors to a BBC couple. Alan's health was deteriorating. One of his eyes had been bad since the First World War, when he had suffered from trench poisoning, and he now had a cataract in the other eye. He also had a weak heart, which was exacerbated by his weight and heavy drinking. Now he resigned from the BBC and took up a new job as educational adviser for the gramophone and record company EMI. This would allow him to be in Ireland more and the current plan was to move most of their furniture to Bowen's Court and to base themselves there.

But for Elizabeth it was a large and dreamy enough house to contain both her actual life with Alan and her imagined life with Charles. Over the course of the summer, she settled down into a routine of sleepily repetitive days, writing, gardening and dreaming. She wrote in the morning; she cut down nettles after tea; and, writing to Charles, she was able to inscribe him in the rhythm of her days. 'It is a drowsy late-August afternoon,' she wrote, ushering him into the scene. 'I am writing in the library with the windows open. One large blue bottle fly is bumbling about the ceiling: outdoors there is a hum of unspecified insects in the trees. The sky is overcast, but there is a sort of sheen of obstructed sunshine on the heavy dark-green trees and the grass.'

In Ireland, Elizabeth could take stock of her feelings since Charles's departure in January. She looked back on her summer in London as a miserable nightmare, which had culminated in the election. Since then she had been feeling aggressive and disaffected: 'I can't dis-obsess myself from the feeling that democracy has celebrated its victory by being had for a mutt in a big way.' In her disappointment about the election, Elizabeth was in line with many of her friends and social class. But the intensity of her reaction was unusual; few of her friends responded to the results by being physically sick. The election had become imbued with all the desperate helplessness of her longing for Charles. This was a summer that she would always remember with repugnance. 'Like when one's inside is upset, everything has disagreed with me. I have desired nothing (that I could have) and enjoyed nothing.' She dated the nightmare as beginning in January, with Charles's departure.

Now, Elizabeth was learning to be happy again. 'Right or wrong, I cannot tell you how well all this agrees with me,' she told Charles in September. She could now admit to him the scale of her unhappiness during the summer. 'I really was getting into a most odd state in London, Charles. I don't know what would have happened if I had stayed there much longer.' She revealed that she had woken up almost every morning in floods of tears. And at times she had caught herself groaning aloud with exasperation.

Escaping to a place where she was able to disassociate herself from English politics, she was also learning strategies to survive Charles's absence. The most effective was to ensconce herself, even more than she had in June, in the imaginary life they shared. 'To one person you are an entire world,' Elizabeth wrote to Charles at the beginning of September. In this letter she admits that, since January, she has been living on the vague hope ('a hope I never openly formulated, but clung to') that he might reappear. Now that she had left London, she could begin to live once again in the present, and it was a present which could include Charles even in his absence. 'I don't know how I should live if it were not for letters,' she told him.

> How would one not (as you say), without the beloved evidence of a letter, come to torment oneself with the fear that love and the entire world of life that surrounds it was an illusion, subjective, brain-spun. As it is, the unfolding of a letter from you, the whole cast and shape of the handwriting on the paper, even before I have begun to read what is written, gives me a sort of rush of nearness.

Writing to Charles enabled Elizabeth to imagine their shared existence at Bowen's Court. Receiving his letters allowed her to picture herself with him in Canada.

> The hour – day or evening – in which you write, the things round you, the Ottawa bells ringing (like when you wrote last) envelops me. Partly, of course, it stirs up an agonising restlessness. But the happiness, the whole sense and aura of you is worth that.

Although she had never been there, she felt nostalgic for the early autumn Ottawa weather, with its crisp air and red leaves. She was also envisaging the life they could share in New York and finding that the fantasy evoked the make-believe lives she had imagined while looking out at the same Irish countryside as an only child; 'a life lived to the last detail, so real one could hear curtains rustle in imaginary rooms, and street-sounds in a city one was not in.'

There is a sense in which, cut off from her London life, Elizabeth was living with Charles. Writing to him, reading and rereading his letters, picturing him in the house in which they had been so happy together, she came close to sharing her life with him. All this time, Elizabeth was in fact living with Alan; but it was a marriage that gave her the mental space to keep Charles almost permanently in her mind. 'I have felt particularly near you all this last week,' she wrote to him; 'so much so that sometimes I can't bear to be spoken to; as though someone else had come into the room when we were together.' She could feel his presence and she could hear his voice: 'It wakes me up, sometimes, in the night when I'm asleep.'

But at the same time, Elizabeth was fighting continued sadness and fear. In the letter where she mentioned being woken by Charles's voice in the night, Elizabeth attempted to advise him on the question of whether to live in Europe or Canada, though she was aware that the 'fors and againsts' were maddeningly complicated and that it was hard for her to be dispassionate. She could see that he needed to use the full force of his brain, and that this was more possible in Ottawa. On the other hand, she could not bear the thought of his suppressing his imagination and sensuality, and was convinced that he had 'a power to live through feeling and apprehension which makes you in nature more an artist or a poet than any orthodox artist or poet I have ever known.' She was worried that in Canada he was losing touch with the artist and the poet and therefore with the lover. 'And, how can you or I live without love? Without that, one feels an exile any place that one is.' She herself felt exiled, even at Bowen's Court. As always, Elizabeth's fears about Charles were entwined with her anxieties about post-war Europe. She longed for the new Europe to crystallise so that Charles could find a home in which his whole nature could be fulfilled, but worried that it would take years. 'War brutalised physical life; post-war seems to dissipate, in a way that is almost brutalising, psychic life.'

Elizabeth was right to worry about the hardening of Charles's heart. On the same day that she was writing this letter, he was reflecting in his diary that he had become inured to life without her. 'I don't think of E as much as I did. I don't even think about myself.' Like her, he feared his own petrification: 'How long can I stand this midday light of commonplace common sense which is the light of middle age? How long can I stand the neatness and emptiness of my life? And in a way I am quite content.' In this first post-war autumn, the pattern of their long-distance love affair was established. There were times when both Elizabeth and Charles believed that they loved each other equally. But Charles, unlike Elizabeth, lost the sense of powerful togetherness during their separations. She could live in the imaginary world created by their letters, reinforcing it through her novels, with their intense, consuming love affairs. He was unable to believe in the fairy tale of their love without her being present to give it a tangible reality. And when his feelings for Elizabeth proved too complicated to assimilate, he diverted himself by indulging in easier liaisons with younger women.

Meanwhile, during the brief periods when she was not thinking about Charles, Elizabeth continued to distract herself with fierce sessions of violent gardening. Even when she felt melancholy and exiled without love, she could be engrossed and soothed by the everyday, concrete problems of the house. Writing to William Plomer, she described this as a process of rejuvenation.

> I came over here feeling like death, full of visitations and repugnances, but am feeling much better now. I have worked like a black out of doors (hewing down nettles and undergrowth, clearing woods) which was just what I wanted, and hardly laid pen to paper or finger to type-writer . . . I think I have the makings of a better forester than gardener: plenty of brute strength and aggression instinct, but the reverse of green fingers – in fact almost anything I plant dies.

Elizabeth was also engaging in the life of her community, as it reawakened after the war. She was decorating the church in preparation for the Harvest ceremony, arraying it with beets, dahlias, turnips, carrots, michaelmas daisies. This was the first successful harvest since the war, and Elizabeth took it seriously. She persuaded her friend Jim Gates to play hymns on the organ, and put considerable energy into singing 'Come ye thankful people, come' to a congregation comprising the farmers and their wives. Despite her long periods of absence, she had a close relationship with many of her neighbours. In October, during a 'cigarette famine' in which no shop for a thirty-mile radius could provide supplies, she reported to Charles that a rumour must have circulated that she was in danger of madness, because a succession of unexpected people suddenly appeared and handed her their private supplies: the blacksmith, the rector, the chemist, the Master of Fox Hounds all sent small parcels of three or four battered, musty cigarettes to restore her sanity.

In the afterword to *Bowen's Court* she describes this first autumn spent in the house as a charmed period, when for the first time she saw the last of the leaves hang glistening in the transparent woods or flittering on the slopes of the avenues.

> The rooks subsided after their harvest flights; in the gale season one or two gulls, blown inland, circled over the lawns. I heard the woods roaring, and, like pistol shots, the cracking of boughs.

This is a description of surprised discovery. For years, she writes, the house had been empty at this season. Elizabeth herself had only spent extended periods in the house in spring, summer and winter. But it is also a description of desolation. Elizabeth's happiness remained fragile, relying, always, on her continued existence in Charles's mind and on his in hers.

'Yes, I have been and am (as you must have felt) infinitely happier here than I am in London,' she admitted to him in November, after he had told her, to her disappointment, that they would not see each other until January. 'At the same time it's a life that must have something in its core – something not it. You and my love for you are in the core, or are the core. If you were dead or lost, or if I were confronted by having no prospect of seeing you again, I could not bear life here.' In Bowen's Court, more than anywhere else, her 'heart and imagination and nerves and senses' were exposed; if the inner part of her life died, she would leave the house and never return. And now, she was praying that nothing would prevent their meeting in January. 'I love you so much. I don't think I can go on living much longer without you.'

Charles did make it to London in January 1946, and stayed for two months, attending meetings of the General Assembly of the United Nations. After a year apart, Elizabeth and Charles once again returned to the ease of a day-to-day relationship. Arriving back in Ottawa at the end of February, Charles abandoned his habitual self-protective hardness and admitted that he believed again in love. 'I see now', he wrote in his diary, 'that what I feel for E with all its imperfections (on my side) is the "Love of my Life" and that I must never hope to find that again. Any other love will have to be of a different kind.' Settling back into London life with Charles removed, Elizabeth returned to letters as 'a substitute for being alive'. 'Yes, certainly you are my life,' she wrote to him matter-of-factly. 'I have felt and still feel as though I were not here – in this room, in this house, in London – at all; but as though I had crossed the air over the Atlantic with you, and were now following you round Ottawa, from place to place.'

For two weeks after Charles's departure, Elizabeth did not leave the house at all, detained inside by jaundice and then by snow and ice. She was dejected and bewildered without him, and she was still depressed by the politics of post-war Britain. There was even a committee set up to decide the future of the Regent's Park Georgian terraces, which she worried would decree that they were too badly damaged to be worth repairing and should be pulled down. 'That they should do so exceeds one's most horrific imaginations of the brave new world,' she complained. She also felt claustrophobic at home. Alan had been through a work crisis, having turned down a job liaising between the Ministry of Education and UNESCO, and was driving Elizabeth crazy 'ramping round and round my room at intervals having regrets and conscience-storms', a 'poor tortured creature' distracted only by a bottle of rye fortuitously posted by Charles from Canada.

Even for those who were not trapped at home with jaundice, London at the start of 1946 was a depressing place. Many of the wartime bomb sites remained in ruins. The economy had been badly hit by the abrupt withdrawal of American Lend-Lease funds the previous August. As a result of the huge debt owed to America all production went for export. Meanwhile, confidence in the government had been reduced by a dockworkers' strike in October, which left food supplies stranded at British ports. When rationing was tightened in February it became clear that it would be some time before the pre-war quality of life resumed. Henry Yorke attempted to cheer himself up by bringing in Goronwy Rees to the London office of Pontifex as a director. This was a time when Yorke was starting to drift apart from many of his close friends. Anthony Powell and his wife had decided to stop trying to see him because of his churlish behaviour at a dinner party shortly after the end of the war. But Yorke remained close to Rees, despite his sympathy for Rosamond Lehmann when Rees jilted her in 1941. Indeed, Yorke had invited Rees to stay in Rutland Gate not long after Rosamond herself had departed, when Rees was posted to London in his work for the GHQ Home Forces in 1942. Rees was one of the few people with whom Yorke was happy to discuss his writing, and his presence at Pontifex now promised to integrate the usually disparate aspects of Yorke's life.

For his part, Rees was happy to spend his mornings at Pontifex. He was now comfortably married to Margie Morris, with whom he had already had two children. Margie, like Dig Yorke, was willing to coun-tenance infidelity, informing her daughter Jenny that she looked on her husband rather like a favourite cat: 'You see, with a cat, you like to see it go out in the garden and enjoy itself and then you are very pleased to see it again when it comes in.' Rees's experiences of lying to multiple women had stood him in good stead for his work at SIS, where each afternoon he was now secretly assessing and evaluating information gathered by British agents for the Political Section. Pontifex provided a useful explanation for his current whereabouts, and the work was not arduous. According to Mark Wyndham, Yorke's cousin, who was also working for the business at this time, Yorke liked Rees to be there because he had a 'much bigger brain than any of us' and was prepared to oppose Yorke's father. Rees moved from job to job within the firm, first handling advertising, then allocating newly made machinery to clients. The work was fuelled by alcohol. Yorke left for the pub every day at 11.30, where he would drink two pints before moving on to gin. By lunchtime Rees would join him. Wyndham described Yorke as sitting sipping his gin and making up stories about the pub regulars, as well as gossiping with Rees about mutual friends and about the typists and accountants in the office. Yorke was getting into a daily pattern which was dominated by drink, though he still managed to write in the evenings.

While Yorke was assuaging his loneliness with drink, Charles Ritchie tried to cheer himself up in Canada with 'Sex Excesses'. That April he catalogued the symptoms in his diary as 'rapid heart action, sense of guilt, feverish erotic spasms', as well as 'coarsening of sympathy' and 'good timing in dancing'. Elizabeth Bowen hid herself away once again in Bowen's Court, though she was becoming so lonely sometimes that she wondered if she was going mad. Day-dreaming that Charles was arriving at the airport and she was driving there to pick him up, she asked him 'why shouldn't one be able to be happy', insisting that 'love does matter more than anything else in the world. If more people were as right-minded and as happy as you or I are capable of being, the world would be a very different place.' But as long as she was in Ireland, she could sustain herself on daydreams. Rereading his letters in bed she found that 'there's extraordinary happiness in the fact of being in love – however much the sufferings of separation are'. She hated leaving Bowen's Court because it meant leaving behind all the vague happy hours in which she had wandered around the house thinking about Charles, and in London she felt frayed and pin-pricked.

In October 1946, Elizabeth and Charles at last spent a week together in Bowen's Court. They met in Paris, where Charles was one of the advisers to the Canadian Delegation at the Peace Conference convened to formulate peace treaties between the wartime Allies and Italy and the Balkan States. Elizabeth was accredited to the Conference as a journalist. Glimpsing her 'bent head and the line of her neck and shoulders through the window', Charles was touched, and felt himself 'sliding back towards her'. Together they wandered around the tree-lined walks of the Luxembourg Gardens and dined in small restaurants on the Left Bank before travelling once again to the more peaceful setting of Bowen's Court. After Charles returned to Canada,

Elizabeth sat in Clarence Terrace picturing him 'forging, with every minute, further and further away' ensconced in the luxury of the RMS *Queen Elizabeth*, and felt torn in pieces, as though she were being drawn after him. 'How happy we have been – and more than happy,' she wrote; 'I feel welded together with you forever.' She commanded him to 'be happy, and keep me inside yourself as I keep you inside myself', supposing that 'eventually we'll grow old together', as at present they were growing up together. She spent the next week reliving their days in Ireland, working away at *The Heat of the Day* and drinking anything to hand. She was also busy with social engagements – with C. V. Wedgwood, Cyril Connolly and Clarissa Churchill, among others – and with her usual journalism and reviews. Indeed, she was amazingly productive during this period, reviewing three books a week for *Tatler* as well as writing her novel. Nonetheless she remained in a state of submerged sadness, waking each day with 'a feeling of loss and fear'.

Elizabeth Bowen's own sadness went into a review of Rose Macaulay's *They Went to Portugal* that was published in her regular column in *Tatler* at the end of October. Here Bowen lamented the decline of civilisation, which Britain had supposedly fought to preserve. 'We are confronted by dilapidation (more depressing, because subtler in its effects, than out-and-out ruin), by long, heart-breaking stories and short tempers.' Civilisation itself was a matter of high spirits and was sustained by a blend of vision and will. The British now needed it for its renewing qualities, which meant that civilised books had a particular value in a disillusioned post-war world. *They Went to Portugal*, which, as Bowen knew, had emerged from just such a moment of renewal, was civilised and could be civilising.

In November Bowen continued her manifesto for contemporary literature with an enthusiastic review of Henry Yorke's *Back*. Here she paid tribute to Yorke as one of the great writers of their day. Unlike other novelists, who were prepared to borrow from their contemporaries or forebears, Yorke was an original writer who seemed to have read no other novels.

Henry Green is one of the living novelists whom I admire most; also, I
consider him to be nearer than almost any other to the spirit and what
one might call the central nerve of our time (though there are, as you
may at once protest, a dozen others who seem more widely topical).

Elizabeth Bowen enjoyed her role as an arbiter of literary taste, but the
effort of reading three books every week could prove exhausting and
unrelenting. And the pleasure of these public pontifications did little to
distract her from private sadness. The only real moment of lucidity
during her stay in London came during a performance of *King Lear*
starring Laurence Olivier. She saw it on her own and emerged 'feeling
dead tired but pure': 'The effect of *Lear* on me or rather on some part
of my sorrow was that of a hot compress on a boil – it "drew" something to the surface and made it burst,' she told Charles. In this period
of grey numbness, *Lear* seems to have offered Elizabeth clarification by
allowing the world to be tragic rather than merely disappointing. Here
was a man bereft of home, love, identity and sight, baring an extremity
of sorrow to the barren heath. Lear's suffering could lend a dignity to
Elizabeth's own. After weeks of tense anguish she could give way to
sadness and wail alongside him. But the clarity enabled by *Lear* was
brief and it was a relief to return to Ireland in December. Existence in
Bowen's Court was now 'all lopsided' without Charles, but he still
seemed to inhabit the house. His voice woke her in the night; he was
present at her writing table in the library.

In January 1947 Charles began a three-year post in Paris as Counsel-
lor to the Canadian Embassy. Elizabeth was now able to visit him
periodically (in February he recorded in his diary a very happy weekend
spent 'huddled over the weak radiator and the whisky bottle or on the
enormous "made for love" bed' of his flat on the Boulevard St Germain)
and Charles became a fairly frequent guest at Bowen's Court. Although
Charles was happy in Paris, he worried that returning to the city of his
student days as a middle-aged official was like paying a social call on a
former mistress. And the city had aged alongside him, her spirit
contracted by sufferings and scarcities. Despite Elizabeth's frequent
presence, Charles was still busy with other love affairs. 'Is it another

illusion or could it be "love"?' he asked in April, shaken by 'the treacherous sweet poison of this spring'. 'Oh God what a fool I am – at forty.' 'The trouble is', he reflected in September, 'that when I begin to ask myself the question: What woman do I love? I am overcome by a sort of mental dizziness.' All along he was writing passionate letters to Elizabeth. 'Your letter came yesterday morning and made me very happy,' she told him in October. 'Most of all, because of you I am happier than I've ever been in my life,' she assured him. She was wondering why it had been accepted by Anglo-Saxon culture that 'being in love should come so early, almost before one is oneself at all, and then be expected to be put behind and done with?'; she felt entitled to this resurgence of joy in her forties.

Charles visited Bowen's Court in November, and Elizabeth was able to sustain herself with memories once again, insisting that he should do likewise. 'Your beloved letter came on Tuesday. How near each other we are. How deeply I love you: this is such a joy, such a joy we share.' 'Love isn't really an illusion,' she told him, addressing his doubts on his own terms, 'it's a reality. As far as I'm concerned, it's you.' For her part, she had lived with him every moment since his departure, and did not feel lonely. Her certainty lasted through into December – 'the feeling of closeness I've had to you here, day and night, since you left has been extraordinary' – though she missed him constantly, and longed to see him again. In December she left for London, and as always she hated shutting up the house in which the continuous daydream of their love could unfold so easily. 'Every time I have to do it I feel as though something died in me – or even as though I became a degree less virtuous.' She was always fearful that she would die in England and not come back.

All this time she was struggling with *The Heat of the Day*. 'Any novel I have ever written has been difficult to write and this is being far the most difficult of all,' she wrote to Charles in March 1945. 'The thing revolves round and round in my brain . . . Almost anything that happens around me contributes to it.' A year later she was back at the novel, grappling with its technical and psychological challenges but finding it absorbing and cheering. That May she was caught up in the 'most cryptic part of my novel – heavens, it is difficult to write. I discard every page, rewrite it and throw discarded sheets of conversation about the floor. Is everything you do as difficult as that? I imagine so. From rubbing my forehead I have worn an enormous hole in it, which bleeds.' This bleeding wound was the price she paid for her dual life: for the intense fulfilment provided by her shared imaginary existence with Charles, which through willpower alone she kept at every moment from subsiding into anguished longing. But of course the longing was always there, pricking away from below the surface of her defiant happiness, and emerging, bloody and tangible in the wound on her head.

Finally, by December 1947, Bowen was halfway through the last chapter of her novel. Her life was lived round the edges of writing; she was working for eight hours a day, returning to the novel after supper in the evenings. Charles had read parts of it and reported that he felt a new growth and strength in her writing. 'If that is so', she replied, 'and I think it is, you know that has come to me from you, don't you? You've given me not only greater comprehension but clearer vision than I had, and made me more fearless. I feel this in my life: it would be strange if it didn't show at least to some extent in my writing.'

The Heat of the Day had taken five difficult years to write and Bowen had come a long way from the hallucinatory descriptions of wartime love of the opening chapters, written in the early days with Charles. The second half of the novel is dominated by suspicion, doubt and betrayal, as Stella confronts the growing certainty that Robert is, as Harrison has alleged, a spy handing over British war secrets to Nazi Germany.

Wearing away at that bleeding wound in her forehead, Bowen was attempting to write a novel in which the romantic hero has voluntarily and unnecessarily gone over to the German side. The Nazis themselves are never named, but are still present as a hinterland of the novel; an evil melodramatically lurking in the background. For Bowen's English readers it was shocking to make Robert a Nazi sympathiser in a novel published only a few years after the war had ended and the worst crimes of the Nazis had been revealed. Rosamond Lehmann, writing Elizabeth an ecstatic letter praising the novel, wondered if she could have made Robert a Communist instead of a Nazi, which would have made it more palatable.

> What bothers me a little is that I cannot see why he shouldn't have been a Communist and therefore pro-Russia and pro-Ally, rather than pro-'enemy'.

The answer is that for Bowen, as an Irishwoman, the possibility of supporting Germany was less unthinkable than it seemed to British readers. She wrote the scenes in which Robert explains his defection from the point of view of someone who had toyed with assuming an English identity and had come down firmly on the side of the Irish. 'Selfishly speaking I'd much rather live my life here,' she wrote to William Plomer from Bowen's Court in September 1945.

> I've been coming gradually unstuck from England for a long time. I have adored England since 1940 because of the stylishness Mr Churchill gave it, but I've always felt, 'when Mr Churchill goes, I go'. I can't stick all these little middle-class Labour wets with their Old London School of Economics ties and their women. Scratch any of these cuties and you find the governess. Or so I have always found.

For the Irish, Robert's politics were less unusual than they seemed to the English. Throughout his poetry, Yeats had bemoaned the 'new commonness / Upon the throne and crying about the streets', asking for Irish heroes who would rise above the masses and cleanse their nation through force. 'What's equality?' he asked in a 'Marching Song' published in the *Spectator* in 1934; 'Muck in the yard'.

> Historic Nations grow
> From above to below.

In Yeats's late poem and personal epitaph 'Under Ben Bulben' Irish poets are invited to learn their trade by scorning:

> the sort now growing up
> All out of shape from toe to top . . .
> Base-born products of base beds

and embracing instead the completion offered by violence. Here Yeats quotes approvingly the nationalist *Jail Journal* of the nineteenth-century activist John Mitchel: 'Send war in our time, O Lord!' And in Ireland, there had been open pro-Nazi sympathisers throughout the war, albeit not as many as some British propagandists would have people believe. That very Irish Irishman, Francis Stuart, used rhetoric not dissimilar to Robert's in the radio broadcasts from Nazi Germany that Bowen would have been exposed to during her wartime fact-finding trips to Ireland. In one broadcast, Stuart explained his motivation for going to Germany on the grounds that 'like I daresay a good many others of us, I was heartily sick and disgusted with the old order under which we've been existing . . . If there had to be a war then I wanted to be among those people who had also had enough of the old system and who moreover claimed that they had a new and better one.'

A decade earlier, in a memoir written in the early 1930s, Stuart railed against democracy itself as 'the ideal of those whose lives as individuals are failures and who, feeling their own futility, take refuge in the mass and become arrogant in the herd'. In the climactic scene of *The Heat of the Day*, Robert echoes Stuart in his insistence that Britain has already 'sold itself out'; that freedom is merely freedom for 'the muddled, mediocre, damned'.

> Look at your mass of 'free' suckers, your democracy – kidded along from the cradle to the grave . . . Do you suppose there's a single man of mind who doesn't realise *he* only begins where his freedom stops? One in a thousand may have what to be free takes – if so, he has what it takes to be something better, and he knows it: who could want to be free when he could be strong?

Bowen herself expressed views not dissimilar to Francis Stuart's or Robert's in her disappointment about the election results. Though she was prepared to accept that a few of the new Labour leaders and their supporters were 'All Right' (possessed of principles 'one may not share but can admire'), she saw them as surrounded by an 'awful entourage of the sissy, the half-baked, the manqués, the people with the chips on their shoulder, the people who've never made any grade and are convinced that it must be the grade's fault'. These are the people Robert describes as muddled, mediocre and damned; they could be Stuart's failures, taking refuge in the herd, or Yeats's base-born products of base beds.

Robert's sense that his country has betrayed him and therefore he must now betray it in its turn is related to Bowen's own sense, at the end of the war, that democracy had failed and that power was in the hands of the weak. Of course Bowen's sentiments were excessive, and Robert's are too; this is because they are filtered through the intensity of love. If the extremity of her distress at the weakness she found in post-war England was the result of her anguish at Charles's departure and her fear that their love too would fail to make the grade, then perhaps Bowen created Robert as a would-be strong man in order to test and to challenge Charles's strength. Another answer to Rosamond Lehmann's objection is that it is a novel about betrayal, and the betrayal needs to be ballasted by the full force of Nazi evil if we are to accept it as tragic. It is a political novel, but the politics are part of the love story, just as Elizabeth Bowen's own political disillusionment was imbued with the strength of her anguished longing for Charles.

The dedication of the novel to Charles Ritchie was double-edged: both a compliment and a warning. The book contains the loving, romanticised portrait that Charles hoped to find when Elizabeth was first planning it in 1942. Those early chapters that she wrote during the war are a celebration of the act of falling in love and of surrendering one's selfhood into someone else's keeping. 'How extraordinarily that is your and my book,' she wrote to him shortly before its publication; 'Short of there having been a child there could be no other thing that was more you and me.' But, ultimately, it is a book about a love that is destined to implode. During those years when she was constantly assuring Charles of the reality and eternity of their shared love, Elizabeth

Bowen was writing about a love affair destroyed by a lack of faith on one side and an obsessive, sacrificial will-to-power on the other. Rereading the novel after Elizabeth's death, Charles found that it was filled for him 'with echoes, reflections (as from a mirror, or a mirror-lined room). Also of premonitions, backward questionings, unanswered, and now unanswerable guesses. It is the story of our love, with a flaw in it, or did she feel a flaw in me?'

In the end, the love story itself is briefly redeemed. During their final confrontation, Stella turns Robert's photograph to the wall, in order to try to picture life without him. Gazing at the blank white back of the mount, Stella is shaken by returning love. She has to hold on to the chimney piece while she steadies her body 'against the beating of her heart – so violent that it seemed to begin again with cruel accumulated force'. She tries to call out to Robert, but has no voice; he appears anyway, thinking he has heard her cry; at once, they are 'in each other's arms'. Although Stella has seen the full extent of the flaw, she remains loyal to her lover. But it is too late: he goes up onto her roof and dies. Whether he dies intentionally or unintentionally, it is possible that with more faith he could have been saved. She could have confided in him earlier; he could have confided in her. He could have chosen to put love before power, or before the peculiar, almost religious self-righteousness of his politics.

Knowingly or unknowingly, Robert has sacrificed their love for a higher ideal. He realises belatedly that the sacrifice was not worth it. 'What do you suppose I thought in my mother's house?' he asks Stella, explaining why he came back to visit her, even though he knew it was dangerous; 'that I'd never be in your arms again. What do you suppose I had to make sure of? That. That, then to tell you.' In this respect, the novel is not so much a lament for a love that has failed as a warning about the tragedy of a love that is wilfully destroyed. In the end, they are left with a lifelong might-have-been. 'Better', says Robert, 'to say goodbye at the beginning of the hour we never have had, then it will have no end – best of all, Stella, if you can come to remember what never happened, to live most in the one hour we never had.' As far as Elizabeth Bowen herself was concerned, the might-have-been, though

moving as melodrama, was tragically wasteful. In the letter she wrote to
Charles while she was finishing the novel, Elizabeth pleaded with him
to 'somehow, some place in the not too far distant future let me see
your beloved face'. 'Love is a life,' she urged, 'and a life does cry out to
be lived.' *The Heat of the Day* is in part a plea for love and life; for a love
accepted and a life lived.

17

'Flying, no, leaping, into the centre of the mainland'

Hilde Spiel's return to Vienna, 1946

In January 1946, Hilde Spiel went back to Vienna. She had been long-ing to go since the end of the war. On a brief visit to London after VE Day, Peter had brought her a branch of jasmine from the Mirabell park in Salzburg which brought tears to her eyes. After the death of her father her homesickness became stronger than ever. It was time to go home.

Hilde had spent the autumn of 1945 envying Peter's excitement at his life on the Continent, where history was being made and the future of Europe was being worked out. She now wanted to be there too, although she was reluctant to give up her hard-won Englishness. In November she met the French novelist and Resistance hero André Chamson, who had recently arrived in London. He complained about the English, and specifically about their indifference to sex and pretty women. Although she was inclined to agree with Chamson, Hilde now realised how glad she was to have been accepted in the English world. She thought that there was a nobility in English reticence which Cham-son had missed. And she told Peter that she had no doubt where civilisation had reached its peak.

Luckily, Hilde was able both to return to Vienna and to retain her Englishness. In fact, during her stay in Vienna she felt the most content-edly English she had ever been. She later wrote that

Kingsley Martin's automatic assumption that we would slip off our newly won identity like a pair of worn-out slippers at first seemed devastating. But what happened was unexpected and astonishing: never before or afterward would we feel such close attachment to the British as during the three years that followed, never feel so accepted by them as on that mainland, but in the shelter and protection of their army.

Hilde was sent to Vienna in January 1946 as a correspondent for the *New Statesman* at the behest of Kingsley Martin. She left Peter to look after the children in Wimbledon and set off from the house at four in the morning on 30 January, wrapped in a coarse military coat, fur gloves and a khaki scarf and feeling drunk from the effects of flu and a high temperature. The departure from Wimbledon seemed like a flight not merely from the gloom of post-war London but from the dreariness of Hilde's own narrowing sense of herself.

I was flying, no, leaping, into the centre of the mainland; five years of winter were now, with this flight, this leap, finally over.

She recorded in her diary that she longed to shake off the last vestiges of a dreary war spent in fire watches, queues and maternity homes; she wanted to test the present against the past, new loyalties against old, and escape the stultifying calm that had gradually come to envelop her.

Initially, Hilde was driven from St James's to Croydon where she boarded a Dakota bound for Frankfurt. Through the cloudless sky she saw the coastline of England and then the metallic morning sea. The muddy green of the winter meadows of Belgium reminded Hilde of her own continental childhood; she was grateful that her children were growing up on lush English lawns. After a bumpy landing, they arrived at Frankfurt, where she had her first, unenticing glimpse of ruined Germany. 'Humid ghostly atmosphere,' she complained in her diary. 'Rain. Ruins. Hatred everywhere. Have bad cold and cough. 8.10 to bed.' She was struck by the physical destruction but also by the bitterness of the people, whom she felt staring at her in her British army uniform with open hostility and a 'furious spirit of revenge and unforgivingness'. She later claimed that she had not seen a single smile during the twenty-four hours she was there. Gazing at the ashen faces of starving people, many of whom were disfigured by injuries, she found herself lacking in pity because she could see only murder and hell in their looks. The next day, after an afternoon of wandering around ruins she spent the evening in the jollity of the transit mess, where rotund waitresses with blonde plaits swung earthenware beer mugs over their shoulders, presenting Hilde with dishes piled high with steak and vegetables. This was her first experience of the contrast between the life of the British occupiers and of the starving natives who surrounded them.

The next day Hilde flew to Vienna. When her plane swept down over the Vienna woods she looked down at the tracks drawn on the hillsides where she once learnt to ski and realised that from now on her steps would be haunted. But she decided at once that she had not come to grieve for her earlier life; she had merely returned to its source, 'with an eye sharpened by absence and a heart disciplined by loss'. Arriving at 2 p.m., she was driven into the city. The approach to Vienna, she wrote in a diary-style account of her trip later that year, had always been one of 'barbaric ugliness'. Now that it was ruined its ugliness had become starker, and she watched uneasily as they passed through an archway hung with pictures of Lenin and Stalin and then through the three great cemeteries of Vienna, one of which Greene would immortalise in *The Third Man*. As in Frankfurt, she was struck by her own lack of compassion for the ruins that surrounded her. Wondering what had caused this, she decided that she no longer belonged.

> These bombs are not my own. Mine painted the sky red over the City on September 8th. Mine extinguished one lovely Wren church after another, sailed over the London nursing home while my son was born, rained down on us during five years, the incidental music to our lives.

Hilde Spiel, unlike Elizabeth Bowen, was not ready to give up her wartime identity as a Londoner; she was in Vienna as a victor occupying the city.

Like Berlin, Vienna was divided up into four zones, controlled by the Russians, the British, the Americans and the French. Greene describes the division of the city in *The Third Man*, where he notes that the boundaries are marked only by notice boards and that the centre of the city is under the rotating control of all four powers. Although it was under military occupation, Austria was given more autonomy than Germany and was treated as a victim rather than an ally of the Third Reich. In their Moscow Declaration of 1943 the Allies had described the 1938 *Anschluss* as an 'occupation', naming Austria as Hitler's 'first victim'. As a result, in October 1945 the Western Allies recognised the provisional Austrian government, which had been set up in April 1945 under the Chancellorship of the Social Democrat Karl Renner and which comprised a coalition of Social Democrats, Conservatives and Communists. This government was known as the Second Republic and retained authority over the entire country, although ultimately its laws could be vetoed by the Allies in the rare event that all four powers unanimously agreed. Meanwhile the occupying powers each attempted to influence public opinion through a mixture of propaganda and censorship.

At the start of 1946, Vienna was a city of ruins. 'Nine months after the war, the city is still in chaos,' Hilde wrote in her diary account. 'Gigantic piles of rubble obstruct doors and thoroughfares, bomb-damaged buildings remain dangerous.' In every district she saw shuttered shops, empty cafés and closed restaurants. Life had retreated from the streets, though here and there a window display included a finely cut decanter or a single elegant shoe on well-draped cloth. And, though devastated, toothless and singed, the face of the city still had its old features. Its Baroque churches and palaces were untouched.

> Whenever the uncertain weather permits, a shy early spring sun glistens on the patina of their roofs and domes. The tower of St Stephen's Cathedral, shrouded in wavering blue-grey mist, rises above the delicate lines of the Vienna woods; at its feet lie empty shells; everything in its immediate surroundings is destroyed.

Vienna in 1946

Hilde was initially installed in the Hotel Astoria on the Führichgasse near the opera house. Looking out onto the once fashionable street she saw that the joke shops of her childhood were still there, selling boxes of magic tricks – 'the spiders which you can slip into people's drinks, the wax apples inviting the guileless bite' – tokens of a whimsicality the Viennese had little interest in at present. On her first afternoon she went to a British press conference and was invited by fellow journalists to live with the other war correspondents in the British Press camp in a dilapidated palace called the Salmschlössl. This was once the home of the aristocratic Salm family and the house was still heavy with the past, its rooms lined with mirrored cupboards and decorated with stags' antlers and stuffed grouse.

From this point, Hilde was immersed in a new and heady world. In leaving war-torn London she had come to a city where the war was even harder to forget, but the result was exhilarating. 'Darling, this is the most exciting thing that's ever happened to me and I'm really quite unable to say what I feel,' she wrote to Peter in Wimbledon. 'I walk about, not in a daze, but aware that every minute is of the utmost importance to me.' 'This is still the most exciting, heartbreaking, enthralling thing that could have happened to me,' she wrote again two days later. 'It's almost worth having gone away into a new life to have this incredible return, an emotional experience unlike anything that might have happened otherwise.' She had spent her time attending press conferences, socialising with the British, meeting the Viennese, and revisiting the haunting landscape of her past.

Hilde cried on her first day while visiting the rather ugly home she had left behind in 1936, at Stanislaugasse 2. It was here that she had spent her teenage years after the First World War, sitting beside her father in his laboratory as he carried out incomplete experiments, or typing in her bedroom. She discovered on the way there that the park and playground of her youth had been bombed out of existence. The next day she visited her old family servant Marie, whom she found surrounded by her parents' *Jugendstil* bedroom furniture, bitter but triumphant, her own socialist convictions vindicated by the defeat of the Nazis. Hilde then returned to her earlier childhood district of Heiligenstadt where, in melting snow in the late afternoon, she encountered a scene 'a hundred times more heartbreaking' than she had expected. Entering the leafy village of Döbling, where generations of her mother's family had grown up, she found that every alley and corner was familiar. She passed the house of her grandmother Melanie, who had been deported and had then died in Theresienstadt concentration camp. She saw the houses of old friends, now dead, and found the narrow street where she had spent the first ten years of her life. Their apartment was now hidden but she could sense the cold hallway, the staircase on the left, the passage leading to the garden where, on the branches of a forked apple tree, she had read her first fairy tales.

In the failing light she entered the church of St Jakob which she had dreamed of during all those lonely nights spent listening to Beethoven and Schubert in wartime Wimbledon. Now, she was returning as an intruder: 'where my roots reach deep into the earth as nowhere else, I

am a complete stranger, as disconnected in time and space as a ghostly
visitor'. But bowing her head over her hands as she listened to a children's service in progress at the front of the church, Hilde still found
herself overwhelmed by 'all the bottled-up emotion, repressed for years,
when courage had to be bought at the price of dulled sensation – all the
misery over the degradation of my home, all the anxiety over my children in the war, all the grief over my father's death'. Boys in the front
pews turned and stared at the foreign woman in military uniform
kneeling near the door and weeping openly. Quietly, the priest continued to read the mass. 'Heiligenstadt unchanged,' Hilde noted in her
diary that night. 'Walked in sinking light. Heartbreak beyond words.'

Returning from these wrenching trips around the city of her childhood, Hilde spent her evenings drinking in bars and going to parties.
On 1 February there was a big party given by Peter Smollett, who in his
former incarnation had been Peter Smolka, Peter de Mendelssohn's
boss at the Exchange Telegraph in London. He was working as a correspondent for the *Daily Express* and encouraged Hilde to meet the
leading Viennese Communists. In 1987 Hilde would discover that
throughout the 1940s Smollett worked as a Russian spy. She nonetheless looked back on him as 'one of the most remarkable persons of this
century that I ever met', despite his inconsistencies. Now his party
provided her with a chance to meet the Viennese intelligentsia alongside the usual Allied officers and correspondents. There was a mixture
of Catholic Communists and returned intellectuals, all of whom had
offered active resistance to the National Socialists and were now imbued
with faith in the Second Republic.

These were people who were involved in the renewed cultural scene.
Already, walking through the ruins, Hilde could see exhibitions of
crafts whose beauty overwhelmed her. And the opera had been revived,
playing each night to packed audiences. Indeed, the opera house and
theatres had been reopened immediately after the liberation of the city,
with the Red Army allocating special rations to the company members
and allowing the black sheep to return where possible. Hilde went to
the opera, now held in the Theater an der Wien, and heard a finer
performance of Verdi's *Otello* than she could imagine hearing anywhere

else. In Vienna, as in London, Shakespeare was providing catharsis amid the ruins; here was tragedy with rhythm, structure and meaning after the sprawling, apparently meaningless tragedy of the war. 'The opera still seems to be the most perfect in Europe outside Italy,' Hilde wrote in a report on Vienna which was published in the *New Statesman* in April. 'The miracle of Austria's cultural rejuvenation is about to repeat itself once more.'

Despite her delight in Vienna as a city, Hilde had very little patience with the Viennese people. She found them more relaxed-looking than the people she had seen in Frankfurt. 'Quite definitely not the same fury and darkness,' she told Peter, assuring him that she had a completely open mind and was 'not balanced towards the Austrians rationally, only emotionally'. The Austrians, she wrote, simply could not take things so seriously and suffer so utterly from them as the Germans. She had seen smiles from the start, even in the most badly bombed areas. But because Austria had been categorised as a victim of Hitler's aggression, denazification had been less stringent than in Germany and the Austrians were now less guilt-ridden than the Germans. Hilde thought they were too self-satisfied and not apologetic enough, and she began to suspect that most of the people she saw in the streets were fascists. In her later account of Vienna she described how all the jackbooted women wandering through the city seemed to resemble concentration camp guards. 'Hungry looks in defiant or lifeless faces. Derisive or obsequious smiles on facing an Allied uniform.' Now, Hilde denounced the opportunism of the Viennese in her *New Statesman* article. They were 'as rude to each other and as rancorous to the Russians as they are sugary to the Western troops'. Their own language had become coarser, resembling a rural dialect. Their urbane graces had gone.

'Everything is lovable here but the attitude of the Viennese,' she wrote to Peter on 7 February, less tolerant than in her initial letters. The people were

either Nazis (whose sting has been completely removed) or charmingly insane Volkspartei, or prosy, bourgeois Sozialdemokraten, or doctrinaire Communists, or charming, but insane Communists . . . They are either

corrupt or fatigued or politically stupid or fanatical, but they've got one
relieving factor, their great interest in the arts.

She was convinced that the only hope for the Austrians was to immerse
themselves in the arts, making the most of their exquisite taste and
artistic sensitivity. If they could learn to behave discreetly and leave
politics to others then they could hope for a future in Europe.

Hilde was particularly irritated by those Viennese citizens who implied
that she had undergone an easier war than they had. Visiting her old
haunt, the Café Herrenhof, she was pleased to find the head waiter, Franz
Hnatek, still there. But immediately he launched into a scene that her
exiled friends had long predicted, congratulating her on escaping and
saving herself a great deal of unpleasantness. 'The Frau Doktor was right
to leave. The air-raids alone – three times they set the city ablaze.' Disdain-
ful, Hilde offered him cigarettes, which he accepted with a subservient
bow. She was depressed by his lack of awareness of the plight of the exile.
'Expropriation, humiliation, arrest and mortal danger, illegal flight across
closed borders, years of exile, life as an enemy alien in a country shattered
by war'; all was annihilated, waved away with a snap of his fingers.

Gradually, she found herself learning to compromise as Peter had
done in Germany, accepting the equivocal nature of the situation of
those who had stayed behind. Meeting an old friend, Stefan B, she was
confronted with a man who had come to terms with the powers who
took control of his country in 1938. Despite opposing their ideology, he
edited a daily newspaper; while bemoaning the vulgarity of the regime
and the likelihood of a victory by the Allies, he profited from the situation, living in freedom while others died in jail. But she now realised
that everyone had been complicit in some way, except those few who
had died as Resistance fighters.

In England, during the war, when we dreamed of seeing our homeland
again, we resolved never to shake the hand of anyone who had been in
any way linked with the regime. Now this decision seems ludicrous to
me; all the borderlines are blurred. Stefan, I feel, cannot be blamed,
except that he was not born to be either a hero or a victim.

Back in London, Peter was jealous of Hilde's expedition but was trying to be gracious about giving her a share of the fun. 'Of course, I'm envious,' he wrote on 2 February, not having yet received any of her letters, 'and should like to be with you but I tell myself that this is your own special province and privilege and I know how necessary it is for you to make this trip all by yourself. I do so hope you have a good and interesting time and rediscover in yourself all the things that you felt were buried these last few years and sometimes gave up for lost, even.' In her absence he was joining the community in Wimbledon, attending Labour party meetings and getting to know a new set of people. 'England suits me down to the ground,' he told Hilde. 'I should never dream of moving us to any country permanently again. It would be suicide.' If they could persevere for a while longer then all their immigrant troubles would be gone. A week later he had still not heard from her, and he was starting to begrudge spending time alone with the children and to sympathise with her resentment during his absences. 'I can just see how it must be for you. Awful, awful, although the winter is rather worse than the summer.'

Hilde too was discovering and affirming her own Englishness. This return to her roots was not a straightforward homecoming. She repeatedly informed Peter that the Viennese were made bearable and enjoyable by the antidote of the English, whom she returned to each night. She was reassured by the comforting incongruity of the khaki army blankets in her Biedermeier Viennese room, which made her feel doubly at home. 'I lead this curious double life you've known yourself, meeting all the important Viennese and then going back to the boys in the mess, drinking and playing darts in the bar at night.' The British were the most beloved of the occupying forces and she was pleased to be among them. Indeed, she could not imagine a return to Vienna being tolerable except under the auspices of the British – 'belonging to them and sharing their company'. She was more enraptured by the English than she had been for years. 'Those that are nice are really infinitely nice and charming, and I do so like to see and live with these clean, good-mannered, gay, witty English people.' On 4 February she described to Peter a drive round the ruins with a 'sweet Major' with whom she had discussed Sitwell and Bowen, neutralising the scenery around them.

Hilde did not name this particular major to Peter, and she did not mention him again in her letters home. In her autobiography she refers to him as 'Sam B' and describes him as 'the pleasant, cultured Welshman who was to be my frequent escort during the next few weeks'. She was less discreet in her diary at the time, where she noted a couple of sentences a day about her activities. Here Sam is introduced as Major Beasley, a fellow press officer, and is then mentioned frequently, first as Beasley, and then, from 9 February, as Sam. 'Cooked at Sam's flat,' she writes here; 'dinner and a prolonged night in the bar until about 1.30 playing darts and drinking heavily. There is a certain danger of forgetting purpose.' The next morning, terribly hungover, she and Sam went to the Ice Rink and Heumarkt Café. The following day it was worthy of mention that 'Sam didn't appear' and then the next evening she recorded retiring to Sam's room after drinking in the bar. 'Quite delightful. Talked.'

Sam wanted to enter the art market when he returned to civilian life, and on 13 February Hilde accompanied him to galleries and introduced him to painters. She encouraged him to buy an Egon Schiele oil painting for only 2,000 schillings. The following day she and Sam got terribly drunk after a party at the Salmschlössl. Her diary cryptically notes 'Sam: end', but the next day there was another picture-buying mission and theatre premiere, followed by supper in Sam's room. 'What an absurd relation,' she now reported. The following morning she took him to the studio of her former friend Josef Dobrowsky, who had drawn her twice before the war, and Sam bought a portrait for 100 cigarettes. That evening at the end of another big party she noted an 'extraordinary scene' with Sam.

In a novel set in this immediate post-war period called *Lisa's Room*, which would be published in 1965, Hilde Spiel gave the character Lisa (based on her own schoolfriend Hansi) a speech expounding the sexual moral codes of twentieth-century bohemian Vienna. 'You don't think I have any morals?' Lisa asks.

Hilde Spiel, painted by Josef Dobrowsky, 1946

You'd be surprised! It is merely a different code altogether . . . I can't agree that one man or woman should be enough for one lifetime when there are hundreds of trees, flowers, mountains and cities to explore . . . It would seem unnatural to me, unholy even, to forgo any possible sensation. This happens to be my religion. But there are also taboos – don't you believe that I can do without them! The taboo of breaking off a mood violently. The taboo of talking off-key, too coyly, too earnestly, too dramatically for any given situation. The taboo of saying the wrong thing, or the right thing at the wrong moment, of play-acting when absolute candour is called for, or of waking someone who is fast asleep. These are deadly sins to me. And there is another one: that of deliberately hurting people – in cold blood.

Hilde Spiel is satirising Hansi's overblown whimsicality here, but there are elements of Lisa's moral code that resemble her own. Before the war, Hilde had experienced no compunction when she embarked on several simultaneous love affairs while gradually committing herself more seriously to Peter. Now that she was married with children her attitude had changed; she had been furiously jealous of Peter's affair with Juliet O'Hea. Nonetheless, she was still capable of a Viennese lightness of touch when it came to affairs of the heart. At this stage she had no intention of leaving Peter and no real desire to prolong this 'absurd relation' with Sam beyond her stay in Vienna. But she was enjoying it as a chance to regain equality with Peter and as another component of the city's passionate intensity. The scenes were part of the drama; her feelings were alive.

Staying up late, pontificating about the future of Europe and feeling that her opinions mattered, Hilde continued to be elated by the experience. 'I feel', she wrote to Peter on 10 February, 'like someone who's been sober for seven years and then gulps down ten whiskies all at once, no wonder I'm quite drunk.' For his part Peter, in a letter of 14 February, was rather patronisingly pleased that she was having a good time – 'precisely the kind of time I wanted you to have' – but convinced that in retrospect she would look on it differently. He was happy now to be in London, despite the fact that he and the children all had flu and that Anthony had a runny nose which Christine kept smearing over his face in a disgusting fashion. He promised that when she returned they would arrange their lives to their mutual satisfaction. 'I don't want you to stand in a fish queue. But what shall we do with the children? Maybe we shouldn't have had any, perhaps? Well, that's too late to change.'

By 20 February Peter was beginning to lose patience. 'Dearest Mummili,' he wrote; 'the more drunk and hilarious your letters become the less informative they get. One doesn't learn an awful lot from them except that you're having a good time – and that's really all one wants to know . . . Now – about coming home. Mummi, for God's sake don't think I want to rush you home or deprive you of a single day of fun.' But their nanny Beate could not be left alone with the children and was starting to ask Peter when Hilde was expected to return. He was afraid to tell her the brutal truth, which was that he was beginning to suspect she was not going to come back at all. He himself had promised to go to Germany at the beginning of March, and besides, it was time for

Hilde to see her children. In his first letter Peter had enclosed a card from Christine which began 'Dear Mummy, when are you going to come back from Vienna? I would so like to know.'

Luckily for Peter and Christine, Hilde's stay in Vienna was curtailed by the arrival of Richard Crossman, a member of the Anglo-American Committee of Inquiry into the Problems of European Jewry and Palestine and assistant editor of the *New Statesman*. He and Hilde met at a party at Smollett's on 17 February, where he impressed her with his brilliance and eccentricity and spent much of the evening praising Peter's Nuremberg reports. Hilde asked Crossman if he was planning to write about Vienna and later informed Peter that he had 'most charmingly and unconcernedly' replied that he was not going to write a serious political article, just four or five good stories with a lot of background. 'In fact, Pumpi, what I wanted to do,' Hilde complained. 'I was crestfallen but didn't show it, and he proceeded to explain to me that what I should do for Kingsley was the story of the migration of the Jews.'

Late on the evening of 19 February, after a rather flat goodbye drink with Sam, Hilde left Vienna for Carinthia, where a crisis was developing for the British in a Jewish refugee camp. These Jews had been rescued from Polish death camps and were now making their way towards Palestine. Crossman, a pro-Zionist Labour MP, was angry with the Labour Foreign Secretary Ernest Bevin, who in the aftermath of war had refused to remove the limits on Jewish immigration to Palestine. He wanted Hilde to expose the difficulties of the Jews and illustrate their need for a new homeland.

Hilde had spent her childhood holidays in the mountains of Carinthia, and this was another act of return. Wrapped in a fur coat, she lay in her sleeping car, leaning out of the open window of the train, smelling the snowy air around the heavy branches of the fir trees, and looking up to the sky, 'as wide and full of cloudy mountains as the dark plateau below'. She arrived at dawn at Klagenfurt, the capital of Carinthia, where she was taken to the press headquarters in Dellach, driving out of the city on the country roads along the Wörther lake. The press quarters were at the Villa Porsche, an old country house very like the Carinthian hotels Hilde had stayed in as a child. Closing her eyes, feeling the hot tiles against her back, touching the planed wood of the bench with her fingertips and smelling the logs in the fireplace, Hilde was transported back two decades.

> I am on a winter holiday with my parents and sit here, while they settle into their bedroom, to come down soon for our first country breakfast together. Outside, the snow, the sun, the mountains, the lake are waiting. The times are still friendly. And I am still secure within them.

Two days later Hilde reported at one of the five Displaced Persons' camps in Klagenfurt. One in ten people in Carinthia was now a so-called DP and many of these were accused of black market dealings and political activity. Among these, a sizeable proportion were Jews. She was shown around a row of shacks where men, women and children were standing around or leaning 'in the limp posture of people who expect nothing from the next day'. The commandant of the camp, an enthusiastic British officer, told her that he was surprised by their attitude. He was keen to plant a garden of spring flowers in the camp but the inmates could not be bothered to help him.

Why, Hilde asked in her diary account of Vienna, did these people refuse to return to their homes? 'Is it fear or idleness, cunning or stupidity?' They did not seem like political conspirators; they were more like tired and mentally lazy people who had got used to their provisional way of life. They had been forced by the Nazis to work hard during the war. Now they had heard about Tito's 'terror' in Yugoslavia and about the new regime in Poland and were reluctant to return home.

> Reality has already disappeared once from their lives. Now they have gained the reality of a little shack, an iron stove and regular meals from the store-room that lies on the other side of the clay path. Stubbornly, these uprooted peasants cling to their wretched camp regime, the only regime that has taken on a continued existence for them.

After surveying the camp, Hilde was taken to the row of shacks housing the Jewish survivors of ghettos and concentration camps who were waiting to move on to Palestine. Some of the Jews had identified themselves as Polish or Romanian citizens and had been placed with their compatriots, but most had declared themselves homeless and refused to say where they were born. They were now housed together. Outside stood young men in their twenties, unshaven, 'with a look of wild despair in their eyes and of that physical sturdiness which has enabled them above all others to survive the stone quarry and the torture chamber'. Inside there were women lying down and children running aimlessly around. According to their spokesperson none of them wanted to stay in Europe. 'Europe is a graveyard, one big graveyard with our mothers, fathers, sisters. For us there is only one country – Palestine.'

Hilde Spiel had mixed feelings about the situation of these Jews. In her article for the *New Statesman* she described their present situation with compassion and horror. 'These people have no documents other than the blue number tattooed on their arms in Nazi prisons. They are unshaven, tattered, with tired, haunted looks in their eyes.' However, Hilde was not convinced by the claims of the Zionists and was sad that so many Jews would rather move to Palestine than return home. She observed in her diary account that 'a worldwide Jewish confederation has come into being that did not exist when Hitler determined to destroy them'. The Jews wanting to emigrate to Palestine were aided by the American army, who helped them at different stages of their journey. Hilde felt that the Zionist agitators were denying the reality of the situation and that the Jewish refugees who possessed merely a rucksack of dirty clothing and the recollection of their murdered family did not realise that quite apart from Arab opposition, 'even with the most modern methods of irrigation and soil cultivation only a fraction of them could hope to settle in Palestine'.

Hilde had always been ambivalent about her own Jewishness. On her mother's side she came from a family of assimilated Jews who were proud to be culturally more Austrian than Jewish. She was angry, now, that the Nazis and the Zionists had combined to create renewed segregation, and that countries like Poland, Hungary, Romania and Slovakia were doing so little to encourage Jews to return. If plans had been

devised for the restitution of these Jews in their original home countries, many more might have stayed. In Vienna, where the situation was
better, only a quarter of the Jewish population had expressed a wish to
emigrate to Palestine. However, given her grandmother's death and her
parents' narrow escape, Hilde did have some personal investment in the
Jewish plight. She, like Peter, had been impatient with her grandmother, who had behaved with culpable innocence, going shopping at
the forbidden time, reprimanding the laundress for starching a delicate
tablecloth and generally regarding the new regime as an insubordinate
uprising which could be countered by stubborn resistance. In the end
Hilde responded to the post-war situation with anxious uncertainty,
stating that 'a solution must be found while it can still be carried out
and before the situation gets irretrievably out of hand'.

Hilde remained in Carinthia for a few more days, sightseeing in Italy
and exploring the Carinthian Alps where she had spent her childhood
holidays. Here she mourned her father once again. Climbing up a
winding path to the peak of a mountain, smelling the Alpine moss and
resinous bark, she was aware that she was surrounded by her father's
favourite climate: 'the ozone that he sniffed with the same delight in
the mountains as in the laboratory, whose floor shook under the
dynamo'. In the mountains, more than in the city, her return had
become a homecoming. 'I seem to sense his presence.'

On 24 February Hilde went back to Vienna, where she had a fort-
night to say goodbye to her friends. She spent this time with the
English, visiting artists' studios and dancing in Kinsky's, the officers'
club. She recorded in her autobiography that 'with my most faithful
escort, Sam, an intimate little drama came about'. He was, she writes,
'no ladies' man and was now at the mercy of contradictory feelings'.
There is no record of what Sam was asking for or what exactly ensued.
Perhaps Sam was too earnest to accept Hilde's sense that one man or
woman was not enough for a lifetime and wanted their relationship to
be formalised. Perhaps he had his own commitments at home. Either
way, on 7 March Hilde returned to London, where she was met by
Peter at the airport and found that he was looking pale and strained
and was in a bad mood.

Hilde was pleased to be reunited with her children but felt restless, wanting to dash off again. While in Vienna she had written to Peter that it was a 'most dreary thought to have to go back to England where, as I read, fats are being reduced and bread about to be rationed, to a life of tedium and boredom, when I could pull my weight this way or the other, and do some work as well as you.' She was sure that he would regret letting her go, now that she had seen what life could be like when it was filled with real things instead of merely the planning of meals. 'I'm sick, sick, of a housewife's life. That doesn't mean that I'm not going back to it meekly, because it's my duty, and I asked for it, anyway. But it's a terrible sacrifice all the same.' Now she found that the housewife's life was indeed as depressing as she had feared, not least because she and Peter spent their time quarrelling before he escaped back to Germany on 11 March.

Initially, Peter was stationed in Buende, where he was bored and lonely. 'A dozen times each day I ask myself why in hell I had to come out here when I had a warm room, a comfortable bed, a good writing desk, all my books, good lighting, a sweet wife and children at home,' he complained to Hilde, who was glad to be missed although the order of his desires was hardly flattering. And he did not ask her to come and join him. He was sure that she would hate it there; it was even worse than Wimbledon; there was only one 'stinking little cinema'. Hilde was not convinced. She was fed up with Wimbledon. Flesch had invited her to the theatre to see a premiere of Sean O'Casey's *Red Roses for Me* but otherwise she had seen no one except her mother and children.

She wrote back, telling Peter that she thought that Smollett was much happier since returning to Vienna and suggesting that they should follow his example. Peter replied that it would be a mistake. 'Our stakes in England are too high. I have invested too much and would really have to write off an enormous potential capital.' He was getting older and the younger generation was catching up, but he was convinced that he could still make it. A few days later he reported that he was now having a very happy time in Berlin and had 'fallen in love a little bit with a very charming girl' called Barbara Ward, who he was taking to the opera on Saturday. She was petite and very pretty, though her legs were not especially desirable. 'Also to my delight I've found out that she isn't quite as clever as I thought she was but says silly things occasionally.' Hilde wept with rage and replied with a furious tirade, blaming him for her current loneliness and isolation and complaining that he had only helped to arrange her trip to Austria in order to keep her quiet.

Peter responded in turn that Hilde's letter had made him unspeakably angry. 'You have set yourself up in Wimbledon, all heated up in furious resentment, spitting poison, and demanding, demanding, demanding – a whole lot of things that are all contradictory.' She was so self-righteous that she was treating him like a slave who simply needed shouting at. Hilde had complained that she was thrown on her own resources and regretted marrying him at all. 'I have never said that you must stay in Wimbledon,' he retorted angrily; 'I'm quite as sick of it as you.' He would take a house in town or farm the children out as she wished. He was even willing to come back and spend every evening in the flat with his 'beloved little muffins' if she would like a year of freedom and independence. 'And if', he added magnanimously, 'you want to go away altogether, again I would say: Mummi darling, it is your own life and I will do everything so that you can live it. I know the price you have been paying these last few years, and I know that it is a heavy one.' For his part he regretted mentioning Barbara Ward; it was merely a joke, and the trip to the opera had not occurred. 'I really saw her only once, during lunch time with six or seven others . . . So much for my love affairs. But it just shows in what a terrible state of nerves you must have worked yourself for this innocent and silly remark to have made such a disastrous effect upon you.'

Hilde did not reply to this letter, and Peter's missives became increasingly plaintive. 'I feel very suspended and unhappy,' he wrote on 10 April, wondering if he should come home at once. On 13 April he received an envelope from her enclosing bills and clippings but no letter. 'I must assume that this is meant to provoke, meant to hurt. It does. Are the children all right?' Finally, she relented. 'Of course, I still think you wrote up that girl affair in a thoughtless mood,' she replied, not quite believing his protestations. 'If there's one thing a woman hates it's to be made the confidante of her husband. You may not believe me, but I'd far rather you'd gone to bed with her and not told me, than to have written about something that didn't even materialise.' Hilde was becoming infuriated with his confessions of minor infidelities which seemed designed to provoke jealousy, using honesty as a pretext for selfishness. She knew that she could not be the only woman in his life. She would not dream of denying him a privilege that she might want to have herself (and had indeed already had). What she minded was the breaking of the taboos she would describe in *Lisa's Room*. He had said the wrong thing, play-acted when candour was called for, and deliberately hurt her 'in cold blood'. 'Thank God,' Peter wrote back. 'I was getting very seriously worried lest we had really drifted apart in such a way that drastic action was needed to restore the front line. But we are still speaking the same language, my Mummi dear, and that is really all that matters.' Meanwhile he had read her Vienna article in the *New Statesman* and hoped she would not mind his saying that 'it wasn't quite as smooth and faultless as it could have been, if we had gone over it together for half an hour'. She should try writing shorter sentences. Normal relations had resumed.

It was becoming clear that Hilde and Peter's marriage would only survive if they could both decamp from Wimbledon together, either to Europe or to a more settled domestic life in central London. That summer, they debated whether to stay in England or to move to Germany. 'I have one firm conviction and that is that from the point of view of a full, animated, amusing life there is nothing like being in the Army of Occupation,' Hilde had written to Peter from Vienna on 7 February. 'Darling, there's nothing I adore more than a Foreign Correspondent's life,' she added a week later. On 10 February she had suggested rather wildly to Peter that they should buy a house in Buende and criss-cross their way across Europe in a car. 'This is such a fascinating time, perhaps the only time we've got before the atom bomb, and we must see and do and write and talk as much as we can, in fact, make the most out of it.'

Peter was less convinced. 'The only thing that attracts me now to the German job,' he wrote on 14 February, 'really the only one, is the prospect of a decent climate.' Every other aspect of German life seemed hateful. Nonetheless on 20 February Peter responded favourably to Hilde's suggestion that they should move to Germany (perhaps relieved that she had abandoned the idea of zigzagging around Europe). 'Absolutely. If that is what you are after – I should have never dared suggesting such a Teutonic horror – I'm delighted – for a while.' But he warned her that the trouble with Germany was that where in Austria you could live and work without having to take the Austrians seriously, in Germany you could not help occupying yourself seriously with 'the bastards and their problems' if you wanted to be of any use. He was worried that he would involve himself too deeply in their affairs and lose the English ground under his feet as a result. You could not laugh off the Germans as you could the Austrians because you never knew what they were going to do next.

Both Hilde and Peter continued to vacillate throughout the rest of the year. Peter was enjoying the powerful position he had created for himself in Berlin. The two newspapers he had founded, *Der Tagesspiegel* and *Der Telegraf*, were both doing extremely well, and he was now responsible for editing *Die Welt*, trying to bring this rather substandard paper up to par with his own. 'Already people are saying: the only two good newspapers in Berlin were founded by Mendelssohn,' he announced to Hilde in May. 'The rest is rubbish.' He felt that he had now built up a platform from which to influence public opinion, and that this would be useful if and when the situation imploded with the Russians. Indeed, he wondered if he even had a duty to continue his public career, and to move from newspapers to politics.

I'm building up a record, and I'm not inclined to abandon it after a year. There is more to come, Mummi. I'm only 38 now, the same age as Crossman and Hugh Gaitskell and the rest. In five years, at 43, I shall have caught up with them, and shall be in parliament. I know I shall, and they're not going to stop me. Good job I joined the Labour Party when I did.

Hilde herself was still keen to be in Europe, but she was anxious about reports of renewed Nazism in Germany and about the risk of spending too long outside Britain and losing their carefully acquired Englishness.

Peter wrote to reassure her that there was no Nazism and that they could return to England whenever they wanted. In fact, living in close quarters with the other British officials in Berlin they could be more intimately connected to the English than in London, where they were often isolated in Wimbledon. In Berlin he worked in a British office, surrounded by the British; 'it is certainly not the Krauts who determine the picture'. And, perhaps more persuasively, he wanted them to be together. 'I should like to give you a big kiss on your big soft lips and sleep with you in the same bed and feel your warm tummy,' he added, in a rare expression of physical affection.

18

'O, maybe we'll live a while in Killala'

The English in Ireland, 1947

Not everyone could contemplate leaving London altogether. However displaced they felt in post-war England, Henry Yorke and Graham Greene had no alternative home to return to, and instead found a respite from the English austerity of the late 1940s in briefer trips abroad. One particularly enticing destination was Ireland, which for them, as for Elizabeth Bowen, seemed to offer a tranquillity and ease that was now lacking in England. In fact the Irish economy was no stronger than the British economy. Unemployment was high and the cold winter of 1946 caused fuel shortages in Ireland as well as Britain. Bread rationing was imposed in January 1947. Strikes were threatened, and in June 1947 de Valera told the trade union representatives that the government would reluctantly 'take whatever steps it felt necessary to protect bread supply'. But for Graham Greene and Henry Yorke as well as for their mutual friend Evelyn Waugh, the country's economic and social problems remained hidden. They appreciated the continued old-world luxury of the Shelbourne Hotel in Dublin and the apparent plenty of rural Ireland.

Evelyn Waugh made several visits to Ireland in the autumn of 1946, hoping to buy a Big House or castle in which to hide away. That November he mentioned 'constantly recurring' thoughts of Ireland in his diary.

Not so much of what I should find there as what I should shake off here. The luxury of being a foreigner, of completely retiring from further experience and settling in an upstairs library to garner the forty-three-year harvest.

He was certain that Britain as a great power was done for and that the loss of possessions and claim of the 'proletariat' to be a 'privileged race' would produce increasing poverty. He told Winston Churchill's son Randolph in December 1946 that he was negotiating to buy a castle in Ireland where he hoped to find 'brief shelter from the Attlee terror'. In the end he did not buy the castle. Six years later Nancy Mitford remarked to him that 'total to me is the mystery why you don't live in Ireland'. It was made for him with its pretty houses, cold wetness, low income tax, polite lower classes and uncompromising Roman Catholicism.

Ireland was made, too, for Henry Yorke, who visited the country twice in 1947. Yorke had always been fond of Ireland, having fished there as a boy. Even the 1938 holiday had been pleasurable until the Munich crisis made it too difficult to continue. Before the war the Yorkes had stayed regularly with the Earl of Rosse at his eighteenth-century Gothic house, Birr Castle, in County Offaly, which some claim as the original of Kinalty, the house in *Loving*. Now Yorke was curious to see how Ireland had fared in the war, having described it from an imaginative distance in his novel.

In *Loving* Yorke shows the English servants to be contemptuous of Irish neutrality. 'The war's on now all right,' Kate says to the other servants, 'and do these rotten Irish care? They make me sick.' 'It's too bloody neutral this country is,' Raunce tells Edith, revealing that his mother thinks they are "iding ourselves away in this neutral country'. And his boy Albert goes so far as to return to England to join up as a soldier. But any patriotism Henry Yorke himself had felt during the war had dissipated by 1947 and he, like Waugh, was keen to make the most of the positive consequences of neutrality. In May, Dig had jaundice, so Henry took her and Sebastian to Dublin for eight days to recuperate. They stayed, like Bowen, Waugh and Greene on their nights in Dublin, in the Shelbourne Hotel. Bowen in particular was fond of the

Shelbourne, reporting to Charles Ritchie after a visit to Dublin in November 1945 that 'the dear Shelbourne was very much the same'. In her 1951 history of the hotel she commended it for carrying on its own 'impassive, cheerful, wonderfully unchanged life throughout changing, sometimes distressful times'. Yorke too welcomed the unchanged luxury of the hotel, which contrasted refreshingly with the seedy London pubs where he now spent a large part of his days.

In September 1947 Henry Yorke took Dig and Sebastian to the Shelton Abbey Hotel in County Wicklow, on the coast between Dublin and Bowen's Court. This was a holiday which he described to Matthew Smith as 'a complete success'. But he remained disengaged, both from the countryside and his family. Since the affair with Mary had waned he had rarely experienced anything passionately. His enjoyment of Ireland was very different from his happiness during that first holiday in Suffolk with Mary and Matthew, where he had felt like a donkey dropping its burden. Now his pervasive sense was one of apprehension. They were living in a large Victorian mansion, eating six-course meals and looking out onto a pageant of every shade of green. But Henry was finding the surroundings eerily desolate. There were no birds, rabbits or fish to be seen, and the only noise was the sound of a railway engine. 'Sebastian and Dig are the only things that hold me to life,' he told Matthew; 'they laugh and giggle all day long and do not notice.' And he blamed Ireland itself for his own troubled detachment: 'The thing about Ireland is that it is cursed. That is probably true about all of us, and we may only notice it when over here.'

Graham Greene's visit to Ireland in April 1947 was one of the defining moments of his life. He flew to Dublin and then drove to Achill Island in County Mayo, just off the coast from Castlebar and a day's drive north-west from Bowen's Court. There he spent a week in a small cottage rented by Catherine Walston, a rich American socialite with film-star looks, impetuous vitality and candid sexuality. For most of the year Catherine was in charge of Thriplow Farm near Cambridge, one of the most extravagantly luxurious houses in post-war England, where

she lived with her five children and her husband, Harry Walston, a rich
gentleman farmer, civil servant and future Labour candidate. But occasionally she would retreat to this small, white, three-room cottage in
Ireland, which looked out onto barren, wind-shorn grass and an empty
bay. Together, Graham and Catherine filled up buckets of turf for the
fire, baked bread, ate boiled eggs and made love on a mattress on the
floor. For the first time in months, Graham was writing without difficulty; for the first time in years he had found peace. In a poem written
in 1949 he depicted this as a revelatory entry into a new world:

> A mattress was spread on a cottage floor,
> And the door closed on a world, but another door
> Opened, and I was far
> From all the world I had ever known.

Graham was ready to close the door on the old world. In his autobiography, he described 1946 as a year when he felt himself at a loss. He was
finding it difficult to write, chiefly because the booby-traps he had
planted in his private life were blowing up one by one. He had always
thought that war would bring death as a solution, but instead he was
alive, causing unhappiness to people he loved and frequenting brothels
once again. Like Scobie in *The Heart of the Matter*, the book he was
struggling to write, Graham Greene contemplated suicide. But in fact
salvation came through love instead of death, and it was a love that
would result in his most passionate novel, *The End of the Affair*, and
that would bring him some of the most intensely happy and also the
most anguished moments of his life.

Catherine was twelve years younger than Graham and had come
into his life the previous summer as his would-be goddaughter. On the
verge of converting to Catholicism, she wrote to tell him how crucial
his novels had been in her decision and to ask if he would take the part
of godfather. Too busy to play more than a nominal role in the proceedings, Graham sent Vivien to the christening in his stead. On 25
September he wrote Catherine a belated congratulatory note, confessing to being a neglectful godfather – he had not even sent her a silver

Vivien Greene (*top right*) at the christening of Catherine Walston (*bottom left*)

mug – and conveying her all best wishes for the future. She replied with an enticing description of Achill Island; Graham suggested that she should come to tell them all about the west of Ireland when she was back. He was in fact genuinely curious about Ireland. Earlier in the year he had written to Evelyn Waugh saying that he was keen to go to Ireland, because he liked the Irish and approved so strongly of their recent neutrality, and complaining that Vivien had an anti-Irish phobia, so he would not be able to go. Soon he would make plans to go to Ireland with Dorothy the following May.

Graham and Catherine finally met in the autumn. They had a drink in London, where Catherine was intrigued by Graham's descriptions of excursions to the nude revues at the Windmill Theatre. Then in December Catherine invited Graham to come to lunch with her family at Thriplow Farm. Evelyn Waugh, visiting Thriplow with Greene in 1948, described it to Nancy Mitford as 'an extraordinary house', which revealed 'a side of life I never saw before – very rich, Cambridge, Jewish, socialist, highbrow, scientific, farming':

> There were Picassos on sliding panels and when you pushed them back plate glass and a stable with a stallion looking at one. No servants. Lovely Carolean silver unpolished. Gourmets' wine and cigars. The house a series of wood bungalows, more bathrooms than bedrooms. The hostess at six saying 'I say shall we have dinner tonight as Evelyn's here. Usually we only have Shredded Wheat. I'll see what there is.' Goes to tiny kitchenette and comes back. 'Well there's grouse, partridges, ham, a leg of mutton and half a cold goose' (literally). 'What does anyone want?' Then a children's nannie dining with us called 'Twinkle' dressed with tremendous starched frills and celluloid collars, etc and everyone talking to her about lesbianism and masturbation. House telephone so that generally people don't bother to meet but just telephone from room to room.

Waugh described Catherine as 'barefooted and mostly squatting on the floor. Fine big eyes and mouth, unaffected to the verge of insanity, unvain, no ostentation – simple friendliness and generosity and childish curiosity.' Her sister Belinda later said that Catherine was someone who people always felt compelled to look at:

> She had a marvellous carriage, for one thing. She held her head high. She was dark-haired, sort of an auburn colour – and wonderful eyes and – short hair – and cheekbones that were fine cheekbones, rather widely spaced eyes, dark eyebrows, and she wore her clothes with great flair. She never showed that she was frightened of anything.

Her style, according to the art historian and director of the Tate Gallery John Rothenstein, who was a mutual friend of Catherine and Graham's, was that of 'a Marie-Antoinette in elegant jeans or (according to the season) jodhpurs'. And Rothenstein described Catherine at this time as an intelligent woman bent on self-improvement. During the war, after remarking on the narrowness of Catherine's reading, he was challenged

© Harlip

Catherine Walston

to produce a reading list. Once he had done so, Catherine read and reread her way through it. At this point, she was not religious. Rothenstein took her to mass occasionally and had to explain to her the differences between Catholicism and Protestantism. There had been signs, though, that she was attracted to Catholicism. Her intellectual and religious education had been furthered by a reading of Greene's novels, and she was now ready to continue her education with Graham himself.

Initially, Graham was impressed by Catherine's glamour and wealth, but assumed that she was too beautiful to love. 'I had no idea whatever of falling in love with her,' Bendrix states of Sarah in *The End of the Affair*. 'For one thing, she was beautiful, and beautiful women, especially if they are intelligent also, stir some deep feeling of inferiority in me.' Love, when it came, was the result of a journey home in a low-flying plane. Lunch finished at three o'clock; it would be eight o'clock by the time that Graham arrived back in Oxford by train. 'Why not fly?' Catherine suggested. 'I'll come over with you and fly back.' They drove to the local aerodrome and boarded a tiny plane. After a 45 minute flight over snowy countryside they landed in Kidlington, just outside Oxford.

Since childhood, Graham had been thrilled by the idea of flying. Aged seven, when asked to state his greatest aim in life for the school magazine, he had responded that it was to go up in an aeroplane. Now, flying in a private plane with a beautiful woman beside him, he succumbed to the erotic charge of the adventure and of her hair, blown against her face. 'The act of creation', he wrote to Catherine the following September, 'is awfully odd and inexplicable like falling in love. A lock of hair touches one's eyes in a plane with East Anglia under snow and one is in love.' Again and again, he came back to the plane journey as a moment of discovery. In April 1949 he told Catherine that he was experiencing the same kind of in-love feeling as after the plane ride to Oxford, as though he had never made love to her and longed instead to hold hands at a movie. Revisiting it a year later, he could not believe that the plane trip was not designed. And in 1955, writing a book called *110 Airports*, he regretted that he would have to omit the most important: Cambridge, snow on the ground and Catherine's hair blown across his nose.

If the moment of falling in love occurred on the plane journey in December 1946, then love itself developed during the April 1947 trip to Achill. Looking back in 1949, he wondered if they would have done more than begin without their time in Ireland. Achill had set a seal of time and place on their love. He would always recall Achill as a place where, removed from the luxury of Thriplow and the paraphernalia of their daily lives, he and Catherine could see each other clearly. He came back repeatedly to the simplicity of the cottage itself as a setting that enabled a shared unmasking of two people who were habitually masked; he by his reticence and shyness, she by the effervescence of her public persona and by the cushioning luxury of her usual settings.

Returning home, Graham missed Catherine intensely and became exhausted by the strain of lying simultaneously to both Vivien and

Dorothy. Since Graham's lunch at Thriplow in December, Vivien had been coldly polite to Catherine and possessive and suspicious of Graham. At Christmas, Catherine had sent the Greenes a turkey as a present. This was a great luxury in an age of rationing, but Vivien, unwilling to accept charity from her husband's beautiful goddaughter, gave it away to the nuns. Dorothy, meanwhile, was more self-righteously demanding than Vivien. Soon after his return Graham reported to Catherine that Dorothy was complaining that he had changed in Ireland, although she still believed it was merely that he had come under the influence of a pious convert. He was dreading taking Dorothy on the long-promised holiday to Ireland, of all places, in the middle of May. He had been dreaming about Catherine ('woke up blissfully happy. You had been with me very vividly saying, "I like your sexy smell" – and of course I had a sexy smell! It had been one of those nights!') and hated the idea of seeing Dublin with someone else.

Greene's visit to Ireland with Dorothy in May coincided with the first of Henry Yorke's post-war trips to Ireland. Greene's mood was not dissimilar from Yorke's; this was a holiday dominated by drink and emotional detachment. Writing to Catherine, Graham complained that this was both a second-rate Ireland and a second-rate squalor. He and Dorothy had lunched at Jammet's and then escaped to the countryside. Before Graham's departure, Catherine had wished jealously that both he and Dorothy would be horribly ill while they were away and now her wish had come true: he had sweated all night with a bad fever and a splitting headache. Despite this, much sense had been talked between coughs; Graham was trying to persuade Dorothy to move on away from him. He asked Catherine if he could have a week at Thriplow on his return to recuperate from his so-called 'holiday' and finish his novel.

Before he could retreat to Thriplow, Graham was hosting a party for the French writer François Mauriac, who was receiving an honorary degree in Oxford. It was a large literary party for which Graham provided the drinks and Vivien was expected to supply the food. For Graham, it was partly a chance to see Catherine, and to introduce her to literary friends such as Rosamond Lehmann. For Vivien, who found it impossible to supply snacks given the stringencies of rationing (they had only two ounces of butter a week), the task was unmanageable. And the difficulty of preparing for the party was compounded by the humiliation she suffered during the party itself, at which Graham was too focused on Catherine to introduce his wife to any of the guests. Vivien later described how Graham led Catherine into the garden where he sat talking to her in front of the French windows. Vivien, who did not know anyone at the party, went to ask him to come and help pouring drinks. 'I'm not the butler,' he retorted.

The next day, Vivien obtained her revenge and forbade Graham from spending the following week at Thriplow. Graham persuaded her to let him go from Friday until Tuesday on condition that he spent all his future weekends in Oxford. He complained to Catherine that he felt like a cornered rat; he did not want to live permanently in hand-cuffs. Rather melodramatically, he was wondering about killing himself, and asked rhetorically if the ban on suicide only lasted for the first three years of an insurance policy.

On Catherine's side, there was no need for negotiation or subter-fuge. Like Graham and Vivien, Catherine and Harry Walston had had no sex for many years. But unlike the Greenes, the Walstons had come to an 'arrangement', allowing both of them (but more often Catherine) to have lovers. This left them happier than they had been to start off with. Initially, Catherine had married Harry without love. On the day of her wedding, Catherine admitted to her sister Bonte that she was only marrying Harry to escape their family and small-town America. In 1969 she told her sister Belinda that at the time she married Harry she had decided that 'if I found anyone I liked better, I would leave Harry and marry X'. But she added that although their 'sex life broke down before it hardly got started', this did not matter as they had become 'very loving friends, almost twins – brother and sister' and she could now 'not live without him, without his compassion, his fondness, justice, humour, willingness'. Certainly, Harry allowed Catherine a tremendous amount of freedom. Their friend Lady Melchett later reported to Greene's biographer that even with Harry in the house Catherine would say things like, 'You know, Graham and I were in bed all day and all night – that's why I'm feeling a bit jaded.'

Graham Greene spent the spring of 1947 longing to return to Ireland and specifically to the peace it had brought him. He was infuriated with both Vivien and Dorothy. The exhaustion that can come of lying to two women who are no longer loved finds its way into *The Heart of the Matter*, which he finished on 11 June, convinced that only the final third, which he had written since the first trip to Achill, was good. Here he observes that it is better to avoid lying to two people if possible, but that it is tempting to lie out of pity. Scobie faces the pain that inevitably shadows any human relationship and is saddened as he sees himself coming to feel the same kind of intense pity for his mistress as he feels for his wife, knowing from experience how pity always remains after love and passion have died.

Scobie, like Greene, has spent his life dreaming of peace. Peace seems to him the most beautiful word there is. 'My peace I give you, my peace I leave with you.' But with his wife and mistress, Scobie fails to find any sort of lasting peace. In the end he commits suicide, submitting himself to an eternity of restlessness in order to provide the women at least with the peace he lacks. Graham, unlike Scobie, had been given another chance. He had found with Catherine the peace that he had failed to find with Vivien or Dorothy. In August he told her that before she appeared he used to have strangely abstract dreams of peace (like Scobie's dream about the moon) but that now he dreamt about her instead. Two days later, he defined the difference between peacefulness (which he experienced with Dorothy) and peace (which he experienced with Catherine). The previous day with Dorothy had been peaceful, but this was simply a negative state, free from scenes and active unhappiness. Peace, by contrast, was positive, and experiences like being in love and making love which were not in themselves peaceful could still bring peace.

On 27 June, Catherine returned to Achill, and Graham wrote her a plangent letter while she was on her way there. 'You are in the air, Caffrin, and I'm – very much – on the earth.' He reminded her that he loved her, missed her ('your voice saying "good morning, Graham" at tea time') and wanted her, returning lovingly to his memories of shared domesticity in Achill by way of involving her in their love. He wanted to be in her cottage, filling the turf bucket, listening to the clank of her washing up as he worked, or helping her to make lunch. He was thirsty for orange juice at 3 in the morning and longed to see her nursing the fire in her pyjama top.

Two days later, after a weekend of being dragged around country houses by Vivien, he wrote despairingly to Catherine that he was missing her obsessively and was learning to hate beautiful houses and beautiful furniture. He was desperate for a few days of happiness and therefore was going to set about pursuing her to Ireland, where he could finish the film script that would become *The Fallen Idol*. He wanted to kiss her, touch her and make love to her; he was longing just to sit next to her in the car. Even mass felt dead and boring without the awareness of her shoulder half an inch from his. He was not a proper Catholic away from her.

The next day he was already making desperate attempts to find transport to Ireland but was finding it difficult. He had received a letter from Catherine, and was pleased that she was missing him and that Achill was filled with memories of him for her as well. Luckily, he was writing *The Fallen Idol* for Alexander Korda, the film mogul who would go on to produce *The Third Man*. Thanks to Korda's influence Graham managed to procure a seat in an American Overseas Airlines plane to Shannon Airport, arriving on 10 July. He wrote to announce the news to Catherine, bubbling with extravagant enthusiasm. Would he really see her there? And where would they spend the night? He would be happy in sleeping bags on a turf field. Graham spent the following week counting down the days and found that he was too excited to read anything except poetry. He wished that they could escape to Romania and live alone together for months or years until they were tired of each other.

Once more, Achill was the setting for intense and straightforward love. Although Graham and Catherine would spend much longer periods of time in other places – most notably in Italy – Graham would always think of Achill as the place where love could flourish most easily. In August he wrote wistfully that he longed to have her beside him lazily reading on the Achill sofa, interrupting her every ten minutes with words and every twelve minutes with kisses. When Catherine

returned to Achill without him in the autumn of 1949, he wished that
he could be with her, watching her make up the fire and wondering
whether to wait to make love again until the next morning or to start
trying to interest her as soon as she had finished the turf. 'Dear dear
dear', he wrote, and the words were enough to conjure an image of a
red dressing gown and of Catherine pushing a comb through her hair
during their first morning on Achill. The red dressing gown, the turf
fire and the mattress on the floor joined her hair against his face in the
plane as indexes of shared passion. In 1951 he told her that after four
and a half years he still loved her as he had loved her on Achill, brushing her hair in her scarlet dressing gown. Even now, he could feel her
hair on his skin and he never boarded a plane without looking for her
in the seat next to him.

Greene on Achill Island, 1947

Graham inscribed not just the interior of Catherine's cottage but the
whole of Irish history and literature into the mythology of their love.
Between them, they got to know several Irish writers. Some years
earlier, Graham had helped Flann O'Brien to find a publisher for *At
Swim-Two-Birds*, which he always regarded as a masterpiece. In 1976,

Sean O'Faolain thanked Graham for sending him to Italy and in the process converting him from his 'Irish faith to ROMAN Catholicism'. For Graham, these friendships with Irish writers now came to be part of his love affair with Catherine.

After arguing with Catherine at the beginning of September 1947, Graham went into a bookshop and was excited to find a list of titles published by the Cuala Press. At once he was in love again and he celebrated by sending her the list to choose any volumes she would like to own. He himself had bought *Arable Holdings* by F. R. Higgins because he had opened it at 'Elopement' and felt his out-of-love mood vanish:

> O, maybe we'll live a while in Killala,
> Whom few things change with tide and tree,
> Where love had been weaned and the streets in mildew
> Just hobble to the lean sea!
> There even my jealousy would believe you –
> Were you ever so dreamy after the men
> Of a town that yawned as the French marched through it
> And never awoke since then!

Collecting Cuala Press editions together was a way for Graham and Catherine to grant a seriousness to a mutual love of Ireland that had begun with a turf fire and a mattress on the floor. And it was earnest for Catherine as well as Graham. In 1951 their friend the priest Father Caraman proposed an Irish number of his Catholic magazine *The Month* and Catherine wrote back enthusiastically, listing writers to approach, including Sean O'Faolain. 'Graham has just come in,' she reported, 'and we have been talking about the Irish Month and he had some good suggestions – at least we think so.'

Graham always associated Irish literature with his love for Catherine. From 1948 onwards, he was making Catherine diaries each year, which he adorned with a quotation for each day. These tended to be grouped around the often related themes of love, death and religion. Large numbers of the quotations describing love and sex were from Irish writers. Early in the first diary (for 1949), Graham included Frank

O'Connor's translation of *The Midnight Court*, which evoked Achill with its description of

> The stack of turf, the lamp to light,
> The sodded wall of a winter's night.

Most frequently quoted in the diaries is Yeats, whether he is describing the painful delights of obsessive love in

> When I clamber to the heights of sleep
> Or when I grow excited with wine
> Suddenly I meet your face.

or

> Lying alone on a bed
> Remembering a woman's beauty,
> Alone with a crazy head

or the more transitory delights of sex itself in

> All creation shivers
> With that sweet cry

or

> I offer to love's play
> My dark declivities.

For Graham, sex had become quintessentially Irish because Ireland was the setting for his defining sexual experiences with Catherine; for those moments when sex and love came together most inseparably.

After the second trip to Achill, Graham missed Catherine more intensely than ever. That summer, they did not meet as often as he would have liked and they bickered frequently when they did. At the beginning of August, Graham asked Catherine despairingly if she thought they only liked each other in Achill. But the tempestuousness was part of the passion. Vivien later said that her mistake with Graham had been to be always quiet or gentle. She thought that he would have preferred her to scream and fight. Later in August, Graham complained to Catherine that his cigarette burn had completely gone and was in need of renewal. Dorothy, too, endowed her lover with cigarette burns during the more passionate phases of their relationship.

Graham's irritation with Catherine never lasted long, and he spent the second half of August longing for her, body and mind. Sitting in his office, he was delighted to have a dull day lightened by a postcard from Catherine with a picture of the Galway harbour on the front. He fell in love, reading five lines and looking at the Galway swans. And he found it cheering but odd that he could keep falling in love with the same person, often several times a day.

Graham informed Catherine half-jokingly that he was willing to renounce Catholicism for her sake, and wished that she was a pagan. He could become a pagan overnight, though he might relapse back into Catholicism after 17 years when he was 60 and she was nearly 50. But two weeks later he complained that casual sex with 'substitutes' was having little effect on his restlessness and he wished that Catherine would stay in the church except when she was with him. He now wanted them both to relinquish other lovers, at least for a few years.

One potential substitute had also brought Graham happily in contact with Ireland. At the end of August, he told Catherine that after dreaming all night of catching a plane to Shannon, he began to cut the leaves of a Cuala Press book by Frank O'Connor that she had given him. At that moment his phone rang and his secretary announced that there was a call from Peadar O'Donnell, the writer and former IRA commander who had taken over the editorship of *The Bell* from Sean O'Faolain in 1946. Ireland seemed to be breaking in on him uncontrollably; he half expected the window to be smashed by someone throwing a bit of turf. In fact it was not O'Donnell himself, but a girl he had passed Graham's way, wanting to have lunch and talk about *The Bell*.

Out of curiosity, Graham met her at the beginning of September and found that she was a friend not just of Peadar but of Ernie O'Malley.

O'Malley was a former IRA Assistant Chief of Staff, now a writer living on Achill Island. He was a lover of Catherine's, and it was thanks to O'Malley that she had found herself on Achill in the first place. In 1935 O'Malley had become engaged to a wealthy American called Helen Hooker and Catherine's grandmother, Sarah Sheridan, was sent to Ireland to give her verdict on the O'Malley family. As a result, Catherine and Harry were introduced to Ernie and Helen in America, and became friends in England and Ireland. By 1946, Ernie was a frequent visitor to Catherine's Achill cottage and his influence, as well as John Rothenstein's and Graham Greene's, was crucial in her conversion to Catholicism. On first meeting Ernie, Graham was impressed. He later wrote that as a boy he had romantically admired the Old IRA; Michael Collins had been a hero of his youth. In 1981 Graham Greene would recall Ernie O'Malley as an enchanting figure, remembering a day in Achill when he had asked Ernie what time high tide was. Ernie hesitated for a while and then began to look cautious, with the attitude of an Old IRA man resolved not to give information away to a potential enemy. 'Well Graham, that depends,' he eventually replied. But even if Graham respected Ernie, he was always a jealous lover. As a result he was particularly pleased to be introduced to Peadar O'Donnell's girl because it might be fun to cuckold Ernie, though it would be even better if Ernie could be supplied with his own bedfellow and stop bothering Graham's own.

———

Peadar's girl did not in fact manage to distract Graham from his longing for Catherine. Although she was lustrous and blonde she had a babyish manner and a tiresome accent, and she wrote poetry, which she inflicted on Graham. He spent the rest of September missing Catherine and looking forward to a third trip to Achill, which they had planned for the end of October. They were in need of time to stretch in, time to quarrel in, time to love in and time to sleep. At the end of September Graham and Vivien went to New York and he felt deadened by the lack of love; he was looking forward to Ireland as a flight from Purgatory. What if they were not pretending but were really in love, he suggested to Catherine. But then at the start of October the proposed trip to Ireland began to look less certain. Graham pleaded with Catherine to go ahead with it, homesick for the feel of the Atlantic blowing in through the top of the door and for the fresh dampness of the salt on his skin. It was not to be. The Walstons' other plans intervened. Although he would spend the rest of his life longing for the rusty gate, the turf fire and the mattress on the floor, and most of all for the peace that they brought, Graham Greene would never visit Achill again.

19

'The returning memory of a dream long forgotten'

Hilde Spiel in Berlin and Rose Macaulay in Spain, 1947

For both Hilde Spiel and Rose Macaulay, 1947 was a year of rejuvenation. In Berlin, Hilde Spiel found renewed excitement among some of the worst ruins of Europe. Meanwhile Rose Macaulay escaped these recent bomb sites to bask in the colours of the Spanish and Portuguese Mediterranean and contemplate the more picturesque ruins of an earlier age.

Hilde Spiel moved to Berlin in November 1946 and was immediately exhilarated by her new life. This was a pleasant surprise given that the decision to leave England had been so difficult. Even in the weeks just before Hilde and the children's departure, she and Peter were still equivocating about whether they should make the move at all. That summer Peter had tried to assuage Hilde's doubts by assuring her that it was only a temporary move. While they were there they could use Berlin as a kind of headquarters from which to see the continent as a whole. But in October 1946 he wrote to her with less conviction from Hamburg, where he was worn out from working on *Die Welt*:

> This life cannot go on. I'm so exhausted, cold, and ill, I really don't know what to do with myself. The food in Hamburg is very bad, there is no heating yet, it rains, is wet and damp, and I'm just a bundle of misery and unhappiness.

He was longing for the sun, for rest, and for enough money to enjoy himself again, and was worried that he would never fulfil his literary ambitions. In this state, even Wimbledon seemed desirable.

I sometimes see myself back in my little study in Wimbledon, in a warm room, with a good lamp, surrounded by my books, and quiet, and I see Christine come in and talk to me – and an overwhelming longing comes over me to be back, only back, and sit with you and my children.

He asked Hilde to decide what to do for him. If she were to announce that she did not in fact want to come out after all, then in his present mood he would be grateful for the excuse to quit Germany altogether.

Hilde wrote back sympathetically, suggesting that they could indeed return to England, as long as they left Wimbledon. They could even rent a house like Elizabeth Bowen's in Regent's Park. There is a sense of relief in Hilde's letter; it is clear that at this stage she would rather stay in London if it could be partly Peter's own idea. But by the time he received his wife's message Peter was again confident about the need to move to Berlin and happy to decide on her behalf. 'My decision is: we are going ahead. I'm in no fear at all of losing England.' He assured Hilde that there were 'more and more nice people' coming out from England and that it was possible to see very little of the Germans. 'I do feel we must not miss the next 12 months in Berlin. They are going to be the most decisive in history. To be able to say, later: we were there, we knew all these people – that will be worth a lot.' And so in November 1946, Hilde, Christine and Anthony joined a ship full of women and children and WAAFs all making their way to Germany. And she quickly came to feel that she was moving with the current of her time once again, looking back on this as 'the richest, most diverse, most exciting and closest to reality' period in her life.

Like Vienna, Berlin had been divided into four zones, with the heart of the old city now in the Soviet-occupied sector. The British and Americans made do with the former entertainment and newspaper districts as well as with the leafier and wealthier suburbs such as the Grünewald, where Hilde and Peter now lived. Germany was still a country of rubble

Berlin, November 1946, photographed by Fred Ramage

and large tranches of Berlin lay in ruins. In her first weeks there, Hilde wandered around the city in disbelief, experiencing again the total destruction she had seen in Frankfurt. In the centre stood the remains of the Chancellery and of the Reichstag, now a vast shell, covered with the scrawls of the Russian soldiers who had first occupied it. Everywhere there were the precarious façades of rows of bombed houses and shops which had still not fallen down or been rebuilt. Even in the central park, the Tiergarten, the trees had been smashed down to jagged stumps and the grass was pock-marked with craters. Dotted around were the remains of statues celebrating Germany's triumphant past, now lying in distorted attitudes with what Kingsley Martin saw as 'an astonishingly bizarre effect, strange prehistoric beasts surveying with stony eyes the abomination of desolation around them'.

The reconstruction of Germany was progressing more slowly than its inhabitants had expected, and there was now a general feeling of despondency amongst the Germans. In an article written for the *New*

Statesman in July 1946, Peter de Mendelssohn described the hopelessness of the 'hungry, discouraged and disgusted millions' who had spent the past year toiling away at their 'mountainous heritage of ruin'. Gradually, the rubble was being cleared, but it would be a long time before enough new buildings could be erected to make the city feel less desolate. And the Allies had failed to solve the catastrophic food situation, which meant that thousands of people were starving. Late 1946 and early 1947 later became known as the 'hungry winter' or the 'winter battle'. Despite tightened rationing in Britain on Germany's behalf, daily consumption in Berlin was below 1,000 calories. There were mass protests about the food situation throughout the early months of 1947.

Hilde and Peter lived a colonial life in the leafy suburbs of west Berlin. They had been given a large apartment in a 1930s housing estate and were, according to Hans Flesch-Brunningen, enjoying their 'satrap days'. Thanks to the black market they had enough food; thanks to the discrepancy between British and German wages they had a household of servants (a cook, a housemaid and a chauffeur). Peter was firm in insisting that they should not use their supply of cigarettes and alcohol to buy black-market consumer goods, but they still lived on a completely different plane from the ordinary Berliners who were starving and begging throughout the city.

If it was possible for Hilde and Peter to ignore the destitution of the Germans around them and to enjoy themselves, it was largely because of the segregation within districts as well as between zones. Their suburb had been commandeered by the British, so they ended up with more friendly British neighbours than there had been at home in London. Indeed, for Hilde the new gregarious community atmosphere meant that the leafy Berlin suburb was a vast improvement on the equally leafy suburb of Wimbledon, which she had thankfully left behind. From the start, they entertained a wide circle of friends. In January 1947 Hilde reported to her mother that they had hosted a party with forty or fifty guests: 'Apart from the British, we had a lot of Americans here and two Russian officers, which counts as a triumph.'

When they were not partying or dining with friends, Hilde and Peter enjoyed the cultural scene that was flourishing amid the ruins. From the moment the war ended, culture had been revived at a faster rate than buildings or food supplies. Although props and scenery had to be carried in wheelbarrows and the theatres were unheated, windowless shells, audiences turned up night after night to makeshift productions of plays, concerts and operas. Visiting Berlin in the spring of 1946, Elizabeth Bowen's friend Clarissa Churchill commented on the 'unnaturally elaborate cultural life' that had been dragged to its feet by the Allies, observing that casts and orchestras had been 'purged, patched up, and sent onto the stage for the benefit of shivering Germans or stolid Allied soldiery'. By 1947, sustained Anglo-American and Soviet investment in the cultural scene in Berlin had made it impressively professional once again. There were plays and operas at improvised theatres throughout the city and an extensive yearly season at the prestigious Deutsches Theater, which had survived the bombing. During the spring of 1947 Hilde herself was involved in helping to commission a production of her Viennese friend Hans Weigel's *Barabas* at the Theater am Schiffbauerdamm, where Brecht's plays were often performed.

In a 1948 almanac celebrating the theatre in Berlin, Hilde Spiel praised the obsession with the stage in the ruined capital.

> In the midst of the most desolate metropolis in the world, among grey and bleached skeletons of houses, theatres of a splendour such as a Londoner might seek in vain at home still rise, and are rising again.

What was the visitor to think? Were these façades intended to simulate a healthy bourgeois life that the Germans could imitate? No. In fact they were reality itself; the only reality that remained.

> The scenery of the theatre has replaced life . . . Here alone there is still eating and drinking, carefree love and needless death, strutting and warbling, cajoling, laughing . . . And the theatre has not been slow to recognise its own power.

Her enthusiasm for the theatre brought Hilde into troubling contact with the Germans who had compromised with the Nazi regime. In

1945, she had dismissed the ease with which Peter socialised with the Germans, remembering those dark years of 'martyrdom, hunger, annihilation' and resisting the easy fraternisation over Caucasian wine. In fact Peter remained less forgiving of his compatriots than did many of his British colleagues. In 1946 he told Hilde that the Allies had decided, if not to forgive and forget, then at least to ignore. 'Otherwise we can never again live together.' At the time he was confused by this solution, maintaining his 'personal disappointment or rather disgust with the Germans, and I mean the so called good, intelligent and intellectual Germans'.

Meeting an old friend who asked him what he planned to do to aid his former acquaintances, Peter announced that he had no interest in helping the Germans, good or bad. 'I came here,' he said coldly, 'to do my own tiny little share to make sure that this people which has murdered my friends, driven my family into despair, devastated the world I loved, ruined the civilization for which I live and blown my windows and walls in for no reason at all, is from now on going to leave me and my folks in peace once and for all.' He was particularly irritated when, in August 1945, he heard Germans saying how much they liked the rival newspapers produced by Hilde's former suitor Hans Habe, on the grounds that they did not contain the usual stories of war guilt, concentration camps and general German atrocities, which they thought were in poor taste. 'What can one do in the face of such an attitude?' he asked Hilde at the time. 'Employ brute force, kick the shit out of the bastards, as the Americans say, bash their goddam krautheads in, or what?'

Almost two years on, both Hilde and Peter remained just as irritated by the lack of compunction displayed by those Germans who had stayed. As an Austrian and a German, they found it easier than the British dispassionately to condemn the Germans for succumbing to a regime they themselves had resisted. They were less bothered than many of their British acquaintances by the oddness of arriving to reconstruct a country they had spent the last five years bombing; they felt entitled to be self-righteous about supporting the right side in the war and arriving in Germany as British subjects. But Hilde Spiel wrote in her autobiography that in this period she became aware 'how many shades and gradations of thought and behaviour there had been toward the Nazi regime on the part of the intellectuals who had remained in Germany'. Gradually, both she and Peter became more accepting. Looking around in the street she found that most Berliners looked trustworthy. And at parties she found herself engaging in friendly conversations with Nazi actors such as Gustaf Gründgens and Käthe Dorsch (who had once had a good relationship with Göring), conversations which she later looked back on with shame.

Hilde's life in Berlin was interrupted by trips abroad. There were returns to both her homes: to Vienna in March, and London in May. 'London is so beautiful, it breaks my heart to have to leave it again,' she wrote in her diary after a few days of seeing friends and rediscovering England in the spring. In June Hilde and Peter went to Zurich for the second congress of International PEN since the war, accompanied by their daughter Christine, whom Hilde was aware she had neglected since arriving in Berlin, gratefully relinquishing her to the care of their nanny. At the congress they saw old friends such as Klaus Mann and became acquainted with more of the European intelligentsia. Christine played on a swing where Stephen Spender was flirting with Darina Laracy, wife of the Italian writer Ignazio Silone. In the summer Hilde had another solitary adventure, visiting her old friend Hansi (the model for Lisa in *Lisa's Room*) in Rome. There she saw Alberto Moravia for the first time since their pre-war romance, but she was less impressed by his cold charm than she had been ten years earlier. Instead, she was beguiled by the more insistent attentions of a young Italian count whom she referred to in her autobiography as Luciano della P. Encouraged by Hansi, she spent her final night with him.

Returning to Berlin, Hilde became more involved in the theatrical scene. Previously she had been working as a freelance journalist writing articles about English themes for the German newspapers and magazines. Now, in August, Peter became the editor of a separate Berlin edition of *Die Welt* and Hilde was appointed as the drama critic. This involved going to first nights in both the western and eastern sectors of Berlin. These were glamorous affairs and Hilde commissioned gowns from Berlin dressmakers, using material sent by her mother, who bought it with her clothing coupons in London.

The transformation Hilde had longed for during her lonely months as a housewife in Wimbledon was now complete. She was a source of influence and admiration; as theatre critic of one of the city's major newspapers she could make or break reputations. She boasted to her mother that she had become 'one of the foremost highbrows and am read everywhere and complimented by all'. Peter had been informed by his cultural editor that Hilde was the most famous woman in Berlin and, she told Mimi, 'they are even calling me beautiful. They must have a strange idea of beauty here.'

Certainly, when Kingsley Martin visited in November their roles had shifted. He was no longer the gracious host bestowing a favour on exiled German visitors as he had been in London. He was now grateful to be escorted around Berlin by one of its most influential women, and for her part Hilde was happy to spend five days looking after him and introducing him to people. She was, she later wrote, 'taken as ever with his charm and vitality and the bold outline of his extraordinary profile'. 'Let's be sensible,' he said with a sigh, when she collected him from his hotel in pouring rain to take him to the airport.

Martin was in Berlin partly to observe the increasing tension between the Western Allies and the Russians. He spent much of his time in discussion with prominent German politicians and with leading representatives of the occupying forces. By this point, relations between the Eastern and Western occupiers were starting to sour as Cold War divisions became entrenched. Dialogue between the powers had been difficult and hostile from the start. When he was first posted to Berlin Peter wrote to Hilde that there were tensions between the Soviet propaganda 'with its blunt slogans, its blatant and unashamed platitudes' and the language of the other Allies. Journalists, he said, were already drawing parallels between the censorship of the Russians and that of the Nazi regime. However, Peter and Hilde did their best to foster consensus. Hilde was particularly proud that Russians had attended that first party they hosted in Berlin in January 1947. 'They hardly ever accept private invitations, and it made a great impression on everyone that they accepted ours,' she told her mother. 'I am fascinated by them, as is Peter, and very pleased that they are not shy with us. They drank quite a lot and must have had a good time, or they would not have stayed the whole evening.'

Peter's British employers encouraged him in attempts to bring together the British and the Russians. They did not expect open conversation between the two sides, but felt that if the British and Russians could simply be present in the same places, hostility might be tempered. Personally, Hilde was loyal to her earlier ideals of Russia and the Russians and so was keen to promote understanding between the two camps. She had grown up on Russian novels and plays. Seeing a stage adaptation of *Crime and Punishment* in London just before moving to Berlin she wrote romantically to Peter that 'nothing goes to one's heart so much, nothing moves one more in one's inner being than the Russians'.

The British had been encouraged to think favourably about the Russians during the later stages of the war. When Hitler invaded Russia in 1941, Churchill announced to Britain that 'Russia's danger is our danger'. In Vienna in February 1946, hearing tales of Soviet atrocities, Hilde thought back to that moment when she heard in England that Hitler had marched into Russia and she knew that the Allies had a chance of winning the war. 'The Red Army saved my life. How can I condemn it lock, stock and barrel, because it repays evil with evil in enemy country?' She had abandoned the youthful enthusiasm for Communism she had evinced in the 1920s, but although she had heard about the Moscow show trials she had not heard about the destruction of the kulaks. If fascism was the incarnation of evil, Hilde saw Communism as merely a fallen angel.

In March 1946 Winston Churchill had announced that an 'iron curtain' had descended across Europe. But Hilde looked back on 1947 as the year before the entrenched nature of the Cold War became apparent. At least at the time, she and her circle still believed that conflict between the two opposing governments and ideologies could be avoided simply through human contact between representatives from each side. Nonetheless, this was becoming harder and harder by

November 1947. 'It is very difficult to keep up one's hopes of reaching an understanding with the Russians,' Hilde wrote to her mother in December. 'Although war is to be avoided at all costs, we can see here that the Russians are really doing everything possible to forfeit the goodwill of their patrons. This is really very sad.'

It was looking possible that the Western Allies would have to withdraw from Berlin. Hilde and Peter carried on their daily lives, attempting to pretend that nothing had changed. She continued to attend first nights in the eastern sector. But in January 1948 the theatre itself was the setting for an outbreak of East–West tensions, when the French staged a production of Jean-Paul Sartre's 1943 play, *Les Mouches* (*The Flies*), an existentialist adaptation of the Electra myth. Sartre himself was expected to attend, and in the lead-up to the first night tickets went for extortionate prices on the black market. The Soviet-controlled press ran a hate campaign against the 'anti-humanism' of the play, while the French-controlled press proclaimed Sartre a moralist and existentialism a new form of humanist ethics. In the theatre – which, after all, was according to Spiel the only reality that still remained – it was becoming evident that it was going to be hard to avoid open hostility.

Elsewhere in Europe, it was easier to escape both memories of the Second World War and the reality of post-war international conflict. Arriving in Spain to research a travel book in the summer of 1947, Rose Macaulay found the same light and ease that she had experienced in Portugal during the war. Spain was struggling economically and politically. Franco's authoritarian fascist government had been ostracised by the Western Allies following a UN resolution condemning the regime. As a result, the country faced severe food shortages and potential political unrest. Writing to her sister Jean, Rose was aware that the Spanish government was nervous about being attacked; there were coastal places where the British could pass through but not stay overnight. She was also disturbed by the outward reminders of fascism, visiting the police station in Barcelona where prisoners were beaten to extricate confessions. But, touring the Mediterranean coast, she generally remained happily oblivious of the country's contemporary politics, immersing herself in the more distant past.

It was during this trip to Spain and Portugal that Rose Macaulay began to find in ruins a form of possible consolation. She had been wandering obsessively through the bomb sites of London since her own flat was bombed in 1941, but so far she had found only confirmation of her own bleak state of mind. Cecil Beaton may have discovered aesthetic beauty in the still smouldering ashes of a frightful wasteland, but Macaulay would write in *The Pleasure of Ruins* that the debris left by the Second World War was too recent to be consolatory. Now in Spain she was soothed by older ruins and by the sense that cities and buildings were capable of recovering the beauty they had lost. She was learning to aestheticise ruins as Beaton, Greene and Yorke had aestheticised both fire and rubble during the war itself. Reporting on her Spanish trip to her cousin Jean that September, Rose lovingly described the profusion of age-old buildings, 'unheralded and unordered', mouldering into faster ruin.

> Of course this has drawbacks as well as charms – but to come on a deserted ruin of an abbey in the mountains, or some wonderful Cartuja [Carthusian monastery] with the grass and trees and weeds thrusting up through the broken arches, untended and luxuriant in hot sunshine . . gives one a breath-taking shock, as of magic, or of a sudden step back into other centuries.

In *Fabled Shore*, the published account of her trip, she mentions the ruins of the town of Figueras, which was destroyed by Saracens and then burnt down in several later disasters and attacks. Each time, 'with its indefatigable powers of recuperation, Figueras built itself and its church up again'. She then gives an account of Malaga, which has been troubled by 'discontented Moriscos in the sixteenth century, discontented liberals in the nineteenth, angry nationalist rebels in 1937' but has still made a good recovery. Debris, she says – and she would know – is seldom:

so widespread as it appears immediately after a bombardment, and neither the destruction of the town by one side in that savage and pernicious dispute, nor of its churches by the other . . . is now very apparent, though valuable things perished in both.

Buildings clearly could and did survive. Witnessing the recovery of these Spanish towns seems to have restored Rose Macaulay's faith in her own equally indefatigable powers of revival.

Recovery also came through the warmth and light of southern Europe. Spain, like Portugal, was a land of colour. Rose Macaulay described the mountains above the Puerto de Selva as evoking the shifting colours on a dove's breast. The houses were painted white; their doors and shutters were vibrant blue and green. There were brightly coloured plants growing all around. It did not matter that parts of the village had been destroyed by both sides during the Civil War; the colours at least remained. Relaxing into the scenery, Rose started to enjoy a sense of irresponsible freedom. She was happy driving carelessly along the coast in her trusted Morris, expressing only mild alarm when the bumper, the exhaust and even the steering axle ('rather startling!') fell off along the way. In *Fabled Shore* she reported that over the course of the 4,000 miles of road she covered in Spain and then Portugal, she learnt that cars were not as firmly held together as she had hoped. Parts of them were liable to fall off. 'If these objects, which I detested, but which were, it seemed, essential to my car's structure, action, and well being, could be fastened on again with straps, I fastened them on with straps, until I reached the next garage'; otherwise she walked off in search of help.

Feisty and self-sufficient, Rose was settling into the persona of the redoubtable English eccentric that friends would remember her as in old age. Twice when inns listed in her out-of-date guide books turned out no longer to exist she inflated her wartime air mattress and bedded down under the open sky. She informed her cousin that she had passed a lovely night in the woods beneath a moon in the Porta Coeli Cartuja, despite getting badly bitten by mosquitoes.

Sleeping outside, diving off rocks into empty bays whenever possible, Rose was also recovering the sensual pleasure that she had lost with the death of Gerald O'Donovan. As always, she swam obsessively. She told a hitchhiker that she would happily drive to any destination but that her passenger would have to wait patiently while Rose stopped off to bathe along the way. One of the most joyful moments of the trip came in the village of Torremolinos near Malaga where Rose swam in the evening, underneath the moon, and then again the next morning, dropping into the green water amid cactuses, golden cucumbers, pumpkins and palms, and swimming out alongside a boat filled with fishermen who were hacking mussels off the rocks and singing. For Rose the beauty of the place and of the hour – the smooth opal morning sea, the spread of the bay, the colourful garden – was like 'the returning memory of a dream long forgotten'. She was learning to experience alone the joy she had found on holidays with her lover.

Nonetheless, Rose remained lonely, especially after her return to London. It would be some time before she could find a more permanent mental equilibrium. She was as distressed by the political situation in Britain as Bowen and Yorke were, complaining to her sister about the Labour mismanagement of the economic crisis following the nationalisation of the coal industry and assuming that a Conservative government would have avoided making so many mistakes. During the winter of 1947 she wrote the account of Spain and Portugal that would be published in 1949 as *Fabled Shore*. This book is for the most part a joyful and eccentric montage of Spanish colour, but it ends with a scene whose bleakness betrays Rose's own.

The final pages take place in the Cape St Vincent in Portugal, which Rose Macaulay describes as 'a desolation of ruins'. There are chapel-shaped, roofless buildings spread about the cliff; the silence and solitude are eerie. This is Rose's second night of bedding down on the ground and it is less peaceful and pleasant than her first. By this point she is fed up with inns that fail to materialise; distressed to find herself 'stranded, supperless and roofless, at the world's end'. She makes her bed in the roofless apse of what was once a chapel and the night is spent among dark and ghost-trodden ruins. All night the wind moans coldly around her; 'the long beams of the lighthouse . . . speared and shafted the desolate wastes of the sea which bounds the known world'.

20

'The place I really did lose my heart to was Vienna'

Graham Greene, Elizabeth Bowen and Hilde Spiel in Vienna, 1948–9

In February 1948 Graham Greene arrived in Vienna to research the story for *The Third Man*, a new film to be directed by Carol Reed. It was freezing cold. As they landed the plane glided across roofs covered with thick snow and then skidded on the sleet-clad tarmac. Greene was met at the airport by a press photographer, waiting to catch him unshaved, and transported to the famous Sacher Hotel, which had been commandeered as the British headquarters. The hotel itself would feature in *The Third Man* as a symbol of the lost world of old Vienna. Here the hero Holly Martins is caught in shadow against the white opulence of the gleaming marble pillars; enormous ornate vases loom into view as he climbs the stairs. Installed amid broken chandeliers and crumbling stucco flourishes, Greene felt desolate and alone; he was missing Catherine more than he had ever done before. Just after he arrived at the hotel he wrote a letter begging her to marry him, in a registry office if necessary. He had her photograph stuck in a letter rack and felt as though he were an undergraduate in love for the first time.

Graham was able to propose to Catherine with confidence because he was finally in the process of separating from Vivien. The previous November, Vivien had learnt about the full extent of Graham and Catherine's relationship after a series of gradual revelations. In June

1947 he had told Vivien formally about Dorothy. He wrote to her afterwards assuring her that he felt closer to her as a result of his confession and that he still loved her. He was now convinced that the marriage could survive and that their estrangement was the result of his own foolishness. That October after an afternoon in Oxford he left a note for Vivien promising her that he was not going back to anyone in London, as Dorothy had been dispatched to West Africa and would not be returning for some time.

But at the same time as Graham was comforting Vivien he was writing to Catherine, longing to push the rusty gate and see it swing, desperate for peace. At breakfast in Oxford on 20 November, Vivien opened a letter addressed to Catherine in New York which had been sent back to Graham marked 'return to sender'. It was the day of the royal wedding of Princess Elizabeth, and Vivien had been looking forward to the celebrations for weeks. The engagement to Prince Philip of Greece had been announced in July, and although much of Britain was ambivalent about this union with a foreigner, people were generally grateful for a moment of glamour amid the continuing austerity. Londoners brought out their Blitz mattresses and spent the night on the pavements waiting for the procession the next day. In Oxford there were street parties and gatherings as people listened to the wedding on the radio. Vivien's son Francis watched while she opened the letter and asked her if anything was the matter. She took the letter to Campion Hall, where a year earlier she had celebrated Catherine's christening, and showed it to her friend Father Tom Corbishley, who was listening to the coverage of the wedding. The priest went against Catholic doctrine and told Vivien to divorce her husband. She returned home and telephoned Graham at Eyre and Spottiswoode. As always, he tried to defuse the situation, insisting that it was only a love letter. 'I know what real feeling is and this is real,' Vivien informed him. Graham acquiesced. 'I am going to leave you,' he replied. 'We'll be going away together.'

The letter was particularly hurtful because it began with a description of a visit to Oxford, where Graham had been comforting Vivien. Her scenes were less violent than Dorothy's, but he felt tired afterwards, and wished he could escape somewhere, somehow. Vivien read Graham's declarations of love for Catherine in his familiar knotty handwriting. He wanted the first drink of the day with her; he was longing to wake beside her at 3am; and he was in love with her and wanted no one else.

Graham arrived in Oxford a few hours later and informed Vivien again that he was planning to leave her. She cried, prostrated on the floor, her head on Graham's knee. Graham assured her, in a moment of cruelty that Vivien would never forget, that he would still send her the proofs of his novels to read. After Graham had gone, Vivien went to mass at Blackfriars and donated her engagement ring to the collection.

There is no account of this day by Graham Greene himself, but it is clear from his subsequent letters to Catherine that he continued to feel guilty about Vivien. What was it, then, that prompted him to behave so callously when it came to the actual moment of separation? Since the first trip to Achill seven months earlier, Graham had become gradually more exhausted from the strain of being responsible for the happiness of three women, all of whom, in different ways, he loved. The letters where he assured Vivien of his continued affection do seem to have been ingenuous. He loved her as a partner and a family member; twenty years of shared history could not be easily forgotten. He would rather have her there, as a comforting presence in his life, than not there at all. He was used to her reading the drafts and proofs of his novels, and he liked to retreat occasionally from his volatile affairs and busy public life into the ordinary domesticity of life in Oxford. If Vivien could only feel the same way about him then he would rather stay married than separate. He was still enough of a Catholic to wish to avoid divorce if possible; it was apparent that it would be better for the children if their parents remained at least nominally together; and besides, he was not confident about his chances of persuading Catherine to leave Harry.

However, in his more honest moments Graham was also aware that Vivien did not share his feelings and that she wanted more love and more loyalty than he was prepared to give her. He was conscious, too, that she had a right to expect this. He had married her knowing that she was hesitant about sex; he had only gained her initially tentative love by overwhelming her with protestations of the intensity and constancy of his own. In assuring her of his continued affections he was attempting to fulfil his duty to her by convincing himself as well as her of his love. But the strain told, again and again, because there was no day or hour when he was not obsessively thinking about, desiring and needing Catherine.

Vivien's phone call on the day of the Royal Wedding came as a surprise, and Graham's first reaction was to attempt to pacify her and to tell her what she wished to hear. When she stopped him from doing this, Vivien offered him a way out which, in the relief of the moment, he accepted. By naming Graham's feelings for Catherine as love, Vivien suggested that she herself had the strength at least to acknowledge the failure of their own marriage. Graham accepted and therefore exacted this strength when he declared that the marriage was over. Because the decision to separate had been precipitated by Vivien's phone call, Graham did not have time to think about how to end the marriage lovingly. And if Vivien's account is accurate, he did not even attempt to be loving. Perhaps he felt that by behaving cruelly he was offering her clarity; that there was more cruelty in his continual, half-hearted attempts to retain her affection while offering her only the dilapidated remnants of a marriage.

By ignoring Vivien's protests, and by failing to clamber down onto the floor and comfort her, Graham perhaps believed that he was behaving honestly at last by no longer offering a love in which he could only periodically believe. By nonetheless promising her that she would still be given his proofs to read, Graham was offering her instead the continued partnership that he wanted and hoped that in time she would come to want too. Of course, it did not seem that way to Vivien. And with more time to think and to accrue guilt, Graham came to acknowledge his own callousness and to feel remorseful about the selfishness of his behaviour. However, although he could regret his own selfishness he could not regret his love for Catherine, which he saw as an unquestionable and unchosen given and as a force for good; for a unique happiness and peace which he felt had to be given a chance to exist.

Released from his immediate obligations to Vivien, Graham spent Christmas with the Walstons in Thriplow, fairly happily accepting his place within Catherine's extended family. On Boxing Day he left a note for Catherine thanking her for a joyful Christmas. He was surprised how little he had thought about his children. The following week he told her that he was feeling happy for ten reasons. The first, he proclaimed insistently, was their mutual love: he was in love with her, and she was in love with him, or would be when they were united again. The second, more contentiously, was his religion. Throughout their affair, both Graham and Catherine were trying to remain 'in the church' where possible, which meant confessing to their adultery when they were apart. He now announced that he had decided to avoid leaving the church for anything or anybody less important to him than she was, even though this would deprive him of stories to tell her (from the start, Graham and Catherine had been unfaithful to each other partly for the sake of exciting and annoying each other through their subsequent accounts). Fourth in the list came Dorothy, whom he believed had become more independent. And last of all came an unexpected sense of indifference about Vivien.

From this point, Graham committed himself fully to Catherine, and found her absences harder to endure. Missing her viscerally and desolately, Graham now saw Vienna itself as bleakly miserable. Like Colonel Calloway, the narrator of the novel version of *The Third Man*, Graham Greene had never been to Vienna and so could not remember the Strauss music and charm of the city that was once the home of Hilde Spiel. For Calloway, Vienna is merely a city of icy ruins, presided over by the broken Prater and littered with smashed tanks that have not yet been cleared. He does not have enough imagination to visualise it as it once was, any more than he can picture the Sacher Hotel as anything other than a transit hotel for English officers, or see Kärntnerstrasse as a fashionable shopping arcade instead of a street which existed only at eye level, repaired up to the first storey. Now, this former boulevard of Old Vienna is inhabited by a Russian soldier in a fur cap with a rifle over his shoulder, a few prostitutes, clustered around the American Information Office, and men in overcoats, sipping ersatz coffee by the windows.

Greene was depressed by the rubble and did not like the complacency of being on the winning side. He complained to Catherine that he found it humiliating to be one of the victors because all the jokes were turned against the winner, never against the defeated. But the next day it started to snow and he found that everything looked suddenly lovely. He was driven to the enormous central cemetery which would provide the setting of the opening scene of *The Third Man*, and discovered that the monuments looked grotesque under the snow: white bonnets protruded over the eyes of naked stone women.

Greene found in the Vienna that he would immortalise in *The Third Man* a new manifestation of Greeneland. Here were the seedy, downtrodden faces, the smoke-filled rooms, the pasty naked dancers and the shabby gangsters of his 1930s novels. In this respect post-war Vienna provided a continuation of wartime London. Indeed, recaptured in the stark black and white of *The Third Man*'s *film noir* cinematography, Vienna acquires many of the visual characteristics of London in the Blitz with its surreal juxtapositions, picturesque ruins and dark, torchlit streets where the surviving façades of grand buildings tower above messy piles of rubble.

Night-time in Vienna in *The Third Man* (1948)

Shown round by a young film assistant called Elizabeth Montagu, Greene was swept into the Viennese social life that had enveloped Hilde Spiel two years earlier. He attended a run of social gatherings organised by the British and was introduced to Peter Smollett, who took him on a tour of the Russian zone across the canal. It was from Smollett that he learnt about the penicillin racketeering that he would use in the plot of *The Third Man*. At this point penicillin was only given to military hospitals, and hospital orderlies were stealing the medicine and selling it on the private and civilian market. The illegal penicillin was often diluted, which meant that children injected with it frequently died (both because it was too weak to have any effect and because they were infected by the polluted water).

Greene dragged Elizabeth Montagu to strip clubs where they were entertained by prostitutes who seemed as ruined as their city. 'Hideous they were,' she reported later, wondering 'where did such hags come from?' In the novel of *The Third Man* Greene described the Oriental as a sordid smoke-filled night club where visitors found the same risqué photographs on the stairs and the same half drunk Americans at the bar as they would find in any squalid bar in a shabby European city. This did not mean that he was not happy to frequent just these haunts himself. And the Casanova Revue bar provided the setting for several set-piece scenes in the film. Holly Martins talks to the shady Baron Kurtz while serenaded by a scruffy violinist; officials in military uniform seem out of place amid the faded decadence of the draped fabrics and dancing girls, and the small tables are watched over by the silhouetted figures of naked women on the wall.

While in Vienna, Greene spent an evening with Elizabeth Bowen, who was there on a British Council lecture tour. During the day, she was busy addressing the kinds of audiences that Greene would satirise in *The Third Man*. Here Martins is hijacked by a taxi which drives off abruptly and hurtles malevolently through the city. In any other thriller it would lead him to a macabre death but in Greene's hands it lands him in a lecture room. Martins (the author of racy thrillers) finds himself called upon to assume the role of an experimental novelist and address a collection of earnest readers on the subject of the contemporary novel. 'Do you believe, Mr Martins, in the stream of consciousness?' he is asked.

Always a practical joker, Graham took Elizabeth to the Oriental and announced that the police would be raiding the club at midnight. 'How do you know?' she asked. 'I have my contacts,' he replied. On cue at the stroke of twelve, a British sergeant friend arrived, commissioned by Graham to stride across the cellar and demand to see Elizabeth's passport. He recounted in his autobiography that Elizabeth had looked at him with respect; the British Council had not laid on such dramatic entertainment.

Elizabeth, like Graham, was staying at the Sacher Hotel. Years later she recalled its atmosphere to Charles Ritchie.

> I was there do you remember when temporarily it was a British Military Transit hotel, full of specially imported black leather armchairs and, as Graham said, decaying marriages (the Occupation people and their wives). It was true that one heard fractious murmuring grumbles behind each door as one walked down the corridors. And they, the Military, wouldn't let one have breakfast in one's room; one jolly well had to come downstairs fully dressed and drink stewed black tea and eat baked beans. At least I didn't eat baked beans, but one was supposed to. And all that among that elegant glory – the whole of Sachers had such a marvellous atmosphere of former grand dukes and parma violets.

Elizabeth Bowen and Graham Greene did not have a close friendship. Recently, together with V. S. Pritchett, they had been collaborating on a public exchange of letters called *Why Do I Write*, in which Bowen described herself as 'fully intelligent' only when she wrote, suggesting that writers wrote chiefly to work off 'the sense of being solitary and farouche', and Greene and Bowen agreed about the necessity of disloyalty in the writer. This had brought them together intellectually, but they were not close enough for him to mention to her his longing for Catherine or for her to admit to him how much she was missing Charles. If they had been, perhaps each might have recognised the other's intense capacity for love; perhaps they might even have changed allegiances. Both writers were courageous enough to make the leap of faith that was proving more difficult for Catherine or Charles; both had the emotional strength to go beyond the long-drawn-out might-have-been. Instead, they both sought refuge in private longing.

Writing to Catherine, whom he had arranged to meet in Rome, Graham complained that the crowds of people made him feel more lonely; he wanted to be alone with her instead. Everything reminded him of Catherine. Even the blotting pad in his hotel room had the symbol 'Ach/ille' pencilled on it by Graham's predecessor. Before leaving Vienna, he lamented that he desired her very badly and could not believe he had seen her only a week ago. He would have forgotten what she looked like, were it not for the photograph on the letter rack. And he was desperate to see a familiar face that was never familiar enough.

Both Graham and Elizabeth were now dependent on letters; both were living as much through letters as they were through the actual events of their days. For her part Elizabeth was more lonely than usual because a month earlier Charles had married his cousin, Sylvia Smellie. Charles had never intended to marry for love, and the union was largely a practical decision. In 1940, shortly before meeting Elizabeth, he wrote to his mother that it would be a mistake for him to marry anyone he was in love with as too much love made him claustrophobic. Instead, he considered that 'the best thing for me would be someone companionable of whom I am fond like Sylvia'. Even during the war, when his relationship with Elizabeth was at its height, he was considering marriage, and never seems to have wished that it was possible to marry Elizabeth. 'And marriage is an idea that I am always playing with in my mind now,' he wrote in his diary in November 1942, feeling rather at a loss with Elizabeth. 'I might do more than play with the idea but for the complete absence of eligible girls in my life at present.'

Given the lack of eligible alternatives, in the autumn of 1944 Charles started considering Sylvia as a serious possibility. Rightly, perhaps, in view of her continual acceptance and patience after the marriage, he never seems to have doubted whether she would marry him. By the time he arrived in Canada in January 1945, Charles was set on the course that would lead to marriage. Quickly, he began to resent Sylvia's hold over him. About to leave for England, in December of that year, he observed that she was becoming a symbol of obligations, which was stripping her of charm in his eyes. 'Now that I am leaving her, I begin to love her.' He spent the gloomy Christmas Day before his departure minding his 'Death of the Heart, this paralysis of the mind', finding the situation with Sylvia sad and familiar: 'I have been frozen in the same trance of indecision between love and doubt for twenty years.' Reawakened by Elizabeth, he returned to Ottawa convinced that Elizabeth was the 'Love of my Life' and that he would never make the kind of charming, domestic, conventional marriage that he once longed for. And at last – 'at long long last' – he had stopped caring much whether or not it would happen. Yet by May, he saw marriage looming ahead. 'It is not so much marriage that frightens me as the necessity for a decision at a given moment at a given date.'

Elizabeth did her best to rationalise the marriage. In November 1946 she assured him that she was not 'going to take your marriage au grand tragique. I can take it how you want me to, and I will.' Certainly, she had no intention of leaving Alan, although this did not stop her imagining married life with Charles. But Charles's marriage still seemed to take him even further away and, arriving in Prague en route to Vienna, Elizabeth missed him bereftly. 'I thought it would make me feel better – I mean, less lonely for you – coming abroad,' she wrote just after her arrival; 'actually up to now it has made me feel worse.' Walking around the small cobbled streets, she returned to memories of wandering around Paris with Charles. Prague seemed ghostly and unreal as a result: a photographic imitation of a real place. 'When there's no sun, or under mistiness, the whole city blots out – it looks like a photograph with just a few details, red-brown roofs, occasional lawns of gardens, tinted in.' Writing to Isaiah Berlin after her return, Elizabeth described this straightforwardly as a miserable period: 'As a matter of fact I spent much of my 3 weeks in Central Europe in floods of tears.'

All the time she was aware that it would only take Charles's presence to turn simulacrum into reality. 'If I were here with you it would be extraordinary: I keep wondering what sort of life you and I would lead here. Actually I think we would get to love it. It is beautiful; and the strangeness itself would grow on one.' She was also imagining his actual life, ensconced in his new marital home. 'I think so much about you. You are happy, my darling beloved, aren't you? And your new house is nice, and everything goes well?' But she could not move beyond the tone of a polite well-wisher in alluding to his married life, because all her passion was invested in her own desolation. 'The fact is I'm lonely: I do not feel quite myself, quite in balance, quite in command of anything apart from you.' Like Graham Greene, she found that the presence of other people only served to make her feel more painfully alone. And, living for their meeting in Paris three weeks later, longing for the sight of one of Charles's blue envelopes, she was already dreading the day when Charles, escorted by Sylvia, would sweep back to Canada, across the Atlantic, in the autumn. 'The idea of your being so far away again torments me.'

Elizabeth's despondency in Prague was also political. Czechoslovakia was currently ruled by an elected predominantly socialist coalition, with the pro-Stalin Prime Minister Klement Gottwald increasingly imposing Communist reforms. This was the closest Elizabeth had come to Soviet-style Communism. She was still horrified by the Labour government in Britain, which had recently nationalised the Bank of England, civil aviation, coal and the railways in what Attlee described as the introduction of a 'planned economy' operated under the 'Socialist principle of placing the welfare of the nation before that of any section'. The immediate results of British nationalisation had been depressing; the coal industry in particular lost many of its former administrators at the same time as supplies were frozen by the appalling snow and flooding. Elizabeth was not alone in linking nationalisation with the fuel crisis in the winter of 1947 and she was not prepared to regard Czech socialism favourably. Returning to London in March, she wrote to thank Charles's mother, Lilian Ritchie, for a parcel sent from Ottawa, and explained her reactions to Czechoslovakia. 'If I lived in Prague,' she wrote, 'I could almost imagine becoming a Communist out of sheer boredom with the drabness already produced by Socialism. No romanticness, no gaiety, hardly a handsome person to be seen!' She admitted to Charles's mother that she found it particularly unpalatable after the 'already sufficient drabness of London under our present regime', which made Prague 'almost impossible for me to take'.

In contrast, Elizabeth, unlike Graham Greene, was entranced by post-war Vienna. 'The place I really did lose my heart to was Vienna,' she continued to Lilian Ritchie, 'as I imagine everybody always has and always will. Even in its present tragic state it makes one catch one's breath with wonder and sheer pleasure.' She had the feeling that all the gallantry and grace that had been gradually fading out of the world since 1914 was still holding out in a last little pocket of resistance in Vienna. And she was far more impressed than Hilde Spiel by the insouciant cheerfulness of the Viennese: 'the way they go on being gay on half a glass of wine, by the light of one candle. Really they are a lesson to one!'

It was a lesson she was finding it hard to learn. On 27 February she had lunch with Charles in Paris on her way back to London. In late March, Charles came to London to see her play, *Castle Anna*, which was premiering at the Lyric Theatre, Hammersmith, and he and Elizabeth spent a day together. But this was not enough, and he seemed less accessible now that he was married. A week after Charles's London visit, Elizabeth wrote to him from Bowen's Court, disappointed because a blue envelope had appeared in the previous day's post which turned out on closer inspection to be not from Charles but from Isaiah Berlin. This letter was itself a source of sadness; a reminder that old friendships had come to matter less, as she and her friends became more successful and so many of the things they used to enjoy together, principally each other, had been crowded out. 'I feel sometimes', she added to Charles, 'I have let the whole weight of my life lean too heavily on you. But you see apart from everything else you are such a friend.'

She went on, talking, she said, as a friend to a friend, to wonder if she had failed Charles in understanding. 'You are extraordinary, I am extraordinary, we have been extraordinary together. I ought (I can see how you could feel it) to be able to take one more extraordinary thing (your marriage).' But she had not bargained on sadness, which 'seems to take away all one's powers – it's like getting something into one's eye so that one can't see properly, or losing teeth so that one can't bite properly on anything, can't bite on what happens. It not only queers one, it somehow dulls one.' As a result of Charles's marriage, Elizabeth's belief in their imaginary togetherness was failing. Now she was a woman before she was a writer, and her imaginative strength was not enough to protect her from loneliness and grief.

Graham Greene flew from Vienna to Prague on 23 February, delayed for hours by heavy snow. He had heard rumours about the possibility of a Communist takeover in Czechoslovakia, but it was not until he talked to two English correspondents on the plane that he realised how serious the situation now was. They told him that they were on their way to report the revolution and asked if he had booked a room. He had not; this turned out to be a mistake. 'Hotels are always full', he was told severely, 'when there's a revolution.' They landed after midnight and Greene managed to procure himself a sofa to sleep on in the correspondents' room.

The so-called revolution had been precipitated by a cabinet crisis on 20 February, when the non-Communist ministers resigned from the government in protest against Gottwald's attempts to purge the security forces of non-Communists and introduce Soviet-style reform. Backed by Stalin, Gottwald was now seizing total power by force. At the time, these events seemed to Western liberals like a people's revolution. Certainly, by arriving in the middle of the coup, Greene had stumbled into a more glamorous side of Prague than Bowen had managed to find on her visit. When he asked the hotel porter where he could find something to eat, he was informed that all the restaurants in Prague were closed. He pleaded, and was told that there was a servant's ball currently taking place in the basement. There he found the Venezuelan Ambassador dancing with the hotel cook, as senior officials and servants celebrated the coup together. For a brief period at least the revolution was looking hopeful; the next morning he went out into the streets and was greeted by processions and red flags.

A week later Graham at last met Catherine for their promised reunion in Rome. Together, they explored the Amalfi coast, finding the same peaceful happiness in Italy that Rose Macaulay had found in Spain and Portugal, despite the fact that parts of Italy had been badly bombed. As always, it was a working holiday for Graham; he was writing the novel version of *The Third Man*, which he would use as a basis for the screenplay. All he had shown to Korda so far was a scrap of paper describing the resurrection of the absent anti-hero, Harry Lime, who has staged his own death in order to avoid detection for his penicillin racketeering. Rollo Martins (whose name would be changed to Holly in the film) arrives in Vienna to see Harry and, innocently mourning the death of his friend, falls in love with Harry's girl Anna. Resurrected, Harry is prepared to betray both his oldest friend and his loyal lover. It was somewhat audacious in the circumstances for Graham to give the villain the name of Catherine's husband. Graham finished the story quickly, and read it to Catherine in bed in Ravello. Graham and Catherine then visited Anacapri, where they found a small villa, Rosaio, which Graham would buy later in the year with the proceeds of *The Third Man*. Here, once again, Graham found the peace he had experienced in Achill. At the end of their holiday he wrote Catherine a poem which compares the 'great peace' offered by the Friars with the quieter peace accessible for ordinary mortals:

> love is a little peace as well as a little death:
> In an hour our pulse shall cease,
> Stopped like a breath.

Returning to London, Graham immediately began to miss both Catherine and peace and to feel guilty about both Vivien and Dorothy. In a later interview with his biographer, Norman Sherry, Graham Greene admitted that he had betrayed several people in his life and singled out Dorothy in particular as a victim of his betrayal. Now he told Catherine that if Dorothy could be happy then he would begin to be happy as well. He wanted Catherine and peace, with no more decisions to be made.

While Graham was in Italy, Dorothy had found out about Catherine. Her previous obliviousness was remarkable, given that most of

Graham's friends now knew about his latest affair, and in a letter to Graham on 14 April Dorothy seems painfully aware of the scale of her own ignorance:

> Everyone from Douglas to the packers it seems know you are behaving like a fool over an American blond as you have made no attempt to disguise it from anyone, everyone you know in London is talking about it too! . . . They also know that you are prepared to break up Oxford for this woman . . . The general idea is that you are going out of your mind as no man in his right senses would behave as you do over an American blond with a yearning for culture!

Graham and Dorothy had been planning to go on holiday together once he was back, but she now released him from this obligation, guessing that a week or two with her would 'fall very flat' after three months with 'a woman you are so madly in love with'. She was writing because she wanted to avoid any more 'revolting utterances' in person; she commanded him not to mention Italy or *The Third Man* once he was back in London.

In fact Graham did decide to take Dorothy on holiday. He wanted to write her a letter explaining his decision to end the relationship and to give it to her while they were away. They went to Morocco, and Graham sent Catherine a daily commentary describing his progress. He delivered his letter on 7 May and Dorothy initially responded with predictable hostility. Eventually, though, they came up with a compromise, which involved Graham renting his own flat but still sleeping in Gordon Square some of the time. He was willing to try it out if Catherine agreed. Five days later there was no longer a chance of avoiding a complete split. By 19 May Catherine was allowed to write or to telephone him whenever she liked because all the deception was over for ever.

While Graham was in Morocco, *The Heart of the Matter* had been published. In April he had been hoping that he would be in Ireland or Thriplow with Catherine when it came out, so that they could drink to it in Irish. He came back to find that the book was an immediate success. There was hesitation from the Catholic press, but the non-Catholics were happy. The *Evening Standard* chose it as their Book of the Month and the first edition of 10,000 copies sold out in six days. Graham had a few days in London before heading back to Vienna, via New York. While he was away Catherine was furnishing his new flat, which was next door to the Walstons' own London residence on St James's Piccadilly. He wrote to her with instructions for the furniture and sending her copies of his reviews, including one by Elizabeth Bowen in *Tatler* which lauded the novel as the culmination of Greene's literary career so far, stating that he now towered above his contemporaries and set a high mark for younger writers to aspire to.

The Heart of the Matter was dedicated to Vivien and the children. This was an ambivalent gesture, given the portrayal of Scobie's wife Louise in the novel, but Vivien wrote to congratulate her husband on his success. On 3 June he replied to her, wanting to clarify their situation. He assured her that he was fond of her and that he was aware of the responsibilities owed to her and the children. But fondness and responsibility were not going to be enough to see them through. For several years they had lived in an unreal world and they now needed to confront the fact that Graham was unsuited for ordinary domestic life. He would have been a bad husband to anyone because of his selfishness, restlessness and depression. And what was more, he had no inclination to change, because it was his melancholia and inner conflicts that sustained him as a writer. He reminded Vivien that for nine years he had also had a second domestic life in London, but that even that had not been a success; during the last four years he had made Dorothy miserable as well.

If Vivien retained any illusions, remaining with Graham would bring only unhappiness and disappointment. It was possible that they could still share a life in which Oxford remained Graham's headquarters, but there would have to be no conditions for either of them. This, he would be prepared to try. But if this arrangement would only make for more misery, he thought that an open separation would involve less strain for both of them than the disguised separation they were engaged in at present.

On 10 June 1948 Greene arrived in Vienna for a three-week trip, which coincided with a visit to the city by Hilde Spiel. Both were shocked by the changes that had taken place since they were last there. Currency reform had been introduced and the value of money was now stable, which meant that consumer goods were to be had in plenty. As a result there were a number of bankruptcies, including several small publishing firms and intellectual periodicals such as *Plan*, which Spiel was previously involved in. 'Vienna has become a little Zurich,' Spiel noted disappointedly in her diary. Greene was accompanied this time by Carol Reed and the film crew, and he was embarrassed by how much the city had changed since he had written the film treatment. The black-market restaurants were now serving legal albeit scanty meals; many of the ruins had been cleared away. He had to keep assuring Reed that Vienna had once really been as he had described it in February.

Only the Russian sector was still as ruined as ever, and it was there that they were going to film the climactic scene in the ruined ferris wheel at the Prater, where Harry Lime contemplates pushing Holly Martins to his death. In her account of her 1946 trip to Vienna, Spiel recollected the Prater as it had been in her youth, when pairs of lovers strolled among pink and white chestnut blossom and large comfortable families enjoyed large comfortable meals in the coffee houses. Throughout the war she had looked forward to taking her daughter to try out the ferris wheel, with its multicoloured cars, lit by lanterns. Visiting it after the war she was shocked by the wilderness that had taken the place of that cheerful landscape.

> Shellfire and a blaze that was allowed to rage unhindered through the wood and coloured lacquer of the booths have obliterated it from the earth as though it had never existed.

The wheel was now bent and twisted and lacking its wagons, towering in poignant solitude above the desert of charred timber. No effort was made to reconstruct the Prater in the immediate post-war period. In the novel version of *The Third Man* Greene describes the shattered Prater with its bones jutting through the snow. Now it was spring, but according to Elizabeth Montagu the wheel looked 'like a sort of nightmare: something out of Hieronymus Bosch'. Montagu was still accompanying Greene on many of his missions, this time following him to the vast network of sewers in which Harry Lime is finally killed in the film. Greene portrays this in the film treatment as a strange unknown world which lies under our feet: an underground city of waterfalls and rivers. Here again was wartime Greeneland, transposed onto post-war Vienna. In the film the sewers are a blacked-out underground world lit by the torches of the trench-coated police, who resemble wardens in the London blackout.

Writing to Catherine, Graham complained about a general feeling of boredom. Apart from Carol Reed, who was getting more and more likable on closer acquaintance, the people were tedious. He was drinking too much and thinking too much and he was missing Catherine. Even the success of *The Heart of the Matter* meant little without her. Graham wondered if there would be more to look forward to if he was a failure instead of a success. There were plenty of other women available, but Catherine made everyone else seem unenticing. Elizabeth Montagu was nice and very friendly, but lacked sex appeal; he was taking the wife of a British Council official out to lunch while her husband was in England, but his heart was not in the game. A few days later he had dispelled a fit of blues with hard drinking and a night at Maxim's nightclub with an attractive dancer. But he had not gone to bed with her because she lived an hour and a half away and Graham wanted an early night.

Graham was longing to return to his flat in St James's and to find Catherine there with a bottle. Most of all he was yearning, as always, for Achill. He had now had enough of being successful and of spending his time in smart hotels and bars. He wished that they could spend a few days in Ireland in her old Ford, motoring from the cottage to the Sound and back. In fact Graham spent the summer and autumn of 1948 not in Achill but in London, New York and Los Angeles. Catherine went to Achill in October and Graham found it painful to think of her in the quiet candlelight of Achill while he was in Harlem. He was disappointed to fly back via Prestwick and not via Shannon, which meant they could not meet in Ireland. In August he wrote to her from

New York where he was finding the glamour stultifying without her. He was tired of being rich and wondered if she would still like him if he was poor and unsuccessful but happy.

Meanwhile Hilde Spiel's June 1948 trip to Vienna had been abruptly curtailed on 23 June by news of the start of the Berlin blockade. That spring America had finalised plans to inject financial aid into the ailing European economies in an effort to combat the spread of Soviet-style Communism. Named after the American Secretary of State George Marshall, the Marshall Plan came as a great relief for Great Britain, enabling Attlee to put aside some of his most stringent plans for austerity cuts. Initially, Marshall Aid was also offered to the Soviet Union, which predictably rejected it; as a result, the plans put in place to enable American aid to be sent to West Germany escalated incipient Cold War tensions. At the beginning of June the Western Allies announced their intention to establish a separate West German state, which would receive the Marshall Aid. On 21 June they introduced a new currency, the *Deutsche Mark*, into their zones in an attempt to stabilise the German economy. Two days later the Russians responded by issuing a new East German mark and by blocking the railway and road access of the Western Allies to their sectors of Berlin, aiming to force the British and Americans to give the Russians total control over food and fuel provisions to the city.

Hilde Spiel immediately returned to Berlin from Vienna, wearing a parachute on the aeroplane in case of interference by Soviet fighter planes, and found herself in a city with rationing and limited electricity. The Western government in Berlin blocked Soviet efforts to extend their new currency to West Berlin and on 26 June they began an airlift, thwarting the Soviet attempts to force them into submission by cutting off supplies. A month later there were over 1,500 Western flights a day landing in West Berlin. There was now great anxiety throughout Europe that the crisis would lead to full-scale conflict, which seemed frighteningly possible to a generation still reeling from one of the most violent wars in history. Nonetheless, the British Foreign Secretary Ernest Bevin insisted that the British should stay in Berlin rather than abandoning it for fear of war.

Hilde wrote to her mother:

> Our relationship with the Russians is over, on our part rather than theirs, for with their hypocrisy they would probably go on making conversation indefinitely. I am dreadfully sorry that they are behaving so badly, I really liked them as individuals. We held different views, but our contact with them was enormously interesting. We really live in idiotic times, and the twentieth century constantly jangles one's nerves.

The aeroplanes overhead reminded them uneasily of the war and Hilde began to have palpitations at night. Mimi was anxious about Hilde's safety and Hilde was irritated that she had to spend so much time reassuring Mimi when she was troubled enough herself. If it should come to war, Hilde insisted, there was no way of knowing where and on what scale it would take place.

> I can only repeat that His Majesty's Government would take the necessary precautions if we had to be evacuated . . . if the entire population of Berlin is not losing control, I don't see why I should panic . . . As long as I keep my head, everything will be all right. I am doing so, but it would be a help, Mimi, if you could be a little bit grown-up now.

The tension was reflected in Hilde and Peter's marriage. Over the course of their time in Berlin they had strengthened as a couple. Now that she no longer felt downtrodden, Hilde had become gregarious and desirable; Peter, meanwhile, was energetically powerful and ambitious. They could recognise in each other the person they had initially married. Although they remained close to the children, they were both putting their careers and social lives before their roles as parents and this had given them a new space in which to get to know each other. Now, though, Hilde was anxious about the safety of her children. She was not naturally heroic and was fearful in the face of danger. As always the presence of her children made it difficult for her to lay aside her fear, and Peter began to find her needy and demanding. She later looked back on this as a time when they came close to breaking up. 'You are the cause of all my misery,' Peter said at one point, 'because you can't think straight.'

But these months were not solely frightening. As in the war, this period was enlivened by intense friendships, with Hilde and Peter becoming close to the English novelist Rex Warner and his wife Frances. Rex Warner was in Berlin working for the educational branch of the Allied Control Commission, based at the Technical University, which was in the British zone. For Hilde, this was a triumphant moment because it was her first proper friendship with a London intellectual. The two couples were soon meeting almost every day. Rex Warner was part of a set in literary London that included Elizabeth Bowen, Graham Greene, Rose Macaulay and Henry Yorke. He had been at Oxford with W. H. Auden and with Cecil Day-Lewis, with whom Rosamond Lehmann was currently having an affair. At the end of the Second World War, Rosamond had reported to a friend that she had got to know Rex and become very fond of him. 'He is a wonderfully nice man, full of goodness and intellectual vigour, pouring down pints and pints of beer all day.' According to Rosamond 'no one ever suffered less from angst, and it's so refreshing'.

In fact, by the time that he arrived in Berlin, Rex was indeed suffering from angst. At Graham Greene's party for François Mauriac the previous spring he had met Catherine Walston's close friend Barbara Rothschild, who had recently divorced Baron Victor Rothschild and was as glamorous, rich and sexually liberated as Catherine Walston herself. Surveying the crowd at the party, Catherine dismissively informed Barbara that there was not a single man worth speaking to in the room. Barbara replied that there was actually one, pointing out Rex Warner, and suggested that the two women had a bet to see who could talk to him first. Rex was as quickly smitten as Barbara was, and they began an intense affair. During his stay in Berlin, Rex was writing to Barbara every day. Frances knew about the affair and knew too that he was planning to leave her when he returned to London. He was convinced that he ought to have the integrity to act on his feelings rather than living a lie, and that he was incapable of having a mere fling with a woman he loved this much. After visiting Barbara in April he wrote to his friend Pam Morris that he had 'at last found everything I want'.

Hilde and Peter were not yet aware of the tension within the Warners' marriage, although they noticed a sadness on Frances's part. They also did not know how much Rex disliked his life in Germany, although he was pleased to have made a few close friends. At the end of June he told Pam Morris that he was planning to leave Berlin as soon as possible, 'never having enjoyed a city less'. The tensions in his marriage were exacerbated by the political situation. 'Perhaps things aren't rather serious, but there is always the chance of the Americans doing something foolish.' The Warner family left Berlin on 14 July and Rex went straight from the airport to Barbara Rothschild's house in the village of Tackley, near Oxford, where he and Barbara would invite Graham Greene and Catherine Walston for weekend visits that summer. At the end of August Graham pleaded with Catherine to arrange another long Tackley weekend.

Given the political situation, Hilde and Peter had also decided that the safest course was for Hilde and the children to return to London, which she planned to do at the end of July. However, she was delayed by Christine contracting appendicitis and could not leave until the end of August. First she took the children for a much-needed holiday to Bellagio on Lake Como in Italy. The peace and the beautiful scenery were a relief after the dangerous summer in Berlin, but Peter had forgotten to send Hilde any money, and she was lonely with just the children for company. However she had told Hansi she was there, and her friend passed on her whereabouts. Luciano, Hilde's Italian count, telephoned from Milan and then arrived in person, hiring a motorboat to take Hilde to an open-air dance across the lake at Lermo. Hilde was charmed by his naive cheerfulness and love of pleasure. He stayed for two days, entertaining the children by the lake during the day, and then departed. Hilde was left with a memory of 'a moment, perhaps the only one in my life, of Baudelairean perfection'. She never saw him again.

At the end of September Hilde returned to Wimbledon, that 'green grave' she had left two years earlier, hoping never to return. 'In Wimbledon', she wrote in her autobiography, where I was to spend the next fifteen years, one grows old before one's time. Time passes so slowly in this green, restful, peaceful place that one pays no attention to it as in the days of youth, while secretly, mercilessly, it takes its course, so that in old age one is amazed to find oneself cheated of a long span of life.

She was enchanted by the green melancholy beauty of her garden, but it was a grave nonetheless.

Hilde's English social life felt extremely narrow after the excitement in Germany. Peter remained in Berlin, reporting that the city was dying and that everybody had given up hope that it could still come right. 'Deep gloom has descended upon everything . . . the city is so over-wrought that before long it will be ripe for the Russians and they will just squash it.' Hilde was relieved to be away from the danger, but she was increasingly lonely and there were few people to see except for Hans

Courtesy of Christine Shuttleworth

Hans Flesch-Brunningen, *c.* 1948

Flesch-Brunningen, who regularly took her to Soho or to the theatre. The previous August, Flesch's wife Tetta had died. Hilde and Flesch had corresponded throughout her time in Berlin and now that she had returned they settled into a companionship that was becoming increasingly necessary to both of them. Hilde later wrote that at this point Flesch became at once 'a male friend, a female friend, a brother; he was a substitute father, only nine years younger than my real father would have been; he was Vienna to me.' Spending time with him, she was transported into an Austria which no longer existed, but which she still desperately needed. She loved and respected Peter for his German intellect and humour, but she could still succumb to the lure of a more gallant and florid old-world charm.

Flesch's appeal also lay in his need for a kind of intimacy that Peter seems not particularly to have desired. Peter wanted to know that Hilde was there; ideally in the same house as he was, or if not, then at least accessible by letter. But he found it relatively easy to go for long periods apart, as long as he knew that ultimately they were a unit, taking on the world together. There were times when Hilde appreciated the freedom offered to her by this kind of marriage. She could go to Vienna and recover the single life of her youth; she could engage in brief love affairs with a British press officer or an Italian count. But in day-to-day life she wanted a more sustained and intimate companionship than Peter was prepared to offer. She needed to be with someone who would enter into her concerns and share them because they were hers. When she wrote to Peter in Berlin worrying about the debts they were accruing in London, she was informed that she should stop fretting because debts were unimportant in the general scheme of things. This was frustrating because it suggested an unwillingness to experience the world on her terms. The fact was that she was worried, and she needed Peter to sympathise with her anxieties. Flesch did, and this came to matter more and more.

However, Hilde and Peter's marriage had not yet run its course. In November they met for a holiday and parted on passionate and congenial terms. Although Peter was not able to return for Christmas he begged Hilde to come out to Berlin, and in February 1949 he was pleading with her to have another child after he finally returned.

I must write something that has gone through my mind all these days during the trip, and it is now becoming an obsession with me: I do so want another daughter. I know you will scream and spit at me and all the rest, but there it is. Please, please, Mummili, think it over, or rather feel it over, if you can. The reason is simply that I'm so missing the child we lost. Anthony is a golden treasure fallen straight from heaven but he is another, a different child, not that one. It may all sound very stupid and illogical and sentimental and it may also be because I'm away from you all and miss you so – there are moments when I feel I simply cannot bear being separated from the children a day longer – but somehow deep down it worries away at me, and I just want to have that child.

He was aware that he had no right to suggest such a thing, given that he had been absent for so long. But he was doing all he could.

I work like blazes, and I shall go on working and we shall be all right. In any case when I get back to England we must get a house. On that my mind is made up. We must get a house with a garden.

And his letters were filled with uncharacteristic affection and longing in the lead-up to his return to London, which was planned for May. 'Love to you, my darling,' he wrote in March; 'I know you're a good wife to me, and much more than that, and I'd never exchange you for anybody or anything else, my sweet. I love you very dearly.'

In fact Peter did not return in May, although there was a brief visit to London in April which he looked back on as a sweet dream; real while it lasted and unreal once it was over. Hilde, he wrote, had been unspeakably good to him; like a mother to a sick child. He was aware that he had behaved childishly and asked her to forgive him. He had noticed and appreciated every moment of her care and love.

In May 1949 the Soviets finally ended the blockade, humiliated by the success of the air lift, which had made it clear that the Western Allies were able to provide Berlin with food and fuel by air indefinitely. But relations between the occupying powers were no less hostile. 'I'm tired, tired, tired of Germany, of this hopeless people, their hopeless stupidity, arrogance and all the rest of it. I cannot live here any longer,' Peter wrote to Hilde at the end of June. The Germans had been acceptable in 1945 and 1946 when they were miserable and defeated. He had felt then that it was possible to improve them, but now he was sure that it was impossible.

> They're lost to humanity, but the dreadful thing is that they're no exception and that humanity is lost to itself. I really think the world is finished. It has become such a bloody awful place. Look at these monstrous Americans! And the Russians – no, no, no – I have sympathy with no one, they are all awful. That we of all people should have to live to witness the triumph of brainlessness and collective idiocy – I find that a bit strong.

Finally, in July, he returned to London, where he joined Hilde in Wimbledon, that green grave that both found at once so alluring and so stultifying.

Peter came back to London just before the release of *The Third Man* in August 1949. The film was an immediate triumph, winning the Grand Prix for best feature film at the International Film Festival at Cannes in September. It immediately imbued the ruins of post-war Vienna with iconic power. Here was the squalor of the sewers, the dreary decadence of the theatre and clubs, the shabbiness of the Sacher Hotel, transformed into a landscape which seemed to typify the post-war world. Elizabeth Bowen was among those who praised the film's portrayal of the city she and Graham Greene had visited together. It was, she wrote in 1955, 'so like Vienna as we saw it at night', though she also had wonderful daylight impressions of the stupendous perspectives of a city that now seemed more spectacular than Rome. The film captured the imagination of Greene's contemporaries partly because it seemed poised between the eras of post-war and Cold War, between ruin and reconstruction, between cultures of decadence and austerity. Greene claimed to be unexcited by the film's success; he was more preoccupied by the relationship with Catherine, who had gone to Achill without him, leaving him with an awful pang as he addressed his letters to the cottage where he had been so happy. But even this was an appropriate response to the triumph of a film which he had written by her side, and which showed love at once as all-conquering and as ultimately solipsistic and doomed.

The Third Man (1948)

PART VI

Mid-century: Middle Age

21

'We could have been happy for a lifetime'
Graham Greene

For Graham Greene and Elizabeth Bowen the approach of the middle of the century was a marker of the narrowing horizons of middle age. At first, Graham Greene sustained the intensity of the immediate post-war years by fighting for love. But it was becoming evident that it was a battle he was likely to lose. Meanwhile, the possibilities offered by war and its immediate aftermath seemed to be lost too. As the world became entrenched in the stark divisions of the Cold War, Britain continued its course of austerity, interrupted only by the 1951 Festival of Britain, which did not make much impact on Bowen, Greene, Macaulay, Spiel or Yorke. Elizabeth Bowen, like Greene, spent this period gradually coming to recognise the limits of love; Hilde Spiel was accepting the failure of her attempt at Englishness; Rose Macaulay was preparing for the death that she suspected would not be long in coming; and Henry Yorke was increasingly inclined to retreat from the daily business of living altogether by remaining indoors.

In February 1949, Graham Greene presented Catherine Walston with the poem called 'After Two Years' where he describes a door closing on his old life and another opening onto a new world. 'And they called *that* virtue and *this* sin', he adds in disbelief, wondering if he ever knew God before. Now his hand is set in stone and he can remain at peace:

> For this is love, and this I love.
> And even my God is here.

If Catherine had come to God through Graham, then Graham's God was now to be found through Catherine. Over the next two years, Graham would conduct an impassioned and ultimately doomed campaign to persuade Catherine to leave Harry and marry him instead. This was in part an attempt to convince her that for humans true virtue lay in ardent, sexual love.

Thirty years later, Graham stated in an interview that he found the idea of mortal sin difficult to accept because it must by definition be committed in defiance of God. He was sure that no man making love to a woman set out to defy God. This was the crux of the argument he propounded to Catherine. According to the teachings of their church, their adulterous relationship constituted a mortal sin. The church did not recognise divorce, and so even if legally they were to separate from their spouses and marry each other, they would be sinning in the eyes of God. But Graham was unwilling to accept that God would want them to stay with their spouses, given the absence of love and desire.

In January 1950 Graham insisted to Catherine that her marriage had failed before they met. Marriage was not a question of friendship or family life but of physical love, which was inscribed in the Catholic marriage service. 'With this Ring I thee wed, with my body I thee worship'; Catherine and Harry had long ceased to worship each other bodily. Three months later Graham complained angrily to Catherine about a priest who had instructed him to go back to Oxford and resume marital relations with Vivien. He had even had to explain to him that it was impossible for a man to have sex with a woman who did not arouse him. Instead, Graham was convinced that he and Catherine served God best by loving each other. He could only offer himself to God through her.

Even if they were in fact sinning through love, Graham had always been convinced that the sinner was closer to God than the saint. And here he had a whole tradition of theological thought to support him. In Catherine's 1949 diary, he quoted T. S. Eliot's remark that 'most people are only a very little alive; and to awaken them to the spiritual is a very great responsibility'. Once awakened, people become capable of 'real Good', but at the same time then and only then do they become capable of Evil. By implication, the true sinner has a greater capacity for saintliness than the ordinary man. 'The greatest saints', Greene wrote in an essay on the writer and would-be-priest Frederick Rolfe, 'have been men with more than a normal capacity for evil, and the most vicious men have sometimes narrowly evaded sanctity.'

Reviewing Greene's 1938 *Brighton Rock*, a novel which explores exactly these ideas, George Orwell had complained that Greene presented hell as a kind of high-class nightclub to which only the intelligent sinner has access. Some years later, Greene became angry with Malcolm Muggeridge when Muggeridge remarked that where he himself was a sinner trying unsuccessfully to be a saint, Greene was a saint trying unsuccessfully to be a sinner. According to Muggeridge the remark annoyed Greene not so much because it credited him with being a saint, as because of Muggeridge's own pretensions to being a sinner. 'What sort of sinner are you?' Greene asked scornfully, as though Muggeridge had claimed some undeserved achievement or beatitude.

Unfortunately, Catherine's Catholicism was more orthodox than Graham's. She, like Graham, did come to God through sex. In her 1950 diary she recorded matter-of-factly that she had dreamt about having an orgasm in the presence of St Thérèse of Lisieux, whose letters she and Graham were both reading. She seems to have had no qualms about having affairs with several of the priests who were also acting as her spiritual advisors. But her religious commitment was nonetheless serious; more so, perhaps, than Graham's. In March 1950 she was delighted to receive a letter from her daughter Anne announcing that she would like to be received as a Catholic. Catherine prayed to St Thérèse before asking Harry for his blessing and was enormously relieved that he agreed to it. 'And to the other 4 as well. To have been given a flower!' Her faith, like Graham's, was elastic enough to allow for adultery. But the adultery was to be followed, always, by confession; it would have been extremely hard for her to make a permanent step towards living in sin with a lover. Offering to come to Thriplow in

April 1949, Graham assured Catherine that he had no wish to spoil Easter for her in any way. He understood how she felt and might have gone to confession himself by then as well.

However, throughout 1949 and 1950 Graham seems to have remained optimistic about his chances of persuading Catherine to marry him. In December 1949 Graham went on a two-week holiday to Freetown, for the first time since the war. He travelled with Basil Dean, who was directing a theatrical version of *The Heart of the Matter* which Graham had just finished adapting himself. Graham was very happy to be back in West Africa, and he began to associate his surroundings with Catherine, inscribing her body onto the landscape he loved:

> You're my human Africa. I love your smell as I love these smells. I love your dark bush as I love the bush here. I want to spill myself out into you as I want to die here.

He went on to outline his plans for the spring, sad that they were not planning their lives together. He even suggested that she could act as his agent, taking time off to write her own books (Catherine had been attempting to write her own novels since 1947). After spending Christmas with the Walstons in 1947 Graham had described Harry to Catherine as exceptionally likeable, but now that he was in direct competition with Harry he began to resent his presence in Catherine's life. He hated going to sleep night after night without her and was jealous of her husband in the bed next to hers. The fact that she and Harry had no sex was not enough to assuage his jealousy; he was envious of Harry for hearing her first words on waking each day. Travelling home, through Paris, he minded being alone in a place where he had been happy with Catherine. He was longing, once again, for death, wishing that his plane would crash.

During the spring of 1950 Graham made explicit attempts to persuade Catherine to leave Harry. At the end of January he wrote the letter maintaining that her marriage had failed before they met, because she and Harry were no longer in a sexual relationship. Graham, unlike Harry, loved her completely, with brain, heart and body. Any time she asked, he would lay out a plan of action for living together; he was certain that he could make her happy without necessarily excluding the church. She would only be unhappy for a time, and could share the children with Harry as Graham shared his with Vivien. Later in the day, longing to put his arms around her, with her face turned to his, and to hear her sleeping, Graham presented Catherine with an 'Order of Battle' setting out the practicalities of their life together. They would base themselves initially on Achill and Anacapri; he would attempt to have his marriage annulled; she would have access to her children; he would give her half of his controlling shares in his company, handing over a third of all his film and theatrical earnings in perpetuity. To solve the religious dilemma, once they were settled they would always have two rooms available, so that at any time without their ceasing to live together and love each other, Catherine could go to Communion. As far as Graham was concerned, Catherine was 'the saint of lovers to whom I pray'. It is clear that Graham was prepared to leave the church altogether if necessary, and that Catholicism had become a doctrine he engaged with largely for Catherine's benefit. He was now far less of a committed Catholic than he had been in the early years with Vivien or while writing *Brighton Rock*, *The Power and the Glory* or even *The Heart of the Matter*. Catholicism had become chiefly a shared interest with Catherine; it had brought them together and continued to unite them as a common pursuit (not least because it was an area of Catherine's life that was not shared with Harry), but Graham would now have liked to relegate it to a subject for intellectual inquiry rather than a binding moral code.

In February, Graham travelled to Boston, where he was needed at rehearsals of the play. Boarding the ship, he could still see Catherine's hand against the window of the car. He had never felt the pain of parting with her more acutely. He was convinced that they would love each other forever and that she should marry him – they were neither of them married. During the voyage, reading, socialising with the other guests and writing (revising the novel that would become *The End of the Affair*), Graham oscillated between missing Catherine unbearably and feeling happy simply because she was alive. He was desperate to go to

Achill in the spring, and wished they did not have to take other people
into consideration. In a few years her children would leave home and
she would just be left with Harry. Graham wanted to grow old with
her; to be with her when even desire was dead.

Graham arrived in Boston to find that his play, seen in rehearsal, was
a failure. He worked hard revising it but the first night at the end of
February was disastrous. Rodgers and Hammerstein, who were producing the play, decided to end its run in Boston. There was talk of reviving
it later in the year but Graham was convinced that it was far worse than
the original and that it had to be abandoned. Basil Dean was bitterly
disappointed, but if Graham felt suicidal it was primarily because he
had not heard from Catherine. He informed her that he was looking
yearningly at the nembutal, wondering about overdosing on sedatives.
He was resentful that if he committed suicide people would say it was
because his play was a failure. In fact, he did not care about the play;
the problem was the working away on a dead piece of writing and hearing so little from Catherine.

Graham and Catherine were reunited in London on 10 March. He
arrived home at 4 a.m. to find her asleep on his sofa. For Graham, still
on American time, it was not yet midnight, so they lit a fire and poured
drinks. Catherine reported to her sister Bonte that it was 'a superb piece
of debauchery drinking whiskey at 6am'. The next day, Catherine and
Graham went to Thriplow to confront Harry about the situation and
suggest a six-month trial separation for Catherine and Harry. This
seems to have been the moment when Catherine came closest to leaving Harry, but the results were disastrous as far as Graham was
concerned. Graham had met Bonte in New York and had been reassured
to find that she was very much in favour of his relationship with Catherine. He now wrote to her describing the events at Thriplow. The three
of them had begun the weekend discussing Catherine's fraught nerves,
without any of them explicitly referring to the cause. Eventually Catherine signalled to Graham that he could tell Harry the truth and
Graham informed Harry that Catherine was being torn apart by her
failure to decide between non-marriage with Harry and marriage with
Graham. No one made a scene and they all went to bed, where Harry

kept Catherine awake by crying all night. The three of them spent a tortured weekend walking, talking and drinking. On the Tuesday, Catherine and Graham went to Paris, where Graham bought Catherine a ring at Cartier, and they also bought caviar for a forthcoming party at the Walstons' St James's Street house – a delicacy that was so expensive that they considered insuring it. The conversations of the previous weekend had evidently failed to clarify the situation. Alone with Graham, Catherine could accept his ring and play the part of his wife. At the same time, she was spending Harry's money, busy preparing for events she would host with him.

Reading Graham's report to Bonte and his letters to Catherine, it seems as though only Catherine's excessive sense of responsibility for Harry was stopping her leaving him for Graham. However, reading Catherine's diaries alongside Graham's letters, a more ambivalent picture of the relationship emerges, which makes Graham's optimistic descriptions of the life they could share seem deluded. She is loyal and concerned, often reporting on Graham's moods and activities, and the number of words he has written that day. But their times together seem less idyllic than they might appear to Graham in retrospect. A picture emerges of continual arguments and depression that would make the prospect of a life together terribly risky, even without the spiritual dangers of eternal damnation. 'Spent the morning with Graham – very nervous and depressed and self pitying,' she recorded in January 1950. On 21 March, at the end of the extravagant dinner party in which they ate the Parisian caviar, she notes a 'violent quarrel with Graham at midnight', followed the next day by another bad quarrel, apparently the result of his jealousy of Catherine's friend and possible lover Evelyn Shuckbaugh.

At the end of March, Graham wrote to Catherine from Germany wondering why he had been so cruel to her on the only two nights they were alone together. He was now missing her desperately and praying every night for either her presence or death. But over the course of his trip to Germany, Graham continued his assault, convinced that Catherine would be happier with him than with anyone else. He had never imagined he could love anyone so completely before. He wanted to die with her at the same moment and for the same reason. And though it was crazy and childish, he loved her more than work, and more than his family; even God could now only be loved through her. At the beginning of April he told her that he was praying to St Thérèse, whom they had now adopted as a joint patron saint. Where some people had a vocation to love God, he had a vocation to love a human being and he was imploring St Thérèse not to let this vocation to be wasted. By marrying Graham, Catherine would be helping God by enabling Graham to fulfil his own vocation.

Nonetheless, the arguments continued once they were reunited in London. In April Catherine recorded that she and Graham had had 'a miserable day with both of us making scenes of equal magnitude at separate times' and that she had gone to bed exhausted and distressed. Graham wrote apologetically that he was sorry he had failed her again, and that he caused such pain to someone he loved so much.

That evening, Graham met his brother Raymond and heard from him about a conversation Raymond had initiated with Catherine, in which Raymond had been trying to mediate in his brother's relationship. This time, Graham made no attempt to be conciliatory. Writing to Catherine the next day, he announced that he felt strongly for both their sakes that the time had come for truth. Raymond had told Graham that Catherine had made up her mind never to leave Harry, that she was sure she would have a more peaceful and happy life without Graham, but that she felt too responsible for him to leave him. Graham's presence at Thriplow apparently caused anxiety and moroseness and she was bothered by his sexual energy. Now Graham needed to know the truth and was no longer going to put up with half measures. But two days later he was apologising once again, and assuring her that they would never part unless she wanted to. Meanwhile Catherine reflected sadly in her diary that 'almost all was repeated correctly but didn't mean what I meant it to mean'.

Catherine's diaries from this period also reveal the importance and reality of her everyday family life. There is no suggestion that she was actually contemplating abandoning her husband and children to be with Graham. Taking the children to school with Harry in February

1950, Catherine observed that Harry had been 'particularly nice'. Over the course of the spring there were frequent entries about her daily life at Thriplow, weeding her son's garden and tidying the children's rooms. On 13 April, the day that Graham called to berate her about her conversation with Raymond, Catherine visited her new home at Newton Hall where she measured the carpets and allocated some of the twenty-eight bedrooms to family members. There seems to have been no possibility in her mind that she might not end up moving in at all.

This was partly a question of the obvious allure of Harry's wealth. It would have been hard to give up the prospect of Newton Hall. In August 1948 Graham had asked Catherine if she would still like him if he was poor and unsuccessful but happy. The answer seems to have been that she would not, and that in fact he was not rich enough as it was. Catherine had acquired a lifestyle and set of tastes that were dependent on Harry's fortune. It is also evident, though, that Catherine was still easily distracted by other lovers. In April 1950 Graham was writing Catherine angrily jealous letters, unnerved by the presence of her old flame, Lowell Weicker, in London. But Graham continued to believe in the possibility of marriage, sending Catherine a colour advertisement for Cartier engagement rings at the beginning of May. Later that month Graham and Catherine went to Anacapri together. Before they left, Graham had assured Catherine that they would be contented together once they were hidden away in Italy, but in fact the arguments continued. On 16 May, Catherine wrote in her diary that Graham was 'not at all happy' but was pretending to be.

> I am certain he no longer likes me, and feels I am always lying and cheating – also colossally selfish and do nothing ever for anyone except myself. And maybe he is right. This possibility is very depressing.

Their Italian holiday continued to be disheartening. She noted an 'unhappy evening' on 19 May, and the worst evening they had ever had on 25 May: 'Graham really hates me but is only partially aware of this: "I hate your friends; I hate you; I hate what you stand for".' The next day they were reconciled and by the end of the holiday Graham was reading parts of *The End of the Affair* (then called *The Point of Departure*) aloud to Catherine on the roof terrace, although he remained cautious and depressed about it.

Both Catherine and Graham were aware that his mood swings and depressions were not necessarily a result of their relationship. But this did not make life with Graham any more enticing as a prospect, and Catherine was not strong enough emotionally to bear the weight of someone else's depression. 'Caught disease of depression from Graham' she recorded in her diary in Capri in 1949. In June 1950, she wrote in despair to her sister Bonte, convinced that it would be better for Graham as well as her if they could separate:

> I am a coward and cannot bear to watch him suffer because of things that I do . . . Were I really nice and good and brave, I would walk out, as I am convinced for HIM that's the best thing. But then, how seldom do I ever behave in the way that I know is best? He is very sweet to me and tries very hard, and occasionally when he fails he is overcome with remorse. But anyway, it's hard to know, and when you know, it's hard to act.

From Catherine's surviving letters to confidantes such as her sisters and to her priest friend, Father Caraman, it seems that she continued to love Graham but that she had no belief in the future of their relationship and, knowing this, wondered if she should leave him for his own sake. In July 1950 she thanked Caraman for visiting Thriplow, where he had brought solace to both her and Graham. 'Graham seemed very happy during those days,' she told him, 'and I have a special feeling, quite apart from my own, for anyone who helps Graham and causes him to be more hopeful and happy.' Her letters to Caraman throughout 1950 reported anxiously on Graham's moods, writing and religious commitment. In August she informed Caraman that Graham seemed 'more peaceful' though it was hard to know whether to trust 'one's own personal judgements'. In October she wrote from Anacapri to tell Caraman that Graham was hard at work in his room and that she was about to read through the first draft of *The Point of Departure*, although

Norman Douglas Collection

Graham Greene and Catherine Walston in Anacapri, *c.* 1950, photographed by Islay Lyons

she was 'no judge on novels or articles written by Graham as to me they all seem so very good'. This time, Graham and Catherine do not seem to have spent their holiday arguing. There are no quarrels referred to either in Catherine's diary or in her letters to Caraman. Catherine herself was ill, and told Caraman that Graham had been 'so good and patient and cheerful while I cough and splutter and am dreary'.

This trip to Anacapri was dominated by the novel that would become *The End of the Affair*. Catherine was reading the typescript; Graham was editing it; on 12 October Catherine's diary records 'a long talk about the virtues and vices of Sarah, Henry and Bendrix'. Given the explicitly autobiographical content of the book, which was Greene's only novel written as a first-person narrative, this would have been a proxy conversation about themselves. The book had been written during the charged period between 1948 and 1950 when Graham was trying to persuade Catherine to marry him. He later stated that the story had germinated in December 1948 in a bedroom of the Hotel

Palma in Capri. At this stage he referred to it in letters to Catherine as 'the Great Sex Novel'. It is a book frequently assumed to describe Greene's relationship with Catherine, although if it is autobiographical then it is often autobiography as wish-fulfilment (or punishment) rather than reportage.

The events in the novel correspond with Greene's own life in numerous, often trivial ways. Bendrix, like Greene, is a writer who works methodically, producing a daily number of words and keeping a running tally of the total word count. Like Greene, he is an ARP warden, and here Greene conflates different periods of his life by making the affair with Catherine (in the persona of Sarah) take place during the war, when in fact he was with Dorothy at that time. He also moves both himself and Catherine to Clapham, the location of his own marital home which was bombed in 1940. By fusing the two time periods, Greene juxtaposes his love for Catherine (arguably the most intense of his life) with the time when he was most easily contented and alive. He was less often depressed during the war than he was during the years with Catherine. Indeed, it is possible that if he had met Catherine in 1939 instead of in 1946 the relationship might have been more successful; the novel explores this alternative reality.

Like Graham and Catherine, Bendrix and Sarah bond over onions. In real life, Graham and Catherine ate garlic at Thriplow because Harry was repelled by it and so would avoid Catherine during the night. They used 'onions' as a code for garlic and ultimately for sex, with Graham sending Catherine a telegram saying 'I love onion sandwiches' in the early part of their affair. In the novel, Bendrix and Sarah fall in love because Sarah mentions that Henry dislikes onions and then proceeds to eat them with Bendrix. 'Is it possible to fall in love over a dish of onions?' Bendrix asks. 'It seems improbable and yet I could swear it was just then that I fell in love.' The lovers then spend the evening in one of the cheap Bayswater hotels to which Graham took Dorothy for their first night together and continue, like Graham and Catherine, to use onions as a code word for sex.

Sarah shares Catherine's language; she describes Bendrix as being 'sweet' to her, as Catherine described Graham in her diaries. She also shares Catherine's beauty, her 'close knotty hair' and her gift for happiness. Bendrix notices her because she is happy in a period when 'the sense of happiness had been a long while dying under the common storm'. Bendrix, like Greene, does not expect to fall in love with Sarah. Traditionally, he is wary of beautiful women. And love comes, as for Greene, suddenly and irrevocably – though here it is over the dish of onions and not in a low-flying plane. Love brings for Bendrix the sense of peace that it brought Greene: a peace explicitly compared to the saints' vision of God. 'The act of love itself', Bendrix writes, 'has been described as the little death, and lovers sometimes experience too the little peace.' And, as in actual life, love and peace are ecstatically embodied. 'There was never any question in those days of who wanted whom – we were together in desire.'

Like Catherine, Sarah can dispel doubt and unhappiness simply by being present.

> I have never known a woman before or since so able to alter a whole mood by simply speaking on the telephone, and when she came into a room or put her hand on my side she created at once the absolute trust I lost with every separation.

Like Greene, Bendrix dreams of Sarah most nights, waking sometimes 'with a sense of pain, sometimes with pleasure', and believing that 'if a woman is in one's thoughts all day, one should not have to dream of her at night'. And like Catherine, Sarah makes the possibility of sexual substitutes impossible. Toying with the idea of picking up a prostitute, Bendrix realises that his passion for Sarah has 'killed simple lust for ever. Never again would I be able to enjoy a woman without love.'

Henry, Sarah's husband, is also drawn fairly accurately from life, although he is made into a more pathetic figure. Where Harry Walston was tolerant but cognisant of Catherine's affairs (and did have occasional affairs himself), Henry is not so much tolerant as wilfully blind; so easy to deceive that he seems to Bendrix 'almost a conniver at his wife's unfaithfulness'. Henry shares Harry's simple delight in his wife. Whenever Sarah walks into a room, Henry's face falls into 'absurd lines of gentleness and affection' which irritate Bendrix by their blandness. And like Harry, Henry has long ceased to feel any physical desire for Sarah, but still comes to feel jealousy at the point when he becomes 'worried and despairing' about his future, anxious that he will lose her companionship.

By writing Harry into the novel, Greene seems to have given himself the opportunity for open hostility that he rarely had in actual life, where he had to keep up the pretence of feeling fond of Catherine's husband. After the relationship has been over for a year, Bendrix bumps into Henry and briefly believes him to be suspicious for the first time since they became acquainted. He realises that he would have been overjoyed to be confronted with his own guilt during the affair itself:

> one gets so hopelessly tired of deception. I would have welcomed the open fight if only because there might have been a chance, however small, that through some error of tactics on his side I might have won. And there has never been a time in my life before or since when I have so much wanted to win. I have never had so strong a desire even to write a good book.

He now sees that Henry, in his very pathos, has all along possessed the winning cards: 'the cards of gentleness, humility and trust'. As a result, it comes as a huge relief when Henry finally learns about Sarah's infidelities and Bendrix can accuse him of being an 'eternal pimp' who 'pimped by being a bore and a fool'.

Graham Greene was a shy and private man, and in some respects it is odd that he chose to expose the actual details of an intimate love affair so publicly. But if he had never chosen to use his life carelessly in the service of his art before, then he did not do it carelessly now either. This is not life in the service of art, but art in the service of life. The novel is fundamentally a tribute to Catherine. In 1950, Harry could offer Catherine the position of chatelaine of Newton Hall. Graham was never going to win her through the promise of riches. She had fallen in love with him as a man of words, and words were ultimately going to be his best offering. In letters to Catherine, Graham talked about the need to invent a new language with which to describe his love; the old words and phrases were tired. His 'Great Sex Novel' goes further than any letter could go in telling her how much, how specifically, and how multifariously she was loved. Just seeing a photograph of Sarah in *Tatler*, Bendrix is overwhelmed by desire:

> Suddenly I wanted to put out my hand and touch her, the hair of her head and her secret hair. I wanted her lying beside me. I wanted to be able to turn my head on the pillow and speak to her, I wanted the almost imperceptible smell and taste of her skin.

She is adored walking into rooms, speaking on the telephone, 'kissing in her own particular way', lying below him on the floor (her 'brown indeterminate-coloured hair like a pool of liquor on the parquet' as they make love), and breathing heavily from an orgasm 'as though she had run a race and now like a young athlete lay in the exhaustion of victory'.

But, like Elizabeth Bowen's message to Charles Ritchie in *The Heat of the Day*, Greene's message to Catherine in *The End of the Affair* is double-edged. The novel may be a tribute to her but it is also both an apology and a warning. Greene acknowledges his own role in jeopardising the relationship by endowing Bendrix with an extreme form of his own jealousy and capacity for self-destruction. Bendrix, like Greene, initiates quarrels, picking on Sarah 'with nervous irritation', and becomes aware as a result that their love is doomed; that love has 'turned into a love-affair with a beginning and an end'. He forces the pace, 'pushing, pushing the only thing I loved out of my life'. If love has to die, he wants it to die quickly, as though their love 'were a small creature caught in a trap and bleeding to death'. He must shut his eyes and wring its neck. He is also excessively jealous. 'I'd rather be dead or see you dead,' he tells Sarah, 'than with another man.' As a result of his jealousy he squanders a rare afternoon in which to make love by quarrelling so that there is 'no love to make'. The self-blame here is partly a form of exoneration. By blaming himself, Greene was asking Catherine to make allowances for him. He knew that he was destroying their relationship, and was asking for help in overcoming his own faults.

At the same time, he was reminding Catherine of how much she had to lose. In letters to Catherine, Graham insisted again and again how much she loved him and was going to love him. The novel is an extension of this, in that there is no doubt that Bendrix is the love of Sarah's life and that she will never be able to love anyone else this much again. Without love, there is only the self-abnegation of religion and then of death. And Sarah dies as a result of a disease which begins with a wrenching cough – an ailment which had already started to afflict Catherine, who would eventually die partly as a result of lung cancer. At mass in Paris in May 1950 she coughed so much that she had to leave the service. That October in Capri, Catherine's cough was keeping her awake at night. And in showing Sarah's extreme unhappiness away from Bendrix, Greene warns Catherine that she should not overestimate her ability to survive without him. Even religion is not enough to make her happy. Writing in her diary, Sarah admits that she is 'not at peace any more. I just want him like I used to in the old days . . . I want Maurice. I want ordinary corrupt human love.'

By maintaining that Sarah can be made happier by Bendrix than she can be made by God, Greene vindicates human love. He endows Sarah with Catherine's ability to evade personal (if not religious) guilt. 'She had a wonderful way', Bendrix recollects, 'of eliminating remorse. Unlike the rest of us she was unhaunted by guilt. In her view, when a thing was done, it was done.' This, he finds, makes her 'a born Catholic'. But although Sarah, like Catherine, is able not to feel guilt, she too doubts her own goodness. In her diaries, she castigates herself as 'a bitch and a fake', much as Catherine chastised herself in her own diary.

In letters to Catherine, Graham wrote again and again that he was convinced of her ultimate goodness, urging her not to give credence to the people who told her she was corrupt. And he leaves us in no doubt of Sarah's goodness in the novel. She shares Catherine's intense gift for love. Bendrix finds that 'she had so much more capacity for love than I had'. She also has an aptitude for monogamous fidelity that exceeds Catherine's. Sarah has had other affairs prior to meeting Bendrix. She is suspiciously good at deceiving her husband, knowing how to avoid discovery by listening out for Henry's step on the stairs, and how best to contact her lovers. But, contrary to Bendrix's suspicions, she has not in fact been unfaithful to him; she has no desire to have sex with anyone else, and even after she leaves Bendrix her attempt to go to bed with another man fails to make her happy. In this respect Sarah resembles the version of Catherine that Graham insisted on in his letters. Soon, you will only want me, he told her again and again. Sarah tries sex with Duncan but it does not work; she finds, like Graham himself, that substitutes are no good.

Greene presents Sarah and Bendrix as passionate lovers who will be faithful to each other until death. In this respect, her sacrifice of Bendrix and her death lead to a tragic waste of mutual love. 'I swear that if we had been married, with her loyalty and my desire, we could have been happy for a lifetime,' Bendrix states in impassioned parentheses. The role of fate in this fateful novel elevates them to the status of operatically doomed tragic lovers. They can never be happy with anyone else and it is tragic that they have not had a chance to live out their relationship together. The novel is an offering of love. It is also a promise to Catherine of the heights they could soar to together if only she will let it happen, and a warning of how much they have to lose.

But if *The End of the Affair* was Graham Greene's final attempt to win Catherine, then it was ultimately a failure. The relationship continued into the 1950s, but by the time that the novel was published in September 1951 it was already becoming evident that they had no sustained future together. The previous March, Graham had sent Catherine the manuscript of the novel as a present, claiming that because the best part of it had been written beside her he was married to her through its pages. That August he sent advance copies to Catherine and her family and was told by Catherine's sister Binnie that he was jeopardising Catherine's marriage and should disappear. Harry was angry about the dedication of the novel to Catherine – 'To C' in the English edition, 'To Catherine with love' in the American edition – and after the publication of the novel he forbade Catherine and Graham to meet. She wrote to Graham suggesting that they could continue to see each other but no longer have sex. Graham replied that she would set up a situation where they would be too self-conscious to be happy together;

aware always of the bodies they were denying. He refused to be with her and not be her lover; if anything, he was prepared to vanish altogether. It was not just Harry who was driving Graham and Catherine apart. That summer Graham had been consistently depressed and Catherine herself was losing faith in her ability to make him happy. At the end of July she had told Father Caraman that Graham was going through the worst melancholia he had experienced in years and that she was wondering if 'this may possibly be the moment for my exit from the life of G.G.' She was sure that she was not the cause of Graham's depression but was 'far from certain that I don't help to increase it a good deal'.

Despite Harry's protestations, Graham and Catherine were able to spend a few days together that September visiting Evelyn Waugh. 'Greene behaved well and dressed for dinner every night,' Waugh reported to Nancy Mitford afterwards. 'Mrs Walston had never seen him in a dinner jacket before and was enchanted and will make him wear one always.' Catherine enjoyed the trip, not least because Graham was cheerful in Waugh's company. But shortly afterwards they separated for six months. Graham was off to dream nightly about Catherine as he sought death once more in the Far East; Catherine was about to move into Newton Hall and wanted to try out life without him. On the aeroplane, Graham began a poem where he described his journey as a retreat into darkness. Flying between the clouds, suspended above the world, he was retracing his steps to a bleak grave he had once hoped to leave behind.

22

'Let us neither of us forget . . .
what reality feels like and eternity is'

Elizabeth Bowen

Where Graham Greene began the 1950s still hopeful because he was fighting for Catherine, Elizabeth Bowen spent the years following Charles Ritchie's marriage feeling increasingly vulnerable. There were moments – weekends in Paris, weeks at Bowen's Court – when both were certain of each other's love. At these points, the time together made the pain of the time apart seem bearable. In September 1948, returning home after dropping Charles at Shannon Airport, Elizabeth felt happy in his absence, 'as though you had left part of yourself behind and were in some way waiting here to greet me'. She was left with 'something better than memory'; 'a feeling of something still going on – don't you think?' Charles, arriving back in Paris, wrote in his diary that in Elizabeth he had for the first time in his life come to a full stop.

> I can go no further. She bounds my horizon . . . She is the goal towards which part of my nature, the deepest laid and most personal part, has always been drawn. She is the meaning of my life.

And he wrote to tell her so. 'Oh, I am missing you,' she replied, though 'like you I am happy, too: I feel so built in to our love'.

However, between these visits, Elizabeth was finding it harder to sustain herself on the shared existence created by their letters. 'Keep me in your mind,' she commanded in the spring of 1949; 'that's where I feel my only real existence is.' She was envious of Sylvia, who was living in the same house as Charles, getting into the same car, driving to the same places. And she had not imagined it would have been possible to be so lonely. Apart from anything else, he was her 'dearest friend'; so much so that he had become her only friend. As a result, every day without him seemed 'meaningless and imperfect'. She had handed over to him her sense of self to such an extent that he often seemed more real than she did. Sometimes, she came close to collapsing under the strain of her longing. One morning in October 1949, in the middle of dressing, she stood still in the middle of her room and cried out 'Oh God, oh God, oh God!'

Charles, meanwhile, vacillated between a strong awareness of Elizabeth's centrality in his life and a detached indifference. There were times when he articulated both positions in the same diary entry. In October 1949, he lamented that if he stopped caring for Elizabeth, he should never care for anything – 'Oh E, how can I live separated from you? What have I done to us?' – and then went on to express more restrained but also more physical longing for Sylvia. 'I miss my wife. I want her. I am waiting for her.' Charles's marriage, like Elizabeth's own, was more than just a practical arrangement. His diary entries about his wife were often more ardent than his entries about Elizabeth. 'I should like to write to Sylvia and tell her how much I wanted to be in bed with her, if we were on those terms,' he observed in November 1951. And then, a month later, he noted that 'the most extraordinary phenomenon seems to be taking place in me. I seem to be falling in love with my own wife . . . I find her beautiful. I want to go to bed with her all the time, and I don't grudge her this hold over me.'

Remarkably, Elizabeth remained secure in her belief in their love, even in the face of Charles's waning commitment. She found his marriage difficult. 'My inability,' she wrote to him in October 1949, 'though this only breaks out from time to time – to "take" the fact of your being married to someone else is a sort of deformity in me, like my stammer.

Help me with it.' But, whatever cause for doubt Charles gave in person, or in his letters, she never lost faith in his love. 'Our love is like something that we have given birth to,' she averred, in January 1950.

> It has an independent existence of its own, outside temporary anguish and loneliness . . . Don't let us let anything, while we are apart, blunt our imagination and tenderness, even if these are sometimes a cause of pain. See me – I wish I were more beautiful – and feel me, even if it hurts . . . don't get a cold in your soul.

In May she asked if he really loved her as much as she loved him, only to answer her own question with an insistent 'Yes, I think you do'.

Elizabeth overcame the sadness of their partings by maintaining that, though they were physically apart, there was an alternative world in which they were eternally together. She saw each of their letters as 'a page or two of what's really a continuous one', stretching across the years. And she insisted that what they had was perpetuity, in which the breaks were merely shadows. 'You are my eternity.' She consolidated this virtual realm by conjuring into being imaginary worlds. In October 1949 she visited a Nash castle near Bowen's Court which seemed to her 'the perfect dwelling for two people who, in love, had deliberately decided to enter forever the world of hallucination, even at the risk of madness'. It was this world of hallucination that their letters provided for Elizabeth, and she sustained it by populating her imaginary world with literary versions of themselves.

Reading Nora Wydenbruck's biography of Rainer Maria Rilke in December 1949, Elizabeth told Charles that she felt certain that Rilke 'would be your and my poet', suggesting that they should learn enough German to read him. She was sure that Rilke 'could be a great strength and stay' to both of them. A month later, she sent the biography to Charles, acknowledging that it was funny to be so involved in a book about a poet whose work she did not know well, but finding the whole story and its outlook fascinating. 'In a queer way,' she wrote, 'something about the man and the story seems like a by-product of your and my experience.'

Wydenbruck's Rilke is a passionate, sensual, self-destructive man, who falls violently and often briefly in love with one woman after another but remains emotionally loyal throughout much of his adult life to a sustaining friendship with an older woman, the Princess Marie von Thurs und Taxis-Hohenlohe. Princess Marie has several obvious parallels with Elizabeth Bowen. She is brought up by remote parents who float into the nursery, festooned with roses. She has a powerful 'feeling for words, for their substance and texture' and is well-known as a great storyteller. And, crucially, she spends much of her childhood in a dreamy Italian mansion called Sagrado, an enchanted castle in which, in Wydenbruck's account, 'the lonely child dreamt her dreams and unconsciously absorbed the loveliness that was to form her spirit'. After the house was destroyed in the First World War, Princess Marie recalled childhood arrivals at Sagrado in a description that could come straight out of *Bowen's Court*:

> I enter the hall, close my eyes and breathe the scent of Sagrado. It was a scent as of fresh flowers, mingling with a faint odour of dust, almost mildew, and a trace of wax with which the mosaic floors were polished – the smell of cool, shady rooms that have been shut up for a long time. And in the rooms and the closets, the vestibules and the corridors, in the halls and on the stairs I have met an invisible presence and heard its soft step, and I have felt it permeating the enchanted house – it was happiness.

In 1910 Rilke visited Princess Marie at her castle in Duino and the pair began an intense friendship that would continue until his death. Marie recalled the 'precious hours' of this first visit as passing in undisturbed harmony. She was attracted by Rilke's unique charm and struck by his humility. He was a dual man, who combined 'proud self-confidence' with the persona of 'a delightful child', abandoned 'to the dark phantoms of night' yet 'open to tremendous visions'. She longed to remove 'everything harsh and sad from his path'. Rilke was immediately drawn to the Princess, enjoying his 'heartfelt' bond of understanding with her. During his next period of depression it was to her that he turned and, according to Wydenbruck, he now learnt the possibility of ordinary happiness through the offices of 'a woman whose warmhearted, natural humanity was expressed in such perfected form that it no longer frightened or offended him'. Quickly, he began to write to the Princess almost every day: 'spontaneous, natural letters which show how much he felt at home with her'. 'How I wish', he wrote in one, 'we could go for walks together here as we did in Venice, you would show me so many things and I would tell you about them.' These visits and letters set the tone for fifteen years of friendship and literary collaboration. Princess Marie became the most important reader of Rilke's work and the pair worked together on a translation of Dante's poems to Beatrice, reading these love poems aloud together in the evenings after listening to music in the afternoon.

In this aspect of their relationship, it is easy to see why Elizabeth Bowen was happy to identify herself and Charles with Princess Marie and Rilke. However, there is also an acceptance of limitation inherent in her identification. In Wydenbruck's account, Rilke's bond with Princess Marie was one of 'intense sympathy', but it was not a love affair. There is no suggestion that it was ever sexual, and instead Rilke told Princess Marie about his love affairs with other women, showing her the letters he received from his beloveds. Wydenbruck commends the Princess for being 'exceptionally free from the slight jealousy that attends most human friendships'; 'big-hearted' in her desire to help Rilke in questions of love. However, it is not hard to read between the lines of the Princess's 'big-hearted' descriptions of her friend and to glimpse her pain. 'Will he never be left in peace,' she demanded in 1921; 'will he never find the woman who loves him enough to understand what he needs – who would live only for him and not think about her own unimportant little life?' He had asked her over and over again whether she believed that 'a loving being might exist somewhere, one who would be prepared to step back when the voice called to him'. He was seeking a woman who could 'give her whole heart and never ask anything for herself'. Even if such a woman existed, Princess Marie asked herself rhetorically, 'how should he find her?' For his part, Rilke failed to see that he had met her already, continuing instead merely to confide in the woman Wydenbruck describes as 'his motherly friend'.

But Elizabeth, like Wydenbruck, could look beyond Rilke's limitations. While reading the biography, Elizabeth was also identifying with the Rilke of the poetry, merging the man and poet in Wydenbruck's title. In the poetry, Rilke is an ardent lover who commands his beloved to accept the pain that is commingled with the delight of love. 'Let us not, in the dark sweet ecstasy, distinguish the direction of our tears. Are you certain whether we suffer delight, or shine from having drunk our fill of sorrow?' In the biography, there is an intensity even to his fickleness; a grandeur of feeling that allows him to remain lovable in his moments of depression, numbness and bleakness. This portrait of Rilke seems to have provided Elizabeth with a way to reconcile Charles's own limitations with her sense of him as a passionate lover.

Another crucial figure in Elizabeth's imaginary world was Gustave Flaubert, whose fervent love letters to Louise Colet expressed a longing equal to Elizabeth's own. 'I look at your slippers, your handkerchief, your hair, your portrait, I reread your letters and breathe their musky perfume,' Flaubert wrote to Louise Colet in much the same spirit that Elizabeth looked around and saw the corduroy armchair near the fire that Charles once sat in and collided with his ghost. At the same time, in his willingness to accept physical distance as a condition of the relationship, Flaubert resembled Charles. For Elizabeth, Flaubert's blending of passion and distance seems to have legitimised Charles's behaviour. In 1947, Bowen published a preface to a collection of Flaubert's work in which, two years after she had explained Charles as a 'dual' man, torn between the intellectual and the imaginative realms, she saw Flaubert's temperament as breeding his art out of dualities. Here she asserts Louise Colet's power over Flaubert ('He loved her, he loved his love for her, and he loved every evidence of her love'), and also details his failures as a lover. From Louise's point of view, 'there were too many letters and too few meetings'; the raptures of Paris were interspersed with 'lengthening months of nothing'. Although ultimately she does not defend Flaubert's part in the relationship, she suggests that it was no less important for him than for Louise. In Flaubert's life, Louise 'had no successor'.

If he hurt her more than she hurt him, 'she entered his life more deeply than he entered hers. He never forgot, as he never repeated, love.'

During the 1950s, Elizabeth Bowen was preparing an edition of Flaubert's correspondence. This was never published, but she did get as far as compiling an extensive index and translating a handful of letters. Among these were letters to friends, describing the strain and joy of writing, and a few letters to Louise, written while Flaubert was working on *Madame Bovary*. Here, after an exhausting day of writing, he sends Louise a 'caress, a kiss, and all the thought left to me'. In one of the longest letters that Bowen translated, Flaubert admonishes Louise for her jealousy, maintaining that their love is too profound to fall at so petty a hurdle. So might Charles have replied to Elizabeth; her decision to translate it seems to contain an act of self-reproof, as well as an assertion of the passion possible in Charles's more detached position. 'I wanted to love you', Flaubert announces grandly, 'in a way that is not that of lovers.' Between them they could have 'put all sex, all decency, all jealousy, all politeness under our feet, low down, to make us a pedestal; so standing we could together have towered above ourselves'. This love 'would have been the whole heart'.

Writing to Charles in 1960, Elizabeth made explicit the identification she had created, since the 1940s, between Flaubert and both herself and Charles. Here, delighted that Charles was reading the Flaubert letters, she described the 'extraordinary feeling one has towards him' as the 'feeling of identification one has in love'. For her, he captured accurately the sensation she herself had in writing, with its feeling that everything else was unreal. She would not have been able to love anyone without 'the Flaubertian quality about them' and Charles, of course, had it himself. Flaubert was one of the people she most wished she had known, but there was a way in which she did in fact know him. Indeed, once late at night in the library at Bowen's Court, working away at the writing table by the window, she thought 'he was away off behind my back, sitting in one of those corduroy chairs by the fire'. Picturing him in that same chair in which she had so often pictured Charles, she felt a 'frisson' in her spine. When she finally turned round and he was not there, 'with his beautiful heavy fair moustache', she was disappointed. In 1946, in daylight, Elizabeth had come down the flight of stairs in the hall and thought she saw someone standing outside the front door. Certain that it would be Charles, she saw the clothes he would be wearing, his attitude, the expression on his face. Opening the door, she found that there was nobody there. There is an intense actuality to Elizabeth's fantasies that suggests she came close to entering that 'world of hallucination, even at the risk of madness' that she had imagined the lovers crossing into in the Nash castle. It was a world that gained veracity through containing not just herself and Charles but Flaubert and Rilke, incorporating the imaginative worlds of their writing.

Meanwhile, in the day-to-day world that Elizabeth shared with her husband, Alan's health and drinking were getting considerably worse. In May 1949 Elizabeth wrote to Charles that Alan had come back to Ireland from London 'rather ill again: more of that wretched heart-trouble'. He was wandering around in a sort of dream; 'deprived of his cat, he is now falling in love with trees, the trees here'. One day, gazing at the trees, he wrung her heart by saying suddenly, 'Do you realise these are being the happiest months of my life?'

Over the next two years, Alan's health deteriorated rapidly. He suffered a heart attack in 1951, and in January 1952 he retired from his job at EMI and Elizabeth and Alan gave up Clarence Terrace, moving permanently to Bowen's Court. On 26 August, Alan died. It was a quiet death; the sun shone, and the Catholic neighbours came to pray beside his coffin. Elizabeth spent the next few months overwhelmed by grief. Writing to William Plomer on 9 September, she described how reading Plomer's memoir had saved what had otherwise been 'terrifyingly empty days'. More openly, in a letter to Isaiah Berlin in October, written on a depressing autumn afternoon with leaves drifting diagonally past her window, Elizabeth wrote that she had been living in a 'queer state of isolation'. 'I never had, till now,' she explained, 'known what it was to mourn. I have felt sorrows, but those are so unlike the state of grief – which is, I find, almost like a state in the geographic sense, with a climate and landscape of its own.' Elizabeth was acutely aware of how much she had lost with Alan's death. He was, she told Berlin, 'not only the anchorage of my life but also the sort of assurance of moral good in it'; he embodied the principle of 'good sense'.

Elizabeth was always clear in seeing Alan as the person whose support made her writing possible. He organised her life, armoured her with practical and emotional security and believed fervently in her work, knowing long passages from her novels by heart. In an autobiographical note written in 1953 Elizabeth made this debt explicit: 'To his belief in my work, and patience with the vagaries of a writer-wife, I owe everything.' Theirs had not always been a passionate relationship, but its day-to-day rhythms had been the rhythms of most of Elizabeth's adult life. The frightening intensity of Elizabeth's vulnerability with Charles had been sustainable largely because of the comforting protection of Alan's love. Now, she was left feeling helpless and disorientated by his death. In the letter to Berlin she says that since August she has been trying to read *The Times* because up to now this has been Alan's role in the relationship and she feels that 'there must be one person in the family who does so'. With him, she has lost 'the feeling of being located, fixed, held by someone else not only in affection but in their sense of reality'. She now lacks 'the feeling of home and of being protected from winds that blow'. Alan was both her father and mother, 'brought nearer by also being a contemporary'. Legally and psychologically, she now has no next of kin – the closest she has to a family is Bowen's Court itself.

In the aftermath of Alan's death, Elizabeth became increasingly aware of her dependency on Charles. Her life was busy without him; in the year after Alan's death she lectured in Italy, Germany and America; she was much in demand at American universities and now had an independent social life in New York. But year after year, Elizabeth hoped that Charles would give more than he turned out to be able to give; instead, there was one disappointment after another as projected visits failed to materialise and love – that life which cried out to be lived – remained locked in the beautiful but intangible world of letters. After Charles left Bowen's Court at the end of a visit in the summer of 1953, Elizabeth felt physically ill, as though his departure had done something to her stomach. Each time they were together, there was 'a world of timeless and complete happiness', interrupted by 'a blade of anguish coming down like a guillotine'. 'Do you know,' she wrote to him in July 1954, 'it sometimes tears at me like one of those iron hooks used (I believe) by medieval torturers, our going on being apart like this, week after week, summer after summer.'

That summer, Elizabeth visited Charles in Germany, where he had been sent as the Ambassador to the Federal Republic of Germany, working in Bonn and living in Cologne. He was now more certain than ever of his love for Sylvia, noting in his diary the 'growing realisation that having married for companionship I am now passionately physically in love'. If anything, it was the companionship that was lacking, and which he still found with Elizabeth instead. He experienced Elizabeth's visit as a time of 'feverish high-pressure' followed by 'emotional emptiness'. Self-indulgently melancholic, he wrote a mock-advertisement in his diary for 'a life to let'; an 'attractive property', encumbered by squatters' rights, with an owner 'willing to rent at sacrifice price' who would consider sale.

In August, Elizabeth returned again, making scenes, distressed by Charles's increasing numbness. Writing to him over the course of the autumn, Elizabeth attempted to retain her hold over him, insisting still on 'the uninterrupted reality of OUR life' – the only life that was a reality 'to me and, you say, to you'. She herself was struggling to keep up this belief. 'Oh I miss you, I miss you, I miss you – till I can hardly bear it,' she wrote in October. Hanging up the telephone after a conversation with him in November, she was left 'so restless and with such an ache', overcome by a 'what's-the-point-of-being-alive-when-we're-not-together feeling'.

In 1953 and 1954 Elizabeth Bowen wrote two essays about disappointment, which she described as 'a harsh emotional blow'. In the first, she talks about the frightening power of the wreck of a hope or plan to cast the adult into the disproportionate world of childhood. Sometimes, she states, disappointment is of a magnitude which cannot be immediately taken in. As we grow older we expose ourselves to disappointment less, but it can still come upon us unawares. In love, we may experience a point-blank reverse. Some disappointments are years in the making; for example, the 'non-achievement of happiness with another person in the course of a love affair'. What is undergone here is not a single blow but a series of 'checkmatings, defeats, rebuffs' which, cumulatively, have the effect of 'undermining morale or corroding character'. It is hard, in these cases, not to see oneself as a victim. There is a danger of becoming 'that sad type, the recognisably "disappointed" person'.

After this painfully personal analysis of the state of disappointment, Bowen goes on to wonder how to survive the pain. She is sure that the answer is not to inure oneself against disappointment by ceasing to feel. Instead, we must learn to surmount disappointment, once it occurs, by asking 'How far may this be my fault?' 'Is it a fact, for instance, that you or I *have* been living in something of a dream world? If so, there was almost bound to be a collision with reality.' Disappointment teaches the fantasist the necessary but hurtful lesson. And this form of disappointment is most painful in a love relationship.

> Self-deception may play a part in romantic love. Have we, through over-idealisation, created as the object of our affections someone who in reality never was? Have we insisted on being blind to the true nature of the man or woman on whom we set our hearts? If so, a false situation has arisen: the loved one sooner or later *must* give us pain by no more than being himself.

In this case, we must admit our own share in what has come about in order to be healed.

This essay reads, if not as an apology to Charles, then as an admission of partial guilt. But, like *The Heat of the Day*, it is also a warning. If Elizabeth is disappointed because she has been blind to Charles's true nature, then it is because he is considerably less loveable than she has believed. If he is going to let her take the blame for her own disappointment, then he must accept that she will lose her high opinion of him. Elizabeth does provide an alternative to delusion. Some disappointments, she says, are not our fault. Sometimes, bewilderingly, 'someone we had the right to trust' backs down. In these cases, the sufferer '*is* a victim truly'; they are 'cases of outrage to tender love'. In situations such as these, we are 'assailed in our sense of justice – the best in us seems to have gone for nothing'. Here she offers Charles another possibility: he can be the man she thought he was, but then he must take all the responsibility for her disappointment upon himself.

Either way, for her, there is no easy solution to this pain. 'Alone we must set out to rebuild ourselves.' Recuperation will be painful and slow. It is crucial to regain a sense of perspective; to view one's own life in the context of the wider world and to see that life contains alternatives to the particular aim or person on which we had concentrated our thoughts and feelings. There is no point embarking on a new course of action just for the sake of it. 'Disappointment has to be faced out.' Indeed, like 'all forms of primal experience', it has 'a sort of dignity', deepening our knowledge of ourselves and others.

This essay remained unpublished and it was only the second, much shorter and less personally revealing essay on disappointment that Bowen allowed to be exposed to public scrutiny. The second essay does not refer specifically to love, and is focused instead on the suffering of children. The personal note intrudes only at the end, where Bowen maintains that we should 'never underrate disappointment', which is 'seldom distant' and 'always hurts'.

In choosing to write about disappointment, Elizabeth was facing the limitations of her relationship with Charles. It was becoming apparent that they would never see each other as much as she would like, and she now needed to decide whether the happiness the love affair brought her was worth the pain. Should she leave Charles and find someone prepared to commit to her more fully? She answered this in part by writing *A World of Love*, which was published in 1955 and is at once a disappointed and an ecstatic novel. Charles read the American edition of the novel while staying at Bowen's Court in December 1954. It was a difficult visit, still shadowed by their scenes in Germany that summer. Arriving in the house, Charles felt as if he was 'looking at life through bi-focals'; he was wary of Elizabeth, who warned him that if his present life continued he would 'go mad or die'. He feared more realistically that he would dry up emotionally, 'cease to care or even notice that this is happening to me'. He did not want his precarious balance to be undermined by the profound unhappiness which she showed only to him.

Gradually, the magic of the relationship returned. The next day, they continued to discuss the numbness of his feelings but he was experiencing 'a sort of exhilaration' in being with her; the gash in their love caused by Bonn was starting to close. A moment of breakthrough came when he read the new novel, convinced that in spite of 'loneliness, sorrow, despair, she has written this masterpiece of her art'. He found it hard to believe that she had written the final chapters 'in the nightmare agitation of that visit to Bonn', thinking that if 'she was as distractedly unhappy over us as she seemed', it was incredible that she could have written so confidently. He gave himself credit for its success. 'It is our book as it contains our shared illusion of life and could not, as they say in prefaces, have been written without me!' The book had come at a price 'paid by her, perhaps even more by me'.

In some ways Charles is still more central to *A World of Love* than to *The Heat of the Day*, where Stella's love for Robert is one of a number of competing plotlines and themes. The new novel portrays a world haunted by the charismatic, fickle personality of Guy, one-time owner of Montefort, the latest incarnation of Bowen's Court. Twenty-five years on from *The Last September*, Bowen's literary Big House has fallen into disrepair. The roof leaks, the house is covered with moss, most of the neighbours believe it to be empty. In fact, it is inhabited by five desultory figures, three of whom are in love with Guy, who was killed in the First World War. There is his cousin Antonia, a childhood playmate and his equal in spirit and haughtiness ('The way you two were, you could have run the world,' her illegitimate cousin Fred tells her). Then there is Lilia, Guy's one-time fiancé whom, after Guy's death, Antonia invited to live at Montefort, which would rightfully have been hers if Guy had made a will. And there is Jane, daughter of a union between Lilia and Fred which Antonia has arranged for the sake of the house. Jane, 'perfectly ready to be a woman but not yet so', is the more beautiful successor of Lois in *The Last September*; the kid whom Sean O'Faolain saw as being ever at the mercy of the cad. And the cad is her dead cousin Guy, a fickle charmer who in his life 'had stirred up too much', scattering round him 'more promises as to some dreamed-of extreme of being than one man could have hoped to live to honour'.

Guy should by rights have been Jane's father, but instead he comes into her life as a ghostly fantasy lover when she finds his love letters in a trunk in the attic at the start of the book. And *A World of Love* is not just a sorrowful tribute to Charles and a paean to love, but also an elegiac testament to the power of letters. In her first appearance, Jane is wandering ecstatically around the garden, rereading a letter which she knows more than half by heart. Guy's letters are written in 'a speaking language', imbued with all the power of love. Described by him, the garden of the house in which he writes and Jane reads the letters becomes poetically immortal. '*I thought*', he writes, '*if only YOU had been here!*' Given the letter's power, Jane finds it impossible that she could be too late. 'Here was the hour, still to be lived!' His letters have been no more than delayed on their way to her. 'But here I am. Oh, here I *am*!' she protests.

Like Charles, Guy haunts the house he once inhabited. Brought back to life by his letters, he appears with a hallucinatory clearness before the women who love him. Jane, at a dinner party at a nearby castle, draws a 'profound breath' and asks a fellow guest if he knew her cousin Guy. Once the name leaves her lips and enters the room, Guy appears among them; the recoil of the others marks his triumphant displacement of their air. The men at the dinner party help to compose Guy, but remain 'tributary to him and less real to Jane – that is, as embodiments' than he is. She sits listening for his voice, hoping never in all her life again to be so aware of him, or indeed of anyone as 'the annihilation-point of sensation' comes into view. Back at home Antonia, overwrought, lectures Jane on the question of 'what memory costs', overcome by 'the annihilating need left behind by Guy'. Looking outside, she sees her youth and Guy's from every direction. He is more present than a ghost: 'time again was into the clutch of herself and Guy'. 'The intensity of a brought-about recollection', the narrator states, speaking from painful experience, 'leaves one worn down; it consumes cells of the being if not the body.' Guy has become immortal through the longings of these women. Lilia, whose life has been marked out by the loss of love, watches herself and Guy come round the corner, both 'deep in love'.

Guy's reappearances prepare the ground for Jane's encounter with an actual lover at the end of the novel. In the final scene she is sent to Shannon Airport to meet the rejected suitor of the hostess at the castle. Their eyes meet and, in the final sentence, 'They no sooner looked but they loved.' As far as Antonia is concerned, Guy 'came back, through Jane, to be let go'. Jane's progression to an actual love affair enables her to dispel his presence. But Jane is merely an inexperienced girl and there remain two disappointed women still grieving in his wake. Antonia, otherwise suave and self-sufficient and endowed with much of Bowen's professional persona, wonders why she was not loved enough; why Lilia swayed him with her beauty. Lilia, who each day confronts 'the day's disillusionment' and finds that 'disappointment for ever is fresh and young', is gradually deteriorating, gaunt with solitude, alone in a lonely house in a lonely novel.

If in writing *A World of Love* Elizabeth was asking herself in part whether the ecstatic fairy tale of their love was enough to make the loneliness worthwhile, then the book's answer is ambivalent. As Charles said, it was a book that contained their 'shared illusion of life'; it was their book as much as *The Heat of the Day*. But this time their love affair emerged as more sad than triumphant. *The Heat of the Day* had germinated from the shared joy of their wartime experiences. As long as Alan had been alive, Elizabeth had a stable base and family in him, and had sought in Charles an imaginative outlet through which she could explore love, and herself as a lover. This resulted in the fairy-tale world which could be sustaining for Elizabeth as a woman and a writer and which generated *The Heat of the Day*. And if the mood of this novel is the mood of Elizabeth and Charles's wartime love affair, then it also came to dominate the mood of their post-war love, allowing their love to amount to far more than the sum of its parts. Yes, they saw each other only a few times a year, they sometimes bickered, Charles was unfaithful, and they both knew that they had no real future. But in Elizabeth's imagination this was transformed into a great and consuming love affair, too beautiful to sacrifice simply because it made her unhappy. And she could overcome the unhappiness. For the five years of writing *The Heat of the Day*, Elizabeth's longing for Charles had been assuaged by her writing; in a sense he was with her all the time. After the novel was published, she could continue this process through writing letters to Charles and through her reading, inscribing Charles into the Rilke biography or the Flaubert letters.

However, once Alan died, this became harder. Charles is as central to *A World of Love* as to *The Heat of the Day* but he is present primarily as an absent figure. The world of love is an isolating one and the memory of Guy is not enough to protect the women who loved him from pain. Yet if the book is partly an exploration of whether Elizabeth would be happier without Charles, then the answer is that in fact life without Charles is inconceivable. Years after his death, Guy is just as present as if he were alive. For Elizabeth there could be no question of leaving Charles, because by this point her entire imaginative landscape was bound up with him. To give him up would be to give up not only seeing him but also writing to him, which would be to renounce a mode of being in which she was never completely alone because she was always living partly in the terms in which she would describe her experiences to him. To leave him and to begin again with someone else would be to relinquish her own inner world. The life that resulted would be far lonelier than a life in which she was merely physically absent from the man she loved much of the time.

And on Charles's side, every time that he rejoined Elizabeth in Ireland or London, he stepped back into her fairy tale. He could escape it in her absence but not in her presence, and he never stopped seeking her presence. He was aware that he was diminished without her; that she offered not only the vanity-pleasing affirmation of intense love, but a version of himself in which he was finer, larger and more imaginative than he could be without her. 'E has a miraculous and terrifying capacity to bring one to life, to awaken other desires and inspire belief in other possibilities in oneself,' he would observe in his diary in November 1956. He was no longer sexually attracted to her, but he was attracted to himself, reflected in her eyes. And though desire had faded, he found her beautiful, and found the beauty all the more compelling because it was a blend of her physical appearance, her voice, her writing and her house, all converging into her luminous presence which allowed any moment in her company to be alive with possibility.

After reading the new novel, Charles felt himself being gradually lured once more 'into her "World of Love"'. He and Elizabeth sat before the fire and drank whisky, sinking into that 'unreal happiness' they shared. Looking back on the remote joy of his visit a week later, Charles was increasingly convinced that this 'middle-aged paradise' was the only paradise which was now not a false one. Elizabeth, meanwhile, told him that she was still living in the happiness of their perfect week. 'Your sweetness, and our hours, and your dear presence.' Yet for Charles, the crisis continued. In April he wrote in his diary the letter he would write Elizabeth if he still dared to tell her everything; 'if your hatred did not frighten me (that hatred is eating into you, you said it was like a cancer)'. He felt possessed by her, worried that their love had 'twined roots of good and evil' and that they would end by destroying each other. This, he wrote in August, was a 'sad, disturbing, fearful love which I half hate and without which I am not alive'. Yet every day they spent together remained precious; 'patches and tatters of complete life together'.

In the months that followed the publication of *A World of Love*, Elizabeth attempted to follow the advice she had given herself in the disappointment essay and to expect less of Charles. In a letter to him in January 1956 she asked how he could ever think that he could disappoint her. 'You must really realise', she commanded him, 'that loving you is like being absorbed in something that though it never changes always moves forward.' In other people's relationships, the first wild flame gave place to something steadier; for her there was always the flame. Yet ten days later, she was so lonely for him that she was 'nearly off my head: it undermines my physical morale'. 'The fact is Charles', she told him in February, 'that saying goodbye to you this last time has made me feel as though my inside had been torn out.' She was walking from room to room by herself, crying out 'Charles, Charles, Charles'.

But her spirits were revived by another of his visits in May, and writing to him afterwards she invoked the continual present they had experienced in wartime to bind him to her once more:

> These last ten days are not the past, they are a sort of eternity. Oh you beloved Charles, you beloved love. Let us neither of us forget, for a single moment, what reality feels like and eternity is.

23

'The world my wilderness, its caves my home'

Rose Macaulay

In July 1949 Rose Macaulay followed Elizabeth Bowen, Graham Greene and Henry Yorke in visiting post-war Ireland. Her trip, unlike theirs, was an act not of hopeful escape but of sorrowful pilgrimage. Accompanied by Marjorie Grant Cook, she was visiting the lost homeland of her dead lover. On 15 July Rose and Marjorie spent a night with Elizabeth Bowen at Bowen's Court. The next day they went to the sea at Glengariff, where Rose was delighted to find 'a lovely little bay, with little islands scattered about it, and woody shores and rocks – lovely for bathing'. They were making their way around the coast towards Loughrea, where she would visit the cathedral where Gerald O'Donovan had begun his career, seeing for herself the stained-glass windows he had commissioned all those years ago.

This journey to Ireland was the first stage in a three-year exploration of the ruins of the world which comprised the research for Rose Macaulay's compendious *The Pleasure of Ruins* (1953). Since Gerald's death, Rose had taken on the desolate persona she had ascribed to herself in 'Miss Anstruther's Letters'. Bereft of both her home and her lover, she was now 'a ghost, without attachments or habitation'. Accepting her own ghostliness, she began to haunt ruins. At first, she scrambled around the ruins of her own flat and of the City of London. The younger novelist Penelope Fitzgerald later recollected alarming experiences of clambering after Rose when she joined her on these expeditions, keeping Rose's lean figure just in view as she 'shinned down a crater, or leaned, waving, through the smashed glass of some perilous window'. At this stage Rose was seeking a physical manifestation for her own spiritual state, but there was already an element of intellectual quest in her explorations. In an article in *Time and Tide* in October 1940 she described wartime Londoners as 'cave-fanciers and ruin-gogglers', morbidly fascinated by ruins. '"There's a good one in my street," we say, proud of our own monuments. "Makes you think, doesn't it," we say. But just what it makes us think, I am not sure.' As a ruin-goggler, Rose Macaulay was attempting to answer this question, and was becoming fascinated by listing and cataloguing the flowers sprouting in the ruins, pressing, preserving and labelling the cuttings she collected during her expeditions. Then, in her 1947 trip to Spain and Portugal, she began to find in ruins a consolation for grief; a

Flowers growing in a bombsite in the City of London, *c.* 1943

reminder that everything eventually passed. The ruins also offered an aesthetic pleasure which gradually enabled Macaulay to move beyond the anguish that made her wish, in 1941, that she could have been bombed herself. 'A seed can lodge and sprout in any crack or fissure,' Henry Yorke had told Rosamond Lehmann during the war. It took Macaulay longer to believe this, but when she did her consolation was more lasting than Yorke's.

Macaulay made her visit to Ireland straight after she had submitted the manuscript for her first post-war novel, *The World My Wilderness* (1950). This is a book built on the ruins of love and set in the ruins of post-war London. It 'is about the ruins of the City', Macaulay wrote to Hamilton Johnson, the priest who became a friend at this time, 'and the general wreckage of the world that they seem to stand for. And about a rather lost and strayed and derelict girl who made them her spiritual home.' Although she ascribed it to Anon, Macaulay wrote the epigraph to the novel herself:

> The world my wilderness, its caves my home,
> Its weedy wastes the garden where I roam,
> Its chasm'd cliffs my castle and my tomb . . .

In 1949 she was still seeking a tomb in which to bury herself and she hoped to find it in the London wilderness, roaming its weedy wastes and chasm'd cliffs.

Typically, Macaulay splits herself between two heroines in this novel, an older and a younger woman, Helen and Barbary. Barbary is the lost and derelict girl, while Helen is her forty-four-year-old mother, an English woman living in post-war France. Here she mourns the death of her second husband, Maurice, who was drowned by the local Resistance for collaborating with the Germans.

Like Macaulay's, Helen's grief is private and unseen. Richie, her elder son, informed of the death in a brief and dry letter, does not know 'if she greatly grieved or not'. In fact, Helen aches with unspoken want. When her small son, Roland, cries out for Barbary after her departure to England, Helen echoes his childish phrases in her mind – 'Want

Maurice. Maurice is coming never' – before turning from the sea that had swallowed him up. Hungering for Maurice, her senses engulfed in an aching void, Helen attempts to fill the void and to stupefy the ache with artistic endeavours, reading, translating, painting and gambling. But the darkness merely deepens about her, 'as if she were in a cave alone'.

The image of the empty cave reflects Macaulay's own post-war mental state. In the novel, as in actuality, the cavernousness in her mind finds a physical reality in wartime London, where Barbary is sent to stay with her father after the war. The ostensible reason for Barbary's departure is that she has become uncivilised. Like so many Macaulay heroines, Barbary wanders scruffily around, failing to turn into a young lady. Her life on the outskirts of the Resistance during the war has trained her to steal, lie and catapult the police – habits which must be unlearned in London. But in fact Helen sends her daughter away partly because she believes that she has some responsibility for the drowning of Maurice. Helen finds Barbary's presence difficult to bear, and has transferred the full force of her maternal love to Roland, who is Maurice's child.

For Barbary, missing her home in France, London is an unfriendly and strange habitat. She can only feel at home in the ruins of the City, finding a retreat in the caves and the wilderness. She enacts the epigraph of the novel, roaming through the 'weedy wastes' of London. These wanderings are sometimes made alone, but more often Barbary is accompanied by Raoul, Maurice's son from his first marriage, who has also been sent off to stay with relatives in the hope of acquiring some civilised English manners. The two flit alongside ghosts 'about dust-heaped, gaping rooms'. The 'gaping shells, the tall towers, the broken windows into which greenery sprawled, the haunted, brittle beauty' evoke the landscape of the French maquis, offering Barbary in particular a 'spiritual home'. She and Raoul play at home-making, domesticating the caves by accumulating broken possessions. Trapped at a dinner party in her father's house, she escapes into the darkness of the Embankment, and wonders what 'the ruined waste lands looked like after dark'. She knows that it would be a strange and frightening landscape, but believes that it would still have the familiarity of 'a place

long known', with the 'clear dark logic of a dream'. Unlike the unshat-
tered streets and squares, the ruins make 'a lunatic sense': 'it was the
country that one's soul recognised and knew'.

Rose Macaulay, consumed by secret, silent grief for Gerald
O'Donovan, sought out landscapes that reflected her internal state of
mind. Restless and anguished, she, like Barbary, recognised the shattered landscape of the London ruins as her spiritual home. In *The
Towers of Trebizond*, she would find a peace in ruins, consoled by their
beauty and longevity. By 1956, Rose's own renewed religious sense
enabled her to find in the ruins an intimation of the eternal which
mitigated the force of intense individual suffering. This consolation is
not yet present in the ruins of *The World My Wilderness*, which act as a
more temporary refuge. Here, the haunted, brittle beauty of the desolate streets is juxtaposed onto the charged landscape of Blitz infernos.
The flames that ignited Rose's flat and brought on her wrenching
knowledge that her lover was about to die become in this novel the
tormenting flames of hell.

Roaming the ghostly London ruins, Barbary is unable to escape the
past. Macaulay herself would observe in *The Pleasure of Ruins* that the
recent ruins wrought by the Second World War were less consoling
than older ruins, caused by forgotten battles or merely by neglect. 'New
ruins are for a time stark and bare, vegetationless and creatureless;
blackened and torn, they smell of fire and mortality.' Barbary's helpless
anger and guilt find a physical reality in the fires of the Blitz, transformed into the landscape of a Catholic vision of hell. She has had very
little exposure to Catholicism. A nominally Anglican childhood was
followed by a period of cheerful paganism while living with Helen in
France. 'I can't think,' Helen says, 'if people want Gods, why not the
Greek ones; they were so useful in emergencies, and such enterprising
and entertaining companions.' But Barbary is increasingly preoccupied
with a Catholic idea of sin. Overweighed with unexpressed guilt about
the murder of her stepfather, she regrets that heathens like herself
cannot be forgiven because 'we sin only against people, and the people
stay hurt or killed', where if she were a Catholic she could repent and
be granted absolution.

However, Catholicism brings with it the possibility of damnation and Barbary frightens Raoul with her obsession with hell. Together, they visit a ruined church where they find fragments of hymn books, torn and charred, which Barbary uses to read the Dies Irae. ' "Day of wrath," she read aloud, "O day of mourning! See fulfilled the prophet's warning, Heaven and earth in ashes burning!" ' She urges Raoul to repent. 'You must repent, so that you don't go to hell.' She then goes on to preach in French about hellfire, making such vehement gestures that she falls and bruises her knee. Later, they come back to the church, armed with a portable radio, a Judgment Day painting and a black cat, to stage a full Sunday morning service. The radio plays jazz, Barbary sings self-abasing hymns from her torn hymn book, and Raoul holds the mewing, struggling kitten before the altar as a symbolic sacrificial offering. Both are unsurprised when a priest enters, instructing them to stop the noise, put down the kitten and swing the censer, because he is going to say mass.

Obediently, Barbary and Raoul genuflect while the priest says the creed and then goes on to preach about hell. 'We are in hell now,' he says, with matter-of-factness comparable to Barbary's own; 'Fire creeps on me from all sides; I am trapped in the prison of my sins; I cannot get out, there is no rescue possible . . . I cannot move my limbs . . . the flames press on; they will consume my body, but my soul will live on in hell . . . Trapped, trapped, trapped; there's no hope.' Eventually his voice breaks, strangled in his throat, and he shudders to his knees, 'his face in his scarred hands'. Barbary, crying, experiences a moment of clarity: 'It was true, then, about hell; there was no deliverance.' This Blitz-inspired vision of imprisonment in hell has confirmed her own.

In *The Pleasure of Ruins* Macaulay goes on to reassure the reader that the Second World War ruins will not continue to smell of fire and mortality for long. 'Very soon trees will be thrusting through the empty window sockets, the rose-bay and fennel blossoming within the broken walls, the brambles tangling outside them.' These are the flowers that Macaulay had catalogued during her wartime scrambles through the City of London. *The World My Wilderness* is set in this moment of transition and the task, for Barbary as for Macaulay herself, is to escape the flames of hellfire and dwell among trees. Macaulay makes this explicit by associating the ruined landscapes with the wasteland of Eliot's 1922 poem, which she quotes throughout the novel. Her own epigraph is followed by an extract from *The Waste Land*, describing bats which 'Whistled, and beat their wings', 'voices singing out of empty cisterns and exhausted wells' and the 'empty chapel, only the wind's home', with no windows and a door that swings. Early on, post-war London's 'broken habitations' are explicitly connected to 'stony rubbish', and later the narrator describes the maze of little streets; the 'scarred and haunted green and stone and brambled wilderness' which, lying 'about the margins of the wrecked world', receives 'the returned traveller into its dwellings with a wrecked, indifferent calm'.

> Here, its cliffs and chasms and caves seemed to say, is your home; here you belong; you cannot get away, you do not wish to get away, for this is the maquis that lies about the margins of the wrecked world, and here your feet are set; here you find the irremediable barbarism that comes up from the depth of the earth, and that you have known elsewhere. 'Where are the roots that clutch, what branches grow, out of this stony rubbish? Son of man, you cannot say, or guess . . .' But you can say, you can guess, that it is you yourself, your own roots, that clutch the stony rubbish, the branches of your own being that grow from it and from nowhere else.

Eliot's prophetic poem has taken on an eerie truth in post-war London. Here is the barbarism of war; here is the wrecked world. Eliot is asking if a redemption is possible within the spiritual wasteland of 1922 Europe. He assembles a plethora of texts and brings together opposed religious doctrines in the hope of shoring fragments against ruins and finding roots that clutch. Both Macaulay and Barbary seem to be searching for a similar consolation as they explore the physical ruins. Barbary, finding in them confirmation of hell, fails to locate any secure roots. Detained by the police for stealing, she becomes dangerously ill, and starts to dream about the ruins. In her dreams, she runs down rocky corridors, leaping chasms, squirming into dark caves where she finds the Gestapo waiting for her. She lies among rocks and brambles and is 'seized, bound, beaten, her arms twisted back, matches lit between her toes'. Always, there is 'fear and blackness and red pain'. Consumed by excessive guilt, she can no longer find a spiritual home in the ruins. As a result, she is grateful to be packed off back to France, leaving the London wilderness behind. If anyone can comfort Barbary, it is Helen, who offers an earthly version of forgiveness: 'It mattered between us once; but I don't mean it to matter any more. I don't think you or Raoul deliberately let Maurice be murdered.'

But Macaulay herself, in the guise of the narrator, offers a more redemptive vision of the stony rubbish. As a self-proclaimed 'Anglo-agnostic', Macaulay had little patience with the Catholic vision of hellfire, and was better placed than Barbary to escape the flames of the Blitz and find the roots that clutch. In November 1949 Macaulay published an article called 'In the Ruins', entirely comprising descriptions from the as yet unpublished *The World My Wilderness*. With Barbary and Raoul removed from the scene, it becomes evident how much of the novel is based on Macaulay's own clamberings and musings. Most of the description in the article comes straight out of the novel, but Macaulay changes the pronouns so that she is guiding her readers on a journey. 'Make your way', she commands, where in the novel they 'made their way'; the cunning of merchants now bumbles 'about us'. The 'stony rubbish' passage remains unaltered. At this point in the novel, Macaulay addresses an abstract 'you', who hovers between the generic son of man and the reader. Gazing abstractly at the ruins, independently of her characters, Macaulay suggests that the post-war ruin climber can, at best, retrieve her own roots in the rubbish. If sufficiently identified with the ruins, 'the branches of your own being' can begin to grow.

In a post-war article on 'The First Impact of *The Waste Land*', Macaulay described the 'sharp sense of recognition' with which she had greeted Eliot's poem.

Here was the landscape one knew, had always known, sometimes without knowing it; here were the ruins in the soul, the shadowy dreams that lurked tenebriously in the cellars of consciousness, in the mysterious corridors and arcades of dream, the wilderness that stretches not without but within.

The landscape of Eliot's poem was metaphorical; as yet in 1922 the stony waste and the empty chapel had no actual presence in London. Brought to ruin-consciousness by the poem, Macaulay greeted with even sharper recognition the actuality of Eliot's landscape as it started to emerge. The question was how best to find the roots that clutch; how to allow the branches of your own being to take hold.

———

The London of *The World My Wilderness* is caught between the forces of civilisation and the primeval power of enjungling nature. Throughout, Helen's elder son Richie attempts to impose a new order of civilisation after the barbarity of war. 'Slim, elegant and twenty-three', he has returned from soldiering longing for the civility of pre-war life. He disapproves of his mother's sexual freedom and of his sister's uncouth ways; he is unable to tolerate the bomb sites that Barbary and her creator find so compellingly beautiful. The book ends with Richie wandering through the ruins of the city, surveying 'the horrid waste'. He is sickened by 'the squalor of ruin', aware 'of an irremediable barbarism coming up out of the earth', and approves of the excavators who are attempting to reinstate order. But Richie and the excavators are not allowed the final word. Men's will to recover strives against the drifting wilderness, 'but the wilderness might slip from their hands, from their spades and trowels and measuring rods, slip darkly away from them, seeking the primeval chaos' as the jungle presses in on the city.

For Macaulay, civilisation is a questionable good. She mocks Richie for preferring mulled claret, drunk in decorative rooms lit by tall candles, to fireweed and pink rose-bay; she mocks Barbary's father Sir Gulliver for thinking that he can banish his daughter's anguish by forcing her to dress properly. Personal grief and the post-war shock at destruction and barbarity are not going to be redeemed by the 'glitter of good talk and good glass'. If redemption is possible it comes in an appreciative contemplation of the aesthetic and spiritual beauty of the ruins; in an understanding that the jungle precedes and succeeds man-made edifices.

The World My Wilderness holds up the ruins as a potential source of consolation, but does not explain how such consolation will be achieved, or how the ruins of a bombed city can be pleasurable. These are the questions asked in *The Pleasure of Ruins*, which Macaulay began to research in Ireland in July 1949 and which she was planning before finishing *The World My Wilderness*. 'I am within sight of the end of a novel,' she wrote to David Ley in April 1949;

> after that I shall tackle a short book I have been asked to write for Contact, on 'The Pleasures of looking at Ruins'. This will be a pretext for describing ruins all over Britain and Europe and elsewhere, and describing also the acute pleasure they gave our ancestors – the Romantics, the Victorians, and others.

'Others' here might include Macaulay's own generation, those ruin-gogglers of the Second World War, and not least Macaulay herself, who was peculiarly alive to that acute pleasure to be found in the lost splendours of past and present civilisation.

Macaulay's mission, while writing *The Pleasure of Ruins*, was to find consolation through aesthetic pleasure. By leaving London to survey the ruins of the world she could escape personal anguish and dwell in the more impersonal beauty of ruins that no longer smelt of fire and mortality. Nonetheless she began her labours with the personal, making the pilgrimage to Ireland. Tellingly, Loughrea itself does not make it into the final book, but there are several pages devoted to Ireland, including a poignant passage on the 'dispossession of the ancient Catholic glory of Ireland', which lends a grief to the Irish clerical and monastic ruins. The Irish church itself is 'demeaned and deflowered by the bitter centuries of persecution which, though they could not crush it out of existence, plucked from it the proud flower of its intellect and breeding, reducing it to a devout provincialism'. Broken abbeys and churches lie strewn along coast and river, hill and plain throughout Ireland. They have been destroyed 'by Danes, by Normans, by Englishmen, by decay, by time, by poverty, vandalism and dissolution'. Now, 'their crumbling arches and portals and fragments of wall stand in reproachful witness to the passing of a murdered culture'. Here Macaulay takes on O'Donovan's reproachful dissatisfaction both with the Irish, who have failed to emerge out of poverty, and with the English, who have rid the country of its ancient glory. Together, the English and the Irish have murdered an ancient culture and broken O'Donovan's own youthful dreams. Mourning her lover, Macaulay stands, like the fragments of wall, in reproachful witness to the country where his ambitions died. These ruins are too melancholy to be pleasurable.

These are the same melancholy ruins that characterise the landscape of *Bowen's Court*, where Bowen describes Ireland as 'a country of ruins'. Lordly or humble, military or domestic, ruins pervade the Cork landscape of Bowen's book. 'Some ruins show gashes of violence, others simply the dull slant of decline.' The religious ruins are repaired or rendered picturesque but the lay ruins are left in a state of unchecked decay, used as shelters for cattle. 'By the roadsides, roofs of abandoned cabins sag in slowly; desolate farms rear chimneys out of brambles, at the end of silted-up boreens.' Ruins stand for error or failure, 'but in Ireland we take these as part of life'.

Having visited the ruins of Ireland, Rose Macaulay moved on to Wales and then Italy. Over the next three years, she engaged in a panoramic exploration of ruins throughout the world and throughout history. The book was originally commissioned as a short survey of 40,000 words, but quickly grew to more than three times that length. Macaulay's non-fiction always had a tendency to proliferate uncontrollably. But there is a particular obsessiveness to this book which testifies to the urgency of its author's quest to find aesthetic and spiritual meaning amid desolation and destruction.

Perhaps the most urgent task for the post-war ruin-goggler was to explore the relationship between war and pleasure in ruins. Macaulay starts the book by supposing that the earliest such pleasure was 'inextricably mixed with triumph over enemies' and with the violent excitements of war. But, she goes on (and this surely is the book's crucial manifesto and self-justification), 'to say that man found pleasure in celebrating such disasters by word and picture is not quite the same as to say that he found emotional joy in the contemplation of the ruinous results'. 'Or', she asks, 'is it?' It is crucial to distinguish aesthetic from vindictive pleasure, and even in the earliest accounts of battles a 'profound, passionate, poetic pleasure in ruin as such' is distinguishable from the separate triumph of victory.

The book is Macaulay's attempt to locate this aesthetic pleasure and, implicitly, to see if it can be applied to the ruins of post-war Europe. She sees ruin-sensibility as essentially blending pleasure and romantic gloom. Pity and self-pity can be enjoyable; 'the darkly ruinous mind of torn Europe' has always loved the desolation it bewailed. Humans are, she states, intrinsically 'ruin-minded'. Ruins lead to a civilisation of mortality and to our part in a long history. This does not sound particularly pleasant. Macaulay describes ruin as part of 'the general Weltschmerz, Sehnsucht, malaise, nostalgia, Angst, frustration, sickness, passion of the human soul'. But the romantic melancholy enables a contemplation of transience, reminding us that our current sorrow will pass. Whatever horrors may befall our current civilisation, that civilisation is itself only a temporary façade; a brief interim between one enjungled state and another.

The Pleasure of Ruins ends in the ruins of post-war London, which Macaulay insists will be 'enjungled, engulfed' and rendered picturesque in their turn. Month by month it will become harder to trace the original streets within the bombed areas, and small yellow dandelions will make their pattern over broken altars. Already, there is a bizarre new charm in the stairway that climbs to the roofless summit where it meets the sky, though the larger ruins are more tragic – the bombed cities and churches and cathedrals of Europe offer 'nothing but resentful sadness'. Macaulay finds that her own contemporaries, bewildered by the Second World War, can currently confront their ruins only through art. John Piper's depictions of the smouldering bomb sites have succeeded the romantic Roman ruins of Piranesi's engravings and the picturesque remnants of a lost age in Poussin's paintings as the 'ruin-poems' of the day. People hanker for wholeness amid the ruins. But, as in *The World My Wilderness*, the longing for wholeness is not granted the final word. 'Such wholesome hankerings are, it seems likely, merely a phase of our fearful and fragmented age.' *Ruinenlust* will return; anger at destruction will fade; and in the meantime one way to confront the sadness of twentieth-century destruction is to contemplate the ruins of the past. Macaulay does not quite dare to offer the consolation of ruin pleasure to her generation. Their ruins are too raw. But by explaining and insisting on the pleasurable nature of ruins in general, she clears the way to allowing aesthetic pleasure to enjungle and engulf the ruins of the Second World War.

———

Between the publication of *The World My Wilderness* and *The Pleasure of Ruins*, Rose Macaulay returned from 'Anglo-Agnosticism' to Anglicanism. She was aided in her renewed faith by her extensive correspondence with Hamilton Johnson. Rose had first met 'Father Johnson' at a retreat shortly before the First World War. He later recalled that the two discussed 'how a young lady living with her family might most suitably conduct herself'. In August 1950, now living in America, he came across a copy of her 1932 novel *They Were Defeated* and wrote to renew their acquaintance. This voice from her Christian past came at a time of great need. 'If you were in England,' she wrote in response to his letter, 'I should probably ask if I might come and talk to you sometimes, and I wish you were.' She regretted how long it had been since she had been on a retreat 'or anything at all of that nature'; 'I have sadly lost touch with that side of life, and regret it. We do need it so badly, in this queer world and life, all going to pieces and losing.' He responded helpfully, and a month later she wrote again, describing her struggle with *The Pleasure of Ruins* and regretting that

> The people I love most have died. I wish they had not. But there is nothing to be done about it . . . This seems one of the many reasons for wanting, so to speak, a link with another sphere of life.

Johnson continued to encourage her to return to the faith, but she initially found it too difficult.

Partly my difficulties are intellectual – I just can't make the grade – partly, I sometimes think, the blindness that comes from the selfish and deplorable life I've led. Who knows? It's all a kind of vicious circle – badness keeps one from the realisation of God; perhaps nothing but that could cure badness – well, so there one is.

However, by January 1951 she had gone to confession, and by February she was enthusiastically attending Grosvenor Chapel, a high Anglican church in Mayfair, and asking Johnson for advice on how much prayer, what churchgoing, and at what hours he would advise. Two years later, she looked back on this as a time when she 'didn't feel jolly': 'I was in a state of darkness and tension and struggle.' She thanked him for providing her with the remedy for her misery, with the result that she was now happy and did not quite believe her good fortune.

The various phases of Rose Macaulay's lifelong comings and goings from Christianity are recorded through the character of Laurie in *The Towers of Trebizond*, a novel written once Macaulay was ensconced in the relative comfort of the church. A religious child, Laurie was an agnostic through school and university and then at twenty-three 'took up with the Church again'. 'But', she says, without apparent regret, 'the Church met its Waterloo a few years later when I took up with adultery . . . and this lasted on and on.' This is a religious novel, written by Macaulay after she had converted back to Christianity and had begun to look on aspects of her life with regret. She is clear that adultery is 'a meanness and a stealing, a taking away from someone what should be theirs, a great selfishness'. But, even now, she does not deny Gerald O'Donovan's arguments; she still sees love as on the side of life, maintaining that 'out of this meanness and this selfishness and this lying flow love and joy and peace, beyond anything that can be imagined'. After Vere has died as a result of the accident in which Laurie believes she has killed him, Laurie reads a carved inscription about salvation from sins. She hesitates to say the prayer because she does 'not really want to be saved from my sins, not for the time being, it would make things too difficult and too sad'.

What Laurie does find is not the consolation of Christianity but the pleasure of ruins. Her journey to the ruined city of Trebizond in Turkey is at the heart of the novel, and it is apparent that she both expects and finds an epiphany. For Laurie, Trebizond is 'the country one's soul recognised and knew' that Barbary found in the London ruins. This is a country that combines beauty with exile. In 1954 Rose Macaulay reported to Hamilton Johnson that she had just returned from Trebizond, the 'last little Byzantine empire', not conquered by the Turks until 1461, eight years after the fall of Constantinople. By the time of Rose's visit, it was completely Turkish, but there was a Byzantine ruined palace and castle on a high crag above the town, and she climbed up there and felt 'forlorn Byzantine ghosts pattering about it'.

Laurie encounters these ghosts as echoes of her own unlived lives. Before arriving at Trebizond, she has conflated the city with her own soul. Trebizond is a corner of a lost empire, slipping into forgetfulness of its own Byzantine origins just as Laurie is forgetting her Christian past. When she first sees the ruined town lying in its splendid bay, it is like seeing 'an old dream change itself, as dreams do', because this seems more a picturesque Turkish port than a Byzantine ruin. The 'brooding ghost' of the fallen Byzantine empire has been banished and it is this ghost that she must find. Returning later, she learns the meaning of Trebizond, and the revelation comes with the first intimations of a return to God. Shattered by Vere's death, she has pondered going back to the church, but is debarred from it less by guilt than by a horror of being divided still further from Vere. Now she makes steps towards accepting the God in whom she seems already to believe: 'Having to do without God, without love, in utter loneliness and fear, knowing that God is leaving us alone for ever; we have driven ourselves out, we have lost God and gained hell.' She is aware that she lives now in two hells, for she has lost God and also love. Laurie resembles Bendrix in Greene's *The End of the Affair*, for whom hatred of God is a first step in belief. She may shut God out, but she has never stopped believing in him; never lapsed into the agnosticism she fears.

But the novel does not end with the consolation of religion; instead, it ends with Trebizond. Thinking about her future without Vere, Laurie anticipates a life that will offer diversions, given that the world is full of beauty and excitement and romance, but will remain hollow and thin like a ghost. Eventually, she will plunge into death, a prospect which drowns her in mortal fear and mortal grief. She is reluctant to relinquish life itself, which for all its agonies of loss and guilt, 'is exciting and beautiful, amusing and artful and endearing, full of liking and love .. and whatever (if anything) is to come after it, we shall not have this life again'. At this point, she has a vision of Trebizond, the fabled city where the towers still shimmer on a far horizon, held in a luminous enchantment. For Laurie, however much she must stand outside the walls, 'this must for ever be'; the vision will remain. This, if anything, is the meaning of Trebizond. The towers will continue to shimmer; the luminous enchantment will remain present. These haunted ruins offer a promise of eternity less desolate than the primeval enjungled ruins in London. But, 'at the city's heart lie the pattern and the hard core', and these Laurie can never make her own: 'they are too far outside my range. The pattern should perhaps be easier, the core less hard.' Here is 'the eternal dilemma'. This is an ambiguous ending, but it seems that this city that has forgotten its own past retains the knowledge of Byzantium in its core. Laurie must struggle to unravel the pattern and break through the core to grasp Byzantium, which for her will involve an acceptance of God.

Where the ruins of London provided a physical equivalent for the pain of grief, the ruins of Trebizond offer a way to move beyond grief to a state where even sadness is endowed with a shimmering beauty. This beauty is crucial to *The Towers of Trebizond*, which is a religious novel that never negates the sensual beauty or the love at its heart. Writing to thank Rosamond Lehmann for a letter commending the novel, Rose Macaulay described it as 'a book I have had in mind to write for a long time, the heart of the matter being my own story'. 'Looking back,' she wrote, 'now I am getting old, I can't not be glad of the past, in spite of knowing I behaved dishonestly and selfishly for so long. Love is so odd. It can't help being everything at the time.'

Coda

In March 1955 Rose Macaulay accurately predicted her own death. 'I have an intuition that I shall die in 3 years,' she wrote to her sister Jean; 'ie in 1958, so must bustle about and do a lot of things in the time. When do you expect to push off? My own death is very credible to me now, though it usen't to be.'

When she wrote this letter, Rose was finishing *The Towers of Trebizond*, the book that she had intended to write for a long time, and she meant it to be her final word. The novel was partly a testament to Hamilton Johnson: a proof of his influence over her, and of her commitment to her new vision of Christianity. Writing to him afterwards she assured him that she was confident that Laurie would encounter some influence to bring her churchwards: 'she would not for very long be outside it'. But at the same time it was her final tribute to Gerald O'Donovan. 'I can't not be glad of the past,' she wrote to Rosamond Lehmann. Laurie may end the novel on the verge of Christianity but, as yet, Laurie, like her creator, accepts love as everything. And the book is dominated by the presence of Vere, with his 'wit and brains and prestige', his 'brilliance and delightfulness', and by that togetherness in which peace flows about them like music. Even after she had written Hamilton Johnson letters regretting 'the long years of low life' she had lived, Rose could recover both the joy of love and the desolation of a

death which had cut her off from life, leaving her 'scattered adrift, lacking the coherence and integration of love'.

Rose Macaulay may have regretted her own lowness, but she did not
regret the joy, the sensuousness or the good-humoured enjoyment of
life, and these were still evident in this novel. Laurie and Aunt Dot
both bathe as enthusiastically as any Macaulay heroine; they inhabit a
world in which camels love alongside humans, grumbling and stamp-
ing at love's pains. And Rose herself continued to laugh and to bathe
until her death in 1958. Indeed, she came to see swimming as a partly
religious experience, diving into the Serpentine every Sunday on her
way home from church. 'A kind of shining peace prevails in both
places,' she informed Hamilton Johnson, happy to fuse her Christianity with good-natured pagan ritual.

In 1955, Rose organised a lunch party at the Lansdowne Club to
celebrate the marriage of her publisher, Mark Bonham-Carter, instructing all the guests to bring their swimming costumes. Only
Bonham-Carter, Rosamond Lehmann and Rose herself actually swam,
and Rosamond later described the manner in which Rose emerged, 'her
ice-blue eyes obliterated beneath a bathing helmet some sizes too large
for her', armed with an inflated rubber mattress which she cast upon
the waters 'with business-like dispatch':

> Another moment, and her brisk commentary is rattling down as it were
> from ceiling-level: she has scampered up, up, out, to the outermost
> verge of the high-diving board. There I still see her figure indomitably
> poised: androgynous tall figure, flat as a shape cut out in white paper
> and blacked in to knees and shoulders; gaunt, comical, adorable – hero-
> ically topped with an antique martial casque. She is off, she has jumped
> feet first, clutching her nose; has cleft the chlorinated blue and sunk
> sheer as a pair of scissors to the very bottom of the white-tiled basin. She
> takes a long time to come up; indeed (having by now immersed myself
> with caution) I become slightly alarmed and haul her upwards by the
> shoulders. She thanks me cheerfully, and paddles round and round,
> sketching an old-fashioned side-stroke. Mark swims noiseless, watchful,

amused, at a discreet distance. I had assumed Rose to be, like myself, an expert swimmer: it is not so. This fanatical amphibian is not at home in water. She explains this to me as if it had never been a bar to full enjoyment. 'I'm the wrong shape, you see – too long, too thin. I never could remain at the correct angle for self-propulsion. Do swing my legs up.' I do so. Down they fall again. Her laughter is so infectious that I laugh too; but I think: She simply isn't *safe*; surely she could just go down and not surface again. How is it that a creature apparently so ill-suited to this element should sport in it so fearlessly? Also, her lips are blue. She clambers on to the mattress, stretches her peeled-wand limbs full length, and allows me to pull her from end to end of the bath. Almost dreamily – for her prim, somehow practical, academic accents had too much wit and crackle ever to sound dreamy – she ejaculates: 'Oh, Rosamond dear, this is extraordinarily pleasant! I feel like Cleopatra in her barge.'

In March 1958, the time Rose had appointed for her death, she was still living at full speed, although she was worried that one day her writing brain would become muddled, leaving her 'unable to put words together properly, and writing awful sentences, and general low-grade nonsense'. In August, she was in Venice, fantasising about converting the native Catholics to Anglicanism. 'What on earth are you doing here?' she asked Anthony Powell, whom she bumped into walking along a canal. 'I might well ask you the same question,' he replied. 'Oh, me?' Rose said insouciantly. 'I'm just on my way to the Black Sea.'

That October, she was dead. On the morning of 30 October she telephoned the doctor to say that she was feeling ill. A few minutes after opening the door to him she suffered a fatal heart attack. 'But we have all just seen her,' Rosamond Lehmann wrote in disbelief; 'just been talking to her!' Rose Macaulay, who had wished in 1941 that she could have been bombed herself, died as a cheerful eccentric. She had lost everything in the war: all her possessions, the only man she ever loved and, with him, the passionate, sensual woman who had surfaced, in private, from beneath the veneer of the androgynous girl or the redoubtable old lady. After the war, the moment for joy had passed. But by clambering around the ruins of the world she had exorcised her

Rose Macaulay on her way to the Black Sea, 1958, photographed by Victor Glasstone

own ghostliness, overcoming desolation through the quiet appreciation of beauty. And it was a vision of beauty that until the end was suffused with ardent human love.

After her death, Rose Macaulay was remembered affectionately by her friends. In a 1959 interview Elizabeth Bowen emphasised Rose's role in contributing to her early success: 'I had immense hope and encouragement from one writer, forever dear to me as a person, and that was Rose Macaulay.' Elizabeth Bowen gave this interview at a time when she herself was beginning to come to terms with solitary middle age and when her life was starting to resemble aspects of Rose's own. She, like Rose, was learning to take pleasure in the everyday and to move beyond her sadness at Alan's death and her anguish at her continued separation from Charles. In 1958 she told William Plomer that she had enjoyed her fifties; it was the first epoch where she had liked being 'grown up' as much as she had expected to as a child. She was successful and she was in demand, though she could never earn quite enough to keep up Bowen's Court, which had consistently drained away the mental and financial resources of the Bowens for the last two hundred years.

Elizabeth Bowen's essays anatomising disappointment were written during a period in which Elizabeth was adjusting her expectations of Charles. After Alan's death, she hoped periodically that Charles would come to replace her husband in her life. The arguments she started in Bonn were pleas for Charles to recognise the significance of the relationship in his own mind. By 1957, Charles felt that he and Elizabeth had become calm. The scenes between them in Germany were not likely to begin again. That first year in Germany 'was the last in which the panics of youth played a part'. Now, their relationship had settled and he believed that they loved each other equally, though it showed in different ways.

Nonetheless, Elizabeth remained bitter towards Sylvia and she continued to hope that Charles could play a more consistent role in her life. Since Alan's death, Elizabeth had seen Bowen's Court as the symbolic centre of her world; as both her home and her family. 'We *are* a family,' she wrote in a 1958 essay about her house, describing the writers congregating in the library at the end of the day. 'In here, conversation sweeps, swoops, takes an unforeseeable course – by now the ribbed velvet arms of the chairs are rubbed to a gloss by the hands of excited talkers.' Elizabeth hoped, always, that Charles saw its centrality too and that it could be both home and family for the two of them. 'Welcome home,' she said to Charles when he arrived at Bowen's Court in May 1956. 'E and I came home here for dinner and it was coming home,' he observed in his diary the next day. 'This is your house, ours, and it's simply a matter of time till you're back again,' she wrote to him after his departure. In an essay on 'The Idea of the Home' she maintained that the 'dependence on home is one of the few dependences which are not a weaning: on the contrary, this is an origin of strength'. As humans, we are completed 'by what the home gives us – location. Identity would be nothing without its frame'. She was committed to the idea of the home and insisted that Charles should be too.

Part of what Elizabeth needed from Charles was a financial commitment to keeping up Bowen's Court. Despite regular stints of lecturing in America and a flurry of reviews and articles for high-paying magazines, Elizabeth was frequently in debt. In June she told him that she was going to have to sell, and that she was not sure 'it really would break my heart if I did'. Now that he was back in Canada, she had less need of the house. 'Its virtue to me these last years (while you've been in Europe) has consisted in its being our home.'

'The trouble is', Charles wrote in his diary after receiving her letter, 'that it IS my home, but that I get the pleasure of it at her expense in money and worry.' He considered offering her $1,000 a year but was worried that she wanted 'to get out of it – out of her life there'. Without Charles's visits, Elizabeth was growing bored in Ireland. 'I suppose it's the effect of hardening my heart,' she wrote; 'when one can no longer afford to support an illusion, one rather welcomes seeing it break down.' The illusion she could no longer afford was a belief in the future of their love; she was hardening herself against disappointment.

Elizabeth Bowen at Bowen's Court, 1962, photographed by Slim Aarons

In 1959 Elizabeth sold Bowen's Court. A few months later, the new owner demolished the house. It was, she wrote in the 1963 afterword to *Bowen's Court*, 'a clean end'. Better that than one more Irish ruin and, through her book, the spirit of the house remained very much alive. The great and calming authority of the light and quiet around Bowen's Court had endured beyond the war, when it had served as an illusion of 'peace at its most ecstatic'. Now, it had also survived the physical demise of the house itself. 'It remains with me now that the house has gone.'

But this was the house that she had branded after Alan's death as her next of kin. Though she would have other homes, she would never regain a family. At the end of her idiosyncratic 1960 travel guide, *A Time in Rome*, Bowen adopts an oddly personal voice as she describes her departure from Rome. Backs of houses waver into mists, stinging her eyes, and she is left feeling displaced and alone. 'My darling, my darling, my darling,' she writes. 'Here we have no abiding city.' In *Bowen's Court*, Bowen recorded how in 1888 her father had put up a white marble memorial to her grandparents in the church next to the house. Below the two names was the quotation from *Hebrews*: 'Here we have no abiding city, but we seek one to come'. In the valediction at the end of *A Time in Rome*, Elizabeth Bowen both mourns the demise of her house and portends the deaths of herself and Charles, united beyond the grave.

While Elizabeth Bowen was facing her own homelessness, Hilde Spiel was coming to terms with the knowledge that she had failed to find a lasting home in London. The 1950s saw the gradual breakdown of Hilde and Peter's marriage and the increasing dependency of Hilde on Hans Flesch-Brunningen. Ostensibly, Flesch remained a family friend. Most weekends, he came to stay on Saturday nights and spent his Sundays visiting parks with Hilde and the children. This was an arrangement fully accepted by Peter, who needed the weekends to make progress with his writing. Indeed, Peter dedicated his book *Der Geist in der Despotie* to Flesch in 1953. But all this time Hilde was starting to rely less on Peter and more on Flesch, coming to value quiet adoration more than the tempestuous passion provided by her husband.

When Hilde was first warned about Peter's violent fits of anger before their marriage, she had felt capable of standing up to him. She was beautiful, talented, desirable; she would rather suffer occasionally for the sake of passion than bind herself to someone who would passively admire her. But as Hilde herself lost strength, she was becoming less equipped to shake off Peter's moods. Guests invited for dinner who disagreed with their host about questions of German literature or British politics would find themselves angrily asked to leave. Hilde's sense of dignity was affronted. She wanted a quieter life in which she could be at the centre of a gentle circle of adoration. Part of Flesch's allure was his chivalrous formality. Until he and Hilde finally married in 1972 they continued to address each other with the formal 'Sie'. Even after their marriage, Hilde called her husband 'Flesch' or 'Fleschy'. But despite this formality, in the 1950s the relationship developed from courtly companionship into a more passionate affair. Hilde's son Anthony was often taken to meet Flesch and instructed not to tell his father about the encounters. Meanwhile Hilde was becoming increasingly vulnerable within her marriage. Questioned abruptly by her husband or son, she was liable to respond with tears.

There were moments when Hilde and Peter's relationship revived. In 1957 Peter wrote to thank Hilde for a holiday in the house she now owned in the Austrian countryside. 'For the first time', he said, 'I was really heartbroken to have to go away.' He had not been so happy for years. 'It was so harmonious and smooth, everything sunny and lovely.' Hearing that Hilde had charmed a group of men at a party, he told her that he was not surprised. 'With every year that passes I'm more strongly attracted and more deeply attached to you. To me, at any rate, you are simply the woman – unlike anything, the thing itself.' But for Hilde this came too late; increasingly, the central relationship of her life was with Flesch.

This eventually became apparent to Peter, who demanded a clear separation in 1963. When Hilde complained that he was leaving her, he accused her of wilfully destroying their shared existence together and then expecting him to take the blame. 'You have systematically, step by step throughout the last few years, taken away your trust. Everything you did you did behind my back; you lied to me and made excuses.' He maintained that his own affairs had been trivial – he would not have embarked on them at all if he had not needed someone to give him 'a little warmth now and then' – and complained that she had told all their mutual friends that she was planning to leave Peter because she could not live without Flesch. Initially, Peter suggested a two-year trial separation, but Hilde insisted that 'our life is too short for that kind of thing and two years are too long'. Instead, they should end the marriage irrevocably. The separation, when it came, seemed to outsiders, including their own children, merely to confirm the existing status quo. But for Peter it took away the secure base he had always taken for granted. He had often found Hilde irritating; he did not especially appreciate her as a woman or a writer; but he had relied on her as his partner. For Hilde, however, it allowed for the formal foundation of a new, more

Hans Flesch-Brunningen and Hilde Spiel, *c.* 1979

Courtesy of Christine Shuttleworth

peaceful existence lived according to the principles of the courteous and artistic city in which she had grown up.

After the separation, Hilde returned to Vienna, where she began a more public relationship with Flesch. By going back to Vienna she acknowledged the failure of her attempts to integrate fully into English society. Her children were growing up to be English, but she would always be an outsider. In 1967, revisiting her diary entries from her 1946 trip to Vienna, Hilde Spiel realised that her ultimate return to Vienna was already inevitable at this point. The slow process of freeing herself from the English sphere had begun. She retained a connection with English literature by translating books by the English authors she loved. In 1958 she published a German translation of Elizabeth Bowen's *A World of Love*, and in the 1960s she translated Graham Greene's novel *The Comedians* as well as a collection of his short stories. But increasingly her home was in Austria, and once she accepted her Austrian identity it brought its own rewards. Hilde Spiel died in 1990 as a distinguished Austrian woman of letters, at last granted the recognition that she had craved during the war in England, though perhaps never again quite so energetically hopeful as she had been in the immediate post-war years in Vienna and Berlin.

———

For Henry Yorke the post-war period offered no new beginnings. Instead the 1950s saw the beginning of a process of gradual retreat from the world which would continue until his death. After the war he decided never to return to his family home, Forthampton Court, even after his brother Gerald inherited it from his father in 1957, on the grounds that it was unhealthy. And he drifted away from friends as well as family. In 1951 Evelyn Waugh invited Henry for a long weekend at his house in Gloucestershire and reported to Nancy Mitford that he looked 'GHASTLY'.

> Very long black dirty hair, one brown tooth, pallid puffy face, trembling hands, stone deaf, smoking continuously throughout meals, picking up books in the middle of conversations and falling into maniac giggles, drinking a lot of raw spirits, hating the country and

everything good. If you mention Forthampton to him he shies with embarrassment as business people used to do if their businesses were mentioned.

Dig meanwhile was gentle, lost behind 'her great moustaches', and employed a whole new proletarian argot with 'an exquisitely ladylike manner'. 'I really think Henry will be locked up soon,' Waugh concluded. Waugh's description was perhaps more amusing than fair. In 1948 Henry Yorke had invited Christopher Isherwood to dinner and Isherwood had found both Yorkes 'really very nice and so much fun', enjoying Yorke's tales of football matches, blondes and the Fire Service. Even in 1951 Nancy Mitford replied to Waugh that she herself had met Henry and Dig recently and had not seen them in the same 'livid light', though that might be because her '(health service) spectacles' were pinker than his.

At this point Henry was still focused enough to be very involved in Pontifex, although even there he felt stifled by his father's continued presence in the business. In 1948 James Lees-Milne met Henry on a bus and asked how he was. Henry replied that he was 'Bloody awful!' and launched into what Lees-Milne described as

> a diatribe of hate against his octogenarian father who, he claimed, refused to retire from the family firm, in order deliberately to retard his son's succession and ruin his prospects . . . It was evident that he was being deeply thwarted in his middle age by a tyrannical and senile parent who would not relax his grip on the wheel, Henry's wheel by rights of nature.

When Henry got off the bus he departed with the words 'It's unmitigated hell, I can tell you.'

Henry Yorke did launch into a few new friendships in this period. He particularly enjoyed time spent with the Hungarian writer Arthur Koestler, who was also now a friend of Hilde Spiel's. According to Koestler's biographer, the two men were brought together by 'a shared fondness for women and alcohol, an intolerance of fools and an admiration for each other's very different novels'. Throughout the 1950s they spent their Sunday mornings together in their shared local pub. Yorke also had more affairs, including one fairly impassioned one with Kitty Freud (then married to the painter Lucian Freud), but this ended in 1952 and in 1955 Yorke published a short account of 'Falling in Love' which, though partly satirical, does seem to reflect his accrued cynicism on the subject. 'A man', he begins here, 'falls in love because there is something wrong with him.' He gets to the point where he cannot stand being alone and may imagine he wants children, although in fact he does not, 'at least not as women do'. And once married with children of his own he longs to be alone again. Love is a weakness and only after his marriage does the man realise how sick he has been. Affairs outside marriage are no more fulfilling. A man in love with another woman who does not have the courage to leave his wife is like 'a man who takes off his belt, ties it round the branch of a tree, and hangs himself to death in the loop while his trousers fall round his ankles'. Yorke states that love comes from a lack within yourself. We are all animals, and are therefore subject to animal attraction, but there is no need for this to transmute into love, and certainly not more than once given that ultimately we are 'all and each one of us, always and always alone'.

By the 1950s Henry was hardly in touch with Mary or Alice Keene. In 1949 Mary wrote to Henry to congratulate him on *Concluding* and he replied that they 'must meet some time if you can put up with it' but added that he was in poor shape at the moment. In 1957 Mary sent Henry a copy of *Mrs Donald* to read and he responded cautiously. He assured her that she was 'a very good writer indeed', but reprimanded her for her atrocious spelling and suggested that she cut the novel down to a short story. He described himself as 'temperamentally incapable' of reading books with children as the central characters, suggesting that the focus of the novel is Rose, Violet's small sister, rather than Violet, and completely failed to comment on his own alter ego, the poet-painter Louis.

Despite his estrangement from Mary, Henry remained on friendly terms with Matthew Smith, with whom Mary was now in a more settled relationship. Matthew had given Henry a portrait of himself in 1950 which Henry celebrated in his thank you letter as 'beyond words wonderful': 'it glows and lives with a great life of its own and is and always will be a Jewel in my heart'. In 1958 Matthew's wife died and Henry wrote to send his 'deepest sympathy for all the feelings that must have been dredged up from the past by this death'. He added that breaking with the past was

> one of the hardest things we all have to learn, and when we have managed this in a fashion it comes as a blow to find the past still inexorably stretching out its cold arms to us, turning one's blood into a pile of, in my case, guilt and regret and shame. But we have our sons to be proud of, and there is still work to be done.

In fact Matthew did not have his sons to be proud of; they had both died in the Second World War. Henry had Sebastian, but that does not seem to have been enough to prevent the guilt, regret and shame. This admission of guilt may have been in part an implicit apology to Mary, whom he could reasonably expect to read the letter, but it also seems to reflect a more endemic bleakness. And for Henry Yorke in fact there remained very little work still to be done in 1958. After his father died he took little interest in the business, despite having waited impatiently all those years for him to retire. He did not write another novel after *Doting* was published in 1952.

Yorke's final three novels, *Concluding, Nothing* and *Doting*, are characterised by a cold detachment. People love, dote and mourn but the narrator does not imbue the world he depicts with anything like the lyricism of the earlier novels. Rosamond Lehmann's 1954 *TLS* tribute to Henry Yorke and to *Loving* in particular can be seen as a generous recollection of a now faded friend. She lauds the unusual tenderness of *Loving* and states that this quality 'is to become a great deal less evident, if not to disappear entirely, in his subsequent novels'. Rosamond's homage was perhaps intended partly to restore to Henry the life and tenderness he had lost, or at least to remind him to look back appreciatively on his wartime self. In this respect it was successful. After the piece was published, Henry wrote a warm letter of thanks to Rosamond Lehmann.

> Darling. I've read your piece in the TLS and haven't been able to think of what to say. Then it came to me. I think it is one of the four nicest things that ever happened to me in my life.

Moments of connection like this were becoming rarer. Henry saw fewer and fewer friends. His former acquaintances continued to meet Dig, who would assure them that Henry was doing fine and would appreciate a visit. But according to Lees-Milne, old friends were given a hostile reception if they did indeed call. In the early 1960s Henry's drinking became more out of control and Arthur Koestler helped Sebastian to check his father into a clinic for treatment. The friendship with Koestler had remained very close throughout the 1950s, but Koestler was maddened by Henry's refusal to wear a hearing aid, despite his deafness, and found Henry unrelentingly gloomy. Cynthia Koestler wrote that in this period Henry suffered from depression, which was made bearable only by gin. 'The dark eyes with winged eyebrows which seemed to dance according to his feelings – one or the other was often raised – were set in a face whose pallor rarely saw the light of day.' Even the friendship with Koestler ended in 1962 when Koestler decided that Henry was anti-Semitic.

In 1963 Henry Yorke wrote a short biographical sketch in which he characterised himself accurately as a hermit. 'Only the other day', he announced, 'a woman of sixty looking after the tobacconist's shop was dragged by her hair across the counter and stabbed twice in the neck. That is one reason why I don't go out any more.' Danger threatened on the street and the best thing was not to go out at all. 'If one can afford it, the best thing is to stay in one place, which might be bed. Not sex, for sleep.'

Henry Yorke remained in bed until his death in 1973, the same year as the death of Elizabeth Bowen. After the sale of Bowen's Court, Elizabeth had based herself in Oxford and then from 1965 in Hythe in Kent, returning to the small section of coastline where she had lived on first coming to England with her mother as a child. The Hythe house was small, modern and practical; she was not going to attempt to compete with the grandeur of the world she had lost. But from the start she entertained friends from London, putting them up at the local hotel, and encouraged Charles to see the house as his home. She also published a novel, *Eva Trout*, set on the Kent coast where she was now living; a strange and original tale of a clumsy and trouble-making childlike woman. And she made forays into her own childhood, starting an autobiography to be called *Pictures and Conversations*, as well as continuing to lecture abroad and to write essays, though without the financial necessity imposed by Bowen's Court.

Elizabeth Bowen lived in Hythe for eight years before dying of lung cancer in hospital in February 1973. In 1961 Charles had written in his diary that 'nothing, I believe, except death or the ghastly attrition of old age can touch us, and when either happen I shall be finished whether I know it or not'. By the late 1960s it had become apparent to him that old age and death did indeed threaten. In 1968 he reread Elizabeth's early letters, awed and saddened by the strength and certainty of her love. 'I had that and it is gone, but its ghost, thank God, remains to haunt me till I die.' Certainly, it haunted him after her death. Desolate, Charles made no attempt to protect himself from his grief.

I do believe in her love for me. I do believe it and in mine for her.

I shall never see her again in this world or the next . . . She will never advance to me across the grass of Regent's Park at any time of day. She is gone from me forever.

I am never to recover or cease to feel the absence and the pain till I cease feeling anything.

Five years after Elizabeth Bowen's death, Catherine Walston died, also of lung cancer. The cough that Graham Greene had immortalised in *The End of the Affair* had indeed killed her in the end. Like Charles

Ritchie, Catherine had come to regret the failure of the love affair with Graham and to see it as the most important relationship of her life. 'I think of you so often and with such pleasure,' she wrote to him in 1975. 'What a vast amount you gave me.' Shortly before her death she wrote to him in shaky handwriting, just home from a period in hospital, looking back on their happiest times together. 'What a vast amount of pleasure you have given me playing scrabble on the roof at the Rosaio . . . and teaching me to swim underwater at Ian Fleming's house; smoking opium and Ankor etc.' She told him that she would always remember their times in Capri, from the day they first walked through the gate of the villa. 'There has never been anyone in my life like you and thanks a lot.'

Graham and Catherine had sustained an intermittent sexual relationship through the 1950s and into the 1960s, but they had drifted apart as both became involved with other lovers and Catherine's health declined. In 1966 Graham had moved to France to live with Yvonne Cloetta, a younger French woman with whom he would remain until his death in 1991. He was happy with Yvonne and these were productive years for him as a writer. 'If she didn't exist I'd put a bullet to my head,' he told a friend in 1990. But he still looked back on the war years and the time with Catherine as the period when he had been most insistently alive.

Bowen, Greene, Macaulay, Spiel and Yorke all saw the arc of their lives as shaped by their experiences in the Second World War and its immediate aftermath. For Rose Macaulay this was a time of intense sadness, mitigated by moments of beauty under the Mediterranean sun that she and Gerald O'Donovan had loved, and among the ruins that served as a reminder of a wider time-frame. But for the other writers these years brought an exhilaration that was unrivalled in the later post-war period. Bowen, Greene and Yorke responded intensely to the peculiar climate of wartime London; to its temporality, its accelerated intimacies and its visual beauty. They all produced extraordinary novels during and in response to this period. In contrast to the suspended present of wartime, the post-war period was predicated on the future. The welfare state imposed taxes in the present designed to improve the world for the next generation. Bowen, Greene and Yorke all found this depressing. In post-war Vienna and Berlin, however, Hilde Spiel found just the climate that the British writers had found in wartime London, and in Ireland Greene and Bowen were both briefly able to forget post-war actualities and find instead a timeless world of love.

In the quiet years before his death, Henry Yorke was writing very little but he did publish a brief account of his time in the fire service in 1960, intended to be the start of a book-length account of *London and Fire, 1939–45*. Retreating into the past, Yorke regained the energy and humour that he had lost in daily life, mocking his firemen colleagues for their preoccupation with their pensions at the same time as he lauded them for their collective bravery, 'ready to take on lions'. During this period, Graham Greene was recording his dreams, and the continued significance of the war for Greene is evident in his posthumously published dream diary, where he makes frequent nocturnal excursions back to the Blitz. In February 1965, after an air raid, German parachute troops land near his London house; in 1972 a large tranche of London is destroyed by bombs.

And for Elizabeth Bowen, most of all, the war remained a charmed pocket of unrepeatable happiness. Her review of Calder's *The People's War*, written not long before her death, insists on the unique importance of the war years for those who experienced them in London. 'Existence during the war had a mythical intensity, heightened for dwellers in cities under attack.' Here she sees the war as defining the lives of her generation, whether it brought exuberance, loss or horror. 'War is a prolonged passionate act, and we were involved in it.' For individuals as well as for their country the stakes of that involvement were high. But the reward was an intensity they would never know again.

Notes

Abbreviations
People and books

CR:	Charles Ritchie
CW:	Catherine Walston
EB:	Elizabeth Bowen
B's C:	*Bowen's Court and Seven Winters*
HoD:	*The Heat of the Day*
LCW:	*Love's Civil War, Letters and diaries from the love affair of a lifetime*
GG:	Graham Greene
EoA:	*The End of the Affair*
HoM:	*The Heart of the Matter*
HG:	Henry Green (where quotations are from work published under this pseudonym)
HS:	Hilde Spiel
DaB:	*The Dark and the Bright: Memoirs 1911–1989*
HY:	Henry Yorke
PdeM:	Peter de Mendelssohn
RM:	Rose Macaulay
ToT:	*The Towers of Trebizond*
WMW:	*The World My Wilderness*
VG:	Vivien Greene

Archives and libraries

Bod:	Bodleian Library
EB HRC:	Elizabeth Bowen archive, Harry Ransom Center, Austin
GG BU:	Graham Greene archive, Boston University
GG GU:	Graham Greene archive, Georgetown University, Washington
GG HRC:	Graham Greene archive, Harry Ransom Center, Austin
HRC:	Harry Ransom Center
HS NLV:	Hilde Spiel archive, National Library of Vienna
HS PdeM:	Hilde Spiel and Peter de Mendelssohn correspondence, private collection, Austria
HY archive:	Henry Yorke archive, private collection, Yorkshire

London Met: London Metropolitan Archive
Nat Arch: The National Archives, Kew, Surrey
PdeM Mon: Peter de Mendelssohn archive, Monacensia Library, Munich
RL KC: Rosamond Lehmann archive, King's College, Cambridge
RM TC: Rose Macaulay archive, Trinity College, Cambridge
VG Bod: Vivien Greene archive, Bodleian Library, Oxford
Westminster: Westminster Archive

Where novels are available in multiple editions, chapter numbers are given instead of page numbers.

More than one chapter or page number may be given where there are several quotations from the same text within a single paragraph.

Introduction

1   'War had made them': EB, *HoD*, ch. 1.
1   'scenery in an empty theatre': see EB, 'London, 1940', *The Mulberry Tree: Writings of Elizabeth Bowen*, ed. Hermione Lee (London: Vintage, 1999).
3   'straight, long in the eye': HG, *Caught* (London: Harvill Press, 2001), p. 47.
3   'pile their mattresses': see HS, *DaB*, p. 127.
4   'lucid abnormality': EB, preface to *The Demon Lover and Other Stories* (*The Mulberry Tree*).
4   'It came to be rumoured': EB, *HoD*, ch. 5.
4   'war time, with its': ibid.
5   'exuberance, during the early': EB, review of Angus Calder's *The People's War* (*The Mulberry Tree*).
5   'saving resort': EB, preface to *The Demon Lover and Other Stories* (*The Mulberry Tree*).
6   'By moonlight': William Sansom, *The Blitz: Westminster at War* (London: Faber, 2010), p. 49.
6   'most beautiful': RM to Jean Macaulay, 6 September 1940 (RM TC).
6   'We at least': EB, review of *The People's War* (*The Mulberry Tree*).
6   'through the particular': EB, preface to *The Demon Lover and Other Stories* (*The Mulberry Tree*).
6   'the only non-groupy': EB to William Plomer, 6 May 1958 (*The Mulberry Tree*).
7   'imaginary but nevertheless': John Lehmann, *I Am My Brother* (London: Longmans, 1960), pp. 169–73.

Newsreel

11 'plywood under his skylight': see GG to VG, 30 August 1939 (VG Bod).
12 'if necessary for years': Winston Churchill, speech, 18 June 1940, *War Speeches, 1939–45*, compiled by Charles Eade (London: Cassell & Co, 1951–2).
12 'The prospect of invasion': HS, diary, 2 May 1940 (HS NLV).
12 'German parachutists': see Juliet Gardiner, *Wartime: Britain 1939–1945* (London: Headline, 2005), p. 222.
12 '1333 people': see Richard Overy, *The Battle of Britain: Myth and Reality* (London: Penguin, 2010), p. 83.
12 'There are two corrections': J. B. Priestley, broadcast, 9 July 1940, *Britain Speaks* (New York: Harper & Brothers, 1940).
13 'Why doesn't he come?': in William Shirer, *The Rise and Fall of the Third Reich* (London: The Folio Society, 1995), vol. 3, p. 170.
13 'many-coloured flares': J. B. Priestley, broadcast, 4 September 1940, *Britain Speaks*.
13 'the Führer has decided': in Juliet Gardiner, *The Blitz: The British Under Attack* (London: HarperCollins 2011), p. 7.

14 'when the western skies': William Sansom, *The Blitz: Westminster at War* (London: Faber, 2010), p. 27.

14 'I've fought fires': HY to Rosamond Lehmann, 11 September 1940 (RL KC).

14 'I hear little by little': RM to Jean Macaulay, 8 September 1940 (RM TC).

14 'Scraps of cloth': Virginia Woolf, diary, 10 September 1940, *The Diary of Virginia Woolf* , ed. Anne Olivier Bell and Andrew McNeillie (London: Hogarth Press, 1977–1984).

14 'We have need of all': Virginia Woolf, diary, 18 September 1940 (*The Diary of Virginia Woolf*).

15 'When your flat went': EB to Virginia Woolf, 5 January 1941, *The Mulberry Tree: Writings of Elizabeth Bowen*, ed. Hermione Lee (London: Vintage, 1999).

15 'Hitler expects': Churchill, speech, 11 September 1940 (*War Speeches*).

15 'momentous sound': Sansom, *The Blitz*, pp. 34–5.

15 'less fearful in dealing with fire': ibid., p. 24.

16 'the quality of service': J. B. Priestley, broadcast, 10 September 1940 (*Britain Speaks*).

16 'To work or think': EB, *HoD*, ch. 5.

16 'How fantastic life has': RM to Jean Macaulay, 11 September 1940 (RM TC).

16 'out in the wide world': Sansom, *The Blitz*, p. 49.

1: 7 p.m.: Blackout

17 'Through the railings': EB, 'London, 1940', *The Mulberry Tree: Writings of Elizabeth Bowen*, ed. Hermione Lee (London: Vintage, 1999).

18 'local authorities had decided': see Westminster, CD114.

18 'walking in the darkness': EB, preface to *The Demon Lover and Other Stories* (*The Mulberry Tree*).

18 'casualties due to blackout': see Vera Brittain, *England's Hour* (London. Continuum, 2005), ch. 4.

18 'new sense somewhere between': ibid.

18 'Greene was based': see GG, *Ways of Escape* (Harmondsworth: Penguin, 1982), ch. 4.

19 'like a street in a city': EB to Noreen Butler, September 1940, in Victoria Glendinning, *Elizabeth Bowen* (London: Phoenix paperbacks, 1993), p. 133.

19 'I had always placed': EB, 'London, 1940' (*The Mulberry Tree*).

19 '200 cigarettes': ibid.

20 'as appalling a night': EB to Noreen Butler, September 1940 (in Glendinning, *Elizabeth Bowen*, p. 133).

20 'after black-out we keep': EB, 'London, 1940' (*The Mulberry Tree*).

20 'I do ap-p-pologise': see John Sutherland, *Stephen Spender: The Authorized Biography* (London: Penguin, 2005), p. 271.

20 'The sound of the Boche': EB to Noreen Butler, September 1940 (in Glendinning, *Elizabeth Bowen*, p. 133).

20 'The very soil of the city': EB, *HoD*, ch. 5.

21 'twinship with one's century': EB, *A Time in Rome* (London: Vintage, 2010), ch. 3.

21 'the fateful course': EB, *HoD*, ch. 7.

21 'a pink, rattled': EB, 'A Year I Remember – 1918', *Listening In: Broadcasts, Speeches and Interviews by Elizabeth Bowen*, ed. Allan Hepburn (Edinburgh: Edinburgh University Press, 2010).

22 'an impression of abounding': Rosamond Lehmann, letter correcting obituary of Elizabeth Bowen (RL KC).

22 'Hers was a handsome face': May Sarton, *A World of Light* (New York: Norton, 1988), p. 193.

22 'It is possible that Elizabeth's': EB, *B's C*, ch. 9.

23 'a kind of protracted debauch': Malcolm Muggeridge, *Chronicles of Wasted Time*, vol. 2: *The Infernal Grove* (London: Collins, 1973), p. 104.

24 'depressive when the bombs': GG, interview, 1975 in Henry Donaghy (ed.),

Conversations with Graham Greene (Jackson: University Press of Mississippi, 1992), p. 95.

24 'which Greene admired': see GG, 'Lightning Tour', *Spectator*, 13 June 1941.

24 'the instant that an individual': John Strachey, *Post D, Some Experiences of an Air Raid Warden* (London: Gollancz, 1941), p. 18.

24 'air raids were much less trying': EB, autobiographical note, 1948 (EB HRC).

24 'we were a generation': ibid., ch. 2ii.

24 'he dreamed that he was Wilfred Owen': see GG, *A World of my Own: A Dream Diary* (London: Penguin, 1993), p. 44.

25 'we young writers': Christopher Isherwood, *Lions and Shadows: An Education in the Twenties* (London: The Hogarth Press, 1938), p. 74.

25 'I can't help wishing': GG to VG, undated (GG HRC).

25 'Russian roulette': see GG, 'The Revolver in the Corner Cupboard', *The Lost Childhood and Other Essays* (London: Eyre & Spottiswoode, 1951).

25 'expected for so long': GG, 'At Home', *Collected Essays* (Harmondsworth: Penguin, 1970).

26 'If war were only': GG, 'One Man's War', *Spectator*, 6 December 1940.

26 'faint susurrus of the': GG to VG, August 1939 (VG Bod).

27 'suffer that word': GG, *Ways of Escape*, ch. 3ii.

27 'scientific formulae scrawled': Muggeridge, *The Infernal Grove*, p. 78.

27 'high heartless buildings': GG, 'Men at Work', *Penguin New Writing*, 1942.

28 'Greene tried to persuade Waugh': see Evelyn Waugh, diary, 28 May 1940, *The Diaries of Evelyn Waugh*, ed. Michael Davie (London: Phoenix, 2009).

28 'the possibility of throwing stigmata': see Muggeridge, *The Infernal Grove*, p. 78.

28 'there was something rather': ibid., p. 103.

28 'for persons of courage': 'Air Raid Precautions Training Manual' (Westminster, CD149.1).

28 'a quite unnecessary': Violet Bonham Carter, 'Air-raid Wardens' Claims', *Spectator*, 8 November 1940.

29 'mere cant': Strachey, *Post D*, p. 23.

29 'Those who don't like scratchy': EB, 'Britain, 1940', *People, Places, Things: Essays by Elizabeth Bowen*, ed. Allan Hepburn (Edinburgh: Edinburgh University Press, 2008).

29 'We wardens were of all': EB, autobiographical note, 1948 (EB HRC).

30 'instantly pop open': EB, draft typescript of *HoD* (EB HRC).

30 'exchange of searching': EB, 'Britain, 1940' (*People, Places, Things*).

30 'This is a people's war': GG, 'The Cinema', *Spectator*, 29 September 1939.

30 'unembittered humour': GG, 'The Theatre', *Spectator*, 1 November 1940.

31 'heroic raconteur': GG, *Ways of Escape*, ch. 4i.

31 'as though the proximity': GG, interview in Marie-Françoise Allain, *The Other Man: Conversations with Graham Greene* (Harmondsworth: Penguin, 1984), p. 129.

32 'Molly Hawthorn': GG, 'The Londoners', *The Month*, November 1951.

32 'dragging, drumming, slowly': EB, *HoD*, ch. 5.

32 'There is the distant drumfire': Harold Nicolson, diary, 24 September 1940, *Diaries and Letters 1939–45*, ed. Nigel Nicolson (London: Collins, 1967).

33 'The incendiaries sounded': see Barbara Nixon, *Raiders Overhead, A Diary of the London Blitz* (London: Scolar Press, 1980), p. 35.

33 'it was possible for one aeroplane': see 'Air Raids: What you must know and what you must do' (Westminster, CD175).

33 'The Home Office had': see Mike Brown, *Put That Light Out! Britain's Civil Defence Services at War 1939–1945* (Gloucestershire: Sutton Publishing, 1999), p. 88.

33 'incendiaries could be regarded': see Strachey, *Post D*, p. 62.

33 'there were a pair of skiing sticks': GG, 'At Home' (*Collected Essays*).

34 'Of course we were painting': Inez Holden, *It was Different at the Time* (London: John Lane The Bodley Head, 1943), p. 69.

2: *10 p.m.: Fire*

35 'Eighty German aircraft': see Nat Arch, AIR 16/432.
36 'Faith in tables': RM to Jean Macaulay, 23 September 1940 (RM TC).
36 'phobia of being buried': ibid.
36 'government decrees had stipulated': see London Met, Ambulance Box 6.
36 'My God, what a world': RM to Rosamond Lehmann, 10 September 1939 (RL KC).
37 'a great stroke of luck': RM to Jean Macaulay, 26 September 1940 (RM TC).
37 'any exercise or instruction': memo, 21 September 1940 (London Met, Ambulance Box 52).
38 'I like my ambulance colleagues': RM to Virginia Woolf, 10 October 1940 (RM TC).
38 'Sub-station 345V': see HG, 'Before the Great Fire', *Surviving: The Uncollected Writings of Henry Green* (London: Harvill, 1993).
38 'an eccentric, fire-fighting': Rosamond Lehmann, 'An Absolute Gift', *Times Literary Supplement*, 6 August 1954.
39 'Quite well but sleep': HY to Rosamond Lehmann, 11 September 1940 (RL KC).
39 'to work myself silly': HY to Mary Strickland, 10 March 1939, in Jeremy Treglown, *Romancing: The Life and Work of Henry Green* (London: Faber, 2000), p. 125.
39 'the seven-thousandth fireman': see HG, 'Before the Great Fire' (*Surviving*).
39 'not likely to fall down': ibid.
39 'a course that no one failed': ibid.
40 'likely enough to die': HG, *Pack My Bag* (London: Vintage, 2000), p. 153.
40 'what seems to be the alternative': HY to Evelyn Waugh, 14 October 1939 (Waugh Archive, HRC).
40 'the AFS was a suicide squad': see HG, 'Before the Great Fire' (*Surviving*).
41 'All that was real to him': HG, *Caught* (London: Harvill Press, 2001), p. 25.
41 'three years after one war': HG, *Pack My Bag*, p. 1.
41 'We who must die soon': ibid., p. 92.
41 'Old ladies gave': HG, *Caught*, p. 47.
41 'His life in the Fire Brigade': Evelyn Waugh, diary, 26 November 1939, *The Diaries of Evelyn Waugh*, ed. Michael Davie (London: Phoenix, 2009).
41 'Fire fighting is a waiting': HG, 'Before the Great Fire' (*Surviving*).
41 'For forty-eight hours': HG, *Caught*, p. 21.
41 'We come here ready for': ibid., p. 93.
42 'the Fire Service, now that': HY, draft typescript of *Caught* (HY archive).
42 'a group of progressive novelists': Evelyn Waugh, *Officers and Gentlemen* (London: Chapman & Hall, 1955), ch. 1.
42 'it was a particular tradition': see William Sansom, *The Blitz: Westminster at War* (London: Faber, 2010), p. 121.
42 'However frightened, they are': HG, 'Before the Great Fire' (*Surviving*).
42 'We're absolute heroes now': HG, *Caught*, p. 176.
44 'judge of my delight': HG, 'A Fire, a Flood and the Price of Meat' (*Surviving*).
44 'Who are you going out with tonight': see *Trapped: The Story of Henry Green* (BBC documentary, 1992).
44 'the writer, our kind': HY to Rosamond Lehmann, in Lehmann, 'An Absolute Gift'.
44 'well-read, articulate': James Lees-Milne, *Fourteen Friends* (London: John Murray, 1996), p. 123.
45 'The men, I loved them': HY, interview with the *Star*, 15 June 1929.
45 'how little money meant': see HG, *Pack My Bag*, p. 154.
45 'Yorke was as happy': see Anthony Powell, *Messengers of Day* (London: Heinemann, 1978), p. 25.
45 'The behaviour of my AFS unit': HY to Mary Strickland, 10 July 1940, in Treglown, *Romancing*, p. 125.
45 'putting the light out': HG, *Caught*, pp. 45, 145.
46 'In his dirt, his tiredness': HG, ibid., pp. 49, 46, 161.

46   'semi-military discipline': see Sansom, *The Blitz*, p. 121.
47   'Shortly after 11 p.m.': see Westminster, CD25.
48   'Everywhere the searchlights clustered': Evelyn Waugh, *Officers and Gentlemen*, ch. 1.
48   'Yorke sat forward in his seat': see HG, 'A Rescue' (*Surviving*).
48   'Three more HEs': see Westminster, CE38.
49   'A 1940 air-raid manual': 'Air Raid Precautions Training Manual' (Westminster, CD149.1).
49   'Yorke always had difficulty': see HG, 'Mr Jonas' (*Surviving*).
49   'This gripped by the throat': HG, 'Before the Great Fire' (*Surviving*).
50   'had come upon a place': HG, 'Mr Jonas' (*Surviving*).
50   'a roaring red gold': HG, *Caught*, pp. 178, 181.
50   'Yelling and receiving instructions': see HG, 'Mr Jonas' (*Surviving*).

3: *1 a.m.: Rescue*

51   'gradually brought under control': see Nat Arch, AIR 16/432.
51   'cars crashed all night': RM, *Life Among the English* (London: Collins, 1942), p. 47.
51   'To propel a car': RM, *Personal Pleasures* (London: Victor Gollancz, 1935), 'Driving a Car'.
52   'the other cars': ibid., 'Fastest on Earth'.
52   'if he dies': Jean Macaulay, interview in Constance Babington Smith, *Rose Macaulay: A Biography* (London: Collins, 1972), p. 151.
52   'I knew about': RM, *ToT*, ch. 25.
53   'he had given me his love': ibid.
53   'an acute irritation': John Strachey, *Post D, Some Experiences of an Air Raid Warden* (London: Gollancz, 1941), p. 78.
54   'Dust liquefies': RM, 'Notes on the Way', *Time and Tide*, 5 October 1940.
55   'very nice and matey': RM to Jean Macaulay, 27 September 1940 (RM TC).
55   'Sorry Miss': RM, 'Notes on the Way'.
55   'fifteen bomber planes returned': see Nat Arch, AIR 16/432.
56   'This adds to his comfort': memo, 22 November 1939 (London Met, Ambulance Box 38).
57   'tended to vomit': Jean Macaulay in Babington Smith, *Rose Macaulay*, p. 78.
57   'an infinitely incapable': RM, *Told by an Idiot* (London: Collins, 1965), part 4, second period, ch. 2.
57   'thinking it led on': RM, *Non-Combatants and Others* (London: Capuchin Classics, 2010), chs 3i, 9v.
57   'A Watford-based volunteer': see Angela Raby, *The Forgotten Service: Auxiliary Ambulance Station 39* (London: After the Battle, 1999).
58   'eight ambulance drivers': see London Met, Ambulance Box 73.
58   'It is all in the night's': RM to Jean Macaulay, 27 September 1940 (RM TC).
58   'It's like this every night': RM, 'Notes on the Way'.
59   'not to be too vivid': RM to Virginia Woolf, 10 October 1940 (RM TC).
59   'mortified elephant': RM to Daniel George, 30 August 1939 (RM TC).
59   'I am improving': RM to Jean Macaulay, 25 June 1940 (RM TC).
60   'it will be hateful': RM to Rosamond Lehmann, 10 September 1939 (RL KC).
60   'fell dumb in the': RM, 'The Garden', *Poems of Today*, 1915.
61   'rich earth': Rupert Brooke, 'The Soldier', *Poems of Today*, 1915.
61   'who walked about': RM, 'Coming to London', John Lehmann (ed.), *Coming to London* (London: Phoenix House Ltd, 1957).
61   'the death at the war': RM to Katharine Tynan, 25 December 1915, in Sarah LeFanu, *Rose Macaulay* (London: Virago, 2003), p. 112.
61   'As I can't be fighting': RM, *Non-Combatants and Others*, ch. 16vi.
62   'on the side of the angels': Victor Gollancz, *Reminiscences of Affection* (London: Victor Gollancz, 1968), p. 82.
62   'I hate party politics': RM in ibid.

62 'a lot of wrongs': RM, *Dangerous Ages* (London: Collins, 1921), ch. 7v.
62 'Our civilisation': RM, *An Open Letter* (London: The Peace Pledge Union, 1937).
63 'Oh it's you that have': RM, 'Many Sisters to Many Brothers', *Poems of Today*, 1915.
63 'things happening across': RM, *Non-Combatants and Others*, ch. 2v.
64 'Oh, what does one mean': RM, *And No Man's Wit* (London: Collins, 1940), pp. 315–16.
64 'If Nazism really': RM to Jean Macaulay, 14 September 1939 (RM TC).
64 'an appalling indictment': RM to Jean Macaulay, undated, 1939 (RM TC).
65 'very well again': RM to Jean Macaulay, 3 October 1940 (RM TC).
65 'blind, maniac, primitive': RM, 'Notes on the Way'.
66 'only in the ambulance services': see RM, unfinished and untitled article, 1940 (RM TC).
66 'I think this is a good thing': RM to Jean Macaulay, 28 August 1939 (RM TC).
66 'I rather wish': RM to Jean Macaulay, 11 September 1940 (RM TC).
66 'There is so little time': RM to Virginia Woolf, 10 October 1940 (RM TC).

4: *6 a.m.: All Clear*

67 '481 fires': see London Met, FB/WAR/3/10.
68 'glaring deficiencies': Dorothea Fox to Ellen Wilkinson, 23 November 1940 (Nat Arch, HO207/995).
69 'since those days': HS, *DaB*, p. 127.
69 'because of the daily example': HS, 'Psychologie des Exils', 1975, *Kleine Schritte: Berichte und Geschichten* (München: Heinrich Ellermann, 1976).
69 'almost sure to collapse': 'Your Home as an Air Raid Shelter' (Westminster, CD174).
69 'Foreign faces about': EB, preface to *The Demon Lover and Other Stories*, *The Mulberry Tree: Writings of Elizabeth Bowen*, ed. Hermione Lee (London: Vintage, 1999).
70 'the socialist torchlit march': see HS, *DaB*, p. 56.
70 'a climate of the most': ibid., p. 41.
71 'definitely the man for me': HS, diary, 1934 (in *DaB*, p. 74).
71 'a man like a tree': HS, *DaB*, p. 80.
72 'queuing at the fishmonger's': see HS, *Return to Vienna*, trans. Christine Shuttleworth (Riverside, California: Ariadne Press, 2011), 30 January.
72 'dreary and wretched': HS, ibid.
72 'split consciousness': HS, 'Psychologie des Exils'.
73 'Peter's zest': HS, *DaB*, p. 124.
73 'France conquered': HS, diary, 25 June 1940 (HS NLV).
73 'never yet so despondent': HS, diary, 8 August 1940 (HS NLV).
73 'exactly how I felt': HS, *DaB*, p. 76 (PdeM's broadcast quoted here).
74 'The SS will march': ibid., p. 115.
74 'It is horrible and unbearable': HS, diary, March 1938 (HS NLV).
75 'At night I dreamt that': HS, diary, 24 June 1938 (HS NLV).
75 'The Czechs are betrayed': HS, diary, 30 September 1938 (HS NLV).
75 'if we ever experienced': HS, *DaB*, p. 120.
75 'avoid treating as enemies': in Cesarani and Kushner (eds), *The Internment of Aliens in Twentieth-Century Britain* (London: Routledge, 1993), p. 83.
76 'In Britain you have': ibid., p. 87.
77 'It's always a stroke': HS to PdeM, 7 October 1939 (HS PdeM).
77 'I have a fascinating idea': PdeM to HS, October 1939 (HS PdeM).
78 'very charming little': PdeM to HS, 9 November 1939 (HS PdeM).
78 'what the PEN club': HS, *DaB*, p. 107.
78 'Some of you are exiles': *PEN News*, February 1939.
79 'don't fuss': HS, *DaB*, p. 105.
79 'I am so happy': HS, diary, 23 April 1940 (HS NLV).
79 'beautiful, green': HS, *DaB*, p. 127.

80   'hesitant courtesy': see HS, *DaB*, p. 110.
80   'whether it makes one happy': HS, *Anna und Anna* (Wien: Kremayr & Scheriau, 1989), p. 68.
80   '*chez nous* syndrome': HS, 'Psychologie des Exils'.
81   'A small village square': HS, *Return to Vienna*, 6 February.
81   'Exile is an illness': HS, 'Psychologie des Exils'.
81   'back in Vienna': HS, *Return to Vienna*, 31 January.

5: 'War, she thought, was sex'

85   'War, she thought': HG, *Caught* (London: Harvill Press, 2001), pp. 119, 46.
85   'Nature tapped out': EB, *HoD*, ch. 8.
86   'You'd always keep': GG to VG, 7 August 1927 (GG HRC).
86   'Twelve years later': there is some controversy about the dating of the beginning of the affair. According to Norman Sherry (in *The Life of Graham Greene* (London: Pimlico, 2004–5), vol. 2, pp. 19–20) it started at the beginning of the war (information based on a statement by Malcolm Muggeridge).   Richard Greene (*Graham Greene, A Life in Letters* (London: Little, Brown, 2007), p. 102) suggests that it started earlier, based on Greene's remark that the affair was four years old in 1942, but most of the evidence confirms Sherry's view.
87   'I miss you so much': GG to VG, 30 August 1939 (VG Bod).
87   'There's one thing': GG to VG, 4 September 1939 (VG Bod).
87   'Dear love': GG to VG, 6 October 1939 (VG Bod).
87   'I mean, not pub': VG to GG, 1 December 1939 (VG Bod).
87   'You are a kitten': GG to VG, 3 November 1925 (GG HRC).
88   'a lot of stars': VG to GG, 13 December 1939 (VG Bod).
88   'rather affectionately': ibid.
88   'in a physical sense the marriage': VG interview in Sherry, *The Life of Graham Greene*, vol. 2, p. 208.
88   'Clearly, Graham did not have the same': arriving in Freetown in 1943, Greene was immediately on the lookout for 'French letters', lamenting that they were unexpectedly hard to acquire. Evidently he had managed to obtain them in London (see Sherry, *The Life of Graham Greene*, vol. 2, p. 138).
88   'it always worked': GG, *HoM*, book 1, part 1, ch. 1viii.
88   'it is so awful': VG to GG, 3 January 1940 (VG Bod).
88   'Darling darling one': GG to VG, 4 January 1940 (VG Bod).
88   'You wouldn't see much': VG to GG, 19 January 1940 (VG Bod).
88   'pretended to Vivien': see Sherry, *The Life of Graham Greene*, vol. 2, p. 25.
89   'my love, you are a saint': GG to VG, 7 November 1925 (GG HRC).
89   'square and small': VG interview in Sherry, *The Life of Graham Greene*, vol. 2, p. 25.
89   'a person who': Muggeridge interview in ibid., vol. 2, p. 23.
89   'find their own way': GG, *HoM*, book 2, part 1, ch. 3i.
89   'happy, small, rather': David Low interview in Sherry, *The Life of Graham Greene*, vol. 2, p. 22i.
89   'From the first raid': GG interview in ibid., vol. 2, p. 60.
89   'Just look at that pair': David Low interview in ibid., vol. 2, p. 51.
90   'devoted': Muggeridge interview in ibid., vol. 2, p. 23.
90   'a special act of penitence': Malcolm Muggeridge, *Chronicles of Wasted Time*, vol. 2: *The Infernal Grove* (London: Collins, 1973), p. 105.
90   'rather heartbreaking': GG to Marion Greene, undated (*A Life in Letters*, p. 104).
91   'in tears on the edge': VG interview in Sherry, *The Life of Graham Greene*, vol. 2, p. 64.
91   'It's sad because': GG to Mary Pritchett, 18 March 1941 (*A Life in Letters*).
91   'a large mortgage': see Muggeridge, diary, 13 January 1949, Malcolm Muggeridge,

Like it was: the Diaries of Malcolm Muggeridge, ed. John Bright-Holmes (London: Collins, 1981).

91 'simply felt relieved': GG interview in Sherry, *The Life of Graham Greene*, vol. 2, p. 64.

91 'To the great scandal': HY to Anthony Powell, 23 August 1928 (in Jeremy Treglown, *Romancing: The Life and Work of Henry Green* (London: Faber, 2000), p. 77).

91 'falling in love by correspondence': see HG, *Pack My Bag* (London: Vintage, 2000), p. 159.

92 'all agreed as to her beauty': see Treglown, *Romancing*, p. 85.

92 'a stupendous intellect': HY to Evelyn Waugh, 11 April 1939 (Evelyn Waugh archive, HRC).

92 'We had been married': HG, 'Before the Great Fire', *Surviving: The Uncollected Writings of Henry Green* (London: Harvill, 1993).

93 'the saving grace': HG, *Pack My Bag*, p. 80.

93 'even resumed the sexual': see Treglown, *Romancing*, p. 310.

93 'It seems so *gauche*': Dig Yorke quoted in HY letter to Mary Strickland, 25 November 1939, in ibid., p. 138.

93 'the most brilliant feyness': Venetia Murray, interview in Treglown, *Romancing*, p. 161.

94 'tall, and holding herself': Stephen Spender, *World Within World* (New York: Modern Library Classics, 2001), p. 156.

95 'Goronwy had visited': see EB to Isaiah Berlin, 23 September 1946 (Isaiah Berlin archive, Bod).

95 'takes an ell': Louis MacNeice, *The Strings Are False* (London: Faber, 1965), p. 168.

95 'Henry concealing the meetings from his wife': see Treglown, *Romancing*, pp. 127, 309.

95 'a goal to get back to': HY to Rosamond Lehmann, 11 September 1940 (RL KC).

95 'Yes, it *was* the core': Rosamond Lehmann to HY, 15 September 1940, in Treglown, *Romancing*, p. 309.

95 'Rosamond herself later claimed': Lehmann told her biographer Selina Hastings that she had not gone to bed with Yorke and also that nothing had happened with Rees at Bowen's Court (see Selina Hastings, *Rosamond Lehmann* (London: Vintage, 2003), pp. 215, 172).

95 'one of the few disinterested': Rosamond Lehmann to HY, undated, in Treglown, *Romancing*, p. 127.

96 'war is entirely': HY to Rosamond Lehmann, 9 January 1941 (RL KC).

96 'it's like swimming': Rosemary Clifford to HY, 25 August 1940, in Treglown, *Romancing*, p. 135.

96 'Have I told you I miss you?': Rosemary Clifford to HY, 25 August 1940, in ibid., p. 135.

96 'You are now old enough': HY in ibid., p. 132.

96 'back in the Lansdowne': Ann Glass to HY, 28 February 1941, in ibid., p. 134.

96 'How wonderful they seem': HG, *Pack My Bag*, p. 39.

97 'Darling, This is very': Rosemary Clifford to HY, 8 November 1940, in Treglown, *Romancing*, p. 135.

97 'gorged with love': HG, *Caught*, p. 47.

97 'hunting for more farewells': ibid., p. 61.

97 'the bloom, as': ibid., p. 70.

97 'everyone's longing': ibid., p. 107.

97 'like the crack': ibid., p. 116.

98 'silly thing with Hilly': HY to John Lehmann, 11 May 1943 (John Lehmann archive, HRC).

97 'DON'T COME UP': HY in Treglown, *Romancing*, p. 138.

98 'hanging limp to door handles': HG, *Caught*, p. 46.

99 'a new year's turn': HY, draft typescript of *Caught* (HY archive).

6: 'Ireland can be dementing'

101   'high bare Italianate house': EB, *B's C*, ch. 1.
101   'an eternal luminousness': EB, *HoD*, ch. 9.
102   'be some good': EB to Virginia Woolf, 1 July 1940, *The Mulberry Tree: Writings of Elizabeth Bowen*, ed. Hermione Lee (London: Vintage, 1999).
103   'As far as Churchill': see Clair Wills, *That Neutral Island* (London: Faber, 2008), p. 116.
103   'Ireland can be dementing': EB to Virginia Woolf, 1 July 1940 (*The Mulberry Tree*).
103   'childishness and obtuseness': EB, report, 9 November 1940, *Notes on Eire, Espionage Reports to Winston Churchill, 1940–2*, Aubane Historical Society, ed. Jack Lane and Brendan Clifford, 3rd edn.
104   'a race inside a race': EB interview by three writers, 1959 (EB HRC).
104   'screen of trees': EB, *The Last September* (London: Vintage, 1998), ch. 3.
104   'kept the country': EB, preface to *The Last September* (*The Mulberry Tree*).
105   'This country': EB, *The Last September*, ch. 3.
105   'I'm not English': ibid., ch. 11.
105   'I had no idea': ibid.
105   'a resolute profile': ibid., ch. 4.
105   'real pleasure': EB to William Plomer, 17 August 1936 (*The Mulberry Tree*).
106   'fallen utterly in love': Sean O'Faolain, *Vive Moi!*, 2nd edn (London: Sinclair-Stevenson, 1993), p. 302.
106   'I find so much': O'Faolain to EB, undated (EB HRC).
106   'love to run down': O'Faolain to EB, undated (EB HRC).
106   'I am, we are': EB to Humphry House, 1937 (private collection).
106   'at one time suffered': May Sarton, *A World of Light* (New York: Norton, 1988), p. 203.
107   'as synecdoche': Julia O'Faolain, introduction to O'Faolain, *Vive Moi!*, p. xii.
107   '*Here* was a': EB, 'Bowen's Court', 1958, *People, Places, Things: Essays by Elizabeth Bowen*, ed. Allan Hepburn (Edinburgh: Edinburgh University Press, 2008).
108   'so complete was': EB, *B's C*, p. 401.
108   'I met some': EB to William Plomer, 5 June 1938 (*The Mulberry Tree*).
000   'He likes her!': O'Faolain, *Vive Moi!*, p. 309.
108   'dropping his head back': EB, 'Bowen's Court' (*People, Places, Things*).
108   'loveliest novel': O'Faolain, *Vive Moi!*, p. 312.
108   'later misremembered this': ibid., p. 301.
108   'an unfair test': O'Faolain to EB, 22 April 1937 (EB HRC).
109   'the kid and the cad': O'Faolain, 'A Reading and Remembrance of Elizabeth Bowen', *London Review of Books*, 4 March 1982.
109   'eloquence was to rush': EB, *B's C*, p. 265.
109   'the chivalric element': ibid., pp. 49, 219.
109   'were bought, to': ibid., pp. 219, 279, 278, 208.
110   'Alan had telephoned her': see EB to Isaiah Berlin, 30 September 1938 (Isaiah Berlin archive, Bod).
110   'wants to meet you': EB to Virginia Woolf, January 1939 (Monk's House Papers, University of Sussex).
110   'the man with the Irish': Virginia Woolf to EB, 29 January 1939, *The Letters of Virginia Woolf*, ed. Nigel Nicolson and Joanna Trautmann (London: Hogarth Press, 1975–1980).
110   'Virginia's exquisitely, delicately': O'Faolain, 'A Reading and Remembrance'.
110   'lay-abed, passion-sated': O'Faolain, *Vive Moi!*, p. 310.
111   'In a 1940 account': see O'Faolain, *An Irish Journey* (London: Longmans & Co, 1940).
111   'Tradition has been broken': O'Faolain, 'Irish Blackout', *Manchester Guardian*, October 1939, in Wills, *That Neutral Island*, p. 80.
111   'in the heart of the': EB, 'Summer Night', *Collected Stories* (London: Vintage, 1999).
112   'that was at least aware': O'Faolain to EB, 22 April 1937 (EB HRC).

112   'one's own point': EB, 'The Big House', *The Bell*, October 1940.
112   'when the best restaurant': Virginia Woolf, diary, 6 May 1934, *The Diary of Virginia Woolf* , ed. Anne Olivier Bell and Andrew McNeillie (London: Hogarth Press, 1977–1984).
113   'gargantuan stories': EB, *The Shelbourne* (London: Vintage, 2001), ch. 7.
113   'a happy lunch': O'Faolain, *Vive Moi!*, p. 310.
113   'I was able': EB, report, 9 November 1940 (*Notes on Eire*).
114   'expressed complete surprise': see Patricia Craig, *Elizabeth Bowen* (Harmondsworth: Penguin, 1986), p. 101.
114   'the very thought': O'Faolain, *Vive Moi!*, p. 311.
114   'She is an Irishwoman': O'Faolain, *The Vanishing Hero, Studies in the Novelists of the Twenties* (London: Eyre & Spottiswoode, 1956), p. 170.
114   'Come Back to Erin': EB, review of *Come Back to Erin* by Seán O'Faolain, *The Bell*, December 1940.
115   'To be here': EB to Virginia Woolf, 5 January 1941 (*The Mulberry Tree*).

7: 'How we shall survive this I don't know'

116   'This morning at 8am': HS to PdeM, Monday 17, otherwise undated (HS PdeM).
117   'My darling': HS to PdeM, undated (HS PdeM).
117   'The Azores would have been': PdeM to HS, 11 October 1940 (HS PdeM).
117   'If England fights': PdeM, 'Bruchstücke aus dem Prolog zu dem unvollendeten Buch "Den ganzen Weg zurück. Aufzeichnungen aus Deutschland 1945–1949"', in Bernt Engelmann (ed.), *Eine Pen-Documentation, Literatur des Exils* (München: Goldmann Wilhelm, 1981).
117   'it would have seemed like': HS, *DaB*, p. 123.
117   'I have not much faith': HS to PdeM, undated (HS PdeM).
118   'We must': PdeM to HS, undated (PdeM Mon).
118   'I know that England': HS to PdeM, undated (HS PdeM).
118   'wherever you are': PdeM to HS, 22 October 1940 (HS PdeM).
119   'the only person': HS to PdeM, undated (HS PdeM).
119   'the Spiel faces': PdeM to HS, undated (HS PdeM).
119   'It happened to me': HS to PdeM, undated (HS PdeM).
120   'I cried about Benjamin': HS, 'Ein anderer Stern', in *Der Mann mit der Pelerine und andere Geschichten* (West Germany: Gustav Lübbe Verlag, 1985).
120   'only once or twice': HS, diary, 3 December 1940 (HS NLV).
120   'The Greeks are driving': Virginia Woolf, diary, 8 December 1940, *The Diary of Virginia Woolf* , ed. Anne Olivier Bell and Andrew McNeillie (London: Hogarth Press, 1977–1984).
121   'Paris is so young': Harold Nicolson, diary, 25 December 1940, *Diaries and Letters 1939–45*, ed. Nigel Nicolson (London: Collins, 1967).
122   'the still smouldering ashes': Cecil Beaton, *Self-Portrait With Friends: The Selected Diaries of Cecil Beaton*, ed. Richard Buckle (London: Weidenfeld & Nicolson, 1979), p. 79.
122   'to see Chaplin's': HS, diary, 3 January 1941 (HS NLV).
122   'Milan is at once overwhelmed': HS, *Die Früchte des Wohlstands* (München: Nymphenburger, 1981), p. 19.
123   'an impertinence': HS, diary, 2 February 1942 (HS NLV).
123   'he is hit by the smell': HS, *Die Früchte des Wohlstands*, p. 198.
123   'the desolate ruins': Virginia Woolf , diary, 15 January 1941 (*The Diary of Virginia Woolf*).
123   'The firemen in particular': see Juliet Gardiner, *The Blitz: The British Under Attack* (London: HarperCollins 2011), p. 268.
123   'a new phase': 'A New Phase in the Air' by our air correspondent, *Spectator*, 24 January 1941.

124   'to intensify the effect': Hitler, in Gardiner, *The Blitz*, p. 267.

124   'far better than most of us': Winston Churchill, speech, 9 February 1941, *War Speeches, 1939–45*, compiled by Charles Eade (London: Cassell & Co, 1951–2).

124   'unless Germany can': Harold Nicolson, diary, 11 February 1941 (*Diaries and Letters*).

125   'the worst attack so far': HS, diary, 20 March 1941 (HS NLV).

125   'fairly over the country': in Gardiner, *The Blitz*, p. 331.

125   'Virginia Woolf had been taken': see Woolf, diary, 25 January 1915 (*The Diary of Virginia Woolf*).

125   'emporium of cakes': C. E. Pascoe, *London To-day: An Illustrated Handbook of the Season* (London: Sansom Low & Co, 1885).

125   'a piece of good old': HS, diary, 16 April 1941 (HS NLV).

126   'in a single night': see Gardiner, *The Blitz*, p. 341 and Gardiner, *Wartime: Britain 1939–1945* (London: Headline, 2005), p. 339.

127   'the real blitz': GG, Blitz notebook, April 1941 (reprinted in *Ways of Escape* (Harmondsworth: Penguin, 1982), ch. 4i).

129   'one's first corpse': GG to Marion Greene, 18 April 1941, in Richard Greene, *Graham Greene: A Life in Letters* (London: Little, Brown, 2007).

129   'I've been leading a chequered': GG to Anthony Powell, 6 December 1940 (*A Life in Letters*).

129   'for someone like me': GG to Mary Pritchett, 18 March 1941 (*A Life in Letters*).

130   'Do you ever *really*': VG to GG, 4 April 1941 (VG Bod).

130   'dreadfully bewildered': VG to GG, undated (VG Bod).

130   'bandied about among strangers': GG to VG, undated (VG Bod).

130   'She has the thin end': GG to Mary Pritchett, 18 March 1941 (*A Life in Letters*).

131   'very young and not at all': Goronwy Rees to Dig Yorke, in Jenny Rees, *Looking for Mr Nobody: The Secret Life of Goronwy Rees* (London: Phoenix Giant, 1997), p. 114.

131   'suffer *one single*': Rosamond Lehmann to Dadie Rylands, 7 February 1941, in Selina Hastings, *Rosamond Lehmann* (London: Vintage, 2003), p. 214.

131   'rejected and isolated': Rosamond Lehmann, interview in ibid., p. 213.

131   'his rota of ridiculously': ibid., p. 215.

132   'your perfect goodness': Rosamond Lehmann to HY, 19 June 1943, in ibid., p. 215.

132   'One writes for about': HY to Rosamond Lehmann, 21 June 1943 (RL KC).

132   'an eccentric, fire-fighting': Rosamond Lehmann, 'An Absolute Gift', *Times Literary Supplement*, 6 August 1954.

133   'these times are an absolute': HY to Rosamond Lehmann, 14 March 1945 (RL KC).

133   'slipping his identity': Rosamond Lehmann, *The Echoing Grove* (London: Collins, 1953), p. 14.

134   'old, stuffy, solid place': HS, diary, 18 April 1941 (HS NLV).

134   'wave of defeatism': Harold Nicolson, diary, 21 April 1941(*Diaries and Letters*).

135   'This war is going to': HS, diary, 23 April 1941 (HS NLV).

135   'very sad war news': HS, diary, 27 April 1941 (HS NLV).

135   'not only reassured': Churchill, speech, 10 December 1942 (*War Speeches*).

8: 'So much else is on the way to be lost'

136   'this time she believed she would not': for a discussion of Woolf's suicide see Hermione Lee, *Virginia Woolf* (London: Chatto & Windus, 1996), pp. 757–67.

136   'a great deal of': EB to Leonard Woolf, 8 April 1941, *The Mulberry Tree: Writings of Elizabeth Bowen*, ed. Hermione Lee (London: Vintage, 1999).

137   'debating suicide during': see Virginia Woolf, diary, 7 June 1940, *The Diary of Virginia Woolf*, ed. Anne Olivier Bell and Andrew McNeillie (London: Hogarth Press, 1977–1984).

137 'personal charm': RM, obituary for Virginia Woolf, *Spectator*, 11 April 1941.
137 'a wretched way': RM to Sylvia Lynd, 23 April 1941, in Sarah LeFanu, *Rose Macaulay* (London: Virago, 2003), p. 231.
138 'continual, disturbing, restless': RM, *What Not: A Prophetic Comedy* (London: Constable and Company, 1918), p. 157.
139 'muddy red of a stained': Gerald O'Donovan, *Father Ralph* (London: Macmillan, 1913), p. 316.
139 'gay, young and enthusiastic': Beryl O'Donovan in LeFanu, *Rose Macaulay*, p. 132.
139 'considerably older': Beryl O'Donovan in ibid., p. 131.
140 'his manners were bad': RM, *What Not*, pp. 24, 7, 82.
140 'so departmental': ibid., pp. 113, 114-15.
141 'decidedly entertaining': ibid., pp. 7, 121, 127.
141 'negligent, foppish': RM, *Told by an Idiot* (London: Collins, 1965), part 1, ch. 4, part 2, ch. 2.
142 'beastly half-way house': RM, *What Not*, pp. 149-53.
142 'The fact remained': ibid., pp. 157, 180.
143 'I'm not going to take you': RM, *Told by an Idiot*, part 2, ch. 3, part 2, ch. 4.
143 'caught into a deep': ibid., part 2, ch. 4, part 2, ch. 5.
144 'his real work': RM to Rosamond Lehmann, 20 August 1942 (RL KC).
144 'weak to think of him': Gerald O'Donovan, *The Holy Tree* (London: William Heinemann, 1922), pp. 145, 152, 161, 163-4.
145 'Beloved, gaze in thine': W. B. Yeats, 'The Holy Tree', *Collected Poems* (London: Vintage, 2009).
145 'the like of which': O'Donovan, *The Holy Tree*, pp. 171, 203, 225-6.
145 'two stunted souls': ibid., pp. 287, 299, 314.
146 'a faint weariness': RM, *Told by an Idiot*, part 2, ch. 13.
146 'the best kept secret': Victor Gollancz, *Reminiscences of Affection* (London: Victor Gollancz, 1968), p. 83.
146 'at immediate impact': Anthony Powell, 'The Pleasures of Knowing Rose Macaulay', in Constance Babington Smith, *Rose Macaulay: A Biography* (London: Collins, 1972).
146 'the clearest case of sexual': Storm Jameson, in Jennifer Birkett, *Storm Jameson: A Life* (Oxford: Oxford University Press, 2009), p. 75.
146 'felt anyone so utterly': Virginia Woolf to Vanessa Bell, 25 May 1928, *The Letters of Virginia Woolf*, ed. Nigel Nicolson and Joanna Trautmann (London: Hogarth Press, 1975-1980).
147 'There *are* other things': RM, *Dangerous Ages* (London: Collins, 1921), chs 3viii, 13iii.
147 'is the important part': RM to Jean Macaulay, 14 April 1927 (RM TC).
147 'It is stupid': RM, in Alan Pryce-Jones, 'The Pleasures of Knowing Rose Macaulay', 1959 (in Constance Babington Smith, *Rose Macaulay*).
148 'While you hold me': RM, *Told by an Idiot*, part 2, ch. 3.
148 'her limbs and every': O'Donovan, *The Holy Tree*, p. 161.
148 'the longer I live': RM, *And No Man's Wit* (London: Collins, 1940), p. 272.
148 'amphibious days': RM, *What Not*, p. 183.
148 'lapped in the clear': RM, 'Bathing', *Personal Pleasures* (London: Victor Gollancz, 1935).
148 'To swim out agin': O'Donovan, *The Holy Tree*, p. 24.
149 'if one is so fortunate': RM, 'In Deep and Shallow Waters', *The Listener*, 30 January 1936.
149 '507 aircraft': see Neil Wallington, *Firemen at War* (Newton Abbot: David & Charles, 1981), p. 172.
150 'at 4 a.m. the fire brigade': see Westminster, SMBC file 584.
151 'it got first an HE': RM to Storm Jameson, in Jameson, *Journey from the North* (London: Vintage, 1984), vol. 2, p. 112.
151 'House no more': RM to Daniel George, 12 May 1941 (RM TC).

151 'Luxborough Towers have fallen': RM to Victor Gollancz, 18 May 1941, in Gollancz, *Reminiscences of Affection*, p. 78.

152 'all my lovely seventeenth': RM to Storm Jameson, in Jameson, *Journey to the North*, vol. 2, p. 112.

153 'a superb and monstrous': RM, *Milton* (London: Duckworth, 1934), p. 10.

153 'I wish one of his wives': RM to Helen Waddell, 1 November 1932 (RM TC).

154 'my darling Dictionary': RM to Victor and Ruth Gollancz, 28 May 1941 (RM TC).

154 'the only objects to survive': see Jameson, *Journey from the North*, vol. 2, p. 112.

155 'very very charming': HS, diary, 5 September 1941 (HS NLV).

155 'I am an Englishman': Peter de Mendelssohn, 'Writers without Language', PEN, *Writers in Freedom: A Symposium based on the 17th International Congress of the PEN*, ed. Hermon Ould (London: Hutchinson & Co, 1942).

156 'You're very tired': Storm Jameson, *Journey to the North*, vol. 2, p. 113.

156 'It happened to me': RM, 'Losing One's Books', *Spectator*, 7 November 1941.

9: 'You are the ultimate of something'

161 'We are puzzled': Harold Nicolson, diary, 17 June 1941, *Diaries and Letters 1939–45*, ed. Nigel Nicolson (London: Collins, 1967).

161 'a monster of wickedness': Winston Churchill, speech, 22 June 1941, *War Speeches, 1939–45*, compiled by Charles Eade, 3 vols (London: Cassell & Co, 1951–2).

161 'War moved from the': EB, *HoD*, ch. 5.

162 'The pay is very good': GG to Marion Greene, 20 August 1941, Richard Greene, *Graham Greene, A Life in Letters* (London: Little, Brown, 2007).

162 'he had been taught': GG to John Betjeman, 18 October 1941 (*A Life in Letters*).

162 'Everyone has a sort of false': HS, diary, July 1941 (HS NLV).

162 'Beloved, I can't believe': EB to CR, 17 January 1945 (*LCW*).

163 'She says it began': CR, diary, 2 September 1941 (*LCW*).

163 'well-dressed middle-aged': CR, diary, 10 February 1941 (*LCW*).

164 'Wartime London': CR, introduction to *The Siren Years: Undiplomatic Diaries 1937–1945* (London: Macmillan, 1974).

164 'symptoms of sexual happiness': CR, diary, 12 January 1941 (*The Siren Years*).

164 'present hectic life': CR, diary, 29 March 1941 (*The Siren Years*).

164 'looking back on': CR, diary, 21 May 1941 (*The Siren Years*).

164 'some woman's name': CR, diary, 30 May 1941 (*The Siren Years*).

164 'We go from one': CR, diary, 4 July 1941 (*The Siren Years*).

165 'It was not that she': EB, draft typescript of *The Heat of the Day* (EB HRC).

166 'As we walked together': CR, diary,29 September 1941 (*The Siren Years*).

166 'great globular roses': EB, *HoD*, ch. 1.

167 'A particular gentle': EB to CR, 13 January 1950 (*LCW*).

167 'Charles recalled': CR, diary, 24 February 1961 (*LCW*).

167 'More, it was a sort of': EB, *HoD*, ch. 5.

168 'My fancy turns': CR, diary, 10 May 1942 (*LCW*).

168 'I and my friends all': EB, 'Pictures and Conversations', *The Mulberry Tree: Writings of Elizabeth Bowen*, ed. Hermione Lee (London: Vintage, 1999).

169 'Do you realise how': EB to Alan Cameron, 1923 (*The Mulberry Tree*).

169 'Why Elizabeth': Humphry House to EB, 23 July 1934 (private collection).

169 'temperament and tastes': Peter Quennell, *Customs and Characters, Contemporary Portraits* (London: Weidenfeld & Nicolson, 1982), p. 88.

169 'He was quite stout': May Sarton, *A World of Light* (New York: Norton, 1988), p. 192.

170 'I believe his love': EB, *B's C*, p. 174.

170 'War makes us more': EB, 'The Christmas Toast is "Home"', *People, Places, Things: Essays by Elizabeth Bowen*, ed. Allan Hepburn (Edinburgh: Edinburgh University Press, 2008).

170   'Alan was like a character': see CR, diary, 19 September 1942 (*LCW*).
171   'to atmosphere': Sarton, *A World of Light*, p. 197.
171   'overwhelming love': EB to Humphry House, 18 May 1935 (private collection).
171   'a middle-class complaint': CR, diary, 22 October 1941 (*The Siren Years*).
171   'engage in extramarital': Sarton, *A World of Light*, p. 213.
171   'Vacuum as to future': EB, *HoD*, ch. 5.
171   'campers in rooms': ibid.
172   'The extraordinary time': EB, draft typescript of *The Heat of the Day* (EB HRC).
172   'to protract itself': EB, publisher's blurb for *The Heat of the Day* (EB HRC).
172   'a' within': CR, diary, 1 June 1941 (*The Siren Years*).
172   'Would I ever have': CR, diary, 2 September 1941 (*LCW*).
172   'his youthfulness': EB, *HoD*, ch. 5.
173   'the tree-lined': see CR, diary, 27 October 1941 (*The Siren Years*).
173   'The capacity for': CR, diary, 10 November 1941 (*The Siren Years*).
173   'Old men in clubs': CR, diary, 1 October 1941 (*The Siren Years*).
174   'The picture is that': CR, diary, 7 December 1941 (*The Siren Years*).
174   'crowded and dead': Evelyn Waugh, diary, December 1941, *The Diaries of Evelyn Waugh*, ed. Michael Davie (London: Phoenix, 2009).
174   'it felt odd': GG, diary, 3 January 1942, in Norman Sherry, *The Life of Graham Greene* (London: Pimlico, 2004–5), vol. 2, p. 98.
174   'Operation Menace': see Martin Gilbert, *Second World War* (London: Fontana, 1990), p. 127.
175   'Dakar has set us': RM to Jean Macaulay, 29 September 1940 (RM TC).
175   'Henry Yorke no doubt': Evelyn Waugh, diary, 19 October 1940 (*The Diaries of Evelyn Waugh*).
175   'Nothing that I ever wrote': GG to Elisabeth Greene, 2 June 1942, in Sherry, *The Life of Graham Greene*, vol. 2, p. 114.
175   'Ambitiously, Greene wondered': see ibid., p. 120.
175   'I suppose': GG, *A Sort of Life: An Autobiography* (Bath: Chivers, 1981), ch. 7iii.
176   'he and his brother': see GG, *A World of my Own: A Dream Diary* (London: Penguin, 1993), p. 24.
176   'Lying awake at night': see GG, preface to *The Ministry of Fear*, collected edition (London: William Heinemann, 1973).
176   'broken glass': see GG, *The Ministry of Fear*, ch. 1i.
176   'After being the centre': CR, diary, 4 December 1941 (*The Siren Years*).
176   'I should hate to lose her friendship': CR, diary, 21 December 1941 (*LCW*).
176   'E is sad': CR, diary, 11 January 1942 (*LCW*).
176   'A little indifference': CR, diary, 21 April 1942 (*LCW*).
177   'I told her': CR, diary, 9 April 1942 (*LCW*).
177   'desolating': CR, diary, 21 April 1942 (*LCW*).
177   'broken her fairytale': EB, 'Summer Night', *Collected Stories* (London: Vintage, 1999).
177   'She holds me by': CR, diary, 29 September 1941 (*LCW*).
177   'One of the luxuries': CR, diary, 24 May 1942 (*LCW*).
177   'I am in love with E': CR, diary, 25 May 1942 (*LCW*).
177   'Of what is her magic': CR, diary, 2 June 1942 (*The Siren Years*).
177   'more and more of her': ibid.
178   'It's not too easy': RM to Jean Smith, 25 February 1942, in *Dearest Jean: Rose Macaulay's Letters to a Cousin*, ed. Martin Ferguson Smith (Manchester: Manchester University Press, 2011).
178   'cut in two': RM, 'Miss Anstruther's Letters', in Constance Babington Smith, *Rose Macaulay: A Biography* (London: Collins, 1972).
179   'Is there anything to be said': RM, 'A Spectator's Notebook', June 1942 (unpublished, in RM TC).
180   'he didn't linger': RM to Rosamond Lehmann, 20 August 1942 (RL KC).

181   'in parts brilliant': RM obituary for Gerald O'Donovan, *The Times*, 10 August 1942.

181   'I always talked': RM to Hamilton Johnson, 16 April 1951, in *Letters to a Friend 1950–1952*, ed. Constance Babington Smith (London: Collins, 1961).

181   'Her want of Maurice': RM, *WMW*, ch. 3.

181   'And now the joy': RM, *ToT*, ch. 25.

182   'how long we should': ibid., ch. 16.

182   'really she bored him': ibid., ch. 25.

183   'Marjorie Grant Cook': see Babington Smith, *Rose Macaulay*, p. 105.

183   'some men and women': RM, 'People who Should Not Marry', in ibid., p. 106.

183   'to be with the beloved': RM, 'Problems of Married Life', *A Casual Commentary* (London: Methuen, 1925).

183   'How does one know': 'Inquiry into the Sanctity of the Home', in ibid.

183   'a fetter on what shouldn't': RM, *Dangerous Ages* (London: Collins, 1921), ch. 10ii.

183   'a handicap': RM, *Potterism: A Tragi-farcical Tract* (London: Collins, 1920), part 6, ch. 2i.

184   'a good one': RM to Sylvia Lynd, 30 July 1942, in Sarah LeFanu, *Rose Macaulay* (London: Virago, 2003), p. 237.

184   'Oh why was there': RM to Hamilton Johnson, 16 April 1951 (*Letters to a Friend*).

10: *'Can pain and danger exist?'*

185   'a painful series': Winston Churchill, speech, 23 April 1942, *War Speeches, 1939–45*, compiled by Charles Eade (London: Cassell & Co, 1951–2).

185   'Even Hitler makes': Churchill, speech, 10 May 1942 (*War Speeches*).

186   'We shall go out to bomb': in Juliet Gardiner, *Wartime: Britain 1939–1945* (London: Headline, 2005), p. 613.

186   'a breathless glory': EB, *HoD*, ch. 9.

186   'the light': EB, *B's C*, p. 248.

187   'Only the wireless': afterword to *B's C*, p. 457.

188   'Harold Nicolson reflected': see Harold Nicolson, diary, 22 July 1942, *Diaries and Letters 1939–45*, ed. Nigel Nicolson (London: Collins, 1967).

188   'a greater degree of cut-offness': EB, report, 31 July 1942, *Notes on Eire, Espionage Reports to Winston Churchill, 1940–2*, Aubane Historical Society, ed. Jack Lane and Brendan Clifford, 3rd edn.

188   'Irish newspapers and radio stations': see Clair Wills, *That Neutral Island* (London: Faber, 2008), p. 274.

189   'Eire feels as strongly': EB, 'Eire', *New Statesman and Nation*, 12 April 1941.

189   'an ocean of indifference': Hubert Butler, 'The Barriers', *The Bell*, July 1941.

189   'not in the true': James Dillon, in Wills, *That Neutral Island*, p. 130.

190   'no responsibility': Éamon de Valera, in ibid., p. 131.

190   'if, in some awful': James Dillon, in Maurice Manning, *James Dillon: A Biography* (Dublin: Wolfhound Press, 1999), p. 173.

190   'even I distrust': EB, report, 9 November 1940 (*Notes on Eire*).

190   'Mr Dillon's uncompromising': EB, report, 9 February 1942 (*Notes on Eire*).

190   'an almost neurotic': EB, report, 20 February 1942 (*Notes on Eire*).

191   'dishonesty, of turning': EB, report, 31 July 1942 (*Notes on Eire*).

191   'stop thinking of': Cyril Connolly, editorial, *Horizon*, January 1942.

191   'fearless lights': EB, *HoD*, ch. 9.

191   'queer feeling of': Sean O'Faolain, in Wills, *That Neutral Island*, p. 277.

192   'general impression of': EB, report, 20 February 1942 (*Notes on Eire*).

192   'live and act in the': O'Faolain, editorial, *The Bell*, July 1942.

192   'small but very vocal': O'Faolain, editorial, *The Bell*, November 1942.

193   'minor errors': D. A. Binchy, review of *Bowen's Court*, *The Bell*, August 1942.

193   'in whose shadow': EB, 'Sunday Afternoon', *Collected Stories* (London: Vintage, 1999).

194   'could do untold good': EB, report, 12 July 1942 (*Notes on Eire*).

194   'aristocrat's capacity': The Bellman, interview with Elizabeth Bowen, *The Bell*, September 1942.
196   'the timidity of an intruder': EB, *HoD*, ch. 10.
196   'somehow less remarkable': CR, diary, 15 August 1942 (*LCW*).
196   'Spent the day with': CR, diary, 14 September 1942 (*The Siren Years*).
196   'It is like their deciding': Stephen Spender to T. S. Eliot, 30 August 1943 (Spender archive, Bod).
196   'It would be true to say': Stephen Spender, journal, 28 December 1942, *New Selected Journals*, ed. Lara Feigel and John Sutherland (London: Faber, 2012).
197   'a childish-looking uniformity': Spender, *World Within World* (New York: Modern Library Classics, 2001), p. 293.
197   'I sit in my swivel': HY, 21 July 1942, in Jeremy Treglown, *Romancing: The Life and Work of Henry Green* (London: Faber, 2000), p. 154.
197   'Yorke had processed orders': see HY to Rosamond Lehmann, 21 June 1943 (RL KC).
197   'if life in a fire station': HG, 'The Lull', *Surviving: The Uncollected Writings of Henry Green* (London: Harvill, 1993).
198   'I have been thinking over': HY to John Lehmann, 18 November 1942 (John Lehmann archive, HRC).
198   'he could not leave': HG, *Caught* (London: Harvill Press, 2001), p. 30.
198   'he could not, this time': HG, draft typescript of *Caught* (HY archive).
199   'There is a great advantage': Churchill, speech, 11 November 1942 (*War Speeches*).
199   'noble Desert Army': ibid.
199   'Montgomery's through': EB, *HoD*, ch. 9.
199   'the best work you have': HY to Evelyn Waugh, 24 December 1942 (Evelyn Waugh archive, HRC).

11: *'Only at night I cry'*

200   '1942, still with no': EB, *HoD*, ch. 17.
201   'First made me': HS, diary, 18 January 1943 (HS NLV).
201   'beastly Luftwaffe': HS, diary, 21 January 1943 (HS NLV).
201   'tiny, perfect, absolutely': HS, diary, 12 February 1943 (HS NLV).
202   'breaking down only': HS, diary, 10 February 1943 (HS NLV).
202   'in a way': HS, diary, 13 February 1943 (HS NLV).
202   'glad to be alive': HS, diary, 15 February 1943 (HS NLV).
202   'nervous breakdown': HS, diary, 17 February 1943 (HS NLV).
202   'Very charming': HS, diary, 22 February 1943 (HS NLV).
202   'Scenes from Dante's': HS, *DaB*, p. 133.
202   'the goodwill': ibid., p. 134
203   'Peter was informed': see HS, diary, 3 December 1942 (HS NLV).
203   'The vision of home': HS, 'Psychologie des Exils', *Kleine Schritte: Berichte und Geschichten* (München: Heinrich Ellermann, 1976).
203   'The memories of home': see HS, *DaB*, p. 132.
204   'I was so pleased': HS, diary, 27 March 1943 (HS NLV).
204   'the community of readers': see HS, *DaB*, p. 128.
206   'Then why did you hit me?': HS, *Die Früchte des Wohlstands* (München: Nymphenburger, 1981), p. 243.
206   'the older woman took it': HS, *DaB*, p. 98.
206   'I should have thought': HS to PdeM, 30 April 1943 (HS PdeM).
207   'The vision of my beloved': HS to PdeM, 3 May 1943 (HS PdeM).
207   'war's being global': EB, *HoD*, ch. 17.
209   'refreshed (not quite as': HY to Matthew Smith, 25 February 1943 (private collection).
210   'the most beautiful English girl': Ruthven Todd, in Jon Stallworthy, *Louis MacNeice* (London: Faber, 1995), p. 238.

210   'Too large in': Louis MacNeice, 'The Kingdom', c.1943, *Collected Poems* (London: Faber, 2003).

210   'in the centre': Louis MacNeice to Mary Keene, undated (private collection).

211   'Lying in bed': Terry Southern interview with HY, 'The Art of Fiction', 1958, *Surviving: The Uncollected Writings of Henry Green* (London: Harvill, 1993).

211   'above her lovely head': HG, *Loving* (London: Vintage, 2000), pp. 2, 8, 17, 64.

211   'her great eyes': ibid., pp. 123, 52, 95, 141.

212   'I'd sell it': ibid., pp. 110, 63, 126, 142, 145.

212   'Mary Keene': for biographical details about Mary Keene and Matthew Smith see Alice Keene, *The Two Mr Smiths: The Life and Work of Matthew Smith* (London: Lund Humphries, 1995).

214   'You know of course': Matthew Smith to Ida Hughes Stanton, in ibid., p. 68.

214   'I have been guessing': Mary Keene to HY, undated (private collection).

215   'I have a great hangover': Mary Keene to Matthew Smith, undated (private collection).

215   'Believe it or not': HY to Rosamond Lehmann, 21 June 1943 (RL KC).

12: 'Alas, what hate everywhere'

216   'As far as I can see': GG to Raymond Greene, 4 January 1943, in Richard Greene, *Graham Greene, A Life in Letters* (London: Little, Brown, 2007).

216   'Kim Philby': see Norman Sherry, *The Life of Graham Greene* (London: Pimlico, 2004–5), vol. 2, p. 130.

217   'I feel it was': GG to Marion Greene, 30 November 1942 (*A Life in Letters*).

217   'He arranged for Mass': see GG, *A Sort of Life: An Autobiography* (Bath: Chivers, 1981), ch. iii.

217   'I felt sick': GG to Marion Greene, 19 January 1943, in Sherry, *The Life of Graham Greene*, vol. 2, p. 154.

217   'not yet touched': GG to Raymond Greene, 4 January 1943 (*A Life in Letters*).

217   'after the North': Kim Philby, in Sherry, *The Life of Graham Greene*, vol. 2, p. 154.

218   'Doll wrote to me': GG to Hugh Greene, 1 August 1942 (*A Life in Letters*).

218   'French letters': see Sherry, *The Life of Graham Greene*, vol. 2, p. 138.

218   'things can be': GG to Elisabeth Greene, 15 October 1942 (*A Life in Letters*).

218   'Won't it be nice': VG to GG, 9 March 1942 (VG Bod).

218   'I don't altogether': VG to GG, 14 April 1942 (VG Bod).

219   'so VERY tired': VG to GG, 21 April 1942 (VG Bod).

219   'You are the best': GG to VG, 8 April 1943 (VG Bod).

219   'pity and responsibility': GG, *HoM*, book 1, part 1, chs 1iii, 2iv.

220   'One forgets the dead': ibid., book 3, part 2, ch. ii.

220   'been torpedoed': GG to VG, undated (VG Bod).

221   'Lisbon, with all': Malcolm Muggeridge, *Chronicles of Wasted Time*, vol. 2: *The Infernal Grove* (London: Collins, 1973), p. 136.

221   'a very thin': James Lees-Milne, diary, 20 January 1943, *Diaries, 1942–1954*, abridged and introduced by Michael Bloch (London: Hachette, 2011).

222   'entailed a good': RM to Hamilton Johnson, 16 April 1951, *Letters to a Friend 1950–1952*, ed. Constance Babington Smith (London: Collins, 1961).

222   'Open your eyes': RM, 'Lisbon day: London day' (RM TC).

222   'Pleasure in this': RM, 'A Happy Neutral', *Spectator*, 9 July 1943.

223   'We cannot doubt': Winston Churchill, speech, 8 June 1943, *War Speeches, 1939–45*, compiled by Charles Eade, 3 vols (London: Cassell & Co, 1951–2).

223   'best spirits': HS, diary, 9 September 1943 (HS NLV).

223   'If they shorten': HS, diary, 24 May 1943 (HS NLV).

223   'the Germans should': Churchill, speech, 14 July 1941 (*War Speeches*).

223   'The result was the bombing': see Gordon Corrigan, *The Second World War: A Military History* (London: Atlantic Books, 2010), pp. 444–52 and Richard Overy, *Why the Allies Won* (London: Pimlico, 2006), pp. 143–9.

224 'unqualified approval': see Juliet Gardiner, *Wartime: Britain 1939–1945* (London: Headline, 2005), p. 612.

225 'this horrible smashing': RM to Jean Smith, 4 July 1943, *Dearest Jean: Rose Macaulay's Letters to a Cousin*, ed. Martin Ferguson Smith (Manchester: Manchester University Press, 2011).

225 'At present I feel': RM to Jean Smith, 4 August 1943 (*Dearest Jean*).

225 'Heart not': RM to Jean Smith, 12 August 1943 (*Dearest Jean*).

225 'lunch with Graham Greene': see RM to Jean Smith, 17 September 1943 (*Dearest Jean*).

226 'both books received': see Jeremy Treglown, *Romancing: The Life and Work of Henry Green* (London: Faber, 2000), p. 163.

226 'too sour and bitter': Stephen Spender, in ibid., p. 148.

226 'Caught mirrored': John Lehmann, *I Am My Brother* (London: Longmans, 1960), p. 219.

226 'two proper novelists': Philip Toynbee, 'New Novels', *New Statesman and Nation*, 26 June 1943.

227 'Poor Rome': RM to Jean Smith, 17 September 1943 (*Dearest Jean*).

227 'Germany is standing': Stalin quoted by Churchill, speech, 24 August 1941 (*War Speeches*).

227 'Very confused': HY to Mary Keene, 11 October 1943 (private collection).

228 'miserable': Mary Keene to Matthew Smith, undated (private collection).

228 'quite dazzled': Mary Keene to Matthew Smith, undated (private collection).

228 'his great world': Mary Keene, *Mrs Donald* (London: Chatto & Windus, 1983), pp. 11–13.

229 'they stood eternally': ibid., pp. 16, 17.

229 'to love what': ibid., pp. 41, 53–5.

230 'Us at your age': ibid., pp. 56, 59.

230 'turning from her': ibid., pp. 85, 81.

231 'I know there is': HY to John Lehmann, 18 December 1943 (John Lehmann archive, HRC).

231 'would not make': Jack Marlowe, 'A Reader's Notebook', *Penguin New Writing*, April–May 1943 (issue actually published in December).

232 'My dear John': HY to John Lehmann, 29 December 1943 (John Lehmann archive, HRC).

232 'full of stories': HS, diary, 21 December 1943 (HS NLV).

232 'one of the loveliest': HS, diary, 8 January 1944 (HS NLV).

232 'I can't stand': HS, diary, 15 January 1944 (HS NLV).

233 'noisy night': RM to Jean Smith, 24 January 1944 (*Dearest Jean*).

233 'All this Rome': ibid.

233 'These contained a device': see William Sansom, *The Blitz: Westminster at War* (London: Faber, 2010), p. 176.

233 'the perverse vivacities': ibid., p. 178.

234 'still hear today': HS, *DaB*, p. 136.

234 'We had not expected': HS, diary, 26 February 1944 (HS NLV).

234 'in contrast to': Evelyn Waugh, diary, 2 March 1944, *The Diaries of Evelyn Waugh*, ed. Michael Davie (London: Phoenix, 2009).

234 'He reported to': see Evelyn Waugh to Laura Wade, 29 February 1944, *The Letters of Evelyn Waugh* (London: Phoenix, 2010).

235 'It felt difficult': HS, diary, 6 March 1944 (HS NLV).

235 'under the blankets': HG, *Pack My Bag* (London: Vintage, 2000), p. 33.

235 'women had men': HY to Mary Keene, 4 April 1944 (private collection).

236 'Darling. I'm so very': HY to Mary Keene, 15 May 1944 (private collection).

236 'sexual intercourse': Legal letter about the Keene divorce case, 14 February 1946 (private collection).

236 'the most compassionate': Rosamond Lehmann, 'An Absolute Gift', *Times Literary Supplement*, 6 August 1954.

13: 'Droning things, mindlessly making for you'

241   'D-Day has come': CR, diary, 6 June 1944, *The Siren Years: Undiplomatic Diaries 1937–1945* (London: Macmillan, 1974).

241   'D-Day!': HS, diary, 6 June 1944 (HS NLV).

241   'John Lehmann held': see Selina Hastings, *Rosamond Lehmann* (London: Vintage, 2003), p. 240.

241   'a memorable and glorious': Winston Churchill, speech, 6 and 8 June 1944, *War Speeches, 1939–45*, compiled by Charles Eade (London: Cassell & Co, 1951–2).

242   'stolid, cheerful': CR, diary, 16 June 1944 (*The Siren Years*).

242   'mysterious rocket-planes': Harold Nicolson, diary, 14 June 1944, *Diaries and Letters 1939–45*, ed. Nigel Nicolson (London: Collins, 1967).

243   'They fly slowly': Harold Nicolson, diary, 16 June 1944 (*Diaries and Letters*).

243   'droning *things*': EB, *HoD*, ch. 17.

243   'As we came out of': HS, *DaB*, p. 136.

244   'A clever, educated': HS, diary, 20 June 1944 (HS NLV).

244   'At the time O'Hea': see HS, diary, 10 February 1944 (HS NLV).

244   'Life is really absurd': HS, diary, 23 June 1944 (HS NLV).

244   'I was incredibly': HS, diary, 24 June 1944 (HS NLV).

244   'Peter and I': HS, diary, 23 July 1944 (HS NLV).

244   'he was confronted': see GG interview in Norman Sherry, *The Life of Graham Greene* (London: Pimlico, 2004–5), vol. 2, p. 184.

245   'one had thought': GG, diary, 22 June 1944 (GG HRC).

245   'I had to put on': ibid.

245   'they could hear a bomb': GG, diary, 23 June 1944 (GG HRC).

246   'We had only': GG, *EoA*, book 2, ch. 5.

246   'must surely have been': GG, diary, 23 June 1944 (GG HRC).

246   'Six down during': GG, diary, 27 June 1944 (GG HRC).

246   'An odd thing': ibid.

246   'Hugh is all right': GG, diary, 30 June 1944 (GG HRC).

246   'This was one of the worst': see Juliet Gardiner, *Wartime: Britain 1939–1945* (London: Headline, 2005), p. 643.

247   'the moment always': GG, diary, 22 June 1944 (GG HRC).

247   'A bad night': GG, diary, 3 July 1944 (GG HRC).

247   'a wonderful figure': Churchill, speech , 6 and 25 July 1944 (*War Speeches*).

247   'we are getting used': CR, diary, 13 July 1944 (*The Siren Years*).

248   'usually to be found': see Sherry, *The Life of Graham Greene*, vol. 2, p. 197.

248   'Nobody who has not': EB, autobiographical note, 1948 (EB HRC).

248   'tied up, sealed up': EB, 'Calico Windows', *People, Places, Things: Essays by Elizabeth Bowen*, ed. Allan Hepburn (Edinburgh: Edinburgh University Press, 2008).

248   'When we just': EB, 'Oh, Madam', *Collected Stories* (London: Vintage, 1999).

249   'I read his letter': EB, *B's C*, p. 440.

249   'Her nerves have': CR, diary, 20 July 1944 (*LCW*).

249   'a new novel': see CR, diary, 19 September 1942 (*LCW*).

249   'I like to think': CR, diary, 18 February 1944 (*LCW*).

250   'fairness, not quite': EB, *HoD*, ch. 5.

250   'How proud Charles': Rosamond Lehmann to EB, 14 February 1949 (EB HRC).

250   'a flash of promise': EB, *HoD*, ch. 5.

251   'high up in a monstrous': CR, diary, 12 August 1944 (*LCW*).

251   'calico stretched and tacked': EB, 'The Happy Autumn Fields' (*Collected Stories*).

252   'All my life': EB to Virginia Woolf, 5 January 1941, in *The Mulberry Tree: Writings of Elizabeth Bowen*, ed. Hermione Lee (London: Vintage, 1999).

252   'Churchill himself': see Churchill, speech, 6 and 25 July 1944 (*War Speeches*).

253   'The anxiety it causes': Harold Nicolson to Ben and Nigel Nicolson, 13 August 1944 (*Diaries and Letters*).

253   'Stephen Spender assured': see Stephen Spender to Christopher Isherwood, 17 August 1944 (Stephen Spender archive, Bod).

253   'Tonight the doodlers': PdeM to HS, undated (HS PdeM).

254   'absolutely brilliant': PdeM to HS, 22 August 1944 (HS PdeM).

254   'the news of Paris had really': see PdeM to HS, 23 August 1944 (HS PdeM).

254   'Isn't the war': PdeM to HS, 24 August 1944 (HS PdeM).

255   'I'll see you in the stove': 'The Horrors of Lublin', *The Times*, 12 August 1944.

255   'What an execrable': PdeM to HS, undated (HS PdeM).

256   'Harold Nicolson heard': see Harold Nicolson, diary, 4 September 1944 (*Diaries and Letters*).

256   'the ear-splitting': HS, *DaB*, p. 137.

256   'conceived among bombs': ibid.

257   'the heroic stand': Churchill, speech, 5 October 1944 (*War Speeches*).

257   'During and dangerous'. HS, diary, 1 December 1944 (HS NLV).

257   'You should comfort': PdeM to HS, 8 December 1944 (PdeM Mon).

257   'the backdrop for': CR, 3 January 1945 (*The Siren Years*).

258   'The baby doesn't': HS, diary, 15 December 1944 (HS NLV).

258   'We were all': HS, *DaB*, p. 137.

258   'so glad to be': EB to Susan Tweedsmuir, in Victoria Glendinning, *Elizabeth Bowen* (London: Phoenix paperbacks, 1993), p. 147.

258   'I wouldn't want to give': CR, diary, 19 December 1944 (*LCW*).

258   'I suppose I could have': CR, diary, 3 February 1945 (*The Siren Years*).

258   'We are so close': EB to CR, 17 January 1945 (*LCW*).

259   'E says she would': CR, 3 December 1944 (*LCW*).

259   'We rush, we storm': EB, 'The Art of Reserve' (*People, Places, Things*).

259   'She said she thought': CR, diary, 12 November 1942 (*LCW*).

259   'E has become': CR, diary, 6 February 1943 (*LCW*).

260   'it was impossible for him': see CR, diary, 27 February 1944 (*LCW*).

260   'Outside us neither': EB, *HoD*, ch. 10.

14: *'A collective intoxication of happiness'*

261   'Let us be of good': Winston Churchill, speech, 18 January 1945, *War Speeches, 1939–45*, compiled by Charles Eade (London: Cassell & Co, 1951–2).

261   'I feel the war': RM to David Ley, 14 February 1945 (RM TC).

262   'People were anxious': see William Sansom, *The Blitz: Westminster at War* (London: Faber, 2010), p. 199.

262   'a huge crash': GG, diary, 20 March 1945 (GG HRC).

262   'It really looks': GG to Marion Greene, in Norman Sherry, *The Life of Graham Greene* (London: Pimlico, 2004–5), vol. 2, p. 205.

262   'His captivating smile': Churchill, speech, 17 April 1945 (*War Speeches*).

262   'Early this morning': HS, diary, 13 April 1945 (HS NLV).

263   'Darling, darling, I'm': HY to Mary Keene, 15 February 1945 (private collection).

263   'I think about you': Mary Keene to Matthew Smith, undated (private collection).

263   'I don't take': Mary Keene to HY, undated (private collection).

263   'I fear they are': HY to Mary Keene, 26 February 1945 (private collection).

264   'Dearest dearest': Mary Keene to HY, undated (private collection).

264   'My dearest darling': Dig Yorke to Mary Keene, undated (private collection).

264   'My darling darling': HY to Mary Keene, 9 March 1945 (private collection).

265   'prepare a "scheme"': HY to Mary Keene, 10 March 1945 (private collection).

265   'slip in a bit': Mary Keene to HY, undated (private collection).

265   'There was a hole': Mary Keene to Alice Keene, undated (private collection).

265   'Loving had been': see HY to Mary Keene, 21 March 1945 (private collection).

265   'Your letters': HY to Rosamond Lehmann, 14 March 1945 (RL KC).

265   'Armies monotonously': Evelyn Waugh, diary, 13 April 1945, *The Diaries of Evelyn Waugh*, ed. Michael Davie (London: Phoenix, 2009).

266 'The war hurries': HS, diary, 28 April 1945 (HS NLV).
266 'Hitler reported dead!': HS, diary, 1 May 1945 (HS NLV).
266 'Now she told Charles': see EB to CR, March 1945, in Victoria Glendinning, *Elizabeth Bowen* (London: Phoenix paperbacks, 1993), p. 155.
266 'There was a breathless': EB to CR, March 1945, in ibid., p. 156.
267 'everyone wondering': EB to CR, 7–8 May 1945 (*LCW* and in ibid., p. 157).
267 'God bless you': Churchill, speech, 8 May 1945 (*War Speeches*).
268 'On a monster': EB to CR, 7–8 May 1945 (*LCW* and in Glendinning, *Elizabeth Bowen*, p. 157).
269 'Having watched the blitz': GG to Marion Greene, undated, in Sherry, *The Life of Graham Greene*, vol. 2, p. 207.
269 'LOVE AND HAPPY': GG to VG, in ibid., vol. 2, p. 206.
269 'huge leaping pyres': VG to GG, May 1945 (VG Bod).
269 'There was precious little': GG to Marion Greene, undated, in Sherry, *The Life of Graham Greene*, vol. 2, p. 207.
269 'It was very quiet': GG, *EoA*, book 3, ch. 5.
269 'just as completely': GG to VG, 3 June 1948 (VG Bod).
269 'it is a mistake': see GG, *HoM*, book 3, part 1, ch. 11.
270 'I felt a sort': VG, interview in Sherry, *The Life of Graham Greene*, vol. 2, p. 208.
270 'Never before or': HS, *DaB*, p. 138.
270 'each one staggered': EB to CR, 7–8 May 1945 (*LCW* and in Glendinning, *Elizabeth Bowen*, p. 157).
271 'I would not have': EB, autobiographical note, 1948 (EB HRC).
271 'deteriorating dead': EB to Cyril Connolly, in Glendinning, *Elizabeth Bowen*, p. 158.
271 'completely incarcerated': EB to William Plomer, 24 September 1945 (*LCW*).

15: 'The days were listless and a flop'

272 'slow motion': EB to CR, June 1945 (*LCW*).
272 'first entering the house': see ibid.
272 'really, focuses internally': EB to CR, 17 June 1945 (*LCW*).
273 'I look round and see': ibid.
273 'No more danger': HS, *DaB*, p. 138.
273 'He does it all': HS, diary, 19 April 1941 (HS NLV).
274 'I would have treated': HS, *DaB*, p. 140.
274 'Everything now is': HS, diary, 10 July 1945 (HS NLV).
274 'At odd moments': PdeM to HS, 22 June 1945 (PdeM Mon).
274 'This is the crowning': PdeM to HS, 8 July 1945 (HS PdeM).
275 'boiling in sweltering': PdeM to HS, 15 July 1945 (HS PdeM).
276 'My darling': HS to PdeM, 23 July 1945 (HS PdeM).
276 'I picked my way': Richard Dimbleby, in Juliet Gardiner, *Wartime: Britain 1939–1945* (London: Headline, 2005), p. 674.
277 'This is the crowning': PdeM to HS, 17 July 1945 (HS PdeM).
277 'I'm quite innocent': PdeM to HS, 21 July 1945 (PdeM Mon).
279 'the problems and pressures': *Let Us Face the Future*, in David Kynaston, *Austerity Britain*, p. 21.
279 'would have to fall back': Winston Churchill, speech, 5 June 1945 (*War Speeches*).
279 'His public appearances': see Kynaston, *Austerity Britain 1945–51* (London: Bloomsbury, 2008), p. 65.
279 'lost cause': EB to CR, 26 June 1945 (*LCW*).
279 'Reluctantly I shall': GG to Marion Greene, undated, in Norman Sherry, *The Life of Graham Greene* (London: Pimlico, 2004–5), vol. 2, p. 214.
279 'For once it feels good': PdeM to HS, 26 July 1945 (HS PdeM).
280 'Damn!': see Walter Allen, *As I Walked Down New Grub Street* (London: Heinemann, 1981), pp. 103–4.

280   'terrific psychic shock': EB to CR, 29 July 1945 (*LCW*).
281   'It is the people's': EB, 'Britain, 1940', *People, Places, Things: Essays by Elizabeth Bowen*, ed. Allan Hepburn (Edinburgh: Edinburgh University Press, 2008).
281   'large quantities': see CR, diary, 22 January 1941, *The Siren Years: Undiplomatic Diaries 1937–1945* (London: Macmillan, 1974).
281   'Let Cartiers and the Ritz': CR, diary, 17 December 1941 (*The Siren Years*).
282   'Another lot': EB to CR, 29 July 1945 (*LCW*).
282   'all about a man': HY to Rosamond Lehmann, 14 March 1945 (RL KC).
283   'crying, dear Rose': HG, *Back* (New York: The Viking Press, 1981), pp. 5, 50.
283   'an echo of his': ibid.
283   'Charley (he is called': Mary Keene, note in her copy of *Back* (private collection).
284   'entirely legitimate': *Manchester Guardian*, in Gardiner, *Wartime*, p. 681.
284   'as often miles': Evelyn Waugh, diary, 7 August 1945, *The Diaries of Evelyn Waugh*, ed. Michael Davie (London: Phoenix, 2009).
284   'further debasement': Juliet Gardiner, *Wartime*, p. 681.
284   'the newspapers': see Evelyn Waugh, diary, 9 August 1945 (*The Diaries of Evelyn Waugh*).
285   'This means the end': HS, *DaB*, p. 141.
286   'I was genuinely': HS to PdeM, 16 August 1945 (HS PdeM).
286   'My sweet, I was glad': PdeM to HS, 9 August 1945 (PdeM Mon).
287   'most cordial': HS, diary, 12 February 1945 (HS NLV).
287   'About the christening': PdeM to HS, 21 July 1945 (PdeM Mon).
288   'Is it possible': PdeM to HS, 23 August 1945 (HS PdeM).
288   'You know how I': EB to CR, 24 August 1945 (*LCW*).

16: 'The magic Irish light and the soft air'

294   'arrived by boat': see EB, *The Shelbourne* (London: Vintage, 2001), ch. 7.
294   'It is impossible': EB, 'Ireland makes Irish', *People, Places, Things: Essays by Elizabeth Bowen*, ed. Allan Hepburn (Edinburgh: Edinburgh University Press, 2008).
294   'belong to a class': EB to CR, 29 July 1945 (*LCW*).
295   'Quite illicitly': EB to CR, 24 August 1945 (*LCW*).
295   'the action of Mr': Winston Churchill, 13 May 1945, *War Speeches, 1939–45*, compiled by Charles Eade (London: Cassell & Co, 1951–2).
295   'but acting justly': Éamon de Valera, speech, 16 May 1945, *Speeches and Statements by Éamon de Valera 1917–73*, ed. Maurice Moynihan (Dublin: Gill and Macmillan, 1980).
296   'The sense of profusion': EB to CR, 2 September 1945 (*LCW*).
296   'The food in all': EB to CR, 9 September 1945 (*LCW*).
296   'This house': EB to CR, 24 August 1945 (*LCW*).
297   'It is a drowsy': ibid.
297   'I can't dis-obsess': ibid.
297   'Like when one's': EB to CR, 2 September 1945 (*LCW*).
297   'I really was': EB to CR, 9 September 1945 (*LCW*).
298   'To one person': EB to CR, 2 September 1945 (*LCW*).
298   'The hour – day': ibid.
299   'I have felt': EB to CR, 17 September 1945 (*LCW*).
299   'It wakes me up': ibid.
299   'fors and againsts': ibid.
299   'War brutalised': ibid.
299   'I don't think of E': CR, diary, 17 September 1945(*LCW*).
300   'I came over here': EB to William Plomer, 24 September 1945, *The Mulberry Tree: Writings of Elizabeth Bowen*, ed. Hermione Lee (London: Vintage, 1999).
301   'cigarette famine': EB to CR, 14 October 1945 (*LCW*).
301   'The rooks subsided': EB, afterword to *B's C*, p. 449.

301   'Yes, I have been': EB to CR, 12 November 1945 (*LCW*).
302   'I see now': CR, diary, 23 February 1946 (*LCW*).
302   'Yes, certainly': EB to CR, 26 February 1946 (*LCW*).
302   'That they should': EB to CR, 6 March 1946 (*LCW*).
302   'ramping round': ibid.
303   'Anthony Powell and': see Jeremy Treglown, *Romancing: The Life and Work of Henry Green* (London: Faber, 2000), pp. 196–7.
303   'You see, with a cat': see Jenny Rees, *Looking for Mr Nobody: The Secret Life of Goronwy Rees* (London: Phoenix Giant, 1997), p. 120.
303   'much bigger brain': Mark Wyndham, in ibid., p. 150.
304   'rapid heart action': CR, diary, 7 April 1946 (*LCW*).
304   'why shouldn't one': EB to CR, 20 May 1946 (*LCW*).
304   'bent head and the': CR, diary, 21 August 1946 (*LCW*).
305   'forging, with every': EB to CR, 6 November 1946 (*LCW*).
305   'a feeling of loss': EB to CR, 18 November 1946 (*LCW*).
305   'We are confronted': EB, review of Rose Macaulay, *They Went to Portugal*, *Tatler*, 23 October 1946.
306   'Henry Green is': EB, review of Henry Green, *Back*, *Tatler*, 27 November 1946.
306   'feeling dead tired': EB to CR, 23 November 1946 (*LCW*).
306   'all lopsided': EB to CR, 12 December 1946 (*LCW*).
306   'huddled over': CR, diary, 20 February 1947 (*LCW*).
306   'returning to the city': see CR, diary, 20 January 1947, *Diplomatic Passport: More Undiplomatic Diaries 1946–1962* (Toronto: Macmillan, 1981).
306   'Is it another': CR, diary, 2 April 1947 (*LCW*).
307   'The trouble is': CR, diary, 9 September 1947 (*LCW*).
307   'Your letter came': EB to CR, 26 October 1947 (*LCW*).
307   'Your beloved letter': EB to CR, 28 November 1947 (*LCW*).
307   'Every time I': EB to CR, 6 December 1947 (*LCW*).
307   'Any novel I': EB to CR, March 1945 (*LCW*).
308   'most cryptic': EB to CR, 20 May 1946 (*LCW*).
308   'If that is so': EB to CR, 6 December 1947 (*LCW*).
309   'What bothers me': Rosamond Lehmann to EB, 4 March 1949 (EB HRC).
309   'Selfishly speaking': EB to William Plomer, 24 September 1945 (*The Mulberry Tree*).
309   'new commonness': W. B. Yeats, 'In the Seven Woods', 1902, *Collected Poems* (London: Vintage, 2009).
309   'What's equality?': W. B. Yeats, third 'Marching Song', *Spectator*, 23 February 1934.
310   'the sort now growing': W. B. Yeats, 'Under Ben Bulben', 1938 (*Collected Poems*).
310   'like I daresay': Francis Stewart, in Clair Wills, *That Neutral Island* (London: Faber, 2008), pp. 370–1.
310   'the ideal of those': Francis Stuart, in ibid., p. 371.
310   'sold itself out': EB, *HoD*, ch. 15.
311   'All Right': EB to CR, 24 August 1945 (*LCW*).
311   'How extraordinarily': EB to CR, 17 June 1948 (*LCW*).
312   'with echoes, reflections': CR, diary, 18 August 1973 (*LCW*).
312   'against the beating': EB, *HoD*, ch. 15.
313   'somehow, some place': EB to CR, 6 December 1947 (*LCW*).

17: *'Flying, no, leaping, into the centre of the mainland'*

314   'a branch of jasmine': see HS, *DaB*, p. 138.
314   'she was inclined to agree': see HS to PdeM, 17 November 1945 (HS PdeM).
315   'Kingsley Martin's': HS, *DaB*, p. 143.
315   'I was flying': HS, *DaB*, p. 154.
315   'the last vestiges': HS, 'The Streets of Vineta' (English draft of *Return to Vienna*), 30 January (HS NLV).

315 'metallic morning sea': ibid.
315 'Humid ghostly atmosphere': HS, diary, 30 January 1946 (HS NLV).
315 'furious spirit': HS to PdeM, 1 February 1946 (HS PdeM).
316 'not seen a single': ibid.
316 'with an eye': HS, 'The Streets of Vineta', 31 January (HS NLV).
316 'barbaric ugliness': ibid.
316 'These bombs are not': ibid.
317 'Greene describes the': see GG, *The Third Man* (London: Vintage, 2001), ch. 1.
317 'In their Moscow': see Hella Pick, *Guilty Victim: Austria from the Holocaust to Haider* (London: Tauris, 2000), p. 17.
318 'Nine months after': HS, *Return to Vienna*, trans. Christine Shuttleworth (Riverside, California: Ariadne Press, 2011), 8 February.
318 'the spiders which': HS, 'The Streets of Vineta', 31 January.
318 'Darling this is the most': HS to PdeM, 2 February 1946 (HS PdeM).
319 'This is still the most': HS to PdeM, 4 February 1946 (HS PdeM).
319 'A hundred times more': ibid.
319 'where my roots reach': HS, *Return to Vienna*, 6 February.
320 'Heiligenstadt unchanged': HS, diary, 2 February 1946 (HS NLV).
320 'one of the most': HS, *DaB*, p. 110.
321 'The opera still': HS, 'Vienna', *The New Statesman and Nation*, 13 April 1946.
321 'Quite definitely not': HS to PdeM, 1 February 1946 (HS PdeM).
322 'The Frau Doktor': HS, *Return to Vienna*, 9 February.
322 'Expropriation, humiliation': ibid.
322 'In England, during': HS, *Return to Vienna*, 10 February.
323 'Of course, I'm envious': PdeM to HS, 2 February 1946 (HS PdeM).
323 'England suits me': ibid.
323 'I can just see how': PdeM to HS, 11 February 1946 (HS PdeM).
323 'I lead this curious': HS to PdeM, 7 February 1946 (HS PdeM).
323 'Those that are nice': HS to PdeM, 15 February 1946 (HS PdeM).
324 'sweet major': HS to PdeM, 4 February 1946 (HS PdeM).
324 'the pleasant, cultured': HS, *DaB*, p. 156.
324 'Cooked at Sam's': HS, diary, 9 February 1946 (HS NLV).
324 'Sam didn't appear': HS, diary, 11 February 1946 (HS NLV).
324 'Quite delightful': HS, diary, 12 February 1946 (HS NLV).
324 'Sam: end': HS, diary, 14 February 1946 (HS NLV).
324 'What an absurd': HS, diary, 15 February 1946 (HS NLV).
324 'extraordinary scene': HS, diary, 16 February 1946 (HS NLV).
324 'You don't think': HS, *The Darkened Room* (English translation of *Lisas Zimmer*) (London: Methuen, 1961), p. 132.
326 'I feel like someone': HS to PdeM, 10 February 1946 (HS PdeM).
326 'precisely the kind': PdeM to HS, 14 February 1946 (HS PdeM).
326 'Dearest Mummili': PdeM to HS, 20 February 1946 (HS PdeM).
327 'most charmingly': HS to PdeM, 18 February 1946 (HS PdeM).
327 'as wide and full': HS, *Return to Vienna*, 20 February.
328 'I am on a winter': ibid.
328 'in the limp': HS, *Return to Vienna*, 21 February.
328 'Is it fear': ibid.
329 'with a look': ibid.
329 'Europe is a graveyard': ibid.
329 'These people have': HS, 'The Trek to Palestine', *The New Statesman and Nation*, 23 March 1946.
329 'a worldwide Jewish': HS, *Return to Vienna*, 21 February.
329 'even with the': HS, 'The Trek to Palestine'.
330 'a solution must': ibid.
330 'the ozone that': HS, *Return to Vienna*, 23 February.

330   'with my most': HS, *DaB*, p. 164.
331   'most dreary thought': HS to PdeM, 7 February 1946 (HS PdeM).
331   'A dozen times': PdeM to HS, 17 March 1946 (HS PdeM).
331   'Our stakes in': PdeM to HS, 20 March 1946 (HS PdeM).
331   'fallen in love': PdeM to HS, 27 March 1946 (PdeM Mon).
332   'wept with rage': HS, *DaB*, p. 165.
332   'You have set': PdeM to HS, 4 April 1946 (HS PdeM).
332   'I feel very suspended': PdeM to HS, 10 April 1946 (PdeM Mon).
332   'I must assume': PdeM to HS, 13 April 1946 (PdeM Mon).
332   'Of course, I still': HS to PdeM, 11 April 1946 (HS PdeM).
333   'Thank God': PdeM to HS, 20 April 1946 (PdeM Mon).
333   'I have one firm': HS to PdeM, 7 February 1946 (HS PdeM).
333   'Darling, there's nothing': HS to PdeM, February 1946 (HS PdeM).
333   'This is such': HS to PdeM, 10 February 1946 (HS PdeM).
333   'The only thing': PdeM to HS, 14 February 1946 (HS PdeM).
334   'Absolutely. If': PdeM to HS, 20 February 1946 (HS PdeM).
334   'Already people': PdeM to HS, 2 May 1946 (PdeM Mon).
335   'it is certainly': PdeM to HS, 4 May 1946 (PdeM Mon).

18: 'O, maybe we'll live a while in Killala'

336   'In fact the Irish': for an account of the Irish economy in this period see J. J. Lee, *Ireland 1912–1985, Politics and Society* (Cambridge: Cambridge University Press, 1989).
336   'take whatever steps': Éamon de Valera, in ibid., pp. 289–90.
336   'constantly recurring': Evelyn Waugh, diary, 9 November 1946, *The Diaries of Evelyn Waugh*, ed. Michael Davie (London: Phoenix, 2009).
337   'brief shelter from': Evelyn Waugh to Randolph Churchill, 22 December 1946, *The Letters of Evelyn Waugh* (London: Phoenix, 2010).
337   'total to me': Nancy Mitford to Evelyn Waugh, 26 April 1952, *The Letters of Nancy Mitford and Evelyn Waugh*, ed. Charlotte Mosley (London: Sceptre, 1997).
337   'The war's on now': HG, *Loving* (London: Vintage, 2000), pp. 29, 192.
338   'the dear Shelbourne': EB to CR, 26 November 1945 (*LCW*).
338   'impassive, cheerful': EB, *The Shelbourne* (London: Vintage, 2001), p. 6.
338   'a complete success': HY to Matthew Smith, 3 September 1947 (private collection).
339   'A mattress was spread': GG, 'After Two Years', *A Quick Look Behind: Footnotes to an Autobiography* (Los Angeles: Sylvester & Orphanos, 1983).
339   'at a loss': see GG, *Ways of Escape* (Harmondsworth: Penguin, 1982), ch. 4ii.
339   'a belated congratulatory': see GG to CW, 25 September 1946 (GG GU).
340   'he was keen to': see GG to Evelyn Waugh, undated, Richard Greene, *Graham Greene, A Life in Letters* (London: Little, Brown, 2007), p. 139.
340   'They had a drink': see Norman Sherry, *The Life of Graham Greene* (London: Pimlico, 2004–5), vol. 2, p. 227.
340   'an extraordinary house': Evelyn Waugh to Nancy Mitford, 4 October 1948 (*The Letters of Nancy Mitford and Evelyn Waugh*).
341   'She had a marvellous': Belinda Straight, interview in Sherry, *The Life of Graham Greene*, vol. 2, p. 220.
341   'a Marie-Antoinette': John Rothenstein, *Brave Day, Hideous Night: Autobiography 1939–1965* (London: Hamish Hamilton, 1966), p. 155.
342   'I had no idea': GG, *EoA*, book 1, ch. 3.
342   'They drove to': see GG to Marion Greene, undated, in Sherry, *The Life of Graham Greene*, vol. 2, p. 227.
343   'to go up in an aeroplane': see GG, in William Cash, *The Third Woman: The Secret Passion that Inspired The End of the Affair* (London: Abacus, 2001), p. 4.
343   'The act of creation': GG to CW, 30 September 1947 (GG GU).
343   'the same kind of in-love': see GG to CW, 12 April 1949 (GG GU).

343   'Cambridge, snow': see GG to CW, 2 September 1955 (GG GU).
343   'they would have done more': see GG to CW, 24 September 1949 (GG GU).
344   'gave it away to the nuns': see VG, interview with William Cash (private collection).
344   'Dorothy was complaining': see GG to CW, 5 May 1947 (GG GU).
344   'woke up blissfully': ibid.
344   'a second-rate Ireland': see GG to CW, 15 May 1947 (GG GU).
345   'Graham led Catherine': see VG, interview with William Cash (private collection).
345   'he felt like a cornered': see GG to CW, 15 May 1947 (GG GU).
345   'if I found anyone': CW to Belinda Straight, 1 January 1969, in Sherry, *The Life of Graham Greene*, vol. 2, p. 233.
345   'You know, Graham': CW in Lady Melchett interview, in ibid., p. 260.
346   'it is better to avoid lying': see GG, *HoM*, book 3, part 1, ch. 11; book 1, part 1, ch. 21v; book 1, part 2, ch. 2ii.
346   'before she appeared he used to': see GG to CW, 25 August 1947 (GG GU).
346   'the difference between peacefulness': see GG to CW, 27 August 1947 (GG GU).
346   'You are in': GG to CW, 27 June 1947 (GG GU).
347   'he was missing her obsessively': see GG to CW, 29 June 1947 (GG GU).
347   'he wanted to kiss': see GG to CW, 30 June 1947 (GG GU).
348   'Would he really see': see GG to CW, 4 July 1947 (GG GU).
348   'escape to Romania': see GG to CW, 5 July 1947 (GG GU).
348   'lazily reading on': see GG to CW, 24 August 1947 (GG GU).
348   'watching her make': see GG to CW, 3 October 1949 (GG GU).
348   'after four and a half': see GG to CW, undated, 1951 (GG GU).
349   'Irish faith to': Sean O'Faolain to GG, 9 February 1976 (GG BU).
349   'At once he was in love': see GG to CW, 3 September 1947 (GG GU).
349   'O, maybe we'll': F. R. Higgins, 'Elopement', *Arable Holdings* (Dublin: The Cuala Press, 1933). GG inscribed the 8 April 1949 entry of CW's diary with this quotation.
349   'Graham has just': CW to Phillip Caraman, undated, 1951 (GG BU).
349   'the first diary': CW's diaries are held in GG GU.
351   'they only liked each other': see GG to CW, 2 August 1947 (GG GU).
351   'always quiet or gentle': see VG, interview with William Cash (private collection).
351   'his cigarette burn': see GG to CW, 25 August 1947 (GG GU).
351   'He fell in love': see GG to CW, 21 August 1947 (GG GU).
351   'He could become a pagan': see GG to CW, 18 August 1947 (GG GU).
351   'Ireland seemed to be': see GG to CW, 27 August 1947 (GG GU).
352   'romantically admired': see GG, interview, 1981 in Henry Donaghy (ed.), *Conversations with Graham Greene* (Jackson: University Press of Mississippi, 1992), p. 156.
352   'an enchanting figure': see ibid., p. 153.
352   'it might be fun': see GG to CW, 5 September 1947 (GG GU).
352   'lustrous and blonde': see ibid.
353   'a flight from': see GG to CW, 28 September 1947 (GG GU).
353   'the Atlantic blowing': see GG to CW, undated, 1947 (GG GU).

19: *'The returning memory of a dream long forgotten'*

354   'was immediately exhilarated': see HS, *DaB*, p. 184.
354   'This life cannot': PdeM to HS, 4 October 1946 (PdeM Mon).
355   'My decision is': PdeM to HS, 12 October 1946 (PdeM Mon).
355   'the richest': HS, *DaB*, p. 197.
356   'the Reichstag, now a vast shell': see Stephen Spender, *European Witness* (London: Hamish Hamilton, 1946), p. 235.
356   'an astonishingly bizarre': Kingsley Martin, 'A German Diary', *The New Statesman and Nation*, 27 April 1946.

357   'hungry, discouraged': PdeM, 'The Dead Cities Revisited', July 1946 (unpublished article in PdeM Mon).

357   'satrap days': see HS, *DaB*, p. 182.

357   'Apart from the British': HS to Mimi Spiel, in ibid., p. 190.

358   'Although props and scenery': see Walter Goehr, 'Art Among the Ruins', *The New Statesman and Nation*, 13 July 1946.

358   'unnaturally elaborate': Clarissa Churchill, 'Berlin Letter', *Horizon*, March 1946.

358   'In the midst of': HS, *DaB*, p. 228.

359   'Otherwise we can never': PdeM to HS, 15 July 1945 (HS PdeM).

359   'I came here': PdeM to HS, 1 September 1945 (HS PdeM).

359   'What can one do': PdeM to HS, 12 August 1945 (PdeM Mon).

360   'how many shades': HS, *DaB*, p. 219.

360   'London is so beautiful': HS, diary, in *DaB*, p. 206.

361   'one of the foremost': HS to Mimi Spiel, in *DaB*, p. 223.

361   'taken as ever': ibid., p. 227.

361   'with its blunt': PdeM to HS, 19 August 1945 (HS PdeM).

362   'They hardly ever': HS to Mimi Spiel, in *DaB*, p. 190.

362   'nothing goes to one's': HS to PdeM, in ibid., p. 191.

362   'The Red Army': ibid.

363   'It is very difficult': HS to Mimi Spiel, in ibid., p. 227.

363   'Writing to her sister': RM to Jean Macaulay, 17 July 1947 (RM TC).

363   'She was also disturbed': RM to Jean Macaulay, 25 August 1947 (RM TC).

364   'unheralded and unordered': RM to Jean Smith, 16 September 1947, *Dearest Jean: Rose Macaulay's Letters to a Cousin*, ed. Martin Ferguson Smith (Manchester: Manchester University Press, 2011).

364   'with its indefatigable': RM, *Fabled Shore: From the Pyrenees to Portugal* (London: Hamish Hamilton, 1950), pp. 32, 171.

365   'evoking the shifting colours': ibid., p. 23.

365   'rather startling!': RM to Jean Smith, 16 September 1947 (*Dearest Jean*).

365   'If these objects': RM, *Fabled Shore*, p. 40.

365   'she had passed a lovely': RM to Jean Smith, 16 September 1947 (*Dearest Jean*).

366   'She told a hitchhiker': see RM, *Fabled Shore*, p. 175.

366   'the returning memory': ibid., p. 175.

366   'the Labour mismanagement': RM to Jean Macaulay, 25 August 1947 (RM TC).

366   'a desolation of': RM, *Fabled Shore*, pp. 245–6.

20: *'The place I really did lose my heart to was Vienna'*

367   'roofs covered with': see GG to CW, 11 February 1948 (GG GU).

368   'not going back to anyone': see GG to VG, 19 June 1947 (VG Bod).

368   'longing to push the': see GG to CW, undated, 1947 (GG GU).

368   'much of Britain was ambivalent': see David Kynaston, *Austerity Britain 1945–51* (London: Bloomsbury, 2008), p. 243.

368   'I know what real': see VG, interview with William Cash (private collection).

368   'comforting Vivien': see GG to CW, undated (VG Bod).

371   'a joyful Christmas': see GG to CW, 26 December 1947 (GG GU).

371   'he was feeling happy': see GG to CW, 30 December 1947 (GG GU).

371   'bleakly miserable': see GG to CW, 11 February 1948 (GG GU).

371   'He does not have enough imagination': see GG, *The Third Man* (London: Vintage, 2001), ch. 1.

372   'white bonnets protruded': see GG to CW, 16 February 1948 (GG GU).

372   'The illegal penicillin': see GG to Wilfred Harrington, 28 July 1950, Richard Greene, *Graham Greene, A Life in Letters* (London: Little, Brown, 2007).

372   'Hideous they were': Elizabeth Montagu, interview in Norman Sherry, *The Life of Graham Greene* (London: Pimlico, 2004–5), vol. 2, p. 252.

372   'a sordid smoke-filled': see GG, *The Third Man*, ch. 11.
373   'How do you know?': see GG, *Ways of Escape* (Harmondsworth: Penguin, 1982), ch. 5i.
373   'I was there': EB to CR, 12 April 1955 (*LCW*).
374   'fully intelligent': EB, GG, V. S. Pritchett, *Why do I Write? An Exchange of Views* (London: Percival Marshall, 1948).
374   'the crowds of people': see GG to CW, 17 February 1948 (GG GU).
374   'He would have forgotten': see GG to CW, 18 February 1948 (GG GU).
375   'the best thing': CR to Lilian Ritchie, April 1940, in *LCW*, p. 41.
375   'And marriage is': CR, diary, 12 November 1942 (*LCW*).
375   'Now that I am leaving': CR, diary, 23 December 1945 (*LCW*).
375   'Death of the Heart': CR, diary, 25 December 1945 (*LCW*).
375   'Love of my Life': CR, diary, 23 February 1946 (*LCW*).
375   'going to take': EB to CR, 23 November 1946 (*LCW*).
376   'As a matter': EB to Isaiah Berlin, Easter Sunday, 1948 (Isaiah Berlin archive, Bod).
376   'If I were': EB to CR, 8 February 1948 (*LCW*).
377   'Socialist principle': Clement Attlee, in Peter Hennessy, *Never Again: Britain 1945–51* (London: Penguin, 2006), p. 198.
377   'If I lived': EB to Lilian Ritchie, 10 March 1948 (*LCW*).
378   'I feel sometimes': EB to CR, Easter Sunday, 1948 (*LCW*).
378   'Hotels are always full': see GG, *Ways of Escape*, ch. 5ii.
379   'a scrap of paper': see GG, *Ways of Escape*, ch. 5i.
379   'love is a little peace': GG, 'Il Pace', *A Quick Look Behind: Footnotes to an Autobiography* (Los Angeles: Sylvester & Orphanos, 1983).
380   'he had betrayed': see GG, interview in Sherry, *Graham Greene*, vol. 2, p. 281.
380   'Everyone from Douglas': Dorothy Glover to GG, 14 April 1948, in William Cash, *The Third Woman: The Secret Passion that Inspired The End of the Affair* (London: Abacus, 2001), p. 169.
381   'drink to it': see GG to CW, 29 April 1948 (GG GU).
381   'lauded the novel': EB, review of *The Heart of the Matter*, *Tatler*, 2 June 1948.
381   'he was fond of her': see GG to VG, 3 June 1948 (VG Bod).
382   'Currency reform': see HS, *DaB*, p. 214.
382   'Vienna has become': HS, diary, in ibid.
382   'he was embarrassed': see GG, *Ways of Escape*, ch. 5i.
383   'Shellfire and a blaze': HS, *Return to Vienna,* trans. Christine Shuttleworth (Riverside, California: Ariadne Press, 2011), 8 February.
383   'the shattered Prater': see GG, *The Third Man*, ch. 14.
383   'like a sort': Elizabeth Montagu, interview in Sherry, *The Life of Graham Greene*, vol. 2, p. 250.
383   'a strange unknown world': see GG, film treatment for *The Third Man* (GG HRC).
383   'more and more likable: see GG to CW, 21 June 1948 (GG GU).
384   'enough of being successful': see GG to CW, 25 June 1948 (GG GU).
384   'tired of being rich': see GG to CW, 4 August 1948 (GG GU).
385   'the British foreign secretary': see Hennessy, *Never Again*, p. 351.
385   'Our relationship': HS to Mimi Spiel, in *DaB*, p. 242.
386   'I can only repeat': ibid.
386   'You are the cause': PdeM, in ibid.
387   'He is a wonderfully': Rosamond Lehmann to Rayner Heppenstall, 26 February 1945, in Selina Hastings, *Rosamond Lehmann* (London: Vintage, 2003), p. 240.
387   'Barbara replied that': for Rex Warner's meeting with Barbara Rothschild, his letters to Pam Morris and his life in Berlin more generally, see Stephen E. Tabachnick, *Fiercer than Tigers: The Life and Works of Rex Warner* (East Lansing: Michigan State University Press, 2002), pp. 239–46.
388   'Tackley weekend': see GG to CW, 1 August 1948 (GG GU).
388   'a moment, perhaps': HS, *DaB*, p. 246.

388   'green grave': see HS to PdeM, February 1946 (HS PdeM).
388   'In Wimbledon': HS, *DaB*, p. 249.
388   'Deep gloom has': PdeM to HS, 12 September 1948 (HS PdeM).
389   'a male friend': HS, *DaB*, p. 252.
390   'I must write': PdeM to HS, 18 February 1949 (PdeM Mon).
391   'Love to you': PdeM to HS, 3 March 1949 (PdeM Mon).
391   'I'm tired, tired': PdeM to HS, 22 June 1949 (PdeM Mon).
392   'so like Vienna': EB to CR, 12 April 1955 (*LCW*).
392   'an awful pang': see GG to CW, 24 September 1949 (GG GU).

21: 'We could have been happy for a lifetime'

397   'And they called *that*': GG, 'After Two Years', *A Quick Look Behind: Footnotes to an Autobiography* (Los Angeles: Sylvester & Orphanos, 1983).
398   'the idea of mortal': see GG, interview in Marie-Françoise Allain, *The Other Man: Conversations with Graham Greene* (Harmondsworth: Penguin, 1984), p. 159.
398   'Marriage was not': see GG to CW, 30 January 1950 (GG GU).
398   'a priest who had': see GG to CW, 13 April 1950 (GG GU).
398   'He could only offer': see GG to CW, 3 April 1950 (GG GU).
398   'most people are only': see CW's diary, 26 February 1949 (GG GU).
399   'The greatest saints': GG, 'Frederick Rolfe: Edwardian Inferno', *The Lost Childhood and Other Essays* (London: Eyre & Spottiswoode, 1951).
399   'Reviewing Greene's': George Orwell, 'The Sanctified Sinner', *Collected Essays, Journalism, Letters*, vol. 4: *In Front of Your Nose*, ed. Sonia Orwell and Ian Angus (Harmondsworth: Penguin, 1970).
399   'What sort of sinner': see Malcolm Muggeridge, *Chronicles of Wasted Time*, vol. 2: *The Infernal Grove* (London: Collins, 1973), p. 105.
399   'she had dreamt about having': CW, diary, 24 March 1950 (GG GU).
399   'And to the other': CW, diary, 28 March 1950 (GG GU).
400   'He understood how': see GG to CW, 11 April 1949 (GG GU).
400   'You're my human': GG to CW, 8 December 1949 (GG GU).
400   'exceptionally likeable': see GG to CW, December 1947 (GG GU).
400   'He hated going': see GG to CW, 18 December 1949 (GG GU).
400   'Order of Battle': see ibid.
400   'see Catherine's hand': see GG to CW, February 1950 (GG GU).
402   'In a few years': see ibid.
402   'looking yearningly': see GG to CW, 28 February 1950 (GG GU).
402   'superb piece': CW to Bonte Durán, 13 March 1950, in Norman Sherry, *The Life of Graham Greene* (London: Pimlico, 2004–5), vol. 2, p. 326.
402   'The three of them had': see GG to Bonte Durán, 19 March 1950, in ibid.
403   'Spent the morning': CW, diary, 11 January 1950 (GG GU).
403   'violent quarrel': CW, diary, 21 March 1950 (GG GU).
403   'another bad': CW, diary, 22 March 1950 (GG GU).
403   'why he had been so cruel': see GG to CW, 28 March 1950 (GG GU).
403   'He had never imagined': see GG to CW, 29 March 1950 (GG GU).
404   'he was praying': see GG to CW, 3 April 1950 (GG GU).
404   'a miserable day': CW, diary, 12 April 1950 (GG GU).
404   'he felt strongly': see GG to CW, 12 April 1950 (GG GU).
404   'almost all': CW, diary, 13 April 1950 (GG GU).
405   'particularly nice': CW, diary, 12 February 1950 (GG GU).
405   'I am certain': CW, diary, 16 May 1950 (GG GU).
405   'unhappy evening': CW, diary, 19 May 1950 (GG GU).
405   'Graham really hates': CW, diary, 25 May 1950 (GG GU).
406   'cautious and depressed': CW, diary, 31 May 1950 (GG GU).

406   'Caught disease': CW, diary, 28 March 1949 (GG GU).
406   'I am a coward': CW to Bonte Durán, 16 June 1950, in Sherry, *The Life of Graham Greene*, vol. 2, p. 318.
406   'Graham seemed very': CW to Phillip Caraman, 17 July 1950 (GG BU).
406   'more peaceful': CW to Phillip Caraman, undated (GG BU).
406   'no judge on': CW to Phillip Caraman, undated (GG BU).
407   'so good and': ibid.
407   'a long talk': CW, diary, 12 October 1950 (GG GU).
407   'the story had germinated': see GG, *Ways of Escape* (Harmondsworth: Penguin, 1982), ch. 5iii.
408   'Is it possible': GG, *EoA*, book 2, ch. 2.
408   'sweet': GG, ibid., book 3, ch. 2; book 2, ch. 3; book 2, ch. 1; book 1, ch .2; book 2, ch. 2.
409   'almost as a conniver': ibid., book 1, ch. 1; book 1, ch. 7.
410   'one gets so': ibid., book 1, ch. 1; book 1, ch. 3; book 2, ch. 4.
411   'Suddenly I wanted': ibid., book 2, ch. 3; book 2, ch. 6; book 2, ch. 1.
411   'with nervous irritation': ibid., book 1, ch. 6; book 2, ch. 2.
412   'not at peace': ibid., book 3, ch. 1.
413   'I swear that if': ibid., book 2, ch. 2.
413   'the best part of it': see GG to CW, 22 March 1950 (GG GU).
413   'a situation where they': GG to CW, undated (GG GU).
414   'this may possibly': CW to Phillip Caraman, 23 July 1951 (GG BU).
414   'Greene behaved': Evelyn Waugh to Nancy Mitford, 19 September 1951, *The Letters of Nancy Mitford and Evelyn Waugh*, ed. Charlotte Mosley (London: Sceptre, 1997).
414   'Flying between the clouds': see GG to CW, 6 October 1951 (GG GU).

22: *'Let us neither of us forget . . . what reality feels like and eternity is'*

415   'as though you': EB to CR, 4 September 1948 (*LCW*).
415   'I can go no': CR, diary, 5 September 1948 (*LCW*).
415   'Oh, I am': EB to CR, 7 September 1948 (*LCW*).
416   'Keep me in your': EB to CR, 14 April 1949 (*LCW*).
416   'dearest friend': EB to CR, 26 May 1949 (*LCW*).
416   'Oh God': EB to CR, 28 October 1949 (*LCW*).
416   'Oh E, how': CR, diary, 16 October 1949 (*LCW*).
416   'I should like': CR, diary, 11 November 1951 (*LCW*).
416   'the most extraordinary': CR, diary, 2 December 1951 (*LCW*).
416   'My inability': EB to CR, 16 October 1949 (*LCW*).
417   'Our love is': EB to CR, 5 January 1950 (*LCW*).
417   'Yes, I think': EB to CR, 6 May 1950 (*LCW*).
417   'a page or': EB to CR, 16 October 1949 (*LCW*).
417   'You are my': EB to CR, 18 June 1953 (*LCW*).
417   'the perfect dwelling': EB to CR, 28 October 1949 (*LCW*).
417   'would be your': EB to CR, 26 December 1949 (*LCW*).
417   'In a queer': EB to CR, 5 January 1950 (*LCW*).
418   'feeling for words': Nora Wydenbruck, *Rilke: Man and Poet; A Biographical Study* (London: John Lehmann, 1949), pp. 171, 166–7.
418   'precious hours': ibid., pp. 181, 185, 187–8.
419   'intense sympathy': ibid., pp. 224, 237, 305.
420   'Let us not': ibid., p. 288.
420   'I look at your': Gustave Flaubert to Louise Colet, 6 August 1846, *The Letters of Gustave Flaubert*, ed. and trans. Francis Steegmuller (London: Picador, 2001).
420   'He loved her': EB, preface to *The Flaubert Omnibus, Collected Impressions* (London: Longmans, Green & Co, 1950).
421   'a caress, a kiss': EB, translation of a letter from Flaubert to Louise Colet (EB HRC).

421   'extraordinary feeling': EB to CR, 6 November 1960 (*LCW*).

422   'In 1946, in daylight': see EB to CR, 30 June 1946 (*LCW*).

422   'rather ill again': EB to CR, 26 May 1949 (*LCW*).

422   'terrifyingly empty days': EB to William Plomer, 9 September 1952, *The Mulberry Tree: Writings of Elizabeth Bowen*, ed. Hermione Lee (London: Vintage, 1999).

422   'queer state of': EB to Isaiah Berlin, 8 October 1952 (Isaiah Berlin archive, Bod).

423   'To his belief': EB autobiographical note, 1953 (EB HCR).

424   'Do you know': EB to CR, 6 July 1954 (*LCW*).

424   'growing realisation': CR, diary, May 1954 (*LCW*).

424   'feverish high-pressure': CR, diary, 18 July 1954 (*LCW*).

424   'a life to let': CR, diary, 29 July 1954 (*LCW*).

424   'the uninterrupted': EB to CR, November 1954 (*LCW*).

424   'Oh I miss you': EB to CR, 14 August 1954 (*LCW*).

424   'so restless and': EB to CR, November 1954 (*LCW*).

425   'non-achievement of happiness': EB, 'Disappointment' 1, *People, Places, Things: Essays by Elizabeth Bowen*, ed. Allan Hepburn (Edinburgh: Edinburgh University Press, 2008).

426   'never underrate': EB, 'Disappointment' 2 (*People, Places, Things*).

426   'looking at life': CR, diary, 8 December 1954 (*LCW*).

427   'a sort of exhilaration': CR, diary, 9 December 1954 (*LCW*).

427   'loneliness, sorrow': CR, diary, 10 December 1954 (*LCW*).

427   'The way you two': EB, *A World of Love* (London: Jonathan Cape, 1957), chs 7, 1, 8.

428   'a speaking language': ibid., ch. 1.

428   'profound breath': ibid., chs 5, 6, 8.

429   'They no sooner': ibid., chs 11, 2, 4.

430   'E has a miraculous': CR, diary, 11 November 1956 (*LCW*).

431   'unreal happiness': CR, diary, 12 December 1954 (*LCW*).

431   'middle-aged paradise': CR, diary, 20 December 1954 (*LCW*).

431   'Your sweetness': EB to CR, 4 January 1955 (*LCW*).

431   'if your hatred': CR, diary, 15 April 1955 (*LCW*).

431   'sad, disturbing': CR, diary, 28 August 1955 (*LCW*).

431   'You must really': EB to CR, 6 January 1956 (*LCW*).

431   'The fact is': EB to CR, 29 February 1956 (*LCW*).

432   'These last ten': EB to CR, 15 May 1956 (*LCW*).

23: *'The world my wilderness, its caves my home'*

433   'a lovely little': RM to Jean Macaulay, 16 July 1949 (RM TC).

434   'shinned down a': Penelope Fitzgerald, introduction to Virago 1983 edition of *WMW*.

434   'cave-fanciers and': RM, 'Notes on the Way', *Time and Tide*, 5 October 1940.

435   'A seed can lodge': HY to Rosamond Lehmann, quoted in Rosamond Lehmann, 'An Absolute Gift', *Times Literary Supplement*, 6 August 1954.

435   'is about the': RM to Hamilton Johnson, 30 August 1950, *Letters to a Friend 1950–1952*, ed. Constance Babington Smith (London: Collins, 1961).

435   'if she greatly': RM, *WMW*, chs 2, 3.

436   'about dust-heaped': ibid., chs 5, 6.

437   'New ruins': RM, *Pleasure of Ruins* (London: Weidenfeld and Nicolson, 1953), p. 454.

437   'I can't think': RM, *WMW*, ch. 2.

438   'Day of wrath': ibid., chs 7, 23.

438   'We are in hell': ibid., ch. 23.

438   'Very soon trees': RM, *Pleasure of Ruins*, p. 454.

439   'broken habitations': RM, *WMW*, chs 5, 18.

440   'seized, bound': ibid., ch. 31.

440   'Make your way': RM, 'In the Ruins', *Spectator*, 18 November 1949.

440   'sharp sense of': RM, 'The First Impact of *The Waste Land*', Braybrooke (ed.), *T. S. Eliot: A Symposium for his Seventieth Birthday* (London: Rupert Hart-Davis, 1958).

441   'Slim, elegant and twenty-three': RM, *WMW*, chs 2, 34.

441   'glitter of good': ibid., ch. 2.

442   'I am within': RM to David Ley, 15 April 1949 (RM TC).

442   'dispossession of the': RM, *Pleasure of Ruins*, pp. 362–3.

443   'a country of ruins': EB, *B's C*, pp. 15, 17.

443   'inextricably mixed': RM, *Pleasure of Ruins*, p. 1.

444   'the darkly ruinous': ibid., pp. 9, 20, 23.

444   'stupendous past': ibid., pp. 40, 84, 165.

444   'enjungled, engulfed': ibid., pp. 454–5.

445   'how a young lady': Hamilton Johnson, in Constance Babington Smith, introduction to Rose Macaulay, *Letters to a Friend*.

445   'If you were in England': RM to Hamilton Johnson, 30 August 1950 (*Letters to a Friend*).

445   'The people I love most': RM to Hamilton Johnson, 28 September 1950 (*Letters to a Friend*).

446   'Partly my difficulties': RM to Hamilton Johnson, 28 October 1950 (*Letters to a Friend*).

446   'didn't feel jolly': RM to Hamilton Johnson, 10 November 1952, *Last Letters to a Friend 1952–1958*, ed. Constance Babington Smith (London: Collins, 1962).

446   'took up with the': RM, *ToT*, chs 7, 20, 14.

447   'last little Byzantine': RM to Hamilton Johnson, 8 July 1954 (*Last Letters to a Friend*).

447   'an old dream': RM, *ToT*, chs 8, 25.

448   'is exciting': ibid., ch. 25.

448   'a book I have': RM to Rosamond Lehmann, 11 September 1956 (RL KC).

Coda

449   'I have an': RM to Jean Macaulay, 22 March 1955 (RM TC).

449   'she would not': RM to Hamilton Johnson, 1 October 1956, *Last Letters to a Friend 1952–1958*, ed. Constance Babington Smith (London: Collins, 1962).

449   'I can't not be': RM to Rosamond Lehmann, 11 September 1956 (RL KC).

449   'wit and brains': RM, *ToT*, ch. 24.

449   'the long years': RM to Hamilton Johnson, 9 January 1951, *Letters to a Friend 1950–1952*, ed. Constance Babington Smith (London: Collins, 1961).

450   'scattered, adrift': RM, *ToT*, ch. 25.

450   'A kind of shining': RM to Hamilton Johnson, 25 May 1951 (*Letters to a Friend*).

450   'her ice-blue eyes': Rosamond Lehmann, 'The Pleasures of Knowing Rose Macaulay', in Constance Babington Smith, *Rose Macaulay: A Biography* (London: Collins, 1972).

451   'unable to put': RM to Jean Macaulay, 17 March 1958 (RM TC).

451   'What on earth': RM, in Anthony Powell, 'The Pleasures of Knowing Rose Macaulay', in Babington Smith, *Rose Macaulay*.

451   'But we have all': Rosamond Lehmann, 'The Pleasures of Knowing Rose Macaulay', in ibid.

452   'I had immense hope': EB interview by three writers, 1959 (EB HRC).

452   'she told William Plomer': EB to William Plomer, 6 May 1958, *The Mulberry Tree: Writings of Elizabeth Bowen*, ed. Hermione Lee (London: Vintage, 1999).

453   'was the last in which': CR, diary, 22 January 1957 (*LCW*).

453   'We *are* a family': EB, 'Bowen's Court', 1958, *People, Places, Things: Essays by Elizabeth Bowen*, ed. Allan Hepburn (Edinburgh: Edinburgh University Press, 2008).

453   'E and I came home': CR, diary, 8 May 1956 (*LCW*).

453   'dependence on home': EB, 'The Idea of the Home', undated (EB HRC).

454   'it really would break': EB to CR, 18 June 1958 (*LCW*).

454 'The trouble is': CR, diary, 23 June 1958 (*LCW*).

454 'I suppose it's': EB to CR, 21 July 1958 (*LCW*).

455 'a clean end': EB, afterword to *B's C*, p. 459.

455 'My darling, my darling': EB, *A Time in Rome* (London: Vintage, 2010), ch. 5.

455 'Here we have': EB, *B's C*, p. 377.

456 'Guests invited for dinner': this and much other information in this paragraph comes from an interview conducted by the author with Anthony Felix de Mendelssohn.

456 'For the first time': PdeM to HS, 4 May 1957 (HS PdeM).

456 'You have systematically': PdeM to HS, 31 August 1963 (HS PdeM) (originally in German).

457 'our life is too short': HS to PdeM, 25 October 1963 (HS PdeM) (originally in German).

458 'her ultimate return to Vienna': see afterword to *Return to Vienna*, trans. Christine Shuttleworth (Riverside, California: Ariadne Press, 2011).

458 'Very long black': Evelyn Waugh to Nancy Mitford, 16 May 1951, *The Letters of Nancy Mitford and Evelyn Waugh*, ed. Charlotte Mosley (London: Sceptre, 1997).

459 'really very nice': Christopher Isherwood, diary, 10 May 1948, *Diaries Volume One: 1939–1960* (London: Chatto & Windus, 1996).

459 'livid light': Nancy Mitford to Evelyn Waugh, 18 May 1951 (*The Letters of Nancy Mitford and Evelyn Waugh*).

459 'a diatribe of': James Lees-Milne, *Fourteen Friends* (London: John Murray, 1996), p. 130.

459 'a shared fondness': Michael Scammell, *Koestler: The Literary and Political Odyssey of a Twentieth-Century Skeptic* (New York: Random House, 2009), p. 495.

460 'A man falls': HG, 'Falling in Love', *Surviving: The Uncollected Writings of Henry Green* (London: Harvill, 1993).

460 'must meet some time': HY to Mary Keene, 21 March 1947 (private collection).

460 'a very good': HY to Mary Keene, 9 December 1957 (private collection).

461 'beyond words wonderful': HY to Matthew Smith, 4 December 1950 (private collection).

461 'deepest sympathy': HY to Matthew Smith, 21 January 1958 (private collection).

461 'is to become': Rosamond Lehmann, 'An Absolute Gift', *Times Literary Supplement*, 6 August 1954.

462 'Darling. I've read': HY to Rosamond Lehmann, 30 August 1954 (RL KC).

462 'The dark eyes': Cynthia Koestler, *Stranger on the Square* (London: Hutchinson, 1984), p. 221.

462 'Only the other day': HG, 'For Jenny with Affection from Henry Green' (*Surviving*).

463 'nothing, I believe': CR, diary, 11 June 1961 (*LCW*).

463 'I had that': CR, diary, 24 December 1968 (*LCW*).

463 'I do believe': CR, diary, 24 May 1973 (*LCW*).

463 'I shall never': CR, diary, 14 June 1973 (*LCW*).

463 'I am never': CR, diary, 30 July 1973 (*LCW*).

464 'I think of you': CW to GG, 13 December 1975 (GG BU).

464 'What a vast amount': CW to GG, 18 May 1978 (GG BU).

465 'ready to take on': HG, 'Before the Great Fire' (*Surviving*).

465 'In February 1965': see GG, *A World of my Own: A Dream Diary* (London: Penguin, 1993), pp. 39, 50.

465 'Existence during the war': EB, review of Angus Calder's *The People's War* (*The Mulberry Tree*).

Bibliography

Allain, Marie-Françoise, *The Other Man: Conversations with Graham Greene* (Harmondsworth: Penguin, 1984)

Allen, Walter, *As I Walked Down New Grub Street* (London: Heinemann, 1981)

Babington Smith, Constance, *Rose Macaulay: A Biography* (London: Collins, 1972)

Beaton, Cecil, *Self-Portrait With Friends: The Selected Diaries of Cecil Beaton*, ed. Richard Buckle (London: Weidenfeld & Nicolson, 1979)

Beckett, Francis, *Firefighters and the Blitz* (Wales: The Merlin Press, 2010)

Birkett, Jennifer, *Storm Jameson: A Life* (Oxford: Oxford University Press, 2009)

Bowen, Elizabeth, *A Time in Rome* (London: Vintage, 2010)

— *A World of Love* (London: Jonathan Cape, 1957)

— *Bowen's Court and Seven Winters*, introduction by Hermione Lee (London: Vintage, 1999)

— *Collected Impressions* (London: Longmans, Green & Co, 1950)

— *Collected Stories*, introduction by Angus Wilson (London: Vintage, 1999)

— *Listening In: Broadcasts, Speeches and Interviews by Elizabeth Bowen*, ed. Allan Hepburn (Edinburgh: Edinburgh University Press, 2010)

— *Notes on Eire, Espionage Reports to Winston Churchill, 1940–2*, Aubane Historical Society, ed. Jack Lane and Brendan Clifford, 3rd edn

— *People, Places, Things: Essays by Elizabeth Bowen*, ed. Allan Hepburn (Edinburgh: Edinburgh University Press, 2008)

— *The Heat of the Day*, introduction by Roy Foster (London: Vintage, 2008)

— *The Last September*, introduction by Victoria Glendinning (London: Vintage, 1998)

— *The Mulberry Tree: Writings of Elizabeth Bowen*, ed. Hermione Lee (London: Vintage, 1999)

— *The Shelbourne* (London: Vintage, 2001)

Bowen, Elizabeth, Greene, Graham and Pritchett, V. S., *Why do I Write? An Exchange of Views* (London: Percival Marshall, 1948)

Bowen, Elizabeth and Ritchie, Charles, *Love's Civil War, Letters and diaries from the love affair of a lifetime*, ed. Victoria Glendinning with Judith Robertson (London: Simon & Schuster, 2009)

Braybrooke, Neville (ed.), *T. S. Eliot: A Symposium for his Seventieth Birthday* (London: Rupert Hart-Davis, 1958)

Brittain, Vera, *England's Hour* (London: Continuum, 2005)

Brown, Mike, *Put That Light Out! Britain's Civil Defence Services at War 1939–1945* (Gloucestershire: Sutton Publishing, 1999)

Bryant Jordan, Heather, *How Will the Heart Endure: Elizabeth Bowen and the Landscape of War* (Ann Arbor: University of Michigan Press, 1992)

Cash, William, *The Third Woman: The Secret Passion that Inspired The End of the Affair* (London: Abacus, 2001)

Cesarani, David and Kushner, Tony, *The Internment of Aliens in Twentieth-Century Britain* (London: Routledge, 1993)

Churchill, Winston, *War Speeches, 1939–45*, compiled by Charles Eade, 3 vols (London: Cassell & Co, 1951–2)

Corrigan, Gordon, *The Second World War: A Military History* (London: Atlantic Books, 2010)

Craig, Patricia, *Elizabeth Bowen* (Harmondsworth: Penguin, 1986)

Demarne, Cyril, *The London Blitz: A Fireman's Tale* (London: Battle of Britain Prints International, 1991)

De Valera, Éamon, *Speeches and Statements by Éamon de Valera 1917–73*, ed. Maurice Moynihan (Dublin: Gill and Macmillan, 1980)

Donaghy, Henry J. (ed.), *Conversations with Graham Greene* (Jackson: University Press of Mississippi, 1992)

Emery, Jane, *Rose Macaulay: A Writer's Life* (London: Murray, 1991)

Engelmann, Bernt (ed.), *Eine Pen-Documentation, Literatur des Exils* (München: Goldmann Wilhelm, 1981)

Flaubert, Gustave, *The Letters of Gustave Flaubert*, ed. and trans. Francis Steegmuller (London: Picador, 2001)

Foster, R. F., *W. B. Yeats: A Life*, vol. 2: *The Arch-Poet 1915–1939* (Oxford: Oxford University Press, 2003)

Gardiner, Juliet, *The Blitz: The British Under Attack* (London: HarperCollins 2011)

— *Wartime: Britain 1939–1945* (London: Headline, 2005)

Gilbert, Martin, *Second World War* (London: Fontana, 1990)

Glendinning, Victoria, *Elizabeth Bowen* (London: Phoenix paperbacks, 1993)

Gollancz, Victor, *Reminiscences of Affection* (London: Victor Gollancz, 1968)

Green, Henry, *Back* (New York: The Viking Press, 1981)

— *Caught*, introduction by Jeremy Treglown (London: Harvill Press, 2001)

— *Loving*, introduction by Sebastian Faulks (London: Vintage, 2000)

— *Pack My Bag*, introduction by Alan Ross (London: Vintage, 2000)

— *Surviving: The Uncollected Writings of Henry Green* (London: Harvill, 1993)

Greene, Graham, *A Quick Look Behind: Footnotes to an Autobiography* (Los Angeles: Sylvester & Orphanos, 1983)

— *A Sort of Life: An Autobiography* (Bath: Chivers, 1981)

— *A World of my Own: A Dream Diary* (London: Penguin, 1993)

— *Collected Essays* (Harmondsworth: Penguin, 1970)

— *Collected Short Stories* (Harmondsworth: Penguin, 1988)

— *The End of the Affair* (London: Vintage, 2004)

— *The Heart of the Matter* (London: Vintage, 2004)

— *The Lost Childhood and Other Essays* (London: Eyre & Spottiswoode, 1951)

— *The Ministry of Fear*, collected edition (London: William Heinemann, 1973)

— *The Third Man* and *The Fallen Idol* (London: Vintage, 2001)

— *Ways of Escape* (Harmondsworth: Penguin, 1982)

Greene, Richard, *Graham Greene, A Life in Letters* (London: Little, Brown, 2007)

Harmon, Maurice, *Sean O'Faolain, a Life* (London: Constable, 1994)

Hastings, Selina, *Rosamond Lehmann* (London: Vintage, 2003)

Hennessy, Peter, *Never Again: Britain 1945–51* (London: Penguin, 2006)

Higgins, F. R., *Arable Holdings* (Dublin: The Cuala Press, 1933)

Holden, Inez, *It was Different at the Time* (London: John Lane The Bodley Head, 1943)

Isherwood, Christopher, *Diaries Volume One: 1939–1960* (London: Chatto & Windus, 1996)

— *Lions and Shadows: An Education in the Twenties* (London: The Hogarth Press, 1938)

Jameson, Storm, *Journey from the North* (London: Vintage, 1984)

Keene, Alice, *The Two Mr Smiths: The Life and Work of Matthew Smith* (London: Lund Humphries, 1995)

Keene, Mary, *Mrs Donald* (London: Chatto & Windus, 1983)

Koestler, Arthur and Cynthia, edited and introduced by Harold Harris (London: Hutchinson, 1984)

Kynaston, David, *Austerity Britain 1945–51* (London: Bloomsbury, 2008)

Lee, Hermione, *Virginia Woolf* (London: Chatto & Windus, 1996)

Lee, J. J., *Ireland 1912–1985, Politics and Society* (Cambridge: Cambridge University Press, 1989)

Lees-Milne, James, *Diaries, 1942–1954,* abridged and introduced by Michael Bloch (London: Hachette, 2011)

— *Fourteen Friends* (London: John Murray, 1996)

LeFanu, Sarah, *Rose Macaulay* (London: Virago, 2003)

Lehmann, John (ed.), *Coming to London* (London: Phoenix House Ltd, 1957)

— *I Am My Brother* (London: Longmans, 1960)

Lehmann, Rosamond, *The Echoing Grove* (London: Collins, 1953)

Macaulay, Rose, *A Casual Commentary* (London: Methuen, 1925)

— *And No Man's Wit* (London: Collins, 1940)

— *An Open Letter* (London: The Peace Pledge Union, 1937)

— *Dangerous Ages* (London: Collins, 1921)

— *Dearest Jean: Rose Macaulay's Letters to a Cousin,* ed. Martin Ferguson Smith (Manchester: Manchester University Press, 2011)

— *Fabled Shore: From the Pyrenees to Portugal* (London: Hamish Hamilton, 1950)

— *Keeping Up Appearances* (London: Methuen, 1986)

— *Last Letters to a Friend 1952–1958,* ed. Constance Babington Smith (London: Collins, 1962)

— *Letters to a Friend 1950–1952,* ed. Constance Babington Smith (London: Collins, 1961)

— *Letters to a Sister,* ed. Constance Babington Smith (London: Collins, 1964)

— *Life Among the English* (London: Collins, 1942)

— *Milton* (London: Duckworth, 1934)

— *Non-Combatants and Others,* foreword by Sarah LeFanu (London: Capuchin Classics, 2010)

— *Personal Pleasures* (London: Victor Gollancz, 1935)

— *Pleasure of Ruins* (London: Weidenfeld and Nicolson, 1953)

— *Potterism: A Tragi-farcical Tract* (London: Collins, 1920)

— *The Towers of Trebizond* (London: Collins, 1967)

— *The World My Wilderness,* introduction by Penelope Fitzgerald (London: Virago, 1983)

— *Told by an Idiot* (London: Collins, 1965)

— *What Not: A Prophetic Comedy* (London: Constable and Company, 1918)

Mackay, Marina, *Modernism and World War II* (Cambridge: Cambridge University Press, 2007)

MacNeice, Louis, *Collected Poems* (London: Faber, 2003)

— *The Strings Are False* (London: Faber, 1965)

Manning, Maurice, *James Dillon: A Biography* (Dublin: Wolfhound Press, 1999)

Mellor, Leo, *Reading the Ruins: Modernism, Bombsites and British Culture* (Cambridge; Cambridge University Press, 2011)

Muggeridge, Malcolm, *Chronicles of Wasted Time*, vol. 2: *The Infernal Grove* (London: Collins, 1973)

— *Like it was: the Diaries of Malcolm Muggeridge*, ed. John Bright-Holmes (London: Collins, 1981)

Nicolson, Harold, *Diaries and Letters 1939–45*, ed. Nigel Nicolson (London: Collins, 1967)

Nixon, Barbara, *Raiders Overhead, A Diary of the London Blitz* (London: Scolar Press, 1980)

O'Donovan, Gerald, *Father Ralph* (London: Macmillan, 1913)

— *The Holy Tree* (London: William Heinemann, 1922)

O'Faolain, Sean, *An Irish Journey* (London: Longmans & Co, 1940)

— *The Vanishing Hero, Studies in the Novelists of the Twenties* (London: Eyre & Spottiswoode, 1956)

— *Vive Moi!*, 2nd edition (London: Sinclair-Stevenson, 1993)

Orwell, George, *Collected Essays, Journalism, Letters*, vol. 4: *In Front of Your Nose*, ed. Sonia Orwell and Ian Angus (Harmondsworth: Penguin, 1970)

Overy, Richard, *The Battle of Britain: Myth and Reality* (London: Penguin, 2010)

— *Why the Allies Won* (London: Pimlico, 2006)

Pascoe, C. E., *London To-day: An Illustrated Handbook of the Season* (London: Sansom Low & Co, 1885)

PEN, *Writers in Freedom: A Symposium based on the 17th International Congress of the PEN*, ed. Hermon Ould (London: Hutchinson & Co, 1942)

Pick, Hella, *Guilty Victim: Austria from the Holocaust to Haider* (London: Tauris, 2000)

Piette, Adam, *Imagination at War: British Fiction and Poetry, 1939–1945* (London: Papermac, 1995)

Powell, Anthony, *Messengers of Day* (London: Heinemann, 1978)

Priestley, J. B., *Britain Speaks* (New York: Harper & Brothers, 1940)

Quennell, Peter, *Customs and Characters, Contemporary Portraits* (London: Weidenfeld & Nicolson, 1982)

Raby, Angela, *The Forgotten Service: Auxiliary Ambulance Station 39* (London: After the Battle, 1999)

Rawlinson, Mark, *British Writing of the Second World War* (Oxford: Clarendon, 2000)

Rees, Jenny, *Looking for Mr Nobody: The Secret Life of Goronwy Rees* (London: Phoenix Giant, 1997)

Ritchie, Charles, *Diplomatic Passport: More Undiplomatic Diaries 1946–1962* (Toronto: Macmillan, 1981)

— *The Siren Years: Undiplomatic Diaries 1937–1945* (London: Macmillan, 1974)

Rothenstein, John, *Brave Day, Hideous Night: Autobiography 1939–1965* (London: Hamish Hamilton, 1966)

Sansom, William, *The Blitz: Westminster at War* (London: Faber, 2010)

Sarton, May, *A World of Light* (New York: Norton, 1988)

Scammell, Michael, *Koestler: The Literary and Political Odyssey of a Twentieth-Century Skeptic* (New York: Random House, 2009)

Schivelbusch, Wolfgang, *In a Cold Crater: Cultural and Intellectual Life in Berlin, 1945–1948*, trans. Kelly Barry (Berkeley: University of California Press, 1998)

Schramm, Ingrid and Hansel, Michael, *Hilde Spiel und der literarische Salon* (Innsbruck: Studienverlag, 2011)

Schramm, Ingrid and Neunzig, Hans A., eds, *Hilde Spiel: Weltbürgerin der Literatur* (Wien: Zsolnay, 1999)

Sherry, Norman, *The Life of Graham Greene*, vols 1–3 (London: Pimlico, 2004–5)

Shirer, William, *The Rise and Fall of the Third Reich* (London: The Folio Society, 1995)

Spender, Stephen, *European Witness* (London: Hamish Hamilton, 1946)

— *New Selected Journals*, ed. Lara Feigel and John Sutherland (London: Faber, 2012)

— *World Within World*, introduction by John Bayley (New York: Modern Library Classics, 2001)

Spiel, Hilde, *Anna und Anna* (Wien: Kremayr & Scheriau, 1989)

— *Der Mann mit der Pelerine und andere Geschichten* (West Germany: Gustav Lübbe Verlag, 1985)

— *Die Früchte des Wohlstands* (München: Nymphenburger, 1981)

— *Kleine Schritte: Berichte und Geschichten* (München: Heinrich Ellermann, 1976)

— *Return to Vienna*, trans. Christine Shuttleworth (Riverside, California: Ariadne Press, 2011)

— *The Dark and the Bright: Memoirs 1911–1989*, trans. Christine Shuttleworth (Riverside, California: Ariadne Press, 2007)

— *The Darkened Room* (English translation of *Lisas Zimmer*) (London: Methuen, 1961)

Stallworthy, Jon, *Louis MacNeice* (London: Faber, 1995)

Strachey, John, *Post D, Some Experiences of an Air Raid Warden* (London: Gollancz, 1941)

Sutherland, John, *Stephen Spender: The Authorized Biography* (London: Penguin, 2005)

Tabachnick, Stephen E., *Fiercer than Tigers: The Life and Works of Rex Warner* (East Lansing: Michigan State University Press, 2002)

Treglown, Jeremy, *Romancing: The Life and Work of Henry Green* (London: Faber, 2000)

Wallington, Neil, *Firemen at War* (Newton Abbot: David & Charles, 1981)

Wasson, Sara, *Urban Gothic of the Second World War: Dark London* (Basingstoke: Palgrave Macmillan, 2010)

Waugh, Evelyn, *Officers and Gentlemen* (London: Chapman & Hall, 1955)

— *The Diaries of Evelyn Waugh*, ed. Michael Davie (London: Phoenix, 2009)

— *The Letters of Evelyn Waugh* (London: Phoenix, 2010)

— *The Letters of Nancy Mitford and Evelyn Waugh*, ed. Charlotte Mosley (London: Sceptre, 1997)

Wheal, Elizabeth-Anne and Pope, Stephen (eds), *The Macmillan Dictionary of the Second World War* (London: Macmillan, 1989)

Wills, Clair, *That Neutral Island* (London: Faber, 2008)

Woolf, Virginia, *The Diary of Virginia Woolf*, vols 1–5, ed. Anne Olivier Bell and Andrew McNeillie (London: Hogarth, 1977–1984)

— *The Letters of Virginia Woolf*, vols 1– 5, ed. Nigel Nicolson and Joanna Trautmann (London: Hogarth Press, 1975–1980)

Wydenbruck, Nora, *Rilke: Man and Poet; A Biographical Study* (London: John Lehmann, 1949)

Yeats, W. B., *Collected Poems* (London: Vintage, 2009)

Acknowledgements

Writing this book has been one of the most enjoyable enterprises I have ever undertaken. This is in part thanks to the five writers whose lives I have been immersed in, and in part thanks to the enthusiasm and generosity of friends, family and colleagues, and of all the people whom the book has brought me into contact with along the way.

Thanks goes first to Alex Harris, over whose kitchen table the idea for the book was born, and to Juliet Gardiner and Hannah Mulder, who both helped sustain my faith in the book in its early stages, and in whose company and cottages much of the book has been written. Alex and Juliet have also been generous readers of the manuscript, as have Lisa Appignanesi and Richard Overy, with whom I have engaged in several years of oddly enjoyable discussions about Second World War bombing.

Many colleagues and students at King's have been supportive friends. Clare Brant and Max Saunders have given Life Writing a home in the English department and me a home in the Centre for Life-Writing Research without which I don't think I would have had the courage to write this kind of book. It is thanks to the inspiration of Neil Vickers that so much of Ireland has found its way into the book. Hannah Crawforth provided happy companionship during our shared months of maternity leave and book finishing. Ellie Bass, Nicola von Bodman-Hensler, Susie Christensen and Natasha Periyan made the final stages of writing into an enjoyable (and energetic) holiday. And Ellie dug out microfilms for me in the British Library while I was buried in Norfolk and clambered through an exceptionally dusty attic searching for Greene letters, while Nicola helped with many of the German translations and references.

I am extremely indebted to the other biographers of my subjects, both for their work and for their generosity in welcoming me into the field. I am especially grateful to William Cash, who not only shared his Greene material with me but allowed me to write part of the book in his beautiful gatehouse, as well as making possible a trip to Achill. Sarah LeFanu and Martin Ferguson Smith have been generous in sharing photographs, sources and archival adventures. Jeremy Treglown has been extremely encouraging throughout the project. I am also indebted to the biographers I do not know personally, especially to Victoria Glendinning and Norman Sherry. The children of Hilde Spiel and Henry Yorke have all been very supportive of my endeavours. Christine Shuttleworth and Felix de Mendelssohn have been munificent in sharing anecdotes, manuscripts and photographs; Sebastian Yorke has been welcoming and helpful, despite some scepticism about the value of biography; Alice Kadel and John House have both been very kind in allowing me access to their parents' archives.

Researching the book has taken me on several archival trips and I am grateful for the grants that made these possible and the friends who made them fun. Mark Turner and Jan Palmowski enabled a research grant from King's College London which funded the trips to America, Vienna and Munich. The Heinrich Böll Foundation funded the trip to Achill. My stay in Austin was made possible by the hospitality of Inga and Richard Markovits. These trips have been turned into holidays by the friends who accompanied and hosted me: Marcel Feigel and Justin Williams in Vienna; Rebecca Welsford, Robert Newell, Vike Plock, Jason Hall and Hannah Crawforth in America; Mary Fairclough and Michelle Kelly in York; Kate Arthur in Cambridge; William Peacock, Julia Schoen and Eveline Kilian in Berlin; and Nicola von Bodman-Hensler in Munich. And I am happily indebted to the staff in numerous archives but especially at the Harry Ransom Center, the Georgetown and Boston University Greene archives, the Bodleian Library, the Wren Library at Trinity College Cambridge and the national libraries of Vienna and Munich, as well as to Georg Fritsch in Vienna who arranged for me to see one of the Spiel archives. I am extremely grateful to Brigitte Petrisch for her meticulous research assistance in Vienna. Several other friends have contributed to this book in their conversation, sharing of knowledge and support. In particular I'd like to thank Katie Graham, Caroline Maclean, Beatrice Pembroke, Stephen Romer, Matthew Spender, John-Paul Stonard, Nick Stargardt, John Sutherland and Matt Taunton.

I have been extremely fortunate in both my agent and my publishers. Zoe Waldie believed in both me and the book from the start and was invaluable in helping to shape it in its early stages and in finding it a home at Bloomsbury. Michael Fishwick has been a superb, visionary editor whose passionate enthusiasm for my writing has imbued me with great confidence and made the writing process all the more enjoyable. My desk editor Anna Simpson has been a model of clarity and calm, turning potential crises into solvable situations. I don't think that I could have had a better experience of publishing.

The book is dedicated to my son, Humphrey, though it might be a while before he can read it. Humphrey's impending birth provided a happy deadline for the first draft of the book and he himself has been a much happier distraction during the year of editing and proofing the book. I couldn't have done all this without the unstinting support of his five grandparents – Ilse, Marcel, Paul, Margaret and Jimmy – and I certainly couldn't have done it without my husband John, who has made this year of books and babies not only possible but fun. Neither husbands nor fathers come very well out of the book but John has excelled as both and I am more grateful than I can say.

Index

Note: page references in *italics* indicate illustrations. The abbreviations WWI and WWII refer to the First and Second World Wars respectively.